NATIONAL BUREAU OF ECONOMIC RESEARCH

STUDIES IN
BUSINESS CYCLES

No. 1

THE PROBLEM AND ITS SETTING

RELATION OF THE DIRECTORS
TO THE WORK OF THE NATIONAL BUREAU
OF ECONOMIC RESEARCH

1. The object of the National Bureau of Economic Research is to ascertain and to present to the public important economic facts and their interpretation in a scientific and impartial manner. The Board of Directors is charged with the responsibility of ensuring that the work of the Bureau is carried on in strict conformity with this object.

2. To this end the Board of Directors shall appoint one or more Directors of Research.

3. The Director or Directors of Research shall submit to the members of the Board, or to its Executive Committee, for their formal adoption, all specific proposals concerning researches to be instituted.

4. No study shall be published until the Director or Directors of Research shall have submitted to the Board a summary report drawing attention to the character of the data and their utilization in the study, the nature and treatment of the problems involved, the main conclusions and such other information as in their opinion will serve to determine the suitability of the study for publication in accordance with the principles of the Bureau.

5. A copy of any manuscript proposed for publication shall also be submitted to each member of the Board. If publication is approved each member is entitled to have published also a memorandum of any dissent or reservation he may express, together with a brief statement of his reasons. The publication of a volume does not, however, imply that each member of the Board of Directors has read the manuscript and passed upon its validity in every detail.

6. The results of an inquiry shall not be published except with the approval of at least a majority of the entire Board and a two-thirds majority of all those members of the Board who shall have voted on the proposal within the time fixed for the receipt of votes on the publication proposed. The limit shall be forty-five days from the date of the submission of the synopsis and manuscript of the proposed publication unless the Board extends the limit; upon the request of any member the limit may be extended for not more than thirty days.

7. A copy of this resolution shall, unless otherwise determined by the Board, be printed in each copy of every Bureau publication.

(Resolution of October 25, 1926, revised February 6, 1933)

BUSINESS CYCLES

The Problem and Its Setting

WESLEY C. MITCHELL

NATIONAL BUREAU OF ECONOMIC RESEARCH, Inc.

NEW YORK, 1927

Reprinted by Offset Lithography, REEHL LITHOGRAPHING CO.,
Bound by H. WOLFF, NEW YORK
Printed in United States of America

PREFACE

Much has been learned about business cycles since 1913, when my first book on that problem was published. Economic theorists have been studying the phenomena with increasing energy and thoroughness—Albert Aftalion and Jean Lescure in France; Mentor Bouniatian and S. A. Pervushin in Russia; Gustav Cassel in Sweden; John Maurice Clark, William T. Foster, Waddill Catchings, Alvin H. Hansen, and Henry L. Moore in America; R. H. Hawtrey, John A. Hobson, A. C. Pigou, and Dennis H. Robertson in England; Emil Lederer, Joseph Schumpeter and Arthur Spiethoff in Germany, to name but a few. Economic statisticians have made rapid progress in analyzing time series—witness the accomplishment of Warren M. Persons and his many co-workers here and abroad. Most important of all in promise for the future, the leading commercial nations are learning to keep more adequate records of their economic activities. Of the extraordinary business fluctuations through which the world has been passing of late, we have fuller knowledge than of any earlier cycles.

For perhaps ten years my unwieldy quarto has been out of print. At least as long it has been out of date. Nor could it be brought abreast of current research by mere revision. It became plain that if I could add anything of value to the work in process it would be only by writing a new book. But single-handed, I could not manage the wealth of new materials, or apply the improved methods of statistical analysis. From this quandary I was rescued by the National Bureau of Economic Research, which offered to collect and analyze the data I needed, and to supply the gaps in my equipment.

Despite the National Bureau's efficient aid, my resurvey of the field is taking more time than the first survey took. This work has been my chief concern since 1923, yet only one volume is ready for publication. It deals, as the sub-title indicates, with "The Problem and its Setting." A second volume on "The Rhythm of Business Activity" will follow as soon as I can finish it.

The present treatise resembles its forerunner in general plan. But the statistical data prove so extensive that they must be published separately in a series of volumes, instead of being included as before with the theoretical discussion. There is the more reason for this change in that the National Bureau's collection of tables promises to be a source book of great value to many workers concerned with other problems than business cycles. Also, the collection of annals, which in the earlier treatise covered only four countries and 23 years, has grown into a survey embracing 17 countries and extending back to 1790 in the United States and England. That collection, made by Dr. Willard L. Thorp, has already appeared in print.

I have not been able to devise a new way of conducting the inquiry which seemed better than the way followed in 1913. My earlier impressions that business cycles consist of exceedingly complex interactions among a considerable number of economic processes, that to gain insight into these interactions one must combine historical studies with quantitative and qualitative analysis, that the phenomena are peculiar to a certain form of economic organization, and that understanding of this scheme of institutions is prerequisite to an understanding of cyclical fluctuations—these impressions have been confirmed by my efforts to treat the subject in a simpler fashion. Hence the new version is not shorter or easier than its predecessor. Much to my regret, it makes even heavier demands upon a reader's time and effort.

From the Staff and the Directors of the National Bureau of Economic Research I have had most generous help. Among the staff members Drs. Frederick C. Mills, Willford I. King, Willard L. Thorp and Simon S. Kuznets have put their technical skill freely at my disposal. Among the Directors, Professor Allyn A. Young and Colonel Malcolm C. Rorty have made especially searching criticisms of the first draft. Dr. Edwin F. Gay, Director of Research, has been my mainstay for counsel from the beginning of the undertaking. Several other friends have read parts of the manuscript and suggested improvements—Messrs. Carl Snyder and Karl Karsten, Professors Walter F. Willcox, Warren M. Persons, Vladimir G. Simkhovitch, and James W. Angell. The Harvard Committee on Economic Research through its chairman Professor Charles J. Bullock, the American Telephone and Telegraph Company through its statistician Mr. Seymour L. Andrew, Sir William Beveridge, Mr. Snyder, and Dr. Dorothy S. Thomas have kindly consented to the free use I have made of their contributions. Miss Edith Handler of the National

Bureau has made most of the charts. My secretary, Miss Catherine Lochhead, has shared in the labors of proof reading and indexing.

To all these men and women, and to the many co-workers by whose criticisms and constructive suggestions I have sought to profit, my hearty thanks are due.

WESLEY C. MITCHELL.

New York City, June 1st, 1927.

P.S. Inasmuch as the National Bureau hopes to publish a second volume of this treatise at no distant date it seems time to place the words Volume I upon the title page. A few typographical errors have been corrected in this printing but no thorough revision has been undertaken.

W. C. M.

December 1, 1936.

Note to the Thirteenth Reprinting

A thirteenth reprinting of this volume was being planned when Wesley C. Mitchell died. In 1942, in compliance with a Government order, the plates for this volume were melted. Therefore this edition is an offset reproduction of the 1936 reprinting. The title pages have been modified to conform with those of the National Bureau series, Studies in Business Cycles, the list of officers and directors brought up to date, and a few typographical errors corrected. On the last three pages National Bureau publications especially concerned with business cycles are listed.

ARTHUR F. BURNS

CONTENTS

PAGE

CHAPTER I. THE PROCESSES INVOLVED IN BUSINESS CYCLES

I. The Plan of Attack 1

II. The Discovery of the Problem 3

III. The Multiplying Solutions 7

IV. The Theories now Current 11
  1. The Weather 12
  2. Uncertainty 16
  3. The Emotional Factor in Business Decisions . . . 17
  4. Innovations, Promotion, Progress 20
  5. The Processes of Saving and Investing 23
  6. Construction Work 26
  7. Generalized Over-Production 29
  8. Banking Operations 31
  9. Production and the Flow of Money Incomes . . . 35
  10. The Rôle Played by Profit-Making 42

V. Plans for Further Work
  1. Problems Raised by the Diversity of Explanations . . 47
  2. A Classification of the Theories 49
  3. The Necessity for Making Measurements 53
  4. Causal Theory and Analytic Description 54
  5. History and Theory 55
  6. The Framework of the Investigation 58

CHAPTER II. ECONOMIC ORGANIZATION AND BUSINESS CYCLES

I. The Historical Connection between Business Cycles and the
  Use of Money 61
  1. A Preliminary Statement 61
  2. The Meaning of "Business Economy" 63
  3. The Evolution of Business Economy 66
  4. When Business Cycles First Appear 75

II. The Modern Organization for Making Money 82
  1. The Money-Making Population 82
  2. The Business Enterprise 86

PAGE

3. The Size of Business Enterprises and Business Cycles 86
4. Economic Resources and the National Dividend . . 90
5. The Interdependence of Business Enterprises . . . 100
6. Profits as the Clue to Business Fluctuations 105
7. Factors Affecting Business Profits 107

III. The System of Prices 108
1. The Prices of Consumers' Commodities 108
2. The Prices of Producers' Goods in Relation to the
Prices of Consumers' Commodities 110
3. The Prices of Producers' Goods in Relation to Antecedent Prices 110
4. The Prices of Business Enterprises 111
5. The Prices of Services to Persons 112
6. The Interrelations Among Prices 113
7. The Rôle of Prices in Economic Life 116

IV. The Monetary Mechanism 116
1. Ambiguity of the Terms "Money" and "Currency" . 117
2. The Relative Importance of Checks and of Coin and
Paper Money in Making Payments 117
3. The Elasticity of the Circulating Medium 119
4. The Velocity of Circulation 122
5. The Quantity Theory and Business Cycles 128

V. The Flow of Money Payments 139
1. Production and Purchasing Power 139
2. The Flow of Money Incomes to Individuals 140
3. The Outflow of Personal Incomes 146
4. The Flow of Payments Among Business Enterprises . 149
5. Saving and Spending 151

VI. The Guidance of Economic Activity 154
1. The Problem of Adjusting Supply to Demand in a
Business Economy 154
2. The Rôle Played by Business Managements 157
3. The Rôle Played by Technical Experts 159
4. The Rôle Played by Lenders 162
5. The Rôle Played by Consumers 163
6. The Rôle Played by Government 167
7. The Alleged "Planlessness" of Production 169

PAGE

VII. International Differences in Economic Organization . . . 174
 1. The Uneven Development of Business Economy . . 174
 2. The Proportion of the Workers Engaged in Farming . 175
 3. Enterprise and Thrift 177
 4. Monetary and Banking Systems 178
 5. Government's Share in Directing Economic Activity . 179

VIII. Conclusion 180
 1. The *Raison d'Être* of Chapter II 180
 2. A Summary 182
 3. The Conception of Equilibrium 186

CHAPTER III. THE CONTRIBUTION OF STATISTICS

 I. The Current Distinction between Theoretical and Statistical
  Work   189

 II. Development of the Statistical Approach 190
 1. Why the Early Writers upon Business Cycles Made
  Slight Use of Statistics 190
 2. The Growth of Statistical Technique 193
 3. The Accumulation of Statistical Data   197
 4. The Present Situation 199

 III. The Analysis of Time Series 202
 1. The Quality and Quantity of Economic Statistics . . 202
 2. Time Series in Their Raw State 205
 3. The Problem of Secular Trends 212
  (1) The Empirical Approach to the Problem . . . 213
  (2) The Interpretation of Secular Trends . . . 221
  (3) The Hypotheses of "Secondary Trends" and of
   "Long Waves"   226
  (4) Conclusion   230
 4. The Problem of Seasonal Variations 233
  (1) The Causes and Pervasiveness of Seasonal Variations 236
  (2) Methods of Measuring Average Seasonal Variations   240
  (3) Efforts to Measure Changing Seasonal Variations   243
  (4) Conclusion   245
 5. The Problem of Irregular Fluctuations 249
  (1) The Concept of Irregular Fluctuations . . . 249

PAGE

(2) Irregular Fluctuations in the Theory of Business Cycles   252
6. The Problem of Isolating Cyclical Fluctuations . . .   255

IV. On Measuring the Relationships Among Time Series . . .   261
1. The Correlation of Time Series and Its Pitfalls . . .   262
2. Transformations of Time Series in the Investigation of their Relationships   265
3. Conclusion   269

V. The Amplitude and the Timing of Cyclical-Irregular Fluctuations in Different Processes   270
1. The Amplitude of Cyclical-Irregular Fluctuations . .   271
2. The Time Sequence of Cyclical-Irregular Fluctuations   280

VI. Indexes of Business Conditions   290
1. A Collection of Indexes of Business Conditions . .   291
(1) Beveridge's Chart of "The Pulse of the Nation," Great Britain, 1856-1907   291
(2) Persons' "Index of General Business Conditions," United States, 1903-1914   293
(3) The American Telephone and Telegraph Company's "Index of General Business Compared with Normal," United States, 1877 to date .   294
(4) Snyder's "Index of the Volume of Trade," United States, 1919-1925   295
(5) Persons' "Index of Trade," United States, 1903-1925   297
(6) Miss Thomas' Quarterly Index of "British Business Cycles," 1855-1914   299
(7) Axe and Flinn's "Index of General Business Conditions for Germany," 1898-1914   302
(8) Annual Indexes of Business Cycles   302
(9) Snyder's "Clearings Index of Business," United States, 1875-1924   304
(10) Frickey's "Index of Outside Clearings," United States, 1875-1914   305
(11) Snyder's "Index of Deposits Activity," United States, 1875-1924   307
2. A Critique of the Indexes of Business Conditions . .   307
(1) Indexes of the Pecuniary Volume of Business .   312

PAGE

(2) Indexes of the Physical Volume of Trade or
of Production 315
(3) Indexes of "General Business Conditions" . . 320
(4) Forecasting Sequences 324
3. What the Indexes of Business Conditions Show about
Business Cycles 326
(1) The "Saw-Tooth" Contour of the Business Indexes 329
(2) Month-to-Month Changes 330
(3) On Identifying Business Cycles by the Use of
the Business Indexes 334
(4) Time Relationships Among the Business Indexes 336
(5) Duration of Periods of Expansion and Contraction 337
(6) The Duration of Business Cycles 339
(7) The Amplitude of Business Cycles 343
(8) The Distinctive Character of Each Business
Cycle 354
VII. The Need of Combining Theory, Statistics and History . 357

CHAPTER IV.　THE CONTRIBUTION OF BUSINESS ANNALS

I. The National Bureau's Collection of Business Annals . . 361

II. The Trustworthiness of the Annals 363
1. Sources and Methods of Compilation 363
2. A Comparison of Business Annals and Business Indexes 365

III. The Cyclical Character of Business Fluctuations 376
1. The "Normal State of Trade" a Figment 376
2. Use of the Term "Cycles" 377
3. The Phases of Business Cycles 378
4. "Crises" and "Recessions" 378
5. "Prosperity" and "Depression" 381
6. The Uniformity and Variability of Business Cycles . 382

IV. The Duration of Business Cycles 383
1. Current Estimates of Average Length 383
2. Measurements Based upon the Annals 386
3. Frequency Distributions of the Measurements Based
upon the Annals 391
4. The Relative Duration of Prosperity and Depression . 407

PAGE

    5. Secular Changes in the Average Duration of Business
       Cycles 412
    6. Conclusions 416
  V. International Relationships Among Business Cycles . . . 424
    1. A Conspectus of Business Conditions in Different
       Countries 424
    2. How Closely the Cycles in Different Countries Agree . 438
    3. Domestic and Foreign Factors in Business Cycles . . 446

CHAPTER V. RESULTS AND PLANS

  I. The Concept of Business Cycles 451
    1. Evolution of the Concept 451
    2. A Working Concept of Business Cycles 455
       (1) Elements Derived from Business Reports . . 455
       (2) Elements Derived from Theories of Business
          Cycles 459
       (3) Elements Derived from Statistical Analysis . 463
    3. Two Criticisms Considered 464
    4. A Definition of Business Cycles 468
  II. Tentative Working Plans 469

ADDENDA 475
INDEX 481

LIST OF TABLES

Table 1. A Conspectus of the Population of the United States in
1920 83

Table 2. Cyclical Decline in the Volume of Employment Offered by
Different Industries, and by Establishments of Different Sizes,
from the Peak of Prosperity in 1920 to the Trough of Depression
in 1921-1922 88

Table 3. The Velocity of Deposit Currency, Estimated from Total
Payments by Check and Average Deposits Subject to Check. The
United States, 1919-1926 126

Table 4. Estimates of Income Received in Money by Individuals.
The United States, 1919-1926 141

Table 5. Personal Incomes Reported to the United States Bureau of
Internal Revenue, Classified by Sources. 1919-1924 142

PAGE

Table 6. Relative Variability of the Flow of Money Incomes from Different Sources. The United States, 1919-1924 144

Table 7. Channels Through Which Family Expenditures Flow . . 147

Table 8. Estimated Proportion of Income Received in Money Spent in Retail Shops. The United States, 1919-1923 148

Table 9. Comparison of the Estimated Volume of Payments, Income Received in Money, and Volume of Retail Sales. The United States, 1919 to 1923 or 1926 150

Table 10. Proportion of Gainfully Employed Males Engaged in Agricultural Pursuits in Various Countries 176

Table 11. Relative Amplitude of the Cyclical-Irregular Fluctuations of Various Economic Processes 273

   A. American Series, 1860, 1862 or 1866 to 1880 273

   B. American Series, 1903-1914 or 1903-1918, by months . . 274

   C. American Series, 1879-1896 and 1897-1913 274

   D. American National Banking Series, 1901-1914, by 5 "calls" yearly 275

   E. Velocity of Bank Deposits in American Cities, by Months, 1919-February, 1923 275

   F. American Series Showing Volume of Wholesale and Retail Trade by Months, 1919-1925 276

   G. British Series, by Quarters, before 1850 276

   H. British Series, by Quarters, 1903-June 30, 1914 277

   I. British Series. by Years, various dates to 1913 277

   J. British Series, by Quarters, various dates to 1914 . . . 278

   K. German Series, by Quarters or Months, various dates to 1913-14 278

Table 12. Time Sequences in the Cyclical-Irregular Fluctuations of Various Economic Series 282

   A. American Series, by Months, January, 1903-July, 1914 . 282

   B. American Series, by Months, January, 1902-December, 1908 283

Table 13. Coefficients of Correlation between the Cyclical-Irregular Fluctuations of Industrial Stock Prices and an Index of "General Business" 284

Table 14. Dates of the Troughs and the Crests of American Business Cycles in 1878-1924 according to Five Monthly Indexes of Business Activity 335

Table 15. Duration of Alternate Periods of Business Expansion and Business Contraction in the United States, 1878-1923, according to Five Indexes of Business Activity 338

PAGE

Table 16. Duration of Business Cycles in the United States, 1878-1925, according to Five Indexes of Business Activity 340

Table 17. Percentage Deviations from their Base Lines of Five Indexes of Business Activity at the Crests and Troughs of Successive Business Cycles. United States, 1878-1923 346

Table 18. Amplitude of the Rise from Trough to Crest and of the Decline from Crest to Trough in the American Business Cycles of 1878-1923, as shown by Five Indexes of Business Activity . . 347

Table 19. Dates of the Most and the Least Violent Cyclical Fluctuations in American Business, 1878-1923, according to Five Indexes of Business Activity 348

Table 20. Amplitude of Combined Rise and Fall in Violent Business Cycles, according to Five Indexes of Business Activity . . . 348

Table 21. Frequency Distributions of 111 Observations upon the Amplitude of the Percentage Deviations of Five Business Indexes from their Respective Trends at the Troughs and Crests of American Business Cycles: 1878-1923 351

Table 22. Frequency Distribution of 106 Observations made from Five Indexes of Business Conditions, upon the Amplitude of the Rise from Trough to Crest and the Decline from Crest to Trough in American Business Cycles, 1878-1923, reckoned in Percentages of Trend Values 353

Table 23. Business Recessions in the United States and Approximate Duration of Business Cycles, 1790-1925 387

Table 24. Business Recessions in England and Approximate Duration of Business Cycles, 1790-1925 390

Table 25. Dates of Business Recessions in Fifteen Countries: Various Years to 1925 391

Table 26. Frequency Distribution of Business Cycles according to Duration in Years 398

Table 27. Frequency Distribution of Business Cycles according to Approximate Duration in Years: by Countries, Groups of Countries and Periods 399

Table 28. Relative Duration of Different Phases of Business Cycles in Seventeen Countries, 1890-1925 408

Table 29. Relative Duration of the Prosperous and Depressed Phases in the Business Cycles of Seventeen Countries during Various Periods. 410

Table 30. Relative Duration of the Prosperous and the Depressed Phases of Business Cycles in Periods of Rising and Declining Trends of Wholesale Prices: England and the United States, 1790-1925 411

PAGE

Table 31. Relative Duration of Phases of Depression and Phases of
Prosperity in Business Cycles Lasting Nine Years or More . . 412

Table 32. Conspectus of Business Fluctuations in Various Countries   425

Table 33. Agreement and Difference of Phase in English, French,
German, Austrian and American Business Cycles. Various
Periods   441

LIST OF CHARTS

Chart 1. Sample Time Series Plotted on a Logarithmic Vertical Scale   211

Chart 2. Examples of Secular Trends of Time Series Fitted by Various
Methods 217

Chart 3. Samples of Time Series Plotted as Deviations from Secular
Trends Represented by Horizontal Lines   222

Chart 4. A Collection of Time Series to Illustrate Differences in
Seasonal Variations 234

Chart 5. Examples of Seasonal Variations which Have Changed in
the Course of Time 241

Chart 6. Indexes of Seasonal Variations Made by the Moving-average
median Method and the Link-relative Method 246

Chart 7. Indexes of Seasonal Variations Made by Various Methods . 248

Chart 8. Residual Fluctuations of Time Series after Elimination of
Trends and Seasonal Variations 258

Chart 9. Sir William H. Beveridge's Chart of "The Pulse of the
Nation" 292

Chart 10. Persons' "Index of General Business Conditions" . . . 294

Chart 11. The American Telephone and Telegraph Company's Index,
of "General Business Compared with Normal" 296

Chart 12. Carl Snyder's Index of the Volume of Trade 298

Chart 13. Persons' Index of Trade 300

Chart 14. Miss Thomas' Index of "British Business Cycles" . . . 301

Chart 15. Axe and Flinn's "Index of General Business Conditions
for Germany" 303

Chart 16. Snyder's "Clearings Index of Business" and Frickey's "Index of Outside Clearings" 306

Chart 17. Snyder's "Index of Deposits Activity" compared with his
"Clearings Index of Business" 308

PAGE

Chart 18. One Business Cycle, United States, 1919-1921, shown by a Plot of 27 of its Components 310

Chart 19. Frequency Distribution of Month-to-Month Changes in Five Indexes of Business Activity 332

Chart 20. Frequency Distribution of 101 Observations upon the Duration of Business Cycles: United States, 1878-1923 . . . 344

Chart 21. Business Fluctuations in the United States, as shown by the Annals and by Two Statistical Indexes, 1875-1925 368

Chart 22. Business Fluctuations in England, as shown by the Annals and Dr. Dorothy S. Thomas' "Quarterly Index of British Cycles," 1855-1914 372

Chart 23. Approximate Duration of Business Cycles, arranged in Chronological Sequence 393

Chart 24. Percentage Distribution of Business Cycles in Various Countries and Various Periods according to their Approximate Duration in Years 402

Chart 25. Logarithmic Normal Curve Fitted by Davies' Method to the Frequency Distribution of 166 Observations upon the Duration of Business Cycles 419

Chart 26. Percentage Distribution of Measurements of the Duration of Business Cycles in the United States, based upon Business Indexes, 1875-1925, and Business Annals, 1790-1925 423

Chart 27. Conspectus of Business Cycles in Various Countries, 1790-1925 444

BUSINESS CYCLES

CHAPTER I.

THE PROCESSES INVOLVED IN BUSINESS CYCLES.

I. The Plan of Attack.

As knowledge of business cycles grows, more effort is required to master it. Formerly, an attack upon the problem required no special preparations. Early writers upon "commercial crises" could assume that they and their readers were familiar with the phenomena to be explained and the methods to be used. They felt no need of collecting statistics, of compiling business annals, of comparing the amplitude and the timing of cyclical fluctuations in different activities, of developing and defining technical concepts. After the briefest of introductions, they plunged into a discussion of the cause of crises, and worked such evidence as they cited into their argumentation. In consequence, their discussions had an agreeable directness, which our generation may envy, but cannot wisely imitate.

Elaborate preparations have become necessary, not because the direct attacks upon the problem proved futile, but because they won so many and such different results. Every investigator of the cause of commercial crises seemed to make out a case for the hypothesis he favored. In trying to prove their divergent explanations correct, successive theorists did prove that business cycles were more intricate phenomena than any of them had surmised. These cycles turned out to be complexes, made up of divergent fluctuations in many processes. Familiarity with the phenomena to be explained came to mean familiarity with the interrelations among cyclical fluctuations in the production of raw materials, industrial equipment and consumers' goods; in the volume of savings and investments; in the promotion of new enterprises, in banking, in the disbursement of incomes to individuals and the spending of incomes, in prices, costs, profits and the emotional aberrations of business judgments. However

1

conversant he may be with practical affairs and economic theory, no competent investigator now supposes that he can explain the fluctuations of these interrelated factors on the basis of his general knowledge.

This lesson from experience in making theories of business cycles has been confirmed in recent years by work with statistics. Serried tables of figures, and charts drawn from them, have made our knowledge of cyclical fluctuations much more definite. Year by year the range covered by statistical compilations has grown wider, the accuracy of reporting has improved, and the technical methods of analysis have become more refined and more powerful. But we have no statistical evidence of business cycles as wholes. What the data show us are the fluctuations of particular processes—producing pig iron, transporting freight, clearing bank checks, selling goods by mail, declaring dividends, and so on. And these fluctuations differ widely. In certain cases we assemble or average the data for various processes, and say that we have "indexes" of cyclical fluctuations in wholesale prices, physical production, the volume of trade, or even "general business conditions." Yet the most inclusive indexes we can make fall far short of showing all that we mean by business cycles. The more intensively we work, the more we realize that this term is a synthetic product of the imagination—a product whose history is characteristic of our ways of learning. Overtaken by a series of strange experiences our predecessors leaped to a broad conception, gave it a name, and began to invent explanations, as if they knew what their words meant. But in the process of explaining they demonstrated how inadequate their knowledge was. From their work we can learn much; the first lesson is that we must find out more about the facts before we can choose among the old explanations, or improve upon them.

An inquiry into business cycles, then, cannot wisely begin by defining the general concept, and proceed systematically to take up one part of the whole after another. It should begin rather with the individual processes which can be studied objectively, seeking to find what these processes are, how they affect each other, and what sort of whole they make up.

The best way to learn what processes are involved in business cycles is to profit by the discoveries of earlier workers. Most of these men found the clue to business cycles in the recurrent fluctuations of some single economic process. All together they may not have covered the whole field. But in no other way can we get so comprehensive a view of business cycles, or such vivid insight into their complexities, as by following a series of persuasive demonstrations that each one of a dozen different processes reveals the factor of crucial importance.

It is not advisable to attack the statistical data until we have made this survey of theories. For while the statistics will come to seem scanty as our demands develop, they are sufficiently abundant and diverse, susceptible of enough transformations and combinations, to make hopeless a purely empirical investigation. At every turn, we shall need working hypotheses to guide our selection of data, and to suggest ways of analyzing and combining them. Our survey of theories will provide us with the most promising hypotheses which have been invented. Not until we are thus equipped can we begin constructive work upon the problem of business cycles, confident that we are not overlooking elements already proved to be important.

II. The Discovery of the Problem.

Serious efforts to explain business crises and depressions began amid the violent fluctuations in trade which followed the Napoleonic Wars. For a century or more Western Europe had been experiencing at intervals speculative manias, glutted markets, and epidemics of bankruptcy. The Mississippi Bubble and the South Sea Scheme which had burst in France and England in 1720, and the commercial crises of 1763, 1772, 1783 and 1793, not to mention less notable cases, had excited much discussion.[1] But the eighteenth-century writers dealt mainly with the dramatic surface events; concerning the underlying causes they developed no arresting ideas. By 1815 progressive changes in economic organization were forcing the problem to the fore, and men were better equipped to attack it. The Physiocrats and Adam Smith had made political economy a branch of philosophy, if not of science, and when the wars ended Ricardo was recasting the theory into the form which is still dominant.

It was not the orthodox economists, however, who gave the problem of crises and depressions its place in economics, but sceptics who had profited by and then reacted against their teachings. From Adam Smith to Mill, and even to Alfred Marshall, the classical mas-

[1] See Mentor Bouniatian, *Studien zur Theorie und Geschichte der Wirtschaftskrisen.*
II *Geschichte der Handelskrisen in England, 1640-1840.* Munich, 1908.

ters have paid but incidental attention to the rhythmical oscillations of trade in their systematic treatises. They have been concerned primarily to elucidate principles which hold "in the long run," or apply to the "normal state." To them crises and depressions have been of secondary interest—proper subjects for special study or occasional reference, but not among the central problems of economic theory.[2] To force into prominence the fact that economic activities are subject to recurring phases of contraction and expansion was the work primarily of men who were critics, not merely of orthodox economics, but also of modern society—men such as Sismondi and Rodbertus.

J. C. L. Simonde de Sismondi was an Italian Swiss who had early become enamored of Adam Smith's doctrines and expounded them for continental readers in a treatise *De la Richesse Commerciale.* After publishing this book in 1803, Sismondi had turned to medieval research and won European celebrity as the historian of the Italian Republics. Then an invitation from the Scotch physicist, Sir David Brewster, to write an article on "Political Economy" for the new *Edinburgh Encyclopædia,* recalled him to his first theme in 1818.

The time was one of widespread distress. As Napoleon's fall drew near, English manufacturers and merchants, anticipating the reopening of hungry continental markets, accumulated large stores of goods for export. Waterloo was fought in June, 1815. There followed several months of brisk trade and optimistic speculation. But before the year was out it became clear that European consumers lacked the means to buy freely. Heavy consignments of British goods overstocked the markets and many of the consignors went bankrupt. The year after Waterloo was one of distress from beginning to end. Recovery began in the spring of 1817 and made rapid progress, so that 1818 showed great industrial activity. But in 1819 fresh difficulties occurred, and depression returned to last through 1820. Not

[2] Thus Adam Smith mentions the "knavery and extravagance" of the South Sea Company's "stock-jobbing projects," (*Wealth of Nations,* Cannan's ed., vol. ii, p. 236); Ricardo speaks of "revulsions in trade" accompanying the outbreaks or the ending of great wars (*Principles of Political Economy,* Gonner's ed., pp. 250, 251); Mill discusses "commercial crises" in his chapters on the Rate of Interest and on the Tendency of Profits to a Minimum, besides mentioning them incidentally in several other passages (*Principles of Political Economy,* Ashley's ed., pp. 561, 641, 644, 651, 709, 734-735, 845); Marshall puts a book on "Fluctuations of Industry, Trade and Credit," not into his *Principles of Economics,* but into his volume on *Money, Credit and Commerce,* London, 1923, pp. 234-263.

until 1821 did a sustained revival begin,—and the prosperity which presently reigned ended in the panic of December, 1825.[3]

Sismondi had accepted Brewster's invitation readily, thinking he had merely to write a brief exposition of "principles universally admitted." But as he studied current developments he was assailed by doubts concerning the theories he had accepted from Adam Smith.

> I was deeply affected, (he wrote), by the commercial crisis which Europe had experienced of late, by the cruel sufferings of the industrial workers which I had witnessed in Italy, Switzerland and France, and which all reports showed to have been at least as severe in England, in Germany and in Belgium.

The case of England was to him particularly significant—that "surprising country which seemed to be undergoing a great experiment for the instruction of the rest of the world." If the land of the economists, the land where the doctrine of economic liberty had freest sway in government, the land where the new methods of machine production had scored their greatest triumphs—if that land was plunged in want by the return of peace, must there not be something wrong in the philosophy of *laissez faire?* When everyone was free to produce as much as he could, it seemed that no one could buy what he needed to consume. How could this be? Sismondi set himself to solve the problem. The result was his *Nouveaux Principes d'Économie Politique,* published in 1819.[4]

We should not expect the first efforts to explain so complicated a phenomenon as a business crisis to be free from crudities. Nor was Sismondi fully equipped to solve the problem he had posed; though an excellent observer, he lacked analytic finesse. Yet he made several suggestions, ill coördinated with each other, which were developed and combated by later writers, and which continue to play rôles of importance in theories now current.

One of these suggestions is that commercial organization is at fault. The business man, as Sismondi phrases it, caters to a "metaphysical public"—customers whose numbers, tastes, consumption and purchasing power are all unknown to him, and all variable. The only guide he has in planning how much to produce is prices. By

---

[3] See the conspectus of English business annals in Chapter IV below, or better the chapter on England in *Business Annals,* by Willard L. Thorp, National Bureau of Economic Research, 1926.

[4] See the prefaces to the first and second editions. The latter appeared in 1827

comparing present prices with costs, he decides whether to increase or restrict his output in the near future.

> Unfortunately this comparison is made by all the producers at the same time . . . and all of them together, ignorant of how much their competitors will undertake, nearly always exceed the limit which they had in view.[5]

A second suggestion is that in periods of industrial activity the income available for buying consumers' goods falls short of the value of the goods sent to market. This idea sounds modern, but Sismondi's supporting analysis offered a broad target to his detractors. The purchasing power available to absorb the produce of any year, he stoutly contended, is the aggregate income of the preceding year—a notion probably suggested by his life among the peasants of Italy. When capacity to produce is increasing rapidly through the introduction of machinery, the markets must become glutted frequently. For the faster the increase in production, the wider will be the gap between last year's income and this year's output.[6]

Still a third suggestion embodies in quaint form the "over-saving" theory of crises. In opulent nations, production often goes astray because its volume is determined by the abundance of capital seeking investment rather than by the demand of consumers. Of course the latter demand is the only safe guide; the fact that merchants and manufacturers have money to invest in new ventures does not guarantee a market for their wares.[7]

Sismondi laid most stress, however, upon an idea often repeated but never clearly worked out in his book: the fundamental cause of crises is inequality in the distribution of incomes.

> It is a serious error into which most of the modern economists have fallen to represent consumption as a power without limits, always ready to devour an infinite output. . . . The needs of the laboring man are narrowly limited of necessity.

The masses do not wish luxuries so much as they wish respite from toil. But when methods of production are improved, our economic institutions, instead of giving the workers leisure, keep them busy as long as ever and increase the volume of products offered for sale.

[5] *Nouveaux Principes,* 2d ed., I, 325-330.
[6] The same, I, 106, 121-124.
[7] The same, I, 367-368.

Who is to buy? After food, clothing and housing on a meager scale have been provided for the wage-earners, the chief market for further goods is the market for luxuries. The desire for such goods is indeed without limit. But the increase of trade in luxuries puts a nation's industry in a precarious position. Domestic consumers of luxuries prefer foreign wares, and domestic producers must seek foreign outlets. Recent experience of unsalable consignments all over the globe has shown the English how undependable is the export trade. Everyone would be better off if the workers had incomes sufficient to give the home demand a broad base.[8]

III. The Multiplying Solutions.

In a generation addicted to economic speculation, events which affected so many fortunes as did the vicissitudes of trade were certain to be explained in different ways. Sismondi was but the most suggestive among a numerous company of writers, most of whom had their own explanations to offer and their own remedies to urge. Nor did the differences of opinion grow less with the passing of time. On the contrary, as later crises brought new men and new materials into the discussion, the explanations multiplied. Gradually the plausible views became standardized into several types of theory, each represented in the growing literature by a number of variants. Before the end of the nineteenth century there had accumulated a body of observations and speculations sufficient to justify the writing of histories of the theories of crises.[1]

A simple form of the "over-production" or "under-consumption" theory was widely held. Through the adoption of modern machinery, it was said, the power of society to produce has outgrown its power to consume. Hence the periodical occurrence of "general gluts"—paradoxical episodes in which superabundance causes want. Unable to

[8] The same, I, 75-78, 357-372. The best modern account of Sismondi's views is given by Albert Aftalion, *L'Oeuvre Économique de Simonde de Sismondi*, Paris, 1899.

[1] The most elaborate of these histories is Eugen von Bergmann's *Die Wirtschaftskrisen: Geschichte der nationalökonomischen Krisentheorien*, Stuttgart, 1895. The best accounts in English and French are Edward D. Jones' *Economic Crises*, New York, 1900, and Jean Lescure's *Des Crises Générales et Périodiques de Surproduction*, 3rd ed., Paris, 1923, pp. 313-412.

See also Harry E. Miller's paper on "Earlier Theories of Crises and Cycles in the United States." *Quarterly Journal of Economics*, February, 1924 (xxxviii, pp. 294-329), and Adolf Löwe's review of recent German contributions, "Der gegenwärtige Stand der Konjunkturforschung in Deutschland," in *Festgabe für Lujo Brentano*, Munich and Leipzig, 1925, vol. ii, pp. 329-377.

sell their increasing output of goods at remunerative prices, employers are forced to close their factories and turn away their hands—a remedy which aggravates the disease by reducing yet further the community's power to purchase for consumption.

To most of the classical economists, the theory of general overproduction was a heresy, which they sought to extirpate by demonstrating that the supply of goods of one sort necessarily constitutes demand for goods of other sorts.[2] But maladjusted production they allowed to be possible, and their brief references to crises usually aimed to show how production becomes maladjusted through the sinking of capital in unremunerative investments. They often held that such misuse of capital was one result of "the tendency of profits to a minimum." When the current rate of profits has fallen to an unaccustomed level, the less sagacious capitalists become dissatisfied and embark on ill-considered schemes. There result the production of goods for which no market can be found, business failures, and loss of confidence—in short, a crisis which extends over all lines of trade.

Another group of writers, among whom Schäffle was prominent, accepted ill-adjusted production as the cause of crises; but accounted for it by the complexity of modern business organization—the first of Sismondi's suggestions. Not only are manufacturers compelled to produce goods months in advance for markets whose changes they cannot forecast, but investors are compelled years in advance to put their funds into enterprises the need of which is uncertain. A close adjustment of supply to demand cannot be maintained. Mistakes are inevitable, and should be ascribed less to bad judgment than to the planlessness of capitalistic production.

The most vigorous attempt to prove that crises are a chronic disease of capitalism, however, was that made by Rodbertus and elaborated by Karl Marx. The germ of this theory also is found in Sismondi and Robert Owen. Wages form but a fraction of the value of the product and increase less rapidly than power to produce. Since the masses dependent upon wages constitute the bulk of the population, it follows that consumers' demand cannot keep pace

[2] Upon this point, as upon many others, Malthus dissented from the "orthodox" opinion. See his *Principles of Political Economy,* 1st ed., London, 1820, 351-375; 2d ed., London, 1836, 314-330. Mill admitted that "there may really be, though only while the crisis lasts, an extreme depression of general prices, from what may be indiscriminately called a glut of commodities or a dearth of money. But (he added) it is a great error to suppose, with Sismondi, that a commercial crisis is the effect of a general excess of production. It is simply the consequence of an excess of speculative purchases." *Principles of Political Economy,* Ashley's ed., p. 561.

with current supply in seasons when factories are running at full blast. Meanwhile the capitalist-employers are investing their current savings in new productive enterprises, which presently add their quotas to the goods seeking sale. This process of over-stocking the market runs cumulatively until the time comes when the patent impossibility of selling goods at a profit, or even at cost, brings on a crisis.[3]

A wider acceptance was accorded to the "inflation" theory. An increase in gold, in irredeemable paper money, in bank notes, or in deposit currency was held to start an advance in prices. The latter in turn stimulates business to great activity, which runs to extremes in reckless investments and foolish speculation, and ends in a crash of credit and widespread bankruptcy.

The "psychological" type of explanation was elaborated in John Mills' paper "On Credit Cycles and the Origin of Commercial Panics," published in 1867.[4] On this view the fundamental cause of crises lies less in the character or abuse of economic institutions, than in the emotional aberrations to which business judgments are subject. Fair trade breeds optimism, optimism breeds recklessness, recklessness breeds disaster. In their turn, the disasters of a crisis breed pessimism and pessimism breeds stagnation. From depression business picks up only when men's spirits recover on finding that matters have gone less badly than they had feared.

As John Mills sought the fundamental cause of commercial fluctuations in psychology, so W. Stanley Jevons sought it in physics. His theory that the activity of solar radiation controls mundane weather, weather controls crops, and crops control business conditions, was first announced in 1875.

Finally, some economists, for example Wilhelm Roscher, despaired of finding any theory which would account for all crises in the same way. To these men a crisis is an "abnormal" event produced by some "disturbing cause," such as the introduction of revolutionary inventions, the development of new transportation lines, wars, the return of peace, tariff revisions, monetary changes, crop failures, changes in fashion, and the like. This view assumes that the equilibrium of economic processes has become so delicate that it may be upset by untoward conjunctures of the most dissimilar kinds, and

---

[3] For a recent statement of the Marxian theory of crises by a sympathetic interpreter, see Otto Leichter, "Zur Analyse der Weltwirtschaftskrise," in *Der lebendige Marxismus, Festgabe zum 70. Geburtstage von Karl Kautsky*, Jena, 1924, pp. 45-100.

[4] *Transactions of the Manchester Statistical Society*, 1867-68, pp. 5-40.

points to the conclusion that each crisis has its own special cause which must be sought among the events of the preceding year or two.

While all these speculations and others unmentioned concerning the cause of crises and depressions were being debated, some progress was made toward more exact observation and description of the phenomena. The most distinguished pioneer in work of this sort was Clement Juglar, whose elaborate treatise *Des Crises Commerciales et de leur Retour Périodique* was published in 1860 and again in 1889. Max Wirth emphasized the international character of the major crises in his *Geschichte der Handelskrisen* (Frankfort a, M. 1858; 4th ed., 1890), Tugan-Baranovski made an intensive study of English crises in the nineteenth century,[5] and numerous observers wrote pamphlets or books on single crises.

In this descriptive work, much freer use was generally made of statistical materials than in the theoretical essays. As the century wore on, the data available concerning prices, currency, banking, interest rates, foreign trade, production and employment grew wider in range, more reliable, and more precise. Meanwhile statisticians like Jevons and Edgeworth were developing a better technique for wresting significant conclusions from masses of seemingly chaotic data. But the use of these methods in theoretical inquiries was slow to develop.

The most fundamental change to which the use of statistics contributed was a change in the conception of the problem to be solved. The earlier writers had sought for the cause merely of crises, or of crises and depressions. It is true that a wider view had been suggested occasionally. In 1833, an English journalist, John Wade, remarked casually that

> The commercial cycle is ordinarily completed in five or seven years, within which terms it will be found, by reference to our commercial history during the last seventy years, alternate periods of prosperity and depression have been experienced.[6]

Presently this idea of cyclical oscillations was amplified by more influential writers—Lord Overstone, Hyde Clark, William Langton.

---

[5] Published first in Russian (1894), then in German (1901) and finally in French under the title *Les Crises Industrielles en Angleterre* (Paris, 1913).
[6] John Wade, *History of the Middle and Working Classes*, 2d ed., London, 1834, p. 211.

John Mills, Condy Raguet and Amasa Walker: [7] it was indeed implied in the numerous discussions of the "periodicity of crises."   One could talk about credit cycles and "periodic" crises, however, without devoting much attention to business revivals after depression, or the process by which revivals grow into prosperity.   But one could scarcely use time series, showing the fluctuations of activity year after year, without seeing that the developments in the non-crisis periods offered quite as much a problem as did the crises themselves.   Thus the use of statistics hastened the time when economists passed on from the theory of crises to the theory of business cycles.   Clement Juglar's great "book of facts" made clear the need of the step.[8]

So bald a statement as the preceding falls far short of doing justice to the nineteenth century writers; but it suffices to indicate the foundations upon which our contemporaries have built their more elaborate theories.   The latter conserve all of permanent value which the older economists achieved, and contain in addition certain fresh contributions to the subject.   Accordingly, a more detailed account of the leading explanations which have been offered recently will put us in possession of the ideas most likely to prove useful in further work.

IV. The Theories Now Current.

Recent writers upon business cycles differ from one another less in principle than in emphasis.   Everyone who studies the problem with care must realize that many processes are involved in the alternations of prosperity and depression.   But each investigator decides for himself the question: What among these many processes is the prime mover in producing cyclical oscillations, and what processes merely adapt themselves as best may be to changes produced elsewhere?

[7] Lord Overstone's statement may be quoted:
"The history of what we are in the habit of calling the 'state of trade' is an instructive lesson. We find it subject to various conditions which are periodically returning; it revolves apparently in an established cycle. First, we find it in a state of quiescence,—next improvement,—growing confidence,—prosperity,—excitement,—overtrading,—convulsion,—pressure,—stagnation,—distress,—ending again in quiescence." *Reflections suggested by a perusal of Mr. J. Horsley Palmers' pamphlet on the Causes and Consequences of the Pressure on the Money Market.* By Samuel Jones Loyd, London, 1837.
On the American observations, see Harry E. Miller, "Earlier Theories of Crises and Cycles in the United States," *Quarterly Journal of Economics*, February, 1924, vol. xxxviii, p. 300.
[8] *Des Crises Commerciales*, 2d ed., Paris, 1889, chapter i and *passim*.

Each gives chief attention to the one or more factors which he believes to play the chief causal rôle; but many writers also show how the changes produced by their chosen causes affect other processes, and in so doing they are likely to find use for the work of men whose distribution of emphasis differs from their own.

Among the factors to which the leading rôle in causing business cycles has been assigned by competent inquirers within the past decade are the weather, the uncertainty which beclouds all plans that stretch into the future, the emotional aberrations to which business decisions are subject, the innovations characteristic of modern society, the "progressive" character of our age, the magnitude of savings, the construction of industrial equipment, "generalized over-production," the operations of banks, the flow of money incomes, and the conduct of business for profits. Each of these explanations merits attention from those who seek to understand business cycles; for each should throw light upon some feature or aspect of these complex phenomena.

We need not, however, review the full analysis of the writers by whose ideas we seek to profit. That would be the task of a treatise upon theories of business cycles. This book deals with the cycles themselves, and to it the theories are tools to be used in constructive work. The following pages, therefore, aim merely to borrow from the recent books and articles upon business cycles those suggestions which promise to enlarge our understanding of the problem as a whole.

1. THE WEATHER.

Most elegant among current explanations of business cycles are the meteorological theories.

In 1801 Sir William Herschel suggested that changes in sun-spots may affect the weather, hence crops, and hence prices.[1] This idea, coupled with Schwabe's discovery (recognized by the Royal Astronomical Society in 1857) that sun-spots are cyclical, fascinated the speculative mind of W. Stanley Jevons, and led him to the hypothesis that business cycles are caused by solar cycles. To test this notion, Jevons studied the records of English trade from 1721 to

[1] Observations tending to investigate the nature of the Sun in order to find the Causes or Symptoms of its variable Emission of Light and Heat; with Remarks on the Use that may possibly be drawn from Solar Observations. *Philosophical Transactions of the Royal Society of London*, 1801, vol. xci, pp. 265-318.

1878 to see how closely the two cycles agreed with each other. He concluded that there had been 16 crises in this period of 157 years. Thus he obtained an average length of 10.466 years for the commercial cycle, which agreed almost exactly with the length then assigned to the sun-spot cycle, 10.45 years. Jevons declared himself

> perfectly convinced that these decennial crises do depend upon meteorological variations of like period, which again depend, in all probability upon cosmical variations of which we have evidence in the frequency of sunspots, auroras, and magnetic perturbations.[2]

Unfortunately for this theory, since 1878 astronomers have revised their computations of the sun-spot cycle (the average now commonly accepted is 11 + years),[3] and commercial cycles have departed still further from the decennial norm. Hence in 1909, Jevons' son, Professor Herbert Stanley Jevons, suggested a modification of the solar hypothesis. He believed that meteorologists had demonstrated the existence of a $3\frac{1}{2}$ year period in solar radiation and in barometric pressure. By analyzing agricultural data he found evidence of a $3\frac{1}{2}$ year periodicity in crop yields also. Trade cycles, he held, are either 7 or $10\frac{1}{2}$ years in length. He tied these two results together by observing that a single period of good crops does not suffice to produce an unhealthy boom in business, but that two or at most three such periods following each other will do so. In this revised form, he concluded that his father's meteorological theory of the business cycle remains valid.[4]

Since Professor Jevons had relied largely upon American data to establish his weather cycle of $3\frac{1}{2}$ years, surprise was felt when Professor Henry L. Moore announced in 1914 that harmonic analysis of rainfall data from the grain areas of Ohio and Illinois shows the existence of a 33-year and an 8-year cycle. His supplemental computations showed high coefficients of correlation between crop yields per acre and other indices of business conditions, such as wholesale

---

[2] Jevons' leading papers on this topic, dating from 1875 to 1882, are reprinted in his *Investigations in Currency and Finance*, edited by H. S. Foxwell, London, 1884, pp. 194-243. The passage quoted is on pp. 235, 236. Jevons' first investigation, by a different method, will be referred to in Chapter IV, section iv, 1, below.

[3] Sir William H. Beveridge, "Wheat Prices and Rainfall in Western Europe," *Journal of the Royal Statistical Society*, May, 1922, vol. lxxxv, pp. 434-437.

[4] See "The Causes of Unemployment: III, Trade Fluctuations and Solar Activity," *Contemporary Review*, August, 1909, vol. xcvi, pp. 165 ff. Reprinted with added preface and summary, as *The Sun's Heat and Trade Activity*, London, 1910.

prices and pig-iron production. Professor Moore formulated his conclusions in the following "law":

The weather conditions represented by the rainfall in the central part of the United States, and probably in other continental areas, pass through cycles of approximately thirty-three years and eight years in duration, causing like cycles in the yield per acre of the crops; these cycles of crops constitute the natural, material current which drags upon its surface the lagging, rhythmically changing values and prices with which the economist is more immediately concerned.[5]

Later, Professor Moore extended his investigations to other parts of the United States, to England and to France, finding confirmation for his 8-year, but seemingly not for his 33-year cycle. He also suggested an astronomical cause for this dominant weather cycle more daring than the sunspot theory. At intervals of 8 years Venus comes directly into the path of solar radiations to the earth. Its magnetic field, thinks Professor Moore, may affect the stream of electrons flowing from the sun and so produce an effect on earthly magnetism and weather.[6]

To complete the record of divergencies among the economists who have utilized meteorological data, it must be added that Sir William H. Beveridge has applied harmonic analysis to European wheat prices for the three centuries from 1545 to 1844, and found evidence that there are, not one or two, but many cycles in the weather. Of these cycles a few of the best accredited have lengths (1) of 5.1 and 35.5 years (shown by harmonic analysis and confirmed by independent meteorological data), and (2) of 5.671, 9.750, 12.840, 19.900, 54.000 and possibly 68.000 years (clearly shown by harmonic analysis, but not yet confirmed by meteorological observations). There is no 8-year period in the cycles for which Sir William Beveridge finds the strongest evidence. But a period of 8.050 years occurs in his third group, for which there is "some, but not first-rate, evidence both in wheat prices and in meteorology."

Sir William's conclusion is that,

Somewhere or other in the solar system there are periodic movements affecting our weather and crops, 10 or 20 or more

[5] *Economic Cycles: Their Law and Cause.* New York, 1914, p. 149.
[6] These later investigations are summed up in Professor Moore's volume, *Generating Economic Cycles*, New York, 1923.

in number, far more regular than had ever been believed, possibly approaching in some cases the regularity and persistence of free orbital motion, subject in other cases to sudden birth and death. These movements may be of one type, or of several types; they may be in the sun or the planets or the moon; in the earth or in the air or water upon its surface.[7]

A novel variant of the weather theories was propounded by Professor Ellsworth Huntington in 1919. Starting to collect statistical evidence of the effect of business conditions upon health, Huntington convinced himself that "Health is a *cause* far more than an effect" of economic conditions.

The statistics from 1870 to the Great War show that a high death rate regularly *precedes* hard times, while a low death rate precedes prosperity.

He also found that his death-rate curve, when inverted, agreed well with the fluctuations of school attendance one year later, New York bank clearings three years later, wholesale prices and National Bank deposits four years later, and immigration five years later.

Business cycles (Professor Huntington concluded) appear to depend largely on the mental attitude of the community, . . . the mental attitude depends on health . . . and health depends largely upon the weather.[8]

Professor Werner Sombart's theory of the dissimilarity in the rhythm of production of organic and inorganic goods may be regarded as a view intermediate between the preceding group of theories which trace business cycles to physical causes and the following groups which trace them to economic factors. He points out that the inorganic industries, typified by the steel trade, can expand enormously within a brief period without being seriously hampered by scarcity of raw materials. The organic industries, typified by cotton-spinning, on the contrary are always in precarious dependence upon the year's harvests. In the organic industries, one may say, the condition of business is determined largely by the yield of raw materials; in the inorganic industries, the condition of business itself determines how

[7] Sir William H. Beveridge, "Wheat Prices and Rainfall in Western Europe," *Journal of the Royal Statistical Society*, May, 1922, vol. lxxxv, pp. 412-459. The quotation is from p. 452.

[8] Ellsworth Huntington, *World-Power and Evolution*. New Haven, 1919, chapters ii-iv. The passages cited are on pp. 29 and 42.

much of the raw materials shall be produced. In a period of prosperity, the organic industries dependent upon uncertain harvests for their supplies may be unable to keep pace with the inorganic trades, which are being rapidly expanded by heavy investments of capital. There results a disturbance of the proportion which must be maintained in the production of the two types of goods, if the current supplies of both types are to find a profitable market. The modern crisis, therefore, is at bottom the result of a clash between the workings of physical and economic processes.[9] *

2. Uncertainty.

Of the theories which trace business cycles to economic rather than physical conditions, the simplest is that which develops Sismondi's indictment of prices as guides to production. A fresh statement of this familiar idea is given by Dr. Charles O. Hardy of the Institute of Economics in his book on *Risk and Risk-Bearing*.

The business man's "principal devices for securing a balanced output," Dr. Hardy points out, "are prices and advance orders." Both are fallible guides.

Prices and orders give information concerning the prospective state of demand compared with the known facts of present and future supply, but they give no clue to the changes in supply which they are themselves likely to cause.

This situation results in "a tendency to alternations of over- and under-production." When prices and orders indicate an expansion of demand,

the tendency is for an increasing number of persons to try to take advantage of the situation, each more or less in ignorance of the other's plans, and no force intervenes to check the continued increase of production till it reflects itself in declining orders and falling prices. By that time, however, investments have been made, contracts let, and operations started which will result in further augmentation of the supply. Time is required to check this increase in the volume of production, and during this time production outruns consumption unless

[9] See Werner Sombart, "Die Störungen im deutschen Wirtschaftsleben während der Jahre 1900 ff." *Schriften des Vereins für Sozialpolitik*, September, 1903, vol. cxiii, pp. 130-133.

* The keynesian analysis of this problem is found on pp. 330-1 of the General Theory.

consumption is stimulated by unprofitably low prices. Moreover, just as was the case on the upswing, the indications that production is being overdone result in curtailment of operations by independent producers in ignorance of each other's intentions, and this tendency continues till output is decreased to a rate below that which is economically justified.

Speculative purchases and sales form a quite independent cause of cyclical fluctuations in business, reënforcing the first cause. For the speculators must base their judgments on substantially the same data as the producers. Hence their operations grow rapidly in prosperity and shrink rapidly in depression.

The effect of this tendency to mass movements of buying and selling is greatly to accentuate the effect of the producers' uncertainty concerning one another's plans. . . . For an increase in middlemen's stocks gives the producers *twice* a false index of the amount of production which is economically justifiable. When the increase in buying takes place it swells the volume of orders and creates a false appearance of expansion in the market, and whenever the excess stock is utilized it again gives a false indication, this time of contraction in the market.

At bottom, then, business cycles result from

uncertainty, chiefly uncertainty on the part of producers and middlemen concerning the conditions that will prevail in the market when they are ready to dispose of their goods.[1]

3. The Emotional Factor in Business Decisions.

Everyone recognizes the uncertainties with which business men must contend in planning their operations; but most writers on business cycles hold that uncertainty merely provides opportunity for the working of other factors to which they attach greater significance. One of these factors is the "psychological," or more accurately, the emotional influences which warp business judgment. The best exposition along this line is that given by Professor A. C. Pigou of Cambridge University. In his opinion "the movement of business confi-

---

[1] Charles O. Hardy, *Risk and Risk-Bearing*, Chicago, 1923, chapter v. The passages quoted are on pp. 72-75.

Dr. Hardy's exposition may be regarded as an elaborated form of "the competition theory" set forth by Sir William H. Beveridge in *Unemployment, a Problem of Industry*, London, 1908, 2d ed., 1910, chapter iv.

dence" is "the dominant cause of the rhythmic fluctuations that are experienced in industry": "optimistic error and pessimistic error, when discovered, give birth to one another in an endless chain."

After stating the conditions which make it difficult to avoid errors in planning production, Professor Pigou attacks the problem why the majority of these errors run in the same direction, instead of cancelling each other. It is at this point that his explanation diverges from the path that contents Dr. Hardy. While the latter relies upon the similarity of the price and order data used by producers and by speculators to account for the similarity of their errors, Professor Pigou has recourse to waves of elation and discouragement which sweep over the business community.

> Let us suppose the business world to be in a neutral position, not suffering from either type of error. On this situation there supervenes some real cause for increase in the demand for business activity.

Then, because business men cannot foresee the results which will be produced by their own and other men's response to the stimulus, errors of the optimistic type will begin to be made. But why should these errors multiply so rapidly and grow so huge?

> When an error of optimism has been generated, (Professor Pigou answers) it tends to spread and grow, as a result of reactions between different parts of the business community. This comes about through two principal influences. First, experience suggests that, apart altogether from the financial ties by which different business men are bound together, there exists among them a certain measure of psychological interdependence. A change of tone in one part of the business world diffuses itself, in a quite unreasoning manner, over other and wholly disconnected parts. . . . Secondly . . . an error of optimism on the part of one group of business men itself creates a justification for some improved expectation on the part of other groups.

Thus the optimistic error once born grows in scope and magnitude.

But since the prosperity has been built largely upon error, a day of reckoning must come. This day does not dawn until after a time long enough to construct new industrial equipment on a large scale, to bring the products of the new equipment to market, and to find that they cannot be disposed of promptly at profitable prices. Then the past miscalculation becomes patent—patent to creditors as well as to debtors, and the creditors apply pressure for repayment. Thus prosperity ends in a crisis. The error of optimism dies in the crisis, but in dying it

> gives birth to an error of pessimism. This new error is born, not an infant, but a giant; for an industrial boom has necessarily been a period of strong emotional excitement, and an excited man passes from one form of excitement to another more rapidly than he passes to quiescence.

Under the influence of the new error, business is unduly depressed. For a time there is relatively slow extension of facilities for production. In consequence,

> a general shortage of a number of important commodities gradually makes itself apparent, and those persons who have them to sell are seen to be earning a good real return. Thereupon, certain of the bolder spirits in industry see an opportunity and seize it.

Business begins to pick up slowly and gradually.

> The first year or two, say, is taken up with a wholly justified expansion. But, after the first year or two, further expansion represents, not a correction of the past error, but the creation of a new one.

And the new error grows until it has betrayed business men into courses which end in a fresh crisis.[1]

Professor Pigou represents waves of elation and depression as arising from changes in the business situation, changes which are magnified into business cycles by the emotions they excite. Dr. Maurice Beck Hexter, Director of the Federated Jewish Charities of Boston, has thrown out the suggestion that these waves of feeling have an origin independent of the business world.

By an elaborate statistical analysis of vital and economic data, Dr. Hexter has reached the conclusion that

[1] A. C. Pigou, *The Economics of Welfare*, 1st ed., London, 1920, Part vi, chapter vi. The quotations are from pp. 833, 839, 840, 843 and 844. In companion chapters, Professor Pigou shows how the results of the "dominant cause" are modified by other factors, such as harvest fluctuations, and the workings of the monetary system. Professor Pigou has dropped this discussion from his second edition, hoping to incorporate it "in the next year or two" in "a study of industrial fluctuations." See preface of the 2d ed., 1924.

. . . fluctuations in conceptions *precede* fluctuations in wholesale prices by about eight months; fluctuations in the birth-
rate *precede* fluctuations in unemployment by about seventeen
months . . . fluctuations in the death-rate *precede* fluctuations in wholesale prices about seventeen months; and . . .
fluctuations in the death-rate *precede* fluctuations in unemployment by about ten months.

A causal explanation of these relations is suggested by the powerful emotional reactions excited in men by the death of friends and
the prospect of having children. Dr. Hexter argues thus:

Business enterprise is the application of mental effort to the
transformation of our physical environment. Anything which
affects the emotions of men must necessarily affect their ability
to make decisions, anticipate decisions, or postpone decisions.
If these times of postponed decisions or accelerated judgments
or stimulated efforts are not isolated, but, on the contrary,
run in wave-like movements, we think that there may be something to (*sic*) the suggestion that varying birth-rates and
fluctuating death-rates can and do affect business cycles. The
errors of optimism and the errors of pessimism may be closely
connected with these variations in human emotions. It may
very well be that these waves of emotion which run through
society from time to time are very closely related to these
variations in births and deaths.[2]

It will be noticed that Dr. Hexter's hypothesis is related to Professor Huntington's quite as closely as to Professor Pigou's. But
Hexter differs from Huntington in that he does not seek to connect
fluctuations in vital statistics with fluctuations in the weather.

4. Innovations, Promotion, Progress.

Professor Joseph Schumpeter of Bonn holds that to explain business cycles by errors bred of uncertainty and nourished by mass
psychology is superficial. That errors are made, that they wax with
prosperity, and that they play a considerable rôle in the cycle he
admits; but, he adds, crises and depressions would continue to run
their round if miscalculation were eliminated.

The fundamental cause of business fluctuations Schumpeter finds

[2] Maurice B. Hexter, *Social Consequences of Business Cycles*. Boston and New York.
1925, Part ii. The quotations are from pp. 169, 174 and 175.

in the innovations made from time to time by the relatively small number of exceptionally energetic business men—their practical applications of scientific discoveries and mechanical inventions, their development of new forms of industrial and commercial organization, their introduction of unfamiliar products, their conquests of new markets, exploitation of new resources, shiftings of trade routes, and the like. Changes of this sort, when made on a large scale, alter the data on which the mass of routine business men have based their plans. These plans doubtless involve a certain element of error; but business innovations produce a far graver situation.

Somehow, all enterprises must adapt themselves to the novel conditions now confronting them, or go to the wall. Considerable numbers do fail. A far larger number manage to work out new plans based on the new data concerning prices, costs, methods and markets. But this process of feeling out the novel conditions and making adjustments to them takes time. While the readjusting is under way, the making of innovations slows down; even the most restless of enterprisers cannot get the capital and coöperation required to carry out their schemes. This is the period of depression. It lasts until the readjustments have gone far enough to produce a fairly stable condition of affairs, stable enough to let men regain confidence in the future.

But the very restoration of quasi-stability makes it possible for the disturbers of the business peace to resume operations on a large scale. By borrowing for their new projects the innovators raise interest rates; by investing capital they raise the prices of industrial equipment and increase payroll disbursements. There follows an increase of demand and a rise in the prices of consumers' goods. The general activity thus initiated brings prosperity to the mass of enterprises—and stimulates further innovations. Prosperity continues until the unsettling consequences of the business changes begin to appear *en masse* in the shape of large supplies flooding the market, high costs of materials and labor, shifting of demand to new products, the supersession of old sources of production by new sources, and so on. Then comes a new crisis and a new period of readjustments.

To complete this theory it is necessary to show why innovations themselves come in waves. Schumpeter explains that the combination of capacities required for conceiving new undertakings and carrying them through all obstacles and hazards is rare among men; but that when a few highly endowed individuals have achieved success, their example makes the way easier for a crowd of imitators. The rising prices, the increasing demand, the spread of optimism make borrowers more eager and lenders less cautious. Men who do not have the capacity to originate new schemes may have the wit to profit by and even improve upon the work of the pioneers. So, once started, a wave of innovation gains momentum—until it is checked by the consequences which it produces.[1]

The "promotion theory" of business cycles, developed by Professor Minnie T. England of the University of Nebraska, rests upon the same foundations as Schumpeter's theory of innovations. While less complete in its formal logic, Mrs. England's exposition runs in more realistic terms and cites more evidence. It should be studied by those who feel that Schumpeter's sketch lacks substance.[2]

While Mrs. England represents promoters and Professor Schumpeter represents a less specialized group of innovators as responsible for business crises, Dr. Emanuel H. Vogel, late of Vienna University, lays the responsibility upon "progress" at large.

In his eyes, crises are accidents which are bound to happen every now and then in a growing society based on private enterprise. For when such a society is expanding year after year, prosperity requires the maintenance of an economic equilibrium which is itself moving. The rates at which the important industries are growing must be kept in adjustment to each other; so also must the rates at which the incomes of all classes of the people and their consumption of goods are growing.

Such a consummation of adjustment, Dr. Vogel argues, is thinkable only in a society whose changes are always in the same direction and at the same pace. It is not thinkable in a society whose fortunes are represented by an ascending saw-toothed curve. We know that expansion at a constant rate never continues unbroken long at a

[1] Dr. Schumpeter's first version of this theory was published in May, 1910: "Ueber das Wesen der Wirtschaftskrisen," *Zeitschrift für Volkswirtschaft, Sozialpolitik und Verwaltung*, vol. xix, p. 271. Successive revisions appear in his *Theorie der wirtschaftlichen Entwicklung*, Leipzig, 1912, chapter vi; "Die Wellenbewegung des Wirtschaftslebens," *Archiv für Sozialwissenschaft und Sozialpolitik*, July, 1914, vol. xxxix, pp. 1-32, and in the second edition of his *Theorie der wirtschaftlichen Entwicklung*, Munich and Leipzig, 1926, chapter vi. This latest version includes replies to several critics of the theory, and is written in the most emphatic tone.

[2] See "Fisher's Theory of Crises," *Quarterly Journal of Economics*, November, 1912, vol. xxvii, pp. 95-106; "Promotion as the Cause of Crises," the same, August, 1915, vol. xxix, pp. 631-641; "Economic Crises," *Journal of Political Economy*, April, 1913, vol. xxi, pp. 345-354; "An Analysis of the Crisis Cycle," the same, October, 1913, vol. xxi, pp. 712-734.

time; every community experiences setbacks which check its economic progress. Unfavorable political events, mistaken forecasts of the future, the disturbances caused by improvements in technical methods, discoveries of new sources of supply, alterations in consumers' tastes, suggest how various are the factors which are changing the pace of growth and occasionally causing shrinkage.

Irregularities of change, then, are rooted deep in modern economic organization. And to these irregularities it is quite impossible that all the different rates of growth should adjust themselves promptly and in such a way as to maintain among themselves a moving equilibrium. A serious rupture of equilibrium produces an economic crisis followed by a period of declining activity. Gradually men work out a fresh series of adjustments, equilibrium is re-established, and progress resumes its course until something new happens to which the rates of growth cannot adjust themselves without losing adjustment to each other.[3]

5. The Processes of Saving and Investing.

One of the explanations of crises most in favor among business men is that they are caused by "scarcity of capital." Investments during prosperity are so heavy that the supply of loan funds is gradually exhausted. When this stage is reached, borrowers are unable to complete their financing and the boom ends in a crisis. This idea has been elaborated by Professor Michel Tugan-Baranovski, whose Russian treatise of 1894 has been repeatedly revised and translated into French and German.

It is necessary to distinguish, Tugan-Baranovski begins, between loan funds and capital invested in production. The loan fund is the aggregate of savings made by individuals belonging to all classes, and by business enterprises. During depressions the savings of business enterprises, business men, stockholders and wage-earners decline. But there is an important class of savers whose incomes are little affected by depression—landlords, bond-holders, salaried officials; indeed their savings are augmented by the lower cost of living. Thus saving continues on a large scale during depression, and (the vital point) if the aggregate declines below the records of prosperity, it certainly declines less than does investing. Hence depression brings

[3] *Die Theorie des volkswirtschaftlichen Entwickelungsprozesses und das Krisenproblem.* By Dr. Emanuel Hugo Vogel. Vienna and Leipzig, 1917.

the gradual accumulation of a huge uninvested fund of loan capital. Evidence of this accumulation appears in the swollen bank reserves and in the low rates of interest and bank discount.

Of course, the reason why these savings are not invested as they are made is found in the disorganized state of business. Few business men wish to borrow on a large scale during depression. But let savers become eager enough to get their funds into profitable use, let the rates of interest which they will accept drop low enough, the dam behind which the loan fund has been accumulating will give way, and money will begin to flow into investment.

When this time comes the huge purchases made with borrowed loan funds bring prosperity. Stimulated by its own effects, investment keeps expanding and presently attains a scale so large as to exceed current savings. Hence the uninvested loan fund is gradually exhausted. When the point of exhaustion is neared, available capital becomes so scarce that pending plans for further business extensions cannot be financed. Interest rates rise to prohibitive levels, bank reserves drop to the danger point, the makers of industrial equipment get no new orders, and prosperity ends in a crisis.[1]

While giving the preceding account of the process by which crises are bred periodically, Tugan-Baranovski holds that the alternate accumulation and exhaustion of the loan fund could not occur were income more evenly distributed.

> It is the inadequate remuneration of labor . . . which is the fundamental cause of the rapid accumulation of social capital, which in its turn provokes crises.[2]

This is the idea which an English publicist, Mr. John A. Hobson, has developed into the theory that business cycles are due to "over-saving" —a theory quite different from Tugan-Baranovski's.

Mr. Hobson holds that at any given time

> there is an exact proportion of the current income which, in accordance with existing arts of production and existing foresight, is required to set up new capital so as to make provision for the maximum consumption throughout the near future.

---

[1] The latest exposition known to me is the French edition of Tugan-Baranovski's treatise, *Les Crises Industrielles en Angleterre*, traduit par Joseph Schapiro (Bibliothèque Internationale d'Économie Politique), Paris, 1913. See especially Part II.

[2] The same, p. 279.

If in a period of prosperity, the rate of consumption should rise *pari passu* with the rate of production, there is no inherent reason why the prosperity might not continue indefinitely. But in modern societies, a large portion of the wealth produced belongs to a small class. In active times their incomes rise more rapidly than their consumption, and the surplus income is perforce saved. There results for the community as a whole a slight deficiency of spending and a corresponding excess of saving. The wealthy class seeks to invest its new savings in productive enterprises—thereby increasing the supply of goods and also increasing the incomes from which further savings will be made. This process runs cumulatively during the years of prosperity until finally the markets become congested with goods which cannot be sold at a profit. Then prices fall, liquidation ensues, capital is written down, and the incomes of the wealthy class are so reduced that savings fall below the proper proportion to spending.

During the period of depression, the glut of goods weighing upon the market is gradually worked off and the prospect of profitable investment slowly returns. Savings rise again to the right proportion to spending and good times prevail for a season. But after a while the chronic impulse toward over-saving becomes fully operative once more; soon or late it begets another congestion of the markets, and this congestion begets another depression.

Proximately then, the cause of alternating prosperity and depression is the tendency toward over-saving; ultimately it is the existence of the surplus incomes which lead to over-saving.[1]

[1] Mr. Hobson has presented his theory in several books, but most fully in *The Industrial System*, London, 1909, chapters iii and xviii, and in *Economics of Unemployment*, London, 1922. The passage quoted is from p. 53 of the earlier volume.

Another form of the savings theory is presented by Mr. N. Johannsen. The act of saving by itself, means the withdrawal of purchasing power from the market, and so always tends to produce business depression. But when the sums saved are promptly invested "in the creation of new productive capital," the deficiency of purchasing power is offset, and the community's wealth is increased. No such offsetting occurs, however, when savings are used to buy property from embarrassed owners, or loaned to people in distress. Those who get the money expend it; but their expenditures merely offset their own losses, and the withdrawal of purchasing power caused by the act of saving is not compensated for. Whether saving tends to sustain prosperity or to cause depression thus "depends upon the manner of investment." "Impair savings," as Mr. Johannsen calls savings which are not used to create new capital, "always hurt business, and if sufficiently large, they cause a general depression." See N. Johannsen, *A Neglected Point in Connection with Crises*, New York, 1908, and *Business Depressions: Their Cause. A Discovery in Economics*, Stapleton, New York, 1925.

Dr. Rudolf Stucken of the University of Kiel argues in a somewhat similar vein that, if a period of expansion in business activity is checked for any reason, savings will not be invested in productive enterprises, but used to repay bank loans. The immediate result is to reduce the purchasing power offered for goods below the current supply seeking sale, and so to convert the check upon expansion into a contraction.

6. Construction Work.

Among the numerous theorists who have been influenced by Tugan-Baranovski are writers who have sought to show what his

But the reduction of bank loans, and the concomitant reduction of demand liabilities enables the banks to increase their credit advances to business men liberally when a revival begins, and thus to convert revival into prosperity. See Rudolf Stucken, *Theorie der Konjunkturschwankungen,* Jena, 1926.

While Mr. D. H. Robertson cannot be classified with the savings theorists, since he believes that other factors have a leading share in producing cyclical oscillations in trade, the most notable feature of his recent book on *Banking Policy and the Price Level,* (London, 1926), is an analysis of the role played by savings in "trade cycles." For this analysis he invents a curious terminology.

"The essence of the activity of providing capital" is "Lacking." "A man is lacking if during a given period he consumes less than the value of his current economic output. . . . The amount of Lacking done in a given period may be measured by the volume of consumable goods lacked. . . . The things in the provision of which Lacking eventuates I propose to call Capital. . . . Long Lacking is directed towards providing society with the use . . . of the fixed and durable instruments of production: Short Lacking towards" providing society with the use of circulating capital, which, like fixed capital, consists of commodities. (Pp. 40-42.)

Equipped with these definitions, Mr. Robertson argues:

"From our present point of view, the fundamental feature of the upward swing of a trade cycle is a large and discontinuous increase in the demand for Short Lacking, occurring as the essential preliminary to an expansion of output . . . the supply of (Spontaneous) Short Lacking is not sufficiently elastic to cope with such pronounced and discontinuous increases in demand, and . . . the responsibility for meeting them rests almost entirely upon the banking-system (Pp. 71, 72) . . . Now the banking-system can, of course, only 'provide' . . . Short Lacking . . . by extorting it from the general public through the multiplication of currency." (Pp. 88, 89.)

The meaning seems to be that current output cannot be expanded freely in a period of prosperity unless there has been an increase in the commodities which constitute circulating capital; that these commodities cannot be provided in sufficient quantity unless the general public is prevented from increasing its consumption as fast as output rises, and that the banks put the necessary brake upon consumption by raising prices through an increase of the currency.

Mr. Robertson holds that most periods of prosperity bring also a rapid increase in the demand for fixed capital, and therefore for the Long Lacking which provides it. Part of this demand is met by investors, but part falls on the banks. The latter can provide Long Lacking only by the means which they use to provide Short Lacking, that is, they must extort Long Lacking from the public by expanding the currency and raising prices. (Pp. 84-89).

But the rise of prices through which the banks extort Lacking, Short and Long, from the public increases the money value of the circulating and fixed capital required by business enterprises, and therefore makes necessary a greater rise of prices. Obviously a self-inflating process of this sort cannot be sustained indefinitely. To keep the process under control, the banks raise interest rates, sell government securities, and, at need, limit new money loans. Despite the skill which modern banking-systems have acquired in promoting equilibrium between the demand for and supply of Lacking, many crises are still characterized by what is popularly called "an acute shortage of capital," and what is properly called "a deficiency in the activity Lacking." (Pp. 79, 90).

I offer this interpretation of Mr. Robertson's analysis with a diffidence which readers of his book will understand. It is certainly incomplete; I hope it is not wrong.

analysis of savings means in terms of production. By so doing they have shifted the emphasis from over-saving to over-production of one type of goods in comparison with another type. This variant of business-cycle theory is represented in Germany by Professor Arthur Spiethoff of the University of Berlin; [1] but it will suffice to cite the less technical exposition given by Mr. George H. Hull, an American business man.

High prices of construction, runs Hull's thesis, is the hitherto "unknown cause of the mysterious depressions" from which the industrial nations suffer. The greater part of modern trade fluctuates within relatively narrow limits. Agriculture provides the necessities of life, commerce distributes them, and finance adjusts the bills. The volume of all this business is fairly constant, because the demand for necessities is incapable of sudden expansion or contraction. Industry, on the contrary, may expand or contract indefinitely, especially that part of industry devoted to construction work. For the sources of booms and depressions, therefore, we must look to the enterprises which build and equip houses, stores, factories, railways, docks, and the like.

Of the huge total of construction, which Mr. Hull believes to make "say 77 per cent of all industrial products of the nation" after "deducting land and the necessities of life," about two-thirds, even in the busiest of years, consists of repairs, replacements, and such extensions as are required by the growth of population. This portion of construction is necessary and must be executed every year. But the remaining portion is "optional construction," and is undertaken or not according as investors see a liberal or a meager profit in providing new building and equipment.

When the costs of construction fall low enough to arouse "the bargain-counter instinct," many of the "far-seeing ones who hold the purse-strings of the country" let heavy contracts, and their example is followed by the less shrewd. The addition of this new business to the volume of "necessity construction" and the provision of consumers' goods, creates a boom. But, after a year or two, con-

---

[1] Professor Spiethoff published his analysis in a series of articles in Schmoller's *Jahrbuch für Gesetzgebung,* 1902, pp. 721-759; 1903, pp. 670-708; 1909, pp. 445-467, 927-951, 1417-1437. See also Spiethoff's article "Krisen" in the 4th edition of the *Handwörterbuch der Staatswissenschaften,* Jena, 1925, vol. vi, pp. 8-91. Mr. Dennis H. Robertson has developed a theory of "constructional relapse" which runs on similar lines. See *A Study of Industrial Fluctuation,* London, 1915, pp. 170-198.

A summary of Spiethoff's theory may be found in the earlier edition of this book, pp. 10, 11.

tractors discover that their order books call for more work than they can get labor and materials to finish within the contract time. When this oversold condition of the contracting trades is realized, the prices of labor and raw materials rise rapidly. The estimated cost of construction on new contracts then becomes excessive. Shrewd investors therefore begin to postpone the execution of their plans for extending permanent equipment, and the letting of fresh contracts declines apace. While the contractors are gradually completing work on their old orders, all the enterprises making iron, steel, lumber, cement, brick, stone, etc., begin to suffer a serious shrinkage of new business. Just as the execution of the large contracts for "optional construction," let in the low-price period, brought on prosperity, so the smallness of such contracts, let in the high-price period, now brings on depression. Then the costs of construction work fall until they arouse "the bargain-counter instinct" of investors once more, and the cycle begins afresh.[2]

Colonel Malcolm C. Rorty has suggested that the over-construction theory should be expanded into an "over-commitment" theory, and strengthened by analysis of financial processes. At an early stage in many periods of prosperity, he points out, simultaneous over-commitments to business extensions and new ventures are made in most, if not in all, branches of industry. Each such commitment involves the creation, through credit extensions, of new purchasing power. Since the additional purchasing power is not offset promptly by a corresponding increase in production, prices rise. This process of extending commitments, expanding credit and raising prices continues until it is checked by shortage of credit facilities, or until prices have reached a level at which experienced business men see danger in making further additions to their stocks of goods. Then comes a contraction of purchases, and a crisis.

Such are the essential features of a typical boom and crisis, arising from causes inherent in the business organization. But Colonel Rorty adds that we have cycles of two other types. The milder periods of prosperity and recession arise from mere current readjustments of production, distribution and consumption. Still other cycles arise primarily from non-business causes, such as wars. Admitting that sometimes it is difficult to decide to which of these three types a

[2] George H. Hull, *Industrial Depressions*, New York, 1911. The passages quoted are from pp. 103-107.

given case belongs, Colonel Rorty holds that this classification clarifies the problem, and explains why no one theory accounts in satisfactory fashion for all cycles.[3]

7. GENERALIZED OVER-PRODUCTION.

The emphasis which Spiethoff and Hull put upon the difference between the rôles played by industrial equipment and consumers' goods in business cycles has become a commonplace in later writings. Two theorists in particular have developed this idea, and in developing it have reached results which differ sharply from those of Tugan-Baranovski and Hull. Against the first they contend that there is and can be no accumulation of uninvested loan-capital; against the second they contend that crises result from a general, not a partial over-production of goods, and that the seat of difficulty is in the industries making consumers' goods rather than in those making industrial equipment. Mentor Bouniatian, professor at the Polytechnic Institute of Tiflis was perhaps the earlier to publish; but the clearer exposition has been supplied by Albert Aftalion, professor at the University of Paris.[1]

When the price level rises after a period of depression—why it should rise will appear later—business men see that current demand for consumers' goods is larger than current supply at the old prices. To secure their shares of the good profits in prospect, manufacturers enlarge the volume of their orders for industrial equipment. These orders increase employment, thus stimulate consumers' demand, and so encourage the placing of still larger orders for equipment.

To construct the equipment which is typical of modern industry, however, requires months and often years. Hence a considerable time must pass before notable additions can be made to the current supply

[3] See M. C. Rorty, *Some Problems in Current Economics*, Chicago, 1922, pp. 73-84, and the report of Colonel Rorty's address to the National Founders Association, in *The Iron Age*, November 25, 1926, pp. 1478-1482.

[1] On the relations between the ideas of these two writers see the preface of *Les Crises Économiques*, par Mentor Bouniatian, Traduit du Russe, (Moscow, 1915) par J. Bernard (Bibliothèque Internationale d'Économie Politique), Paris, 1922. Bouniatian's first book on the subject was *Wirtschaftskrisen und Ueberkapitalisation*, Munich, 1908. Aftalion published first a series of articles on "La réalité des surproductions générales" in the *Révue d'Economie Politique*, 1908-09 (vol. xxii, pp. 696-706; vol. xxiii, pp. 81-117, 201-229, 241-259); then an *Essai d'une théorie des crises générales et périodiques*, Paris, 1909, and finally a treatise, *Les Crises périodiques de Surproduction*, 2 vols., Paris, 1913.

of consumers' goods. During this "period of gestation,"[2] the supply of consumers' goods continues inadequate, prices keep advancing, employment grows fuller, large incomes are disbursed and prosperity reigns.

After prosperity has grown at an increasing pace for some time, however, large quantities of new equipment are ready for use and the current supply of consumers' goods is augmented. Then trouble begins. For, according to "the laws of value," these increments added to the supply of consumers' goods cannot be sold at prices such as have recently prevailed. When the supply of any commodity increases, the wants satisfied by consuming new increments are less intense than the marginal wants recently satisfied. The later days of prosperity are therefore characterized by a decline in the marginal utility of consumers' goods. This decline brings with it a reduction in the prices consumers are willing to pay—a fall which is rendered greater by the concomitant rise in the marginal utility of money, caused by the increasing demands upon the circulating medium made by active trade. Presently it becomes clear that general over-production prevails. The fall of prices extends from one field to another and prosperity ends in a crisis.

General over-production accompanied by a declining price level lasts for a year or so after the crisis, because the new equipment has cost so much money that it must be kept running, if that is anywise possible. Indeed, over-production increases for a time, since part of the equipment ordered in the latter part of the boom is not finished until after the crisis, and when it is delivered it must be made to give some return upon the capital locked up in it. The fall of prices is now opposed by a decline in the marginal utility of money, which is less needed in depression; but the decline in the marginal utility of consumers' goods more than offsets this factor.

Recovery from depression comes after three or four years, because, while prices are falling, there is little inducement to order new equipment. It is true that some new orders are placed even in the

[2] The phrase is borrowed from Mr. D. H. Robertson, who has developed this point more fully than Aftalion or Bouniatian. In particular Mr. Robertson suggests that the recurrence of business cycles may be due in large part to the more or less simultaneous wearing-out and re-ordering of large masses of equipment made in an earlier period of prosperity. See *A Study of Industrial Fluctuation*, pp. 13-25, London, 1915.

Professor Pigou, who also makes much of the "period of gestation," ventures the statement that "ten years seem to be, not merely the average, but also the markedly predominant" length of life of machinery. *The Economics of Welfare*, 1st ed., pp. 827-830, 841-848.

worst of times; but the volume shrinks greatly in comparison with that of the preceding period of prosperity. Meanwhile the demand for consumers' goods continues to grow, though at a slightly slower pace than in prosperity. Let this situation persist for a few years, and gradually the current demand for consumers' goods at the low prices which depression causes will come to exceed current supply. When this happens, prices turn upward again. Then business men seek to increase their output and begin ordering equipment more freely. But while their orders are being executed, the current supply of consumers' goods becomes scantier in comparison with the growing demand, prices rise further, and another period of prosperity dawns.

8. Banking Operations.

All the explanations summarized in the preceding sections take for granted that the processes which they trace run in communities equipped with modern monetary and banking systems. From their viewpoints, however, money and bank credit are simply mechanisms through which the economic forces causing business cycles work their effects. At most these theories admit that the monetary mechanism accentuates the wave movements which are started by more fundamental factors.[1] The explanations which make business cycles a direct consequence of banking operations therefore constitute a distinct variety of cycle theories.

No one has contented himself with a briefer statement of the reason for adopting this type of explanation than Professor Alvin H. Hansen of the University of Minnesota.

Demand, (he argues), is based on purchasing power. The source of purchasing power is income, and the source of income is the production of material goods and services. . . . In short, goods and services are exchanged against goods and services. On this basis one would expect production to run an even course, and not to run in cycles. And indeed in the barter economy there were no business cycles.

But how does the rise of money economy produce cyclical oscillations? Under modern conditions, Professor Hansen answers,

[1] See, for example, Professor Pigou's chapter on "Accentuation of Wave Movements due to the Working of the Monetary System." *The Economics of Welfare*, 1st ed., pp. 849-864, and Mr. Robertson's chapter on "The Wage and Money Systems," *A Study of Industrial Fluctuation*, pp. 206-238.

The nominal purchasing power obtaining in any society at any given moment may be measured substantially by the amount of money in hand-to-hand circulation and the volume of bank credit in the form of deposit currency.

The amount of purchasing power, and therefore of demand, made available by the banks is limited

by two things: first, by the quantity of reserves; second, by the desirability of converting personal credit into bank credit, and this depends upon the discount rate and the profitableness of the employment of capital in industry.

Plainly neither these limits themselves nor the closeness with which they are approached is fixed; hence the purchasing power which the banks provide can fluctuate through a wide range.

When the banks increase nominal purchasing power by granting more credit, they add to the circulating media.

The effect is an increase in prices and therefore no increase in real purchasing power. The nominal incomes of people generally are as before, but their real purchasing power is reduced because of the increase in prices. The issuance of bank credit simply redistributes purchasing power, reducing the real purchasing power of income receivers generally, and increasing the purchasing power of entrepreneurs able to secure bank credit. It is this redistribution of purchasing power, accomplished through the instrumentality of banking institutions, that changes demand, upsets prices, affects the profit margin, and therefore production. Here, in short, may be found the fundamental cause of the business cycle.

To complete the theory, it is necessary to follow the round of events:

When accumulated stocks have run out, when costs are falling, when labor is easily obtainable, when loanable funds are plentiful and interest rates run low, then prospects for profit-making are bright and entrepreneurs apply for bank credit. The issuance of bank credit increases the purchasing power of entrepreneurs. The result is increased bidding for raw materials, capital equipment, construction work, etc., with a consequent increase in prices.

The business men, who profit by the increased demand, in their turn apply for bank loans and so the process runs expansively for a time. "This upward movement comes to a close only when bank credit can no longer be further extended, for the reason that it has already reached the limit of banking safety." But this limit can hardly be reached without being overrun; for the activity of trade causes more money to be drawn into hand-to-hand circulation, at the expense of bank reserves. "It therefore becomes necessary not merely to stop the expansion of bank credit, but actually to reduce the outstanding volume." The resulting contraction causes prices to fall, the volume of business to shrink, and the demand for bank credit itself to slacken —once more a self-propagating process.

> But as the upward movement culminated because of the strain placed upon bank reserves through an undue extension of bank credit, so the downward movement comes to a close because of the great accumulation of bank reserves due to the reduction of outstanding bank credit and the return of money from hand-to-hand circulation following the decline of prices. This continued accumulation of reserves leads bankers progressively to lower discount rates to a point low enough to make the employment of bank credit again profitable. New securities are freely issued, bank loans are readily obtainable, and the purchasing power of business enterprises increases. Thus the upward swing returns and the cycle repeats itself.[2]

Like Professor Hansen, Mr. R. G. Hawtrey of the British Treasury thinks he has "proved that there is an inherent tendency toward fluctuations in the banking institutions which prevail in the world as it is." But Hawtrey lays more stress than Hansen upon the importance of changes in discount rates.

"An expansion of trade occurs," Mr. Hawtrey explains, "when the amount of credit money in existence is less than the bankers think prudent, having regard to their holdings of cash, and they lower the rate of interest in order to encourage borrowing." This reduction in the cost of loans starts a long train of consequences: dealers give larger orders to producers, producers increase output and raise prices, employment becomes fuller and wages rise, the increase of incomes augments retail demand, the prosperous business classes borrow more

---

[2] *Cycles of Prosperity and Depression in the United States, Great Britain and Germany*, by Alvin H. Hansen (University of Wisconsin Studies in the Social Sciences and History, No. 5). Madison, 1921. The quotations are from pp. 104-108.

freely—and so on progressively, until the banks, having lent all the credit they think prudent,

> no longer need to keep down the rate of interest. The rate of interest is then raised to the "profit rate," and the inducement (for dealers) to increase stocks of goods is removed.

Trade expansion is followed by trade depression, because the high rates of interest tempt the banks to lend as much as possible. For a time they can expand loans without losing much cash; but when the lagging rise of wage rates gets under way, bank reserves are reduced. Further, high prices are likely to stimulate imports, check exports and so cause an outflow of gold from the country enjoying prosperity. When their reserves decline appreciably, the banks are forced to contract outstanding loans. For this purpose they raise the rate of interest still further and withdraw funds loaned on the investment market. Then securities fall and dealers in commodities seek to reduce stocks on which the carrying charge has become heavy. They give fewer orders to producers; producers decrease output and cut down their working forces; retail demand falls off; stocks threaten to become redundant again because of fewer sales, and the process starts all over again. During this period of depression business men need less credit and the reduced wage disbursements allow cash to accumulate in the banks. Thus the banks win back to an easy condition, and "no longer need to keep up the rate of interest." By the fall in interest rates the way is prepared for a new expansion of trade.[3]

[3] *Good and Bad Trade. An Inquiry into the Causes of Trade Fluctuations*, by R. G. Hawtrey, London, 1913. The quotations are from pp. 3, 199, 268 and 269.

In a later volume, Mr. Hawtrey seems to have changed his fundamental thesis somewhat. "Far from causing the cyclical fluctuations," he says on p. 425 of *Currency and Credit* (2d ed., London, 1923), "a banking system diminishes their violence and facilitates their control." The "instability of credit" is due "not so much to the banker as to the merchant and the promoter." (p. 423). But he adds, "though credit institutions are not themselves the cause of this phenomenon, yet where such institutions exist it is through them that the fluctuations take effect." (p. 425). For present purposes, it is Mr. Hawtrey's analysis of the process by which cyclical fluctuations come to pass in modern communities, rather than his brief discussion of their causes, which is helpful. To this analysis he adheres in *Currency and Credit* (see p. 130 and chapters ix, x), with minor modifications, of which I have incorporated the most important into my summary made from his *Good and Bad Trade*.

Mr. Hawtrey's theory has much in common with views formerly held by Professor Irving Fisher. But there is a significant difference. Professor Fisher built upon what he believed to be a statistically demonstrated fact that changes in interest rates lag behind price movements. This lag increases the profits of business borrowers when prices are rising and stimulates activity. When prices are falling, the lagging of interest rates reduces profits and augments depression. Mr. Hawtrey, on the other hand, repre-

9. Production and the Flow of Money Incomes.

In a sense, all of the theories so far reviewed are ways of explaining why the people of a country sometimes cannot or will not buy at profitable prices all they produce; or, what comes to the same thing, why they produce more than they can sell.   But the most direct way of solving the problem when stated in this way has still to be noticed.   It consists in giving new reasons for Sismondi's contention that in periods of activity money incomes lag behind the money value of the goods produced. *

The suggestion of Mr. R. E. May introduces the subtle recent theories which follow this line.   May builds upon two corner stones: (1) in a modern industrial community wages form by far the largest of the income streams, (2) wages increase less rapidly in prosperity than the aggregate value of goods produced.   Thus the purchasing power of the most important class of consumers fails to keep pace with the volume of goods seeking sale.   Let the resulting excess of dollar supply over dollar demand accumulate for a year or two, and it is inevitable that the market for consumers' goods will be glutted.   Then come a crisis and depression which restore the body economic to health, by forcing down prices to the point where the wage-earning consumers can buy what is offered.   And Mr. May

sents changes in bank-discount rates as themselves the active force in initiating trade fluctuations, with their concomitant price fluctuations.

For Professor Fisher's theory, see *The Purchasing Power of Money*, New York, 1911, chapters iv and xi, sections 15-17; and "Gold Depreciation and Interest Rates," *Moody's Magazine*, 1909, pp. 110-114 (a summary statement).   As late as December, 1923, Fisher still suspected "that the principal force affecting the cycle is the *real* rate of interest, the sum of the *money* rate of interest and the rate of appreciation (positive or negative) of the purchasing power of the dollar."   (See "The Business Cycle Largely a 'Dance of the Dollar'," *Journal of the American Statistical Association*, vol. xviii, p. 1024). Recently, however, Professor Fisher has come to believe that "the" business cycle is a myth.   Fluctuations in "trade," (which remain genuine in his eyes), are due primarily to "price-change"; but the next most important influence "is probably that of the rate of interest."   See "Our Unstable Dollar and the So-called Business Cycle," *Journal of the American Statistical Association*, June, 1925, vol. xx, pp. 191, 198.

Professor Wilhelm Röpke of Jena has suggested an interesting combination of the savings and the banking theories of business cycles.   The "real cyclical bacillus" he finds in periodic variations in the ratio between accumulation and consumption, which cannot be altered much without producing serious disturbances in the process of exchange.   But these periodic variations in the ratio between accumulation and consumption are due in large part to periodic changes in the volume of credit—changes which appear in discrepancies between the real and the nominal rates of interest, in the liquidity of the credit-granting banks, and in their operating policies.   See his paper on "Kredit und Konjunktur," in *Jahrbücher für Nationalökonomie und Statistik*, March-April, 1926, vol. cxxiv, pp. 243-285.

* The Keynesian explanation will be seen as something which was put in sharper, more precise terms than the thoughts of the economists discussed in this section. Keynes exemplifies Pope's couplet from "The Essay on Criticism":

    True wit is nature to advantage dressed;
    What oft was thought, but ne'er so well expressed

follows the logic of his diagnosis to the point of recommending a legal limitation of profits, in order that producers may be forced to reduce selling prices as they increase output.[1]

A more adequate development of this theme has been provided by Professor Emil Lederer of Heidelberg.

Depression is characterized, he begins, by a decline in physical production and in prices. Though general, the price decline is not uniform. The prices which constitute the incomes of the propertied and salaried classes shrink but little. Nor do wage cuts and unemployment reduce the money incomes of the working masses so much as the cost of living falls. Farmers, also, as a rule lose less than they gain by the price movements. Thus, the discrepancies characteristic of the decline in prices enable consumers to buy perhaps a larger physical quantity of commodities, certainly a larger quota of the current output. Business profits, on the other hand, fall heavily, just because wages, rent and interest charges lag behind the decline of selling prices. The unprofitableness of business, and the consequent reduction of savings check the expansion of industrial equipment. But the increasing purchasing power of the majority of income receivers gradually absorbs whatever stocks of consumers' goods were carried over from the prosperous phase of the cycle in addition to the reduced current output, and so produces a condition which favors a resumption of activity.

A business revival, as it gets under way, reverses the trend of prices. Rising prices and the growing volume of trade call for larger payments. To a limited extent, the increase in payments can be effected by quickening the circulation of money and credit, which had become sluggish during depression. Further expansion may be provided for by additions to the gold supply. Seldom, however, are these resources adequate to the need. Broadly speaking, periods of prosperity are made possible only by "additional credit"—that is, purchasing power, provided chiefly by banks, which is not based upon previous production.

Supported by "additional credit," the advance of prices gains momentum as activity waxes. But the advance is no less unequal than the decline had been. The prices which make up the incomes of the propertied, the salaried, and the wage-earning classes lag

[1] R. E. May, *Das Grundgesetz der Wirtschaftskrisen und ihr Vorbeugensmittel im Zeitalter des Monopols*, Berlin, 1902.

behind the prices of commodities. Hence the buying power of these classes is reduced, or, at least, fails to keep pace with the expansion of output. Meanwhile the lagging of those prices which constitute costs to business enterprises behind the prices which constitute receipts is enhancing profits. Larger profits lead to larger savings, larger investments in industrial equipment, and, when this equipment is ready for use, to larger supplies of consumers' goods, for which the demand is growing less rapidly, if not actually shrinking. Under such circumstances a crisis is inevitable, and a crisis reverses the trend of prices once more, starting the processes with which the analysis began.

According to Lederer, then, the most important cause of business cycles lies in the inequalities characteristic of price movements—inequalities which alter the distribution of purchasing power among income classes, the demand for different types of products, the rate at which industrial equipment grows, and the trend of price movements themselves. "Disproportionality of production" is as characteristic of business fluctuations as "disproportionality of income"; but the two developments have quite different effects. Over-production of certain goods in comparison with others leads to price changes, which affect profits, force alterations in production schedules, and so restore proper balance. "Disproportionality of incomes" is not self-rectifying; its consequences cumulate until they reach the critical point at which they convert depression into prosperity, or prosperity into depression.[2]

Like Professor Lederer, Messrs. Catchings, Foster and Hastings of the Pollak Foundation for Economic Research hold that prosperity is checked by the failure of consumers' incomes to keep pace with the output of consumers' goods. But the Pollak group give an explanation of this deficiency of consumer buying which differs from Lederer's theory of the inequalities in the rates at which different prices advance.

To keep business active, the Pollak theory begins, consumers must receive and spend incomes equal to the full value, at current retail prices, of the consumers' goods sent to market. Were industry confined to providing consumers' goods, this requirement would mean (1) that the total selling value of all products must be paid out

[2] Emil Lederer, "Konjunktur und Krisen," *Grundriss der Sozialökonomik*, Part iv, Section i, Tübingen, 1925, pp. 354-413.

promptly by business enterprises as costs (that is, as wages, salaries, rent, interest, taxes, etc.) or as dividends; (2) that all the money received by individuals must be paid back promptly to business enterprises for their products.

In the real world, of course, many business enterprises make goods which are not offered to consumers, and in so doing disburse incomes to individuals. It may seem that these disbursements, plus the incomes disbursed by industries making consumers' goods, must exceed the value of consumers' goods sent to market. But in so far as producers' goods are raw materials or supplies used up currently in contributing toward the making of consumers' goods, their full selling prices must be charged into the prices of the latter products, and the incomes disbursed for making the materials and supplies can do no more than equal this element in the prices of consumers' goods. There remain some things which consumers are not called upon to buy on completion; for example, public works and industrial equipment. Incomes disbursed in making such goods add to consumer purchasing power without adding an equivalent supply of consumers' goods. In periods of active construction, income payments on this account, plus the payment of wages before products are sent to market, for a time provide consumers with incomes exceeding the supplies of consumers' goods then on sale. Such a situation, however, soon produces consequences which end it. Prices of consumers' goods rise, that rise stimulates production at once, and the difficulty reappears of maintaining consumer purchasing power adequate to absorb the larger output at the higher price level. The difficulty is further accentuated as soon as the new industrial equipment on which men have been working begins adding its quota, directly or indirectly, to the consumers' goods flowing to market.

Thus "overproduction—a supply in excess of demand—is a purely monetary phenomenon," and, as such, might be prevented by monetary adjustments.

If corporations went on forever increasing their output, and, in the process, expanding the volume of money in circulation *at a sufficient rate,* and if the flow of the output to the markets sufficiently lagged behind the flow of the new money as wages to consumers, consumers might continue to buy all that the markets actually offered. Such an expansion of money, however, does not long take place. Business men always fear a slump in demand; and when they doubt the capacity of consumers to buy current output, they have no incentive for increasing output—no motive for using bank loans for that purpose.

But why should not business enterprises pay out the full values received for their products, and thus prevent a deficiency of consumer purchasing power? Because under modern conditions, a thriving enterprise must provide for expansion, and the safest way to finance expansion is "to plough part of the profits into the business." Messrs. Foster and Catchings believe that, on the average, American corporations do not disburse as dividends much over half of their profits. Nor would the situation necessarily be better if corporations paid out all their profits as dividends, and financed their extensions by selling stock to their shareholders. For in that case, consumers would divert income which is needed to sustain the demand for consumers' goods into demand for equipment, in order to make still more consumers' goods in the future. Even as matters stand, consumers are continually saving current income, for reasons as sound as those which justify the financial conservatism of corporations. And their savings are as much responsible for the deficient demand for consumers' goods as is the dividend policy of business enterprises.

To sum up:

Progress toward greater total production and resultant higher standards of living is retarded because consumer buying does not keep pace with production. Consumer buying lags behind for two reasons: first, because, on account of corporate savings industry does not disburse to consumers enough money to buy the goods produced, without a fall in the price-level; second, because consumers, under the necessity of saving, cannot spend even as much money as they receive. Partly on account of these savings, there is not an even flow of money from producer to consumer, and from consumer back to producer. Furthermore, the savings of corporations and individuals are not used to purchase the goods already in the markets, but to bring about the production of more goods. The expansion of the volume of money does not fully make up the deficit, for money is expanded mainly to facilitate production, and the product must be sold to consumers for more money than the expansion has provided. Consequently we make progress only while we are filling the shelves with goods which must either remain on the shelves as stock in trade or be sold at a loss, and while we are building more industrial equipment than we can use. Inadequacy of consumer income is, therefore, the main reason, though not the only reason, why we do not long continue to produce the wealth which natural resources, capital facilities, improvements in the arts and the self-interest of employers and employees would otherwise enable us to produce. Chiefly because of shortage of consumer demand, both capital and labor restrict output, and nations engage in those struggles for outside markets and spheres of commercial influence which are the chief causes of war.[3]

While the Pollak group were developing their theory of business cycles in this country, Mr. P. W. Martin of the International Labour Office was working on similar lines in Switzerland. Martin holds that the factor which ends phases of prosperity, and, he adds, the factor which keeps production even in prosperous years far below its attainable levels, is the impossibility of selling what we desire to produce. In turn, the lack of markets is due to lack of "buying power." But Martin differs from Foster and Catchings in paying slight attention to the distinction, which they stress, between consumers' and producers' goods. To maintain prosperity, it is quite as necessary to have an adequate market for industrial equipment as for clothing. And Martin ascribes the deficiency of buying power, not to saving by corporations and individuals, but to the need of larger "liquid capital" which prosperity brings. His summary runs:

> So long as the community's buying power is used exclusively to pay for goods, the price system works. But from time to time industry must increase its liquid capital. This means that part of the community's buying power, which is needed to pay for goods if equilibrium between the flow of buying power and the flow of prices is to be maintained, goes instead

[3] A brief sketch of this theory was given in 1923 by William T. Foster and Waddill Catchings in chapter xx of *Money* (No. 2 of the Publications of the Pollak Foundation for Economic Research). A more elaborate exposition was worked out by Hudson B. Hastings in *Costs and Profits* (No. 3 of the same series), 1923. A later and somewhat different statement is found in Foster and Catchings, *Profits* (No. 8 of the Pollak series), 1925. The quotations are from p. 320 of *Profits* and pp. 16, 17, 28, and 29 of "The Dilemma of Thrift," a summary of their theory by Foster and Catchings, reprinted from the *Atlantic Monthly*, April, 1926. *Business Without a Buyer*, Foster and Catchings' latest exposition, appeared after this chapter had been set up. (No. 10 of the Pollak series).

The Pollak theory relates to crises rather than to business cycles: it does not explain how activity revives after depression, or how revival grows into prosperity.

to induce the production of more goods for sale. As a consequence, goods are produced for which no buying power exists.

This "flaw in the price system" can be remedied by supplying buyers with money enough to purchase what is offered for sale.

The first step will be for the Government, acting in agreement with the banks, to increase buying power how, when, where and to what extent the best available information shows to be advisable, until unemployment is reduced to its minimum. From that time on the Government and the banks will endeavour to adjust the additions to the community's buying power so that it shall always be exactly sufficient to provide an adequate market for the goods offered for sale. Their guide in this will be the price level. If the price level falls, the natural indicator of a lack of markets, they will pump in additional buying power until the lack of markets is completely obviated (as shown by the price level regaining its former position). If prices rise, the signal of inflation, additions to buying power will be made more slowly (if necessary buying power will be drained out even), until the price level is brought back to "normal," until, that is to say, all symptoms of inflation have been totally eliminated. These measures will be applied by special offices using the best knowledge and most scientific instruments available. Supporting their efforts at every turn will be the automatic action of the psychological factor in industry, tending to be, not as now, an inflationary agency during prosperity, a depressing agency during depression, but an automatic stabiliser of both prices and markets.[4]

Still another variation upon the income theme has been composed by Dean Arthur B. Adams of the University of Oklahoma. An increase in the buying of consumers' goods may lead to recovery from depression; but it cannot initiate a period of prosperity. For business in consumers' goods cannot give rise to money incomes which exceed the sales value of the current output, and prosperity requires that consumers be able to buy an increasing output at rising prices. Therefore, it is an error to think that "recovery generates a period of

[4] See P. W. Martin, *The Flaw in the Price System*, London, 1924, and *The Limited Market*, London, 1926. The quotations are from the later book, pp. 53, 54, 69, 70.
   The theory expounded by Major C. H. Douglas of the Royal Air Force in a series of books seems to be an adumbration of the ideas worked out by the Pollak Foundation group and by Mr. Martin. See, for example, Major Douglas' volumes, *Credit Power and Democracy*, London, 1921, and *Social Credit*, London, 1924.

prosperity," or that "business is always going through some phase of a business cycle." The end of one cycle is sometimes separated from the beginning of the next by a prolonged period of "oscillating equilibrium." A new cycle does not start until something happens to give consumers incomes exceeding the value of the consumers' goods on sale. The factor which most often plays this rôle is "rapid expansion of capital equipment," financed by expansion of bank credit. Periods of prosperity, initiated by such developments, grow more intense for a time, but are finally terminated by the following "forces," working singly or together: (1) the output of consumers' goods eventually overtakes and exceeds the volume of consumers' incomes, (2) costs of production per unit eventually rise faster than selling prices, (3) the banks eventually reach the limit of their ability to increase loans.[5]

10. The Rôle Played by Profit-Making

There remain the theories which explain business cycles by the fact that the producing, transporting and distributing of goods are conducted mainly by business enterprises which aim at making money. Of course the theories already reviewed take the quest of profits for granted; but they treat business enterprise as an organization through which more fundamental forces operate. The distinguishing characteristic of the theories now to be noticed is that they represent the alternations of prosperity and depression as arising from certain technical exigencies of profit-making itself. This view was developed in 1904 by Dr. Thorstein Veblen, of the New School for Social Research, and in 1906 by Professor Jean Lescure of the University of Bordeaux.[1]

Dr. Veblen begins his discussion of "the theory of modern welfare" by pointing out that prosperity, crisis, and depression

are primarily phenomena of price disturbance, . . . They affect industry because industry is managed on a business footing, in terms of price and for the sake of profits.

A period of prosperity is ushered in by a rise of prices, caused, for example, by an increased supply of gold, or by heavy government

[5] See A. B. Adams, *Economics of Business Cycles*, New York, 1925.
[1] *The Theory of Business Enterprise*, New York, 1904, chapter vii; *Des Crises Générales et Périodiques de Surproduction*, Paris, 1906, 3rd ed., 1923. A summary of Lescure's version is given in the first edition of the present book, p. 13.

purchases. This rise affects first some one industry or line of business, which responds with a burst of activity and increased investment by business men eager to exploit the profitable field. Partly by actual increase of demand, partly by lively anticipation of future increases, aggressive business enterprise extends its ventures and pushes up prices in remoter branches of trade.

Now the growing demand and enhanced prices increase the prospective profits of the business enterprises in each trade as they reach it. Larger prospective profits lead to higher market capitalization of the business enterprises, and, of course, higher market capitalization means an increased value of the properties as collateral security. Thus the way is paved for the marked extension of credit on which the active trade is largely dependent.

This sequence of growing demand, rising prices, increasing expectations of profit, swelling capitalization of business enterprises, and expanding credit keeps repeating itself on an ever growing scale so long as its basis lasts—an anticipated increase in demand or selling prices greater than the anticipated increase in costs. But eventually the process undermines its basis. For the expense of doing business rises with the increasing cost of labor, and with the gradual extension of the advance in prices to all the commodities which business enterprises buy. In the end, these costs gain so much upon prospective selling prices as to narrow the anticipated margins of profit. Then the enhanced market capitalization of the business enterprises begins to seem excessive. Consequently, the security behind the loans which have been granted shrinks in the estimation of the business community, and ceases to be regarded as an adequate guarantee of repayment. The confident tone of business expectations which characterized the period of prosperity yields to nervousness. To bring on a general crisis, it needs but that some considerable creditor should conclude that the present earning capacity of his debtors no longer warrants the capitalization upon which their collateral is appraised. When this happens liquidation begins, extending from one industry to another and converting prosperity into depression.

Veblen differs from most writers in holding that, once begun, business depression tends to perpetuate itself, instead of tending to produce a resumption of activity. The financial reorganization of embarrassed enterprises reduces their fixed charges, and turns the weakest competitors into the most dangerous. Yet more important is the unceasing advance in technical perfection which characterizes modern machine industry, and which enables the new plants which are built from time to time to start with a marked initial advantage in equipment over their partially antiquated predecessors.[2] The difficulty of earning a fair profit without submitting to a reduction of capitalization is made chronic by these conditions. Hence periods of prosperity are taking on the character of episodes, initiated by some extraordinary increase in the demand for goods, and running out presently into the normal state of depression through the sequence of events which has been recited.

To Veblen, then, the important factor in determining the character of a business period is the relation between current capitalization and anticipated earning capacity. When prospective profits rise, business has a season of prosperity, during which capitalization expands rapidly. But rising costs always undermine the basis for anticipating high profits and then capitalization is left higher than prospective profits warrant. The latter situation characterizes depression.

The "profits theory" of business cycles has been accepted, or independently arrived at, by several writers since the publication of Veblen's and Lescure's books. These recent versions differ from the earlier models and from each other in the emphasis which they put upon various factors affecting profits. Thus Professor Gustav Cassel of the University of Stockholm ascribes especial importance to the fluctuations in both interest rates and construction work.[3] Mr. F. Lavington of the University of Cambridge, following Professor Pigou, emphasizes fluctuations in business confidence.[4] Major J. R. Bellerby of the International Labour Office stresses the expansion of the currency as a factor in breeding booms, and the reduction of surplus stocks of commodities and the artificial support of consumers' demand as factors in starting revivals of activity.[5] Professor John Maurice Clark of Columbia University has fitted into the profits theory his acute analysis of the relation between the orders for new industrial equipment and the *rate* of growth or shrinkage in the demand for

[2] Dr. Robert Liefmann suggests that this factor, the introduction of technical improvements in production and the consequent "scrapping" of equipment not yet amortized, is the most fundamental cause of crises. See his *Grundsätze der Volkswirtschafts-lehre*, 2nd ed., Stuttgart and Berlin, 1922, vol. ii, pp. 840, 841.

[3] *The Theory of Social Economy*, New York, 1924, Fourth Book. (First published in Leipzig, 1918, *Theoretische Sozialökonomie*.)

[4] *The Trade Cycle, an Account of the Causes Producing Rhythmical Changes in the Activity of Business*. London, 1922.

[5] *The Controlling Factor in Trade Cycles*. Reprinted with additions from the *Economic Journal*, September, 1923, vol. xxxiii, pp. 305-331.

finished products.[6]   Finally, Mr. Lawrence K. Frank has given a "behavioristic" interpretation of business cycles which has so definite a bearing upon current statistical work that it must be summarized.

> The 'cause' (Mr. Frank remarks), if we wish to use that term, of business cycles . . . is to be found in the habits and customs (institutions) of men which make up the money economy, with its money and credit, prices, private property, buying and selling, and so on, all loaded, so to speak, on the industrial process.

This institutional situation gives rise to alternations of "over-buying" and "under-buying" by business men in this way: In a depression retail purchases of consumers' goods do not shrink greatly, certainly not so much as the current production of these goods shrinks. Hence depression sees a gradual dwindling of current stocks of finished goods, and also a dwindling of the stocks of materials carried by producers. Given that situation, it is merely a question of time when retail merchants will find their assortments growing meager and will be forced to increase their current orders for goods, even though their current sales remain constant or contract slowly. When this time does come, production of consumers' goods will pick up a bit. Before long, the producers from whom the retailers or wholesalers bought will exhaust their supplies of materials and must increase the orders they place with other producers. So an increase of buying, started by retail merchants, spreads from group to group, and grows as it spreads.

Each business man, as he sees his sales increasing, thinks it well to acquire a larger stock of the goods he sells or uses. "Moreover, speculator-traders place orders for future delivery and begin to accumulate stocks." The consequence is that rates of production are increased. Statistical evidence seems to show that this acceleration of production becomes more rapid as it travels back from consumers' goods through semi-finished commodities to raw materials and industrial equipment. But just as retail trade did not shrink greatly during the depression, so now it does not expand greatly during prosperity. Presently the rate of production exceeds the rate of

[6] *Studies in the Economics of Overhead Costs,* Chicago, 1923, chapter xix. See also Professor Clark's paper, "Business Acceleration and the Law of Demand: A Technical Factor in Economic Cycles." *Journal of Political Economy,* March, 1917, vol. xxv, pp. 217-235.

consumption, and so produces an accumulation of stocks which grows larger as long as the processes in question continue.

But these accumulations are limited by storage capacity and the willingness of banks to lock up their funds in doubtfully liquid loans. As these limits are approached, purchases decline. Then the stocks of commodities are discovered to be overlarge for the reduced volume of sales. To reduce stocks, men fill their current orders from goods on hand and curtail production or orders from producers. Current production then falls below current consumption. The business groups which have accumulated the largest stocks—those furthest from the retailers—will almost stop buying.

Hence the rates of production in the several stages will decrease progressively faster going backward to raw materials, until the end of the ensuing depression brings a revival again.[7]

To this exposition of Mr. Frank's, Dr. Thomas Warner Mitchell of the Federal Trade Commission has made an important addition by explaining how fluctuations in demand are amplified as they run back through the channels of trade from consumers to producers of raw materials. His explanation runs as follows:

(1) Because of the length, in time, of the whole production process from the natural resources to the ultimate consumer, and the length of time required for selecting and training personnel in building up a production organization, production rates that have fallen below demand rates cannot quickly be augmented to equal the demand rates, but require many months to be so augmented. (2) There is deception and illusion all along the line as to the real extent of demand, due to over-ordering by customers. (3) The illusion is accentuated under our atomistic competitive system by counting the same demand several times over as it is presented to different atoms in the industrial organization. All three operate together to produce a grossly exaggerated measurement of demand in the boom period, followed automatically by a crisis and by a gross under-measurement of demand during the crisis and depres-

[7] "A Theory of Business Cycles," by Lawrence K. Frank, *Quarterly Journal of Economics*, August, 1923, vol. xxxvii, pp. 625-642.

Before Mr. Frank wrote, Mr. Henry S. Dennison had sketched a similar theory. See "Management and the Business Cycle," *Journal of the American Statistical Association*, March, 1922, vol. xviii, pp. 20-31. Dr. Simon S. Kuznets enriches the analysis and shows its statistical support in his volume on *Cyclical Fluctuations, Retail and Wholesale Trade, United States, 1919-1925*, New York, 1926.

sion; and that followed automatically, in turn, by another boom. Consumers' psychology, manifested in the form of resistance to the rising cost of living and a slowing-up of their demand near the end of a boom period, accentuates the effect of the superabundance with which the merchants' orders for goods are eventually filled, and materially assists in precipitating a crisis. The cyclical movement, once started, tends to complete and repeat itself automatically and perpetually.[8]

V. Plans for Further Work.

1. PROBLEMS RAISED BY THE DIVERSITY OF EXPLANATIONS.

We began the preceding survey of current theories to find what economic activities are involved in business cycles, and to get working hypotheses for use in a fresh attack upon the problem. It may seem that we have been too successful: we have found so many processes involved and have collected so many explanations that the materials threaten to be confusing rather than illuminating. What we sought was aid toward solving one problem: we now find on our hands a new puzzle—to determine the relations among a lot of theories. What explanations are incompatible with each other, what are complementary? Each theory taken by itself seems plausible; but how can we work with so many hypotheses? Is it necessary to test each hypothesis in turn? Must we plan an eclectic theory, selecting useful elements from several different writers? Or can we find some way of developing a thoroughly unified explanation of business cycles, and yet incorporate the seemingly diverse hypotheses with which we have become acquainted?[1]

[8] "Competitive Illusion as a Cause of Business Cycles," *Quarterly Journal of Economics*, August, 1924, vol. xxxviii, pp. 631-652.

[1] The humorous reader is invited to observe at this point what care has been taken to economize his effort. In place of ten types of theories in some twenty variant forms, twice or five times that number might have been put forward as having claims on his attention. A look at the table of contents in von Bergman's *Geschichte der National-ökonomischen Krisentheorien* (Stuttgart, 1895), or at the catalogue of any large library of books on economics will show how much literature has been omitted. The list of theories reviewed above is a most exclusive list, admitting only (with one diverting exception) those explanations which can show the best of credentials.

Among the recent books passed over for one reason or another are the following:

Ludwig Pohle, *Bevölkerungsbewegung, Kapitalbildung und periodische Wirtschaftskrisen.* Göttingen, 1902.

Pierre Vialles, *La Consommation et les Crises Économiques.* Paris, 1903.

Hugo Bilgram and Louis E. Levy, *The Cause of Business Depressions.* Philadelphia, 1914.

Daniel Bellet, *Crises Économiques,* Paris, 1918.

Wilhelm Röpke, *Die Konjunktur.* Jena, 1922.

Embarrassing as the multiplicity of explanations may seem at this stage, it is an embarrassment which must be faced, because it arises from the complexity of the problem itself. Everyone who has had practical experience in business knows that business is affected by numberless factors physical, psychological, political, economic or social in origin; local, national or world-wide in scope; obvious or obscure in character and working; temporary or enduring in effect. And everyone who has studied economics realizes that business activity depends upon the smoothly coördinated functioning of many processes, the extraction or growing of raw materials; the fabricating, distributing, transporting and consuming of goods; the paying and spending of money incomes; the saving and investing of capital; the granting and canceling of credits. Any of these factors or any of these processes can be made to yield a plausible theory of business cycles, provided some investigator can show that it is an independent source of recurrent fluctuations in the activity of trade. And that is what each of our theorists believes himself to have done with reference to the factor of his choice. Nor can we be sure in advance that any one of them is wrong.

An easy affirmation that business cycles are exceedingly complex phenomena is not an adequate preparation for constructive work. To plan this work wisely we need to know what the complexities are. Such knowledge we get in the most convincing way from the conclusions reached by earlier investigators. It is for this reason that study of current theories forms the best introduction to the subject, at its present stage of development. Knowing what we now do, we should be effectually guarded against the besetting sin of theorists in this

Hugh W. Sanford, *The Business of Life,* New York, 1924. Vol. i, pp. 1-222.
Paul Mombert, *Einführung in das Studium der Konjunktur.* Leipzig, 1925.
Moreover, several important contributions have been mentioned but incidentally, because they stress the joint importance of two or more processes which are exploited separately in other writings. Comprehensiveness of view is certainly no defect; but the complexity of business cycles can be exhibited most effectively by following many leaders, each of whom focuses attention upon some single process and represents all other developments as subordinate to, or as contributing to, his chosen chain of cause and effect. If this chapter were intended to evaluate recent studies of business cycles, the following books would have conspicuous places:
Dennis H. Robertson, *A Study of Industrial Fluctuation,* London, 1915; *Banking Policy and the Price Level,* London, 1926.
Gustav Cassel, *The Theory of Social Economy,* Translated by Joseph McCabe, New York, 1924. (First published in German, Leipzig, 1918.)
John Maurice Clark, *The Economics of Overhead Costs,* Chicago, 1923.
Arthur Spiethoff, "Krisen," *Handwörterbuch der Staatswissenschaften,* 4th ed., Jena, 1925. Vol. vi, pp. 8-91.
Simon S. Kuznets, *Cyclical Fluctuations,* New York, 1926.

field—neglecting phenomena which do not fit neatly into preconceived schemes.

Realizing how many lines of analysis we must be ready to test and perhaps to accept, we cannot regard the planning of our work as an easy, or a brief task. We must provide a place for every line of analysis which may prove important in the sequel, and yet not lose our way in a maze of interactions. How to draw up such a plan is our next concern.

2. A Classification of the Theories.

As the first step in this systematic planning of our work, we must set our collection of working hypotheses in order. The exposition given above proceeds as far as feasible from the simpler to the more intricate theories. Now we can rearrange the theories on logical lines, according to the processes which they stress.

First, the different theories may be classified as physical, emotional and institutional explanations.[1] The large third class may then be subdivided into (1) theories which find the source of fluctuations in institutional change, and (2) theories which find the source of fluctuations in the functioning of institutions in their present form. Finally, the last named group may be further divided into four or five species according to the economic processes in which fluctuations are held to start: namely, theories concerned with (1) the quest of profits, (2) the flow of incomes from business enterprises to indi-

[1] Compare E. M. Patterson, "The Theories Advanced in Explanation of Economic Crises," *Annals of the American Academy of Political and Social Science*, May, 1915, vol. lix, pp. 133-147.

Since this chapter was written, Professor Warren M. Persons has published a classification of "theories of business fluctuations" which resembles the present classification of theories of business cycles. See *Quarterly Journal of Economics*, November, 1926, vol. xli, pp. 94-128.

Persons' classification is the first stage of a critical examination of "the theories of business fluctuations." My classification is the first stage of a constructive study of business cycles. Persons is interested primarily in the causes of business fluctuations stressed by different writers: I am interested primarily in those parts of a theory which offer working hypotheses which I can use. This difference between our aims leads us at times to classify the same writer under quite different heads. To give a single example: Professor Persons ranks Dr. Veblen among those who emphasize "factors other than economic institutions," because Veblen holds that revivals "are pretty uniformly traceable to specific causes extraneous to the process of industrial business proper." However, Persons notes that Veblen's analysis of prosperity, crisis, and depression runs in terms of economic activities. For my purposes, it is this analysis which is most significant in Veblen's theory. I therefore rank Veblen among the writers who treat business cycles in terms of institutional factors, and merely mention his view that some "disturbing cause" from outside the system of business dealings is necessary to revive activity after a depression. (See above section iv, 10).

viduals and frcm individuals back to business enterprises, (3) the balance between rates of production and of consumption at large, (4) the special balance between personal consumption and the production of industrial equipment (the under- and over-savings, as well as the construction theories), and (5) the functioning of the banks in relation to the rest of the community.

For ready reference from time to time, it will be convenient to have this classification, with some elaboration of detail, set out in tabular form.

A CLASSIFICATION OF CURRENT THEORIES OF BUSINESS CYCLES.

I. Theories which trace business cycles to *physical* processes
1. Three-and-a-half-year cycles of solar radiation produce similar cycles of crop yields, and so seven- or ten-year cycles of business activity. H. S. Jevons.
2. Eight-year periods in the conjunction of Venus produce similar cycles in mundane weather, crop yields, and business. Henry L. Moore.
3. Weather cycles affect health, health affects mental attitudes, and mental attitudes affect business. Ellsworth Huntington.
A theory intermediate between the groups stressing physical and institutional processes.
Industries which depend upon organic, and industries which depend upon inorganic materials have unlike rhythms. The resulting disturbances and restorations of balance produce business cycles. Werner Sombart.

II. Theories which trace business cycles to *emotional* processes
1. "Optimistic error and pessimistic error, when discovered, give birth to one another in an endless chain." A. C. Pigou.
2. The fluctuations of birth rates and death rates are chiefly responsible for mass alternations of optimism and pessimism, and thus indirectly responsible for alternations of prosperity and depression. M. B. Hexter.

III. Theories which trace business cycles to *institutional* processes
1. Cycles arise from the change of institutions.
(1) Social progress is by nature jerky: changes in its pace and direction produce disturbances from time to time in the moving equilibrium of economic processes. Emanuel H. Vogel.
(2) Innovations come in waves, and initiate periods of activity followed by crises and depressions. Joseph Schumpeter, Minnie T. England.

2. Cycles arise from the functioning of existing institutions.

    (1) From the technical exigencies of money-making:

Fluctuations in prospective profits cause fluctuations in business capitalization and confidence; the latter in turn give rise to new fluctuations in prospective profits. Thorstein Veblen, Jean Lescure.

The money economy leads to fluctuations in mercantile orders, manufacturing and the production of raw materials which are progressively larger than the fluctuations in consumers' purchases, upon which all business depends, directly or indirectly, for its market. Henry S. Dennison, Lawrence K. Frank, Simon S. Kuznets.

The reason why the aforesaid fluctuations grow wide as one passes from consumer demand toward the production of raw materials lies in the competitive illusion to which our business system gives rise. Thomas W. Mitchell.

    (2) From lack of equilibrium in the processes of disbursing and spending incomes and of producing values:

Incomes paid to wage earners lag behind changes in the money value of goods produced, thus making consumers' demand alternately larger and smaller than current supply. R. E. May.

Inequalities in the rates at which prices rise and fall cause consumers' incomes to lag behind the output of consumers' goods in prosperity, and to exceed that output in depression. Emil Lederer.

Incomes disbursed by business enterprises to individuals are alternately less and more than the full value of the goods produced for sale; the fluctuations thus initiated are enhanced by the savings of individuals. Waddill Catchings, William T. Foster and Hudson B. Hastings.

Prosperity requires an increase of liquid capital, which can be provided only out of funds which must be spent for consumers' goods if prosperity is to continue. Recovery comes because depression checks the growth of liquid capital. P. W. Martin.

Consumers' incomes can be made to exceed the value output of consumers' goods only by expansion of capital equipment, financed by expansion of bank credit. But this condition, which characterizes prosperity, works its own undoing. A. B. Adams.

    (3) From lack of equilibrium in the process of producing and consuming goods in general:

Waves of general over-production result from "the well-nigh

universal fact of industrial competition." Sir William H. Beveridge.

The uncertainty involved in all business planning leads to alternate over- and under-production of goods. Charles O. Hardy.

Good trade leads to rapid increase in industrial equipment and later in output, and finally to a decline in the marginal demand prices for consumers' goods. A depression follows in which the growth of industrial equipment and output is checked. The marginal demand prices for consumers' goods finally rise again, and a new period of activity begins. Albert Aftalion, Mentor Bouniatian.

(4) From lack of equilibrium in the processes of consuming, saving, and investing capital in new construction:

In prosperity the demand for capital exceeds current savings; the resulting scarcity of capital brings on a crisis. In depression, investment falls below current savings; free capital accumulates until investing becomes aggressive once more and starts a new period of activity. Michel Tugan-Baranovski.

Large incomes, which grow rapidly in prosperity, lead to over-saving and over-investment in new plants, so that supply exceeds current demand. Depression follows, in which the large incomes are reduced, and over-saving ceases, so that consumption catches up with output and starts a revival. John A. Hobson.

Crises are caused by over-production of industrial equipment and concomitant under-production of the goods necessary to use that equipment. Arthur Spiethoff.

Relatively slight changes in demand for consumers' goods and in costs of construction cause far more violent changes in the volume of construction work: the latter changes react to heighten and propagate changes in the demand for consumers' goods. George H. Hull.

Over-commitments to business extensions of all sorts involve additions to purchasing power not counterbalanced by increased production. Prices rise until they reach a level at which men see danger in adding to their stocks. Then purchasing contracts and a crisis comes. Malcom C. Rorty.

(5) From the processes of banking:

Banks increase the purchasing power of business men, when prospects are favorable, by lending credit; the activity thus stimulated grows cumulatively until the banks are forced to restrict advances. Then comes a crisis and depression, during which idle funds accumulate in the banks and enable them to start a new movement of expansion. Alvin H. Hansen.

When banks have large reserves they reduce discount rates, and thus encourage borrowing and business expansion, which grows cumulatively until the banks find that larger cash requirements are impairing their reserves. Then banks raise discount rates, restrict loans and thus reduce business activity. Funds again accumulate in the banks because cash requirements are now smaller, and the cycle starts afresh. R. G. Hawtrey.

The exceedingly condensed summaries in this table do no more than suggest the central theses maintained by the writers named. One who has not read the books drawn upon, or at least read the preceding section on "Current Theories of Business Cycles," will find the entries scarcely intelligible and may well distrust his own guesses at their meaning. Of course the classification provides no single niche for men like Mr. Robertson, Mr. Lavington, Professor Cassel, Professor J. M. Clark and Major Bellerby who make large use of several different causes of fluctuations. Nor does the table show the effective supplementary use made by many writers of ideas other than their leading theses.

3. The Necessity for Making Measurements.

Regarding the technical methods to be used in the investigation one broad conclusion is already clear. The conception of business cycles as congeries of changes in numerous processes running abreast or following each other—a conception made vivid by the review of current theories—shows the need of quantitative knowledge. What is the relative importance of the factors represented as causes of fluctuations? What is the relative amplitude of the fluctuations characteristic of these factors and of the effects which they are said to produce? In what sequence do the fluctuations appear and at what intervals of time? These are but samples of the quantitative problems which become crucial in an effort either to test a given theory or to do constructive work. Such problems can be solved only by appeal to statistics.

Indeed, our best chance of improving upon the work of earlier writers lies in this direction. Because each year as it passes extends the record for study, because of the widening scope of statistical compilations and the progressive refinement of statistical technique, the latest investigator has a quasi-mechanical advantage over his predecessors, plus the advantage of profiting by his predecessors' ideas. Nor is this advantage of more precise knowledge limited to recent cycles. To-day we have better data concerning the trade fluctuations after the Napoleonic Wars than were available to Sismondi, or Jevons, or Tugan-Baranovski. Obviously we should exploit this advantage to the full, not forgetting that the figures are of little use except as they are illuminated by theory.

4. Causal Theory and Analytic Description.

The next step in planning our work is to drag into the light for inspection the tangled problem of cause and effect which most of the theorists have tried to solve.

The usual aim of writers upon business cycles is to show where and how wave movements start—that is, to discover "the cause" of business cycles. A second aim, followed in the full-length discussions, is to show how the original wave movement spreads from its source over all the processes of industry, commerce, and finance. This spread is also treated in terms of cause and effect, but the causal relations grow intricate. The first effects become causes producing new effects, which act as new causes, and so on. Often the analysis moves consciously in a circle or a spiral; the final effects reënforce the first cause, or after a lapse of time start the first cause into activity again, or even produce the first cause afresh.[1]

This broadening of business-cycle theories from the effort to discover causes into an effort to explain the full round of events is demanded by both our scientific and our practical interests. But as our knowledge grows wider and more intimate, our attitude toward the discussion of causes undergoes a subtle change. When we have accounted in casual terms for each stage in a lengthy series of actions and reactions, we find that our analysis deals with many causes, each one of which is logically indispensable to the theory we have elaborated. On reflection, we see the application to our work of the old contention that the idea of causation has pragmatic, rather than

[1] Of course there is nothing "vicious" in a circle of this sort. The argument is not circular in the sense of depending upon itself, but in the sense of following a process which is conceived to be rhythmical.

scientific, warrant.   All the conditions which are indispensable to produce a certain result stand on much the same footing from the viewpoint of science.   But there may be practical reasons why, from the many conditions indispensable to produce certain results, we should single out some one or more for special attention, and call them "the cause" or "the causes."   We stand a better chance of making a wise selection of factors for special attention, however, if we have already gained a scientific understanding of the process as a whole.

In the progress of knowledge, causal explanations are commonly an early stage in the advance toward analytic description.   The more complete the theory of any subject becomes in content, the more mathematical in form, the less it invokes causation.   In business-cycle theory, the transformation from causal explanations into analytic description is being hastened by free use of statistical materials and methods.   What time series can be made to show are functional relationships.   We are always reading something into statistics, when we assert that the process represented by one series exercises a causal influence upon the process represented by a second series.   Yet a stiff refusal to employ causal expressions in the detail of our investigation might often hamper us.   In the present stage of our knowledge, we can probably make more rapid progress toward attaining insight into business cycles, by using the thought-forms of daily life than by trying to express ideas at which we are grasping in the form which may ultimately prevail.

5. History and Theory.

A few business-cycle theorists not only work forward from "the cause" of wave movements to its effects, but also work backward from "the cause" to its cause.   As already noted, Professor Tugan-Baranovski, after expounding his theory of the alternate accumulation and exhaustion of uninvested loan funds, adds,

> . . . it is the inadequate remuneration of labor, and the consequent misery of the working classes, that is the fundamental cause of the rapid accumulation of social capital which provokes crises.[1]

Similarly, Professor Aftalion, after tracing the origin and development of general over-production through two volumes, remarks at the end,

[1] *Les Crises Industrielles en Angleterre*, p. 279.

It is to the conditions established by the capitalist technique of production that we must attribute the great difficulty of avoiding error. It is this technique, after all, which must bear the responsibility for the appearance of over-production.[2]

And Mr. Frank, after exploiting the difference in the rhythms of consumption and production, concludes by saying,

The 'cause,' if we wish to use that term, of business cycles . . . is to be found in the habits and customs (institutions) of men which make up the money economy . . .[3]

Presumably, this contention, that business cycles arise from that peculiar form of economic organization which has come to prevail in England within the last two centuries, and over much of the world in more recent times, would be admitted by most theorists. On this view, of course, the cause of business cycles lies enmeshed among the causes that produced modern money economy, or capitalism.

Needless to say, our theorists have not followed the logical implications of this historical perspective. No one writes an economic history of mankind as a prolegomenon to a theory of business cycles. The current practice is to take the existing scheme of institutions for granted, and to show how cyclical oscillations come to pass under this régime.

Nor do our theorists treat business cycles as episodes each of which is to be fully accounted for on historical grounds. On the contrary, they consciously endeavor to abstract from the peculiarities of particular cycles, in order that they may arrive at a clearer understanding of the generic features. The statistical investigator does the best he can to segregate the cyclical oscillations in his time series from all complicating features, and for this purpose he has developed an elaborate technique.[4] The man of speculative temper does his abstracting in bolder fashion. Surveying the phenomena of concrete experience, he seeks to fasten on the factors of chief moment, and to isolate these factors in his thoughts. By a series of imaginary experiments, he develops a synthetic account of cyclical oscillations which contains enough of reality to be enlightening and not so much as to be confusing.

---

[2] *Les Crises Périodiques de Surproduction*, vol. ii, pp. 359, 360.
[3] "A Theory of Business Cycles," *Quarterly Journal of Economics*, August, 1923, vol. xxxvii, p. 639.
[4] See Chapter III below.

Of course, there is no logical opposition between the theoretical and the historical viewpoints, any more than there is opposition between causation and analytic description.   On the contrary, history and theory supplement each other.   The theorist who wishes to analyze the workings of current economic institutions needs a vivid, objective view of their characteristics.   That view he can obtain most effectively by a study of their evolution.   Nor is current history less important to him than history of the past.   It is only by historical observations that he can determine what features of business cycles are common and what are occasional, a matter upon which he should satisfy himself before he devises his imaginary experiments.   So, too, the statistical worker appeals to history for help in performing the most difficult of his technical tasks—separating "irregular" from cyclical fluctuations.   And by whatever methods a theorist works, he may—and should—check his explanations by seeing how far they account for the cycles of history.

Several distinguished theorists have prepared themselves for explaining cyclical phenomena by elaborate historical investigations. For example, Tugan-Baranovski wrote the history of English crises from 1825 to 1910; Bouniatian carried the account back to 1640; Lescure begins his treatise with a history of French, German, English, and American crises from 1810 to 1922.[5]   Doubtless many theorists, without making first-hand historical researches for themselves, have studied such historical accounts.   To follow the precedent is an obvious piece of common sense.   Indeed, we should strive to achieve a closer blending than our predecessors have accomplished of the data and the suggestions afforded by history with the hypotheses suggested by economic theory.   The statistical series we shall analyze are fragments of the historical record.   The business annals summarized in a later chapter are a condensed account of cyclical fluctuations in numerous countries at different stages of development. These collections of historical materials, and economic history in its more elaborate form, we can use to exhibit the general characteristics of modern economic organization, to aid in determining what features are common to business cycles at large, to suggest hypotheses, and to test our conclusions.

[5] See M. Tugan-Baranovski, *Les Crises Industrielles en Anglete.re*, Paris, 1913, Part i: M. Bouniatian, *Geschichte der Handelskrisen in England, 1640-1840*, Munich, 1908; J. Lescure, *Des Crises Générales et Périodiques de Surproduction*, 3d ed., Paris, 1923, pp. 3-312.

6. The Framework of the Investigation.

Another step in planning our work is to decide whether we shall use a framework provided by the theories we have reviewed, or a framework provided by the subject matter.

It is possible to take up the theories one by one, make a critical examination of the evidence offered in support of each, at need devise new tests, and treat conclusions regarding the validity of each theory as our main objective. It is also possible to take up the successive phases of business cycles one by one, collect facts regarding periods of prosperity, crisis, depression and revival in different countries at different times, use the theories to suggest facts which should be gathered and relations looked for, and make conclusions regarding the fluctuations our main objective, treating verdicts upon the theories as by-products to be turned out when convenient.

Between these two procedures it is easy to choose. What we want is insight into the facts. We care about the theories only as aids toward attaining such insight. The plan of testing theories would indeed lead to work with the facts, but in an artificial order, and one involving much repetition. At best it would turn into a study of one or two processes at a time in successive phases of the cycle, whereas we are concerned primarily with these phases, and wish to discover the relations among different processes which give each phase its character and at the same time transform it into the following phase.[1]

But if we are to use the phases of business cycles as a framework, we run grave risk of getting hopelessly confused in a maze of interacting processes. That danger the review of current theories has made startlingly clear. The physical processes of making and consuming goods of numberless kinds, the business processes of buying and selling, the flow of money incomes to and from individuals, the circulation of money and credit, borrowing and lending, saving and investing must all be watched in relation to each other—and each of these processes is itself a complex of variables.

To guard against losing our way in this tangle, we must get as clear a view as possible of the organic relations among these various

[1] There is the less need for making a critical study of the several theories because Professor Warren M. Persons has promised to perform that arduous task. See the first paper in the series, "Theories of Business Fluctuations," *Quarterly Journal of Economics*, November, 1926, vol. xli, pp. 94-128.

processes before we begin to study their fluctuations from phase to phase of the cycle. That is, we must survey that form of economic organization which has come to prevail in all "advanced" communities as if it were a curiosity instead of our familiar environment. In particular, we must get what light existing statistics shed upon the relative magnitude of those factors which our survey of current theories has pointed out as playing important rôles in business cycles.[2]

[2] In his recent critique of current German studies of business cycles, Dr. Adolf Löwe makes the following comment upon the treatment of facts and theory in my earlier book upon business cycles:

As in all social-economic work, so in our narrower field, the analysis of facts forms the second chapter of an exposition. It must be preceded by a chapter on the theory of business cycles. Such is always the order in truth, even though the first chapter remains unwritten, and though (worse still) the writer is not conscious that his mind harbors a theory. For it is theory which provides the principles by which the irreproducible fullness of reality can be set in order; it is theory which formulates the questions which the facts must answer. (See "Der gegenwärtige Stand der Konjunkturforschung in Deutschland," in *Die Wirtschaftswissenschaft nach dem Kriege, Festgabe für Lujo Brentano*, Munich and Leipzig, 1925, vol. ii, p. 367. I have translated freely in an effort to preserve the vigor of the original.)

I cannot claim to heed Dr. Löwe's counsel in the present volume, unless my vague impressions concerning what phenomena should be looked into deserve to be called a theory. Of course Chapter I does treat theories of business cycles, but it uses these theories to reveal certain facts—that is, to show how many processes run side by side in cyclical fluctuations. In the light of these results, I pass on in Chapter II to discuss modern economic organization, in Chapter III to treat statistical problems, and in Chapter IV to draw conclusions from business annals, all before I undertake in Chapter V to formulate a definite conception of business cycles. As for a theory of the subject, that is deferred to Volume II. This order seems to me more likely to lead to the discovery of new truth than a treatment which begins with a "theory" and then looks for "facts."

Dr. Löwe's view of the relations between facts and theory in scientific work is a common one. But it seems to me over-schematic. Against the statement, "One cannot set economic facts in order unless one has a theory" (I should prefer to say "hypothesis"), can be put the statement, "One cannot form an economic theory unless one knows some facts." And both these statements overlook the fact that the two categories are not mutually exclusive. The theories with which science works cannot be conceived as existing apart from the facts of human experience, and men can apprehend facts only in terms of the notions with which their minds are furnished. The more thoughtfully one considers the relations between these two phases of knowing, the less separable they become. Even on the basis of the crude usage which contrasts fact and theory, it is futile to debate which of the two comes first in the history of the race, in the life of an individual, in the growth of a science, or in the progress of an investigation. What is clear is that in scientific work these two blends, knowledge of fact and theoretical conceptions, keep stimulating, extending and enriching each other. An investigator who starts with what purports to be an exposition of theory is tacitly using the facts by which the ideas have been molded. And one who starts with what purports to be an exposition of facts, is tacitly using the theoretical conceptions by which facts have been apprehended. Whether it is better to begin a particular task by elaborating upon the theoretical conceptions employed, saying little about the facts for the moment; or to begin by elaborating upon the facts, saying little about theories for the moment, depends upon the problem in hand and upon the contribution which the investigator hopes to make toward its solution. In an investigation of moment, both

This survey is the most important step in preparing for the constructive work we hope to accomplish. To it is devoted the next chapter.

the theory and the facts are elaborated at various stages of the proceedings, each by the aid of the other, and later workers start with a fact-theory blend improved by the new contribution.

CHAPTER II.

ECONOMIC ORGANIZATION AND BUSINESS CYCLES.

I. The Historical Connection Between Business Cycles and the Use of Money.

1. A PRELIMINARY STATEMENT.

That business cycles occur only in communities having a distinctively modern type of economic organization is explicitly recognized by several of the writers cited in Chapter I, and is implied by all who trace these cycles to institutional factors of recent development. Even the theories which resort to physical causes need not be taken as dissenting opinions. Whatever cycles occur in the weather produce cycles in economic activities only where economic activities are organized upon a business basis.

This dependence of business cycles upon a particular scheme of institutions must be a fact of the highest theoretical significance. But what we can learn from it will depend upon our understanding of the institutional scheme in question. Modern economic organization is so bewildering a complex that it explains nothing. Before we can make the historical connection illuminate our problem, we must find some way of breaking the complex into comprehensible elements, related to each other in a comprehensible fashion. Is there not, then, some feature of the economic organization found in all communities subject to business cycles, which will help us to plan our inquiry into the various processes marked for investigation in the first chapter?

Two suggestions are provided by Chapter I. Many economists have held that crises and depressions are a result of "capitalism," or, as others phrase it, "a disease of capitalism." A few recent writers have preferred to say that business cycles are produced by "money economy." [1] Neither of these statements professes to be a theory of business cycles. But both statements suggest working programs

---

[1] For illustrative citations, see the section of Chapter I called "Causal Theory and Analytic Description."

which we might follow. Can we organize our inquiry into the various processes involved in business cycles more efficiently if we relate these processes to "capitalism," or if we relate them to "money economy"?

The view which will be developed here runs as follows: The feature of modern economic organization which throws most light upon business cycles is that economic activities are now carried on mainly by making and spending money. This condition is characteristic of capitalism; but that term puts its stress upon other features of the present scheme of institutions—such as the ownership of the means of production—features of primary importance in certain problems, and not to be neglected here, but features of less service in the effort to understand alternations of business prosperity and depression than the feature stressed by the term "money economy." Accordingly, we shall seek a less ambiguous term for this concept, analyze its meaning, and use it in exploring the maze of processes which we have found to be involved in business cycles.

One reason why the connection between business cycles and pecuniary organization was long overlooked is that the difference between the use of money in communities which do not and in communities which do suffer from business cycles is a difference in degree, not a difference in kind. Economists accustomed to depend upon what Alfred Marshall called "qualitative analysis" were prone to overlook the significance of differences in degree, and to concentrate attention upon differences in kind, or what they took to be such. Capitalism seemed to many men in the nineteenth century, men not versed in economic history, a new portent in economic life. They fastened upon it as an explanation of many phenomena which seemed to them equally new—commercial crises among others.

As will be shown below, the coming of business cycles is a gradual development. It can be explained only by some change which proceeds by degrees. Communities slowly become subject to recurrent alternations of prosperity and depression as a large proportion of the people begin to rely upon making and spending money in a large proportion of their activities. We lack the data which might enable us to assign a critical point, or a critical range, in the growth of money economy at which business cycles appear. But we can tell in what period the critical range was reached in various countries.[2]

[2] Capitalism also developed gradually, and, so far as that goes, might serve as well to explain the coming of business cycles as does the cumulative growth of pecuniary

Just because its development has been so gradual, "money economy" has many meanings. It calls to mind certain features in the dissimilar economic organizations of states which have flourished at various times through several thousand years of history. A term which can be taken to cover all the successive stages in a long and checkered evolution is not an apt term to characterize the peculiarities of the latest stage in the series. To suggest the differentiating features of that highly developed form of money economy within which business cycles occur, we shall do well to use words which have modern associations in our minds. Perhaps the combination "profits economy" or "business economy" is most suggestive and least misleading. The second of these terms will be used in this discussion, but with frequent reminders that what seems to count in producing business cycles is the common practice of money-making and money-spending by the population as a whole, not merely by a limited class of business men.

2. The Meaning of "Business Economy."

To repeat: we do not say that a business economy has developed in any community until most of its economic activities have taken on the form of making and spending money. That way of organizing production, distribution and consumption is the matter of importance —not the use of money as a medium of exchange.[1]

Instead of making the goods their families need, men "make" money, and with their money incomes buy for their own use goods made by unknown hands. The exceptions to this rule presented by the domestic work of housewives, by the consumption of their own produce by farmers, by the raising of vegetables in family gardens,

organization. As said above, the reason for organizing the present inquiry around the use of money, rather than around the ownership of the means of production, is that the former plan puts the problems to be faced in a way which makes them more open to attack. Of course no contention of this sort can be justified in advance. It must stand or fall by the results to which it leads.

[1] One of the objections to the term "money economy" is that it is often contrasted with a "credit economy." Thus Bruno Hildebrand, who seems to have introduced the terms, distinguished three stages of economic development: *Naturalwirtschaft*, *Geldwirtschaft*, and *Kreditwirtschaft* (*Jahrbücher für Nationalökonomie und Statistik*, vol. ii, pp. 1-24). But Hildebrand's stages have not proved of much use either in economic history or in economic theory, and his term *Geldwirtschaft* seems now to be used in Germany much as "business economy" is used here. In this sense, of course, the predominant use of credit instruments in effecting payments is merely one feature of a highly developed money economy.

and by agricultural leases for shares of the crops, are continuations of an earlier order, in which most families subsisted chiefly upon goods produced by their own efforts and themselves consumed most of what they produced.

It is characteristic of the dominating rôle played by money in economic planning that the nation collects hardly any data concerning these surviving elements of "real" income which families produce for themselves. Housewives form by far the largest occupation group, outnumbering farmers three to one, and the group whose work affects welfare most intimately. Yet the census of occupations does not count the number of housewives working at home. Enumerators are instructed to include only "gainful occupations," those from which people get money incomes. When the National Bureau of Economic Research made its first studies of income, it could do no more than estimate the number of housewives, and apply to this number the average wages of a group of paid workers consisting mainly of women who do some of the multifarious tasks of the housewife. The rough results thus obtained ran above 18 billion dollars in 1919, more than a quarter of the total money income. But the whole procedure was so conjectural that the National Bureau did not venture to add the housewife item to its other figures.[2]

The other elements of family-produced income can be priced without hesitation, because they consist of goods such as pass through the markets. Yet we know their magnitude but vaguely. In 1914, Mr. W. C. Funk of the Department of Agriculture made a careful study of the incomes of 483 farm families, and estimated the value of their own produce which these families consumed.[3] With the aid of Funk's data, Dr. W. I. King has figured that the non-monetary income of American farmers amounted to nearly 2 billion dollars in 1913 and nearly 4½ billions in 1920—say 6 per cent of the national income in the latter year. Much smaller values, not reaching half a billion, are produced for their own consumption by urban and village

[2] See *Income in the United States,* by the Staff of the National Bureau of Economic Research, New York, 1921, vol. i, pp. 57-60.
[3] See United States Department of Agriculture, *Farmers' Bulletin* No. 635, December, 1914. More recently Messrs. L. M. Bean and O. C. Stine of the United States Bureau of Agricultural Economics have estimated that the income "consumed on farms for family living" has varied between 21.6 per cent of "operators' *gross* income from agricultural production" in 1919-20 and 27.6 per cent in 1921-22. "Income from Agricultural Production," *The Annals of the American Academy of Political and Social Science.* January, 1925, vol. cxvii, p. 33.

families which cultivate kitchen gardens, or keep cows, pigs and poultry.[4]

Finally, as the most important survival of exchange by barter, it may be noted that rather more than a quarter of the 6,450,000 farms in the United States were cultivated in 1920 by tenants who paid as rent a share in the produce.[5]

Despite the considerable importance of these continuations of an earlier order, the economic comfort or misery of a family now depends more upon its ability to command an adequate money income and upon its pecuniary thrift, than upon its efficiency in making useful goods and its skill in husbanding supplies. Even in years when crops are short and mills are idle, the family with money need not be uncomfortable. The family without money leads a wretched life even in years of abundance.[6]

To the family, then, prosperity and depression appear less as problems of the adequacy of the goods produced by itself or by the community as a whole, than as problems of the adequacy of its money income. To the nation, the making of money is important in a way quite different. Comfort and misery do not depend upon the aggregate of money incomes received by its citizens; they depend upon the abundance of useful goods. Efficiency in producing goods is important to an individual chiefly because of its bearing on his ability to make money; money-making is important to a nation chiefly because of its bearing upon efficiency in production. Natural resources, mechanical equipment, workmanlike skill, and scientific technique are factors of fundamental importance under any form of organization. But where business economy prevails natural resources are not developed, mechanical equipment is not utilized, workmanlike skill

---

[4] See *Income in the United States*, vol. ii, p. 231. There are other items of income, particularly, the rental value of owned homes and the use of other consumption goods such as furniture, which do not figure in the money income and outgo of a family each year. But most of these goods have been bought for money in the past, and the real income derived from them cannot be regarded as produced by the recipients. The estimate of the non-monetary income of farmers given in the text does not include the rental value of farm homes.

[5] *Fourteenth Census of the United States*, Agriculture, Washington, 1922, vol. v. p. 124.

[6] Compare Dr. Robert L. Hale's statement: "All incomes, in the last analysis, whether derived from ownership of property or from personal services, are not 'products' created by the recipients; they are payments derived from the rest of the community by the exertion of some sort of pressure. To say this is not to condemn the exertion of such pressure; it is the only means a man has under present arrangements, and perhaps under any workable scheme of things, for keeping alive." "Economic Theory and the Statesman," *The Trend of Economics*, edited by R. G. Tugwell, New York, 1924, p. 216.

is not exercised, scientific discoveries are not applied, unless conditions are such as to promise a money profit to those who direct production.

The elaborate coöperative processes by which a nation's people provide for the meeting of each other's needs are thus brought into dependence upon factors which have but an indirect connection with the material conditions of well-being—factors which determine the prospects of making money.

3. THE EVOLUTION OF BUSINESS ECONOMY.

To grasp the rôle played in our lives by this form of organization is difficult, because we who have grown up in a business economy have had our minds molded by it. In studying the institution as it now exists, we are practicing a sort of introspection into our own mental processes. To get an objective view of the present situation, our best course is to trace the stages by which the uses of money have grown. What is so familiar and organic a whole to us that we hardly see the need of analyzing it, will dissolve into thought-suggesting parts as we note how our race has slowly evolved one element in the complex after another.

The faltering first steps toward the use of money were taken in those dim stretches of time when men were beginning to exchange gifts and then to barter for the sake of goods, to evolve the concept of ownership, to express values in a common denominator, to use some commodity as currency, to hold markets, to develop specialized occupations, and to mix trading as a business with cattle lifting, man stealing and town sacking. Of all these slow developments what little information is available comes mainly from anthropologists and archæologists and is loosely tied together by conjecture.

When written history begins in Babylonia and Egypt, in China and India, in Europe, in Mexico and Peru, it shows us a more advanced stage. Men are using copper, silver or gold as currency; they are making contracts involving the future; they are buying and selling, borrowing and lending on a considerable scale; they are keeping rude accounts. Very slowly these practices diffuse from the centers of cultural achievement, and quite as slowly the shifting cultural centers score advances. The epochal invention of coinage was probably made in western Asia Minor about 700 B. C., and was carried by Phœnician traders round the Mediterranean world.

Having passed through these earlier stages, the uses of money entered a phase of rapid development in Phœnicia, Carthage, and Greece and upon a still more notable expansion in Rome. Money changing, letters of exchange, simple banking, production of staple goods on a large scale for a wide market, speculation, business enterprises not only in trading, but also in mining and manufacturing, became common. Large fortunes were built up by private people and invested for profit. Despite the prevalence of slavery, many men worked for wages. It was, indeed, a business-like society that flourished under the Pax Romana.

But with the disintegration of Roman culture, pecuniary organization declined as decisively as any other phase of civilization. In economic, as in political life, a sharp contrast appeared between East and West. Over those parts of the empire which were later to assume leadership in culture, central authority dissolved into a shifting multitude of local controls; petty warfare became a chronic misery; the admirable Roman roads fell into disrepair; commerce shrank to a dribble of luxuries for the powerful and a local exchange of indispensables like iron, salt and tar for the commonalty; manufacturing for a wide market almost disappeared; coinage became scanty, irregular, and incredibly confused; the use of money was superseded in large part by the payment of feudal and manorial dues in personal services and commodities. The vast majority of the population lived in village communities, each of which produced most of the things its low standard of living required, and consumed most of its own products. Even the kings and other magnates spent much of their time moving about from one manor to another, eating up the local produce on the spot. All the more elaborate achievements of pecuniary organization had to be won over again.

Quite different was the situation in the area dominated by Constantinople. There the money economy suffered no such eclipse as in western and northern Europe. Gold coinage, a banking system, manufacturing on a considerable scale, a commerce which tapped the Orient on one side and the western Mediterranean on the other side were maintained and in some respects elaborated. It was due largely to this continuation that the reëstablishment of money economy in western and northern Europe was a far more rapid process than its original growth, requiring scarcely a thousand years. What the Byzantines had conserved they, and the Saracens, passed on. After the sack of Constantinople by crusaders and Venetians in 1204, and more decisively after the capture of Constantinople by the Ottoman Turks in 1453, commercial leadership passed to the Italian cities. Many merchants emigrated to Venice, Amalfi, Genoa, and other towns, carrying with them their capital, as well as their skill in commerce and finance. A vigorous development of money economy began in the lands bordering the western Mediterranean and spread by degrees to northern countries.

The stages of this revival are imperfectly known, though they have been lived through so recently. Economic history is a young specialty, and the men devoted to it have not been fully alert to the importance of pecuniary institutions. Nor do the surviving materials on which their work is based pay much attention to the homely details of the life of the peasant, the craftsman and the merchant, except as these humble people had relations with their lords. Yet enough is known, particularly regarding England, to reveal the broad features of the story.

In economic development, the leaders were successively the Italian cities, Spain, Southern Germany, France and the Low Countries. England lagged behind until the 18th century, when London finally displaced Amsterdam as the greatest financial center, and the English began to live by making and spending money incomes as generally as the Dutch. In a history of money economy, English developments would form but one strand in a complicated fabric—a strand which does not fairly represent the whole. But the very slowness of English developments serves the present purpose. For that purpose is not to sketch the history of pecuniary organization as a whole; but to make clear the complex character of the institutions which we are wont to take as a simple matter of course. Also, the English have peculiar interest for us, because, when they finally took the lead, pecuniary organization was just reaching that stage which ushers in the business cycles of our historical record.

Even in Anglo-Saxon times, the English kings were finding that the use of money was a more efficient method of administration than levying upon commodities and requiring feudal services. They early began to commute the duties in kind upon exports and imports, for example, so many tuns of wine or bales of wool in a cargo, into money payments, and to collect in money as much of the internal taxes, fines, and dues as their officers could. The Danegeld, for instance, was levied and paid in silver. The Anglo-Saxon kings struck a currency of silver pennies based on the Carolingian pound. (It was not until 1343 that gold coins were issued in England and the gold standard was not established until nearly 400 years more had passed.) Besides taxing, the English kings borrowed on a considerable scale from religious establishments, from the Jews until their expulsion in 1290, and later from Italian merchants and bankers who did business in London.

Another great step in pecuniary organization was taken when the kings began to replace the unreliable feudal levies with paid professional soldiers. This change involved commuting the tenant's obligation to render military service in person with his retainers at his back into money payments by the tenant-in-chief and his knights. And a similar change was effected gradually in the management of the crown lands. On royal manors the villeins were allowed to commute their dues in labor and commodities into sums of money which constituted a revenue the king could use where convenient.

Meanwhile the reorganization of life among the common people on the basis of buying and selling was proceeding spontaneously in the towns. Here the differentiation of crafts could develop only so fast as the exchanging of products increased. As they devoted more and more time to their specialties, the master craftsmen had to buy their raw materials and most of the food for their families, apprentices and in-working journeymen. The towns were also the centers of what foreign or inter-regional trade was carried on, and the volume of such trade grew unsteadily larger with each generation. Thus the towns came to be "islands of money economy" in a sea of customary duties and rights—*foci* from which organization on a monetary basis diffused itself gradually over the countryside.

In the rural districts the epochal change was the extension of commutation into money rents of the week-work, boon-work and commodity payments required of the masses of villeins and cotters. From the manors held by the crown and the great religious houses, this change spread slowly and unevenly to manors held by lesser magnates. The process was piecemeal, marked by pauses and spurts, but cumulative. It was accompanied by the rise of estate management for revenue, instead of for subsistence. More slowly still the masses of the peasantry moved, or were shoved, into a new manner of life. Holdings of scattered strips in the common fields were amalgamated into blocks. The waste lands, the commons and the common fields themselves were enclosed. On many manors, the old three-

field system of cultivation was abandoned in favor of the more lucra-
tive grazing of sheep for the export commodity, wool, and later for
methods involving more use of fertilizers and the rotation of crops.[1]
Specialization in animal husbandry and crops increased. Those of
the old population who could not master the new arts of making and
living on money, sank to the position of wage-workers on the land,
or drifted away to the towns. The more adaptable men turned into
business-like farmers, paying money rents, using hired laborers and
selling most of their produce. So slow and so uneven was the process
of transformation that over much of England these changes were still
going on in the 18th and early 19th centuries. Perhaps four-fifths
of English acreage was enclosed after 1760.

Even by the 16th century, however, the uses of money had developed far enough in England to make the inflow of Mexican and Pe-
ruvian silver from Spain produce grave social results. The "price
revolution" of the 16th and 17th centuries reduced the value of the
money payments into which many dues had been commuted and so
forced a reorganization of estate management upon many reluctant
landlords. On the other hand, it gave increased opportunities for
profit by dealings between the districts where silver was abundant
and the districts where it was scanty. Thus the new supplies of the
precious metals (for presently gold began to come in considerable
volume from the Brazilian placers) gave a powerful impetus to
commercial enterprise. England, which had been mainly a self-contained agricultural state, entered upon a career of colonizing, developed a mercantile marine, and in the 18th century became the
foremost commercial power.

As commerce increased, financial organization became more elaborate. Lending at interest, which had been permitted only under conditions carefully stipulated by the Church, became a legalized
practice as the benefits of investment of capital grew clearer. Presently banking arose in England. During the 17th century the London
goldsmiths, whose business with precious metals made strong boxes
necessary, were resorted to more and more frequently by merchants
and other wealthy men for the safekeeping of moneys. The goldsmiths who accepted deposits found that they were never required to

---

[1] Dr. Harriett Bradley in *The Enclosures in England*, New York, 1918, cites evidence
to show that wool growing became more profitable than wheat raising only on lands
whose fertility had been depleted by long continued cropping. The price of wool was
low in comparison with the price of wheat during the enclosure period of the 15th and
16th centuries. See chapter ii. and pp. 97-100.

pay back more than a fraction of the total in any day or week. They could make profits by lending part of the sums in their hands. To increase the funds which they could lend, they presently began to pay interest upon deposits. Soon they discovered that it was as easy to lend their promises to pay as it was to lend coin. Goldsmiths' notes became familiar currency among well-to-do people, and London had a flourishing set of banks of deposit, lending, and issue some decades before the Bank of England was established in 1694.

With the increased scale and growing intricacy of business dealings, there was need for more accurate bookkeeping. On large estates the stewards had perforce kept simple accounts of the work done and the commodities received from the numerous tenantry. Doubtless merchants and many craftsmen had made more elaborate records of their transactions. But the mystery of double-entry bookkeeping—an Italian invention first published in 1494—was both a marked technical advance in itself and an incitement to the further improvements which led to modern accounting. That mystery the mercantile classes of England began to acquire in the 16th century.

Commerce came home to the mass of English people while it was extending to the ends of the earth. The periodical markets and fairs, which made such a picturesque feature of medieval life, became inadequate to meet the needs as communities became less self-sufficient. Weekly markets became common, then daily markets, then retail shops. By 1700 not only London but also several other towns had a variety of shops doing business with a wide clientele.

Lagging not very far behind the development of new economic practices came their recognition and enforcement at law. Through their dealings with foreign traders abroad and at home, English merchants early became acquainted with the law merchant—a highly developed commercial code which had grown up during the Middle Ages in the great continental fairs. In his *Legal Foundations of Capitalism,* Professor John R. Commons has shown how the English judges gradually reshaped the old feudal conceptions of suzerainty to fit the nascent conception of private property in land; how side by side with the law of prerogative they built up the common law to regulate the relations among individuals; how they legitimized property in promises to pay, in good will, in going concerns. The great development of mercantile law by Chief Justice Mansfield came in the middle of the 18th century.

Trade, and to a less extent mining and colonial schemes, had been the favorite field of what business enterprise appeared in the 16th and 17th centuries. Manufacturing, banking and insurance were added to this list in the 17th and 18th centuries. Capitalistic organization of various industries, as opposed to the earlier craft organization, developed with the widening of markets, and the consequent opportunity for mass production and standardization of products. Thus it antedated the "Great Inventions" by two or three generations. But the introduction of power machinery and the building of factories quickened and broadened the process. Adam Smith could take it for granted that a capitalist employer was the typical figure in industry, just as he took it for granted that a capitalist farmer paying money rent was the typical figure in agriculture. The proportion of men working on their own account shrank in all fields of enterprise, as did the number who consumed their own products, while the proportion of men working for wages increased.

As the scale of business undertakings grew, the one-man enterprise, and even the partnership, became inadequate. Large and hazardous ventures in foreign trade were carried on in the 15th and 16th centuries commonly by "regulated companies" enjoying certain privileges conferred by government, but composed of merchants each of whom traded on his own account. In the latter half of the 16th century, the joint-stock form of organization began its conquering career in England with the Russia Company and the Adventurers to Africa. The Bank of England (preceded by several continental institutions) adapted this form to banking and it spread slowly to other fields. But in 1776 Adam Smith argued that, in most lines of business, the joint-stock company was necessarily less efficient than the simpler organization in which one man or a few partners were giving strict attention to their personal interests. The enlarged capital needs of factories, however, the coming of railroads and the rapid growth in the volume of business, so altered the situation that within a century after the *Wealth of Nations* was published the joint-stock company in some of its proliferating variants became the dominating form of business organization outside of farming, retail trade, and the professions. The spread of this form was much more rapid after 1862, when Parliament accepted the principle of limited liability of stock holders.

An investment market evolved with the growth of capital. Stockbrokers had long been known in London before the great outburst of speculation in the shares of the South Sea Company in 1720. The development of their business owed much to the rise of high-grade investments, particularly the manifold forms of government obligations.   In 1773 the London brokers organized the Stock Exchange, and so had the financial machinery ready to handle the great increase of investment and speculative transactions in securities which came with the Napoleonic Wars, the spreading of joint-stock companies, and the building of railways.   These facilities gave a stronger impetus and a wider scope to two processes already familiar to Englishmen. A new leisure class of people who had inherited "money" developed in each generation from the families of successful business men, and the old leisure class of landowners could strengthen their position by participating silently in business ventures or by intermarrying with the new rich.

When European settlers came to America they brought with them the monetary usages of their various home countries in the 17th century.   But under the rough conditions of frontier life the colonists suffered a temporary recession to simpler forms of organization.   They were short of coin and had to use commodity currencies at times— tobacco, wampum, beaver skins.   They had to live more on their own, somewhat after the fashion of medieval villagers; the differentiation of occupations was simpler; financial machinery was scarcely needed and scarcely existed; the chief business of life was to get enough food and clothing, to build houses and clear land, to keep off the Indians.

This recession was relatively short-lived on the Atlantic seaboard, but it remained characteristic of life on the westward-moving frontier as long as the frontier lasted.   Always the fur traders, the trappers and hunters, the early settlers, had to get or make much of what they consumed, though they could draw upon trading posts for their arms, tools and firewater, and barter or sell such of their products as were easily transportable.   Even the more thickly-settled Eastern colonies, despite their rapid progress in economic matters, continued to lag behind England in the drastic thoroughness with which they practiced monetary habits, and the refinement with which they developed financial organization.   It was not until late in the nineteenth century that the United States drew fairly abreast of the mother country in this respect.   Even to-day our farming is not quite so business-like as the English, except for our large-scale ventures in coöperative marketing of agricultural products.   Our investors have not evolved or borrowed all of the British institutions to look after their interests our foreign financial connections are less perfect, and our technique in foreign trade is inferior. But on the other hand, retail trade on the whole is more highly organized than in England, and our industrial corporations probably excel the English not only in the scale of their operations but also in systematic organization.

This sketch is all too brief and too simple to give an adequate impression of the way in which the developing uses of money have altered the life of mankind, and how they have fitted into the growth of other institutions, checking some and stimulating others. Still less does it show how the development of monetary practices in England was related to the larger growth in Europe. But with all its omissions, the sketch suggests how "fearfully and wonderfully made" is the complex of pecuniary practices which seems to us so natural. The commutation of feudal dues into money payments, the corresponding commutation of labor and commodity rents into money, the development of crafts with exchange of products, the rise of towns as trading centers, the invention of banking, the growth of retail shops, the excogitation of business law, the organization of joint-stock companies and their rise to dominance in most fields of business enterprise, the adoption of accounting as the technique for controlling economic ventures, the evolution of special organizations to provide for investment and speculation, the differentiation of the whole population into those who live on wages, on profits, on income from investments, or on an income which combines these types, the shifting of power from men of prowess or high birth to men of great wealth or marked business ability, the discomforting of those whose talents are not such as to command considerable incomes in a money-making world—all these developments have combined to produce the current form of business economy. Nor can we assume that this current stage is the final pattern. On the contrary, it is probable that pecuniary institutions are now changing as rapidly as at any period of their long history.[2]

---

[2] Although the literature of money is reputed to be more extensive than that upon any other branch of economics, we have no comprehensive treatise upon the development of pecuniary institutions. In default of adequate guidance, I have had to compose the best sketch I could by piecing together bits drawn from many sources. To give a list of the books used would take much space and render little help to anyone acquainted with economic history. My heaviest obligations are to Dr. Edwin F. Gay who made many critical and constructive suggestions concerning my first draft.

I hope that better equipped investigators will presently take up the study of this subject, which is as fascinating as it is important, and which promises large returns to

4. When Business Cycles First Appear.

It is not until the uses of money have reached an advanced stage in a country that its economic vicissitudes take on the character of business cycles.

This remark does not mean that the economic life of communities with simpler organization is free from crises, or from alternations of good and bad times. On the contrary, life seems to have been more precarious, economic fortune more fluctuating, in a medieval town than in a modern city. But until a large part of a population is living by getting and spending money incomes, producing wares on a considerable scale for wide markets, using credit devices, organizing in business enterprises with relatively few employers and many employees, the economic fluctuations which occur do not have the characteristics of business cycles described in the preceding chapter.

If the coming of business cycles depends upon the gradual development of a specific form of economic organization, it must be difficult to date their first appearance in any country with precision. And so it is. To take the best explored case: Dr. William Robert Scott of St. Andrews has made a minute study of British business records in manuscripts, official reports, books, pamphlets and newspapers from the middle of the 16th century to 1720. From these materials he has compiled a summary showing the periods of good and bad trade and of crisis during the 163 years he has covered. The table on pages 76 and 77 gives Scott's list of crises, and his "remarks" concerning each. In a few cases where his entries are very brief, I have added in brackets explanations drawn from his text. Also, I have inserted a column showing the number of years from the beginning of one crisis to the beginning of the next.

With Dr. Scott's remarks upon English crises from 1558 to 1720, we may compare Dr. Willard L. Thorp's concise descriptions of English crises from 1793 to 1925, published in the National Bureau's volume of *Business Annals*. Several differences appear.

competent workers. Anyone who contemplates an investigation will find that Georg Simmel's *Philosophie des Geldes* (2d ed., Leipzig, 1907) is a most suggestive book to read before plunging into the historical sources. An interesting sidelight upon developments in Europe is thrown by a forthcoming monograph in the Columbia University Studies in History, Economics and Public Law: *The Penetration of Money Economy in Japan and its Effects upon Social and Political Institutions*, by Matsuyo Takizawa.

A LIST OF CRISES IN ENGLAND FROM 1558 TO 1720

From William R. Scott, *The Constitution and Finance of English, Scottish and Irish Joint-Stock Companies to 1720*, vol. i, Cambridge, 1912, pp. 465–467.

"Serious crises" are marked with an asterisk

The "number of years between crises" is counted from the beginning of one crisis to the beginning of the next.

Dates of Crises	No. of Years between Crises	Remarks
1558–9	..	Famine 1556–8.
1560	2	English bills refused abroad [because of the financial difficulties of Government].
1563 (Aug.) to 1564 (Aug.) *.	3	Plague (the number of deaths said to be 20,000), interruption of trade with Flanders, famine.
1569 (Jan.) to 1574 *	6	Seizures of English goods in Flanders, January, 1569, followed by failures. Norfolk's insurrection, December, 1569, followed by failures. Bad harvests from 1571 to 1574. It is slightly uncertain whether the years 1570–4 should be classed as a part of the crisis or of the subsequent depression.
1586–7 *	17	Babington plot, failures, bad harvest, 1587.
1596–7 *	10	Famine, 1595–8.
1603 *	7	Plague, deaths in London, 30,561.
1616–17	13	Crisis in cloth trade [disorganized by manipulations of James I].
1620–5 *	4	Effects of crisis in cloth trade, Dutch competition in foreign trade, default of East India and Russia companies, bad harvests, plague, deaths in London, 35,403.
1630 *	10	Famine, tonnage dispute, plague, deaths in London, 1,317.
1636–7	6	Depression through the monopolies of Charles I, plague, deaths in London, 10,400.
1640 *	4	Seizure of bullion by Charles I. (July), of pepper (Aug.), plague, deaths 1,450.
1646–9 *	6	Exhaustion of the country through the Civil War, great dearth, high taxation.
1652–4	6	Losses of shipping in the Dutch War, possibly too effects of the Navigation Act.
1659–60	7	Losses in Spanish War, especially in cloth trade, strain of continued high taxation.
1664 (Winter) to 1667 (July)*	5	Dutch War, plague (deaths 68,596), Great Fire, Dutch fleet in the Thames, 1667. Run on bankers.
1672 *	8	Stop of the Exchequer, failure of bankers.
1678	6	Prohibition of trade with France, expectation of war with Holland, run on bankers.
1682	4	Run on bankers occasioned by state of home politics foreign trade little affected.

A List of Crises in England from 1558 to 1720—*Continued*

Dates of Crises	No. of Years between Crises	Remarks
1686.....................	4	Depression in cloth trade, failure of Corporation bank [1685, on news of Monmouth's rebellion], foreign trade still fairly prosperous.
1688.....................	2	Revolution—run on bankers.
1696-7 *.................	8	The financial strain of the war, exaggerated ideas of the nature of credit, bad harvests, suspension of cash payments by Bank of England, failure of Land bank schemes.
1701 (Feb.) *.............	5	Tension between East India companies, political situation, run on banks and consequent failures.
1704 (Oct.) to 1708 (Feb.) *.	3	Losses in the war, financial strain, tension between England and Scotland, fears of a French invasion, run on Bank of England.
1710–11 (Winter)..........	6	Financial strain of the war, change of ministry.
1714 (Jan. to April)........	4	Fears as to the succession, reported death of Anne, run on Bank of England.
1715 (Oct.)................	1	Rebellion.
1717 (Jan. to March)........	2	Walpole's conversion scheme.
1718 (Oct.)................	1	Fears of an invasion.
1720 (Sept.) *.............	2	Panic, following the collapse of speculation [South Sea Bubble].

(1) Dr. Scott connects almost all of the early crises with famines, outbreaks of the plague, wars, civil disorders, irregularities of public finance, or high-handed acts of Government. Dr. Thorp notes the occurrence of bad harvests, epidemics, wars, political unrest, and changes in public policy from time to time in 1790-1925, and now and then suggests a connection between such events and a crisis. But disasters of non-business origin, which occupy the foreground in Dr. Scott's remarks, recede into the background of Dr. Thorp's account. They continue to influence economic activities; but the sources which Dr. Thorp condenses put developments within the world of business foremost among the factors responsible for crises.

It may be that, because of shortcomings in his sources, Dr. Scott over-stresses the influence of "disturbing causes." He has checked contemporary opinions by actual business records and by such statistics as he could find. But these materials are less abundant in his period than they have since become, and he must depend in part upon commentators who were prone to hold Government or nature responsible for whatever went amiss. To make sure that our conclusions concerning the character of earlier and of later English crises are not warped by differences between the economic insight of observers in 1558-1720 and of observers in 1790-1926, we may note further contrasts between the pictures drawn by Scott and Thorp.

(2) Dr. Scott represents a fifth of his crises as lasting three years or more—1569-74, 1620-25, 1646-49, 1652-54, 1664-67, and 1704-08. Since periods of "depressed trade" are entered in a separate column of Scott's summary, the implication is that trade continued to be not merely dull, but seriously disturbed during the periods cited. Reference to the fuller accounts given in Scott's earlier chapters justifies this interpretation. In Thorp's annals, it is difficult to find a parallel to these long crises.

(3) In modern business cycles, the crisis or recession follows a period of prosperity. It still happens occasionally, that a season of acute strain, such as Dr. Scott presumably would enter as a crisis, occurs in a period of depression. The most striking recent instance is the trouble caused by the outbreak of war in 1914—an episode which Dr. Thorp does not list as a crisis, just because it came in the trough of a cycle which had culminated in 1913.[1] In Scott's summary, no less than 12 out of 30 crises listed were preceded by periods, not of prosperity, but of "depressed trade."

Of course, this difference between the earlier and the later crises is connected with that first noted. It confirms Scott's conclusion concerning the dominant rôle played in business fluctuations of 16th- to 18th-century England by non-business factors. Crises which are due primarily to such economic processes as are considered in Chapter I can occur only after prosperity has produced certain stresses within the business system. Crises which are dominated by events of a non-business character can occur equally well in any phase of a cycle. Whether crises due to wars, famines, epidemics, or the like will occur more often when trade is good or when trade is poor, must depend in the long run upon the relative number of fat and lean years. The number of crises listed by Scott as following years of depressed trade is greater than the ratio of lean years to fat years would lead one to expect.[2]

[1] For other cases of financial strain occurring during depressions, see below, Chapter IV, section iii, 4.

[2] As closely as I can reckon from Scott's table, the periods of good trade in 1558-1720 covered about 64 years, the periods of depressed trade about 38 years. On this basis, the crises breaking out when trade is good should have exceeded in number the crises breaking out when trade was bad by 1.8: 1. The actual excess was not over 1.5: 1.

This computation cannot be made with precision. Scott does not report the con-

(4) Dr. Scott calls attention to the fact that

> a time of good trade tended to persist, once it had set in, with a long interval between crises, while in the converse case the interval between them was reduced. For instance, in the eleven good years from 1575 to 1585, there was, as far as is known, no crisis, again in seventeen prosperous years (1603 to 1620), there was only one, whereas in an equal number of bad years (1586 to 1603) there were three, and again from 1696 to 1708, there were only four years free from very great disturbances of trade.[3]

Modern business history does not run in such considerable stretches of good times free from crises, serious or mild, and of bad times in which serious crises crowd one another. The longest period of prosperity revealed in Thorp's English annals for 1793-1920 lasted only four years. Nowadays it is periods of depression which "tend to persist"—if that expression is permissible at all. Yet the longest English depression in our record lasted less than six years.[4]

(5) The intervals between the beginnings of crises in Scott's list and the intervals between recessions (which include both mild and severe crises) in Thorp's annals give similar averages: 5.6 years in 1558-1720, 5.8 years in 1793-1920. But the intervals are decidedly more irregular in the earlier period. They run from 1 to 17 years in Scott's list, from 2 to 10 years in Thorp's. The coefficient of variation—perhaps the best measure of variability for this comparison—is 63 per cent in the one case and 39 per cent in the other.[5]

(6) In a business cycle, the order of events is crisis, depression, revival, prosperity, and another crisis (or recession). That Scott does not enter revivals separately in his summary means little; for scant attention has commonly been given to that least dramatic phase of the recurrence. But it is significant that in only 5 cases out of his 29 does Scott report a crisis as followed by depression, prosperity

dition of trade preceding the first of his crises, 1558-9; he does not always show the month or quarter of a year when business conditions changed; there are several intervals scattered through his summary, totaling some 7½ years, for which he makes no report.

The time covered by Scott's 30 crises is 49 years—more than all his periods of depressed trade put together.

[3] W. R. Scott, *Constitution and Finance of English, Scottish and Irish Joint-Stock Companies to 1720*, vol. i, Cambridge, 1912, p. 470.

[4] Chapter IV, section iv, below, "The Duration of Business Cycles."

[5] The coefficient of variation in a statistical array is the standard deviation expressed as a percentage of the arithmetic mean. On the standard deviation see Chapter III, section v, 1, "The Amplitude of Cyclical-Irregular Fluctuations."

and another crisis, in the modern order. Eleven of his intervals between crises contain no period of "good trade"; 12 intervals contain no period of depression; one interval runs: crisis, "good trade," "depressed trade," crisis. No reasonable discount for the stereotyping influence which the concept of business cycles exercises upon the minds of modern business annalists will reduce the record of English business since 1790 to such irregularity of sequence as Dr. Scott records.

It seems clear, then, that the English crises of 1558-1720 were not business crises of the modern type, and that the intervals between these crises were not occupied by business cycles.[6]

Were Dr. Scott's investigations carried backward in time, they would doubtless continue to show frequent crises of a sort as far as records of business transactions could be followed in England. And since England lagged behind other countries in developing business traffic, crises of the type Scott describes must run back to earlier times in the Low Countries, France, Southern Germany, and the Italian towns.[7] Still earlier chapters in the same story appear in the economic histories of Constantinople, of Rome, of Athens. Indeed, we may feel sure that crises, in the sense of serious trade disturbances, are just as old as trade itself. They must have been familiar phenomena in ancient Babylonia and ancient Egypt. But if the crises of 17th- and even 18th-century England differed from the crises of 19th- and 20th-century England as much as Dr. Scott's results suggest, it seems most improbable that the crises of earlier date in any country resembled recent crises closely. Such accounts as I have read of early crises strengthen the inferential doubt. In certain respects interest-

[6] In view of the differences pointed out in the text, it is not surprising that Dr. Scott finds the modern theories of crises inapplicable to his period. "Occurrence of the unforeseen" is the explanation which best fits the facts in his opinion.

It is when the forecast of the majority of traders is in error that a crisis results. The cause of the miscalculation may lie either mainly in the men who judge or in the events to be judged. . . . At later periods the importance of man's judgment and calculation becomes marked in the period of speculative activity which precedes a crisis. But, prior to the development of banking, such intense activity is scarcely to be expected. . . . Analyzing the crises up to 1720 . . . it will be seen that, owing to defective intelligence in the form of news or to bad government, the objective aspect tends to predominate.

See *Joint-Stock Companies,* vol. i, pp. 469-471.

[7] For example, the second volume of Richard Ehrenberg's *Das Zeitalter der Fugger* gives a most interesting account of the great 16th century crises in Antwerp and Lyons, precipitated by the debt repudiations of the Spanish, French and Austrian monarchs. Not less vivid is Alfred Doren's history of the checkered fortunes of business in Florence at the height of her prosperity in the 13th and 14th centuries. *Studien aus der Florentiner Wirtschaftsgeschichte,* Stuttgart, 1901; *Entwicklung und Organisation der Florentiner Zünfte in 13. und 14. Jahrhundert,* 1896.

ing parallels can be drawn between the business difficulties with which we are familiar, and the business difficulties of which we read in early modern times, in the Middle Ages, or even in classical antiquity. But the differences are striking—most obviously, the difference in the rôle played by events of a non-business type.

The difficulty of deciding when the transition from crises dominated by crop failures, epidemics, wars, public finance and political struggles, to recurrent cycles dominated by business processes took place in England is increased by a gap in our detailed knowledge. There is no adequate record for the years between 1720, when Dr. Scott stops, and 1790, when Dr. Thorp begins. Jevons' list of English crises in the 18th century is too meager and too uncertain to be of much service.[8] The chief study of later date, Mentor Bouniatian's *Geschichte der Handelskrisen in England, 1640-1840,* is based on no such thorough examination of the original sources as Scott made, and mentions only the most impressive cases.[9] Possibly a close year-by-year record of developments would give a more modern impression than does an account limited to half-a-dozen dramatic episodes. That must remain uncertain until some thorough investigator closes the gap between Scott and Thorp. Meanwhile, we have Bouniatian's opinion that no crisis of really modern type can be found before the close of the 18th century.

According to this authority, the next memorable crisis after 1720 occurred in 1745, when the Pretender with his Highlanders got within 120 miles of London. The end of the Seven Years War was followed in 1763 by lively speculation and collapse. Again in 1772, England and Scotland suffered a banking crash after a period of wild speculation—a crash which extended next year to Holland, Hamburg and other continental centers of trade. Six years later, losses brought on by war with the American colonies caused serious difficulties in England. When the war ended in 1783, peace once more gave rise to a sudden expansion of business, and expansion led to a crisis. Finally, in 1793, came what Bouniatian ventures to call the first of England's great industrial crises, followed by depression in general business.[10]

[8] "The Periodicity of Commercial Crises and Its Physical Explanation." 1878. See W. S. Jevons, *Investigations in Currency and Finance,* London, 1884, pp. 207-215.

[9] Bouniatian's book was published at Munich in 1908. During the period treated by both Bouniatian and Scott (1640-1720), the former includes only five crises, the latter nineteen.

[10] Bouniatian, as cited above, p. 171.

As further evidence of the historical connection between business cycles and an advanced stage of pecuniary organization, I may refer to the National Bureau's collection of *Business Annals* at large. These annals show that in the countries which lag furthest behind in pecuniary organization—China, India, Brazil, South Africa, Russia —the vicissitudes of economic life have least of business character. Droughts and floods, epidemics among men and cattle, or civil disorder are responsible for a large part of the economic troubles which are recorded. Indeed, Thorp's record for China in 1890-1925 is curiously like Scott's record for England in, say, 1558-1660. Such misfortunes have consequences more serious in the less business-like communities than similar events have in western Europe or in North America. But, mingling with these phenomena of the natural economy, we find even in China indications that the nascent business activities of the people are subject to fluctuations arising from other sources. The merchants of the coast cities, at least, have their share of troubles with fluctuating commodity prices and exchange rates; some producers find the export demand for their produce falling and rising with conditions in other countries; the banks feel the reaction of developments in Lombard and Wall Streets. Thus the beginnings of business cycles in the laggard countries appear largely as reflections of the cycles in more advanced countries, and are perhaps overemphasized by foreign observers. But these beginnings promise to grow in significance as the backward lands organize a larger and larger part of their economic life on the basis of making and spending money incomes.

II. The Modern Organization for Making Money.

1. The Money-Making Population.

Table 1, compiled from the Fourteenth Census eked out by an estimate, shows broadly how the American people use their time.

Children under ten years of age form more than a fifth of the population. Their chief business is to develop into future citizens; for the time being they must be cared for and trained by adults in the family and the school. Any contributions they may make toward the community's support are incidental.

Leaving out this group of young children, the census indicates that 95 people in the hundred are either getting educated, or are contributing to the country's real income. The money makers form 50 per cent of this group, the home makers form 27 per cent, the students form 17 per cent, and those not accounted for in the table form 5 per cent.

The 4,610,000 persons not accounted for include some 400,000 children over 9 neither at school nor at work, a much larger number of the infirm in body or mind,[1] the "leisure class" among the rich and among the poor, those reported as following disreputable occupations, together with workers concerning whom the enumerators learned nothing but their names and residences.

TABLE 1

A CONSPECTUS OF THE POPULATION OF THE UNITED STATES IN 1920

	Total Number	Attending School	Keeping House (estimated)	Gainful Workers	Not accounted for, 10 years of age and over
Totals...................	105,700,000	21,800,000	22,500,000	41,600,000	4,610,000
Under 10 years of age					
Under 5 years..........	11,600,000				
5–9 years..............	11,400,000	7,800,000			
10–19 years of age					
10–14 years............	10,600,000	9,800,000		600,000	200,000
15–19 years............	9,400,000	3,700,000	1,100,000	4,400,000	200,000
20–64 years of age					
Males.................	29,800,000	280,000		28,300,000	1,220,000
Females...............	28,000,000	210,000	20,100,000	6,600,000	1,090,000
Over 64 years of age					
Males.................	2,500,000			1,500,000	1,000,000
Females...............	2,400,000		1,300,000	200,000	900,000
In Percentages of the Total Population					
Totals...................	100.0%	20.6%	21.3%	39.4%	4.4%
Under 10 years of age					
Under 5 years..........	11.0				
5–9 years..............	10.8	7.4			

[1] "The Department of Commerce announces that on or about January 1, 1923, there were 893,679 persons confined in Federal, state, city, county and private institutions for defectives, dependents, criminals, and juvenile delinquents, hospitals for mentally diseased, institutions for feebleminded and epileptics, homes for adults and dependent or neglected children, institutions for juvenile delinquents, penal institutions and almshouses." Of this total 229,780 were children. Needless to say a large, though unknown, number of the infirm in body or mind are cared for by their families and do not appear in a census of institutions. The quotation is from an official press release of July 14, 1924.

TABLE 1 — *Continued*

A Conspectus of the Population of the United States in 1920

	Total Number	Attending School	Keeping House (estimated)	Gainful Workers	Not accounted for, 10 years of age and over
10–19 years of age					
10–14 years............	10.0	9.3		.6	.2
15–19 years............	8.9	3.5	1.0	4.2	.2
20–64 years of age					
Males.................	28.2	.3		26.8	1.2
Females..............	26.5	.2	19.0	6.2	1.0
Over 64 years of age					
Males.................	2.4			1.4	.9
Females..............	2.3		1.2	.2	.9
In Percentages of the Age and Sex Classes					
Under 10 years of age					
Under 5 years..........	100.0				
5–9 years..............	100.0	68.4			
10–19 years					
10–14 years............	100.0	92.4		5.7	1.9
15–19 years............	100.0	39.4	11.7	46.8	2.1
20–64 years of age					
Males.................	100.0	.9		95.0	4.1
Females..............	100.0	.7	71.8	23.6	3.9
Over 64 years of age					
Males,................	100.0			60.0	40.0
Females..............	100.0		54.2	8.3	37.5
In Percentages of the Occupation Classes					
Totals..................	100.0%	100.0%	100.0%	100.0%	100.0%
Under 10 years of age					
Under 5 years..........	11.0				
5–9 years..............	10.8	35.8			
10–19 years of age					
10–14 years............	10.0	45.0		1.4	4.3
15–19 years............	8.9	17.0	4.9	10.6	4.3
20–64 years of age					
Males.................	28.2	1.3		68.0	26.5
Females..............	26.5	1.0	89.3	15.9	23.6
Over 64 years of age					
Males.................	2.4			3.6	21.7
Females..............	2.3		5.8	.5	19.5

Persons of unknown age are included in the group 20–64 years of age.
Notes on Table 1 continued on page 85.

The 14,000,000 students 10 years of age and over are made up mainly of children under 15. About that age half or more of the children drop out of school and begin earning money or helping with housework. Less than half a million persons over 19 years are reported as attending school, and not a few of them are also doing other work.

The 22,500,000 housewives are mainly women in the middle years of life; but there seem to be over a million girls and a somewhat larger number of elderly women who devote themselves primarily to maintaining homes for their families.

Finally, the 41,600,000 money earners include nearly half of the children between 15 and 19 years, not quite a quarter of the women of 20-64, nearly all of the men within these ages, more than half of the older men and a small part of the older women. Arranged in another way, the data show that of the gainful workers 12 per cent are under 20 years, 16 per cent are adult women, and 72 per cent are adult men.

Our concern, as students of business cycles, is mainly with this group of money makers. But we must not conceive the money makers as "supporting" the whole population; housewives contribute a large slice of real income. For the matter of that, the work young people do in school is of vital concern to economic welfare in the long run. And as consumers, the whole population comes into our reckoning.

Notes on Table 1 continued:

The number of women entered as "keeping house" without pay is based on estimates kindly made at the writer's request by Dr. Alba M. Edwards of the Bureau of the Census and by Dr. Ralph G. Hurlin of the Russell Sage Foundation. One of Dr. Edwards' methods, utilizing various population returns, yielded 23,000,000 housewives; the second, starting with the number of "homes" reported by the census, deducting for institutions enumerated as homes, and for family homes maintained by single men, paid housekeepers and by women having gainful occupations, and adding for homes managed by two women, yielded 22,300,000 housewives. Dr. Hurlin also tried two ways of approximating the number of unpaid housewives. His first method was to estimate the number of women occupied in other ways; by elimination, there seemed to be some 21,900,000 housewives. A second method, which Dr. Hurlin prefers, applies the American ratio of private to census families in 1900 and the British ratio of private families to "all occupiers" in 1911 to the 1920 count of homes, and after deductions for homes not managed by unpaid women, yields 22,500,000 housewives. The round figure adopted in the table is a little higher than the mean of these four estimates.

Some persons are reported both as attending school and as having gainful occupations. These cases are counted twice in the table. Their number is not known; but probably is not large enough to affect the results seriously. The gainfully-occupied women who also keep house are not counted as housekeepers.

The gainful workers include persons temporarily unemployed, and inmates of institutions who have specific work to perform. They do not include people of independent means who report no regular money-making occupation.

2. The Business Enterprise.

In spending money, the family is still the dominant unit of organization. But as the dominant unit of organization for making money, the family has been definitely superseded by the business enterprise, except perhaps in farming, petty trade, and the professions. The business enterprise commonly draws its members from several or many families, paying each individual a money income, and welding them into a new unit organized to make profits.

A business enterprise is an organization which seeks to realize pecuniary profits upon an investment of capital, by a series of transactions concerned with the purchase and sale of goods in terms of money.[1] The goods dealt in may be commodities of any vendible kind from coal to newspapers; they may be services, such as transportation, storage, or technical advice; they may be rights, such as bank credit, securities, or insurance against specified risks. The enterprise may "produce," or fabricate, or store, or transport, or distribute, or merely hold the title to the goods in which it deals.

3. The Size of Business Enterprises and Business Cycles.

Business enterprises of a highly organized type have come to occupy almost the whole field in railway and marine transportation. They dominate mining, lumbering, construction work, warehousing, most branches of manufacturing, the public utilities not managed by government, wholesale trade, insurance, banking and finance at large. They play an important, if not a controlling, rôle in retail trade, journalism, market gardening, fishing, hotel keeping, and various amusement trades. They are invading dairying, fruit raising, general farming, and the learned professions—engineering, architecture, law, education, medicine.

Of course, everyone who is working on his own account—the peddler, the cobbler, the farmer, the doctor and lawyer, the boardinghouse keeper, the newsboy—may be regarded as running a business enterprise. All these people, and those whom they suggest, get their money incomes by buying and selling goods, or by selling their services to numerous buyers. But there are broad differences between the

[1] Compare Werner Sombart, *Der Moderne Kapitalismus*, 1st ed., Leipzig, 1902, vol. i p. 195.

industries dominated by small-scale and those dominated by large-scale enterprises. In commercial alertness and business method, in complexity of organization, in dependence upon the money market, the typical farm, repair shop, neighborhood store, and boarding house are in a different class from the enterprises typical of mining, manufacturing, commerce and finance. Most professional men engaged in private practice hold, what some business men deny, that there is also a significant difference between professional and commercial aims.

In the study of business cycles, this uneven development of business enterprise in various fields is important. It is within the circle of full-fledged business enterprise that the alternations of prosperity and depression appear most clearly and produce their most striking effects. All of the authorities whose theories were reviewed in Chapter I seem to agree tacitly, if not explicitly, upon this fundamental point. They deal primarily with processes that run their rounds within the centers of commerce, industry, construction work, transportation, and finance. Farming, the professions, personal service, repair work, and petty trade are in the background of the picture. Even the writers who regard changes in crop yields as the cause of business fluctuations are no real exception; for while they hold that cyclical fluctuations arise in agriculture, they recognize that these fluctuations manifest themselves chiefly in commercial dealings, manufacturing activity, transportation, and financial operations.

Statistical evidence for this view that business cycles are primarily phenomena of large-scale enterprise was provided incidentally in 1923 by one of the investigations made by the National Bureau of Economic Research for the President's Conference on Unemployment. The pertinent results are assembled in Table 2. While the figures in this table are estimates based upon rather slender samples; while they refer to but one cycle in one country, and cover but one aspect of business—shrinkage in the hours worked by employees in depression—they give the most comprehensive statistical view yet presented of the relation between scale of organization and degree of cyclical fluctuations.

Two conclusions are indicated by the table. (1) When arranged according to the severity of the decline in employment after the crisis of 1920, the leading industries form three groups. Manufacturing, railroading, mining, and construction work were most disastrously affected by the depression. A second group, in which the shrinkage of employment was far less serious, but substantial, included finance. wholesale trade, and transportation other than by railroad. These two groups of industries constitute the sphere of business par excellence. The remaining industries, among them agriculture and retailing, are characterized by small-scale organization, or by the prominence of non-commercial aims, or by both features. These industries

TABLE 2

CYCLICAL DECLINE IN THE VOLUME OF EMPLOYMENT OFFERED BY DIFFERENT INDUSTRIES, AND BY ESTABLISHMENTS OF DIFFERENT SIZES, FROM THE PEAK OF PROSPERITY IN 1920 TO THE TROUGH OF DEPRESSION IN 1921–22.

	All establishments Per cent decline	Establishments with 0–20 employees Per cent decline	Establishments with 21–100 employees Per cent decline	Establishments with over 100 employees Per cent decline
All Industries	16.50	3.08	13.84	28.23
All Factories	29.97	8.21	19.21	38.56
Steam Railways	29.68	a	a	29.68
Extraction of Minerals	29.66	a	a	30.18
Building and Construction	18.92	14.66	a	a
Finance	7.14	0.00	0.00	25.58
Transportation other than railways	6.77	3.72	9.80	8.17
Wholesale Trade	5.64	0.00	12.31	7.77
Public and Professional Service	4.57	a	a	a
Domestic and Personal Service	4.11	5.40	4.48	3.92
Agriculture	3.18	2.15	a	a
Retail Trade	2.75	1.31	4.66	10.84
Hand Trades other than Building	0.00	2.11	4.67	a

a Reports received from less than 20 enterprises.
The comparisons are based upon quarterly reports from 9,289 enterprises, and cover the full years 1920 and 1921, and the first three months of 1922.
Adapted from Willford I. King, *Employment, Hours and Earnings in Prosperity and Depression. United States, 1920–1922.* National Bureau of Economic Research, New York, 2d ed., 1923, pp. 55–58, 60. (I have corrected a misprint in the source.)

reduced the amount of employment offered but slightly. (2) The correspondence between scale of organization and violence of fluctuations holds not merely among industries as wholes, but also among the establishments within an industry. As a rule, large establishments were more affected by the depression than medium-sized establishments, and the latter were more affected than small establishments.

These conclusions cannot be regarded as definitely proven, until they have stood the test of further investigations. They harmonize, however, not only with the assumptions of theoretical writers, but also with what is known about the fluctuations of prices, production, stocks, and the like in different industries. At a later stage, these fluctuations will be analyzed at length. In the meantime it is important to inquire what proportion of economic activity is exposed to a large business-cycle hazard and what part to a slight one.

Well over one-half of all employees in the United States seem to depend for work upon manufacturing, mining, railroading and building and construction, the industries in which the cyclical oscillations appear to be most violent.[1] Within these industries probably three-fourths or more of the employees are in concerns which have over 100 hands—the subdivision most exposed to the business-cycle hazard.[2] The middle group of industries shown in Table 2 has a much smaller body of employees, perhaps as much as one-tenth, perhaps as little as one-twentieth of the total. There remain in the industries least exposed to cyclical fluctuations something like a third or two-fifths of all wage and salary earners. And a large majority of these workers are employed in the smallest and least-affected class of enterprises.[3]

Very different is the distribution of men working on their own account. Estimates based upon the 1920 census of occupations indicate that the number of such persons in the United States was a little more than 10,000,000.[4] Certainly less than one-tenth, perhaps not

[1] See Dr. King's estimate of the number of employees working in various industries in 1920, *Employment, Hours and Earnings*, p. 20.

[2] The Fourteenth Census gives definite data for manufactures, mines, and quarries, which may be summarized thus:

MANUFACTURING ESTABLISHMENTS AND MINES AND QUARRIES: CLASSIFIED ACCORDING TO NUMBER OF EMPLOYEES: UNITED STATES, 1919

Number of Employees per Establishment	Manufacturing Establishments		Mines and Quarries	
	Per cent of Number	Per cent of Total Employees	Per cent of Number	Per cent of Total Employees
20 or less	81	10	73	6
21–100	13	19	17	18
Over 100	6	71	10	76
	100	100	100	100
Actual numbers	290,000	9,096,000	21,300	982,000

Compiled from *Fourteenth Census of the United States*, vols. viii, *Manufactures*, p. 90, and xi, *Mines and Quarries*, p. 31.

All the operating railroads, of course, employ more than 100 men. Concerning building and construction, the data are meager; but Dr. King has made a very rough estimate that in 1920, not quite one-third of the employees were working for concerns having more than 100 persons on the payrolls. See *Employment, Hours and Earnings*, p. 20.

[3] Once more see Dr. King's estimates on p. 20 of *Employment, Hours and Earnings*.

[4] See the three estimates compared by Dr. Leo Wolman in *The Growth of American Trade Unions, 1880-1923*. New York, National Bureau of Economic Research, 1924, pp.

one-twentieth, of these enterprisers [5] were in those branches of business most exposed to the business-cycle hazard. About nine-tenths, on the other hand, were in the least exposed group of industries,—farming, retail trade, and professional, domestic and personal service.[6]

4. Economic Resources and the National Dividend.

Of the vast array of natural resources and man-made equipment used by our 41,600,000 money-earners and our 22,500,000 housewives —to keep the 1920 census figures of Table 1—many writers upon business cycles have emphasized one category, and taken the others for granted. Hobson's theory of over-savings and over-investment in industrial equipment, Tugan-Baranovski's theory of the alternate accumulation and exhaustion of loan-funds, Hull's theory of the changing costs of construction work, the numerous theories which stress the effects of extending plant capacity, Foster and Catchings' theory of the inability of consumers to buy the goods offered them, all build in one way or another upon a contrast between the process of supplying current income and the process of increasing the appliances for future production.[1]

To lay a factual basis for testing these views, we should find out what we can about the relative magnitude of (1) the value of the equipment with which the population works, (2) the income produced, and (3) the annual additions made to working equipment out of income. The present section deals with the first two magnitudes; a later section will deal with savings.

For summaries of the resources which the population uses in its work, we must turn to inventories of the national wealth. Two esti-

---

78-81. Mr. Carl Hookstadt's figures cited here are raised well above 10,000,000 by including 1,850,119 "home farm laborers" with the employers. *Monthly Labor Review,* July, 1923, vol. xvii, p. 2, footnote.

[5] Of the various aliases under which the man who is doing business on his own account passes in current economic literature (entrepreneur, undertaker, capitalist-employer, business man), the name enterpriser seems least objectionable. It is an old English word, recently brought back into current use at almost the same time by Professors Frank A. Fetter (*Principles of Economics,* New York, 1904), and H. Stanley Jevons (*Essays on Economics,* London, 1905).

[6] Compare the estimates given by Dr. W. I. King in the first chapter of Dr. Maurice Leven's *Distribution of Income by States,* New York, National Bureau of Economic Research, 1925, and by Dr. Leo Wolman in his monograph cited above, p. 77.

[1] See the references to the writers named in Chapter I, section iv. Among the men who assign much importance to the construction of additional equipment are Veblen, Spiethoff, Bouniatian, Aftalion, J. M. Clark, Robertson, Cassel, and A. B. Adams.

mates for the United States as of December 31, 1922, have recently
been made by the Bureau of the Census and the Federal Trade Commission. Both organizations recognize that their results are rough
approximations at best. The concept "national wealth" is so vague
that statisticians differ about the items to be included, and about the
proper methods of ascertaining values. Also, the data with which
they must work leave much to be desired in comprehensiveness and
accuracy. Under such circumstances, it is not to be expected that
different estimates will agree closely, or that any estimate can command full confidence. The Federal Trade Commission's total for
1922 is some 10 per cent greater than that of the Census, primarily
because the Commission includes "land and improvements in streets
and public roads," which the Census omits, and because the Commission values "public service enterprises" at 46 billion dollars, while
the Census values them at 35 billions.[2] But the 10 per cent difference
between the two totals does not represent the margin of uncertainty
surrounding both results. Accordingly, I shall use the figures only in
the broadest fashion to indicate the great classes of resources with
which the population works, the order of magnitude among these
classes, and the relative value of man-made equipment and of annual
income.

[2] See *Estimated National Wealth*, Bureau of the Census, Washington, 1925; *National
Wealth and Income, A Report by the Federal Trade Commission* (Senate Document
No. 126, 69th Congress, 1st session), Washington, 1926. The Federal Trade Commission's estimate is rather a reworking of and supplement to the basic Census figures
than an independent investigation of the whole field.

With these official estimates compare the inventory of "Physical Property in the
United States" in 1920, made by Dr. Walter Renton Ingalls, *Wealth and Income of the
American People*, 2d ed., York, Pennsylvania, 1923, p. 79. Dr. Ingalls' total of 273
billion dollars is 18 per cent less than the Census total and 29 per cent less than the
Federal Trade Commission total. These differences are smaller than one would expect
in view of the facts that (1) Ingalls' estimates are for 1920, the Census and Commission
estimates for the end of 1922; (2) Ingalls used 1913 values, so far as possible, the
Census and Commission tried to use current values; (3) Ingalls made relatively freer
use of estimates as contrasted with enumerations, than did the Census and Commission.
(For example, to arrive at the value of manufacturing machinery, Ingalls estimated
that 7,750,000 workers used plant of average cost of $2,000 per worker, while the Census
summed up many thousands of reports from manufacturing enterprises concerning
the value of their machinery.) On the other hand, it should be noted (1) that the
period 1920-22 included a severe crisis and depression, during which the increase of
wealth was retarded; (2) that the money values of real estate, buildings, heavy machinery, and the like were far less affected by price fluctuations than our current index
numbers might lead one to think, and that none of the estimators can hold rigorously
to values of a given date; (3) that several of the items must be guessed at, and it may
make little difference (as in the machinery item) whether the guess is based on elaborate
study of a sample, or on the estimate of an expert who has had long experience in
valuation work. Needless to say, in some items the percentage differences among
the three estimates are far larger than the differences among the three totals. But it
is not feasible to enter into details in this place.

Since our national inventories refer to the end of 1922, it seems well to compare them with the mean income of the two calendar years, 1922 and 1923. For national income in these years, we have three estimates, one made by the Federal Trade Commission, one made by Dr. W. R. Ingalls, and preliminary figures made by Dr. W. I. King for the National Bureau of Economic Research. These estimates are not strictly comparable; for the Federal Trade Commission and Dr. Ingalls omit two items which Dr. King includes—the rental value of homes occupied by their owners and interest upon the value of consumers' goods owned by families. Since the inventories we are using include both family dwellings and personal effects as considerable items of national wealth, consistency requires that we include the services rendered by these goods in the income estimates which we compare with the wealth estimates. This consideration points to the use of King's figures. But King's figures for 1922-23 are preliminary estimates, while the Federal Trade Commission's figures are the result of elaborate investigation. It seems best, therefore, to use the Commission's estimate as basic, but to add King's figures for the two items in question. This procedure gives 70 billion dollars as the average income for 1922-23.[3]

We may begin our canvass of economic resources with an item on which no one can set a price—the knowledge which enables men to use other resources as they now do. What count here are not merely the engineering applications of modern science, but also the organiz-

[3] For the three estimates, see Walter Renton Ingalls, "An Estimate of National Income for 1925," *The Annalist,* September 24, 1926, p. 395, and the National Bureau's *News-Bulletin,* February, 1927.
  The figures for 1922-23 are as follows:

Estimates of National Income in the United States
In billions of Dollars.

	Ingalls	National Bureau	Federal Trade Commission
1922	60.5	65.6*	61.7
1923	71.9	76.8*	69.8

  * Preliminary estimates, subject to revision.

King's estimates for the two items omitted by the other authorities are, in billions of dollars:

	Rental value of homes occupied by owners.	Interest upon value of consumers' goods owned by consumers.
1922	1.8	2.6
1923	1.9	2.8

The addition of these items to the Federal Trade Commission estimates brings their average for 1922-23 within 1¼ per cent of King's corresponding figure (70.3 billions in one case and 71.2 billions in the other).

ing capacity of business men, the skill of mechanics, the ability of housewives as both managers and manual workers—indeed the whole mass of commonplace and of specialized knowledge which enables people to work in disciplined harmony for each other and to make use of each others' products.

In a discussion of secular trends in economic life, past or future, this resource would take first place. Man's ability to multiply and to raise his standard of living, in a world where many natural resources appear to be exhaustible, depends upon the progress of his knowledge. In treating business cycles we need not face this issue at large. Yet several of the working hypotheses which other investigators have suggested show that we cannot set knowledge aside as a factor of no concern to us. Vogel, Schumpeter, Mrs. England, and Cassel regard business cycles as by-products of progress in the arts of production and of business organization.[4]

Though we cannot value the inestimable, we can make contact between the maintenance cost of knowledge and our measuring stick, the national income. Knowledge is one of the resources which must be continuously renewed. According to the occupation tables, one money-earner in every fifty is a school or college teacher, and according to the Educational Finance Inquiry one fiftieth of our national income is spent upon schools.[5] But these figures give a most inadequate impression of the effort we make as a nation to educate ourselves. The census figures of Table 1 show that more than a fifth of the total population are attending school. For every two persons earning money, one person is studying. The discount upon this comparison for the brevity and irregularity of school attendance by many children is partly offset by the irregularity of the work done by many adults. It is a common aim of state laws to give every child eight or nine years of schooling. There must be several millions of Americans who have spent fifteen years or more primarily in study.[6] Nine years make a fifth, and fifteen years make a third of an active working life of 45 years. And besides the years we devote to formal training, each

[4] See Chapter I, section iv.
[5] Mabel Newcomer, *Financial Statistics of Public Education in the United States*, (Educational Finance Inquiry, vol. vi) New York, 1924, pp. 11-29.
Dr. Newcomer estimates the governmental expenditures upon schools (1.220 million dollars in 1920) at 1.6 per cent of the national income in 1910, 2.0 per cent in 1915, and 1.7 per cent in 1920. No one knows how large are the educational expenditures of endowments and private schools. I take one-fiftieth of the national income to indicate merely the order of magnitude of the money outlay upon this item.
[6] Table I shows that in 1920, 490,000 persons over 19 years of age were reported as "attending school."

of us spends much time in learning and in teaching others how to do specific jobs at home or where we are employed.

To all this effort spent upon imparting our inherited store of knowledge must be added a further item, much smaller in amount, but doubtless involving a direct money outlay of hundreds of millions annually upon efforts to improve and extend knowledge. Here be-longs all the energy put into research proper, and the endless experimenting with new devices and methods for doing the world's work.[7]

To come to the tangible resources: (1) In the national inventories for 1922, an item of nearly 40 billion dollars is entered as "furniture and personal effects." If we add a rough figure for pleasure automobiles, this item rises to 42 or 43 billions—say two-thirds of one year's national income.

How rapidly the goods in question are worn out and replaced on the average, we do not know. But family budgets throw some light on that problem. In 1924, the Federal Bureau of Labor Statistics published tables summarizing the expenditures of over 12,000 white families living in 92 industrial centers, and having incomes which averaged about $1,500. Of their total outlays, 23 per cent was spent for clothing, furniture, furnishings, and miscellaneous items which can be classified as "personal effects."[8] The representative value of these figures is open to question. Negro and farm families probably spend a smaller proportion of their money for clothing and personal effects than do white urban families; but well-to-do families probably spend more than wage-earners.[9] Also, the period covered by the Bureau of Labor Statistics' budgets—mainly the calendar year 1918— was peculiar in several ways. Hence we cannot trust wholly the

[7] Secretary Hoover has recently ventured the following estimates:
"We are spending in industry, in government, national and local, probably $200,-000,000 a year in search for applications of scientific knowledge—with perhaps 30,000 men engaged in the work . . . the whole sum which we have available to support pure science research is less than $10,000,000 a year, with probably less than 4,000 men engaged in it, most of them dividing their time between it and teaching."
Herbert Hoover, "The Nation and Science," Science, January 14, 1927, vol. lxv, pp. 26, 27.
[8] See "The Cost of Living in the United States," Bulletin of the U. S. Bureau of Labor Statistics, No. 357, p. 5, and last section of Table G. The largest miscellaneous item is "automobiles, motor cycles, bicycles." The budgets were collected in 1918-19 from places scattered over 42 states.
[9] In the Bureau of Labor Statistics' table the percentages of outlay for clothing, furniture and furnishings, and miscellaneous objects all rise with family income. Also see the table on p. 26 of the National Bureau's report on Income in the Various States, 1925. These figures, compiled by Dr. King, indicate that expenditures on automobiles

conclusions that upwards of a quarter of family income is spent for quasi-durable consumers' commodities, and that the stock of these commodities on hand is between two and three years' purchases. But such are the indications of what data we have.

(2) At all times there is a huge stream of raw materials, partially-fabricated products and finished goods flowing through the country's industrial and commercial enterprises on its way toward family or business consumers. The 1922 inventories value this flow at about 36 billion dollars. That sum is equivalent to half of the national income in the year concerned, and is not much smaller than the value assigned to the furniture and personal effects owned by families.

The contrast drawn by writers like Henry S. Dennison, Lawrence K. Frank, T. W. Mitchell, and Simon S. Kuznets between the fairly even pace of consumer purchasing and the fluctuating course of production suggests that the volume of merchandise and materials on hand, on wheels, and in process, undergoes large changes. The rough comparison which the national inventories let us make between the value of "products, merchandise, etc." at a given time and the national income for one year indicates that a check upon production need not check consumption at once. But we need more continuous, specific, and reliable data than an occasional inventory can give. Fortunately, we have a clear view of the flow of goods in at least one industry.

By checking the input of copper by smelters against the deliveries of copper by refiners, the American Bureau of Metal Statistics is able to make a continuous record of the flow of copper through the metallurgical system. This record commands the confidence even of its compilers—a virtue rare in industrial statistics. The reports show for the first of each month the quantity of copper at five successive stages of its trip toward consumers—blister at smelteries, blister in transit, blister at refineries, metal in process of being refined, and refined copper on hand at refineries. The total tonnage reported at these five stages month by month varies considerably—for example, it shrank in 1922 from 427,000 tons at the beginning of the year to 344,000 tons at the close. The general level of the tonnage in this flow is about one-third to one-half of the annual output of virgin copper.

(including tires), books, clothing, diamonds, furs, house furnishings, and pianos made up about 28 per cent of the outlays of urban employees, 29 per cent of the outlays of families spending $5,000 annually, and 32 per cent of the outlays of families spending $25,000 annually.

All this refers solely to the metallurgical system, which is con strued as ending at the exit gates of the refineries. After passing through these gates into the manufacturing system, copper travels to mills wherein by itself, or as brass, bronze, or nickel silver, it is made into sheets, rod, wire, tubing, or castings. From the mills, basic fabricated products go partly into direct consumption (for example, electrical transmission wire), but more largely to other manufacturers who make finished goods, such as electrical motors and automobiles. Many products (for example, hardware and house fittings) pass from secondary manufacturers through jobbers to the shelves of retailers. A complete report would show copper in transit, in stock, in process, and ready for delivery at each of these supplemental stages before it passes into actual use in a myriad of forms. Moreover, in the manufacturing processes a considerable proportion of the copper worked up passes into scrap, turnings, borings, etc. This scrap is reworked, so that an appreciable fraction of our copper is continuously going round and round in the manufacturing system. It is computed that in 1923 the quantity of such scrap was about one-third of the manufacture, which would mean a lockup of about four months' supply in this form alone, in addition to the lockup of from three months' to six months' supply in the metallurgical system. The copper in transit, in processes, and in stock in the manufacturing and distributing systems, for which there is no statistical accounting, should be added. The director of the American Bureau of Metal Statistics, Dr. W. R. Ingalls, believes that "the normal stock of copper in the United States is equivalent to something between six months' and twelve months' production, and more nearly the latter than the former." [10]

How representative the copper industry is in this respect, we shall not know until other industries develop similar statistical services. Meantime, we may take this case as illustrating, though not as measuring, a feature of economic activity too often overlooked.

(3) Business-cycle theorists have concentrated their attention primarily upon the next item—movable equipment—though its value in the inventory is a little smaller than the value of "furniture and personal effects," and only a little larger than the value put on "products, merchandise, etc." As movable equipment we count some 16 billion dollars worth of manufacturing machinery, tools, and im-

[10] See W. R. Ingalls, *Wealth and Income of the American People,* 2d ed., 1923, p. 150. It is to Dr. Ingalls that I am indebted for information concerning the work of the American Bureau of Metal Statistics

plements; 11 to 14 billions of public service equipment (apart from improvements upon land); 6 billions of live stock; 2½ billions of farm implements and machinery, and 1 or 2 billion dollars worth of motor trucks and cars used wholly or largely for business. The total runs to about 37 billion dollars according to the Census, and to about 40 billions according to the Federal Trade Commission—somewhat over half of one year's national income.

(4) The value of "improvements upon land," including much besides buildings, is a highly conjectural figure.[11] Doubtless we are safe in accepting the conclusion that this item is much larger than any of the preceding, and is every year larger than the current national income. The Census figures give a total of 89 billion dollars; the Commission figures mount to 108 billions.

(5) The value of land itself is estimated by the Census method at 112 billion dollars in 1922, and by the Commission method at 122 billions. With these imposing sums we have little concern. Land values are unquestionably influenced by changes in business activity, and excited real-estate speculation is a familiar feature of "booms." But what men get out of land year by year, and what improvements they make upon it, are matters of greater moment in the study of business cycles than are the money values imputed to land.

One point, however, we should notice. On the face of the returns, agriculture is capitalized at a higher figure than manufacturing. According to Dr. King's figures, by 1920 the number of money-earners who depended upon manufactures for their living had become decidedly larger than the number who depended upon agriculture— 11,500,000 persons against 8,900,000.[12] Of machinery and implements, the factory workers used in 1922 a value six times that of the farm workers—15.8 billion dollars against 2.6 billions. Adding 5.8 billions for live stock still leaves the farm workers with far less movable equipment. But the value assigned to farm real estate is more than double that assigned to the real estate used in manufacturing—53 billion dollars against 24 billions. Of course, the farm is a home as well as an income-making enterprise; but even if we subtract a fifth from the real-estate value of farms to cover this item, we have left a difference of 17 or 18 billions between agricultural and manufacturing real estate—more than enough to offset the excess in the value of

[11] On its derivation, see the Federal Trade Commission's report on *National Wealth and Income*, pp. 31-34.
[12] See his introduction to *Income in the Various States*, National Bureau of Economic Research, 1925, pp. 21 and 23.

movable equipment used in manufacturing.[13]   Of the real estate used
in these two great branches of industry, it is safe to assume that improvements constitute a larger percentage in manufacturing than in
farming.   Thus the high capitalization of agriculture is due wholly to
the greater value imputed to land itself.   If we could separate the
value of all man-made equipment (including live stock) from the
value of natural resources, we would find that the average factory
worker uses a far larger stock of the first in his work than does the
average farm worker, but that the nominal value of the average farm
worker's total equipment is the greater.

(6) Finally, our inventories include a small item, 4.3 billion dollars, representing the value of gold and silver coins and bullion.   From
the national viewpoint, this resource must be regarded as part of the
permanent equipment for production.   But it is a peculiar type of
equipment.   It renders its service as it changes ownership, or as it
lies in vaults as a "reserve" supporting a larger volume of credit
currency.   It is one of the most durable man-made resources, so that
the supply consists mainly of past accumulations.   The changes in
any country's stock during a year are usually due more to a redistribution of the world stock than to fresh production minus wastage.
Both the redistribution and the annual production of the precious
metals bear upon price fluctuations.   That fact secures this item, small
as it is in comparison with other resources, a leading place in studies
of business fluctuations.

The chief conclusion to be drawn from this survey of economic
resources is that the physical, man-made equipment with which the
American population works represents a value equivalent to between
three and four years' effort of its money-earners.   Barring land, the

[13] The estimates used are given in a footnote on p. 29 of the Federal Trade Commission's report on *National Wealth and Income*.   Even the 1920 Census figure of 44
billion dollars for the "capital" of manufacturing establishments—a figure against which
the Bureau of the Census itself warns us—falls far short of the value of farm property
minus an allowance for farm homes.   A third figure showing the "estimated value of
wealth used in *corporate* business" by manufacturing industries (33.7 billions of dollars)
is derived by the Commission from tax reports made to the Bureau of Internal Revenue
(see p. 135 of *National Wealth and Income*).   According to the Census of Manufactures
in 1920, incorporated enterprises produced 87.7 per cent of the total value of manufactured goods.   If we apply this ratio to the above estimate of "the value of wealth
used" by manufacturing corporations, we get some 38 billion dollars as "the value of
wealth used" by all manufacturing enterprises.   That figure agrees fairly well with
the estimates used in the text (15.8 billion dollars worth of movable equipment, plus
24 billion dollars worth of real estate).

The estimate of the value of farm real estate in 1922 (53 billions) was made by the
Department of Agriculture.

Bureau of the Census values our tangible man-made resources at 209 billion dollars in 1922. The Federal Trade Commission puts the figure at 231 billions.[14] To raise the first estimate to three times the national income of 1922-23, we should have to add to it a billion dollars. To raise the second estimate to four times the national income we should have to add 49 billions. But though our conclusion is protected by these margins (one of which is narrow), we should view it as no more than a rough approximation based upon imperfect data.[15]

[14] A tabular recapitulation of the figures may be useful. I have rearranged the items to serve the present purpose, but have not altered the figures. The slight discrepancies between the totals entered and the sums of the items are due to the dropping of fractions.

ESTIMATES OF THE NATIONAL WEALTH OF THE UNITED STATES IN 1922
In billions of dollars

		Census	Federal Trade Commission
Land		112	122
Improvements on land		89	108
Movable equipment			
Live stock	5.8		5.8
Farm implements and machinery	2.6		2.6
Manufacturing implements and machinery	15.8		15.8
Public service equipment	10.6		13.6
Motor cars and trucks	2.0		2.0
		37	40
Products and merchandise		36	36
Furniture and personal effects (including automobiles)		42	42
Gold and silver coin and bullion		4	4
Total man-made equipment		209	231
Grand Total		321	353

For more detailed estimates, see the Federal Trade Commission's report on *National Wealth and Income*, 1926, pp. 28 and 34.

[15] One would expect to find the accumulated stock of wealth larger in proportion to current income in western Europe than in the United States. This surmise is supported by computations based on the data collected by Sir Josiah Stamp in "The Wealth and Income of the Chief Powers," *Journal of the Royal Statistical Society*, July, 1919, vol. lxxxii, pp. 441–493. From Sir Josiah's summary table (p. 491) and from land values given in his text (pp. 455, 467 and 475), the best figures I can make run as follows:

RATIO OF ONE YEAR'S NATIONAL INCOME TO:

		National Wealth	National Wealth minus value of land
United Kingdom	1914	1:6.4	1:5.9
Germany	1914	1:7.7	1:6.1
France	1914	1:8.0	1:5.9
Australia	1914	1:5.9	....
United States	1914	1:5.8	....
United States	1922–23	1:5.0	1:3.3

Although the results answer expectations, and although I have included only the countries for which tolerably good estimates of wealth and income are available, the comparison is hazardous. In particular, it seems that the valuation of lands must be

The possession of this equipment gives a modern community not only vastly enhanced power of producing income, but also power to consume for a time more than it produces. Even a private family can fall back at need upon its store of "furniture and private effects" —a store which our estimates make equal to nearly two-thirds of a year's income on the average. They can suspend renewals and repairs upon such goods, and even turn some goods into food at a pinch— though seldom without heavy loss. A farmer can sell part of his live stock, let his buildings run down, and make shift with his old implements—not to speak of depleting the fertility of his land. A business enterprise can pursue the same policy—particularly it can reduce its inventories of materials, products or merchandise on hand. Of course, neglect of maintenance usually incurs heavy economic penalties; but there are times when families and business men have no choice in the matter. They must live "on their fat" for a while.

Nor is that all. While current net additions to man-made equipment are probably smaller in value one year with another than are current renewals, these additions can be nearly suspended at need, and made in large volume when conditions are favorable. In practice, the fluctuations in extension and betterment work doubtless have far larger amplitudes than the fluctuations in repairs and renewals. Added to the latter, they make the cyclical swings in production considerably greater than the cyclical swings in consumption.

What the present section adds to common knowledge is that, in dealing with business cycles, (1) attention should be paid to several types of resources besides buildings, machinery, and public-utility equipment, (2) account should be taken of fluctuations in outlay upon maintenance, as well as of fluctuations in outlay upon extensions, and (3) the value of all tangible man-made resources in use at a given time seems in the United States to be less than four times the value of one year's national income, as that income is usually reckoned.

5. The Interdependence of Business Enterprises.

Every business enterprise for which a set of books is kept may be treated as an independent unit. Indeed, the Bureau of the Census made on different principles in the four countries for which figures are given. On the face of the figures, land values make 8 per cent of total wealth in the United Kingdom, 21 per cent in Germany, 26 per cent in France, and 35 per cent in the United States. Probably the ratios of income to total wealth are less reliable approximations than the ratios of income to wealth minus land values.

accepts this test of separate bookkeeping as its chief criterion in deciding how many "establishments" to recognize in its enumerations of mines, factories and farms. Yet all business enterprises are so bound to each other by industrial, commercial, and financial ties that none can prosper and none can suffer without affecting others.

As an industrial plant handling commodities, the typical enterprise is one wheel in a great machine. Our wants are supplied by series of nominally independent plants which pass on goods to each other in succession. One series, for example, embraces wheat farms, elevators, railways, flour mills, wholesale dealers in provisions, bakeries, and retail distributors. Each set of members in such a series is dependent upon the preceding set for its chief supplies and upon the succeeding set for its chief vent. The wheat, as grain, flour and bread, flows through the successive sets of enterprises in an unceasing stream, though the volume of flow is far from steady.

Further, no industrial series is self-sufficing. Each set of enterprises in the example, from farms to retail shops, is dependent upon other industrial series for buildings, machinery, fuel, office supplies, transportation, insurance, professional services, and sundries. An especially intimate dependence exists between all other industrial enterprises and the railways. Coal mining and the steel trade also serve almost all industrial enterprises in one way or another. So far, indeed, have industrial differentiation and integration been carried that "the whole concert of industrial operations is to be taken as a machine process, made up of interlocking detailed processes, rather than as a multiplicity of mechanical appliances each doing its particular work in severalty." [1]

To the public the unbroken flow of goods from plant to plant until they finally reach consumers is the matter of prime concern. But business men are concerned more with the commercial than with the industrial aspects of this flow. The movement of goods through successive sets of enterprises which form industrial series, and between enterprises which belong to different industries, is maintained by purchase and sale. Hence the commercial bonds which unite business enterprises to one another in varying degrees of intimacy. Each enterprise is affected by the fortunes of its customers, its competitors, and the purveyors of its supplies.

[1] Thorstein Veblen, *Theory of Business Enterprise*, New York, 1904, p. 7.

Financial interdependence is in part but a third aspect of these industrial-commercial bonds. Complicated relationships of creditor and debtor arise from the purchase and sale of goods upon credit, and make the disaster of one enterprise a menace to many. On this financial side of their operations, the banks bear a relation to all other enterprises not unlike that which the railways bear on the industrial side; for most enterprises need bank credit not less than they need freight service. As a serious congestion of railway traffic applies the brake to industrial operations, so any hampering of banking operations applies the brake to business dealings.

There is a further set of financial bonds which need not run parallel with industrial-commercial relationships. The corporate form of business organization facilitates the acquisition of common ownership in enterprises nominally independent of each other. The same capitalist or group of capitalists often owns a large or even a controlling interest in companies doing different kinds of business, or the same kind in different places. Thus the selling agent may acquire an interest in the factory whose output he handles; the manufacturer may open his own retail stores, or buy stock in a competing company, or secure his raw materials by taking over timber lands or mines; the large capitalist may invest in steel and real estate, in railways and banks, in newspapers and hotels, in mines and moving pictures. Thus also we have our chain shops, chain banks, chain newspapers, chain theaters, chain lumberyards, and the like. Often the financial bond is made less personal, but more direct, by one corporation holding stock in tributary or even in rival companies.

How dominant the corporate form of organization has become in certain fields, the census shows. In 1920 corporations owned 32 per cent of American manufacturing establishments, employed 87 per cent of the wage-earners and turned out 88 per cent of the value produced. In mining, corporations were even more important, owning 51 per cent of the mines, employing 94 per cent of the men, and producing 94 per cent of the product.[2] Of course in railway transportation corporations cover the whole field, and they probably do more than half of the business in all branches characterized by large-scale organization. In 1920, 345,600 corporations filed tax returns showing an aggregate gross income of some $126,000,000,000.[3] Even

[2] *Fourteenth Census of the United States*, vol. viii, *Manufactures*, p. 119, and vol. xi, *Mines and Quarries*, p. 29.

[3] *Statistics of Income from Returns of Net Income for 1920.* United States Internal Revenue, p. 61. The gross income of all corporations has been increased as suggested on

in agriculture, retail trade, domestic, personal and professional service, corporations cut an appreciable figure.[4]

The tangle of financial relationships among business enterprises which has arisen from the prevalence of corporate organization is so complicated that it never has been, and perhaps cannot be, adequately represented in figures. Many corporations are owned, in whole or in large part, by some parent company or holding concern. In other cases, formerly independent enterprises have cemented a financial alliance by exchanging stocks. In still other cases, two or more companies are owned largely by a common group of stockholders. Some of these financial bonds are close and permanent, others are loose and shifting. The reasons for the financial alliance, whatever its form, are sometimes far from obvious—business makes strange bed fellows as well as politics.[5] The alliance may be used to safeguard the interests of all the participants, or it may result from and be used to enhance the power and profit of some preponderating interest. Under the corporate form of organization an investor may reduce his risks by spreading his holdings among numerous enterprises and industries; a corporation may enlist the interest of thousands of customers or employees in its welfare by seeking a wide distribution of its shares; a group of financiers which has won prestige may control the use of business capital far larger than its members own; unscrupulous managers may run an enterprise primarily for their personal advantage through stock-exchange operations in its securities or through corrupt bargains with other concerns in which they hold shares. These are indeed but suggestive examples of the many opportunities, wholesome or injurious, which the rise of joint-stock companies has brought to the denizens of a business economy.

The one fact of commanding importance for the present purpose which emerges from this tangle of relationships and opportunities is that interlocking ownership organizes many nominally independent enterprises into communities of interest. While such bonds are far less comprehensive than the industrial-commercial-credit bonds which

p. 8 of this document, to correct the incomplete returns of railroad and other public utility corporations.

[4] The number of corporations reporting in these fields were as follows: farming, 12,376; retail trade, not including department stores, 50,604; domestic service, 7,298; amusements, 5.258; professional and other service. 10.510. See as above, pp. 62-69.

[5] Compare the diverse reasons found by Dr. Willard L. Thorp for the formation of "central-office concerns"—groups of industrial establishments operated from a single office. *The Integration of Industrial Operation*, Census Monographs, iii, Washington, 1924, pp. 159-265.

embrace practically all enterprises, they are important, both because they affect particularly the largest corporations, and because they give to close-knit groups enhanced strategic influence upon business activity as a whole.

Besides the close bonds based upon commercial dealings, credit arrangements and ownership, there are looser ties which make the fortunes of business enterprises interdependent.

(1) Business enterprises must buy what they need in a common market, and compete against each other for possession of the common stock of the numerous goods which almost every enterprise requires. Among these goods we must list not only railway transportation, coal, steel and bank credit, but also many other widely used commodities, investment funds, land, common labor, and certain highly skilled services, for example, those of business executives, salesmen, engineers, lawyers, and accountants. When business is slack this interrelation through dependence upon a common source of supply is scarcely noticed; but at the peak of an intense boom its importance becomes manifest.

(2) Business enterprises must also sell in a common market, bidding against each other for the money of customers. This tie becomes closest in periods of depression. It is not simply that the clothier feels the competition of his trade rival, but also that the clothing industry feels the competition of the automobile industry, theaters fear the inroads of motion pictures and radios upon their market, insurance companies find their claims upon family incomes endangered by the claims of landlords, labor unions and the makers of automatic machines contest for the same work, and so on.

(3) If in these two respects the relations of business enterprises are competitive, it is not less true that business enterprises draw their support from one another. All business depends in the last resort upon the demands of personal consumers—even the enterprises which make products like mining machinery or bank equipment. And the bulk of the incomes which enable consumers to buy are incomes disbursed by business enterprises as wages, rents, interest or profits. Any serious reduction in the flow of incomes from business enterprises to consumers reacts promptly upon the concerns which provide consumers' goods and through them upon the concerns which cater to business needs.

All the interrelations among business enterprises here spoken of are matters of common knowledge. But since the study of business cycles is concerned with the spreading of given changes from their points of origin, it is well to note explicitly the variety of the bonds which unite all the enterprises of a country into a loose system. For these bonds are also channels through which the quickening or slackening of activity in one part of a business economy spreads to other parts.

6. Profits as the Clue to Business Fluctuations.

Not less important for the present purpose than the interrelations among all business enterprises, is the relation between the making of goods and the making of money within each enterprise. A business enterprise can serve the community by making goods only on condition that, over a period of years, its operations yield a profit.[1]

The subordination of service to money-making is not grounded in the mercenary motives of business men, but is one of the necessary results of pecuniary organization. A business man may be as public spirited or as scientifically minded as any one in the community, he may get his personal satisfaction chiefly from the contribution his enterprise renders to human well-being; yet he must so order affairs that his receipts exceed his expenses, or he will be put out of business and lose his chance to render service. Probably in the long run scrupulous maintenance of quality of output, avoidance of all misrepresentation, fairness in dealing with customers, liberal treatment of employees, and similar policies conducive to well-being are more profitable in dollars and cents than are sharp practices. Probably the man who thinks of little else than the money he is making on each deal is less likely to achieve large business success than the man who thinks much about the wants of others and how they can be satisfied. But the fact remains that the survival or extinction of a business enterprise or policy is determined by a financial test. Only Government and philanthropy can provide services which do not

---

[1] Of course there are ways of making money which contribute nothing toward human welfare, and ways which are detrimental to welfare. Business men themselves, social reformers, legislators, and the courts are continually striving to check abuses as they develop, or as they are recognized, by amending the rules of the business game. In this process of modifying the business economy, the results of economic analysis play a rôle. But in trying to understand how business cycles develop, it is confusing to mix considerations of welfare with considerations of process.

pay. In business the useful goods produced by an enterprise are not the ends of endeavor, but the means toward earning profits. And the business economy ruthlessly enforces that subordination.

The profits which count in determining solvency are not merely the profits or losses realized in the recent past, but also the profits anticipated in the near future. Indeed, business looks forward more than it looks backward. Even a concern which has been losing money for several years is likely to get the financial support required for continued operations, if its principals and backers believe that its fortunes will mend. And anticipated profits play the decisive rôle in fixing the direction to be taken by business expansion. It is the enterprises with faith in their future which finance extensions out of their own funds or out of funds borrowed from investors. Among the new ventures continually being organized by promoters, it is the ones which people with money to invest think likely to prove most profitable that get beyond the paper stage.[2] Finally, it is at those stages of business cycles when the profits anticipated from such operations are most attractive that extensions of old and launchings of new enterprises reach their highest points.

It follows that an account of economic fluctuations in a business economy must deal primarily with business conditions—with the pecuniary aspect of economic activity. This conclusion runs counter to one of the traditions of economic theory. Most economists have explicitly subordinated the pecuniary aspect of behavior, on the ground that money is merely a symbol the use of which makes no difference save one of convenience, so long as the monetary system is not in disorder.[3] The classical masters and the masters of utility analysis thought that they were delving deeper into the secrets of behavior when, with scarcely a glance at the "money surface of things," they took up the labor and commodities, or the sacrifices and utilities, which they held to be the controlling factors. When followed in the present field of study, this practice diverts attention

[2] Men can often be induced to put money into ventures in public welfare which promise only a meager return—for example, model tenements or liberty bonds;— but such mixing of philanthropy or patriotism with business is limited in scale, except in great national crises.

[3] Compare John Stuart Mill's dicta to this effect, *Principles of Political Economy*, book iii, chapter vii (Ashley's edition, 1909, pp. 483-488). See also Wesley C. Mitchell, "The Rôle of Money in Economic Theory," *American Economic Review*, Supplement, March, 1916, vol. vi, pp. 140-161.

from the way in which business cycles come about, and concentrates attention upon alleged non-business causes of fluctuation.

Of course, business prospects are continually being influenced by changes in crops, and in methods of manufacturing, storing, shipping and distributing goods—as well as by changes in politics, fashion, education, recreation, and health. But it is only as these changes affect the prospects of making money that they affect business activity. To take profits as the leading clue to business cycles does not rule out in advance causes of fluctuation which arise from non-business sources; what it does is to focus attention upon the process through which any cause that stimulates or retards activity in a business economy must exercise its influence. And that is a desirable result. For it is only by study of the processes concerned that we stand much chance of discovering how recurrent business fluctuations come about.

7. Factors Affecting Business Profits.

Economic activity in a money-making world, then, depends upon the factors which affect present or prospective profits. Profits are made by connected series of purchases and sales of goods—whether in merchandising or manufacturing, mining or farming, railroading or insurance. Accordingly, the margins between the prices at which goods can be bought and products sold are one fundamental condition of business activity. Closely connected with price margins is the second fundamental condition—the present and prospective volume of transactions.

Just as the ever-recurring changes in prices affect business activity and through it the volume of goods produced and distributed, so do changes in the volume of business react upon prices. A period of expansion starts an interminable series of readjustments in the prices of various goods. These readjustments in their turn alter the pecuniary prospects of the business enterprises which buy or sell the commodities affected and lead to new changes in the volume of trade. As the latter changes take place, the whole process keeps starting over again. Prices once more undergo an uneven readjustment, prospects of profits become brighter or darker, the volume of transactions expands or contracts, prices feel the reflex influences of the new situation—and so on without end.

III. The System of Prices.

The prices ruling at any moment for the infinite variety of commodities, services, and rights which are being bought and sold constitute a system in the full meaning of that term. That is, the prices paid for goods of all sorts are so related to each other as to make a regular and connected whole. Our knowledge of these relations is curiously inexact, for a matter so important and so open to investigation.[1] What follows is merely a sketch designed to indicate the organic character of the relationships among different parts of the system of prices.

1. The Prices of Consumers' Commodities.

The prices which retail merchants charge for consumers' commodities afford the best starting-point for a survey of this system.

For most commodities in a given market at a given time, there is not a single retail price, but a variety of retail prices. It is only by an elaborate policy devised for the purpose, that a uniform price can be maintained, and the frequent infractions of price-maintenance schemes attest the strength of the commercial forces which make for price variety. Yet the differences among the prices charged for the same article by various shops are kept within fairly definite limits. For inexpensive articles, the differences may form a large percentage of the mean price, but they seldom amount to many cents. For costly articles, the differences may amount to many dollars, but they seldom form a large percentage of the mean. In other words, though the retail prices at which a given article is sold by different shops on the same day in the same town are not identical in the majority of cases, they are closely related to each other.

A much looser, but still significant, bond connects the retail prices charged for goods of unlike kinds. An advance in the price of any commodity usually diverts a part of the demand for it to other commodities which can be used as substitutes in certain of its uses, and thus creates business conditions which favor an advance in the price of the substitutes.

[1] At the present time, the National Bureau of Economic Research is carrying on certain studies in this neglected field. The investigator in charge, Dr. Frederick C. Mills, hopes to have his first results ready for submission to the directors with a view to publication before the end of 1927.

Retail prices are also related to the prices for the same goods which shopkeepers pay to wholesale merchants and the latter to manufacturers. In most cases, the wholesale prices for a given article, also constitute arrays rather than single quotations. The series of successively smaller prices' for the same commodities in different hands often has more or less than three members, because of the intervention of more than one wholesaler or jobber, or of an importer in the traffic, or because of direct selling by manufacturers to retailers or even to consumers.

There is wide diversity in the margins between the successive prices in these series. The margins are generally wider in retail than in wholesale trade; wider in "charge-and-deliver" than in "cash-and-carry" shops; wider on goods limited in sale, slow in turnover, perishable, sold in small lots, requiring a large assortment, subject to changes in fashion or season, than on durable, standardized staples handled in bulk.[1] A manufacturer who sells directly to consumers must charge a wider margin than does any one of the several dealers who commonly intervene. Perhaps also the margins average wider when a large advertiser or quasi-monopolist dominates a trade than under conditions of keen competition; that is not certain, for competition may be carried to a pitch which leaves each enterprise with so small a volume of business, or with such heavy selling expenses, that wide margins between buying and selling prices are made necessary for all concerned. It is notorious that wide margins do not always mean large profits.

These diversities in the margins are themselves established and kept tolerably regular by the quest of profits. Controlled in this way, the margins between the successive prices in the series for each kind of consumers' commodities form a feasible basis for making money out of the process of supplying the community with the goods it uses.

---

[1] Recent investigations by the Bureau of Agricultural Economics and the Port of New York Authority have shown that the factor of chief moment in fixing retailers' margins upon perishable food products is the average size of the package sold. Seemingly, the retailer must impose a service charge, which varies little from the mean, 10 cents, upon every package handed to a customer. On goods usually sold in small lots, for example fresh onions, this service charge constitutes a much larger percentage advance upon the jobbers' price, than on goods (like potatoes) sold in larger lots. Perhaps this generalization will be found to apply to many other branches of retailing.

See Dr. Charles E. Artmån, *Food Costs and City Consumers* (Columbia Studies in History, Economics and Public Law, No. 280), New York, 1926, chapter iii.

2. The Prices of Producers' Goods in Relation to the Prices of Consumers' Commodities.

The business enterprises engaged in squeezing money profits out of these price margins are seldom, if ever, able to keep the whole differences between their selling and buying prices. From retailers back to manufacturers, unless they are operating on a minute scale, they must purchase various commodities, services and rights for the efficient conduct of their business. For such producers' goods they have to pay out prices which commonly absorb the greater part of the price margins on the consumers' commodities in which they deal. The most important classes of these producers' goods are raw materials and such current supplies as coal and stationery, buildings with proper machinery or other equipment, manual and clerical labor, loans, leases, transportation, advertising and insurance.

To all business enterprises, the prices which they pay for these producers' goods are important factors in fixing the margins between the buying and selling prices of the commodities in which they deal. But, save in the case of transportation and certain kinds of labor, men who handle a variety of goods require elaborate accounting systems to connect the prices which constitute costs with the margins upon which they sell particular goods. For the cost prices of producers' goods are paid for the advantage of the enterprise as a whole, and the accruing benefits extend to many transactions and often cover a long time.

3. The Prices of Producers' Goods in Relation to Antecedent Prices.

With the exception of labor, producers' goods are provided, like consumers' commodities, chiefly by business enterprises, large or small, operating on the basis of margins between buying and selling prices. Hence the price of any given producers' good is related not only to the prices of the consumers' commodities to the production or distribution of which it must finally contribute in some way, but also to the prices of the various other producers' goods employed in its own manufacture and distribution. Thus the prices of producers' goods do not end the series of price relationships; at most they begin new series of relationships, which run backward with countless ramifications and never reach definite stopping points. Even the prices of raw materials in the hands of first "producers" are related systematically to the prices of the labor, current supplies, machinery, buildings, land, loans, leases, and so on, which the farmers, miners, quarrymen, lumbermen, and fishermen employ.

Concerning the prices of such producers' goods as consist of material commodities no more need be said. And most of the less tangible services—loans, advertising, transportation, insurance—require but a word. They are the subjects of an organized business traffic, in which price margins play the same rôle as in the buying and selling of commodities. Therefore, the prices charged by the bank, the advertising agency, the railway and the insurance company, are systematically related both to the prices which these enterprises must pay for their own producers' goods, and to the prices of the wares dealt in by the enterprises which borrow money, use publicity, ship goods and carry insurance.

The prices of labor—manual, clerical, professional and managerial —may seem to bring the series to a definite stop, at least along one line. For men do not have a business attitude toward the production of their own energy, and not wholly a business attitude toward the acquisition of their own training. But the prices which wage- and salary-earners can command are indubitably connected with the prices of the consumers' goods which established habit has made into standards of living for the classes to which they belong, as well as with the prices of the goods they help to make. Along this line, therefore, analysis of the interrelations among prices brings us, not to a full stop, but back to our starting point—the prices of consumers' commodities.

4. The Prices of Business Enterprises.

Connected with the prices of consumers' commodities, of raw materials, and of other producers' commodities or services, are the prices of business enterprises.

Occasionally, established business enterprises are sold outright as going concerns. Promoters are also constantly offering for sale new business organizations or reorganizations of old enterprises. But far the most numerous transactions of this type are dealings in the shares of corporations.

Closely associated with the prices of such shares are the prices of corporate notes, bonds and debentures. Theoretically, a sharp line may be drawn between ownership of common stock in an enterprise (carrying no right except to vote at its meetings, and to share in its dividends, if any), and ownership of its mortgage-assured bonds. But many types of securities have been invented intermediate between these extremes—stocks "preferred" in various ways, convertible bonds, voting bonds, bonds secured by second or third mortgages, and so on through a long list. All of these securities carry an interest in the corporation with them, some risk, and the possibility of having to assume control under certain contingencies. Indeed, the common stocks of some corporations are rated a safer investment than the first-mortgage bonds of others. An effort to classify all these securities on logical lines would involve much elaboration. In a summary view of the system of prices it is permissible to pass over such details and treat the traffic in corporate securities of all kinds under one head.

That the prices of whole business enterprises, of shares in them, and of their promises to pay are intimately related to the prices already discussed, is clear. For the value of an enterprise is determined primarily by capitalizing its present and prospective profits. Profits depend primarily upon price margins times the volume of business transacted. The rate of interest at which prospective profits are capitalized is determined by the going price for the use of investment loan funds, and as such is related to the whole complex of prices which affect the investment markets.

5. The Prices of Services to Persons.

There remains one other grand division of the system of prices—a division which has much in common with the price of consumers' commodities on the one hand, and with the prices of personal services to business enterprises on the other hand. It consists of the prices of the heterogeneous services which are rendered to persons. Here belong the prices of domestic service, medical attendance, most life insurance, much instruction, some legal advice, many forms of recreation, passenger transportation, hotel accommodation, and so on.

In part, this field is cultivated by large-scale business enterprises, conducted methodically for the profit to be made out of price margins. Hotels, amusement places, travel bureaus, life-insurance companies, standardize their goods, watch their operating expenses, and compete for custom on a price basis in much the same way as department stores. But in other parts of the field, business traffic can scarcely be said to exist. Contacts are made and maintained largely on a personal basis, the services are not and often cannot be standardized, the sellers often deprecate commercial motives, and prices are often varied according to the individual buyer's capacity to pay. Consumers do not shop about for the services of family lawyers, doctors, or even cooks, as they shop for shoes. Hence, the prices of non-business services to persons form the most loosely organized and irregular division of the system of prices.

6. The Interrelations Among Prices.

The aim of this classification of prices is not to set up different categories, but rather to emphasize the relations which bind all prices together and make of them one system. The close relations (1) between the prices of consumers' commodities in the hands of retailers, wholesalers and manufacturers; (2) between these prices and those of producers' goods, whether used directly or indirectly in making consumers' commodities, and (3) between the buying and selling prices in any branch of trade and the prices of securities of the business enterprises engaged in it, are sufficiently clear, and enough has been said about (4) the looser bonds which unite the prices of services to persons with the larger field of business dealings. But several other lines of relationship should be called to attention.

(5) On the side of demand, almost every good has its possible substitutes in some or in all of its uses. Through the shiftings of demand among commodities thus made possible, changes in the price of one commodity are passed on to the prices of its substitutes, from the latter to the prices of their substitutes, and so on. An initial price change usually—though not always—becomes smaller as it spreads out over these widening circles.

(6) Similarly, on the side of supply, almost every good has genetic relationships with other goods, made from the same materials, or supplied by the same set of enterprises. Along these genetic lines also, price changes radiate from the points of disturbance over a wide field. Particularly important because particularly wide are the genetic relationships arising from the use of certain producers' goods in many lines of business. Land, loan funds and transportation most of all; with somewhat less universality, coal, steel, certain types of

labor, and insurance enter into the cost of most commodities. Accordingly, a changed price established for one of these well-nigh universal producers' goods in any important use will extend to a wide variety of other uses, and may produce further price changes without assignable limit.

(7) Closely connected with this genetic relationship through common producers' goods, is the relationship through business competition, both actual and potential. Price margins which make one trade decidedly more or less profitable, all things considered, than other trades in the same market area cannot long continue in the lines of business which anyone controlling capital really can "break into" if he so desires. For, after a time which varies with technical and business conditions in the trade which is out of step, the influx or efflux of capital changes the supply of commodities in question and brings the price margins into closer adjustment with those prevailing in other trades.

This familiar proposition does not mean that competition tends to bring the price margins on which all goods are handled to a common level. On the contrary, the tendency is to make these margins differ from each other,—differ in whatever way is necessary to keep the prospects of return to capital and enterprise, everything considered and over whatever periods men think of in planning their ventures, so nearly alike that no one of the lines open to investment seems much more attractive to the average enterpriser than its alternatives.

Nor does this proposition imply that there is a tendency toward an equality of profits in business. Whatever such tendency exists is limited to equalizing the prospective opportunities for making profits on fresh investments. In every branch of business followed by numerous enterprises, and in every year, experience shows a marked diversity of returns, running from liberal profit percentages to substantial losses. There seems to be no tendency for these divergencies to disappear, except perhaps when a trade becomes concentrated in the hands of very few concerns. Where there are many concerns, the tendency toward equalizing the prices of similar producers' goods and similar products—and in the given market areas this tendency is real—makes profits depend upon the skill of managements and the particular circumstances under which each management operates. Since neither skill nor circumstances are uniform, the differences in profit rates which they produce tend to recur indefinitely.

(8) Present prices are affected by prices of the recent past and also by the anticipated prices of the near future. Indeed, present prices are determined largely by past bargains, many of which established time contracts still in operation. Over a wider field, our ideas of what is a "fair price" to ask come from past experience to affect present and future conduct. Thus the price system has no definable limits in time. No analysis can get back to the earliest term in the endless series of bargains which helped to make the prices of to-day, nor can anyone say how much influence is exerted to-day by the anticipations of what prices will be to-morrow, or how many to-morrows are taken into business reckonings.

(9) Nor has the price system any logical beginning or end. At whatever point analysis may begin tracing the interlocking links of the price chain, to that point will it come round again if it proceeds far enough. The above analysis, for example, started from the prices of consumers' commodities at retail. These prices are paid out of personal incomes. But personal incomes are themselves aggregates of prices received for labor, for the use of loan funds, or for the use of rented property; or they are aggregates of the net price differences which yield profits.

Thus all the prices in a business economy are continually influencing one another. To account for any one item in the system, one must invoke the whole. Realization of that fact has made economic theorists dissatisfied with efforts to explain the prices of particular goods in terms of their respective costs, or utilities, or supply and demand. In 1874 Léon Walras showed how any number of prices can be conceived as simultaneously determined, under certain imaginary conditions. Mathematical economists are now seeking to make his method of approach (the use of several sets of simultaneous equations equal in number to the number of the "unknowns") applicable to real life.[1] These efforts may provide students of business cycles with a better technique than they now possess for treating the problem of price changes. But even as matters stand, we can trace the main channels through which price fluctuations propagate themselves by using statistical data in ways suggested by the preceding analysis.

[1] See Walras, *Éléments d'Économie Politique Pure,* 1874; 4th ed., Lausaunne and Paris, 1900; Gustav Cassel, *Theory of Social Economy,* New York, 1924; Henry L. Moore, "A Theory of Economic Oscillations," *Quarterly Journal of Economics,* November, 1926, vol. xli, pp. 1-29.

Among writers who make no use of mathematical symbols, Herbert J. Davenport has faced the mutual interdependence of all prices perhaps more frankly than anyone else. See his *Economics of Enterprise,* New York, 1913.

7. The Rôle of Prices in Economic Life.

Prices, then, form a system—a highly complex system of many parts connected with one another in divers ways, a system infinitely flexible in details yet with a fairly stable equilibrium among its parts, a system like a living organism in its capacity to repair the serious disorders into which it recurrently falls.

So much for the structure of the system of prices; concerning its functions in economic life a few words must be added. The system of prices is our mechanism for regulating the process of producing, and distributing goods. Prices make possible the elaborate exchanges, and the consequent specialization and coöperation in production which characterize the present age, and so are one of the factors contributing to its relative comfort. They are the means by which all consumers in concert make known what goods the community wants and in what quantities; the signs which enable all business enterprises in concert to come as near as they do toward achieving a satisfactory allocation of productive energies amidst the million channels into which these energies might flow. Prices are the source from which family income is derived, and the means by which goods are obtained for family consumption; for both income and cost of living—the jaws of the vise in which the family feels itself squeezed—are aggregates of prices. Prices also render possible the rational control of economic activity by accounting; for accounting is based upon the plan of representing all the unlike commodities, services and rights with which an enterprise is concerned as buyer or seller in terms of a money price. Most important of all for the present purpose, the margins between different prices within the system hold out that prospect of money profit, which is the motive power that drives our business world.

IV. The Monetary Mechanism.

Monetary and banking systems are such obvious features of the business economy that they require little attention here. It is well, however, to state the sense in which certain terms will be used, to note the relative magnitude of important variables, and to indicate the bearings of a famous controversy upon the problem of business cycles.

1. Ambiguity of the Terms "Money" and "Currency."

Business men, economists at large, and writers upon business cycles in particular, use the word money in a confusing variety of meanings. The variants important here are illustrated by Professor Irving Fisher on the one side and by Messrs. Foster and Catchings on the other. Fisher defines money as "what is *generally* acceptable in exchange for goods," thus distinguishing money from bank deposits subject to check. "Currency" is Fisher's broad term for all the common media of exchange. On the contrary, Foster and Catchings use the word money in the broad sense assigned by Fisher to currency, and the word currency in the narrow sense assigned by Fisher to money.[1]

Needless to say, both of these opposing usages can be defended by abundant precedents, drawn from the world of books and from the world of affairs. To follow either usage, however, is to invite misunderstanding by those accustomed to the other. Care in stating definitions in one chapter and consistency in adhering to them in later passages may be a logical defense against the misinterpretations of readers who have "skipped" or forgotten the formal definitions; but it is better to give no opening for mistake when that is feasible. The shortest unambiguous term for what Fisher calls money and what Foster and Catchings call currency seems to be "coin and paper money." We must choose between the unattractive alternatives of using some such cumbrous expression or of facilitating misunderstanding. Of these two evils, the latter seems the greater.

Accordingly, in the chapters which follow, the terms "coin and paper money" and "deposit currency" will be used. All the common means of making monetary payments taken together will be called the "circulating medium."

2. The Relative Importance of Checks and of Coin and Paper Money in Making Payments.

Our knowledge on this head has not been advanced materially since 1909, when Professor (now President) David Kinley of the University of Illinois superintended an investigation made by the Comptroller of the Currency for the National Monetary Commis-

[1] See Irving Fisher, *The Purchasing Power of Money*, New York, 1911, pp. 8-13; W. T. Foster and Waddill Catchings, *Money*, Boston and New York, 1923, pp. 17-18.

sion. The Comptroller secured reports from some 11,500 banks of all kinds concerning the character of the funds deposited with them on Tuesday, March 16, 1909, by retail merchants, wholesale merchants, and customers of other occupations. From these returns, supplemented by estimates of deposits in the non-reporting banks and vaguer approximations to the transactions of people without bank accounts, Kinley concluded that we may "safely accept an average of 80 to 85 per cent as the probable percentage of business in this country done by check." In wholesale trade the percentage was above 90, in the business of non-mercantile depositors it was "close up to that of the wholesale trade," in retail trade it was 50 to 60 per cent, and even of the pay rolls made up by banks 30 per cent were in checks. On comparing the 1909 returns with those secured in a similar investigation which he had supervised in 1896, Kinley also concluded "that the percentage of the volume of ordinary payments made by check has been increasing somewhat." [1]

Of course estimates based upon the transactions of a single day are especially unsatisfactory to students of business cycles, since they are much concerned with the magnitude of seasonal, cyclical, secular and random fluctuations in business processes. Probably the percentage of payments made by checks is higher on dates when rents, salaries, dividends, bond coupons, and income taxes are being paid in large amounts than on a mid-month day, like March 16th. Full records over a period of years might show fairly regular seasonal variations in the percentage, corresponding in timing to the seasonal variations in bank clearings. There may also be cyclical fluctuations in the relative use of checks and coin or paper money, as well as a rising secular trend for the first and a declining secular trend for the second. But all this is surmise. What we know with certainty is that the great bulk of payments in the United States is made with checks. Probably coin and paper money do not more than a tenth or at most a fifth of the "money work." The figure intermediate between these limits, 15 per cent, seems to fit well with the run of the estimates presented in the following sections.

---

[1] David Kinley, *The Use of Credit Instruments in Payments in the United States.* National Monetary Commission. 61st Congress, 2d session, Senate Document 399, Washington, 1910, pp. 197-201. (The critical reader may be warned that the percentage of pay rolls in checks is misstated on p. 200; the correct figures are given on p. 103). Kinley gives percentages for checks on p. 198 which run somewhat higher than his final conclusions quoted above. It is these higher figures which Professor Irving Fisher uses in his *Purchasing Power of Money,* revised ed., p. 491, to support his own estimate that 91 per cent of all business in 1909 was done with checks.

3. The Elasticity of the Circulating Medium.

How far the money mechanism responds to the changing requirements of business from phase to phase of a cycle, and how far the money mechanism may start, augment or limit business fluctuations, are among the problems raised in Chapter I. Presumably, these problems have no single solution, since so much depends upon what the changing requirements of business are, upon how the money mechanism is arranged, and upon the skill with which it is managed. All three conditions differ from country to country, and in any one country they may differ from time to time. Close attention must be paid to this factor in business cycles later on. At present it will suffice to show that the currency which the business community provides for itself through the banks rises and falls with the activity of trade more regularly than coin and paper money provided through government agencies.

The fluctuations in the amount of gold in monetary use in any country during a given year depend mainly upon (1) the current output of such gold mines as it possesses, (2) the country's gain or loss of gold by international shipments, and (3) the quantity of gold which goes into industrial uses. No one of these factors can be depended upon to increase the supply of gold currency when trade is brisk, or to diminish the supply when trade is dull.

(1) Changes in gold production are controlled mainly by the discovery and exhaustion of deposits, by improvements in the arts of mining and metallurgy which make it possible to work lower grade ores at a profit, and by conditions which facilitate or hinder industrial operations in the mining districts. None of these factors are organically related to business fluctuations. Of secondary importance are financial conditions which affect the raising of capital for investment in gold mining, and price conditions which affect the cost of operating mines. Prosperity facilitates the raising of capital, but increases operating costs. In turn, high operating costs give mining engineers a stronger incentive to develop improved methods of work, and thus may lead presently to increased output. All in all, one would not expect a close correspondence between business cycles and gold production, and when one examines the statistics over a period of years this negative expectation seems to accord with experience. Over periods much longer than those typical of business cycles,

however, there seems to be an organic relation between gold production and the rate of economic expansion. The periods of large additions to the world's gold supply have been accompanied or followed by periods in which the prosperous phases of business cycles have been relatively long and intense and the depressed phases have been relatively short. The reverse also seems true: periods of declining gold production have been accompanied or followed by periods in which the phases of prosperity have been relatively short and the phases of depression relatively long. Thus the fluctuations of gold output are important in the study of business cycles; but important as a part of the economic environment in which cycles run their course, rather than as part of the cycles themselves. But this relationship we can study to better advantage after we have won such insight as we can into the character of cyclical fluctuations.

(2) The industrial demand for gold is decidedly sensitive to business conditions; it rises in prosperity and falls in depression. Since the general level around which this percentage fluctuates seems to approximate a quarter of the annual output, and since the plus and minus departures from this average are considerable, we have here a not unimportant factor of "perverse elasticity" in the monetary supply of gold.

(3) The amount of gold shipped into and out of any country in the course of a year is the net resultant of a multitude of factors. Among the more important are the relative magnitudes of payments and receipts on merchandise account, freight account, travelers' account, migration account, and banking account. While every one of these items may be directly affected by the state of trade in the country in question, it is hard in most cases to be sure whether the state of trade will affect the credit side more than the debit side of that item. Moreover, the problem is never limited to the influence exercised by the state of trade in any one country; it includes also the influence exercised by the state of trade in every one of the other countries with which the first has extensive dealings. Of especial importance to the Western world is the highly variable flow of gold to the Orient, especially to British India—a flow which depends less upon business conditions in the West than upon conditions in the East. The net resultants of all these complicated factors, as summed up by official statistics, show that no simple conclusion can be drawn concerning the relation between international gold movements and business conditions, except in severe crises.

The exception is important. In times of peace, any nation menaced by a credit collapse has usually been able to secure within a few weeks a large inflow of gold from the "free gold market" of London, or, in recent years, New York. International business has developed a rudimentary centralized gold reserve, which any commercial nation can draw upon, after negotiation and somewhat tardily, to meet emergencies. Perhaps this constitutes the world's most considerable achievement toward adjusting the supply of gold currency to the demands of business.

As for government paper money, it is notorious that the large changes in issues are controlled by the exigencies of public finance. Paper standards occur as episodes in monetary history. The suspensions of specie payment, by which they are ushered in, are usually forced by wars, political revolutions, or national bankruptcies. A return to specie payments becomes an aim of fiscal policy after the emergency has passed, though an aim which is often pursued in a wavering and dilatory fashion. Of course, the developments which lead to suspensions, the depreciation of the monetary unit which usually follows suspensions, and the appreciation which usually precedes resumption, all influence the activity of trade. But these influences, like the influence exerted by marked changes in the rate of gold production, must be classed among the "disturbing causes," by which theorists explain the divergencies characteristic of different business cycles.

Government paper money as an element of monetary systems having a metallic standard is seldom controlled in such a way as to make its volume regularly responsive to changing needs. But much as the gold supply of a country has often been increased in severe crises by huge importations, so governments have sometimes aided business in emergencies by increasing their paper issues, or by shifting paper money from the public treasury to the banks.

The broad conclusion from the preceding analysis is that, except in severe crises, business must depend primarily upon bank notes, checking deposits, and bills of exchange to keep the supply of the circulating medium adjusted to its changing pace.

This adjustment is made possible within certain limits by the fact that bank notes are issued and bank deposits created chiefly by the granting of bank loans, while bank notes are retired and bank deposits are canceled chiefly by the repayment of bank loans. The drawing of a check against his deposit by the customer of a bank no more reduces the volume of deposit currency than the payment of a bank note by one man to another reduces the volume of notes in circulation. In both cases a part of the circulating medium is merely transferred from one holder to another—unless the check or note is used to repay bank loans. Now a period of prosperity, during which production expands, prices rise, and profits swell, increases the money value of the security upon which banks make their loans, and so provides a basis for the increase of bank currency which is required by trade. A period of depression, on the contrary, diminishes the business demands for bank loans, and through their repayment contracts the volume of notes and deposit currency as the requirements for means of payment decline. The qualifications to which these sweeping statements must be subjected in later chapters prevent the adjustment of bank currency to the needs of business from being always prompt and precise; but the broad contrast between the responsiveness to changes in business activity of bank currency and the unresponsiveness of coin and government notes remains valid.

Of course, the limits within which bank notes, checking deposits, and bills of exchange can be thus adjusted to the changing volume of trade depend upon the organization and management of a country's banking system. Mistakes in adjustment disastrous to business can be made within these limits, as well as by failure to heed them. Hence we may expect to find that the development of banking legislation and of banking practice has played an important rôle in the history of every country's business cycles.

4. The Velocity of Circulation.

Fluctuations in the activity of business lead to changes not only in the volume of deposit currency and bank notes, but also in the average rate at which all forms of circulating media pass from hand to hand. An increase in the volume of payments can be effected in either of these ways, and in practice is usually effected both by an expansion in the quantity of bank currency and by a quicker turnover of coin, paper money and deposits. Changes in the velocity of circulation are not limited by technical factors as are changes in the quantity of the circulating medium. Broadly speaking, anyone in receipt of current funds can spend them again as quickly or as slowly as suits him. But like most phenomena produced by the actions of millions of men, the average velocity of circulation is markedly regular in its changes.

It is only of late that we have attained even rough measurements of this factor in business processes. In 1907 Professor E. W. Kemmerer summed up a few preceding studies and made the best estimate of velocity which the data then permitted. Kinley's study of credit instruments for the National Monetary Commission enabled Irving Fisher in 1911 to improve upon Kemmerer's results. In turn, certain recent investigations of the Federal Reserve Bank of New York have made it possible for Dr. W. Randolph Burgess to supersede Professor Fisher's figures.[1]

The New York Reserve Bank has collected monthly data concerning the volume of individual demand deposits and the debits to individual accounts in the banks of eight cities, ranging in size from New York to Syracuse and in location from Boston to San Francisco. The data, beginning in January, 1919, and extending by months to February, 1923, when they were analyzed by Dr. Burgess, covered somewhat more than one full business cycle, and so gave a basis for approximating not only the mean velocity of bank deposits but also the variations about the mean.

Dr. Burgess found that there is a close relationship between the amount of bank deposits in a city and the rapidity of their turnover. In New York the velocities ran six to eight times as high as in Syracuse. Between these extremes, the velocities in other towns (excepting Albany) varied so neatly with the volume of deposits that it seemed justifiable to use this relationship as a basis for estimating the average velocity of deposits in the United States. Computations following the line thus suggested indicated that a reasonable estimate would place the velocity of circulation for the country as a whole at a rate somewhere between 25 and 35 times a year, and probably under rather than over 30.

Not less important for our purpose than the general average reached by Dr. Burgess, are the seasonal and cyclical variations which he found to characterize deposit velocities. The seasonal swings ranged from 12 per cent of the annual mean in San Francisco and 14 per cent in Chicago to 29 per cent in Boston and 31 per cent in Albany. After these seasonal changes had been eliminated from the

[1] See E. W. Kemmerer, *Money and Credit Instruments in their Relation to General Prices*, New York, 1907, pp. 108-119; Irving Fisher, *The Purchasing Power of Money*, New York, 1911, pp. 441-477; W. Randolph Burgess, "The Velocity of Bank Deposits," *Journal of the American Statistical Association*, June, 1923, vol. xviii, pp. 727-740.

series, the cyclical swings remaining were even larger. They ranged from 22 per cent of the average value for the whole period in Chicago, and 26 per cent in San Francisco to 63 per cent in Syracuse and 68 per cent in Albany. New York, which is often thought of as subject to exceedingly wide seasonal and cyclical variations in all financial matters, was near the center of the range in both the seasonal and cyclical array.[2]

Certain of Dr. Burgess' results can be tested by using other recent data. The Federal Reserve Board now compiles the total "debits to individual accounts" in the banks of many cities. These figures come far closer to showing the volume of payments made by check in the United States than do any earlier data:—among other advantages, debits include the millions of checks which are deposited in the banks against which they are drawn, and which therefore do not pass through a clearing house. By careful analysis of these returns from 240 cities in 1922, Mr. Carl Snyder has shown that the total debits for the whole country in that year were about 534 billion dollars. This is probably a close approximation as such matters go; for the actually recorded amounts not only cover banks holding more than

[2] The leading results of this important paper may be presented in tabular form as follows:

VELOCITY OF BANK DEPOSITS, JANUARY, 1919, TO FEBRUARY, 1923

	New York	Albany	Buffalo	Rochester	Syracuse	Boston	Chicago	San Francisco
Original data								
Average........	73.7	29.9	19.7	20.2	9.9	34.1	46.1	39.9
Maximum......	91.3	49.0	25.1	23.6	15.3	47.6	51.5	44.9
Minimum.......	62.1	21.6	16.1	16.7	7.0	24.7	38.4	34.0
Range..........	29.2	27.4	9.0	6.9	8.3	22.9	13.1	10.9
Range as per cent of average....	39.6	91.6	45.7	34.2	83.8	67.2	28.4	27.3
Seasonal Fluctuations								
Average month..	100	100	100	100	100	100	100	100
Maximum......	112	117	112	109	113	113	106	106
Minimum.......	91	86	92	92	89	84	92	94
Range..........	21	31	20	17	24	29	14	12
Cyclical Fluctuations (Seasonals eliminated)								
Average........	73.7	29.9	19.8	20.2	9.9	34.1	46.0	40.0
Maximum......	84.8	43.0	26.1	22.8	13.5	42.1	52.0	45.9
Minimum.......	63.4	22.7	16.3	16.9	7.3	29.0	41.7	35.5
Range, per cent of average.......	29.0	67.9	50.0	29.2	62.6	38.4	22.4	26.9

W. Randolph Burgess, "Velocity of Bank Deposits," *Journal of the American Statistical Association*, June, 1923, vol. xviii, pp. 727–740.

All of the velocities in this table are computed on a yearly basis.

four-fifths of the total deposits, but also afford a good basis for making estimates for the missing banks.[3] If we had equally trustworthy figures of the average volume of deposit currency to compare with this total, we could compute its velocity of circulation with confidence. Once a year the Comptroller of the Currency does compile a nearly complete table of deposits in all kinds of banks in the country; but the portion of these deposits subject to check is not stated for all kinds of banks and must be estimated in part. Then these partially estimated figures for June 30th must be made into annual averages as well as may be by using an index based upon a comparison between the individual deposits of the National Banks on June 30th and the average of such deposits in the five (or four) reports to the Comptroller. Figures made in this fashion must be accepted as subject to a margin of uncertainty; but an error of a billion dollars one way or the other would not make 5 per cent of the total. Indeed, this method of approximating the velocity of deposit currency involves less estimating than Dr. Burgess' more elaborate method, which builds upon returns that are more precise, but include only 8 cities.

Table 3 shows that the results to which this method leads agree well with Dr. Burgess' conclusion that the average turnover of deposit currency for the country as a whole is somewhere between 25 and 35 times a year, and probably under rather than over 30. In view of its firmer foundation, this estimate has better claim to acceptance than the pioneer figures of Professor Irving Fisher, who had set the velocity of bank deposit currency at nearly 37 in 1896, 53 in 1909 and 96 in 1918.[4] The table also confirms the conclusion that the velocity of deposit currency rises and falls with business activity, though of of course these annual figures do not move through nearly so wide a range as the data which Dr. Burgess presents by months.

If 80-85 per cent of the country's payments are made with checks, if the volume of checking deposits rises and falls with the activity of trade, and if the circulation of these deposits is quickened in prosperity and retarded in depression, it may seem that the money

[3] Compare Carl Snyder, "A New Index of the General Price Level from 1875," *Journal of the American Statistical Association,* June, 1924, vol. xix, pp. 189, 190.
[4] See his *Purchasing Power of Money,* New York, 1911, p. 304, and "The Equation of Exchange for 1918," *American Economic Review,* June, 1919, vol. ix, p. 407. Even before the Federal Reserve Bank data on bank-deposit velocity were gathered, Professor Fisher had become skeptical of his own values, at least for years far from his basing points, 1896 and 1909. See the article just cited.

TABLE 3

THE VELOCITY OF DEPOSIT CURRENCY, ESTIMATED FROM TOTAL PAYMENTS BY CHECK
AND AVERAGE DEPOSITS SUBJECT TO CHECK

The United States, 1919–1926

	Estimated Volume of Payments made by Check Billions of Dollars	Estimated Average Volume of Deposits Subject to Check Billions of Dollars (As of July 1st)	Estimated Average Velocity of Deposits
1919	546.8	18.99	28.8
1920	587.7	21.08	27.9
1921	484.0	19.63	24.7
1922	533.9	20.47	26.1
1923	570.3	22.11	25.8
1924	600.1	23.53	25.5
1925	653.4	25.98	25.1
1926	695.3	25.57	27.2

NOTE: The data used in this table were supplied by Mr. Carl Snyder of the Federal Reserve Bank of New York. For the 1922 estimate of payments by check, see text. The figures in other years for the country outside of New York were made from the 1922 estimate by means of an index based upon debits in 140 cities. Mr. Snyder believes that the margin of error in these estimates may be 10 per cent.

economy has developed a mechanism adequate to the changing requirements made upon it from phase to phase of business cycles. Whether this impression is sound depends, of course, upon the relative magnitudes involved. And these magnitudes vary from cycle to cycle and from country to country. Here, then, is another problem which we must treat on a quantitative basis, with the expectation that the results will not be the same in all cases, or in all phases of the cycle.

While the payments made in coin and paper money seem not to exceed one-tenth or one-fifth of the total, these payments must be made, and they cannot be made in checks without a mass change in monetary habits and arrangements. The velocity of coin and paper money is, therefore, a highly important variable. Concerning its average magnitude and its limits of fluctuation scarcely anything has been learned since 1911 when Professor Fisher was studying the equation of exchange. His final result for 1909 was that coin and paper money changed hands against goods on the average 21.1 times, as compared with 52.8 times for deposit currency.[5] Our next problem is whether the first of these figures is as far out of the way as later data show the second to be.

[5] *The Purchasing Power of Money*, p. 304.

Professor Fisher's method of approximating the velocity of coin and paper money involved (1) an estimate of the amount of coin and paper money flowing into and out of the banks in a year—an estimate built up from the deposits made in a part of the banks in one day; (2) an estimate of the sums withdrawn from the banks which are paid to non-depositors, and (3) estimates of the average number of times the cash received by depositors and by non-depositors exchanges against goods before it is redeposited in banks. Fisher's final picture of the circulation in 1909 is as follows:

Coin and paper money withdrawn from banks	Use made of the funds withdrawn	Average circulation of the funds withdrawn before they are redeposited	Volume of payments made outside of banks by coin and paper money
8 billions	Paid to depositors	Once	8 billions
12 "	Paid to non-depositors	Twice	24 "
1 "	Paid to non-depositors	Three times	3 "
21 billions			35 billions

To get the average velocity of coin and paper money in this year, he divided this total of 35 billions by his estimate of the amount of money in circulation, 1.63 billions, and thus got 21.5—a figure which he scaled down in the final adjustments to 21.1.[6]

Little confidence can be felt in results resting upon so many conjectural estimates. And the best test that we can make by the use of later data, while somewhat less conjectural, yields but vague results. As said above, Mr. Snyder has shown that the check payments in the United States in 1922 totaled about 534 billion dollars. If we accept Kinley's estimates that payments made by check constitute 80-85 per cent of all payments, then we must put the payments made by coin and paper money in 1922 at from 94 to 133 billions. If, as Professor Fisher thinks proper, we take at least 90 per cent as the proportion of payments by check, the payments in coin and paper money shrink to 59 billions. The average amount of money in circulation that year outside of the treasury and the banks was 3.67 billion dollars.[7] Division gives the average velocity of coin and paper money

[6] For the details of this elaborate computation, see *The Purchasing Power of Money*, pp. 448-477.

[7] On the assumption that the coin and paper money in all commercial banks on June 30th, bore the same ratio to the average for the year as is borne by the coin and paper money outside the Treasury and the Federal Reserve System to the average for the year.

in 1922 as 16, 26, or 36 times, according as we take 90, 85, or 80 as the percentage of payments by check. Professor Fisher's figures—21.1 in 1909 and 30 in 1918—fall within this range. There seems to be no such difference as he surmised between the velocity of deposit currency and of paper money and coin. The middle figure in the range, 26, seems the most plausible. It coincides with the velocity of deposit currency in 1922 shown by Table 3. But of course this is a most uncertain guess. Whatever figure we accept as representing the average velocity of coin and paper money, we may suppose that the annual rate rises and falls with the activity of trade, though probably in less degree than the velocity of bank deposits.

5. The Quantity Theory and Business Cycles.

So far we have been concerned with the way in which the circulating medium responds to the changes which business cycles bring in the volume of trade. We cannot leave this topic, however, without noting the contention that fluctuations in the quantity of the circulating medium are causes of price changes and so of business cycles, rather than adaptations to the needs of business. This view is most picturesquely put in the title of one of Professor Fisher's recent articles, "The Business Cycle Largely 'A Dance of the Dollar.'" [1]

The problem can best be presented by using the equation of exchange as formulated by Fisher: $MV + M'V' = PT$. M stands for the quantity of coin and paper money in circulation and M' for the amount of deposits subject to check. V and V' are the respective velocities at which these media are exchanged for goods. P represents the price level and T the physical volume of goods exchanged. Thus the equation means that the total volume of payments made in coin, paper money and checks in a given time equals the money value of the goods bought and sold.

For the moment we are not concerned with the conditions under which this equation is valid, but with the causal relationship among the several magnitudes represented in the equation. Professor Fisher holds that

The price level is normally the one absolutely passive element in the equation of exchange. It is controlled solely by the

[1] See *Journal of the American Statistical Association*, December, 1923, vol. xviii, pp. 1024-1028.

other elements and the causes antecedent to them, but exerts no control over them.[2]

In this proposition the word "normally" is important: for Professor Fisher admits that *"to a limited extent during transition periods, or during a passing season* (e.g. *the fall)"* the "price level is an independent cause of changes" in other magnitudes in the equation.[3]

What, then, are "transition periods," and what fraction do they make of time? Professor Fisher's answer begins as follows:

> The change which constitutes a transition may be a change in the quantity of money, or in any other factor of the equation of exchange, or in all.[4]

The discussion of transition periods, thus introduced, gives him occasion to expound a theory of "credit cycles," which stresses the lag in the adjustment of interest rates to changes in the price level. And

[2] *The Purchasing Power of Money*, p. 172. Italics as in original.

Through a most ingenious statistical study, of which some account will be given in the next chapter, Professor Fisher has recently come to the "conclusion that changes in price level almost completely explain fluctuations in trade, for the period 1915-23," and that they "dominate" fluctuations in trade from 1877 to 1914 See "Our Unstable Dollar and the So-called Business Cycle," *Journal of the American Statistical Association*, June, 1925, vol. xx, pp. 191 and 201.

Without inquiring for the moment into the significance of Professor Fisher's statistical researches, it is pertinent to ask whether his two conclusions (1) that the price level is normally "absolutely passive" and "exerts no control over" other elements in the equation of exchange, and (2) that changes in the price level "dominate" fluctuations in the volume of trade, are consistent with each other.

The two conclusions can be reconciled formally by putting a strict construction upon the word "normal." My understanding is that Professor Fisher draws a sharp line between what is normally true and what is historically true. What is normally true is that which would happen under certain hypothetical conditions which are never fulfilled absolutely. What is historically true is that which actually happens under conditions which combine the factors represented in the theorist's imaginary case with a continually changing host of other factors. Hence relations which hold normally may never be realized historically.

Granted the logical validity of this distinction, the question remains how an investigator should choose the hypothetical conditions to be assumed in his theorizing. One who is interested in pure theory for its own sake may choose any hypothetical conditions which provide the basis of an interesting argument, whether that argument will illuminate experience or not. But I take it Professor Fisher is not interested in pure theory for its own sake; he desires that his theorizing shall give insight into actual experience. On this interpretation, it seems doubtful whether hypothetical assumptions are well chosen for his purposes when they lead to conclusions concerning what is normally true which run counter over long periods to the results of his statistical studies of historical processes. By altering the assumptions underlying his theorizing about the relations among the factors in the equation of exchange, Professor Fisher might draw a different set of conclusions concerning what is normally true which would harmonize better with his version of historical truth.

[3] *The Purchasing Power of Money*, p. 169. Italics as in the original.

[4] The same, p. 55.

while he is dealing with this subject, Professor Fisher observes that "periods of transition are the rule and those of equilibrium the exception."[5]

On this showing, there seems to be no reason from the viewpoint of a quantity theorist, why a student of business cycles should treat the price level as a "passive element" in the equation of exchange. His business is with "transition periods," these periods are "the rule," and during them the price level may be "an independent cause of changes" in other factors of the equation of exchange. Thus, the quantity theory interposes no bar to following any leads which the analysis of business dealings may suggest.

We cannot rest content, however, with so negative a conclusion. What we need is insight into the relations between changes in prices and changes in the circulating medium under modern business conditions. Our best chance of getting such insight is to follow the process of determining prices, transferring goods, and making payments.

The three quantities represented in the equation of exchange as simultaneous—payments, prices, and physical volume of trade—are in fact three stages through which business transactions pass in time. When a sale is made, the parties agree, tacitly or explicitly, upon the price, upon the quantity of goods to be transferred, upon the date of delivery, and upon the date when payment is due. In retail trade, all three stages are frequently completed in a few minutes—the customer assents to the price, receives his bundle, and pays cash. But delivery is deferred when consumers' goods are made to order, and payment is often deferred to the end of the month, or spread over several months on some "installment plan." In wholesale trade, weeks or months commonly elapse between the date when a sale is made at an agreed-upon price, the date when the goods are delivered to the buyer, and the still later date when the seller receives a check. In other types of business the time relations between the three stages present a wide variety, ranging from prepayment for goods to be delivered in the future to long deferred payments for goods delivered in the past. How long are the average lags of deliveries behind price agreements, and of payments behind deliveries; how these lags vary from trade to trade, from district to district and from period to period, are matters about which little is known; but that such lags play a prominent rôle in business planning is certain. Time is therefore a

[5] The same, p. 71.

factor which cannot be disregarded in studying the relations between prices and the circulating medium.

In terms of the equation of exchange, these observations mean that of the payments $(MV + M'V')$ made to-day, the bulk are payments for goods transferred (T) some time ago, at prices (P) most of which were agreed upon still earlier; a considerable fraction are payments for goods transferred to-day at prices now agreed upon; a minute fraction are payments for goods which will be transferred later. Similarly, of the goods transferred (T) to-day, a few have been paid for in advance, more are paid for now, but the bulk will be paid for in the future. Once more, of the prices (P) agreed upon to-day, a part are paid at once, but a larger part will be paid in weeks, months, and years to come.

Though merely a suggestion of the complications of business practice, what has been said suffices to show that on every business day the payments then made, the transfers then effected, and the prices then agreed upon refer to three different aggregates of transactions. In other words, the day-by-day relations between $MV + M'V'$ and PT are indeterminate—the payments made to-day are most unlikely to equal the prices quoted to-day multiplied by the goods exchanged to-day.[6] The only way to maintain the equation for such brief intervals is to interpret the PT of a given day as meaning the exchanges for which payments are then being made, instead of the current exchanges and prices. But on that interpretation, the relation between the time intervals covered by the two parts of the equation becomes indeterminate. An expression which shows nothing about time gives slight help toward solving problems in which time relations are important.

Quite different is the position when we test the equation of exchange as summarizing the transactions of a large community for some such interval as a year—the longer the interval, the better for the equation. On that basis, we can say both that the payments, prices and transfers represented all refer to approximately the same period of time, and that the two sides of the equation are nearly equal in fact. To be concrete, the payments made each year in the United

[6] Indeed, on a day-to-day basis the expression PT is nonsense; for only a part of the goods which change hands on a given day change hands at the prices which are current on that day—the P's then quoted refer in large part to T's which will come later. Also the expression $MV + M'V'$ may have a different interpretation on a day-to-day basis from that assigned it on an annual basis. Of course, the equation was not made to represent the transactions of a single day, and its inadequacy for that purpose is not surprising.

States are mainly payments for goods transferred within that year at prices then current. Some tranfers and some payments are made under price agreements entered into before January 1st; some price agreements are made before December 31st in transactions which are not completed by transfers and payments until the following year or later. But the difference between these two "carry overs" is small in comparison with the aggregate volume of transactions completed within the year.

So much seems clear. The critical question is: What period of time should we consider in trying to discover the relations between prices and the circulating medium? If we consider periods of a year's duration, we shall have the equation of exchange to aid us. But we cannot follow business processes in annual summations. To learn how changes in prices, physical volume of trade, and dollar volume of payments are related to each other, we must watch these changes going on as they go on in every hour of every business day. Accordingly we must concentrate attention upon what happens in, or rather through, brief intervals of time. If an analysis of the day-by-day processes of agreeing upon prices, transferring goods, and making payments is sound, we can be sure that it will prove consistent with the relations which the equation of exchange reveals over longer periods.

Consider, then, a business man buying raw materials or goods for resale—one of those commercial transactions which reach a money total far exceeding the volume of retail trade. How are such a man's decisions regarding prices related to the quantity of coin, paper money and deposit currency in his possession?

The one definite remark we can make in answer is that, if our business man must pay in cash and cannot borrow, the means of payment in his possession set an upper limit upon the dollar volume of his purchases. Note that the price he can offer per unit is not limited, unless the price of a single unit would exhaust his funds. Nor is the number of units he can buy limited, with the same exception. The limit is imposed not upon prices as such, nor upon physical volume of trade as such, but upon prices times physical volume. Below this limit, even our cash-paying, non-borrowing business man has free play for judgment concerning what price to pay and how much to buy. His range of discretion is further enlarged by the factor of time. He can increase or diminish the scale of his purchases according as he thinks prices will rise or fall in the near future; he need not spend his funds as he receives them, but can buy on a hand-to-mouth schedule for a while and wait for a favorable opportunity to make a large purchase. Yet we must note, also, what our business man is not likely to forget, that the more goods he can buy and sell at given margins the more money he will make. Thus he has a standing incentive to expand his transactions to the limit set by his circumstances. These limiting circumstances are numerous and shifting; but among them the amount of his funds is a factor of the first rank under the conditions we are discussing.

Of course, these conditions are not typical; nearly every business man can both buy on time and borrow. That fact makes the relations between prices and the quantity of the circulating medium still more elastic. The upper limit upon an individual's purchasing power is set by the funds in his hands plus the credit he can get from sellers and banks. The credit he can get depends not merely on his financial position at a given moment, but also on his financial prospects over a period which varies considerably from case to case, and on the financial position and prospects of those from whom he seeks credit. Thus the consideration of an individual business man's ability to buy widens out into consideration of the business community's ability to provide him with the means to pay.

If the financial positions and prospects of both seekers and grantors of credit are important factors in determining the purchasing power of business men, then the problem of prices and the circulating medium will change its complexion as these positions and prospects shift. For the business community as a whole, we know that the financial position and prospect changes from phase to phase of business cycles. Therefore in dealing with the problem of prices and the circulating medium, we must not merely consider brief intervals of time, but must recognize also that what is true of one brief interval may be false of another. What present knowledge enables us to do is to discuss the problem with reference to intervals characterized by business depression, revival, prosperity, and recession. Of the facts required for such a discussion, the more important have been suggested by the preceding sections, or by the "banking theories" of business cycles summarized in Chapter I.

During a period of depression, the quantity of coin and paper money which was in hand-to-hand use toward the close of the preceding period of prosperity, exceeds current requirements. The velocity of circulation declines; "idle money" accumulates in the banks, swelling their cash reserves; if the bank-note currency is elastic, it is contracted; if business remains more active in other countries, gold is likely to be _exported_. What happens to coin and paper money happens also to deposit currency and to commercial credits. Business men turn over their funds less rapidly, require less working capital, repay part of their bank loans (despite the lower discount rates), and reduce their accounts payable. The reduction of bank loans commonly exceeds the net flow of idle cash to the banks, so that deposits subject to check decline somewhat. Accordingly, the limit upon coin and paper money in circulation is fixed, not by the monetary stock and bank-note policy, but by the current demands of trade. Similarly, the limit upon deposit currency is fixed, not by what the banks can provide, but by what business men care to use. In Professor Fisher's terms, the fall of prices and the concomitant shrinkage in the physical volume of trade are, for the time being, the "active" factors in the equation of exchange. To the conditions which they produce, the monetary and banking factors adjust themselves in whatever way the organization of the monetary and banking systems permits.

These banking and monetary adjustments to business depression are among the developments which facilitate a revival of activity. The low discount rates, the reserve lending-power of the banks, the redundant quantity of coin and paper money, the low velocities of circulation mean that an increase in business transactions will encounter no check from the inadequacy of the circulating medium. Business men who see a prospect of profit in enlarging their purchases have no difficulty in securing means of payment if their bankers share their confidence. The physical volume of trade and prices can enter an ascending spiral, every increase in the one promoting an increase in the other. As the dollar volume of business expands, a new series of adjustments is worked out in the distribution of coin and paper money between the banks and the public, in the issue of bank notes, perhaps in the international distribution of gold, certainly in the volume of deposits subject to check, and in the velocities of circulation. Monetary and banking conditions may be said to "permit" these developments, and even to "favor" them; but the "active" rôle is still played by prices and the physical volume of trade.

Not until the dollar volume of business has grown so large that it taxes the elasticity of the monetary and banking system, do the monetary factors in the equation of exchange begin to dominate business transactions. That point is sure to be reached in business cycles, however, provided some non-monetary factor does not put an earlier close upon the expansion of trade. Even in the centers of finance, the velocity of circulation cannot be increased indefinitely. There is little assurance that the monetary stock of gold will grow with the need of bank reserves, and there is full assurance that prosperity will draw an increasing quantity of coin and paper money into hand-to-hand circulation. If bank reserves do not decline, at least they fail to expand as rapidly as do demand liabilities. There are limits, more or less definite, fixed partly by law, partly by practical experience, upon the minimum ratios between bank reserves on the one hand and bank notes and deposits on the other hand. When these minima are approached, bankers must check the expansion of loans. On the development of such conditions it ceases to be true that the business man can count upon obtaining funds to finance what promise to be profitable transactions. It then becomes true that both prices and the physical volume of trade are "passive" factors, controlled for the time being by monetary and banking conditions. And this domination becomes more absolute if the stringency develops into a financial panic, and many business men fear lest they cannot obtain funds to meet their maturing obligations.

In numerous business cycles, we shall find that prosperity wanes from other causes before the dollar volume of trade has attained dimensions which overtax the monetary and banking systems. Many recessions show slight traces of monetary stringency. Thus the periods when monetary and banking factors dominate prices and the physical volume of trade are brief, and they recur less regularly than the periods of depression, revival, and moderate prosperity, when prices and the physical volume of trade play the "active" rôles. Nevertheless, the intervals of monetary domination have had critical importance in the history of prices.[7] How that has come about may be stated in terms of the foregoing analysis, though not without some repetition.

The net shifts of price levels between two dates separated by decades depend upon the relative duration of the several intervening periods of prosperity and the corresponding periods of depression,

[7] This whole discussion relates to metallic-standard monetary systems, supplemented by banks of deposit and issue. Inconvertible paper-money standards present certain special problems which it is not necessary to consider here.

together with the rates at which prices rise in the first set of periods and fall in the second set. Hence, a factor which helps to lengthen the prosperous periods of successive cycles, to shorten the periods of monetary stringency, and to provide financial conditions which favor early revivals, tends to give the undulating curve of prices a rising secular trend. Under gold-standard monetary systems, an increase in the current output of gold is such a factor. A large flow of gold into bank reserves and general circulation postpones the time when an expansion in the pecuniary volume of trade will overtax the monetary and banking resources for making payments.* When a monetary stringency does occur, such a flow brings quicker relief, and hastens the day when a revival of activity becomes financially possible. A dwindling of the current additions to the monetary stock of gold has the opposite effects, and tends to give the undulating course of prices a declining secular trend. We now have index numbers of wholesale prices covering some century and a half in countries which most of that time have had gold standards. The correspondence between the secular trends of these index numbers and the secular trends of gold production has been fairly close. When the world output of gold has been increasing rapidly, or has been fluctuating about a high level, prices have moved up and down with the alternations of business prosperity and depression; but they have risen more than they have fallen. When the annual output of gold has declined, remained on a relatively low level, or increased slowly, prices have continued their cyclical oscillations; but the declines have exceeded the advances.[8]

To sum up: the lag of deliveries behind price agreements, and of payments behind deliveries, gives business men time to arrange the financing of their transactions. In periods of depression, revival, moderate prosperity, and even mild recession, the man who buys skillfully knows that the possession of goods which can be sold at a profit will help him to borrow part of the funds wherewith to make pay-

[8] To enter into further details concerning this well-known correspondence would divert attention from what is at present the main issue. Yet it may be noted that there are grounds for hoping that men may free themselves from dependence upon fortuitous changes in the annual output of gold by more skillful management of their monetary and banking systems. Whether such policies as have recently been adopted by the Federal Reserve Banks of the United States to prevent a huge supply of gold from producing such an inflation of prices as might have been expected from historical precedents can be generally applied and further developed is a matter for the future to determine. Seen in historical perspective, these experiments appear as the current stage in that long and gradual process by which men are learning to keep money, the good servant, from becoming at times a bad master.

*A continuing govt. deficit financed by sales of bonds to the Federal Reserve Banks would have the same effect.

ment. It is the current and prospective money value of merchandise that counts to the credit man. Thus an increase of P, which swells the value of inventories, becomes a basis for an increase of M', and of that part of M which consists of bank notes. An increase of T (physical volume of trade) plays the same rôle, unless it is offset by a decline of prices. Usually, though not always, these two factors rise and decline together—a close study of their shifting relations from phase to phase of business cycles is one of the leading problems for later chapters. When the pecuniary volume of business expands, it not only swells the volume of credit currency, but also quickens the velocities of circulation. Thus, most of the time, P and T are the "active" factors in the equation of exchange; they bring about changes in M', V and V'; to a less extent they affect even M.

Modern monetary and banking systems provide a considerable measure of elasticity in all the factors which affect payments, except gold and certain types of government paper money. Gold is particularly important because under monetary systems of the approved type it provides the critical reserve for M'. The free movements of P and T are confined within the range provided by this elasticity. When the pecuniary volume of trade has reached limits which tax MV + M'V', then monetary and banking factors assume the "active" rôle, and force a reduction in PT. Not every business cycle reaches a pitch of intensity which brings on a financial stringency. But in the past that point has been reached with regularity sufficient to let the secular trends of gold production control the secular trends of wholesale prices.

These conclusions may be repeated in slightly different form: Because of the lag of deliveries behind price-agreements and of payments behind deliveries, the payments made on a given day are most unlikely to equal the prices then current times the transfers then in process. But in buying goods, business men must plan to pay for them by the dates set by trade practices or formal contract. This means that the equation of exchange, which, as commonly interpreted, does not hold for short periods, is substantially valid for periods such as a year or more. Nor does it matter whether the years be years of depression or prosperity, crisis or revival, save that the proportion of bad debts may become appreciable in a year of severe crisis. All the time, business men have an incentive to buy as many goods as they can resell at a profit, and to charge prices as high as the traffic will bear. In depression, revival, moderate pros-

perity and mild recessions, the effective limit upon their transactions
is set by commercial demand.   Monetary and banking conditions
would permit a larger volume of business.   But in intense booms,
the commercial demand may become so active that transactions reach
the limit set by the monetary and banking systems.   Over long periods
of time, prices and the physical volume of trade have tended to expand up to these limits—not steadily, but in recurrent spurts of activity.   And that fact has given changes in the annual output of gold
a dominant influence upon the secular trends of wholesale prices, and
seemingly some influence upon the secular trends of the physical
volume of trade.

Time, then, is of the utmost consequence in considering the relations between prices and "the quantity of money."   Relations which
hold in long periods do not hold in short ones.   Nor are all short
periods alike; what is true in certain phases of business cycles is not
true in all phases.   Yet most of the seemingly contradictory statements which fill the long controversy over this problem can be reconciled when put in their proper relation to time.   For example, I do
not think that anything said here is incompatible with Professor
Fisher's exposition of the causal relations between the factors in his
equation of exchange, provided his term "normally" is not taken in
the sense of usually.   Nor is the present discussion inconsistent with
the celebrated theorem: "Other things being equal, prices vary directly as the quantity of money in circulation."   That theorem is
formally valid.   Equally valid are a number of other theorems similar
in form: for example: "Other things being equal, the quantity of the
circulating medium varies directly as prices:" "Other things being
equal, the quantity of the circulating medium varies directly as the
physical volume of trade."   Any of these propositions can be developed into an adequate theory of the "relations between money and
prices" by analyzing the "other things" which are supposed to remain equal.   Yet it is an awkward way of working to start with a
proposition which suggests so limited a view of the problem, and it is
misleading to end with a proposition which contains so limited a version of the truth.   The orthodox formulation of the quantity theory
owes its prominence to the fact that economists have given most attention to the long-period relations between gold-supply and prices
at wholesale.   For that particular problem, the proposition "other
things being equal, prices vary directly as the quantity of money in

circulation" is both valid and important. But for the periods with which the theory of business cycles is concerned, we need a far more discriminating statement of the relations among prices, the physical volume of trade, the quantity and the velocity of the circulating medium—a statement which takes into account changes in these relations produced by depression, revival, prosperity and recession.[9]

V. The Flow of Money Payments.

1. PRODUCTION AND PURCHASING POWER.

To make the business economy function smoothly, it is necessary not only that the volume and velocity of the circulating medium shall respond to the changing pace of business, but also that coin, paper money, and deposit currency shall keep flowing through the hands of business enterprises and individuals in exchange for goods. The flow, moreover, must be kept adjusted to the counterflow of goods offered for sale, in detail as well as in gross. If the dollar volume of any kind of goods flowing to market exceeds the flow of purchasing power which the prospective buyers are receiving and expending for that kind of goods, business troubles result—troubles that are trifling or grave as the quantities involved are small or large.

As we saw in Chapter I, two sets of theorists have found an explanation of cyclical fluctuations in this feature of the business economy. The Pollak Foundation group contend that in prosperity the flow of money incomes to consumers, and from consumers to the sellers of consumers' goods, lags behind the dollar volume of the consumers' goods poured into the markets. Mr. P. W. Martin holds a similar thesis with regard to money incomes at large and goods of all kinds. The over-production theorists look at the process from the other side; they offer a variety of reasons why the flow of goods to market exceeds the markets' ability or willingness to buy at profitable prices. To make use of these hypotheses in interpreting business

[9] Much the best survey of the literature concerning the quantity theory of the value of money known to me is given by Professor James W. Angell's recent treatise on *The Theory of International Prices,* Cambridge (Massachusetts), 1926. Although he shows that attention has frequently been called to the factor of time in discussions of the relations between money and prices, Angell notes that writers upon monetary theory have neglected the problems presented to them by cyclical fluctuations in trade. (See pp. 127, 134, 181.) The leading exception is Mr. R. G. Hawtrey, whose *Currency and Credit* (2d ed., London, 1923) deals acutely with the topic. Writers upon business cycles have done little to supply what the monetary theorists have omitted.

activities we need to know the basic facts about the flow of purchasing power.

Our knowledge on this head is just beginning to attain quantitative form. Every year, the volume of monetary payments vastly exceeds the money value of the goods produced—that is a matter of course. Some progress has been made toward tracing and measuring the currents which are parts of this general circulation. One current of especial importance is the disbursement of money incomes to consumers and the spending of these incomes by consumers. Large as it is, this current is but a minor part of the total circulation of purchasing power. Much greater are the payments made by business enterprises to each other, as they pass products through the successive links of the chains which connect producers of raw materials with retail shops, or with final business buyers. Even the "savings" of individuals and business enterprises are almost all paid out for goods in some form, constituting another current of strategic interest. There are also the payments from one individual to another for personal service, and the payments involved in collecting government revenues and making government disbursements. Finally, not only current products and services, but also a portion of the accumulated property rights in real estate, business enterprises, government loans and the like change hands each year. So huge is the aggregate value of these properties, that a shift of ownership in a minor fraction creates a current of payments running in the tens of billions of dollars.

2. The Flow of Money Incomes to Individuals.

The magnitude we have now to measure as best we may—incomes received by individuals in money—is considerably smaller than the country's income as estimated by the National Bureau of Economic Research. It does not include the value of their own produce consumed by farm families; commodity income from family gardens, poultry and cows; the rental value of homes occupied by their owners, or any allowance for the use of household furnishings and personal effects. As estimated by Dr. King, these items have an aggregate value which ranges from nearly 7 to slightly over 8 billion dollars per annum in 1919-26. By subtracting the sums in question from the corresponding estimates of current income, we get estimates of income received in money. Table 4 shows these results, together with King's estimates of total payments to employees as wages, salaries, pensions, compensation for injuries, and the like. It should be noted that all the figures for 1922-26 are preliminary, and subject to revision on the basis of a more detailed analysis of the underlying data, which is now being made in the National Bureau.

TABLE 4

ESTIMATES OF INCOME RECEIVED IN MONEY BY INDIVIDUALS
UNITED STATES, 1919–1926

	Total Income Received in Money Billions of Dollars	Payments to Employees Billions of Dollars	Percentage of Total Paid to Employees
1919.................	59.9	34.8	58 per cent
1920.................	65.9	41.6	63 " "
1921.................	55.4	34.7	63 " "
1922.................	58.9 *	35.3 *	60 * " "
1923.................	69.7 *	39.4 *	57 * " "
1924.................	72.0 *	39.6 *	55 * " "
1925.................	78.9 *	43.0 *	54 * " "
1926.................	82.1 *	44.5 *	54 * " "

* Provisional figures, subject to change.
All the entries are estimates made by the National Bureau of Economic Research under the supervision of Dr. Willford I. King.

According to these estimates, payments to employees must be by far the largest of the income streams. Supplementary studies of the National Bureau indicate that salaries of officials average between 7 and 9 per cent of total payrolls in the highly organized branches of trade (where they are most important), and probably less than 3 per cent of all income received in money.[1] Even if we subtract such salaries from payrolls, the remainder exceeds all the other money-income streams put together. Another conclusion of importance for students of business cycles is that the ratio of wages and salaries to total income paid in money rises decidedly in depression and declines in prosperity.

A less comprehensive, but more detailed, view of the relative magnitude of the several money-income streams can be had from the statistical reports of the Tax Division of the Bureau of Internal Revenue. Table 5 summarizes the pertinent data. Of course these figures must be considered critically. (1) They include less than half of the aggregate money incomes of individuals, according to

[1] See *Income in the United States*, vol. i, p. 99, National Bureau of Economic Research, 1921.

the estimates of the National Bureau, mainly, though by no means solely because tens of millions of small incomes are exempt from the tax, and are not reported to the federal authorities. (2) Since these small incomes are composed largely of wages, the percentages of wages and salaries in Table 5 run somewhat lower than in Table 4, though not so much lower as one might expect. (3) Relatively few farmers and other small business men report. The deficiency in profits which results is believed to be offset in part by the inclusion under this head of considerable interest payments. (4) Interest is rather low, not only for the reason just suggested, but also because interest upon the large sum of tax-exempt bonds is not reported fully. (5) Finally, efforts to avoid and to evade taxation distort the

TABLE 5

PERSONAL INCOMES REPORTED TO THE UNITED STATES BUREAU OF INTERNAL REVENUE, CLASSIFIED BY SOURCES

1919–1924

Billions of Dollars

	1919	1920	1921	1922	1923	1924
Total	22.4	26.7	23.3	24.9	29.3	29.6
Salaries, wages, commissions, bonuses, directors' fees, etc	10.8	15.3	13.8	13.7	14.2	13.6
Business, trade, commerce, partnerships, farming, and profits from incidental sales of property	6.7	5.9	4.2	5.3	7.6	8.0
Dividends	2.5	2.7	2.5	2.7	3.1	3.3
Rents and royalties	1.0	1.0	1.2	1.2	1.8	2.0
Interest, investment, and fiduciary income	1.5	1.7	1.7	2.0	2.6	2.6

Percentages of the Total

	1919	1920	1921	1922	1923	1924
Total	100	100	100	100	100	100
Salaries, wages, commissions, bonuses, directors' fees, etc	48	57	59	55	49	49
Business, trade, commerce, partnerships, farming, and profits from incidental sales of property	30	22	18	21	26	27
Dividends	11	10	11	11	11	11
Rents and royalties	4	4	5	5	6	7
Interest, investment, and fiduciary income	7	6	7	8	9	9

Compiled from *Statistics of Income from Returns of Net Income for 1924*, Washington, 1926, pp. 8, 32–33.

income returns to an unknown extent, and one which may vary appreciably with changes in tax rates, efficiency of administration, and perhaps with business conditions.

Even in incomes large enough to be subject to the federal tax, wages and salaries average slightly more than half of the total one year with another. Profits come second, despite the omission of nearly 99 per cent of the farmers, and equal or exceed dividends, rent and interest added together in the years of business activity. Interest payments are smaller than dividends, but that appearance may be due to a difference in the degrees of under-reporting. Finally, of the commonly recognized sources of incomes, rent is the smallest according to these figures.

A second question can be answered in general terms by rearranging the data in Table 5: How are the money incomes of individuals from different sources affected by business cycles? If we reduce the yearly figures for the various income streams to relatives based upon their respective average values, and also compute the percentage change from one year to the next, we can see which streams have been fairly steady and which have been highly variable. Table 6 serves this purpose.

In view of the extraordinary price gyrations of 1919-21, the figures in Table 6 have no claim to stand as typical of the changes in money incomes which accompany the business cycles of less disturbed times. A supplementary table covering pre-war years would be useful; but the data for making estimates of money income command less confidence prior to 1914 than the data for recent years, and the latter require confirmation. Under these circumstances, we must make the most of the fact that a case which magnifies the changes has its advantages.

When an individual is considering the investment of his funds, he thinks of bonds as yielding a fixed rate of interest (in dollars), and of stocks as yielding dividends which may change in any quarter year. If he buys real estate, he may be expecting an income fixed by a long lease as rigidly as interest on a bond; or he may be expecting an income subject to many fluctuations—all depends upon the character of the property he acquires. If he goes into business on his own account, he expects a higher average return upon his investment than he could get from income yielding bonds, stocks or

TABLE 6

RELATIVE VARIABILITY OF THE FLOW OF MONEY INCOMES FROM DIFFERENT SOURCES
UNITED STATES, 1919–1924

Based upon Table 5

Percentages of the Average Values during the Period Covered

	Average Values in Billions of Dollars	Percentages of the Average Values					
		1919	1920	1921	1922	1923	1924
Total.....................	26.0	86	103	90	96	113	114
Salaries, wages, commissions, etc.....................	13.6	80	113	102	101	105	100
Business, trade, profits on sales of property, etc.....	6.3	107	94	67	84	121	127
Dividends................	2.8	89	96	89	96	111	118
Rents and royalties........	1.4	73	73	88	88	132	146
Interest, investment, and fiduciary income..........	2.0	74	85	85	99	129	129

Percentage Rise (+) or Fall (−) from Value in Preceding Year

	1919–1920	1920–1921	1921–1922	1922–1923	1923–1924
Total...........................	+19%	−13%	+7%	+18%	+1%
Salaries, wages, commissions, etc...	+42	−10	−1	+4	−4
Business, trade, profits on sales of property, etc..................	−12	−29	+26	+43	+5
Dividends......................	+8	−7	+8	+15	+6
Rents and royalties.............	0	+20	0	+50	+11
Interest, investment, and fiduciary income......................	+13	0	+18	+30	0
Total income from dividends, rents, and interest..................	+8	0	+9	+27	+5

The percentages have been computed from figures carried to more places than are shown here.

real estate; but he must expect that his profits will vary widely from year to year.

These expectations regarding the relative steadiness of incomes from interest, dividends, rents, and profits are based upon the returns per dollar invested in different ways. That is not what Table 6 shows. It purports to give changes in the total incomes received under various captions by all individuals who report to the Internal Revenue. The total receipts are affected each year by the investment of new funds in bonds, stocks, real estate, and business. More than that, the tax returns include "investment income" and "fiduciary income" with interest, they include royalties with rents, and they include gains from the shifting of investments with business profits. Hence differences between prevailing opinions regarding the relative steadiness of returns upon investments of the various sorts on the one hand, and the conclusions suggested by the totals on the other hand, need not be taken as discrediting either the opinions or the statistics. In studying the flow of incomes to individuals, we are concerned with the total payments, rather than with the returns per dollar invested.

(1) Profits appear to be, as one expects, much the most variable type of income. They fall nearly 30 per cent in one year and increase over 40 per cent in another year. (2) Rents and royalties rank next in average variations; but these figures may not be representative, because, during the years covered, rents seem to have been undergoing a belated adjustment to the change in the general level of prices brought about by the war. They make spasmodic advances in 1921, 1923 and 1924, while in two other years they show no change. (3) Interest, investment and fiduciary income varies much more than one would expect. All the changes are increases. Even in the severe depression of 1921, interest receipts did not fall off. (4) Dividends, while moving up or down every year, proved decidedly the stablest type of money income in this period. That is, the changes, though frequent, were small in comparison with the maximum changes in the other types of income. Particularly striking, and particularly important for our problem, is the contrast between the extreme variability of profits and the relative steadiness of dividends. Nor does Table 6 bring out this contrast in full. The profits there shown are the profits of individuals and partnerships, while dividends are paid by corporations. If we subtract the deficits reported each year to the Internal Revenue by the corporations which lost money from the profits reported by the corporations which made money, we get net corporate incomes of 8.4 billion dollars in 1919, 5.9 billions in 1920, 0.5 billions in 1921, 4.8 billions in 1922, 6.3 billions in 1923 and 5.4 billions in 1924.[2] Dividends reported by individual taxpayers were far less than net corporate incomes as computed here in the relatively good business years, and far more than net corporate incomes in 1921.

[2] See the appropriate text tables in the official *Statistics of Income* for these years.

While the differences in variability of dividends, interest, and rent are interesting, they are not of great importance to us. Most men of property diversify their investments, holding some bonds, some stocks, and perhaps some real estate. Hence the changes in the money incomes of the investing classes are best ascertained by adding together interest, dividends and rents. On so doing we get an income stream whose average volume (according to the Internal Revenue figures) is about equal to the volume of profits, but which varies not much more than dividends. This is the flow which we should compare with profits on the one hand and wages on the other.

That comparison indicates that the largest of the income streams, payments to employees, as wages, salaries, commissions, bonuses, pensions, and the like, was decidedly less variable than profits in 1919-24, and decidedly more variable than income from investments in securities and real estate. More precise statements would have little meaning, because we know that our data are open to question and that the period covered is peculiar. But it seems improbable that the variations of wages and salaries in this period were more exaggerated than the variations of interest and rents. Thus the conclusion is probably valid that the largest of the money-income streams are also the most variable in flow. According to Table 6, wages, salaries and profits, added together, make over three-quarters of taxable income; of total income received in money they probably make four-fifths. And their aggregate volume may change by 15, or 20 per cent, or, in extreme cases even more, in a single year.

3. The Outflow of Personal Incomes.

All business enterprises disburse money incomes directly to individuals; but only a few classes of enterprises share directly in the reflow of purchasing power from individuals. By far the greatest collectors of consumers' funds are the retail merchants. A much smaller stream flows to the landlords, who may or may not be business enterprises, and still smaller streams to enterprises which render personal services of various descriptions, and to public utilities.

Our most detailed information on this head comes from the analysis of family expenditures. In 1918-19 the United States Bureau of Labor Statistics collected budgets from over 12,000 families. On rearranging the data according to channels of expenditure, we get the following results:

TABLE 7

CHANNELS THROUGH WHICH FAMILY EXPENDITURES FLOW. BASED UPON BUDGETS OF 12,096 AMERICAN FAMILIES IN 1918–19, COLLECTED BY THE U. S. BUREAU OF LABOR STATISTICS.

	Average Expenditures	Percentage of Total
Payments made to		
Retail shops...	$994.37	66.1
Service agencies (insurance, laundry, amusement, etc.)....	83.03	5.5
Public utilities......................................	56.07	3.7
	$1,133.47	75.3
Landlords...	186.55	12.4
Professional men (doctors, dentists, nurses, etc.).........	43.42	2.9
Organizations (churches, trade unions, lodges, etc.).......	18.22	1.2
Servants..	4.01	.3
Government (postage, taxes)..........................	3.62	.2
Undistributed ("patriotic," gifts, vacations, etc.)........	36.98	2.5
Surplus...	78.93	5.2
Total..	$1,505.20	100.0

Compiled from *Cost of Living in the United States,* Bulletin of the U. S. Bureau of Labor Statistics, No. 357, Washington, 1924.

While these data are doubtless representative of the important class whose expenditures the Bureau of Labor Statistics wished to cover (white families in industrial centers, depending mainly upon wages or small salaries), they are certainly not representative of the population as a whole. The budgets collected by Dr. King for the income studies of the National Bureau indicate that, as incomes increase, families devote larger percentages of their expenditures to housing, to domestic service, to travel and amusement, and smaller percentages to purchases from retail shops and public utilities. The expenditures of farmers probably follow still a different pattern, but the data available do not suffice to show details.[1] In short we lack budgets representative of the population as a whole.

We can, however, get at the point most important for us—the proportion of money income spent at retail shops by the population as a whole—in a different way. Mr. Lawrence B. Mann, formerly of the Federal Reserve system, Professor Paul H. Nystrom of the Retail

[1] See the weights used in making index numbers of the prices of consumers' goods bought by families which expend $25,000 per year and $5,000 per year; by families of urban employees, and by farm families; introduction to *Income in the Various States,* National Bureau of Economic Research, 1925. These figures do not profess to be complete budgets; but they do cover the main heads of family expenditure, and justify the statements made in the text.

Research Bureau, and the Federal Trade Commission have made estimates of the money volume of retail trade in the United States, estimates which we can compare with the estimates of money income made by the National Bureau. The results, given in Table 8, show what the preceding paragraph makes one expect—that the proportion of money income which flows to the retail shops is somewhat smaller in the case of the whole population than in the case of urban wage earners.

TABLE 8

ESTIMATED PROPORTION OF INCOME RECEIVED IN MONEY SPENT IN RETAIL SHOPS
UNITED STATES, 1919–23

| | Estimated Income Received in Money | Estimated Volume of Retail Trade | | Percentage of Money Income Spent in Retail Shops | |
| | Billions of Dollars From Table 4 | Billions of Dollars | | Per Cent | |
		Nystrom-Mann	Federal Trade Commission	Nystrom-Mann	Federal Trade Commission
1919.........	59.9	32.6	34.8	54	58
1920.........	65.9	38.3	38.3	53	58
1921.........	55.4	33.6	30.7	61	55
1922.........	58.9 *	33.5	32.5	57	55
1923.........	69.7 *	35.0	38.2	50	55

* Provisional figures, subject to change.

NOTE: I have taken Paul H. Nystrom's figure for 1923 (35 billion dollars) as basic, and used Lawrence B. Mann's figures for 1919–22 as an index for carrying the series backward. The connecting link is an estimate, which Professor Nystrom made at my request, that the volume of retail trade was 4 or 5 per cent larger in 1923 than in 1922. See Mann, "The Importance of Retail Trade in the United States," *American Economic Review*, December, 1923, vol. xiii, pp. 609–617; Nystrom, "An Estimate of the Volume of Retail Trade in the United States," *Harvard Business Review*, January, 1925, vol. iii, pp. 150–159.

The Federal Trade Commission's estimate is part of their report upon *National Wealth and Income*, Senate Document No. 126, 69th Congress, 1st Session, Washington, 1926 pp. 306–313.

Of the three estimates, Professor Nystrom's seems to rest upon the broadest study of the relevant materials. The Federal Trade Commission figures are built up by a bold combination of various bits of evidence which may not be an adequate foundation for the superstructure. It seems improbable that the percentage of money income spent at retail shops fell off in the bad year 1921, as the Commission figures indicate. An increase in this percentage, such as Mann's estimates show, is more plausible.

The general conclusions which seem justified by the data may be put in this form: (1) More than half of the money incomes received by individuals flow back to the world of business through retail merchants, (2) probably this proportion rises somewhat in dull times,

(3) other business enterprises, such as public utilities and service agencies, collect probably less than a tenth of the money income, (4) more than a quarter, perhaps nearly a third, is paid to landlords (some of whom are corporations), professional men, voluntary organizations, servants, and the government, or is invested as savings.

4. THE FLOW OF PAYMENTS AMONG BUSINESS ENTERPRISES.

Business-cycle theorists have concerned themselves more with the circuit flow of payments from business enterprises to consumers and from consumers back to business enterprises than with the flow of payments from one enterprise to another. Yet the latter flow is certainly several times as great as the former. In preceding sections we have obtained rough estimates for recent years of the payments made by check in the United States, of the volume of money income, and of the volume of retail trade. These figures, supplemented by a new (and hazardous) estimate of payments made in coin and paper money, are assembled for comparison in Table 9.

Inspection of these figures may inspire more confidence in their accuracy than is merited. The percentage relationships among the quantities are fairly stable; but such is likely to be the case when one expresses any set of figures as percentages of much larger sums. A considerable margin of uncertainty surrounds every series in the table—a margin which is broadest in the estimates of payments made in coin and paper money. Yet the estimates are probably trustworthy concerning the order of magnitude of the three quantities, and that is the point at issue.

On the face of the figures, retail sales account for not much more than one-twentieth of the aggregate volume of payments, and the payment of money incomes to individuals for about one-tenth. Even the round-flow of money incomes to individuals and from individuals seems to make only a fifth of the aggregate payments in average business years. While these rather precise ratios may be faulty, it seems certain that the payments arising from other business transactions are several times the volume of payments involved in receiving and spending personal incomes.

All business is said to depend in the last resort upon consumers' demand, and the statement is doubtless valid in a broad sense. Yet there is no mystery in the fact that retail trade itself is but a small

TABLE 9

COMPARISON OF THE ESTIMATED VOLUME OF PAYMENTS, INCOME RECEIVED IN MONEY,
AND VOLUME OF RETAIL SALES

UNITED STATES, 1919 TO 1923 OR 1926

	Estimated Volume of Payments in			Estimated Incomes Received in Money	Estimated Retail Sales	Percentages of the Estimated Total Volume of Payments	
	in Checks	Coin and Paper Money	Total			Income Received in Money	Retail Sales
	Billions of Dollars	Billions of Dollars	Billions of Dollars	Billions of Dollars	Billions of Dollars	Per Cent	
1919.......	547	106	653	59.9	32.6	9.2	5.0
1920.......	588	121	709	65.9	38.3	9.3	5.4
1921.......	484	97	581	55.4	33.6	9.5	5.8
1922.......	534	93	627	58.9 *	33.5	9.4	5.3
1923.......	570	102	672	69.7 *	35.0	10.4	5.2
1924.......	600	98	698	72.0 *		10.3	
1925.......	653	95	748	78.9 *		10.5	
1926.......	695	105	800	82.1 *		10.3	

* Preliminary estimates, subject to revision.

The estimated payments in checks are taken from Table 3.

The estimated payments in coin and paper money are computed by assuming that the average volume of these media outside of the Treasury and the banks has the same velocity of circulation each year as is shown by the estimates of deposit velocity in Table 3. This assumption is as plausible as any other, but it may be considerably in error. The results it yields happen to agree with the view that 85 per cent of American payments are made in checks. That is, sums of the above estimates for 8 years make the payments in coin and paper money 14.9 per cent of the grand totals. On Mr. Carl Snyder's advice, I have used the official statements of coin and paper money in circulation, except in 1919 and 1920. Adjustments of the official figures for certain bank holdings of coin and paper money give respectively 3.67 and 4.33 billion dollars in these two years.

The estimated incomes received in money are taken from Table 4.

The estimated retail sales are the Nystrom-Mann figures from Table 8.

fraction of business. In most cases the components of the goods which the consumer finally buys have been bought and sold several times over by wholesale merchants, jobbers, manufacturers, and producers of raw materials. These successive turnovers much more than counterbalance the higher prices which consumers pay.[1] Then there

[1] Kinley found the deposits of wholesalers to be more than twice the deposits of retail dealers—$124,824,000 against $60,447,000 on March 16, 1909. He also found that "all other deposits" were upwards of three times the volume of retail and wholesale deposits added together—$502,817,000. *The Use of Credit Instruments in Payments in the United States* (Senate Document No. 399, 61st Congress, 2d session). Washington, 1910; pp. 85, 133, 171.

Building upon admittedly questionable taxation returns from Pennsylvania, the Federal Trade Commission estimates the dollar volume of wholesale trade at 63.22 per cent of the dollar volume of retail trade in 1923. Presumably this estimate takes account only of the sales by wholesale merchants to retailers. See *National Wealth and Income*, 69th Congress, 1st Session, Senate Document No. 126, pp 308, 314, 315 are all the incidental payments involved in running an enterprise which deals in consumers' goods, from freight and insurance to repairs and credit transactions. Next we must add in the business in producers' goods, including the construction of industrial equipment. Changes in the ownership of securities and real estate call for another vast sum of payments. So also does the investment of fresh savings, and the making and repaying of loans. These items are not independent of each other—for example, the investing of fresh savings is largely the paying for new industrial equipment—and we cannot measure them as yet. But the list, though incomplete, shows that there is no reason to discredit the conclusions drawn from Table 9.

For the smooth working of the business economy it is as necessary that the immensely larger flow of payments among business enterprises shall be maintained as it is necessary that the smaller flow of payments from consumers to retail merchants shall continue unchecked. The strategic importance of the two flows, however, cannot be judged from their relative volumes. Indeed, the greater the volume of all business payments in comparison with the volume of retail trade, the more delicate may become the equilibrium, if all types of business are really concerned indirectly with satisfying personal wants. Here we have developed yet another problem which we must face when we come to study the interrelations among the processes of business expansion and contraction.

5. SAVING AND SPENDING.

We commonly think of spending money and saving money as activities the opposite of each other. But every kind of saving except actual hoarding involves spending. In the business economy, indeed, the process of saving is one current in the flow of money payments.

This process, also, has been made to yield theories of business cycles. Professor Tugan-Baranovski contends that crises come because people do not save enough money to meet the huge capital requirements of prosperity. Professor Spiethoff holds that crises come because people put their savings into too much industrial equipment and not enough consumption goods. Mr. Hobson says simply that, when incomes expand in prosperity, rich people save too much, and by their investments in productive enterprises overstock the markets with wares.

Data concerning saving are among the most difficult of economic

records to obtain with precision. The very word "saving" has half
a dozen different meanings. The most ingenious effort so far made
to surmount these difficulties, conceptual and statistical, is that of
Dr. Willford I. King. Taking as his basic data the doubtful census
returns of wealth, and subtracting or adding the estimated foreign
debits or credits of the country, Dr. King finds a total increase of
wealth between 1909 and 1918 of 122 billion dollars. But correction
for price fluctuations reduces that huge sum to 46 billions. These
savings equal 14 per cent, or one-seventh of the estimated income of
the country during this nine-year period. We might doubt this result
because of the admitted inaccuracies of the census data, inaccuracies
which may or may not be sufficiently different in the reports for 1909
and 1918 to make the estimate of increase in wealth far wrong. But
Dr. King has made a second, quite independent, estimate which confirms the first. He has computed the percentage of increase in all the
important items of wealth for which he could get reliable data in
physical units over the same years, and found that the average increase was even higher than his first method indicated. He concludes,
accordingly, that "The normal fraction of the national income saved
is about one-seventh."

If this percentage seems large, it must be remembered (1) that
about 40 per cent of the country's savings are made by business enterprises, through the retention and reinvestment of profits which might
otherwise have been distributed to individuals, and (2) that about 9
per cent more seems to consist in the accumulation of larger stocks
of clothing, personal ornaments, furniture, and automobiles. Thus
only half of the total corresponds to what many have in mind when
they speak of the savings of people. Finally it should be said that
defects of the data lead Dr. King to present his results as rough approximations, which require confirmation or revision in the light of
later and fuller statistics. Certainly his estimate covers an exceptional period; in 1916 Dr. King finds that savings jumped to twice the
pre-war average even after he had allowed for the rise of prices, and
in 1918 he finds that the war wastes more than offset savings. While
these exceptional cases tend to cancel each other, there is small assurance that ten years of post-war experience will yield averages agreeing closely with 1910-18.

Little can be gained by attempting to refine upon rough approximations; but it must be pointed out that Dr. King's average of 14
per cent of income saved means 14 per cent of income as estimated by

the National Bureau in its first report. If the savings were compared with money income, the percentage would run somewhat higher. On the other hand, Dr. King quite properly treats an increase in the stock of durable consumption goods as savings. But we have just been considering what part of money incomes is spent in buying goods at retail, without reference to the problem of saving. Subtracting the increase of consumption goods (9 per cent of savings, according to Dr. King), would make the savings which flow into revenue-producing investments a lower percentage of money income. In view of the partial offsetting of these two items, we have no clear reason for saying that the proportion of money income invested to produce income is greater or less than one-seventh.

On the basis of Dr. King's estimates, it seems that on the average employees "save" about 5 per cent of their annual wages and salaries; farmers, together with owners of farm lands and mortgages, "save" about 12 per cent of their net income from agriculture; other business men "save" about 33 per cent of their annual incomes. That is, these classes spend the respective percentages of their income in ways which increase their stocks of semi-durable consumption goods, or better their equipment for making money, or buy securities which enable some enterpriser to better his equipment, or acquire revenue-bringing claims against other people. Of the total savings in his period Dr. King attributes 20 per cent to employees, 12 per cent to the agricultural interest, and 68 per cent to business men and property owners in non-agricultural lines. Two-fifths of all the saving is done directly by business enterprises, without the funds ever passing into the hands of individuals. Dr. King also finds, and this point is of especial interest here, that "the volume of saving by business concerns varies directly with the waves of business activity," but that "the extent of private saving is much less closely correlated with the economic cycle." [1] *

Another study of American savings, made on a different plan by Dr. Walter Renton Ingalls, confirms King's chief results. Using the National Bureau's and his own estimates of national income from 1912 to 1922 on the one side, and on the other side David Friday's and his own estimates of savings, Dr. Ingalls computes that, before the war, savings made about 15 per cent of annual income, one year

[1] Willford I. King, "The Net Volume of Saving in the United States," *Journal of the American Statistical Association,* September and December, 1922, vol. xviii, pp. 305-323 and 455-470.

* Hansen stresses this. See his chapter on the Cyclical - Consumption Pattern in "Fiscal Policy + Bus. Cycles."

with another. This percentage agrees closely with Dr. King's fraction —one-seventh. Again like King, Dr. Ingalls finds that nominal savings were greatly enhanced by the war, but that the war savings were mostly spent in destroying lives and property, or lost in the post-war readjustments. Finally, in 1920-22, Dr. Ingalls thinks that savings shrank to about half their pre-war proportion—say 7 or 8 per cent of the national income.[2] Of course, a marked decline of savings in a three-year period which includes a great crisis followed by a severe depression is not out of line with Dr. King's results.

Both of these investigations indicate that saving, whether measured in dollars or in percentages of national income, belongs among the highly variable factors in our problem. Any average which we may take to represent the general run of affairs will differ widely from the figures for years of great prosperity and deep depression. Yet we must use some average in order to compare current savings with the accumulations of the past. If we take Ingalls' pre-war estimate of 15 per cent, or King's estimate of one-seventh, as a fair average of the part of income saved annually, and if we accept the estimate presented in an earlier section that the value of man-made equipment possessed by our people is equal to the national income of three or four years, it follows that, in the United States, the man-made equipment on hand represents a value equivalent to the average savings of between 20 and 30 current years.[3]

VI. The Guidance of Economic Activity.

1. The Problem of Adjusting Supply to Demand in a Business Economy.

The discussion of the flow of money payments in the preceding section provides a basis for treating one aspect of the protean problem of supply and demand in a business economy. Another aspect of this problem must now be faced—the difficulty of keeping the rate at

[2] See W. R. Ingalls, *Wealth and Income of the American People*, 2d ed., York, Pennsylvania, 1923, pp. 202-204, 252-254, and *Current Economic Affairs*, 1924, pp. 82, 152.

[3] Professor Cassel believes that in Sweden annual savings average approximately one-fifth of national income, and that national income averages approximately one-seventh of national wealth. I judge that the estimate of wealth used includes the value of land. On this basis, the accumulated wealth of Sweden equals the average savings of some 35 years. The National Defense Commission estimated the average annual increase of wealth in 1885-1908 at 3.18 per cent. See Gustav Cassel, *Theoretische Sozialökonomie*, 3d ed., Erlangen and Leipzig, 1923, p. 52.

which each kind of goods is being produced adjusted to the rate at which each kind is being bought.

Within the hundred years since Sismondi wrote about the uncertainties of catering to a "metaphysical public," this problem has been growing ever more intricate. Factory production has taken over one household industry after another, market areas have widened, the variety of products has multiplied, industrial equipment has become more elaborate and more specialized. On one side of the market stand the millions of money-income receivers, who provide for most of their families' want by buying goods which others make. On the other side stand these same millions with their diversified capabilities as workers, their diversified properties in natural resources and industrial equipment, and their fluid investment funds, seeking the most profitable markets for all these productive energies. The buyers of goods and the sellers of goods are the same persons; but this identity does not enable them to keep their efforts as producers, organized in business enterprises, adjusted to their wants as consumers, organized in families.

So pervasive is this problem in a business economy and so constant its pressure, that generation by generation a large part of the routine shrewdness and a large part of the innovating energy of business men are absorbed in keeping abreast of it. Many-sided progress has been achieved in the course of this effort. Communication has become incomparably more rapid within the century, and made to yield vastly better reports of demand in widely separate markets. Improvements in transportation have rendered possible a more satisfactory distribution of supplies. The collection and analysis of commercial statistics are beginning to aid the distribution of goods through time, as the telegraph, railway and steamship aid distribution in space. Trade associations make competition less blind, and industrial integration makes planning of production more systematic. Insurance has expanded to equalize the burden of carrying a vast variety of economic risks. The standardization of goods, which comes with mass production, partially offsets the diversification of products. One use of advertising is to control demand for goods, so far as may be. Combined with all these technical improvements, is the day-by-day effort of every responsible business man to follow current demand with vigilance, to take advantage of every favorable change, to guard against every decline, with all the skill which mother wit and practical experience can muster.

Yet it is not certain that those efforts all put together have gained upon the growing difficulties of the problem. For, on the side of business administration itself, there are forces which keep the markets from attaining equilibrium. So long as free enterprise prevails on a competitive basis, there cannot be a stable adjustment of supply to demand. As Dr. Schumpeter has pointed out, every business innovation disturbs the preceding basis of adjustment.[1] New products and new styles or brands of old goods, new sources of supply, new methods of production, even new competitors turning out familiar goods by familiar methods, keep forcing changes in the production and marketing schedules of established houses. And there is no evidence that the current of business innovations is becoming less swift.

In the trades which cater to personal needs, the trend seems to be toward offering to consumers an ever wider variety of wares and services ready for immediate delivery. Trade goes largely, perhaps increasingly, to enterprises which enable consumers to buy "what they want when they want it." To make such buying possible, some business enterprise must provide goods in anticipation of the demand. If the manufacturer does not make to stock, then the wholesale merchant or the retailer must assume the hazard.

Nor is the case widely different in trades which make goods only to order. There the business enterprise must provide facilities for executing orders before it can get them. Inventory hazards may be reduced; but not the larger and longer hazards upon investment of capital and time. Business men who embark in any productive enterprise, investors who advance capital, and wage-earners who learn trades are all taking a chance that the demand for their services at a satisfactory price will prove less than the supply they offer. This hazard is faced even in an enterprise which has a complete monopoly of its special field.

"Uncertainty," to use Dr. Hardy's term, is thus an all-pervading phase of every business undertaking.[2] Its tap root is uncertainty concerning what people will buy at what prices. Its lateral roots are uncertainty what competitors, direct and indirect, will sell at what prices; uncertainty what supplies of all the needed kinds can be bought at what prices, and uncertainty what will happen within the enterprise, or within its business connection, to affect its profits.

[1] See Chapter I, section iv, 4.
[2] See Chapter I, section iv, 2. On the distinction between risk and uncertainty, see Frank H. Knight, *Risk, Uncertainty and Profit*, Boston, 1921.

The fruits of uncertainty appear in the emotional aberrations of business judgments and competitive illusions, by which Professor Pigou and Dr. T. W. Mitchell explain business cycles.[3] And under the pressure of uncertainty men have evolved that elaborate co-operative system of guiding economic activity, which we have next to consider.

2. The Rôle Played by Business Managements.

The most active rôle in determining what use shall be made of the country's natural resources, industrial equipment, investment funds, brains and brawn is played by business men.

When the earliest theories of crises were being formulated, economists could assume that there stood at the head of the typical business enterprise a capitalist-employer, who provided a large part of the invested funds, carried the brunt of the hazard, performed the "work of superintendence," and pocketed the profits. Millions of enterprisers of this versatile type are still in business; but they are most numerous in industries where the scale of organization has remained what it was in the days of Sismondi and Ricardo. These are industries in which the business-cycle hazard is small.[1] In the industries dominated by large-scale organization, the single capitalist-employer has ceased to be typical; though in mining, manufacturing, and construction work such men can be counted by the tens or the hundreds of thousands. In this field which particularly concerns us, because of the wide oscillations in business activity to which it is subject, quite a different form of business leadership has evolved.

The corporations, which now handle the bulk of large-scale business, are usually owned by a miscellaneous and shifting body of stockholders. The funds required for fixed investment are provided in some measure by these owners, but in large part by bondholders, who may or may not own shares as well as bonds. The immediate pecuniary hazards are borne by the shareholders; but ordinarily under provisions which limit their liability to loss of the sums which they have put into their shares, and under conditions which enable them to throw a large part of the business-cycle hazard upon the employees. The work of management is largely dissociated from ownership and financial responsibility. The stockholders delegate the super-

---

[3] See Chapter I, section iv, 3 and 10.
[1] See above in this chapter, section ii, 3.

vision of the corporation's affairs to a committee—the directors—
and the directors turn over the task of administration to a set of
general officers. The latter are paid fixed salaries, though they may
receive in addition a percentage of the profits, or hold stock in their
own right.

In such an organization it is difficult to find anyone who corresponds closely to the capitalist-employer. Certainly stockholders
who take no part in managing the corporation beyond sending in their
proxies to be voted at the annual meeting, do not fill the bill. Neither
do directors who confine such attention as they may give the corporation's affairs to passing on questions of general policy, selecting
officers, criticizing or approving reports, and the like. Finally, the
general officers, dependent on the directors, remunerated largely if
not wholly by salaries, and pi acticing among themselves an elaborate
division of labor, have no such discretion and carry no such responsibility as the capitalist-employer. The latter, in fine, has been replaced by a "management," which includes the more active directors
and high officials, often with the addition of one or two financial advisers, legal counsel, and large stockholders. Practically, it is this
group which decides what the corporation shall do.

There are, however, many small and a few large corporations in
which a single person dominates affairs. The stockholders elect his
candidates to office, the directors defer to his judgment, the officials
act as his agents. His position may be entrenched by outright ownership of a majority of the voting shares, or it may rest upon his influence with those who "own the control." In these "one-man" corporations, the theoretical division of responsibility and function becomes a legal fiction. Yet the position of such a captain of industry
usually differs from the position of the old capitalist-employer, in
that he furnishes a smaller proportion of the capital, assumes a
smaller proportion of the detailed labor of superintendence, and shares
the uncertainties and the profits with more associates. Instead of
restricting, these limitations enhance his power; they mean that the
individual who controls a corporation can determine the use of a
mass of property and labor vastly greater than his own capital would
permit.

Thus, while the corporate form of organization has produced a
division of the leadership of business enterprises among several parties
at interest, it has made possible greater centralization of power. The
captains of finance and industry wield an influence increased by the

capital which their prestige attracts from thousands of investors, and sometimes augmented still further by working alliances among themselves.

Another development to be noted is the partial differentiation of a class of enterprisers who play an exceptionally active rôle in guiding economic activity—promoters. The promoter's special province is to find and bring to the attention of investors new opportunities for making money; new natural resources to be exploited, new processes to be developed, new products to be manufactured, new organizations of existing business enterprises to be arranged. But the typical promoter is merely an explorer who points out the way for fresh advances of the army of industry. When an enterprise of his imagination has been organized and begun operations, the promoter seldom retains the leadership for long. As permanent officers, men of more cautious temper and more systematic habits commonly take command.

3. The Rôle Played by Technical Experts.

The "labor of superintendence" which men like Richard Arkwright and Robert Owen undertook in the early nineteenth century involved oversight of industrial, as well as commercial and financial, plans and operations. But under the impetus of scientific discoveries and mechanical inventions, the technique of industrial processes rapidly became so elaborate that this combination of functions ceased to be feasible. A few, very few, men possessed the versatility and the energy to keep abreast both of the increasingly exacting business problems and of the increasingly exacting industrial problems. Almost with the start of the Industrial Revolution, there began a division of labor between the men skilled in designing and operating machinery, and the men skilled in dealing with the markets for wares and money. While the old capitalist-employer has evolved on the one side into a business management, he has evolved on the other side into a set of technical experts.

As early as the middle of the 18th century, the civil engineers in England had branched off from the military engineers. The civil engineers were concerned mainly with the construction of roads, bridges, aqueducts, canals, harbors, docks and lighthouses. From this parent stock, there were differentiated successively the mechanical, mining, marine, sanitary, gas, chemical, and electrical engineers. By applying the results and the methods of modern science to the everyday work of the world, these men led that rapid advance in the making of goods which characterizes the present age. They became the chief directors of productive energies, on the technical side.

The prompt rise of the engineering professions must be ascribed to the relatively advanced stage of physical science, and the obvious advantage of applying its discoveries to industry. The social sciences lag far behind mechanics, chemistry and electro-physics in certainty and precision, and hence in the practical usefulness of the knowledge they convey. But in recent years they too have begun to yield results applicable to practice. At least as rapidly as they have grown ripe for the task, these sciences have been put to work by new groups of experts, who are gradually gaining something of the self-confidence and the recognition enjoyed for decades by engineers. Personnel managers are being trained to select and deal with employees, to study the requirements of different jobs, and to supervise working conditions, with the double object of increasing output and diminishing friction. Marketing—the art of winning and keeping customers—is becoming a field for specialists in advertising and selling. Business statisticians give advice on many phases of planning and current operations. "Scientific management" calls for a combination of so many kinds of expertness that perhaps it will contribute to the growth of half-a-dozen professions rather than one. Indeed, these developments are all so recent, so much in process, that one can be sure of little except that new professions are growing up which offer guidance to economic activity based on the still modest achievements of the social disciplines.

Thus a business management is now able to command supposedly expert advice in the direction of its affairs, not only from its old counsellors in law and accounting, but also from a bewildering array of talent versed in the sciences of nature and man. Perhaps the time is coming when the chief function of the business executive will be deciding whose advice to ask and what advice to accept, what experts to enroll in his staff and what to consult on occasion. If the multiplication of technical professions continues, that function itself may evolve into a profession.

In 1923, the National Industrial Conference Board made an effort to estimate the number of men in the United States who can fairly be "included in the category of those who plan, supervise and administer the business of the nation." As such it counted major officials, managers, superintendents, technical engineers, designers, draftsmen, inventors, architects, chemists, assayers, metallurgists, and auditors, together with one-quarter of the number of foremen, overseers and inspectors in agriculture, mining, construction, trade, transportation and public service.

Even with this liberal definition of business and industrial guides, the Board found, on analyzing the census data for 1920, that only a million and a half persons could be included. This number is much smaller than the number of men engaged in business on their own account—some 10,000,000.[1] But the proportion of all persons having gainful occupations who are "administrators, supervisors and technical experts" has been rising steadily each decade; it stood at 1.25 per cent in 1870 and 3.80 per cent in 1920. And this percentage is decidedly higher in the large-scale industries subject to a considerable business-cycle hazard, than in small-scale industries like agriculture.[2]

While the technical experts who build upon the natural sciences know most about the making of goods and the technical experts who build upon social sciences are coming to know most about the managing of men, they remain for the most part merely advisers to the

[1] See above, section ii, 3.
[2] The chief results of this report are shown in the following table:

THE GAINFULLY OCCUPIED COMPARED WITH ADMINISTRATORS, SUPERVISORS AND TECHNICAL EXPERTS

THE UNITED STATES, 1920

	Total Persons Gainfully Occupied Thousands	Administrators, Supervisors, and Technical Experts Thousands	Percentage
Agriculture and animal husbandry	10,953	200[a]	1.83
Extraction of minerals	1,090	44	4.00
Manufacturing and mechanical industries	12,819	600	4.68
Transportation	3,064	105	3.42
Trade	4,243	229	5.39
Public service	770	34	4.41
Professional service	2,144	265[b]	12.36
Domestic and personal service	3,405	5	.14
Clerical occupations	3,127	30	.95
Total	41,614	1,510	3.63

[a] Rough approximation.
[b] Includes engineers and other technical persons.
See *Engineering Education and American Industry*, Special Report No. 25, National Industrial Conference Board, New York, 1923, p. 6.

captains of industry.   Higher authority belongs to the business men.
That is an inevitable result of economic organization on the basis of
money economy in its present form.   For the crucial factor in deciding
the fate of a business enterprise is not the perfection of its mechanical
processes, the excellence of its personnel work, or even the cleverness
of its selling methods.   All such excellencies contribute toward business success, and it is on this ground that the technical professions
get their chance to share in the guidance of economic activity.   But
the final test is the ability of an enterprise as a whole to make profits.
This fact entrenches the business men in their position as the authori-
tative leaders of the industrial army.

4. The Rôle Played by Lenders.

Business managements, however, must often submit their decisions
to review by a higher court.   Most enterprises need to borrow, and
this fact gives the lenders an effective veto power over proposals which
do not meet their approval.

Whenever an enterpriser applies to an individual capitalist to take
an interest in some project, to a bank to discount his notes, or to the
investing public to buy bonds, he must satisfy the lenders of his
ability to pay the interest and to safeguard the principal.   Even when
the applicant can provide collateral security for the loan, and obviously when he cannot, the lender's decision depends largely upon
his own judgment regarding the business prospects of the intended
venture.   To aid their officers in forming intelligent decisions, banks
require applicants for loans to make statements of their financial
position.   In addition, the banks and the houses which grant mercantile credits subscribe to commercial agencies and maintain credit de-
partments of their own, to collect and analyze information about the
business prospects of their customers.   Similarly, corporations which
offer bonds or stocks for sale furnish circulars setting forth their financial records, the purposes for which money is being raised, and the
anticipated profitableness of the extensions in view.   Affidavits from
certified public accountants, legal counsel, and consulting engineers
are often appended to lend these statements greater force.   Credit
men perform a technical function for large lenders similar to the
function performed by engineers for industrial companies.

This review of the projects of enterprises by lenders, then, is no
perfunctory affair.   Nor is its practical influence upon the guidance of

economic activity slight. There are always being launched more schemes than can be financed with the available funds. In rejecting some and accepting other schemes, the men of money are taking an important, though not a conspicuous, part in determining how labor shall be employed, what products shall be made, and what localities built up.

Not all lenders, however, are able to make intelligent decisions. The great mass of small investors, and not a few of the large, lack the experience, or ability, or time to discriminate wisely between profitable and unprofitable schemes. Many such folk put their funds into savings banks, rely upon the advice of friends who are better equipped, consult with their banks and lawyers, study the financial press, employ investment counsel, or follow what they suppose to be the lead of some conspicuous figure in high finance. Investors who lack independent judgment are peculiarly subject to the influence of feeling in the matters where feeling is a dangerous guide. The alternating waves of confidence and timidity which sweep over the market for securities are among the most characteristic phenomena of business cycles. Even those who are relied upon for advice are not wholly immune from the emotional contagion. Thus the guidance of economic activity by the investing class is only in part an intelligent review of plans by competent experts.

A more vigorous and more intelligent leadership is exercised by the larger capitalists. They excel the investing public not only in means of securing information and in business sagacity, but also in the efficiency with which they follow up their investments. The greatest lenders become perforce much more than lenders. Over the enterprises in which their fortunes and their prestige are at stake they keep close watch. On the highest levels of business success, indeed, the functions of the investor and the enterpriser merge into each other.

5. THE RÔLE PLAYED BY CONSUMERS.

The court of last resort in deciding what goods shall be made is the whole body of consumers with money incomes to spend. Since retail merchants, public utilities, personal service agencies, and professional men strive to supply what the public will buy, this rule applies immediately to the production of goods which gratify personal wants. Less strictly, the rule applies also to the production of the materials from which consumers' goods are made, to the production of all producers' goods used in making consumers' goods, and even to the production of producers' goods used in making producers' goods. But the farther the remove from personal wants, the less is the control of consumers over demand and the larger the element of business discretion. Business managements and their technical advisers have considerable leeway in choosing what locations, what materials, what equipment and what services they shall use in production, and in what proportions they shall combine the several factors. Nor is the timing of business purchases rigidly bound by the timing of consumers' purchases. Thus the accurate form of statement is: production is guided by forecasts of what consumers will buy, supplemented by judgments concerning profitable methods of providing both consumers' goods and the endless variety of producers' goods which modern technique requires.

What proportion of current effort goes directly to the making of consumers' goods, and so falls most strictly under the rule of consumers' demand, we do not know. Of course, the preceding estimate that some such fraction as one-seventh of the total money income of the American people is "saved" on the average does not mean that six-sevenths of productive effort is spent directly upon consumers' goods. Still less does the estimate that the receipt of money incomes constitutes only a tenth of business transactions mean that nine-tenths of productive effort goes into making producers' goods. But where between these wide limits consumers' control fades into a mere sphere of influence we have no means of telling. The one certainty is that the development of modern technique directs an even larger amount of energy to the production of goods for making goods, and to the training of men to plan and supervise the directly productive efforts of other men.[1]

Even within the range where their control is most direct, consumers exert their authority as guides of production in a passive fashion. Usually they reveal what they want made only by buying briskly certain of the finished goods offered them, and by buying

[1] Mr. H. Gordon Hayes has estimated from the American Census of Occupations that about a quarter of "gainfully occupied" persons are engaged in the production of "durable goods"—including "all household furnishings and all household equipment that is made of wood or metal." He also estimates that about 4.25 per cent of the gainfully occupied are engaged in the construction and repair of factory buildings, machinery, railway roadway and rolling stock, and agricultural implements. "Production After the War," *Journal of Political Economy*, December, 1918, vol. xxvi, pp. 941-951.

other goods slowly.   Producers follow the leads thus given as closely as they can, but also endeavor to stimulate demand and to direct it into profitable channels.   Indeed, it seems that consumers often learn what they want by looking over the wares displayed in the shops. People are conscious of the general character of their needs, rather than of the specific goods which they desire.   To decide precisely what foods, garments, furnishings, ornaments, or amusements one will buy is a difficult task.   The picture given by so many economic treatises of buyers coming to market with their minds already made up about what goods they wish, and what price they are willing to pay at need for successive units of each kind, is an undeserved compliment to the mental energy of mankind.   Even to canvass the market's offerings thoroughly takes more time and thought than the average shopper will devote to the task.   So people follow an easier course, buying what they have bought before, what they see others using, or what advertisements and salesmen urge them to buy.   The psychological categories important to the understanding of consumers' demand are habit, imitation and suggestion—not reflective choice.   In particular, new products are seldom called for by consumers conscious of ungratified wants; they are pushed upon consumers by business enterprises, which often spend large sums in "educating the market," or "creating demand."

One reason why spending money is a backward art in comparison with making money was suggested early in this chapter;—the family continues to be the dominant unit of organization for spending money, whereas for making money the family has been superseded largely by a more highly organized unit.   The housewife, who does a large fraction of the world's shopping, is not selected for her efficiency as a manager, is not dismissed for inefficiency, and has small chance of extending her sway over other households if she proves capable.   She must buy so many different kinds of goods that she cannot become a good judge of qualities and prices, like the buyers for business houses. She is usually a manual laborer in several crafts, as well as a manager—a combination of functions not conducive to efficiency.   From the sciences of most importance to consumption, physiology and psychology, she cannot get as much practical help as the business man can get from the more mature sciences of physics and chemistry. Above all, she cannot systematize all her planning on the basis of accounting like the business man; for while the dollar is a satisfactory unit for reckoning profits as well as costs, it is not a satisfactory unit for expressing family welfare. Under these conditions, it is not surprising that what the world has learned in the art of consumption has been due less to the initiative of consumers, than to the initiative of producers striving to win a market for their wares.[2]

Yet with all their puzzles, consumers are in a strong market position. Their formal freedom to spend their money incomes as they like, combined with their massive inertia, keeps producers under pressure to solicit custom, to teach the public to want more goods and new goods. This task of stimulating demand is never done; for the march of technical improvement is ever increasing our capacity to produce, and before we have learned to distribute and to use what has just been added to our output, new advances have been scored. Hence the chronic complaint of business men that our industries are "over-built." The classical economists had logic of a sort on their side when they argued that general over-production is impossible in an exchange economy, because a supply of one kind of goods constitutes demand for goods of other kinds. But keener insight was revealed by Sismondi, and by Malthus who said,

> That an efficient taste for luxuries and conveniences, that is, such a taste as will properly stimulate industry, instead of being ready to appear at the moment it is required, is a plant of slow growth, the history of human society sufficiently shows.[3]

If anyone falters at reviewing the evidence which Malthus airily cites, he can try the conclusion by work-a-day business experience. Testimony abounds that the crucial difficulty in modern business lies in the "selling end," and the sincerity of this opinion is attested by the rapidly-increasing volume of selling costs.[4]

This pressure passively put by consumers upon producers is relaxed occasionally by the wasteful consumption of wars, and more frequently in booms, when the volume of demand is speciously magni-

---

[2] Compare Wesley C. Mitchell, "The Backward Art of Spending Money," *American Economic Review*, June, 1912, vol. ii, pp. 269-281; Henry Harap, *The Education of the Consumer*, New York, 1924 (a demonstration of how much a consumer needs to know), and Hazel Kyrk, *A Theory of Consumption*, Boston, 1923 (a demonstration that the economic theory of consumption is as laggard as the practice).

[3] T. R. Malthus, *Principles of Political Economy*, 2d ed., London, 1836, p. 321. For Sismondi's similar views, see above, Chapter I, section ii.

[4] For an effective presentation of the sellers' problem in modern business by an economist who has had practical experience, see George Binney Dibblee, *The Laws of Supply and Demand*, London, 1912, chapters x-xv.

fied for a while by business illusions. But most of the time the pressure is felt to be severe by the bulk of business enterprises. And that fact keeps consumers' demand the final arbiter of production, both in amount and in kind.

Back of consumers' demand, of course, stands the congeries of factors which control the distribution of income and the habits of spending. But this remark means merely that society's ways to-day are conditioned by its ways yesterday, coupled with its inability to make quick adjustments to altered conditions. To follow this fascinating line of analysis further would not be irrelevant, but the bare suggestion must suffice.

6. THE RÔLE PLAYED BY GOVERNMENT.

Concomitantly with the growth of money economy in Europe after the Middle Ages, the rôle which Government played in guiding economic activity became less active. The time had been when all men believed that the state should direct and regulate the economic life of its people for the good of the commonweal, quite as much as it should provide for the common defense. But as money economy extended, it began to appear that the merchant and the craftsman, in order to make money for themselves, must provide goods which the public wanted, and that in competing with each other for trade these private agents would keep down prices. The economic theory of *laissez faire*, as expounded by the Physiocrats, Adam Smith and the classical school, was an intellectual reflection of these accumulating facts of experience. By rationalizing the policy of private initiative in search of profits, which had developed spontaneously within the old scheme of governmental control, the economists expedited the transition in progress. Matters moved so fast, indeed, that the beginnings of reaction against extreme *laissez faire* appeared within the generation of Ricardo. The unrestricted pursuit of profits led at certain points to shocking ills, which Parliament intervened to check. England, and after her the world, in the fumbling fashion characteristic of social experimentation, presently attacked the problem of finding in detail what part of economic activity is best left to the guidance of business managements, and what part is best directed by the state. With that problem the leading nations are wrestling to-day as vigorously as ever. They seem to be no nearer a uniform and satisfactory solution than they were in the transition days of Adam Smith; for, though progress is doubtless made, the problem keeps developing new difficulties.

Of course, the great argument for confiding economic activity to the Government's guidance is that Government aims at promoting public welfare, while business enterprises must make money. Government can consider what needs it is most important to satisfy and can assess the cost upon those most able to bear it; whereas business enterprises must consider what demands it is profitable to meet, and cannot serve those who cannot pay. Were that the whole story, Government would to-day play a more active rôle in economic life than it played in the era of Mercantilism. But most people prefer to buy what they like, rather than to pay for what the authorities think ought to be produced. And most men are skeptical of Government's efficiency in pursuing its aims. Hence the scope of Government activities varies from country to country and from time to time with changes in public opinion—not to say public sentiment—on these fundamental issues.

At present Government in the United States, including the federal, state and local authorities, constitutes one of the leading branches of production. Government owns a huge amount of property, employs about 9 per cent of all wage- and salary-earners, and pays about 8 per cent of the current income of individuals. These are post-war figures.[1]

The few services which are almost everywhere performed by Government are services in which management for profit is deemed incompatible with public welfare. Schools run for profit would not teach the children of the very poor; sanitary bureaus run for profit could not force their services upon communities which need attention. The longer list of services which in some places are assumed by Government and in others left to business enterprises fall mainly into four classes: undertakings like water supply, street cars, and railways which are most economically managed as monopolies, and are therefore open to the suspicion of practicing extortion; undertakings like the management of forests, in which the community is interested in conserving sources of supply over a longer period than competing business enterprises find it profitable to regard; undertakings like the

---

[1] The percentage for incomes is an average for the years 1919-21. The percentage for employees refers to 1921. Both figures are drawn from Dr. King's estimates. See his introductory chapter to Dr. Leven's *Income in the Various States*, National Bureau of Economic Research, New York, 1925.

improvements of rivers and harbors, the reclamation of waste lands, and the buildings of canals in which the prospects of profits are not sufficiently bright to attract the requisite amount of private capital; and undertakings like the salt, tobacco, mining and lottery monopolies of Europe, which are frankly exploited by Government for the sake of raising revenue.

Over a far wider field, Government affects the guidance of economic activity by trying to prevent the pursuit of private profit from clashing with public welfare. Factories are required to adopt expensive safeguards for the benefit of their employees or patrons; they are forbidden to employ the cheap labor of young children, to keep women at work more than eight hours a day, and so on, with many variations from country to country and state to state. Certain products are often forbidden, such as impure foods and drugs. So too, in this country, are business practices restrictive of competition.

Most economic regulations of Government are negative in character; but Governments sometimes attempt to direct business enterprise into undertakings which are believed by the majority of the moment to be socially advantageous, though unprofitable without assistance from the state. Protective tariffs upon imports, bounties upon the production of sugar, and ship subsidies are examples in point. In other cases, the Government provides producers with expert technical advice—exporters and farmers, for example.

Still more in general, the whole plan of raising public revenues and apportioning public expenditures, the methods of providing for the public defense and maintaining domestic order, the monetary system and even the form of political institutions, in short, everything Government is and does, influences the direction of economic activity. For the business economy is so flexible a form of organization that the prospects of profits, and therefore the direction of economic activity by private initiative, are affected by a thousand acts of Government done for other than economic ends. Indeed, it is mainly as a "disturbing factor" that Government figures in the theory of business cycles. Its own economic operations are perhaps freer from cyclical fluctuations than those of any industry.

7. The Alleged "Planlessness" of Production.

With technical experts to plan the processes of production, business experts to guide the making of money, lenders to review all projects requiring large investments, Government to care for the public welfare, and with the whole buying public as a final arbiter, it may seem as if the business economy provides a staff and a procedure adequate to the task of directing economic activity, vast and intricate as that task is.

This impression is strengthened by observing that each class of guides is spurred to efficiency by hope of gain, and deterred from recklessness by fear of loss. The engineer who blunders is discharged, the enterpriser who blunders goes into bankruptcy, the lender who blunders loses his money, and even the administration which blunders may lose office—though that is less sure. Thus the guides who misdirect the industrial army are always being eliminated from the number of those who lead. On the other hand, those who succeed are always being promoted to posts of wider power.

Nor does all this apply merely to the leaders of economic activity. In theory, every adult is free to choose whatever lawful ways of making a money income he thinks wise, and to change as often as he likes. Thus every worker is supposed to have a modest share in directing production. In practice, of course, the range of occupations for which anyone can qualify is limited both by his native capacity and by his opportunities to get the requisite training and social connection. But the pressure which the business economy applies to the rank and file of the industrial army to develop efficiency in working and spending money is certainly not less severe than the pressure it applies to the captains. The older writers who expounded the philosophy of individualism emphasized the need of such pressure to make men work and save, at the same time as they argued that each man is the best judge of his own interests. Later writers, who credit men with less rationality than was the fashion a century ago, hold that economic individualism, involved in the current money economy, is a safeguard against failures to recognize where self-interest lies. Professor John Maurice Clark's remark on this head is whimsical only in part:

> Individualism may be regarded, not so much as the system calculated to get the utmost out of a people of extremely high intelligence, as the system in which human stupidity can do the least harm.[1]

[1] "The Socializing of Economics" in *The Trend of Economics,* edited by R. G. Tugwell, New York, 1924, p. 97.

With this powerful stimulation of individual efficiency, the business economy unites an opportunity for coöperation on a grand scale. By paying money prices, the leaders can enlist the aid of laborers who contribute work of all kinds, of expert advisers who contribute special knowledge, of landlords who contribute the uses of their property, and of investors who contribute the uses of their funds. And all these classes can be made to work in disciplined order toward the execution of a single plan. The fusing of incitements to individual efficiency with opportunity for wide coöperation is the great merit of the business economy.

That men like making and spending money as a way of organizing economic activity on the whole better than any other system they have yet practiced on a large scale, is indicated by history. The first section of this chapter suggests that the business economy grew out of the preferences of millions of men in successive generations in all quarters of the world. The medieval king and his tenants, the lord of the manor and his serfs, seem all to have gained by substituting monetary payments for the rendering of personal services. No one forced the housewife to give up making her own bread and her candles; no one forced the frontiersman to buy clothing in place of dressing in buckskin. It was because they preferred the new way of providing for their wants when the opportunity to choose was presented, that consumers patronized the retail shop selling factory products. So, too, banking could develop only as great numbers of people year after year found it useful. Not that the growth of money economy has involved no coercion, loss, and injustice—witness, for example, the tragic side of the enclosures which made possible farming for profit, the sufferings of peasants who could not learn the art of living on money, the oppressions exercised by money lenders, and the tragic struggle of the hand-loom weavers against the power loom. But broadly speaking, it seems clear that this feature of culture could have attained such general acceptance by the most advanced peoples of the world after so thorough a trial only because it seemed to meet their needs more adequately than the other forms of economic organization with which they have had experience.

Nevertheless, the business economy has obvious limitations as a system of organizing economic effort for the satisfaction of wants—limitations which must be noticed because they bear on the problem of business cycles.

1. The business economy provides for effective coördination of effort within each business enterprise, but not for effective coördination of effort among independent enterprises.

The two schemes of coördination differ in almost all respects. Coördination within an enterprise is the result of careful planning by experts; coördination among independent enterprises cannot be said to be planned at all; rather is it the unplanned result of natural selection in a struggle for business survival. Coördination within an enterprise has a definite aim—the making of profits; coördination among independent enterprises is limited by the conflicting aims of the several units. Coördination within an enterprise is maintained by a single authority possessed of power to carry its plans into effect; coördination among independent enterprises depends on many different authorities which have no power to enforce a common program, except so far as one can persuade or coerce others. As a result of these conditions, coördination within an enterprise is characterized by economy of effort; coördination among independent enterprises by waste.

In detail, then, economic activity is planned and directed with skill; but in the large there is neither general plan nor central direction. The charge that "capitalistic production is planless" therefore contains both an important element of truth and a large element of error. Apart from the transient programs of economic mobilization adopted under stress of war, civilized nations have not yet developed systematic plans for the sustenance of their populations; they continue to rely on the badly coördinated efforts of private initiative. Marked progress has been made, however, in the skill with which the latter efforts are directed, and also in the scale on which they are organized. The growth in the size of business enterprises controlled by a single management is a gain, because it increases the portion of the field in which close coördination of effort is feasible.

2. But the managerial skill of business enterprises is devoted to making money. If the test of efficiency in the direction of economic activity be that of determining what needs are most important for the common welfare and satisfying them in the most economical manner, the present system is subject to a further criticism. For, in nations where a few have incomes sufficient to gratify trifling whims and where many cannot buy things required to maintain their own efficiency or to give proper training to their children, it can hardly be argued that the goods which pay best are the goods most needed

It is no fault of the individual business leaders that they take prospective profits as their own guide. On the contrary, they are compelled to do so; for the men who mix too much philanthropy with business soon cease to be leaders. But a system of economic organization which forces men to accept so technical an aim as pecuniary profit cannot guide their efforts with certainty toward their own ideals of public welfare. And Government can remedy this defect only in part.

3. Even from the point of view of business, prospective profit is an uncertain, flickering light. For profits depend upon two variables —on margins between selling and buying prices and on the volume of trade—related to each other in unstable fashion, and each subject to perturbations from a multitude of unpredictable causes. That the system of prices has its own order is clear; but it is not less clear that this order fails to afford certainty of business success. Men of long experience and proved sagacity often find their calculations of profit upset by conjunctures which they could not anticipate. Thus the business economy confuses the guidance of economic activity by interjecting a large element of uncertainty into business ventures.

4. The hazards to be assumed grow greater with the extent of the market and with the time which elapses between the initiation and the fruition of an enterprise. But the progress of industrial technique is steadily widening markets, and requiring heavier investments of capital for future production. Hence the share in economic leadership which falls to lenders, that of reviewing the various chances offered them for investment, presents increasing difficulties. And, as has been shown, a large proportion of these lenders, particularly of the lenders on long time, lack the capacity and training for the successful performance of such work.

These defects in the system of guiding economic activity and the bewildering complexity of the task itself allow the processes of economic life to fall into those recurrent disorders which constitute crises and depressions. To recognize this fact, however, is but the beginning of wisdom. Much patient analysis is required to discover just how these disorders arise, and why, instead of becoming chronic, they lead after a time to the return of prosperity.

VII. International Differences in Economic Organization.

1. The Uneven Development of Business Economy.

All the highly civilized nations of the world to-day have substantially the same form of economic organization. The business economy, sketched in this chapter with particular reference to the United States, prevails in Great Britain, France, Belgium, the Netherlands, Switzerland, the Scandinavian countries, Germany, Austria, and the great British colonies with white populations. A somewhat less mature stage of the money economy has been reached by the other European countries, by the Spanish- and Portuguese-speaking peoples of South America, and by the European colonists in South Africa. A still less mature stage prevails in the Orient, aside from Japan.[1]

In no country is the development of the business economy uniform over all sections. Everywhere the city dwellers carry on more of their activities by making and spending money incomes than the country folk. Nearly every country, even in the Orient, has its centers of large-scale industry and trade, and every country has its areas where production is organized rather on a family basis than on the basis of full-fledged business enterprises.

This uneven development of business economy influences the course run by business cycles in different parts of the world. It has been shown that alternations of prosperity and depression occur with increasing regularity as business economy extends in scope, and seem to arise more from economic processes and less from political or physical events.[2] It will be shown in the fourth chapter that the business cycles of countries which have highly developed business economies correspond to each other in timing and intensity rather closely; between countries where pecuniary organization is less mature the correspondence is distinctly less close. Finally, within every large country, there are measurable differences in the timing and the intensity of cyclical fluctuations in different sections—differences which appear to correlate with the differences in thoroughness of pecuniary organization.

---

[1] These statements are based upon rather vague and general impressions. Perhaps the grouping suggested is not quite fair in all cases; certainly it is subject to revision as conditions develop in the countries which we now count laggard.

[2] See section i, 4, of this chapter.

The history of the past two hundred years suggests that the international and sectional differences in economic organization are gradually becoming less. In all quarters of the globe business economy has been gaining ground. But the approach toward uniformity is slow, not only because the laggard peoples learn new habits deliberately, but also because the advanced peoples keep elaborating their pecuniary institutions. For as long a time as we can envisage, differences will maintain themselves on a scale sufficient to prevent business cycles from reaching in all quarters of the world even the measure of uniformity which they now possess among the central European nations, Great Britain, Canada and the United States.

2. The Proportion of the Workers Engaged in Farming.

A second set of conditions which make business cycles differ from country to country is found in the character of the occupations followed by their peoples. Of course, all the major industries are represented in every large population; but the proportions of the people engaged in agriculture, manufacturing, mining, transportation, trade, and the professions, vary widely. Because of the divergencies noted above in the business-cycle hazards to which various industries are subject,[1] it is pertinent to make international comparisons of occupation groups.

Unfortunately, occupations are classified in such unlike ways by different countries that close comparisons are out of the question. But the point of most importance—the percentage of male workers engaged in farming[2]—can be ascertained roughly for the countries whose business annals will be presented in a later chapter. The figures are given in Table 10. While the foreign data have been rearranged to fit the American census classification as nearly as may be, the percentages can be trusted only as showing the existence of very wide differences in dependence upon agriculture, and, by inference, upon other industries, particularly manufacturing.

England and Wales here stand in a class by themselves, with only one-ninth of their workers on farms. This does not mean that business cycles in England are more exempt from agricultural influences than business cycles in the European countries or the United

---

[1] See section ii, 3, of this chapter.
[2] Much better figures can be found for men than for women in several of the countries included.

States which have from a quarter to a third of their men in the fields, but that the harvests which affect English cycles are the harvests in

TABLE 10

PROPORTION OF GAINFULLY EMPLOYED MALES ENGAGED IN AGRICULTURAL PURSUITS IN VARIOUS COUNTRIES

Country	Date	Per Cent in Agriculture
China	1911	75.0[a]
India	1911	71.4
Russia	1897	61.6[b]
Japan	1908	58.5[c]
Union of South Africa	1911	55.4
Italy	1911	53.8[d]
Sweden	1910	49.1[e]
Austria	1910	45.5
Brazil	1920	45.0[d]
Canada	1911	41.0[f]
France	1911	40.0
United States	1910	35.8[f]
Argentina	1914	30.0[g]
Netherlands	1909	29.4
Australia	1911	29.0[h]
Germany	1907	28.3
England and Wales	1911	11.0[f]

NOTES:

[a] Estimated. See *China Year Book*, 1916, p. 3; *Journal of the American Asiatic Association*, 1911, vol. xi, p. 203; *Statesman's Year Book*, 1923, p. 771.

[b] Data for the entire Empire, including Siberia and the Caucasus.

[c] Percentage represents the proportion of all households engaged in agriculture to the total number.

[d] Males over 10 years of age.

[e] Males over 15 years of age.

[f] Males 10 years of age and over.

[g] Occupation data do not include workers in occupations not sufficiently specified, such as day-laborers, which tends to lower the percentage of agriculturally employed. The surprisingly low percentage is somewhat substantiated by the fact that 55 per cent of the population is classed as urban. A considerable part of the town and city dwellers consists of landlords and their dependents.

[h] "Exclusive of full-blooded aboriginals."

Compiled by Willard L. Thorp from censuses or official year books of the several countries, except in the cases of China and Russia. For the Chinese sources, see above note ([a]). The Russian data were obtained from the French population census of 1911, I, part iii, p. 176.

The occupation data in the various censuses have been regrouped to conform as nearly as may be to the category in the United States *Census of Occupations*, 1910, entitled "Agriculture, Forestry and Animal Husbandry," not including fishermen and oystermen. In order to make the records as comparable as possible, the data were taken from the census nearest to 1910 for each country.

the countries from which England buys the bulk of her foodstuffs and to which she sells the bulk of her exports.

At the other extreme are the great Oriental populations of China and India, followed by the Russian Empire and Japan. Several of the European countries in the list depend more upon farming than does the United States. More surprising are the low percentages for Argentina and Australia. Defects in the original data (particularly from Argentina, which omits from her occupation tables workers whose trades are not definitely specified) may be partly responsible for this result; but few North Americans realize how large a proportion of the people in these two southern lands live in cities.

3. ENTERPRISE AND THRIFT.

Observers generally agree upon two temperamental differences which are revealed in the business behavior of the foremost commercial nations. The French are held to show less business enterprise than the Americans (who are inclined to credit themselves with pre-eminence in this quality), or the English, or the Germans. Their railways could not be built without a state guarantee of dividends; their merchant marine relies upon bounties; their great credit companies, founded largely to aid in establishing new enterprises, have gone over mainly to the less hazardous business of accepting deposits and handling investments for customers; their private banks are concerned chiefly with transactions in foreign exchange and short-time credits. The Frenchman seems to have no great fondness for the game of business. He aims to secure a competency by the thrifty conduct of his affairs along conservative lines, then to retire and invest his accumulations in *rentes*. It may be largely for this reason that the cyclical fluctuations in French business are relatively narrow in scope, and seldom marked by severe crises.[1]

On the other hand, the French are believed to surpass Americans, English, and even Germans in thrift. In the years preceding the war, France seemed to be displacing England as the world's greatest lender. The relative lack of domestic business enterprise, combined with an enormous aggregate of small savings, provided each year hundreds of millions of francs which sought investment in foreign securities. And in the selection of their investments the French preferred what they believed to be a conservative policy. Occasionally they might buy freely of speculative stocks, like "Kaffirs"; but the bulk of their sav-

[1] Compare K. Wiedenfeld, "Das Persönliche im Modernen Unternehmertum," *Schmoller's Jahrbuch für Gesetzgebung*, 1910, pp. 229-233,

ings went into government obligations, high-grade railway and industrial bonds, or into shares long established as dividend payers.[2]

It would be easy to elaborate by pointing out various contrasts between the business traits commonly believed to characterize the North and the South Americans, the Japanese and the Chinese, or the Russians and the Scandinavians. Nor can it be doubted that whatever differences exist among national temperaments have their bearing upon the whole economic life of the peoples in question. But such elaboration would not sensibly promote the present inquiry. For, after showing in the fourth chapter what relations exist among business cycles in different parts of the world, we shall concentrate attention upon the United States, England, France, and Germany. And about the differences in their business traits what has been said will suffice.

4. MONETARY AND BANKING SYSTEMS.

Before the Great War it was thought that all the commercial nations of the world would soon have monetary systems of the same type. One country after another had gone over to the single gold standard, with supplementary use of silver coins, and of paper money issued by the Government, by the banks, or both. China was the greatest nation remaining on the silver basis; there were no bimetallic standards, and irredeemable paper standards seemed to be rare episodes. While the war produced wild confusion in monetary systems and forced many of the European nations to suspend specie payments, it now seems probable that within a few years the earlier uniformity will be restored in large measure. If so, the old facility of international transactions will return, and the financial bonds which connect the business fortunes of the great commercial nations will become closer than they have been since 1914—unless non-business forces again intervene to prevent.

Banking systems, also, had been growing more alike before the war, as various countries strove to adapt features which had succeeded elsewhere to their peculiar needs. The last great step in this direction was the establishing of the Federal Reserve System by the

---

[2] Compare, for example, A. Neymarch, *French Savings and Their Influence*, pp. 163-181; publications of the National Monetary Commission (Senate Document No. 494, 61st Congress, 2d Session).

United States in 1914—a measure which introduced a modified form of centralization into a system theretofore composed of some 29,000 independent banks. But banking systems and banking usages had never attained such similarity as characterized monetary systems. The difference of chief moment to the student of business cycles is between the preponderant use of bank checks in making payments among the Anglo-Saxon communities, and the relatively slight use of checks in other countries. But it should also be recalled that outside of Europe, North America and Australia, the use of banking facilities is confined mainly to the commercial centers and so touches the bulk of the people only by indirection.

5. Government's Share in Directing Economic Activity.

Finally, there are considerable differences even among those modern nations whose pecuniary institutions are most alike, in the share which central and local Governments take in directing economic activities.

Partly because of limitations placed by constitutional law upon the powers of Government, partly it would seem because of a temperamental restiveness under control, Americans have made fewer and less bold experiments in municipal operation of public utilities, or in state operation of railways, telegraphs, telephones, mines, and the like, than have the Germans, French, or British. Perhaps, however, this difference is growing less decade by decade. Certainly, the rise of public commissions as agencies for regulating privately-owned enterprises has given the federal, state and municipal Governments of the Union a share in directing several branches of business.

While later chapters will show that all the international differences in economic organization and practice which have been pointed out possess some significance, by far the most important is the uneven development of business economy. There are, indeed, close organic relations between this uneven development and the proportion of men engaged in agriculture, the prevalence of an enterprising spirit in business affairs, the use of banking facilities, and perhaps even the share which Government takes in directing economic activity. Yet all these differences together account only for a part of the divergencies which the fourth chapter will show among the business annals of various countries. Another part must be ascribed to factors of a political or physical type. About the relative importance of the forces which produce divergencies among business cycles, however, and about their interactions, our knowledge is meager. Perhaps we are overlooking forces which will some day be found to play dominating rôles. But the way to hasten the day of fuller understanding is to make the best use we can of our present insights, imperfect though they are.

VIII. Conclusion.

1. The RAISON D'ETRE of Chapter II.

Taken one at a time, most of the theories of business cycles reviewed in Chapter I seem plausible, not to say convincing. Certainly each theory, this time without exception, illuminates some angle of the problem. Taken all together, the theories render a different service—one which is welcome only to the man who has the courage and time to enter upon a thorough investigation. They show that business cycles are congeries of diverse fluctuations in numerous processes—physical, psychological, and economic. Indeed, upon reflection the theories figure less as rival explanations of a single phenomenon than as complementary explanations of closely related phenomena. The processes with which they severally deal are all characteristic features of the whole. These processes not only run side by side, but also influence and (except for the weather) are influenced by each other. Thus the diversity of explanations, which at first seems confusing, becomes an aid toward envisaging the complex character of the problem.

Complexity is no proof of multiplicity of causes. Perhaps some single factor is responsible for all the phenomena. An acceptable explanation of this simple type would constitute the ideal theory of business cycles from the practical, as well as from the scientific, viewpoint. But if there be one cause of business cycles, we cannot make sure of its adequacy as an explanation without knowing what are the phenomena to be explained, and how the single cause produces its complex effects, direct and indirect. Neither on the single-cause hypothesis, nor on the hypothesis of multiple causes, are we equipped to deal with the problem of causation until we have learned what are the processes characteristic of business cycles, and how these processes are related to one another. Chapter I indicated what the leading processes are. The way to discover their relations is to study the development and the functioning of the economic organization within which business cycles run their courses. Hence the sketch of the business economy drawn in this chapter.

Few writers upon business cycles deem such an introduction necessary. None of them question that most processes of modern life, social and political as well as economic, have some share in the alternations of prosperity and depression. But most investigators take the complexities for granted, credit themselves and their readers with a knowledge of economic organization sufficient for their purpose, and concentrate upon demonstrating the source from which comes the dominant impetus to cyclical fluctuations. A theorist who has satisfied himself upon that central issue is prone to adduce only the evidence and arguments which seem to prove his explanation, spending little time upon processes which adjust themselves to his ruling cause. A skillful exposition of this type is likely to convince the reader also, unless he is acquainted with one or several equally confident demonstrations that some other cause is primarily responsible. In the latter case, the reader must give up the puzzle, or choose among the explanations on inadequate grounds, or study for himself the interrelations among the processes exploited by his various authorities.

Our debt to men who have written, and even thought, in this summary fashion is heavy. It profits us less to dwell upon their lack of circumspection than to dwell upon their positive achievements. When the problem of business cycles was first attacked it was inevitable that the hypotheses offered would be inadequately worked out. The complexities of the problem, the possibility of making numerous hypotheses, had to be discovered. Contemporaries who still follow out a single line of causation without careful examination of other lines, may seem a trifle quaint; yet they too may add new discoveries to the growing stock of knowledge, or new ideas on which to work. We must choose, however, between following their methods and making use of their results. If we see a promise of usefulness in the seemingly divergent conclusions reached by several different groups of investigators, we must set about our own constructive work with more care than our guides deemed necessary.

2. A Summary.

Now that the sketch of economic organization is completed, we may sum up the leading results in form for future use.

Business cycles do not become a prominent feature of economic experience in any community until a large proportion of its members have begun to live by making and spending money incomes. On the other hand, such cycles seem to appear in all countries when economic activity becomes organized predominantly in this fashion. These observations suggest that there is an organic connection between that elaborate form of economic organization which we may call "business economy," and recurrent cycles of prosperity and depression.

As a money economy attains high development, consumption continues to be carried on mainly by families; but production comes to be carried on mainly by a new unit—the business enterprise. Further, there is evidence that business cycles are most pronounced in those industries which are dominated by full-fledged business enterprises, and that within these industries they affect large enterprises more seriously than small ones.

According to the best available estimates, the man-made equipment which American workers now use has an aggregate value of about three years' current income. This equipment includes not only buildings, transportation system, factories, and implements of all kinds, but also roads, the products and merchandise on their way toward consumers, and the personal effects owned by individuals. The possession of this stock of accumulated wealth makes it possible for the population to consume for a time more than it is producing. Every year the population eats about the same amount of food per capita; but the expenditure upon maintaining and extending the equipment used for business purposes need not be, and in practice is not, kept so nearly uniform. Thus modern industrial methods and modern business organization in combination open the door to wide cyclical fluctuations in at least one important field of economic activity.

To prosper, even to survive, business enterprises must make profits—not every year, but on the average. Hence the making of profits is of necessity the controlling aim of business management. The industrial processes which enterprises carry on in producing, transporting, storing, and distributing goods are means toward this end.

In other phrases: industry is subordinated to business, the making of goods to the making of money.

Yet the quantity of goods handled within a given period is a matter of primary concern, even from the strictest business viewpoint. Profits are the difference between the prices which an enterprise pays for all the things it must buy, and the prices which the enterprise receives for all the things it sells. Thus profits depend upon the physical volume of goods bought and sold, as well as upon the margins between buying and selling prices.

The prices of the innumerable kinds of goods made and consumed in a business economy constitute an orderly system. The active agency in maintaining the relations among the various parts of this system is the quest for profits itself. Business men are ever looking for opportunities which promise a large volume of trade at wide price margins. Where the margins seem wide and demand active, new enterprisers crowd in if they can, and their competition presently raises buying and lowers selling prices. When margins seem narrow, new investments are avoided, and such of the old investments as can be withdrawn are shifted to more promising fields. In consequence, buying prices are likely to fall and selling prices to rise. The result of these shiftings of investment, which are always in progress, is not to make uniform the percentage margins on which all classes of goods are handled; but so to adjust buying and selling prices that the net price margins, together with the volume of trade which can be handled with a given investment, will hold out similar prospects of profits in all branches of business open to newcomers. This uniformity never is attained in fact; but the plus and minus departures from the prevailing level of prospective profits are the guides which business men try to follow in planning investments.

In our analysis of business cycles, then, we must recognize that profit making is the central process among the congeries that constitute the activities of a business economy. Weather conditions count in so far as they affect profits, so do emotional aberrations, so do the production and consumption of consumers' goods, and so do a thousand other factors. On the other hand, the prospects of making profits react upon all these other processes, in so far as they are affected by human behavior. Even the factors which we classify as political or social rather than economic are influenced in varying measure by the profitableness of business. But, of course, attention must be concentrated upon the relations among the processes which are of outstanding importance as affecting and affected by prospective profits. In this chapter, an effort is made to get as good estimates as possible of the relative magnitude of a few fundamental factors.

The elaborate exchanges required by the system of "production for the use of others and acquisition for the use of self" are managed in relatively small part by the use of coin and paper money, and mainly by the use of credit instruments. In the United States it seems that something like 85 per cent of payments are made by check. Deposit currency is adapted to the varying activity of business, because both its volume and its rate of turnover rise and fall with prosperity and depression.

The goods produced by business enterprises are distributed among the community by the continual paying and spending of money incomes. Of the several income streams, wages and salaries is much the largest, averaging over one-half of total money income. Profits ranks second, and is approximately equal to dividends, interest, and rents put together. From the money incomes received by individuals, upwards of 60 per cent seems to be spent at retail shops in average years; the rest is distributed among various channels, of which rent is the most important.

It is characteristic of the business economy that the process of providing goods to meet human needs gives rise to business transactions which far exceed current income. Recent data indicate that the total volume of payments in the United States is perhaps ten times the aggregate money incomes of all individuals, or five times the transactions involved in both receiving and spending personal incomes.

A not inconsiderable fraction of current income is "saved" every year—that is, expended in ways which increase the community's stock of fairly durable consumers' goods or increase its capacity to produce future income. The best available estimate for the United States, which is none too certain, makes this fraction average about one-seventh of current income. Two-fifths of the saving is done not by individuals, but by business enterprises. The indications are that the accumulated wealth of the United States (excluding the value of land) is equal to the savings of some 20 to 30 years.

An economic organization which distributes incomes in money, and lets the recipients spend the money in any way they like, makes extremely difficult the task of adjusting the supply of each kind of goods to the profit-paying demand for it. To cope with this task of directing production in detail, the business economy has evolved an elaborate system. Business managements play the most active rôle in guiding production; but they have the assistance of technical experts of various sorts, and they must submit most of their important projects to review by lenders of credit or investment funds. In the last resort consumers determine what shall be made, by buying certain products freely and others sparingly; their choices, however, can be and are influenced in considerable measure by business enterprises, and business managements decide the technical question what producers' goods, direct and indirect, they had best use in making consumers' commodities.

As the money economy developed in Europe, the share which Government took in guiding economic activity gradually shrank. The turning point seems to have come in the 17th century in England, early in the 18th century in France and late in the 18th century in Germany. Governments now render certain services which the community will not confide to commercial exploitation—a list that varies considerably from place to place—and for the rest endeavor to check methods of making money which are deemed incompatible with public welfare. Aside from schemes of economic mobilization during wars, no country has developed a comprehensive plan for the direction of its economic energies. The scheme of guidance by business managements, technical experts, lenders, and consumers, which has been evolved in the later stages of the money economy, is confined within the limits of single business enterprises, or groups of enterprises dominated by a common control. The relations among the undertakings of independent money-makers are not planned, but are established and altered by the mutual competition of these enterprises—in which anyone who can command the necessary capital is free to join, and in which some enterprisers win more or less monopolistic advantages. Business cycles are among the unplanned results of this scheme of organization.

Business economy nowadays prevails in much the same form among the nations in which Euro-American culture is highly developed. It seems also to be making headway in other countries; but in the Orient, aside from Japan, and in less civilized regions, it has not reached the point at which business cycles attain marked significance. Even among the great commercial nations there are minor differences in economic organization, respecting such matters as the percentage of the population engaged in farming, the relative development of thrift and enterprise, monetary and banking habits, and the economic policy of Government. These differences combine with a multitude of non-economic factors to prevent the business cycles of any two countries from being precisely alike.

3. THE CONCEPTION OF EQUILIBRIUM.

To repeat once more: by showing that business cycles are intricate complexes made up of diverse fluctuations in numerous activities, Chapter I forced us to seek some orderly scheme for conceiving the relations of these processes to each other. The scheme which Chapter II presents centers on the pursuit of money profits. All the "causes" of business cycles stressed by the theories reviewed owe whatever influence they exert upon economic activity to their bearing upon profits, and the like must hold concerning any other "causes" which future investigation reveals. Thus we have a pattern to follow in future chapters, a pattern which should enable us to discuss the wide diversity of processes involved in business cycles without falling into confusion.

A further device for keeping order in the discussion is to treat the detailed problems marked out by our pattern as having all the same form—problems of equilibrium. The conception that business cycles consist in rhythmical ruptures and restorations of balance in some fundamental process is explicitly presented by several of the theories reviewed, and may be read into others. Can we make use of this idea?

Doubtless it was a mechanical analogy which gave its vogue to the notion of economic equilibria. Everyone admits that analogies, though often most suggestive in scientific inquiries, are dangerous guides. The usefulness of the analogy in question was greatest and its dangers least when economists were treating what they called "static" problems. Such problems can be given a quasi-mechanical character, for they are not taken from life, but made in an inquirer's head to suit his purposes, and mechanical analogies are appropriate to mechanical problems. But the problems of business cycles are the opposite of "static." If we are to conceive of them in terms of an equilibrium of mechanical forces, we must conceive of an equilibrium among numerous forces which are constantly changing, changing at different rates, and influencing one another as they change. Perhaps an ingenious person who thought the game worth while might design a mechanical contrivance which would work somewhat after the fashion of cyclical business fluctuations. If he did so, however, most economists would find his machine so difficult to understand, and the real similarity of its operations to business processes so uncertain, that they would leave its intricacies to the pleased contemplation of the inventor.

Yet there is a different conception of equilibrium which may help us—the equilibrium of a balance sheet, or better, of an income and expenditures statement. Such a statement has nothing to do with mechanical forces, and that is a safeguard against false analogies. It deals with pecuniary quantities, and they are genuine elements in our problem. It sums up the results of numerous processes which concern us, through periods of time which we can divide according to their business characteristics. More than that, the statements for successive periods of time link into each other, as they should do for our purposes. The statement for one period shows what has happened to certain items included in its predecessor, and shows also certain items the disposition of which will appear in its successor. Finally, the balance which is struck is really a device for finding how much the expenditures and the receipts are out of balance. The difference between these two aggregates of items is put down on the income side as profit or loss, a positive or a negative sum. That feature, too, serves our needs. We have no more warrant for assuming in advance that business processes "tend" to maintain an equilibrium than to assume that they "tend" to get out of balance. What we need when we employ the concept of equilibrium, is a device for showing the relations between the aggregates which stand opposite each other in various processes, as expenditures and receipts stand opposite each other in bookkeeping. Having found equality, or having found one set of items in excess of the other, our problem is to trace the consequences. It is not a foregone conclusion that these consequences will always be of the sort which tend to restore a balance, any more than losses suffered by a business enterprise one year tend to give it profits in the year following. Yet we know that the modern business system does not function smoothly when the aggregates of the opposing items in certain pairs get too much out of balance.

To indicate the uses of this conception of equilibrium in discussing business cycles is to review again the leading conclusions of the present chapter. The central proposition is the one to which the statement of receipts and expenditures applies directly: business enterprises cannot "carry on" unless in the long run their incomes exceed their outlays by a satisfactory margin of profits. In order that this relation (which the bookkeeper expresses as a balance) may be maintained, an indefinite number of other changing aggregates must be kept in due relation to each other. For example, the selling prices of each of the million kinds of goods produced and sold must be adjusted severally to their costs of production. So, too, the physical quantities of each kind of goods turned out must be adjusted severally to the physical quantities that can be sold. That payments may be made, the quantity and turnover of coin, paper money, and deposit currency must be adjusted to the pecuniary volume of trade, or the pecuniary volume of trade to the circulating medium. Also, the means of payment must be disbursed to buyers as money incomes, or as loans, in proportions duly adjusted to the value of goods sent to market. To provide for expansion of industrial equipment, a portion of the income and loans must be saved and invested, but that proportion must not be excessive.

So we might go on indefinitely, translating perhaps all of the theories of business cycles into terms of equilibrium. Clearly that form of statement has advantages, and may be resorted to freely without danger, if we remember that the equilibria in mind are akin to the balances of bookkeeping rather than to the equilibria of mechanics. Our balances take place in time, over periods which vary from case to case, and which are seldom definite. The balances need not be exact; business plans seek to provide liberal factors of safety; if results fall out in the neighborhood of expectations, all is well. When balances fail persistently by wide margins for a considerable period of time, men can restore them in many cases by writing certain constituents up or writing them down. For business balances usually combine both estimates of certain values and records of certain transactions; they look to the future as well as the past; they are used to control plans quite as much as to register results; their reliability depends upon judgments not less than on arithmetic.

CHAPTER III.

THE CONTRIBUTION OF STATISTICS.[1]

I. The Current Distinction Between Theoretical and Statistical Work.

The review of current theories in Chapter I barely mentions the type of work upon business cycles which is most characteristic of the present and seems most promising for the future—analysis of statistical data. A few of the theorists—notably Henry L. Moore—make skilled and elaborate use of quantitative methods, and almost all cite statistical evidence upon occasion. But most theories of business cycles are still built up by methods which would have seemed familiar to Sismondi and Ricardo.

On the other hand, there has recently appeared a group of business-cycle statisticians who as yet have sought, not to construct general theories, but to establish more precisely the facts concerning cyclical fluctuations in particular economic processes. By their detailed researches, the statistical workers are building up a literature more like the current literature of the natural sciences than like that of economic theory. It contains few treatises, but a multitude of technical papers; it is mathematical in form and empirical in spirit; it deals with restricted problems, lays stress upon measurements, and aspires to prediction.

Between these two groups of workers, the theorists and the statisticians, there has been less communion than their mutual interests require. Many of the statisticians pay little heed to current theories of business cycles, and many of the theorists make little use of statistical methods. A similar divergence of outlook, associated with a similar division of labor, seems not uncommon in modern science. Experimentalists and pure theorists often have difficulty in understanding each other; but in the long run each group provides grist for the other's mill, and scientific progress is a joint product of the

[1] In writing this chapter, I have had generous help from the Staff of the National Bureau, particularly from Dr. Frederick C. Mills, and from the Directors, particularly from Professor Allyn A. Young.

two lines of attack upon the unknown. Such must prove to be the
case in work upon business cycles.

Statistical analysis affords the surest means of determining the
relations among and the relative importance of the numerous factors
stressed by business-cycle theories. In turn, rational hypotheses are
the best guides of statistical research, and theoretical significance
is the ultimate test of statistical results. Aside from the limitations
of investigators or of their resources, the line commonly drawn between statistical and theoretical work has no justification.

II. Development of the Statistical Approach.

1. Why the Early Writers Upon Business Cycles Made Slight Use of Statistics.

A promising beginning of statistical work upon social problems
had been made in England by contemporaries of Sir Isaac Newton.
The most conspicuous figure in the group, Sir William Petty, dealt
with "Political Arithmetick," sought to express himself in "Terms of
Number, Weight, or *Measure,*" and to "bottom" his discourses upon
quantitative "Observations or Positions" which are "either true, or
not apparently false . . . and if they are false, not so false as to
destroy the Argument they are brought for." [1] But political arithmetic had not prospered greatly. "Observations . . . expressed by
Number, Weight, or *Measure*" were scarce, and the "Positions,"
"either true, or not apparently false," upon which Petty's followers
bottomed their discourses sometimes led to contradictory conclusions. While Adam Smith was writing the *Wealth of Nations,* Dr.
Richard Price was proving that the population of England and Wales
had decreased near a quarter since the Revolution, and Arthur Young
was proving that the population had increased. It is not surprising
that Adam Smith had "no great faith in political arithmetic," and
made sparing use of it in expounding "the obvious and simple system of natural liberty." [2]

Yet it is an exaggeration to picture the generation which developed the first theories of business cycles as virtually destitute of

---

[1] From the preface to *Political Arithmetick,* 1690. See *The Economic Writings of
Sir William Petty,* edited by Charles H. Hull. Cambridge, 1899; vol. i, pp. 244, 245.
[2] *The Wealth of Nations,* Cannan's edition, vol. ii. pp. 36 and 184.

significant statistics. One has but to look into such volumes as George Chalmers' *Estimate of the Comparative Strength of Great Britain,* 1782, Sir Frederick M. Eden's *State of the Poor,* 1797, the second edition of Malthus' *Essay on the Principle of Population,* 1803, or Thomas Tooke's *Thoughts and Details on the High and Low Prices of the Last Thirty Years,* 1823, to assure himself that men who had an aptitude for that type of inquiry could gather and use critically a considerable quantity of data covering a considerable range of problems.   And the books mentioned are but prominent examples of a type of work which was rapidly increasing in volume, improving in quality, and gaining public support.   In 1801 the first census of Great Britain was taken, and in 1832 a Statistical Department was added to the Board of Trade.   How voluminous and how varied were the statistical materials which had been quietly accumulating in official sources between these two dates was shown in 1833, when John Marshall published his quarto *Digest of all the Accounts Relating to the Population, Productions, Revenues, Financial Operations, Manufactures, Shipping, Colonies, Commerce, etc., etc., of the United Kingdom, diffused through more than 600 volumes of Journals, Reports, and Papers presented to Parliament during the last Thirty-five Years.*

It is also a mistake to think of the early nineteenth century as altogether lacking in statistical technique.   In *Chronicon Preciosum,* published in 1707 and more than once reprinted, Bishop Fleetwood had shown how to treat changes in the purchasing power of money on a quantitative basis.   A definite plan for making index numbers of prices had been put before the Royal Society by Sir George Schuckburg-Evelyn in 1798.[3]   William Playfair had used graphic methods of presenting time series in the successive editions of his *Commercial and Political Atlas, representing, by Means of Stained Copper-plate Charts, the Progress of the Commerce, Revenues, Expenditures, and Debts of England, during the whole of the Eighteenth Century* (1786, 1787, and 1801).   Joseph Fourier had developed harmonic analysis in a memoir crowned by the *Academie des Sciences* in 1812.[4]   Most important of all, Laplace had published his *Essai Philosophique sur les Probabilités* in 1814.   In this charming essay, the most celebrated mathematician of the age summed up the analytic methods de-

---

[3] "An Account of Some Endeavors to Ascertain a Standard of Weight and Measure," *Philosophical Transactions of the Royal Society of London,* 1798. Part I, art. viii, pp. 132-186, especially pp. 175, 176.
[4] *Théorie des mouvements de la chaleur dans les corps solides.*

veloped by his predecessors and himself, and proposed their use in dealing with social problems.

> Let us apply to the political and social sciences (he wrote) the method founded upon observations and calculus, a method which has served us so well in the natural sciences.

And to that end, Laplace urged that the compilation of social statistics be made systematic. It is highly important to keep in every branch of

> public administration an accurate record of the effects produced by the various measures taken, which are so many experiments tried on a large scale by governments.[5]

Thus it is an over-simple explanation to ascribe the neglect of measurements by early business-cycle theorists wholly to the lack of pertinent data or to the immaturity of statistical technique. Had they taken the line suggested by Laplace, these writers might have used and added to the available data; they might have learned and developed the analytic methods which had been suggested. But like other economists of the day, most writers upon crises had an easier, a quicker, and, as it seemed to them, a more effective method of working. Observers had no trouble in conceiving plausible explanations of crises, and they could rapidly expand their conjectures into imposing theories by selecting from the facts generally known those which accorded with their leading ideas. In this way they avoided a host of doubts and difficulties which would crop up if they tried to bottom their work upon the stubborn data of statistics. With the contemporary writers of economic treatises, they might admit, when discussing problems of method, that their "deductive" reasoning required "inductive verification"; but they somewhat easily excused themselves from going through the second and more arduous operation.[6] Perhaps still more important is the fact that writers who practiced the "deductive" method were apt to formulate their problems in ways which raised obstacles to "inductive verification,"—obstacles

---

[5] *Essai Philosophique*, 6th ed., Paris, 1840, p. 135.
[6] Note, for example, the difference between the procedure which John Stuart Mill recommended in his *System of Logic*, 1843, and the procedure which he practiced in *The Principles of Political Economy*, 1848. In but few chapters does Mill really carry out the "concrete-deductive method."

which might have been avoided by a different approach.[7] Statistical method could not develop its full efficiency so long as it was called in only at the end of an inquiry, and asked to answer questions it had no share in framing.

2. The Growth of Statistical Technique.

The mathematical statisticians of the early 19th century did not enter the economic field. The social phenomena to which Laplace applied the theory of probabilities in his *Essai Philosophique* were such matters as the credibility of the evidence given by witnesses, the decisions of assemblies, mortality, and the average duration of marriages. Adolphe Quetelet dealt with physical, intellectual and moral qualities in his two volumes *Sur l'Homme*, 1835. Henry Thomas Buckle sought to introduce statistical method into historical research, holding in his *History of Civilization in England* (1857 and 1861) that human actions are ruled by laws as fixed and regular as those which govern the physical world; but that these laws can be discovered only by a survey of the facts so comprehensive that disturbing factors will cancel one another. Meanwhile, the chief contributions to statistical technique continued to come from mathematicians proper. Gauss published the method of least squares in 1823. In 1837, Poisson made the theory of probability more applicable to social problems by showing how the curve of distribution is modified

[7] Consider Ricardo's contention that it is impossible to determine "the value of a currency" by its "relation, not to one, but to the mass of commodities."
"To suppose that such a test would be of use in practice," Ricardo argued, "arises from a misconception of the difference between price and value.
"The price of a commodity is its exchangeable value in money only.
"The value of a commodity is estimated by the quantity of other things generally for which it will exchange.
"The price of a commodity may rise while its value falls, and *vice versa*. A hat may rise from twenty to thirty shillings in price, but thirty shillings may not procure as much tea, sugar, coffee, and all other things, as twenty shillings did before, consequently a hat cannot procure so much. The hat, then, has fallen in value, though it has increased in price.
"Nothing is so easy to ascertain as a variation of price (*sic*), nothing so difficult as a variation of value; indeed, without an invariable measure of value, and none such exists, it is impossible to ascertain it with any certainty or precision." ("Proposals for an Economical and Secure Currency," 2d ed., 1816. Ricardo's *Works,* edited by J. R. McCulloch, p. 401.)
Nowadays, economists apply to money Ricardo's definition, "The value of a commodity is estimated by the quantity of other things generally for which it will exchange," and proceed to the construction of price indexes. Then they can compare the price fluctuations of single commodities with this general index, and approximate Ricardo's conception of measuring variations in value, without having an "invariable measure of value."

by dropping the assumption of equal *a priori* probabilities at every trial, and directed attention to "the law of great numbers."

The only economist concerned with the theoretical uses of statistics in this period was Augustin Cournot. In considering the old problem of variations in value, he made a casual suggestion that "Here, as in astronomy, it is necessary to recognize *secular* variations, which are independent of *periodic* variations." More important was Cournot's discussion of demand curves. While his own dealings with this subject were confined to mathematical analysis "by means of an indeterminate symbol," he emphasized the need of statistical inquiry into the relations between demand (D) and price (p). In this connection, he suggested the technique by which statistical laws defining the relationships between economic variables may be discovered.

> Since so many moral causes capable of neither enumeration nor measurement affect the law of demand (he wrote), it is plain that we should no more expect the law to be expressible by an algebraic formula than the law of mortality, and all the laws whose determination enters into the field of statistics, or what is called social arithmetic. Observation must therefore be depended on for furnishing the means of drawing up between proper limits a table of the corresponding values of D and p; after which, by the well-known methods of interpolation or by graphic processes, an empiric formula or a curve can be made to represent the function in question; and the solution of problems can be pushed as far as numerical applications.[1]

Yet Cournot made no use of statistical data in his *Theory of Wealth,* and in his *Exposition de la Théorie des Chances et des Probabilités* (published in 1843), he did not apply the theory to a much wider range of social problems than Laplace had considered in 1814. It was left for W. Stanley Jevons to give the first powerful impetus to statistical work in economic theory.[2]

[1] *Researches into the Mathematical Principles of the Theory of Wealth.* Translated by Nathaniel T. Bacon. New York, 1897, pp. 25, 47-49, and 53, 54. Originally published in 1838.

[2] In 1833 the British Association for the Advancement of Science had set up a Statistical Section, and a Statistical Society had been formed in Manchester. But both organizations sought to avoid discussions of the theoretical implications of their data. "Several men of eminence in statistics chafed at being thus relegated to the position of 'hewers and drawers for political economy and philosophy,' so they joined in promoting the Statistical Society of London, now the Royal Statistical Society, with the view of providing therein a wider scope for their inquiries. Their hopes were frustrated, for a time at least, by the same spirit of caution which dictated the limitations imposed upon

While still a student in the University of London, Jevons began studying "periodic commercial fluctuations"—or, as we now say, "seasonal variations." He passed on quickly to an investigation of the changes in the "value of gold" which had followed the Californian and Australian discoveries.

> It has been abundantly shown by Quetelet and others (he remarked), that many subjects of this nature are so hopelessly intricate, that we can only attack them by the use of averages, and by trusting to probabilities.

To ascertain what changes had occurred in the "value of gold," Jevons made index numbers of the wholesale prices of 39 commodities by years from 1845 to 1862. He discussed the best type of average to use; tested his results by taking a larger sample of 118 commodities, and invoked the theory of probabilities to find the cause of the advance in prices, computing that

> the odds are 10,000 to 1 against a series of disconnected and casual circumstances having caused the rise of prices—one in the case of one commodity, another in the case of another— instead of some general cause acting over them all.[3]

And we may regard Jevons' book on *The Coal Question* (1865) as an important contribution to the study of secular trends.

The theory and the use of index numbers made slow progress for a generation after Jevons' pioneer work in 1863. But in 1887 Professor F. Y. Edgeworth began his long series of distinguished contributions to the problem, and about the same time Adolf Soetbeer, Augustus Sauerbeck, and Roland P. Falkner began providing index

the earlier institutions." For their *Journal* expressed its policy by the self-denying motto, *Aliis exterendum,* which was not dropped until about 1857, although the society had re-defined its aims in a wider style by 1840.

See Sir Athelstane Baines, "The History and Development of Statistics in Great Britain and Ireland," in *The History of Statistics,* edited by John Koren (Seventy-fifth anniversary volume of the American Statistical Association), New York, 1918, pp. 385, 386.

[3] *On the Study of Periodic Commercial Fluctuations,* 1862; *A Serious Fall in the Value of Gold Ascertained,* 1863; *The Depreciation of Gold,* 1869. Reprinted in *Investigations in Currency and Finance,* by W. Stanley Jevons, London, 1884. The quotations are from the paper of 1869, pp. 155-157 of the *Investigations.*

Later writers have questioned the applicability of the theory of probability to index numbers. For citations and discussion of the problem, see Professor F. Y. Edgeworth, "The Element of Probability in Index Numbers," *Journal of the Royal Statistical Society,* July, 1925, Vol. 88, pp. 557-575.

numbers for England, Germany and the United States.[4] Thereafter
this bit of statistical technique rapidly became current among economists, though skepticism concerning the trustworthiness of the results
lingered long in certain quarters.

As slow in winning general recognition was the contribution of
another economist—Wilhelm Lexis. Approaching the theory of probability from the statistical side, Lexis showed in a series of investigations that the birth rates of different populations are not distributed
around their mean values in accordance with the so-called "normal
curve," and developed a mathematical-statistical explanation of the
divergencies. Thus the way was opened for the empirical study of
actual distributions—a type of work which spread gradually from
vital statistics into other fields.[5]

The theoretical justification for applying the theory of probability
to economic data at large was worked out mainly by Professor Edgeworth. In 1885 he directed attention to the fact that

> the distribution of averages will be approximately normal even
> though the distribution of the items composing the averages
> deviate considerably from normal.

Later he showed that the observations subjected to the probability
analysis

> need not be perfectly independent of each other, "it suffices
> that there should be a considerable amount of independence";
> that they need not be of the same order of magnitude, "it
> suffices that no two or three preponderate"; that the condition
> for the absence of systematic errors is not necessary, "it suf-
> fices that the center of gravity for the series of observations

---

[4] Edgeworth's early contributions were published in the *Reports of the British Asso-
ciation for the Advancement of Science,* 1887, 1888, 1889 and 1890 (reprinted in *Papers
Relating to Political Economy,* by F. Y. Edgeworth, London, 1925, vol. i, pp. 195-343).
Soetbeer's index numbers appeared first in 1885, Sauerbeck's first in 1886, and Falkner's in
1893. For more explicit references, see "Index Numbers of Wholesale Prices in the
United States and Foreign Countries," *Bulletin of the United States Bureau of Labor
Statistics,* No. 284, October, 1921.

[5] See Wilhelm Lexis, *Die französischen Ausfuhrprämien in Zusammenhange mit der
Tarifgeschichte und der Handelsentwicklung Frankreichs seit der Restauration,* Bonn,
1870; *Zur Theorie der Massenerscheinungen in der menschlichen Gesellschaft,* Freiburg,
1877; *Abhandlungen zur Theorie der Bevölkerungs- und Moralstatistik,* Jena, 1903
Eugen Altschul gives an interesting account of Lexis later views concerning the application of statistical method to social problems in a paper on "Konjunkturtheorie und
Konjunkturstatistik," *Archiv für Sozialwissenschaft und Sozialpolitik,* January, 1926,
vol. lv, pp. 77-82.

indefinitely prolonged should coincide with the true point which forms the quaesitum." [6]

Another technical contribution for which the economists presently found use was the theory of correlation. Invented by Sir Francis Galton as a method of studying the inheritance of characteristics, it was developed in the early 1890's by Professors Karl Pearson, F. Y. Edgeworth and G. Udny Yule, and later applied to measuring the relationship between paired items in time series.[7]

3. The Accumulation of Statistical Data.

The cumulative growth of statistical technique adapted to the treatment of economic problems in the second half of the 19th century was paralleled by a cumulative growth of statistical data. The impetus toward the collection of statistics came from practical activities rather than from scientific inquiries. Most of the ever-shifting issues in the political life of modern nations have had their economic aspects. Those who urged or those who opposed "reforms," and often both parties, sought to strengthen their cases by instituting special inquiries to show the extent of the evils to be remedied, or of the evils which the proposed remedies would produce. And as changes were made in public policy, administrative agencies were set up which had to keep continuous records not unlike those for which Laplace had called in 1814.

Thus the history of statistics in every country bears the impress of its social struggles. The United States owes its relatively abundant statistics of money and banking to the currency problems which the country has faced in different forms from the days of Alexander Hamilton to the days of the Federal Reserve Board. The relative backwardness of vital statistics in the United States arises from the fact that the population problem has been less pressing in this country than elsewhere. Our statistics of immigration and emigration remained meager until the country became exercised about the millions of newcomers from Southern Europe. So, too, our statistics of income

[6] Warren M. Persons, "Statistics and Economic Theory," *Review of Economic Statistics,* July, 1925, vol. vii, pp. 185-186.
This paper contains the best account known to me of the development of statistical methods now utilized by economists. I have drawn upon it freely.
[7] See Galton's *Natural Inheritance,* 1889, and, for later contributions, Karl Pearson, "Notes on the History of Correlation," *Biometrica,* October, 1920.

were vastly improved by the adoption of the federal income tax. Doubtless one might cite similar examples for any other country.

While Governments were being forced by practical exigencies to increase the scope of their statistical work decade after decade, private business was expanding its quota of statistics. On this side, also, practical needs dominated. The closer integration of business activities, the increasing dependence of every section and industry upon other sections and industries, created a widespread interest in business news. Reports of transactions and prices upon the stock and produce exchanges, reports of money-market conditions, bank clearings, security issues, bankruptcies and the like were wanted by a wide public, and numerous agencies collaborated to meet the demand. Trade journals found that statistical data of technical interest to their clientele attracted subscribers. Later, many trade associations began offering statistical service to their members.

In the various branches of economic activity, the progress toward making an adequate statistical record was influenced by the relative ease of collecting data. Highly organized central markets, like the produce and stock exchanges, made the statistician's task relatively simple. In the commodity field, price quotations were easier to get than production statistics, wholesale prices were easier to get than retail prices, and market prices were easier to get than contract prices. On the side of production, it was easier to compile reports for the highly standardized raw materials like coal, petroleum, and agricultural produce, or for partially fabricated materials like pig iron, spelter and cotton sheetings, than for the vast variety of finished goods like machinery, clothing and household supplies. In comparison with production, transportation presents a comparatively simple problem. On the contrary, statistics of stocks on hand, of orders booked, of mercantile operations, of costs and of profits have been very difficult to obtain.

Though the obstacles in the way of collecting adequate data remain formidable, economic evolution is facilitating the task. The organization of workers in trade unions gave the first opening for collecting significant and regular statistics of unemployment, while the concentration of an increasing proportion of employees in large establishments facilitated the collection of the more significant data concerning numbers on payrolls. The rise of department and chain stores made it feasible to gather the first reliable data concerning retail sales. Obviously, the trend toward standardization of technical processes and of products favors the statistician. So does the trend toward the standardization of accounting methods, a trend which is most marked in such fields as banking, railway transportation, and public utilities, where financial reports must be submitted on official forms to government bureaus. The trend toward publicity of corporate accounts, observable in business circles, promises to give us in the future more accurate knowledge of costs and profits. In the not distant future we may know more about the arcana of business than Sismondi's generation knew about market prices. A policy which combines standardization with publicity is favored by modern methods of producing by automatic machinery, selling by national advertising, and financing by appeal to a large circle of investors. Standardization and publicity give the statistician what he wants.[1]

4. The Present Situation.

Thus it happened that by the time writers upon business cycles began to make systematic use of statistics—say in the decade beginning in 1900—they could utilize many methods already developed by mathematicians, anthropometrists, biologists and economists, and many data already collected by public and private agencies. As their work progressed, these men encountered problems which required special adaptations of the methods used in other fields and problems which required data not yet collected. Yet so well had the way been paved for them that they could make rapid progress toward establishing the study of business cycles upon a quantitative basis.

To analyze time series was the central problem. First, the recurrent cyclical fluctuations had to be isolated so far as possible from the other fluctuations to which time series are subject. Second, the relationships among the cyclical fluctuations of many different series had to be ascertained.

Jevons had made a beginning upon the first task by his studies of what are now called seasonal variations, a beginning which George Clare had continued in his brief treatise upon the London money

[1] The details concerning the increase of statistical data since the opening of the 19th century are far too intricate to sketch. Perhaps the best general view of developments on this side is given by the volume published by the American Statistical Association in commemoration of its 75th Anniversary: *The History of Statistics, Their Development and Progress in Many Countries,* Collected and edited by John Koren, New York, 1918.

A more detailed view of the British, French, German and American data relevant to business cycles is afforded by the collection of statistics which the National Bureau of Economic Research has made in preparation for the present book and which the Bureau hopes to publish.

market.[1] Another step was taken by J. H. Poynting and R. H. Hooker, who attacked the problem of determining secular trends, using for that purpose moving averages.[2] The second task, finding the relationships among quantities varying in time, was undertaken by Professor G. Udny Yule in 1899 and Mr. Hooker in 1901, both of whom applied Pearson's methods of correlation to economic data.[3]

In 1902, Dr. John Pease Norton combined and improved upon these various methods in his *Statistical Studies in the New York Money Market*.[4] Norton measured secular trends by fitting exponential curves to his data; he considered the dispersion as well as the averages of seasonal variations, taken as percentages of his trends; he used lines of regression as well as coefficients of correlation in examining the relations among his variables. Another notable step was taken by Professor Henry L. Moore, who in 1914 applied harmonic analysis to time series.[5] The following year, Professor Warren M. Persons made the first of his business barometers,[6] and in 1917 the Harvard Committee on Economic Research enabled him to begin a more elaborate analysis of economic statistics than had been possible for any of his predecessors. By establishing the *Review of Economic Statistics* in January, 1919, this committee provided an organ devoted primarily to the quantitative study of business cycles. The models which Persons and his colleagues have set in this journal have been studied and imitated widely, not only in the United States, but also in Europe.

This list of men who shared in adapting statistical methods to the analysis of economic time series is far from complete; it mentions only a few of the most noteworthy contributors. Still less justice can be done to recent work. Of late the number of economic statisti-

[1] *A Money-Market Primer and Key to the Exchanges,* London, 1891; 2d ed., 1903.

[2] See J. H. Poynting, "A Comparison of the Fluctuations in the Price of Wheat and in the Cotton and Silk Imports into Great Britain," *Journal of the Royal Statistical Society,* 1884, vol. xlvii, pp. 34-64; R. H. Hooker, "On the Correlation of the Marriage-rate with Trade," the same, 1901, vol. lxiv, pp. 485-492. A sketch of the progressive improvements in ascertaining secular trends will be given in Dr. Simon S. Kuznets' forthcoming monograph on that subject.

[3] Hooker as cited in preceding note; Yule, "An Investigation into the Causes of Changes in Pauperism in England," *Journal of the Royal Statistical Society,* 1899, vol. lxii, p. 249 f.

[4] Published for the Department of Social Sciences, Yale University; New York, 1902.

[5] *Economic Cycles: Their Law and Cause,* New York, 1914.

[6] "Construction of a Business Barometer Based upon Annual Data" (presented in part to a meeting of the American Statistical Association, August 11, 1915), *American Economic Review,* December, 1916, vol. vi, pp. 739-769. See a supplemental paper "On the Variate Difference Correlation Method and Curve-fitting." *Publications of the American Statistical Association,* June, 1917, vol. xv, pp. 602-642.

cians has grown rapidly. Efforts to improve the technique in detail, and efforts to win fresh knowledge by more intensive and more extensive analysis are being made constantly. In later sections I must attempt a critical summary of the constructive achievements of the whole campaign. Here it suffices to remark that recent contributions are to be found in the *Journal of the American Statistical Association,* the *Review of Economic Statistics,* the *Harvard Business Review,* the *Journal of the Royal Statistical Society,* and less frequently in the journals devoted to economics at large.

On the side of data, the Department of Commerce has rendered valuable service by extending the collection of statistics into fresh fields, and by establishing the *Survey of Current Business* in 1921. In this source are assembled most of the current series, old and new, collected by public or private agencies, which are useful to students of business cycles. Of scarcely less interest are the *Federal Reserve Bulletin* and the bulletins issued by the several Reserve Banks. Many of the most significant series, or indexes made from them, are regularly published in "adjusted" form by the *Review of Economic Statistics.*

As the preceding references indicate, the statistical study of business cycles has had its headquarters in the United States. This country continued to suffer from severe crises for a generation after they had been transformed into mild recessions in Europe and Canada. Thus the problem was especially intriguing to Americans. Further, Americans had rather fuller statistics to work with than were available in any other country, partly because of the prominence of economic issues in American politics, partly because of the highly standardized character of American products. The development was much stimulated and colored by a widespread demand for business forecasts. To improve the statistical technique of forecasting was Professor Persons' chief aim, and the hope of finding trustworthy indexes to the future has animated and secured financial support for many ingenious investigations.

Since the war, interest both scientific and practical in this type of work has been spreading to other countries. Since 1921, the *Economic Bulletin of the Conjuncture Institute,* edited by Professor N. D. Kondratieff, has been compiling, analyzing and interpreting Russian data. In Great Britain, the London and Cambridge Economic Service, cooperating with the Harvard University Committee on Economic Research, began the publication of a *Monthly Bulletin* in 1923. The Institute of Statistics of the University of Paris has a similar plan of coöperation with the Harvard group, and publishes *Indices du Mouvement Général des Affaires en France et en Divers Pays*. Germany has an Institut für Konjunkturforschung under the direction of Dr. Ernst Wagemann, which began publishing *Vierteljahrshefte zur Konjunkturforschung* in January, 1926. Two Institutes of Statistics connected with the Universities of Padua and of Rome have joined forces to publish *Indici del Movimento Economico Italiano* under the direction of a Committee presided over by Professor Corrado Gini. The League of Nations has appointed a "Committee of Experts on Economic Barometers," Professor A. W. Flux, chairman, which held its first meeting at Geneva in December, 1926. Finally, in January, 1927, an Oesterreichisches Institut für Konjunkturforschung was organized in Vienna, with a scientific staff directed by Dr. F. A. von Hayek.

The present chapter aims neither to give a full exposition of the statistical methods which have been applied to the study of business cycles—that would fill a volume and exceed my competence,— nor to show what the statisticians have contributed toward our knowledge of cyclical fluctuations—that will be attempted in a second book. It aims rather to show what problems the statistical workers have attacked, how far they have pushed their researches, and what light they shed upon the character of business cycles.

III. The Analysis of Time Series.

1. THE QUALITY AND QUANTITY OF ECONOMIC STATISTICS.

A biologist or anthropologist working upon statistical problems is often able to collect his own data by measuring material in his laboratory. Such measurements can be made to fit the requirements of the problem, and their accuracy can be controlled within assignable limits. A meteorologist is dependent upon data collected mainly by other observers; but these observers are men with at least a modicum of training, using scientific apparatus, and working under scientific direction. The quantitative worker upon economic problems is less fortunate in respect to his raw materials. Seldom can he make in his statistical laboratory a significant collection of measurements. He deals not with "material," but with the behavior of men, and that behavior must be observed and recorded "in the field." Because his phenomena are highly variable, he usually needs a large array of cases, more than he can collect by himself or through the trained assistants at his disposal. Forced to rely upon observations made by others, he must often adapt his problem to the data, when he wishes to adapt his data to the problem.

Economic statistics are usually a by-product of governmental or business administration, collected in a form, at intervals, and by methods determined by some statute, official ruling, or business practice. Even when a public bureau plans a statistical inquiry with an eye to the scientific use of the results—and that happens with increasing frequency—it is usually necessary to fit the results for a variety of uses, and hence not feasible to adapt them precisely to any specific use. Finally, the accuracy attainable in most economic measurements leaves much to be desired. Often the data consist of estimates or rough approximations, and when precision is attainable with reference to the items counted there may be grave uncertainty regarding the representative character of the sample.

It is sometimes suggested that what economic statistics lack in quality they make up in quantity. There are grounds for arguing that a large number of observations compensates for lack of precision in each single observation, and the volume of economic statistics is certainly imposing—it is even intimidating at first sight. But on closer inspection the mass proves to consist less of a multiplication of independent observations upon particular phenomena, than of observations upon a vast variety of phenomena, and of the infinite detail in which certain processes must be observed.

To take the last point first: A student of business cycles is concerned largely with aggregates, for example, bank clearings in the United States, the wheat crops of the world, pig-iron output. On each of these topics and a hundred like them he can find a huge quantity of figures. But the mass is not for all his purposes a large number of observations upon one variable; it consists of many separate items which must be added to get one series of totals. The investigator is glad to have the figures in detail, for he may find occasion to examine the fluctuations (say) of wheat yields in different countries. But he has only one or two estimates for each country each year. Another type of problem is exemplified by efforts to measure changes in the "level" of wholesale or retail prices. Again a huge quantity of raw data is available—the prices of particular commodities, in particular markets, at particular dates. In Professor Edgeworth's phrase, the task is

> to extricate from fallible observations a mean apt to represent the "general trend of prices." [1]

But the investigator has to take the changes between every pair of dates in every country or smaller area as a separate problem, and for no such problem is his number of "fallible observations" very large. The War Industries Board's index number of wholesale prices in 1913-18 included nearly 1500 commodities; but that collection was a *tour de force,* and the largest of the currently published series cover only some 400 commodities, while in many cases the commodities quoted number less than 50.[2]

Hardly less responsible for the bulkiness of economic statistics is the variety of activities covered. Every new attempt to systematize business operations—and such attempts seem endless—involves the making of new records, more and more of which emerge from bookkeeping into statistics. Only a tiny fraction of the records kept appears in published tables; yet in a country like the United States that fraction spreads over a bewildering diversity of processes. Nor can students of business cycles be sure that they are safe in ignoring any section of the record. Certainly they are concerned with the production, exchange, transportation, and distribution of commodities; with wages, rents, interest rates, profits, bond yields, and dividends; with family incomes and expenditures; with prices of all sorts, financial operations, savings, orders, bankruptcies, the launching of new enterprises, patents, construction work, banking in its various aspects, unemployment, migration, imports, exports, and tax receipts. In many cases they need detailed data for particular industries or localities. And they cannot properly neglect pertinent figures from any country which collects them. Even the fact that certain series show slight traces of cyclical fluctuations hardly lessens their task; for that fact may be highly significant in a general view of the problem. They

---

[1] F. Y. Edgeworth, *Papers Relating to Political Economy,* London, 1925, vol. i, p. 405.

[2] See *History of Prices during the War, Summary,* by Wesley C. Mitchell, (War Industries Board Price Bulletin, No. 1) Washington, 1919, p. 5. For the number of commodities contained in the leading wholesale price indexes of various countries at present, see *Institut International de Statistique, Bulletin Mensuel.* The issue for October, 1925, for example, pp. 76, 77, credits the United States Bureau of Labor Statistics with quoting 404 commodities, and the Canadian Department of Labour with quoting 271. Most of the series for the 31 countries represented are made from quotations for less than 100 commodities.

It may be noted that the question, "What shall be counted a distinct commodity in a price index?" is difficult to answer.

cannot even confine their researches within the field of economic statistics. Hypotheses concerning the causes of business cycles carry them back into meteorological data, morbidity rates, and what not, while interest in the consequences of business cycles carries them forward into the fields of vital statistics, criminal statistics, statistics of dependency, philanthropy, poor relief. And the more they learn about the problem, the wider grows the range of data which they deem it pertinent to study.

As an investigator gets deeper into a quantitative analysis of business cycles, his first impression that the statistical data to be dealt with are embarrassingly abundant turns into a conviction that they are painfully inadequate. Each business cycle becomes to him one case, one chance for observation. His method is to make measured observations upon as many cases as he can, and to draw such generalizations from the array of observations as his skill permits. For a very few of the recent cycles in the United States he finds data which allow him to observe with varying degrees of precision a good many of the processes involved. But seldom do the observations of a given process show marked uniformity from case to case. Hence the investigator becomes eager to increase the number of his cases. But as he passes from recent cycles in the United States to earlier cycles, or as he passes from American to European cycles, he finds the supply of statistics rapidly diminishing, and his doubts increasing about the trustworthiness of what statistics there are. In the end he must content himself with such data as practical needs or accident have preserved, make the best use of what he finds, and hope that his efforts may at least help toward getting for his successors better figures than are available to him.

If such an investigator does not give up the effort to frame a general theory of business cycles, he at least gives up the effort to base his theory wholly upon measurements. What statistical results he does attain, he presents as tentative. These results he prefaces, strings together, interprets, and supplements with analysis based upon non-quantitative observations.

2. TIME SERIES IN THEIR RAW STATE.

Since business cycles follow one another in time, the statistical data of chief concern to us are time series—data which show the value of some variable at successive points, or during successive periods, of time. Occasionally surveys showing the magnitude of some factor, or the distribution of certain phenomena at a given moment are drawn upon, but the analysis of time series remains the outstanding task.

These time series have many forms:—prices, aggregate money values, physical quantities (in units of number, weight, length, area, volume, energy), percentages of a total which changes with time, percentages of a total at some past date, ratios to some other quantity, and so on. The intervals vary from the day, week or month to the year or the decade. Many such series cover but a year or two, some have been kept in fairly uniform fashion for a generation, a very few quasi-continuous series run back or can be pieced back, for a century, two centuries, or even more.[1] Some series are available in comparable form for several different countries—for example, wheat production, coal and iron output, discount rates;—some are available only for one country—for example, the valuable German series showing receipts from the tax on bills of exchange, the American data concerning retail sales, the British statistics of outdoor relief. It is indeed a most miscellaneous collection which the investigator of business cycles must use as his raw materials.

A few of the series which such an investigator uses report the variations in factors which are indivisible units in the business situation. For example, the official minimum discount rate of the Bank of England is a single figure, known with precision for every week through long years. Many different matters have been weighed by the bank's directors in deciding upon the rate announced each Thursday; but once announced there is no analyzing the rate into constituent parts. Most time series, however, are aggregates, or averages, which the investigator can, and frequently should, analyze. For example, if bank clearings in the United States fall five per cent between July and August, it may be that in a majority of the clearing houses transactions increased; and in the minority of towns where transactions shrank, the declines may have varied from a fraction of one per cent to half the July volume. Similarly, an index number of

[1] For example, Sir William H. Beveridge has compiled an index number of "Wheat Prices in Western and Central Europe" by years for the whole period, 1500-1869. See his paper on "Weather and Harvest Cycles," *Economic Journal*, December, 1921, vol. xxxi, pp. 449-451. I understand that he has now secured data which will enable him to carry this table much further back than 1500.

wholesale prices shows for each date merely the net resultant of most diverse changes in the prices of individual commodities—changes which nearly always run the gamut from a considerable decline to a considerable rise.[2]   In thinking graphically of price changes we should

[2] By way of illustration consider the following charts of price changes. The first chart (adapted from the *Bulletin of the U. S. Bureau of Labor Statistics*, No. 284) shows the mixture of diversity and concentration in the fluctuations of the wholesale prices of the commodities included in the B.L.S. index number, by years, from 1891 to 1919.   Each year the fluctuations are ranked in order of their magnitude, and then divided into ten groups containing equal numbers of commodities. The dividing points, called decils, and the extreme fluctuations of each year are represented on the chart by dots.   By an arbitrary convention the 11 dots for each year are connected by slanting lines with the middle point of the distribution of the preceding year. The vertical scale is logarithmic. While the chart gives a lively impression of the variety of price changes

occurring every year, it over-simplifies the situation by picturing the annual changes as all starting from the same point. A chart which did not over-simplify some aspect of the changes would be a hopeless tangle of lines.

The second chart (adapted from *History of Prices during the War, Summary*, War think, not of the movements of a single curve, such as represents adequately the Bank of England rate, but of a broad, irregular band, within which many lines are moving, some up, some down, some horizontally—lines which are rather far apart near the edges of the band but thickly congregated near the middle, and which keep crossing each other as they shift their relative positions.

It is true that an investigator often writes of series like bank clearings or price indexes as if they represented magnitudes not less definite than the Bank of England rate. Doubtless there are problems which justify the practice—problems in which the one matter of significance is the net resultant of a complicated mass of movements. Yet such problems are rare, and it is always wise to ask explicitly whether the hypothesis in use does not require that notice be taken of the diversity

Industries Board Price Bulletin, No. 1) is another device for illustrating the diversity and concentration of price changes. It shows the distribution of the relative prices of 1437 commodities in 1918, computed on the base average prices, July, 1913, to June, 1914 equal 100. Here the horizontal scale is logarithmic. The chart shows, for example, that one commodity fell 64 per cent in price from the pre-war level to 1918, another commodity rose 2,991 per cent, but that nearly 600 commodities (over two-fifths) were concentrated in the range of 50 to 109 per cent advance.

1918 DISTRIBUTION OF 1437 COMMODITIES
ACCORDING TO THE MAGNITUDE OF THEIR RELATIVE PRICES

of movements which are hidden in the simple-seeming aggregates or averages. Certainly we do not get the full benefit of the statistical approach to the study of business cycles, unless we keep in mind the range and variety of the changes which most of our time series represent.

The first step toward using any series is usually to represent the figures by a line drawn on a chart. The invention of this device in 1786 is claimed by William Playfair, who set forth its advantages as follows:

As the eye is the best judge of proportion, being able to estimate it with more quickness and accuracy than any other of our organs, it follows, that wherever *relative quantities* are in question, a gradual increase or decrease of any . . . value is to be stated, this mode of representing it is peculiarly applicable; it gives a simple, accurate, and permanent idea, by giving form and shape to a number of separate ideas, which are otherwise abstract and unconnected.[3]

A variant of Playfair's method of charting time series was introduced by Jevons in 1863-65—the use of a logarithmic vertical scale for showing degree of variation, combined with an arithmetical horizontal scale for showing intervals of time.[4] By this device equal percentage changes occuring at equal intervals in a time series are represented by lines of the same slope. Further, two or more different series, expressed in non-comparable units, when plotted upon a ratio chart, will have equal percentage changes in the several series represented by lines of the same slope. Since students of business cycles are usually interested in the relative changes which economic processes undergo recurrently, rather than in the absolute quantities involved in the changes, the "ratio chart" is particularly useful to them.

[3] *The Commercial and Political Atlas,* 3d ed., London, 1801, p. x.
Playfair's claim to be "actually the first who applied the principles of geometry to matters of Finance" is made on pp. viii and ix.
[4] *A Serious Fall in the Value of Gold Ascertained* (1863), and *The Variation of Prices, and the Value of Currency since 1782* (1865). Reprinted in *Investigations in Currency and Finance,* by W. Stanley Jevons, London, 1884. See especially pp. 53, 128, 150 and the charts which follow pp. 56 and 150.
This method of making charts did not come into common use among economists until its merits had been explained by Professors Irving Fisher, "The 'Ratio' Chart for Plotting Statistics," *Publications of the American Statistical Association,* June, 1917, vol. xv, pp. 577-601, and James A. Field, "Some Advantages of the Logarithmic Scale," *Journal of Political Economy,* October, 1917, vol. xxv, pp. 805-841.

To illustrate the materials and problems before us, samples of the time series most useful in studying business cycles are given in Chart 1.[5] These series run in units of long tons of pig iron, pounds of copper, changing percentages of unemployment among members of British trade unions, bushels of wheat, miles of railway track, percentages of the average prices of commodities in 1867-77, billions of dollars, and percentages which the interest received forms of the changing purchase price of bonds. The vertical logarithmic scale of the chart makes comparable the percentage fluctuations in all these different quantities. The only bar to close comparison is that some of the series give data only by years, while others give data by quarters or months.

Looked at broadly, the curves show striking differences. American pig-iron output, copper output and wheat crops present one type of changes. The characteristic of this type is its upward trend more rapid in the two metal curves than in the other, and frequently broken in all three curves by brief reactions. Bank clearings give a similar picture from 1875 to 1914; but the great inflation of the war period introduced a sudden change of trend less marked in the series representing physical production unmixed with prices. American railway building presents a second type of changes. After rising to a peak in the 1880's, it declined unsteadily to a level comparable with that of the 1850's. A third type, characterized by several changes in the direction of movement, is presented by British prices at wholesale. They rise from the 1850's to 1873, fall from 1873 to 1896, rise from 1896 to 1913 at a rate then thought rapid, accelerate their rise in 1914 to 1920, and later fall precipitously. The bond-yield curve also shows several changes in trend; but changes less marked than those of the price curve. Finally, the British unemployment percentages fluctuate about the same general level through the whole 70 years for which they have been compiled.

Except in the unemployment series and perhaps that showing railway construction, these long-period shiftings of level, or "secular trends" as they are technically called, are the most conspicuous features of the chart. But the conspicuous feature of the unemployment

[5] The numerical data used in drawing the charts in this volume are taken, with a few exceptions noted in the proper connection, from the collection of statistical materials which the National Bureau of Economic Research is making and hopes to publish in the near future. Since that collection will have a full index, and will state the original sources from which all the series are obtained as well as the methods of compilation. it seems needless to publish the tables here.

CHART 1.

SAMPLE TIME SERIES PLOTTED ON A LOGARITHMIC VERTICAL SCALE.

Only the Relative Slope, Not the Vertical Position, of these Curves Is Significant.

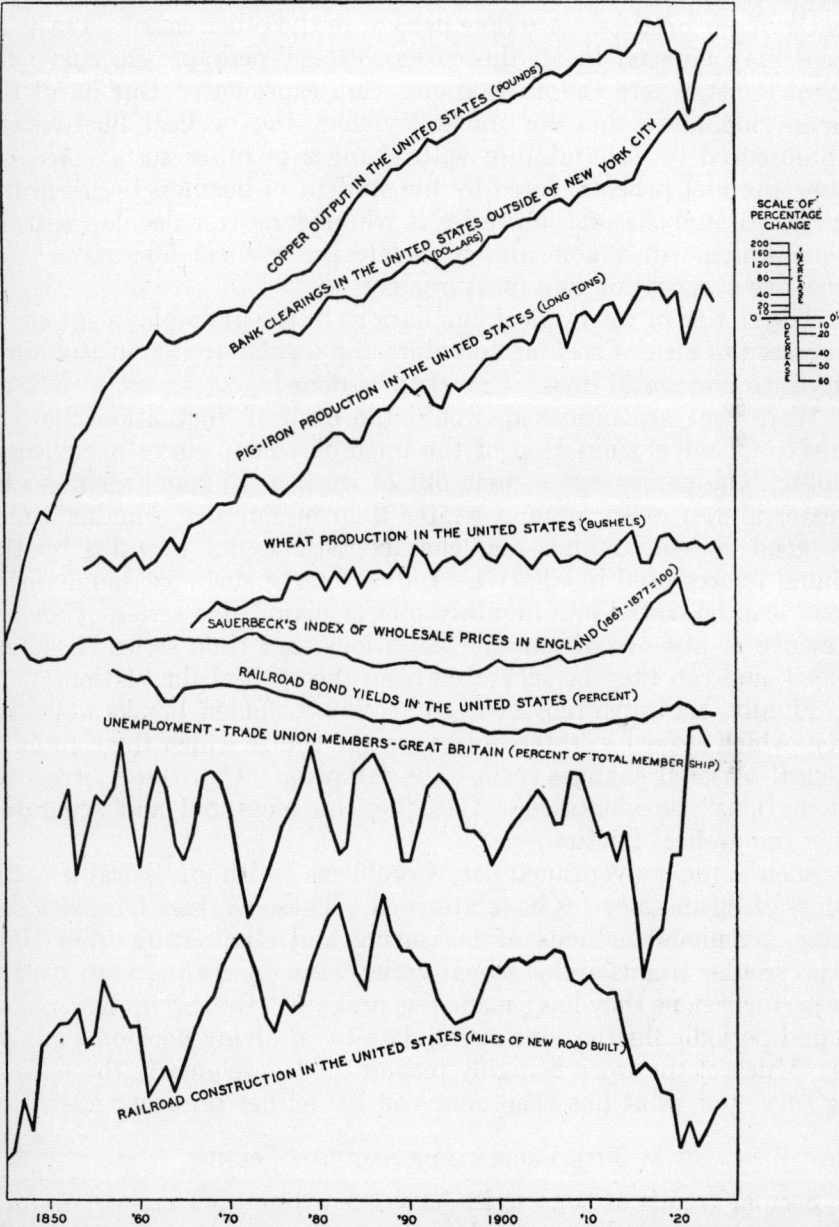

curve is its wavelike movement about a nearly constant level. Of course, these wave-like movements, or "cyclical fluctuations," are the center of our interest. Are they present in the other cases? Traces of them may be seen in all the curves, except perhaps the curve for wheat crops, where the fluctuations seem capricious. But in all the curves, including that for unemployment, the cyclical fluctuations are obscured by intermixture with changes of other sorts. Accordingly, the first problem faced by the student of business cycles in the statistical analysis of time series is whether he can develop a technique which will enable him to isolate the cyclical fluctuations for intensive observation and measurement.

The clarity of the cyclical fluctuations in the unemployment curve suggests the idea of seeking to reduce the secular trends in the other curves to horizontal lines. Can that be done?

Were that accomplished, would the cyclical fluctuations be isolated? Closer examination of the unemployment curve itself raises doubt. The percentage of men out of work in England seems to be greater almost every year in winter than in summer, whether times are good or bad, though that characteristic is not revealed by the annual figures used in Chart 1. Indications of such "seasonal variations" can be traced in a monthly plot of many time series. Can the presence or absence of seasonal variations in a time series be determined, and can they be separated from the cyclical fluctuations?

Finally, the unemployment curve shows sudden breaks now and then, which appear as interruptions in the course which the combined cyclical-seasonal changes seem to be following. Can these "irregular fluctuations" be identified? Can they be measured and separated from the cyclical fluctuations?

Such is the conventional list of problems which statistical investigators of business cycles have attacked. These workers have devised many ingenious methods of measuring and eliminating from time series secular trends and seasonal variations. In dealing with irregular perturbations they have made less progress. One group has sought to find periodic fluctuations in the data by applying harmonic analysis. Much of the work is highly technical. Consequently the following survey of what has been done can be neither brief nor easy.

3. The Problem of Secular Trends

Secular trends of time series have been computed mainly by men who were concerned to get rid of them. Just as economic theorists have paid slight attention to the "other things" in their problems which they suppose to "remain the same," so the economic statisticians have paid slight attention to their trends beyond converting them into horizontal lines. Hence little is yet known about the trends themselves, their characteristics, similarities, and differences. Even their relations to cyclical fluctuations have been little considered. Here lies in obscurity a heap of problems, waiting for properly equipped investigators to exploit.[1]

(1) The Empirical Approach to the Problem.

The procedure adopted in ascertaining secular trends is usually empirical in high degree. Starting with a time series plotted to a convenient scale on a chart, the statistician seeks to find for that one series, within the period covered by his data, the line which best represents the "long-time tendencies" shown by the plotted curve. In cases like that presented by British wholesale prices in Chart 1, he splits the whole period into sections, and seeks to find lines of secular trend for each section separately, or else to find a function which changes direction in the manner of the data.

The technical process usually consists in (1) fitting a "mathematical curve" (for example, a straight line or a third-degree parabola) to the data, or to the logarithms of the data, by the method of least squares or of moments; (2) computing moving or progressive arithmetic means or moving medians, including in the averages whatever number of items seems to give satisfactory results; (3) first computing moving averages and then fitting trend lines to the results; (4) drawing a free-hand curve through the data representing the investigator's impression, formed from careful study, of the long-time tendency; or (5) using ratios between the paired items of series which are believed to have substantially the same secular trends.[1]

[1] So far as I know, the only one working upon secular trends as a problem in its own right is Dr. Simon S. Kuznets, one of the Research Fellows of the Social Science Research Council. Dr. Kuznets has generously allowed me to profit by his results in advance of publication.

[1] Technical directions for computing secular trends by the commoner methods are given in most of the recent textbooks of economic statistics. For example, see Frederick C. Mills, *Statistical Methods*, New York, 1924, chap. vii, W. L. Crum and A. C. Patton, *Economic Statistics*, Chicago, 1925, chap. xx, or Edmund E. Day, *Statistical Analysis*, New York, 1925, chap. xvii.

Among the recent contributions to the subject are Warren M. Persons, "Indices of Business Conditions," *Review of Economic Statistics*, January, 1919, Preliminary vol. i, pp. 8-18; and the following papers in the *Journal of the American Statistical Associa-*

When a secular trend has been fitted by any of these methods or their variants, how can the agreement between the line of trend and the plotted data be determined?

It might be thought that a trend can be tested by breaking a series into two parts, computing trends for the separate sections and seeing whether they agree. But lack of agreement would not prove that the trend for either section of the data was wrong for the period it covered. Secular trends are "subject to change without notice," and it is a common experience that a line which gives an excellent fit to the data for one period ceases to fit well when carried backward in time, or projected for a few years. Thus the failure of a trend fitted now to mark the line followed by developments in the near future need not mean that to-day's work is wrong. Perhaps our successor who computes a new trend for the longer series of data available to him will not be able to improve upon our fit for the period we analyzed.

Then why not break long series into relatively brief segments and compute the secular trends for each separately? That is a device to which the statistical student of business cycles resorts at need; but to go far in that direction is to give up the problem of secular trends rather than to solve it. Unless it is possible to find trends which are satisfactory throughout long periods—long in comparison with business cycles—the distinction between secular and cyclical fluctuations is blurred and the whole analysis loses its point. Just how far the process of subdividing periods for the computation of trends shall be carried is a question to be decided by the character of each series and the uses to which the results are to be put.

There is, indeed, no single criterion for determining "goodness of fit." A mathematical test can be applied only in certain cases. Provided one is choosing between two lines of trend whose equations contain the same number of constants, one can compare the standard deviations of the actual values from the trend lines. A test of wider application is to consider the "reasonableness" of the values shown by projecting trend lines into the future, and to choose lines which

tion: W. L. Crum, "The Determination of Secular Trend," June, 1922, vol. xviii, pp. 210-215. and "The Least Squares Criterion of Trend Lines," June, 1925, vol. xx, pp. 211-222; Holbrook Working, "The Determination of Secular Trend Reconsidered," December, 1922, vol. xviii, pp. 497-502; Willford I. King, "Principles Underlying the Isolation of Cycles and Trends," December, 1924, vol. xix, pp. 468-475; Lincoln W. Hall, "A Moving Secular Trend and Moving Integration," March, 1925, vol. xx, pp. 13-24; Olin Ingraham, "The Refinement of Time Series," June, 1925, vol. xx, pp. 231-233.

indicate results judged to be probable. In forecasting work this test is important for projections within the period to which the forecast applies. For the rest, statisticians fall back upon a visual comparison between the actual values and the trend lines within the time limits of the data. Their confidence in a fitted curve seems to be greater the simpler is its equation and the longer the period within which it gives a reasonable fit. But published expressions of opinion show that a fit which seems good to one man would be called poor by another. Personal equations play a large rôle in such judgments.

Nor is there any general method of deciding in advance what one among the several ways of determining trends will yield the best fit to a given time series, according to these rather indefinite criteria. In the same piece of work, an investigator may fit a straight line to one series and a parabola to a second, compute three-year moving medians of a third and seven-year moving arithmetic means of a fourth, run a free-hand curve through a fifth, use ratios to some other series for a sixth, and devise some novel method for a seventh. He may even use two or three unlike methods of determining the trend in different sections of the same series. Nor will he hesitate to compare the deviations of the actual data from the trends measured in these different ways, if he believes that each of the trend lines expresses the long-time tendency of its data better than would one of the other devices.

Each method has technical advantages, which should be considered with reference to the problem presented by each investigation. Subsequent uses of the data may make it desirable to have a trend which can be expressed by a simple equation, as can curves of known properties. The purpose in view may, or may not, make it important to reject curves which, though they may fit the data admirably for a long period in the past, would indicate results deemed absurd in the future. Ease of construction counts in favor of free-hand curves, and ratios to other series. Of course, the last device is of limited use, for it can be employed only when two series are found which seem to have nearly the same trend. Moving averages are controlled by the data as free-hand curves are not, and this independence of the investigator's personal equation gives comfort to many minds. In business-cycle work, moving averages will yield a satisfactory line of trend, if the trend is linear, if the period of the average corresponds to the duration of the cycles, and if the cycles are regular both in duration and intensity. These conditions are seldom strictly satisfied. If the true trend is a convex curve, a moving average lies above the curve, and so produces errors in the cyclical deviations, the magnitude of which increases with the convexity of the curve and the period of the moving average. If the true trend is concave, errors of opposite sign result. Finally, moving averages seldom yield trends that look satisfactory unless they are centered, and such averages cannot be kept up to date except by the hazardous practice of estimating figures for future years.[2] The advantage claimed for combining moving averages with curve fitting is that it minimizes the influence of the extreme years, which "may represent either the accident of the particular phase of the business cycle with which the series begins or ends, or a change in the real secular trend."[3] Free-hand curves, drawn with care, are preferred by some statisticians of wide experience, not merely because they are easier to make than any other trend lines, but also because they meet the test of visual comparison with the plotted data quite as well as the more pretentious mathematical constructions.

To illustrate the results obtained by applying different methods, Chart 2 has been made. The first section of the chart shows several different trends fitted to a single series—pig-iron production in the United States; the second section shows the application of the same method to several different series, and the third section shows different methods applied to different series.

Having ascertained the secular trend of a time series, the investigator's next step is "to eliminate the trend" from the original data.[4] To that end he finds the numerical value represented by the trend line at each successive interval of time, through computation or by readings from the scale of his chart, and then determines the plus and minus deviations of the actual data from those values in actual amounts or in percentages.[5] Finally, he draws a new chart in which he represents the secular trend by a horizontal line, and the devia-

[2] For example, the trend figure for 1927 in a seven-years' moving average, centered, is computed by adding actual and estimated data for 1924-30 and dividing by seven.
[3] Olin Ingraham, "The Refinement of Time Series," *Journal of the American Statistical Association*, June, 1925, vol. xx, p. 233.
[4] Frequently this elimination is postponed until the seasonal variations have been computed. But of that later.
[5] Professor Allyn A. Young has called attention to the fact that the cyclical deviations from a secular trend are likely to be least trustworthy toward the extremities of the period for which the trend is fitted. Further, it is at the extremities that the differences among the various curves which may be employed as trends commonly become most marked. See "An Analysis of Bank Statistics for the United States," *Review of Economic Statistics*, January, 1925, vol. vii, p. 28.

CHART 2.

Examples of Secular Trends of Time Series Fitted by Various Methods.

Section 1.

Different Trends Fitted to the Same Series. Pig-Iron Production in the United States.

I
A ·——— PIG IRON PRODUCTION
B ——— LEAST SQUARES STRAIGHT LINE FITTED TO LOGARITHMS (1854-1926) Y=6.7849 +.027542X ORIGIN 1890
C ········ TWENTY YEAR BINOMIALLY WEIGHTED MOVING AVERAGES OF LOGARITHMS
D ------ SEVEN YEAR MOVING AVERAGES

II
A ·——— PIG IRON PRODUCTION
B ——— MODIFIED GOMPERTZ EQUATION FITTED TO LOGARITHMS - SUGGESTED AND FITTED BY
F. R. MACAULAY $\log\left(Y + \frac{40,738,000}{199.526}\right) = \log 40,738,000 - (1.025)^{(1.0387)^X} \log 199.526$ ORIGIN 1790
C ········ THIRD DEGREE PARABOLA FITTED TO LOGARITHMS $Y = 6.8531 +.032769X -.0015364X^2 -.0000065417X^3$
ORIGIN 1890
D ------ LOGISTIC CURVE $Y = \dfrac{50,403}{1 + 10^{1.80987 - .17431X}}$ ·ORIGIN 1860

217

CHART 2 (*Continued*).

EXAMPLES OF SECULAR TRENDS OF TIME SERIES FITTED BY VARIOUS METHODS.

Section 2.

The Same Method Applied to Different American Series. Straight-Line Trends from the *Review of Economic Statistics.*

CHART 2 (*Continued*).

EXAMPLES OF SECULAR TRENDS OF TIME SERIES FITTED BY VARIOUS METHODS

Section 3.

Different Methods Applied to Different Series.

I

SAUERBECK'S INDEX OF BRITISH WHOLESALE PRICES (1867-1877=100) WITH TREND
FITTED BY STRAIGHT LINES (LEAST SQUARES) TO LOGARITHMS, BY PERIODS

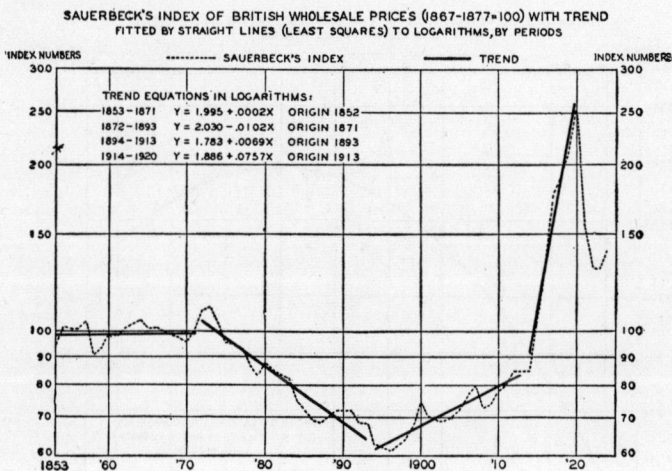

TREND EQUATIONS IN LOGARITHMS:
1853-1871	$Y = 1.995 + .0002X$	ORIGIN 1852
1872-1893	$Y = 2.030 - .0102X$	ORIGIN 1871
1894-1913	$Y = 1.783 + .0069X$	ORIGIN 1893
1914-1920	$Y = 1.886 + .0757X$	ORIGIN 1913

II

RAILROAD BOND YIELDS, UNITED STATES, WITH TREND
FITTED BY A TWENTY YEAR BINOMIALLY WEIGHTED MOVING AVERAGE
CENTERED OPPOSITE THE ELEVENTH YEAR (F.R.MACAULAY)

CHART 2 (*Continued*).

EXAMPLES OF SECULAR TRENDS OF TIME SERIES FITTED BY VARIOUS METHODS

Section 3 (Continued).

Different Methods Applied to Different Series.

III

RAILROAD CONSTRUCTION IN THE UNITED STATES WITH TREND
FITTED BY A SECOND DEGREE PARABOLA

TREND EQUATION IN LOGARITHMS:
1831-1916 Y = 2.046+.0542X -.00045X²
ORIGIN 1830

IV

PRICE INDEX OF BUSINESS CYCLES, U.S.(HARVARD-10 SENSITIVE COMMODITIES) WITH TREND
REPRESENTED BY BRADSTREET'S WHOLESALE PRICE INDEX X 16.54

tions by a curve which fluctuates about the horizontal. Several examples of such construction are given in Chart 3.

When a statistical inquirer into business cycles has reached this point in his work, he commonly goes on at once to ascertain the seasonal variations left in his curve of deviations from the trend, or to use the deviations as they stand. But preoccupation with theory requires us to pause here, and to look at the problem from another angle.

(2) THE INTERPRETATION OF SECULAR TRENDS.

What meanings have the secular trends fitted to time series by empirical methods? As Dr. Kuznets remarks, every mathematical curve used as a trend has definite implications, whether the statistician notices them or not. To take the simplest example: a straight line sloping upward implies future increase without limit. Its constant rate of increase per unit of time implies that the size of the variable at one moment does not affect the size of the increment between that moment and the next. Its percentage rate of increase diminishes along a hyperbolic curve. When we find that a straight line trend fits a given series well, do we accept these mathematical implications as characteristic of the economic process represented by the data? Are successful fits of mathematical curves discoveries in economics?

These questions suggest another way of treating the whole problem of secular trends. We form various hypotheses concerning the long-time tendencies of economic developments in population, production, transportation, exchange, and the like. These hypotheses are derived from and linked to causal explanations; but ordinary reasoning does not enable us to test them adequately. Can we choose curves whose mathematical implications correspond to our causal hypotheses, fit them to time series, perhaps modify the hypotheses in the light of the first results, experiment with other curves, and when finally we have secured good fits argue that we have thrown new light upon the characteristics of economic evolution?

A step toward such a conception is represented by the frequent interpretation of certain trend lines as showing the "growth factor." Statisticians dwell with satisfaction upon their demonstrations that certain industries have expanded decade after decade at a substantially uniform rate, or at a rate which has changed in some uniform way. They take almost as much pleasure in contemplating the somewhat similar rates at which different industries have grown in given

CHART 3.

SAMPLES OF TIME SERIES PLOTTED AS DEVIATIONS FROM SECULAR TRENDS REPRESENTED BY HORIZONTAL LINES.

(Selected from Chart 2).

RAILROAD BOND YIELDS – UNITED STATES

DEVIATIONS FROM TWENTY YEAR BINOMIALLY WEIGHTED MOVING AVERAGES (MATERIAL AND METHOD FROM F.R. MACAULAY)

SAUERBECK'S INDEX OF WHOLESALE PRICES IN ENGLAND

DEVIATIONS FROM STRAIGHT LINES FITTED TO LOGARITHMS BY PERIODS

PIG-IRON PRODUCTION IN THE UNITED STATES

DEVIATIONS FROM SEVEN YEAR MOVING AVERAGES

PRICE INDEX OF BUSINESS CYCLES, UNITED STATES: 1890-1899=100

(HARVARD INDEX OF TEN SENSITIVE COMMODITIES)
DEVIATIONS FROM BRADSTREET'S INDEX OF WHOLESALE PRICES X 1854

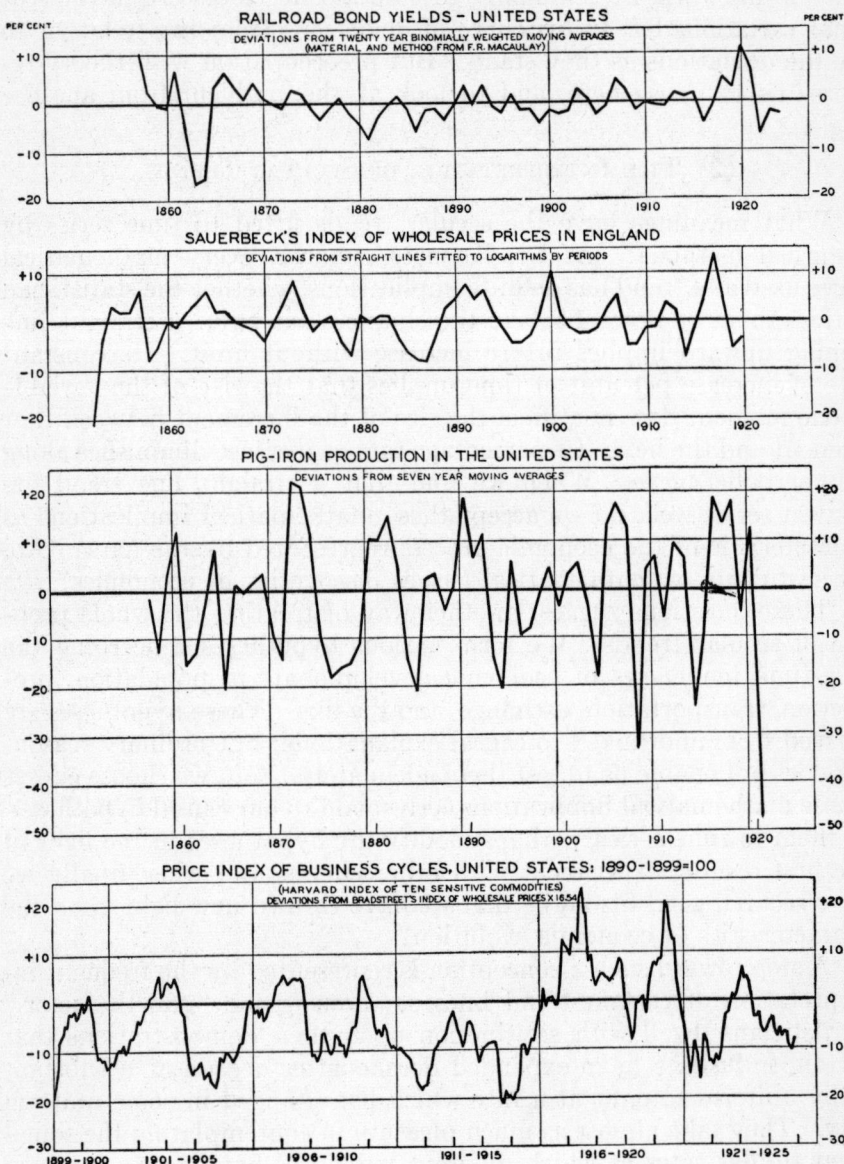

CHART 3 (*Continued*).

EXAMPLES OF TIME SERIES PLOTTED AS DEVIATIONS FROM SECULAR TRENDS
REPRESENTED BY HORIZONTAL LINES.

(Vertical Scale—¼ of scale on opposite page).

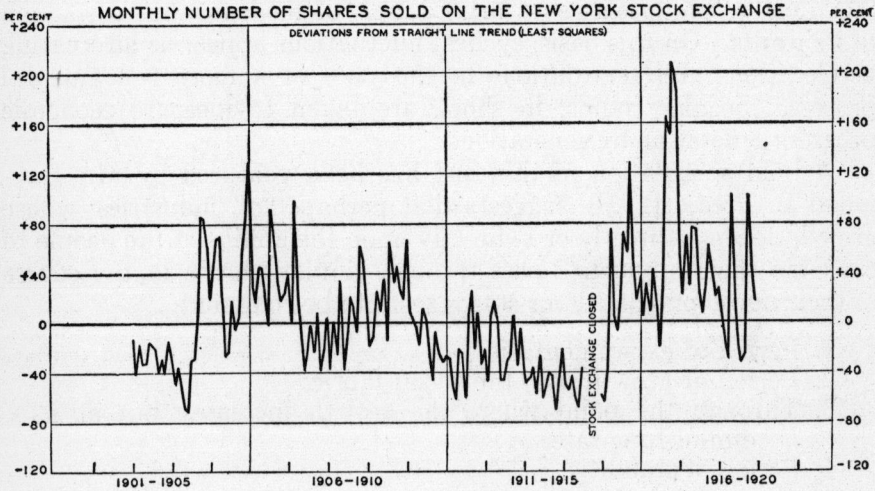

MONTHLY NUMBER OF SHARES SOLD ON THE NEW YORK STOCK EXCHANGE

DEVIATIONS FROM STRAIGHT LINE TREND (LEAST SQUARES)

RAILROAD CONSTRUCTION (MILES OF NEW ROAD BUILT) UNITED STATES

DEVIATIONS FROM A SECOND DEGREE PARABOLA FITTED TO LOGARITHMS periods and countries. Nor are they at a loss for explanations of these uniformities. In view of the increase in population characteristic of the great commercial nations, and of the advance in industrial technique, it seems scarcely fanciful to think of modern society as "tending" to produce an ever larger supply of goods for the satisfaction of its wants. On this basis, cyclical fluctuations appear as alternating accelerations and retardations in the pace of a more fundamental process. Secular trends, in short, are taken to measure economic progress generation by generation.

A bold speculation of this sort has been ventured by Mr. Raymond B. Prescott. He suggests that perhaps "all industries, whose growth depends directly or indirectly upon the ability of the people to consume their products," pass through similar phases in the course of their development. Four stages seem to be common:

1. Period of experimentation.
2. Period of growth into the social fabric.
3. Through the point where the growth increases, but at a diminishing rate.
4. Period of stability.

On this basis, Mr. Prescott suggests that the secular trends of all such industries may be represented by a single type of curve—that yielded by the Gompertz equation.

> Every country (he adds) may have a different rate of growth, and so may every industry, because no two industries have the same combination of influences. They will trace the same type of curve, however, even though the rate of growth is different.[1]

[1] "Law of Growth in Forecasting Demand," *Journal of the American Statistical Association,* December, 1922, vol. xviii, pp. 471-479.

To illustrate his suggestion, Mr. Prescott publishes the following copyrighted diagram, of which the caption is significant.

CURVE OF PROGRESS OR LAW
OF GROWTH (R. B. PRESCOTT)

Dr. Simon S. Kuznets, who has fitted more Gompertz or "logistic" curves (with three constants) to economic series than anyone else known to me, finds that the Gompertz curve gives good fits to a number of series, but that in more cases he gets good fits by using the three-constant "logistic curve." The important properties of this curve are: (1) Finite limits, zero and an upper value to which the curve is asymptotic. (2) The rate of increase per unit of time is directly proportioned to the size of the variable at a given point, multiplied by the distance between that point and the upper limit. This implies that (say) the output of an industry grows in physical units at a rate which increases from the start to the point of inflection of the curve, and then decreases gradually to zero as the curve approaches its upper asymptote. (3) The percentage rate of increase declines steadily from the beginning. These three characteristics, Dr. Kuznets supposes, appear in the history of the many economic processes, whose long-time statistical record is well described by a logistic curve.

The use of logistic and Gompertz curves is not limited to describing the secular trends of growing industries. They can be adapted also to the conditions of industries with a shrinking output. Such industries are not unimportant, even in a highly prosperous country like the United States. Conspicuous examples are canal traffic, gold mining, shipbuilding, bicycle manufacturing, and lumbering. Indeed, a declining phase may be anticipated for most industries, if we define an industry somewhat strictly in terms of its specific output and its geographical location. The cause of the decline may be competition from some other industry (for example, canals *versus* railways, bicycles *versus* automobiles); the depletion of natural resources (for example, lumbering and gold mining), or the approximate satisfaction, at least for a time, of a non-recurrent need (for example, railway building). In adapting his analysis to such cases, Dr. Kuznets takes the maximum output reached by the industry as the upper limit of the variable, and supposes a decline toward zero along an inverted logistic curve. By introducing an additional constant into his equations at need, he is able to secure satisfactory fits.

There remain numerous time series to which the idea of growth and decay is not applicable. Such is the case with all series of prices whether of commodities or other goods, and with many series of ratios, such as interest rates, bond yields, percentages of bank reserves to deposits, marriage rates, and credit ratios. Some of these series are highly important in the study of business cycles. It is a simple task to find empirical trend lines which fit the data reasonably well. For example, in Chart 1 the British unemployment series suggests the use of a horizontal line, and the British index of wholesale prices suggests a series of oblique lines which meet each other at certain well-known dates. But it is exceedingly difficult to rationalize the procedure, as one can in devising trends for quantities which grow or decay. Yet it may be that certain recent investigations are laying foundations on which can be built a rational analysis even of changing price trends.

(3) The Hypotheses of "Secondary Trends" and of "Long Waves"

In studying the relations between the data points of his industrial series, and the logistic or Gompertz trend lines he had fitted, Dr. Kuznets observed that the annual deviations tended to have positive values during the periods when wholesale-price indexes followed rising trends, and to have negative values when the trend of the price indexes was declining. Of course, this observation seems to be a statistical version of the familiar statement that a long-period rise of wholesale prices stimulates, and that a long-period fall of wholesale prices retards, industrial progress. But Kuznets went further, extending his analysis to the wholesale prices of various great staples. In dealing with these series he had to use empirical trends. Again he found that the annual deviations swerved upward from their long-period trends when the general level of wholesale prices was rising, and swerved downward when the general level of prices was sagging.

To test these observations, Kuznets removed the cyclical fluctuations of the annual deviations from the primary trends so far as possible by taking moving averages with periods slightly longer than business cycles, and measured the duration of the swerves, which he called "secondary trends." He found that the swerves averaged a little shorter in the production series than in the corresponding price series—about 11 years in the one case and about 12 years in the other. Doubling these periods to get the full period from crest to crest, or trough to trough, of these fluctuations, he concluded that the average duration since say the middle of the 19th century has been a little less than 25 years.

Dr. Kuznets inclines to treat these secondary trends as a distinct species of business fluctuations, intermediate between the much longer primary trends and the much shorter business cycles. To account for them he thinks economists must develop a special theory. His tentative explanation combines emphasis upon factors of a non-business origin with emphasis upon the fact that certain cyclical developments in business activities have effects which persist from one cycle to the next.

In 1913, a Dutch economist, J. van Gelderen, called attention to what he named "large cycles" in economic development, covering about 60 years. A compatriot, S. de Wolff, confirmed van Gelderen's results in 1924 by the use of more technical statistical analysis. Meanwhile the Russian investigator, N. D. Kondratieff, had developed the same idea independently in 1922. Not content with his first results, Kondratieff collected and analyzed all the time series he could find which covered long periods. The results of his work, which agree substantially with those of van Gelderen and de Wolff, were published in Russian in 1925 and summarized in a German article of last December.[1]

Kondratieff starts with the "long waves" of British wholesale price indexes; the rise from 1789 to 1814, the fall to 1849, the rise to 1873, the fall to 1896, the rise to 1920. Similar waves appear in the interest yields upon French *rentes* and British consols; also in French and English wages. Turning to series which show aggregate values or physical quantities, Kondratieff adjusted them to his needs by reducing the original data to a per-capita basis, fitting mathematical trend lines, computing deviations from the trends, and smoothing the deviations with 9-year moving averages. Such smoothed deviations show "long waves" in French imports, exports, and total foreign trade; British exports; French savings-bank balances; the portfolio of the Bank of France; coal production (or consumption) in France, England, the United States, Germany, and the world; iron production in England, the United States, and the world; lead production in England; and the area planted to oats in France and to cotton in the United States. On the other hand, "long waves" are not found in

[1] See Van Gelderen (using the pen-name "J. Fedder"), "Springvloed Beschouwingen over industrielle ontwikkeling en prijsbeweging," *De Nieuwe Tijd*, 1913, pp. 253-277, 369-384, 445-464; de Wolff, "Prosperitäts- und Depressionsperioden," in *Der lebendige Marxismus, Festgabe zum 70. Geburtstage von Karl Kautsky*, Jena, 1924, pp. 13-43; Kondratieff, *The World Economy and its Conjunctures during and after the War* (in Russian), Moscow, 1922; "The Problem of Economic Conditions," *Monthly Economic Bulletin of the Conjuncture Institute*, 1925, Supplement, pp. 28-79 (in Russian); "Die langen Wellen der Konjunktur," *Archiv für Sozialwissenschaft und Sozialpolitik*. December, 1926, vol. lvi, pp. 573-609.

French cotton consumption, American wool and sugar production, or "in the movement of certain other elements."

Surveying the whole body of his results, Kondratieff concludes that the western world has seen two-and-a-half "long waves" since the closing years of the 18th century.[2] The turning points are as follows:

	Trough of the wave	Crest of the wave	Trough of the wave	Approximate duration
1st long wave.......	Late 1780's or early 1790's	1810–17	1844–51	50–60 years
2nd long wave.......	1844–51	1870–75	1890–96	40–50 years
3rd long wave.......	1890–96	1914–20	.....	....

While Kondratieff believes that his statistical results make the existence of "long waves" highly probable, he offers no hypothesis to account for them. But he does regard these waves as cyclical phenomena, and believes that they arise from causes inherent in "capitalistic economy"—not from accident. Like van Gelderen and de Wolff, he rejects the easy explanation that the "long waves" in prices, and hence in other processes, are due to accidental discoveries of gold deposits combined with improvements in mining and metallurgical methods. To these economists it seems more probable that the business conditions characteristic of the ebbing of a "long wave" offer strong incentives to prospecting for new gold deposits and to improving the technical processes of exploiting known deposits. Thus the ebbing of a "long wave" tends to produce effects which favor a rise in prices and a mounting wave. *Vice versa,* the business conditions which characterize the rising of a "long wave" tend to make gold production unprofitable, hence to check the output, to stop the rise of prices, and so to reverse the direction of the whole movement once more. In other words, they treat the long-period swings in gold output as themselves an organic part of the 40-50-60-year cycles. But

[2] De Wolff suggests that each half of the long waves is composed of 2½ smaller cycles, and that the latter cycles are growing briefer according to this schedule:

10 years	10 years	10 years
9 "	9 "	9 "
8 "	8 "	8 "
7 "		

Beginning with 1825 (de Wolff's starting point), this scheme works out as follows:

			Beginning	Duration in years	Ending
1st cycle	Declining phase..........		1825	10+10+5=25	1850
2nd "	Ascending "		1850	5+ 9+9=23	1873
	Declining "		1873	9+ 8+4=21	1894
3rd "	Ascending "		1894	4+ 8+7=19	1913

See *Der lebendige Marxismus,* pp. 37, 38.

Kondratieff, at least, does not regard this suggestion as an adequate theory of the mechanism by which long cycles are alternately initiated and ended.

Until some adequate reason has been shown why we should expect more or less regular recurrences of "long waves" in economic activities, we shall have nothing beyond empirical evidence concerning their existence. We may admit the probable validity of Kondratieff's statistical argument that two-and-a-half "long waves" have occurred in various economic processes since the end of the 18th century, and yet hold open the question whether the series will be continued. Two-and-a-half recurrences do not suffice to establish empirically a presumption that any feature of modern history will repeat itself.

Another uncertainty is presented by the difference in order of magnitude between the duration of the "long waves" found by van Gelderen, de Wolff and Kondratieff, and the duration of the "secondary trends" found by Kuznets. It may be that the difference in the results is due to differences in methods of fitting trends, and computing and smoothing deviations. Or perhaps the European investigators, looking for replicas of the major swings of wholesale prices, paid slight attention to swerves which attract notice in a less preoccupied mind. Or it may be that there really are two sets of long-term fluctuations in economic activities, one of which averages double the duration of the second. Further research is needed to settle these issues.

But whether there be two sets of long-term fluctuations or only one set, whether (if there be but one set) the typical length is about a quarter or about half a century, and whether these fluctuations are merely historical episodes of considerable interest or an inherent characteristic of "capitalist economy," the investigations of van Gelderen, de Wolff, Kondratieff and Kuznets open an alluring perspective of future work. Starting with the study of commercial crises, the realistic students of economic activities have discovered successively several types of fluctuations which, at least for more than a century, appear to have been recurrent—the seasonal variations to which Jevons directed attention in his youth, the inter-crisis cycles of Juglar and others, the shorter business cycles of later writers, the secular trends of empirical statisticians, the 22-24-year "secondary trends" of Kuznets, and "long waves." Of course, some of these discoveries may prove to be invalid; but, on the other hand, recurrences of other periods may be revealed   Sismondi's problem was merely to explain crises: now the problem is to ascertain how many types of fluctuations are intermixed in economic experience, to differentiate these types from each other, to measure the wave-length of each type and to ascertain its regularity of recurrence, finally to construct a theory which will account adequately for all the types of fluctuations and make clear their relations to each other. As treatises upon crises, or crises and depressions, are giving place to treatises upon business cycles, so the latter may in turn give place to treatises upon economic oscillations.

While the time for undertakings of such scope has not quite come, we should keep constantly in mind the probable interconnection between business cycles and the less-studied fluctuations of shorter or longer duration. One connection is clear. Our writers on secular trends confirm an old contention when they point out that during the ebbing phase of a "long wave" years of depression predominate in the inter-crisis cycles, while during the mounting phase of a "long wave" years of prosperity predominate.[3]

We stand to learn more about economic oscillations at large and about business cycles in particular, if we approach the problem of trends as theorists, than if we confine ourselves to strictly empirical work. The trends which promise the most important additions to our knowledge are those which correspond to rational hypotheses, although they may not "fit the data" so well as empirical constructions which are difficult to interpret. For it may prove possible to integrate the rational hypotheses which yield instructive trends with the theory of business cycles.

(4) CONCLUSION.

The upshot of this discussion is that lines of secular trend show the effects of causes which, though subject to change at any moment, have influenced an economic process in some regular, or regularly changing, way through periods of time long in comparison with business cycles. What these causes have been, and whether they are still in operation, are matters for further inquiry. The empirical inquirer measures something which he knows merely as secular trend; that something is a set of net resultants; he may or we may not try to find out to what that something is due.

If we embark upon a search for causes of secular trends, we must

[3] See, for example, Kondratieff's article cited above, *Archiv für Sozialwissenschaft und Sozialpolitik*, December, 1926, vol. lvi, p. 591.

expect to find not one cause peculiar to each series, but a peculiar combination of a multitude of interrelated causes. These causes may be classified as (1) causes related to changes in the number of population, (2) causes related to the economic efficiency of the population—its age, constitution, health, education, technical knowledge and equipment, methods of coöperation, methods of settling conflicts of interest, and many other matters; (3) causes related to the quantity and quality of the natural resources exploited by the population.

Not only the second, but also the first and the third of these categories consists of a complex of factors which sustain all sorts of relations to each other. Even kinds of causes which the classification separates are interacting. The growth of population is influenced by changes in industrial technique and in natural resources; the growth of population also influences the development of technique and of resources; finally, changes in technique produce changes in resources (the iron-ore ranges and water powers of North America did not exist for the red men), and changes in resources are ever stimulating changes in technique. All of which means that we must think of every type of economic activity in a country as conditioned by a concert of fundamental factors, albeit a concert in which the ranking of the factors differs endlessly from case to case.

Another approach may make the conclusion clearer and more significant. There are secular causes which affect many economic activities in much the same way, for example, changes in gold output, depletion of soil fertility. There are secular causes which affect economic activities in different ways: the extension of the railway net over the United States checked canal building, diminished river traffic, and led to the abandonment of many eastern farms; but it stimulated the settlement of western lands, built up interior cities, and fostered the expansion of the coal and steel trades. There are secular causes whose direct effects are confined mainly to some single line of activity: —a series of inventions which cheapens the cost of producing some article of secondary importance is an example. Those secular causes which influence many activities in much the same way produce a measure of likeness among the secular trends of different time series. Those secular causes which influence various activities in opposite ways, and those secular causes whose perceptible influence is limited in scope introduce diversities in secular trends. There can scarcely be any time series whose trend is not a joint product of factors which tend toward uniformity and factors which tend toward diversity.

The most valuable contributions toward an understanding of the trends empirically established by statisticians have been made by the economic historians. These workers have studied in detail such great movements as the Agricultural and the Industrial Revolutions, the evolution of capitalism, the world-spread of the European races, the discovery, utilization and impairment of natural resources. They have sought not merely to record but also to explain these long-period changes in human affairs, using such statistics as they could gather and such hypotheses as their materials suggested. But they have been kept so busy mastering a vast mass of materials that they have not yet begun a systematic attack upon the problem of secular trends. Nor have they equipped themselves with the statistical technique needed for the most effective use of numerical data.

Economic theorists also have shown some interest in secular trends, but their contributions have been speculations concerning the future, rather than analysis of the past. The "pure" economic theory of recent years has dealt mainly with "static" problems, from which secular changes are barred. Economic "dynamics" has been regarded as more treacherous ground, and the mischances of eminent men who have walked thereon by the light of theory have been discouraging. Ricardo, for example, expected that mankind would be forced to resort to ever poorer soils and ever more intensive cultivation to get food for their increasing numbers; that in consequence real wages would remain at best constant, profits would decline unsteadily, and rents rise until "almost the whole produce of the country, after paying the laborers, will be the property of the owners of land and the receivers of tithes and taxes." [1] Of the numerous speculations of this type, those of Karl Marx are of especial interest here, because they include the increasing frequency and increasing severity of business crises among the secular trends which are to usher in the socialistic state. [2]

It is no wonder that a field which requires the fusion of statistical technique with historical learning and theoretical finesse has not yet

[1] *Principles of Political Economy,* ed. by C. K. Gonner, London, 1891, p. 99.

[2] Marx's theory of crises runs through all three volumes of *Capital,* not to speak of his other writings. For a brief statement of the rôle of crises in the scheme of economic revolution, see the preface which he wrote in 1873 for the first volume of *Capital* (English translation by Moore and Aveling, Chicago, 1915, p. 26.)

John R. Commons, H. L. McCracken, and W. B. Zeuch have made a systematic study of the ideas concerning secular trends propounded by economic theorists. They hold that the conceptions of trends and business cycles have been derived from the theories of value entertained by the writers they discuss and from the types of organization these writers had in mind. See "Secular Trends and Business Cycles: a Classification of Theories," *Review of Economic Statistics,* Preliminary vol. iv, pp. 244-263.

been explored. Yet the time may be near when the problem of secular trends will have as definite a standing in economic research, attract as many investigators, and yield as interesting results as the problem of business cycles. In the meanwhile, students of the latter problem suffer the grave disadvantage of having to deal with a factor which is both important and obscure. They cannot anticipate the results of researches not yet made; they cannot make adequate studies of secular trends as an incident in their studies of cyclical fluctuations, and they cannot let the problem alone.

One set of questions is particularly insistent. Is there a definite relation between secular trends and cyclical fluctuations? Are activities characterized by a rapidly rising trend subject to more frequent, or more violent, cycles than activities whose trend is nearer the horizontal? And more at large, can the trends of time series, after they have been measured, be discarded as of no further interest? Or must the trends themselves be brought into the explanations of cyclical fluctuations, as is suggested by those theories which connect business cycles with "progress"?[3] Are the trends themselves generated by cyclical fluctuations, as Mr. Lawrence K. Frank has argued?[4] While these questions arise at this point, they cannot be answered by any process short of considering the pertinent evidence in detail. But the mere fact that such problems must be faced by the business-cycle theorist suffices to show that he cannot imitate the business-cycle statistician in merely eliminating secular trends.

4. THE PROBLEM OF SEASONAL VARIATIONS.

Chart 4, drawn on a larger scale than the charts illustrating secular trends, shows how time series differ in respect to seasonal variations. As in Chart 1, the data are plotted in their original form, in order to make clear the varied difficulties which confront the statistician who is trying to isolate cyclical fluctuations.

There are series in the chart which undergo seasonal changes each year of much the same sort, and of an amplitude so large as to obscure the cyclical fluctuations, if not the secular trends. There are series in which the seasonal variations, while fairly regular, are not wide. There are others which suggest the presence of seasonal factors

---

[3] Compare Chapter I, section iv, 4.
[4] See Mr. Frank's paper, "Long-Term Price Trends," *Journal of the American Statistical Association*, September, 1923, vol. xviii, pp. 904-908.

CHART 4.

A COLLECTION OF TIME SERIES TO ILLUSTRATE DIFFERENCES IN SEASONAL VARIATIONS.

GROUP I - LARGE AND REGULAR SEASONAL VARIATIONS

FIVE-AND-TEN-CENT CHAIN-STORE SALES (5 CHAINS) IN THE UNITED STATES
AVERAGE MONTHLY SALES 1919=100

PORTLAND CEMENT PRODUCTION IN THE UNITED STATES

GROUP II - SMALL AND FAIRLY REGULAR SEASONAL VARIATIONS

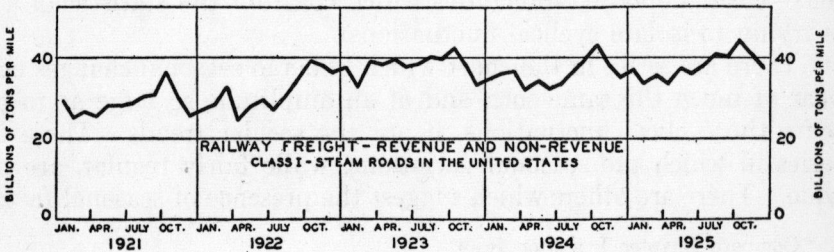

CIGARS - CONSUMPTION IN THE UNITED STATES
(TAX-PAID WITHDRAWALS)

RAILWAY FREIGHT - REVENUE AND NON-REVENUE
CLASS I - STEAM ROADS IN THE UNITED STATES

234

CHART 4 (*Continued*)

A COLLECTION OF TIME SERIES TO ILLUSTRATE DIFFERENCES IN SEASONAL VARIATIONS

GROUP III – RATHER IRREGULAR SEASONAL VARIATIONS

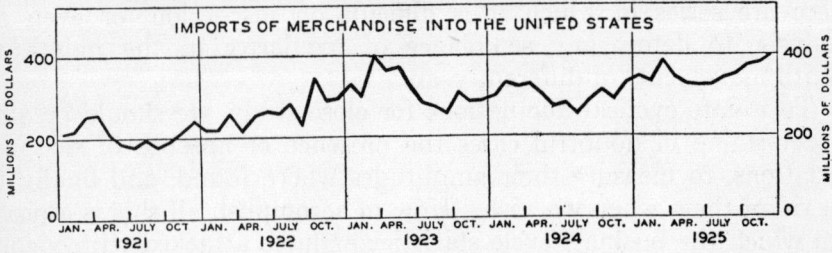

IMPORTS OF MERCHANDISE INTO THE UNITED STATES

AUTOMOBILE PRODUCTION IN THE UNITED STATES

GROUP IV – NO PERCEPTIBLE SEASONAL VARIATIONS

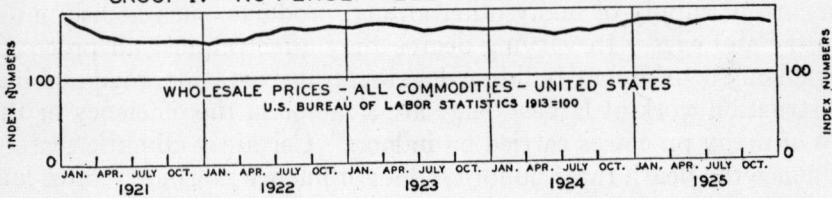

WHOLESALE PRICES – ALL COMMODITIES – UNITED STATES
U.S. BUREAU OF LABOR STATISTICS 1913=100

PIG-IRON PRODUCTION IN THE UNITED STATES

rather irregular in themselves, or so combined with changing conditions of other types as to produce rather irregular results. Finally, there are series in which it is difficult on inspection, or even on analysis, to detect any semblance of regularity in the month to month movements of different years.

To isolate cyclical fluctuations for close study, we should be able to determine in doubtful cases the presence or absence of seasonal variations, to measure their amplitudes where found, and finally to get rid of them when we wish. How to accomplish all this is a problem which the business-cycle statisticians have attacked with vigor.[1] Business-cycle theorists, on the contrary, have paid little attention to these short-period oscillations—an omission which it is unwise to imitate.

(1) The Causes and Pervasiveness of Seasonal Variations.

Two types of seasons produce annually recurring variations in economic activities—those which are due to climates and those which are due to conventions. Upon some activities these seasons act directly, upon others indirectly.

(1) In the temperate zones at least, where lie the areas of chief concern to us, climatic seasons control the growth of crops and of such animal products as wool. They exercise a marked influence upon the current supply of many other animal products, such as fish, milk, poultry and eggs. In varying degree they affect almost all processes carried on out-of-doors, building, logging, transportation, road making, construction work at large. They are a factor in the efficiency or the cost of many processes carried on indoors. Certainly climatic seasons influence the death rate; doubtless they influence morbidity rates and so affect almost all activities in some measure.[1]

Upon the demand for certain types of goods, the effect of climatic seasons is not less clear than its effects upon certain types of produc-

[1] The earliest studies of seasonal variations known to Jevons were made in 1854 to 1856 by J. W. Gilbert (bank-note circulation, *Statistical Journal*, vol. xvii, pp. 289-321, and vol. xix, pp. 144-168) and Charles Babbage (bank clearings, the same, vol. xix, p. 28). Jevons began his own economic studies with a paper, "On the Study of Periodic Commercial Fluctuations," which he sent to the meeting of the British Association in 1862. In 1866 he read a much more elaborate paper, "On the Frequent Autumnal Pressure in the Money Market," to the Statistical Society of London. See *Investigations in Currency and Finance*, by W. S. Jevons, London, 1884, pp. 1-12, and 160-193.

[1] On the seasonal variations of the death rate, see Maurice B. Hexter, *Social Consequences of Business Cycles*, Boston and New York, 1925, pp. 55-57.

tion. The sort of clothing we wear, our sports, the amount of fuel we use, undergo radical changes from winter to summer.

Market supply is kept far steadier than the rate at which goods subject to strong seasonal influences are produced. This steadiness is a triumph of economic planning. It is won by arranging compensatory seasonal variations in the activities which intervene between producing and consuming. The processes of preserving, storing, transporting and distributing goods are purposely made to vary in such a way that a highly unstable rate of production is converted into a fairly even rate of market supply, or into a rate of market supply which varies with seasonal changes in demand. Some efforts are made to counteract also the variations in demand produced by climatic seasons. For example, a seasonal change is made in the price of coal to stimulate buying during the summer, and most seasonal goods can be had cheaper in their "off seasons." Thus the effects of climatic seasons are extended by man's contrivance over a wide variety of economic processes.

(2) Conventional seasons have many origins—ancient religious observances, folk customs, fashions, business practices, statute law.

The most pervasive of all the seasonal variations in time series is due to the calendar. February is nearly 10 per cent shorter than January, except in leap years when it is about 6 per cent shorter, and April is nearly 3 per cent shorter than March. Series of monthly aggregates are thus made to show a spurious seasonal variation—spurious in the sense that it bears no relation to the current rate of activity. And this spurious variation is made irregular from year to year by the different ways in which Sundays and holidays are divided among the months.

Many of the conventional seasons have considerable effects on economic behavior. We can count on active retail buying before Christmas, on the Thanksgiving demand for turkeys, on the July demand for fireworks, on the preparations for June weddings, on heavy dividend and interest payments at the beginning of each quarter, on an increase of bankruptcies in January, and so on. One of these conventional seasons is especially troublesome to statisticians, because it is movable. Easter may come as early as March 22d or as late as April 25th. Seasonal variations in series affected by Easter buying are decidedly different in the March and the April years.

From the activities directly affected by climatic or conventional seasons, acting separately or in unison, seasonal influences radiate to all other activities, probably without exception. In part these radiations are due to the conscious efforts already spoken of to counteract seasonal changes in demand or supply; in part they are unplanned consequences of these changes. For example, the fact that American crops are harvested largely in the autumn gives rise to a seasonal demand for currency in the farming districts, to seasonal changes in interest rates (and sometimes stock prices) in the financial centers, to seasonal changes in railway traffic, to seasonal changes in farmers' receipts, to seasonal changes in their payments to creditors, to seasonal changes in the business of country merchants, and to seasonal changes in wage disbursements. So, too, the expectation of heavy buying by consumers in the holiday season leads retailers to increase their stocks at earlier dates. In turn, the prospect of these large orders injects still earlier seasonal variations into manufacturing, into the demand for raw materials, into employment, and into wage payments, thus tending to produce secondary seasonal variations in retail buying itself.

It seems probable that these reflex effects of the primary seasonal disturbances grow smaller in most cases as they radiate to other processes. For example, manufacturers of goods for which the demand is largely concentrated in a few weeks seek to spread the production over a longer period. It is far less costly to provide a moderate equipment which can be used continuously in making a year's supply of goods than to provide a large equipment which must stand idle most of the time in order to produce a year's supply in a rush. Of course the ideal of continuous production is seldom attained in seasonal trades; but the business motives for stabilizing operations are clear enough and strong enough to moderate the effect of seasonal factors in a notable degree.[2]

Not less important, is the fact that both the original and the derived impulses toward seasonal activity are well scattered over the months of the year. For example, coal mining and logging grow brisk while construction work is falling off and farming requires fewer hands. In Great Britain employment reaches its maximum in

[2] Dr. N. I. Stone has pointed out that efforts to stabilize operations usually begin with seasonal variations, and later may or may not extend to cyclical variations. See his chapter on "Methods of Stabilizing Production of Textiles, Clothing, and Novelties," in *Business Cycles and Unemployment*, National Bureau of Economic Research, 1923, pp. 116-133.

References to the rapidly growing literature upon methods of mitigating seasonal and cyclical variations may be found in the bibliography given by Lewisohn, Draper, Commons and Lescohier in *Can Business Prevent Unemployment?* New York, 1925, pp. 217-226, and in the footnotes of H. Feldman's *The Regularization of Employment*, New York, 1925.

March for shipbuilding; in April and May for the furnishing trades; in June and July for engineering; in August for building; in September for iron mining and iron and steel making; in November for tin-plate and sheet-steel work, the miscellaneous metal trades, and printing; in December for coal mining.[3] This diversity of dates makes the business of a country as a whole far steadier from month to month than are most of the component parts. As the seasonal impulses produced by any factor radiate from the center of disturbance, they encounter the radiating effects of the seasonal variations which have occurred or are expected in other factors. If some time series, like the Bureau of Labor Statistics index number of prices at wholesale or stock prices, seem to be nearly or quite free from seasonal variations, it is presumably because they are affected by many different seasonal influences which cancel one another.

Reflection upon the causes which we assign for seasonal movements suggests that few of them will produce precisely the same effects year after year. An exceptionally cold winter will increase the seasonal swing in coal consumption, in the sale of woolen underwear, and in construction work. The conventional seasons which have not a fixed date in the calendar—particularly Easter—are responsible for other deviations from the seasonal pattern. In careful work, the months with five Sundays must be treated differently from months with four Sundays. And even the conventions tied to fixed dates— like holiday shopping and January and July interest payments— produce different effects when they occur in combination with different phases of business cycles. Over long periods, also, changes in industrial technique, communication, transportation, and business organization alter seasonal oscillations. The autumnal drain upon the money markets for moving the crops, for example, has become decidedly less of a bugbear to operators on the New York Stock Exchange than it was before the organization of the Federal Reserve System. Hence statisticians who break long time series into briefer periods often find that the seasonal variations of the parts differ appreciably. Chart 5 gives two examples of this sort, one taken from

[3] See A. L. Bowley and K. C. Smith, "Seasonal Variations in Finance, Prices and Industry," *London and Cambridge Economic Service,* Special Memorandum, No. 7, July, 1924, pp. 14, 15. The seasonal variations are derived from data for the years 1900-1913.

CHART 5.

Examples of Seasonal Variations Which Have Changed in the Course of Time.

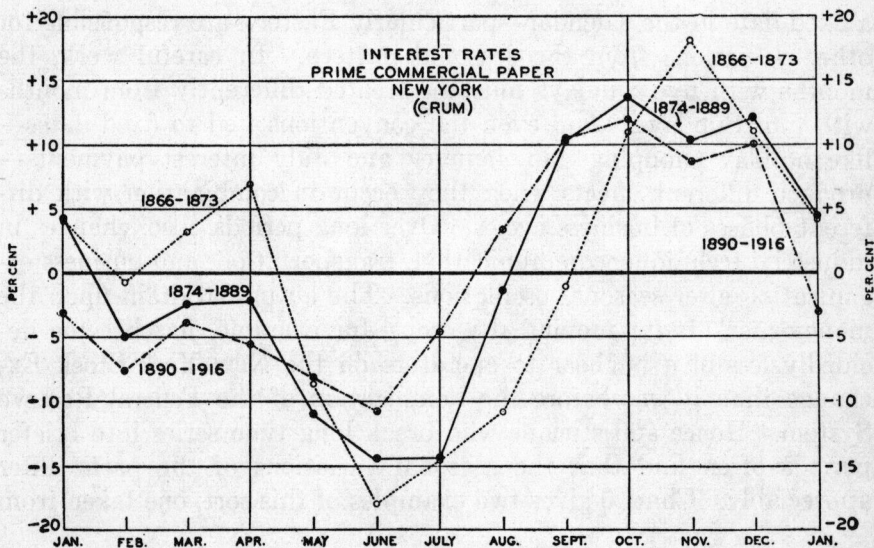

UNEMPLOYMENT IN BRITISH TRADE UNIONS
(BOWLEY-SMITH)

INTEREST RATES
PRIME COMMERCIAL PAPER
NEW YORK
(CRUM)

the British unemployment data, the other from interest rates on prime commercial paper in the New York market.[4]

(2) Methods of Measuring Average Seasonal Variations.

Of ways of measuring seasonal variations, perhaps the most widely used is the ingenious "link-relative" method invented by Professor Warren M. Persons. This method requires six successive operations upon the original data. (1) Compute the link relatives for each successive month (week or quarter), that is, find the percentage of each item to the preceding item. (2) Arrange the link relatives for all the Januaries in a frequency table. Make similar tables for the other months. (3) Find the median in each of these twelve tables. (4) Forge the medians into a chain with January represented by 100. Carry the chain through the twelve months back to January. (5) If, as usually happens, the second January figure differs from the first one, adjust the figures for all the months to make the second January figure 100. (6) Readjust all the figures once more so that the arithmetic mean of the twelve monthly figures shall equal 100.[1]

[4] See the paper of Messrs. Bowley and Smith cited above, and W. L. Crum, "Cycles of Rates on Commercial Paper", *Review of Economic Statistics*, January, 1923, Preliminary vol. v, p. 29.

The data from which Chart 5 is drawn are as follows:

Seasonal Variations of

	Percentage of Members Unemployed in British Trade Unions			Interest Rates on Prime Commercial Paper in New York		
	1887–95	1896–1904	1905–13	1866–73	1874–89	1890–1916
January............	+1.0	+.4	+.5	+ 4.1	+ 4.4	− 3.0
February..........	+ .5	+.1	+.2	− .7	− 4.9	− 7.6
March.............	0	−.4	+.2	+ 3.2	− 2.4	− 3.9
April.............	− .4	−.5	0	+ 6.9	− 2.3	− 5.6
May..............	− .3	−.5	−.3	− 8.7	−11.0	− 8.1
June..............	− .6	−.4	−.2	−18.0	−14.4	−10.8
July..............	− .4	−.4	−.2	−14.6	−14.3	− 4.6
August............	0	0	0	−10.9	− 1.4	+ 3.3
September.........	0	+.3	+.1	− 1.1	+10.2	+10.5
October...........	+ .1	+.3	+.1	+10.9	+13.6	+11.8
November.........	− .1	+.2	−.1	+18.0	+10.3	+ 8.6
December.........	+ .3	+.8	+.4	+11.1	+12.1	+10.0

[1] For examples of this method see Professor Persons' papers in the *Review of Economic Statistics*, particularly Preliminary volume i. Later expositions are given by Professor Persons in "Correlation of Time Series," *Journal of the American Statistical Association*, June, 1923, vol. xviii, pp. 713-726, and in his contribution to the *Handbook of Mathematical Statistics*, edited by H. L. Rietz, Boston, 1924, chapter x.

A technical improvement upon Persons' method has been suggested by Professor W. L. Crum. Instead of using the medians given by the frequency tables, take "the

It will be noticed that Professor Persons measures the seasonal variation of a series before he has computed its secular trend. It is primarily because of the trend that his second January figure usually differs from the first, and that his fifth step has to be taken. Dr. William L. Hart has argued that it is better first to determine the trend of a series by whatever method is most appropriate; second to eliminate the trend, by subtracting the magnitude it indicates from the original item for each month, and then to compute the arithmetic means of all the Januaries, all the Februaries, etc., as shown by the data in this corrected form.[2]

Several statisticians have pointed out that Dr. Hart's method of "monthly means" does not guard against the influence upon the seasonal index of extreme and irregular deviations.[3] As a remedy for this defect, Dr. Lincoln W. Hall and Miss Helen D. Falkner proposed what the latter calls the "ratio-to-ordinate" method. Like Dr. Hart, they start by determining the secular trend. Next they compute the percentage of each original item to the corresponding value given by the trend line, make frequency tables of these percentages for each month, select from the frequency tables a typical value (usually the mean of a middle group of items), and finally adjust the twelve typical values so that their average for the year is 100.[4]

Still another method, devised by Dr. Fred R. Macaulay, is to make 12-months moving averages of the original items centered at the seventh month, compute the ratio of the original item for each month to its moving-average value, find medians of these ratios for

mean of a middle group of items (two or four if the series contains an even number of items, three if an odd number)." "Use of the Median in Determining Seasonal Variation," *Journal of the American Statistical Association*, March, 1923, vol. xviii, pp. 607-614.

Criticisms of this method may be found in several of the papers presently to be cited, and on p. 26 of the paper by Bowley and Smith cited above. "It is very doubtful . . .," say these writers, "whether the comparison of each month with the preceding is as appropriate for the measurement of seasonal influence as the comparison of each month with the position determined by the general average or by the line of trend." They regard Professor Persons' method as "specially suitable for correcting records for seasonal variation" (since it reveals irregularities in the frequency tables), but hold that the most accurate method of "measuring the seasonal effects" is to use deviations from a 12-months moving average.

[2] William L. Hart, "The Method of Monthly Means for Determination of a Seasonal Variation," *Journal of the American Statistical Association*, September, 1922, vol. xviii, pp. 341-349.

[3] See, for example, W. M. Persons in the *Handbook of Mathematical Statistics*, edited by H. L. Rietz, pp. 155-158.

[4] See Lincoln W. Hall, "Seasonal Variation as a Relative of Secular Trend," *Journal of the American Statistical Association*, June, 1924, vol. xix, pp. 155-166, and Helen D. Falkner, "The Measurement of Seasonal Variation," in the same issue, pp. 167-179.

all the Januaries, Februaries, etc., and convert the medians into percentages which total 1200 for the year.[5]

Choice among these methods is to be guided, of course, by the characteristics of the series to be dealt with and the specific purpose in view. As Messrs. Bowley and Smith point out in their systematic discussion of the problem, the first question to be asked is whether the seasonal variation of any month from the annual average is more appropriately considered as a given amount, or as a given proportion. For example, do the October imports of wheat into England tend to be 50,000 tons more than the average of all months, or do they tend to be 11 per cent above the average? If greater regularity is secured by considering amounts, then seasonal variations should be expressed in percentages borne by the absolute difference between the average amount in each month shown by the data (in their original form or adjusted for trend) and the arithmetic mean for the whole year. If greater regularity is secured by considering proportions, then seasonal variations should be computed from ratios, and geometric means should be used. A second question to be considered in either case is whether the series shows an upward or downward trend. If not, the absolute differences or the relative differences may be computed directly from the original data. If there is a trend to be eliminated, that can be accomplished by using moving averages or by fitting curves, and the absolute or relative differences ascertained from the data corrected for trend. Thus Bowley and Smith discuss and use in different series six methods—three based on amounts and three on proportions, one of each set without correction for trend, one with the trend removed by moving averages, and one with the trend removed by the method of least squares. Of these methods they think the two which use moving averages are the most accurate, though the most laborious. In a few cases they make use also of Persons' link-relative method.[6]

(3) Efforts to Measure Changing Seasonal Variations.

In all the preceding methods the object is to find one set of monthly figures which measures the average seasonal influence. Oc-

[5] See "Index of Production in Selected Basic Industries," *Federal Reserve Bulletin*, December, 1922, vol. iii, pp. 1414, 1415.

[6] A. L. Bowley and K. C. Smith, "Seasonal Variations in Finance, Prices and Industry," *London and Cambridge Economic Service*, Special Memorandum, No. 7, July, 1924.

casionally statisticians who use one of these methods notice that the seasonal fluctuations of their series seem to undergo a change between the beginning and the end of their period. They may then break the whole period into two or more parts, and compute fixed seasonals for each segment in the fashion of Chart 5. A more ambitious plan, that of measuring seasonal variations as they change from one year to the next, has been suggested by Dr. Willford I. King. His successive steps are as follows: (1) Plot the data. (2) Draw a free hand curve through the data representing the cyclical fluctuations. (3) Read from this "preliminary cycle curve" the numerical values which it indicates each month, and (4) divide the actual data by these values. The quotients give the first approximation to the seasonal variations. (5) Smooth out the irregularities of this rough approximation by using 9-period moving averages of all the Januaries, all the Februaries, etc. Plot the results and smooth out the small irregularities which may still remain. (6) Adjust the results so that the sum of the twelve seasonal indexes for each year shall equal 1200.[1]

Dr. King's effort to take account of the changes which seasonal variations undergo from time to time has commended itself to other statisticians; but his method has been questioned because of the free play given to the investigator's personal equation.[2] Dr. W. L. Crum has devised a method of showing progressive changes in seasonal variations which is not open to this objection. The essential feature of his plan is to find the secular trend of all the January items in a series, all the February items, and so on, and to use the ordinates of these 12 monthly trends as the basis for determining the seasonal variations in each successive year.[3]

This method is designed primarily to yield "seasonal *standards* applicable to the study of current phenomena." It applies to series

[1] Willford I. King, "An Improved Method for Measuring the Seasonal Factor," *Journal of the American Statistical Association,* September, 1924, vol. xix, pp. 301-313.
[2] Compare O. Gressens, "On the Measurement of Seasonal Variations," *Journal of the American Statistical Association,* June, 1925, vol. xx, p. 205.
[3] The details of this method differ according as the investigator works with link relatives or with monthly means of the data. See W. L. Crum, "Progressive Variation in Seasonality," *Journal of the American Statistical Association,* March, 1925, vol. xx, pp. 48-64. As Dr. Crum points out, similar suggestions have been made by Dr. E. C. Snow, "Trade Forecasting and Prices," *Journal of the Royal Statistical Society,* May, 1923, vol. lxxxvi, p. 334, and by Mr. Harold Flynn, quoted in *The Problem of Business Forecasting,* Boston and New York, 1924, p. 104.
For an interesting application of the method, see Edwin Frickey, "Bank Clearings Outside New York City, 1875-1914," *Review of Economic Statistics,* October, 1925, vol. vii, pp. 258-262. Mr. Frickey found seasonal variations in the terminal years of a period by fitting straight line trends to link relatives for each month, and then made progressively changing seasonals for the intervening years by straight line interpolations.

whose seasonal variations change slowly and progressively for considerable periods.[4] But it does not take account of yearly changes in seasonal factors, such as are produced, say, by warm and cold winters, or by March and April Easters. Mr. O. Gressens has proposed a method which will show changes of the latter type. He computes the ratio of a variable each month to the average monthly value for its year, corrects these monthly ratios when necessary for the trend within the year, smooths them by the use of moving averages, moderates any widely divergent items which may remain, and adjusts his ratios for each year so that their sum shall be 1200. This method he believes to have the merits of Dr. King's procedure, and to be "mechanically more definite." [5]

(4) Conclusion.

The preceding review shows how much labor statisticians have devoted to the measurement of seasonal variations. That problem has an interest of its own, apart from its bearing upon the isolating of cyclical fluctuations. Efforts to mitigate seasonal reductions in employment, and to reduce costs of production by "budgeting" production and marketing are stimulated and made more effective by knowledge of the magnitude and regularity of the seasonal variations in the numerous activities which have to be considered in laying plans. Happily for us, it is often possible to turn results worked out for practical ends to theoretical uses.

A few illustrations of seasonal variations, as measured by statistical investigators have already been given in Chart 5. Additional illustrations are presented in Chart 6, which shows the same method applied to different series, and Chart 7, which shows various methods applied to the same or different series.

Non-technical readers who feel a bit confused by the variety of methods which have been sketched may take comfort in Chart 7. It illustrates a remark made by Messrs. Bowley and Smith. Having experimented with different ways of measuring seasonal variations perhaps more elaborately than any other investigators, they observe

[4] W. L. Crum, as cited, pp. 60, 61.
[5] O. Gressens, "On the Measurement of Seasonal Variation," *Journal of the American Statistical Association,* June, 1925, vol. xx, pp. 203-210.
Dr. King, on the other hand, points out that it is difficult to apply either Crum's or Gressens' method to time series in which the seasonal variations are relatively slight and the cyclical fluctuations relatively violent.

CHART 6.

INDEXES OF SEASONAL VARIATIONS.

Made by the moving-average-median method (F. R. Macaulay).

PIG-IRON PRODUCTION-U.S.

COTTON CONSUMPTION-U.S.

BITUMINOUS COAL PRODUCTION-U.S.

CALVES SLAUGHTERED-U.S.

WHEAT FLOUR PRODUCTION-U.S.*

CIGARETTE PRODUCTION-U.S.

SUGAR MELTINGS-U.S.

HOGS SLAUGHTERED-U.S.

CEMENT PRODUCTION-U.S.

COMPUTATION BASED ON DATA FROM JAN. 1913 TO DEC. 1921
*COMPUTATION BASED ON DATA FROM JAN. 1914 TO DEC. 1921

CHART 6 (*Continued*).

INDEXES OF SEASONAL VARIATIONS.

Made by the link-relative method (W. M. Persons).

IMPORTS OF MERCHANDISE-U.S.
(TOTAL VALUE)

JAN.1903 – JAN.1917

INTEREST RATE ON FOUR-To-SIX
MONTHS COMMERCIAL PAPER
NEW YORK CITY

JAN.1890 – DEC.1915

AVERAGE RESERVES
OF THE NEW YORK CITY
CLEARING HOUSE BANKS

JAN.1879 – JAN.1914

BANK CLEARINGS
NEW YORK CITY

JAN.1903 – JAN.1917

BANK CLEARINGS
OUTSIDE NEW YORK CITY

JAN.1903 – JAN.1917

GROSS EARNINGS OF
TEN LEADING RAILROADS
U.S.

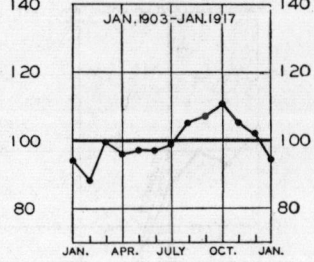

JAN.1903 – JAN.1917

VALUES OF BUILDING PERMITS
ISSUED FOR
TWENTY LEADING CITIES-U.S.

JAN.1903 – JAN.1917

BRADSTREET'S
BUSINESS FAILURES
U.S.

JAN.1893 – JAN.1917

DIVIDEND PAYMENTS
BY INDUSTRIAL CORPORATIONS
U.S.

DEC.1902 – DEC.1917

CHART 7.

Indexes of Seasonal Variations Made by Various Methods.

I
RATIO-FROM-TREND-AND-CYCLE CURVE (KING);
ADJUSTED MEAN; LINK-RELATIVE
(PIG-IRON PRODUCTION-U.S.)

II
RATIO-FROM-TREND-AND-CYCLE CURVE,
CHANGING SEASONAL (KING)
(PIG-IRON PRODUCTION-U.S.)

III
SIMPLE MONTHLY MEAN (RUBINOW);
ADJUSTED FOR SECULAR TREND (CHAPIN)
(MUNICIPAL LODGING HOUSE REGISTRATION, NEW YORK CITY)

IV
ADJUSTED RATIOS TO ORDINATES OF SECULAR TREND,
CHANGING SEASONAL (GRESSENS)
(GROSS ELECTRIC SALES OF THE PUBLIC SERVICE ELECTRIC CO. OF N.J.)

V
RATIO-TO-ORDINATE METHOD (FALKNER);
AND MEDIAN-LINK-RELATIVE METHOD
(RATE OF INTEREST, 60-90 DAY COMMERCIAL PAPER IN N.Y.)

VI
PROGRESSIVE LINK-RELATIVE METHOD (CRUM)
(COMMERCIAL PAPER RATES)

that "in fact, these methods give nearly identical results in most cases."[1]

5. The Problem of Irregular Fluctuations.

While less progress has been made in dealing with the irregular fluctuations of time series than in dealing with secular trends and seasonal variations, we are not at liberty to dismiss this topic quite so summarily as do most statisticians. The conceptual difficulties with which the problem bristles are significant for the theory of business cycles. In considering them, we shall find ourselves confronting certain issues fundamental to our further work.

(1) The Concept of Irregular Fluctuations.

So far as known, all social time series without exception present irregularities of contour in their raw state. Statisticians take these irregularities for granted without attempting to define them, as they define secular trends, seasonal variations, and cyclical fluctuations.[1] What little they say upon the subject concerns the causes of irregularities in particular series. For example, they point out that wars or civil insurrections may disturb many economic processes for a considerable period. Less serious disturbances may be caused by such events as earthquakes, conflagrations, floods, droughts, epidemics, insect pests, strikes and lockouts, railway embargoes, inventions, changes in trade routes, discoveries of fresh resources, changes in laws, judicial rulings, and so on through an interminable list. Nor should we forget the effects of changes in the method of compiling statistics, and of inaccurate reporting. The addition of a new town to the list for which bank clearings are published, the disruption of a trade union which had made unemployment returns, changes in the lists of commodities used in a price index, the failure of customs-house clerks to include all July invoices in their July statement of imports, revisions

[1] "Seasonal Variations in Finance, Prices and Industry," *London and Cambridge Economic Service*, July, 1924, Special Memorandum, No. 7, p. 3.

[1] The nearest approach to a definition has been made by Professor Edmund E. Day, who proposes to divide irregular fluctuations into two classes—namely,

"Episodic movements due to specific causes, ordinarily reflected in sharp, pronounced breaks in the record of the variable. . . .

"Fortuitous or accidental movements, of unknown origin, quite irregular in character, but involving only minor disturbances of the general course of the variable."

See Day's *Statistical Analysis*, New York, 1925, pp. 285, 302-306, and 310-312.

in the estimates of monetary stocks to take account of losses, re-classifications of railroad freight, errors in addition, misprints—a thousand such matters may produce purely artificial irregularities in time series.

The idea suggested by this practice of listing causes is that we may classify as an irregular fluctuation any movement of a curve which we do not ascribe to secular, seasonal or cyclical changes. If we had clean-cutting methods of ascertaining what changes in our curves are due to these three sets of factors, the treatment of irregular fluctuations as residuals would be satisfactory. On that basis we might rationalize our procedure as follows: The activities represented by a time series are influenced every day by a host of factors which are not secular, cyclical, or seasonal in character. Most of these random factors are known vaguely, if at all. But the theory of probabilities justifies the assumption that the random factors acting at a given moment cancel one another when they are very numerous, independent in origin, and of the same order of magnitude. Indeed, Professor Edgeworth has shown that these strict conditions may be relaxed:—there will be much canceling if the random factors are not few, if there is a considerable measure of independence among them, and if no two or three preponderate over the rest.[2] It often happens, however, that even the relaxed conditions are not complied with. At any time a group of mutually related factors may dominate the complex, or one or two factors far more powerful than the other random influences may crop up. Under such circumstances, the random factors cease to cancel one another, even roughly. Instead, they produce a large or small deviation from the undulating curve marked out by the secular trend, seasonal variations, and cyclical fluctuations in combination. It is deviations caused by such failure of mutual canceling of the random factors which we call irregular fluctuations.

One doubt concerning this conception can be met by an extension of the argument. As we saw in the last section, some of the causes of seasonal variations vary from year to year. Likewise all secular trends are admitted to be subject to change without notice, and those trends which are ascribed to growth may be inconstant by nature for aught we know. Finally, among the numerous causes of cyclical fluctuations reviewed in the first chapter, there is not one which we should expect to produce perfectly regular cycles. Thus, once we

[2] Compare section ii, 2, above.

adopt the current practice of the statisticians and start discussing irregular fluctuations in terms of their causes, we seem forced to admit that irregularities may occur in the movements which we classify as secular, cyclical and seasonal. In other words, an attempt to treat secular, seasonal and cyclical changes as regular runs counter to much that we know and more that we suspect.

This conclusion may be admitted, and treated as a reason, not for abandoning the classification of fluctuations in time series into the regular and the irregular, but for making it more rigorous. That is, we may conceive the causes of seasonal, secular, and cyclical changes as so many complexes, each made up of one or more causes which act regularly according to some "law," and of random factors which more or less often fail to cancel each other. Then we may throw the irregularities which are connected with the seasons, with the factor of growth, and with business cycles into the same box as the irregularities which we ascribe to wars, earthquakes, epidemics and misprints. In contrast to this heterogeneous collection of irregularities, we have left secular trends which, if not constant, change in some regular way, seasonal variations which, if not uniform, change in some regular way, and what one who took this view would probably call "normal" cycles.

From the theoretical viewpoint this conception seems clear, whatever difficulties might be encountered in applying it to time series. But is it the conception with which business-cycle statisticians work? Perhaps such an idea is implicit in the application of periodogram analysis to time series.[3] Perhaps there are champions of the "40-month cycle" who would accept the notion.[4] The majority of the business-cycle statisticians, however, find certain features of the idea ill adapted to their needs.

The men who analyze time series primarily with an eye to forecasting the future commonly accept the notion of regular trends and seasonal variations. They need standards by which they can test current developments and on which they can base reasoned expectations. Such standards they can make with trends and seasonals which change according to some rule, but not with irregular seasonals and trends. The forecasters believe themselves justified by the past behavior of many time series in setting up the standard trends and

[3] See the remarks on periodogram analysis at the end of the next section.
[4] See below, section vi, 3, (6) "The Duration of Business Cycles."

seasonals they need, and judging what departures from these standards seem probable in the near future. For while they admit that actual trends have altered and actual seasonals have differed in the past, they seldom find these changes very sudden, or very great. But when they come to cyclical fluctuations, they find less warrant in the past behavior of time series for setting up similar standards. The past changes in these fluctuations have been so sudden, so frequent, and so considerable as to make the notion of a "normal cycle" inappropriate. Not feeling justified in imposing a "normal cycle" upon their data, they have no means of distinguishing the regular from the irregular changes in cycles, as they distinguish the regular from the irregular changes in trends and seasonal variations. Nor can they distinguish clearly between the cyclical fluctuations and the irregular fluctuations of a non-cyclical character. All they can do is to note occasional marked departures from the course of events which it seemed reasonable to expect, and to search through descriptive materials for plausible explanations of these gross irregularities.[5]

The statistical analysts who are not attempting to make business forecasts hesitate to accept even the idea of "normal" trends and seasonals. As shown above, they have suggested methods for measuring seasonal variations which change from year to year. Also, secular trends pursue a meandering course when made by the use of freehand curves or moving averages; they become unsteadier still when obtained by taking ratios to items in other series. Such methods absorb into the seasonals and trends of time series a part of the movements which the methods commonly practiced by forecasters intermingle with the cyclical fluctuations. But even when changing seasonal variations and meandering trends have been eliminated, the residuals show many irregularities.

(2) Irregular Fluctuations in the Theory of Business Cycles.

No method seems to have been devised for segregating and eliminating from the cyclical fluctuations the irregularities not absorbed in seasonals and trends. The nearest approach to such a method is to distribute the irregular fluctuations by the use of moving averages or free-hand curves. Such operations do not show what the cyclical fluctuations would have been in the absence of irregular fluctuations;

[5] Compare Warren M. Persons, "Indices of Business Conditions," *Review of Economic Statistics*, January, 1919, Preliminary vol. i, pp. 33-35.

they merely show the combined cyclical and irregular fluctuations distributed in a new way among the months which are averaged together. And of course we cannot find out what the irregular fluctuations really were by subtracting the successive values of such a smoothed curve from the corresponding original items.

Yet Professor Persons has obtained one result of much theoretical interest by an operation of this character. Taking the value of building permits granted in twenty American cities in the 156 months of 1903-16 (a series in which the irregular fluctuations are marked), he subjected the original data to the following operations: (1) He eliminated the secular trend and the seasonal variations by his favorite methods. The residuals showed the cyclical and irregular fluctuations of the series in combination. (2) He computed the percentages which the twelve months moving averages make of the corresponding ordinates of the secular trend. This process (by averaging) presumably eliminates the irregular variations and seasonal variations, and (by taking ratios) the secular trend; but it does not eliminate the cycles. (3) He subtracted the items found in (2) above from the items described in (1). The irregular variations were present in (1) but not in (2). The resulting differences were, presumably, approximations to the irregular fluctuations. (4) He made the differences thus ascertained into a frequency table. . . . From the data in this table, he drew a rectangular diagram. Finally, to this diagram he fitted a normal curve. From the closeness with which the normal curve fitted the data, Professor Persons concluded that "the distribution of the irregular fluctuations of building permits is normal." [1]

May we not draw a further conclusion? If the irregularities of economic time series over a considerable period are distributed in the same way that errors of observation are distributed, can we not take the combined cyclical and irregular fluctuations of a time series without regard to the temporal order of their occurrence, interpret each fluctuation as one observation upon the behavior of the cyclical factors distorted in some measure by an error, and base our results upon averages drawn with due caution from the array of observations? The confidence we can put in such averages will depend of course upon the number of observations which each time series yields, and upon the way in which the observations in each array are distributed about their central tendency. This procedure is certainly less hazard-

[1] Warren M. Persons, "An Index of General Business Conditions," *Review of Economic Statistics*, April, 1919, Preliminary vol. 1, pp. 137-139.

ous than the attempt to decide what part of a given change in any time series should be ascribed to the failure of random factors to cancel each other. It enables us to utilize all the available statistics, and it gives some basis for judging the probable reliability of the inferences we may draw from them.[2]

In Chapter V, this suggestion will be elaborated, with the aid of the more adequate materials which will then be in hand. Of course, there is no thought of returning to the idea of a "normal cycle." For between the conception of an average empirically determined from the study of statistical arrays, and the conception of "normal" phenomena employed by economic theorists there is a vital difference. The theorist's normal is that which complies with certain conditions which he has laid down. It may approximate average experience, or it may be far removed from the facts of life—all depends upon the manner in which the theorist has chosen the ground for his argument. Even when the two agree closely, they remain conceptually unlike. To speak of average conditions as "normal" is to introduce needless confusion.[3]

In our dealings with irregular fluctuations as theorists, we are confronted again by the problem mentioned at the end of the section

[2] It may be asked: If Professor Persons is justified in computing the irregular fluctuations of building permits in order to find how they are distributed about their central tendency, would he not be justified in eliminating these irregular fluctuations from the residuals left by taking out the trend and the seasonal variations? Would he not thus isolate the cyclical fluctuations? And might not his methods, with this development, be applied freely to other time series?

The reason why statisticians hesitate to follow this obvious line is that in dealing with cycles they cannot accept the rough approximations to irregular fluctuations which will serve in testing the types of distribution to which the latter conform. With 156 irregularities in his frequency table, Professor Persons can suppose that the imperfections of his measurements of irregularities will cancel each other in large degree. He could not make such an assumption regarding the irregular fluctuations which accompanied any specific business cycle. In trying to get a curve representing a succession of cycles, it is small comfort to say that a distortion at one point in one cycle, caused by inaccurate measurement of irregular fluctuations, is probably matched by a distortion of the opposite sort at some unknown point in the same, or another cycle.

The only way in which we can invoke the canceling of random effects in eliminating irregular fluctuations from cyclical fluctuations is the way suggested in the text: namely, by collecting numerous cases showing cyclical and irregular fluctuations in combination, and ascertaining the central tendencies of these arrays.

[3] There is, however, one accredited use of this term in statistics, illustrated in the preceding quotation from Professor Persons: namely, the "normal curve of error" and "normal" distributions, that is, distributions which are described approximately by the "normal" curve. As pointed out by Professor Karl Pearson, who first applied the term "normal" to the curve developed by Laplace and Gauss, the choice was not a happy one. (See Karl Pearson, *Biometrica*, October, 1920, p. 25.) But the usage is so firmly established by this time that more confusion might be caused by departing from than by conforming to it.

upon secular trends. While we desire to discriminate as clearly as we can between the irregular and the cyclical fluctuations of time series, we cannot discard irregular fluctuations offhand as irrelevant to the understanding of business cycles. By doing so we should be tacitly rejecting without investigation some of the working hypotheses presented in Chapter I. Dr. Veblen, for example, holds that in the period from, say, 1816 to 1873 liquidation was "apparently always brought on by some extraneous disturbance," whereas since the 1870's seasons of prosperity "are pretty uniformly traceable to specific causes extraneous to the process of industrial business proper." [4] So also, Professors Arthur B. Adams of Oklahoma and S. A. Pervushin of Moscow argue at length that revival cannot blossom into full prosperity without the aid of some favoring cause which the revival itself does not generate.[5] Several other authorities assign an important though less systematic rôle to "disturbing circumstances" as factors in shaping the course of business cycles. In view of these considered opinions we cannot take it for granted that irregular fluctuations are to be eliminated from our theorizing, much as we should like to eliminate them from our curves. Even statistical elimination is desirable only in the sense that we should like to isolate the irregular as well as the cyclical fluctuations, in order to study intensively both types of changes.

6. The Problem of Isolating Cyclical Fluctuations.

From what has been said regarding the other types of changes found in time series, it is clear that the ambition to isolate cyclical fluctuations has not been attained. Our review of methods of computing secular trends and seasonal variations showed that even for these movements we have approximations rather than measures. Our discussion of irregular fluctuations showed that no statistician ventures to do more than smooth out irregularities in his curves by using moving averages or free-hand constructions. Inability to measure the net effects of secular, seasonal, and random factors separately, or in combination, means that we cannot isolate the cyclical fluctuations of time series by eliminating the three other sets of changes recog-

[4] Thorstein Veblen, *Theory of Business Enterprise*, New York, 1904, pp. 249-255.
[5] Arthur B. Adams, *Economics of Business Cycles*, New York, 1925, pp. 111-158; S. A. Pervushin, *The Business Conjuncture*, Moscow, 1925, pp. 54-61. I am indebted to Dr. Simon S. Kuznets for a synopsis of Professor Pervushin's discussion.

nized by our classification. And no one has yet devised a satisfactory method of measuring the cyclical fluctuations directly.[1]

What we can get from the statisticians, then, are the residual fluctuations of many American and some foreign time series after the secular trends and the seasonal variations (determined by some variant of the methods described above) have been eliminated. The process of eliminating these two types of movements consists in computing, or reading from a chart, the values which the trend, corrected for seasonal variations, would have at successive intervals of time, and then subtracting these values from the corresponding items of the original data, or expressing the deviations of the original data from the corrected trend in percentages.[2]

Chart 8 gives three examples of the results obtained in this way. To apply what has just been said to the chart: the deviations of the

---

[1] It is true that in his plan for ascertaining seasonal variations which change from year to year, Dr. King draws a "preliminary cycle curve" directly from the raw data— "a free-hand curve representing what was assumed to be the course of the cycle." But neither this curve, nor the "final cycle curve" which Dr. King gets after eliminating his varying seasonal indexes, purports to separate the cyclical from the secular and irregular changes. "An Improved Method for Measuring the Seasonal Factor," *Journal of the American Statistical Association,* September, 1924, vol. xix, pp. 301-313.

[2] To illustrate: Suppose that we have obtained the following results by analyzing a series showing the production of commodity X by months.

Ordinate of secular trend January, 1926, 900 tons.
Monthly increment of secular trend, 5 tons.
Seasonal variations expressed as percentages of mean monthly production:

January	90
February	100
March	110
April	80

Suppose also that the production reported in the opening months of 1926 runs as follows:

January	800 tons
February	1000 tons
March	1100 tons
April	700 tons

Then we can make the following computations:

1926	Ordinates of secular trend		Seasonal variations		Trend adjusted for seasonal variations		Original data
January	900 tons	×	.90	=	810 tons		800 tons
February	905 "	×	1.00	=	905 "		1000 "
March	910 "	×	1.10	=	1001 "		1100 "
April	915 "	×	.80	=	732 "		700 "

Results after eliminating the secular trend corrected for seasonal variations.

1926	In tons	In percentages of adjusted trend
January	−10 tons	99
February	+95 "	110
March	+99 "	110
April	−32 "	96

curves from their base lines do not show the cyclical fluctuations of the series included. What they do show are the cyclical fluctuations combined with the irregular fluctuations, among which are included the deviations of the actual seasonal and secular changes from the curves chosen to represent them.

Thus statistical technique in its present state enables us to picture cyclical fluctuations only in a distorting combination with irregular fluctuations which we cannot measure. It seems legitimate to believe that the cyclical factor or factors operate with greater regularity than the curves suggest. But we are not entitled to believe that, were the effects of all non-cyclical factors excluded, the deviation and amplitude of all cyclical fluctuations would be uniform. For cyclical factors influencing time series may vary from year to year, as many of the seasonal factors vary. Just as our conviction that many seasonal variations are not uniform from year to year rests upon what we know about their causes, so the opinions we may finally form concerning the uniformity or variability of cyclical fluctuations must be based upon what we can learn about their causes, rather than upon study of such curves as are presented in Chart 8.

Graphically we can represent these successive steps by the following segments of charts:

Although the statistical segregation of the factors influencing time series stops short of our desires, a comparison of the refined curves of Chart 8 with the "raw-data" curves of Chart 1 shows that the cyclical

CHART 8.

RESIDUAL FLUCTUATIONS OF TIME SERIES AFTER ELIMINATION OF SECULAR TRENDS AND SEASONAL VARIATIONS.

Percentage deviations of original items from secular trend corrected for seasonal variations.

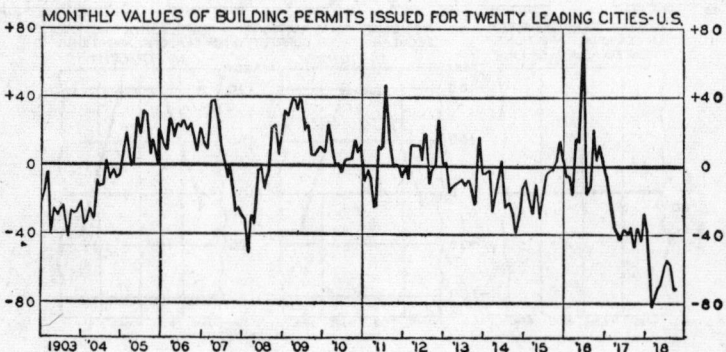

fluctuations stand out more clearly after the statistical trends and seasonal variations have been eliminated, however roughly. We shall therefore make such use as we can of these eliminations in our further work; but instead of ignoring trends and seasonals we shall study them both in their original combinations with cyclical and irregular fluctuations, and in their segregated form.

To readers trained in the natural sciences, it may seem that periodogram analysis should be substituted for the cumbersome and inexact procedure which has been described as the standard method of determining cyclical fluctuations. A few economists, notably Henry L. Moore, Sir William H. Beveridge, and William L. Crum, have made significant experiments with this method.[3] It yields excellent results in many physical processes which show strictly periodic fluctuations of a symmetrical type, and it should reveal any similar periodicities which exist in economic time series. Nor is the method limited to the discovery of simple movements. A periodogram analysis may indicate the existence of several or many periodicities, which when combined with each other give a curve so complicated that the uninitiated reader would not suppose it to be made up of periodic elements.[4] Perhaps it will be found that many of the time series used

[3] For explanations of this rather elaborate method of analysis, and illustrative results, see H. L. Moore, *Economic Cycles: Their Law and Cause,* New York, 1914, and *Generating Economic Cycles,* New York, 1923; Sir W. H. Beveridge, "Wheat Prices and Rainfall in Western Europe," *Journal of the Royal Statistical Society,* May, 1922, vol. lxxxv, pp. 412-459; W. L. Crum, "Cycles of Rates on Commercial Paper," *Review of Economic Statistics,* January, 1923, Preliminary vol. v, pp. 17-29, and "Periodogram Analysis," chapter xi in *Handbook of Mathematical Statistics,* edited by H. L. Rietz, Boston, 1924.

[4] For an example, see the "synthetic curve" made by adding eleven cycles of different lengths, in Beveridge's paper referred to above. (Opposite p. 453.) A section of this curve is reproduced here.

by the business-cycle statisticians can be usefully described by "synthetic curves" formed by adding together several periodic fluctuations which differ in length.

But the systematic application of periodogram analysis to economic series encounters serious obstacles. Comparatively few of the series which we wish to utilize have been maintained over a period long enough to yield satisfactory results when treated in this way. To establish the rather brief cycles in which the business-cycle statistician is most interested, it is necessary to have monthly, or at least quarterly, data, and long series of that character are few. When materials are available in this form, the seasonal variations and the irregular fluctuations so characteristic of economic processes tend to blur the periodograms. To leave out the periods in which irregular fluctuations seem to alter the cyclical movement limits the data available for study still more narrowly, and gives the investigator's personal judgment a considerable influence. To eliminate secular trends and seasonals before applying periodogram analysis is often necessary, but it may bias the results.[5] There remain two doubts more fundamental. Can we assume that the cyclical fluctuations of economic processes are, or tend to be, strictly periodic? If there are tendencies toward periodic fluctuations in given processes at a given point in economic evolution, do such tendencies maintain themselves under changing conditions over a period long enough to be revealed by periodogram analysis?

The most obvious of these obstacles to the systematic use of the periodogram method in business-cycle work—the brevity of the majority of the series which must be analyzed—presumably will shrink with the lapse of time. If the future is less checkered by catastrophes than the past has been, the troubles caused by irregular fluctuations will diminish also. The doubts now harbored about the propriety of adjusting series to get rid of trends and seasonal variations before beginning periodogram analysis may be set at rest by further work. Fuller knowledge may make us readier to accept the working hypothesis that there are true periodicities of various lengths in economic processes, and that these periodicities maintain themselves for long periods of time. Certainly we cannot say that periodogram analysis will not play a large rôle in future economic work. But it seems

[5] Compare Sir W. H. Beveridge's remarks upon this point in the article cited above, pp. 414-415.

equally certain that we cannot yet make it the standard procedure for studying cyclical fluctuations.[6]

IV. On Measuring the Relationships Among Time Series.

While the isolating of cyclical-irregular fluctuations is the end of one set of statistical efforts, it is the beginning of a new set. As we look at Chart 8, we grow eager to attack the problems it presents. The curves resemble each other in that all show at least the major fluctuations in business conditions which occurred during the periods they cover. But this resemblance, though clearer than in Chart 1, before the secular trends and seasonal variations had been eliminated, is still overlaid by striking and persistent differences. If a larger collection is taken than that offered by Chart 8, it is found that the waves in the several curves differ widely in amplitude. They differ also in timing; that is, the crests and troughs come several months later in some curves than in others. They differ finally in shape— some curves have roughly symmetrical waves, others suggest a very choppy sea. What use can we make of these results?

One course is to compile a general index of business cycles from as large and varied a collection of curves as we can assemble, all of them in the form illustrated by Chart 8. If that is our next step, ought we reduce the varying amplitudes of the cyclical-irregular fluctuations characteristic of different series to a common scale? Ought we try to get rid also of the differences in timing, and in shape? Or are the differences in amplitude, timing, and perhaps shape, matters which we do not wish to get rid of, but rather to investigate and use in framing a theory of business cycles? Do we, indeed, wish to make a general index of business cycles? Shall we not gain more by

[6] Colonel M. C. Rorty adds the following comment:

"The harmonic analysis can fairly safely be used to segregate periodicities which are known to be compounded in any series of observations; but I do not believe it can be trusted to establish the existence of periodicities as to the reality of which there is no other definite evidence. The fundamental defect in the harmonic analysis is that it will resolve any ordinary business time series into definite regular periodicities, regardless of whether any real periodicities exist or not. The probability that such resolution has any real meaning would seem to be infinitesimal when the number of cycles subjected to analysis is small and the number of periodicities required for, say, a 90% resolution of the time series exceeds two. Furthermore, when the element of lag is introduced, the value of the harmonic analysis becomes still more tenuous. I doubt whether it is possible to set up a complete and direct mathematical test of the method. Probably the best indirect proof of the lack of value of the harmonic analysis is to create an artificial time series by throwing dice and then analyze this series with and without assumptions as to lag."

concentrating attention upon the fluctuations of particular processes, bringing back into the discussion even the secular trends and the seasonal variations which we have eliminated?

These rhetorical questions suggest their own answers. If we are to make the most of the statistical contribution to business cycles, we must learn all that we can by studying time series separately and studying them with reference to all their characteristics; we must also learn all that we can by studying them in combination, or rather in varying combinations.

For either purpose we need a special technique. Whether we set about comparing the fluctuations of different series, or combining different series into general indexes, we must have some standard method of measuring the relationships among the fluctuations. Such a method has been devised, and we have merely to note how carefully it must be used. But attempts to apply the method lead us on to a subtler problem which statisticians are but beginning to grasp: Precisely what relations among the fluctuations of time series do we wish to measure?

1. THE CORRELATION OF TIME SERIES AND ITS PITFALLS.

Inspection of such curves as are shown in Charts 1 to 8 suggests various conclusions regarding their relationships. But experience has shown that conclusions reached by visual study are strongly biased by the investigator's personal equation. Everyone is likely to see in the curves what he looks for, and not to see relations of which he has no image in his "mind's eye." Moreover, visual comparisons are influenced much more by the conspicuous turning points in the curves—the peaks and the troughs—than by the intermediate segments. Finally, the conclusions yielded by such comparisons are at best vague, and quite incapable of numerical expression. Statisticians have therefore sought some method of measuring the relationships among the fluctuations of time series—particularly among their cyclical-irregular fluctuations—which will be objective, precise, and which will allow due influence to every segment of the curves compared.

Such a method they have found in the correlation calculus invented by Sir Francis Galton for the study of inheritance, developed by Karl Pearson, F. Y. Edgeworth, and G. Udny Yule, and applied to time series by J. Pease Norton and others. The coefficient of correlation expresses the relationship between two series on a scale which runs from + 1.00 (signifying perfect positive agreement), through 0 (meaning no agreement), to — 1.00 (signifying perfect inverse agreement).[1] In adapting this device to measuring the relationship between two time series, the temporal order of the items must of course be kept—a fact which renders the theory of probabilities inapplicable to the data and to the interpretation of the results.[2] Comparisons are made between the deviations of each successive pair of items from the arithmetic means of their respective series. Thus every item in each series has its influence upon the result, and this result is a mathematically precise average, unaffected (so far as the computation is concerned) by the personal equation of the investigator.

Yet the use of coefficients of correlation does not substitute mathematics for personal judgment, or make less necessary the visual study of charts. Just as the representative value of an arithmetic mean must be judged by the distribution of the array from which it is computed, so the significance of a coefficient of correlation must be judged by critical study of the materials combined in getting it.

This critical study should begin with the original data. When secular trends and seasonal variations have been eliminated in order to correlate the cyclical-irregular fluctuations of two series, the "fit" of the two trend lines requires close scrutiny.[3] For in this operation the correlation coefficient averages the relationship between two sets of cyclical-irregular deviations from two trends, and it will show close agreement between the two sets of deviations if the two trend lines misfit their data in similar fashion. One might expect similarity in misfits to be a rare occurrence. On the contrary, it happens often, and the "spurious correlation" it produces vitiates numerous

---

[1] Compare Warren M. Persons' chapter on "Correlation of Time Series" in the *Handbook of Mathematical Statistics*, edited by H. L. Rietz, Boston, 1924, pp. 160-165. Directions for computing coefficients of correlation can be found in almost all recent textbooks of statistics. For a fuller treatment see A. A. Tschuprow, *Grundbegriffe und Grundprobleme der Korrelationstheorie*, Leipzig & Berlin, 1925.

[2] Hence the significance of the "probable error" of a coefficient of correlation between two time series is not known. It certainly does not represent, as in other applications, an equal chance that a second computation, based upon a different sample, would deviate from the coefficient first found by no more than the limits which the probable error sets. See Persons, as above, pp. 162-163.

[3] There is, indeed, little point in correlating two time series from which the trends have not been eliminated, except when both trends can be representd by horizontal straight lines. For the results will show primarily the relations of the trends themselves—an aim which can be attained less ambiguously by simpler devices. Compare F. C. Mills, *Statistical Methods*, New York, 1924, pp. 410-412.

investigations in the business-cycle field. Similar misfits of trend lines are especially likely to occur in correlating

> economic series covering both the period of declining prices previous to 1897 and the period of rising prices following that year. Nearly all economic series dip below the linear trend in the nineties so that a correlation coefficient between their deviations would indicate that fact rather than the general correspondence of their fluctuations.[4]

Since there is seldom an objective criterion for determining the goodness of a trend line's fit, there is seldom an objective criterion for determining the representative value of a coefficient of correlation between two sets of deviations from two trends. All that correlation coefficients can do for us is to make more precise the comparisons which are warranted by careful study of the original data, the fit of the trends, and the character of the deviations.

There is another source of error in interpreting coefficients of correlation which statisticians are prone to overlook. The time relations between the cyclical-irregular fluctuations of economic processes may shift from phase to phase of business cycles. For example, the production of industrial equipment may lag behind the production of consumers' goods during the phase of recuperation after a depression, and yet decline earlier than the production of consumers' goods when prosperity begins to wane. Again, New York clearings have usually begun to decline after periods of prosperity some months before outside clearings drop; in the opposite phase of recovery the New York clearings show no such lead.[5] When such changes in timing occur, a coefficient of correlation gives an average relationship which not only has little significance, but may actually put the investigator off a promising trail. The only safeguard against being misled in this way is to study charts with close attention to the regularity with which fluctuations in one curve precede or follow fluctuations in the second. This warning is needed, because the chief use of coefficients of correlation in business-cycle work has been to determine the lag of one series in relation to another.[6]

[4] W. M. Persons, in *Mathematical Handbook of Statistics*, p. 164, note.
[5] See section v, 2 below, "The Time Sequence of Cyclical-Irregular Fluctuations.
[6] See Professor Allyn A. Young's discussion of the interpretation of correlation coefficients in his introduction to *Social Consequences of Business Cycles*, by M. B. Hexter, Boston and New York, 1925.

2. Transformations of Time Series in the Investigation of Their Relationships.

When economists began to study time series they took the data in their original form, whatever that happened to be. The difficulty of incommensurable units—for example gold production in million ounces and bank discount rates in percentages—could be met by drawing charts on which two arbitrarily adjusted scales were laid off. A neater shift was to turn the original data into the form of "relatives," with 100 to represent the values of both variables in some period chosen as the base. Another plan was to chart the logarithms of the two series. Still another was to drop the original data and compare the percentage differences between the successive items in each series.

Once started upon this career of transforming time series into new shapes for comparison, statisticians have before them a limitless field for the exercise of ingenuity. They are beginning to think of the original data, coming to them in a shape determined largely by administrative convenience, as concealing uniformities which it is theirs to uncover. With more emphasis upon statistical technique than upon rational hypothesis, they are experimenting with all sorts of data, recast in all sorts of ways. Starting with two series having little resemblance in their original shape, they can often transmute one series into "something new and strange," which agrees closely with the other series. In work of this type, they rely upon the coefficient of correlation to test the degree of relationship between the successive transformations.

Two recent examples of such researches may be cited. (1) Mr. Karl G. Karsten has studied the relations between the American data for freight-car surplus and shortage and for interest rates on 60-90 day commercial paper in New York. Between the two series in their original form there appeared to be no correspondence, for the coefficient of correlation was nearly zero (+.02). By making the freight-car data lag behind interest rates eight months, Mr. Karsten got a coefficient of +.402. By cumulating the deviations of the freight-car data from their trend, he obtained a curve which gave a coefficient of +.914 when correlated with the interest curve. By using logarithms of interest rates, he raised the coefficient to +.926, and by omitting the nine months, March to November, 1918, when interest rates were purposefully kept from rising above six per cent, he obtained a coefficient of +.950 between the cumulatives of car shortages and the moving annual averages of interest rates.[1]

(2) Professor Irving Fisher has studied the relation between wholesale-price fluctuations in the United States and the volume of trade. Starting with the Bureau of Labor Statistics index of wholesale prices and Persons' index of the physical volume of trade by months from August, 1915, to March, 1923, he smoothed the latter by a moving average, and found a correlation coefficient between the two series of +.54. Then Fisher turned the price index into figures which showed the rapidity of change in prices, gave this derivative series a seven-months lead over the trade index, and got a coefficient of +.727. Next he made an elaborate set of experiments in distributing this fixed lag over varying numbers of months weighted in different ways "according to the principles of probability." He finally found a scheme of distributing the lag which raised his coefficient to +.941.[2]

These interesting experiments may be the beginning of a long series of efforts to obtain high coefficients of correlation between various pairs of time series by casting them into new forms. Work of this sort is fascinating to the statistical technician. While very expensive, because of the endless experimental computations required, the possibility of finding marketable forecasting series may enable investigators to secure the necessary funds. And such work may yield results of theoretical interest as well as practical value. But it may also lead to grave mistakes, unless soberly controlled.

The proposition may be ventured that a competent statistician, with sufficient clerical assistance and time at his command, can take almost any pair of time series for a given period and work them into forms which will yield coefficients of correlation exceeding ±.9. It has long been known that a mathematician can fit a curve to any time series which will pass through every point of the data. Performances of the latter sort have no significance, however, unless the mathematically computed curve continues to agree with the data when projected beyond the period for which it is fitted. So work of the sort which Mr. Karsten and Professor Fisher have shown how to do must be judged, not by the coefficients of correlation obtained within the periods for which they have manipulated the data, but by

[1] See Karl G. Karsten, "The Theory of Quadrature in Economics," *Journal of the American Statistical Association*, March, 1924, vol. xix, pp. 14-29.

[2] Irving Fisher, "Our Unstable Dollar and the So-called Business Cycle," *Journal of the American Statistical Association*, June, 1925, vol. xx, pp. 179-202. The method devised for distributing the lag will be described below in section v, 2.

the coefficients which they get in earlier or later periods to which their formulas may be applied. Mr. Karsten points out that his co-efficient of correlation between adjusted cumulatives of freight-car shortage and the logarithms of the moving average of interest rates sinks from +.95 in 1915-23 to +.856 in 1907-14. Similarly Professor Fisher shows that his coefficient between the rate of change in prices with a distributed lag and the physical volume of trade sinks from +.941 in 1915-23, to +.58 in 1877-99, to +.67 in 1903-15, and to +.78 in 1923-24.[3] Controlled by such tests, the methods of Karsten and Fisher, or rather an endless variety of methods not _ess intricate, may be applied to the study of the relations among time series *ad libitum* without scruple—provided investigators are chary of in-terpreting their coefficients as demonstrating causal connections.

This caution is important. Statisticians know that such an aver-age of relationships between paired items of two time series as the coefficient of correlation yields does not prove that the changes in one of the series produce the changes in the second series, even when the latter series has been made to lag in the pairing of dates. Care-ful workers bear this fact in mind. Mr. Karsten, for example, though he obtained a high coefficient of correlation between his two series for years preceding his trial period, did not suggest that the number of idle freight cars is controlled by interest rates in New York. Nor would a coefficient of correlation, however high, warrant such an inference, unless independent evidence of causal connection could be adduced. Professor Fisher has reason to believe that the rate of change in prices influences the physical volume of trade, and gives a causal interpretation to his results.[4] But even in Professor Fisher's position an investigator should be cautious. It is not unlikely that by taking equal pains another worker studying the relations between the physical volume of trade and (say) reserve ratios, interest rates, profits, or payroll disbursements within Professor Fisher's period might get very high coefficients of correlation, and argue that he too had found "an almost complete explanation of fluctuations in the volume of trade,"—or several "almost complete" explanations.[5]

[3] See the two papers cited above, pp. 23 (Karsten) and 201 (Fisher).
[4] Something will be said about the causal relationship later in the present chapter (see footnote on p. 286); but the problem will be treated more fully in the second volume.
[5] Compare Professor Fisher's conclusion, "These correlations are so high as to leave little or no doubt that changes in the price level afford an almost complete explanation of fluctuations in the volume of trade for the above period beginning in 1915 and ending in 1923. . . . With a correlation of nearly 100 per cent between trade and pro-jected price-change, there is little left to explain." As cited above, p. 191.

While we cannot account for more than 100 per cent of the variations in one time series by any combination of causal relationships, it is not absurd to have several coefficients of correlation adding up to more than 1.00 between a given series and a number of other series which are regarded as exercising a causal influence over the first. Were such a set of results before us, we should have two quite different lines of explanation. The more obvious explanation is that the several variables correlated with the series whose fluctuations we are trying to account for are not independent of each other. In other words, the same causal influences are represented in two or more of the variables. There is much overlapping of this sort among economic time series. The second explanation is that in a theoretically perfect case of causal explanation by the joint action of two or more strictly independent factors, the two or more coefficients of correlation between the various series which represent causes and the one series which represents effects will add up to more than 1.00. Coefficients of correlation are not percentages, though the fact that they run on a scale from -1.00 to $+1.00$ has seemed to Professor Fisher sufficient warrant for calling them percentages. In the perfect case of exhaustive explanation referred to, it is not the several coefficients which equal 1.00 but the sum of their squares.[6] In con-

---

[6] To illustrate by Fisher's case: Waiving all question about the significance of a relation made to fit one period which does not maintain itself in other periods, let us accept his coefficient of "94 per cent" between price-change with a distributed lag and the volume of trade in 1915-23, and ask what part of the fluctuations in trade is left unaccounted for. The answer is not given by the formula 100 per cent $-$ 94 per cent $=$ 6 per cent; but by the formula $k^2 + r^2 = 1$, in which k stands for the "coefficient of alienation" and r for the coefficient of correlation. The coefficient of alienation measures the lack of agreement between two variables, as the coefficient of correlation measures the degrees of relationship. Substituting .94 for r in the equation, we get $k^2 = 1 - .8836 = .1164$, and $k = .34$. Of course, the coefficient of alienation is no more a percentage than the coefficient of correlation. We must not add 94 per cent and 34 per cent, concluding that we have accounted for 128 per cent of the variability of trade! But we may add $.94^2$ and $.34^2$, and say that their sum, 1.00, represents a theoretically complete explanation. If we insist upon using a percentage scale it should be that of the squared coefficients: $.8836 + .1156 = 1.00$.

Similarly with the results which Professor Fisher gets on applying his method of connecting price-change with volume of trade in other periods than 1915-23. The significance of his correlation of "58 per cent" in 1879-99 is to be judged from the equation $.58^2 + .82^2 = .3364 + .6724 = 1$; the significance of his correlation of "67 per cent" in 1903-15 is to be judged from the equation $.67^2 + .74^2 = .4489 + .5476 = 1$; and the significance of his coefficient of "78 per cent" in 1923-24 is to be judged from the equation $.78^2 + .63^2 = .6084 + .3969 = 1$.

Though calling his coefficients of correlation percentages, Professor Fisher does not commit the error of saying that a coefficient of "94 per cent" explains all but 6 per cent of the variations of the series which lags; he says merely that this coefficient affords "an almost complete explanation." (See preceding note.)

On the coefficient of alienation and its uses, see Truman L. Kelley, *Statistical Method*, New York, 1923, pp. 173, 174.

sidering how much significance attaches to a given coefficient of correlation, therefore, one should take the square of that coefficient, rather than the coefficient itself, as indicating the degree of relationship between the two variables, and compare with it the square of the "coefficient of alienation" as indicating the lack of relationship. And one should always remember that coefficients of correlation, however high, do not suffice to establish relationships of cause and effect.

3. Conclusion

All these cautions about the interpretation of results do not mean that one should hesitate to turn any series into a form which will agree better than the original figures with some variable one wishes to explain. On the contrary, search for relationships which are hidden by the form in which series happen to be compiled is one of the most promising, though one of the most arduous, lines of statistical research. Simple transformations into relatives, logarithms, and first differences have long been practiced with general approval; more elaborate transformations need no justification beyond fruitfulness.

Some hidden relationships between time series may be discovered by accident or by strictly empirical work. But the search is most likely to prosper if guided by rational hypotheses. These hypotheses usually occur to our minds in terms of cause and effect. What we know from non-statistical sources about business processes may suggest that the activities represented by one time series lead to consequences shown by one or more other series. Before plunging into the computations which such a notion suggests, it is wise to think out the hypothesis with care. Precisely what feature of the first series is causally important—the actual magnitudes as reported, the changes in these magnitudes from date to date, the percentage rates of change, the accumulated changes, the excess beyond some critical range, the ratio of the causal factor to some other variable, or what? Similarly: upon what feature of the series regarded as showing effects is the causal effect exercised? The suggestions just listed are possible answers to this question also. Is the relationship direct, or inverse? Is the effect immediate or postponed? Is the effect cumulative? Does the effect change with the phases of business cycles? All these matters, and in many cases others, should be considered. Often it is only by trial computations that one can decide the issues raised; but they are best raised before computations are begun, and then thought out again in the light of what the computations suggest.

In judging the relationship between any two series, how low a coefficient of correlation should one accept as "significant"? That is a question which statisticians often raise, but to which they do not give categorical answers, because much depends upon the character of the data and the purpose in view. When the aim is merely to find whether two phenomena are unrelated to each other, or related in some degree, interest centers less in the absolute size of the coefficient obtained, than in its size compared with that of its standard (or probable) error. Provided a coefficient is several times its standard error, a figure in the forties, or even in the twenties, suffices to show the existence of some relationship. But when the coefficient of correlation is used in estimating the value of one variable from given values of other variables—the problem usually met in correlating time series—a much higher standard must be set. Coefficients ranging from .40 to .50, which often pleased earlier students of cyclical fluctuations, and even coefficients of .60 to .70, are not very imposing when squared, as they should be in thinking about their significance for making such estimates. In many cases a result of this order is best taken as a sign that the investigator has found a promising trail, but is not close to his goal. A reconsideration of the causal relationships involved, and further experimental computations, may lead to much higher coefficients. An expert in research of this type becomes exacting; Mr. Karsten, for example, remarks: "in my own forecasting work I do not consider of much value a coefficient below .90." [1]

V. The Amplitude and the Timing of Cyclical-Irregular Fluctuations in Different Processes.

From the preceding discussion of methods of analyzing time series and their relations we score two gains. One is understanding of and ability to use the results reached by other investigators. The second is guidance in analytic work of our own.

Anyone who takes the statistical approach to business cycles develops a longing to assemble all the pertinent series and analyze them afresh upon some consistent plan, which shall incorporate the best ideas of his predecessors with improvements of his own. But, as must be clear by this time, the analysis of time series is a laborious

[1] Karl G. Karsten, "The Harvard Business Indexes—A New Interpretation," *Journal of the American Statistical Association,* December, 1926, vol. xxi, p. 409.

and expensive process, only less expensive and laborious than compiling the original data. Moreover, the changes made in results by
alterations in method are often slight. Hence every investigator does
well to go as far as he can in utilizing the results obtained by others,
even when these results are not precisely adapted to his needs. Limits
are set upon such borrowings by radical differences in methods, in
periods covered, and in data treated. When he approaches these
limits, the investigator must give up the quantitative approach for
the qualitative, or he must undertake the heavy burden of making
statistical analyses for himself.

On three topics of great interest we can learn much by the simple
process of assembling and comparing the results reached by others:
the relative amplitude of the cyclical-irregular fluctuations characteristic of different economic activities, the temporal order in which
different activities increase or diminish, and the way in which series
differing in amplitude and timing can be combined to throw light upon
the cyclical movement as a whole.

1. THE AMPLITUDE OF CYCLICAL-IRREGULAR FLUCTUATIONS.

While Chart 8 makes it plain that economic processes differ widely
in the amplitude of their cyclical-irregular fluctuations, it leaves us
with rather vague impressions, and we want measurements. A considerable variety of such measurements, however, lies ready to hand.
Analytic statisticians often compute the standard deviations of the
cyclical-irregular fluctuations of their time series expressed as percentages of the ordinates of secular trend corrected for seasonal
changes.[1] These standard deviations may be used as measures of the
average amplitude of cyclical variations in the economic processes
concerned, if certain precautions are observed. Technical defects in
the method of fitting trends and ascertaining seasonals affect the
percentage magnitudes of the cyclical-irregular deviations, and therefore of their standard deviations. Differences in the periods covered
also may influence the results; for the cyclical-irregular fluctuations
of a given time series are likely to vary somewhat from decade to
decade, even in percentage form. Still further doubts are raised by

[1] The standard deviation of a statistical series, conventionally represented by sigma
(σ), is computed by taking the arithmetic mean, finding the deviation of each item from
this mean, squaring the deviations, adding the squares, dividing the sum by the number
of items, and extracting the square root of the quotient. All modern text-books of
statistics discuss this device.

differences in the form of the original data analyzed, of which more presently. But if we make a considerable collection of standard deviations computed in similar ways for various periods and countries, confine our observations to broad differences, and avoid some obvious pitfalls, we can reach conclusions of importance.

In computing the standard deviations which we shall borrow, the aim of statisticians has usually been to get similar units in terms of which they can express the cyclical-irregular fluctuations of their time series, in order to make these fluctuations more comparable. Logically, the procedure is analogous to expressing the prices of the different commodities used in constructing an index number as relatives of the actual quotations for each commodity at some base period. Our aim is different. Several of the theories of business cycles reviewed in Chapter I, notably those of Mr. Lawrence K. Frank and Dr. T. W. Mitchell, rely largely upon differences in the amplitude of the cyclical fluctuations characteristic of different processes to explain the origin or the propagation of cyclical impulses. Like certain other features of time series which give trouble to statisticians, these differences of amplitude may give help to the theorist. At least we must learn what we can about them.

In Table 11 there are assembled several collections of standard deviations of cyclical-irregular fluctuations measured by percentage deviations from ordinates of secular trend corrected, when necessary, for seasonal variations. The rather miscellaneous array is classified first by countries, secondly by periods, and thirdly by the magnitude of the standard deviations themselves.

A glance over the various sections of the table shows that economic activities are characterized by marked differences in the amplitude of their cyclical-irregular fluctuations. In part these differences are due to the form in which the original data are gathered. The most notable case is the extreme variability of employment, which is represented in sections H, I and J of the table by percentages of reporting trade-union membership unemployed at successive periods. If the same data were converted into percentages employed, the standard deviations would be greatly reduced. Again, the standard deviations of the British series showing the market values of certain types of securities outstanding are not strictly comparable with the standard deviations of American series showing the average market prices of similar types of securities. Once more, standard deviations computed from data in monthly, quarterly, and annual form are not strictly comparable. Finally, there are differences of business usage between the United States, Great Britain and Germany which interfere with the comparison of, say, bank clearings, bank loans, and discount rates in the three countries. Most of our comparisons must be limited to items within a given section of the table.

Observing these restrictions does not much reduce the spread of the standard deviations; for the differences between economic processes in the same country and period are much wider than the differences between analogous processes in different countries and periods. In several sections of the table, the standard deviations run from 2 or 3 per cent of the ordinates of secular trend to 30, 40, 50 or 60 per cent. Even in closely related processes, like various banking operations, wholesale and retail trade, the prices of different types of securities, the more variable series of cyclical irregular fluctuations have standard deviations which are two or three times the standard deviations of the stabler series. This table is the statistical justification for the remark made in Chapter I, that we must conceive of business cycles as congeries of cyclical fluctuations in different processes which have widely different amplitudes.

TABLE 11

RELATIVE AMPLITUDE OF THE CYCLICAL-IRREGULAR FLUCTUATIONS OF VARIOUS ECONOMIC PROCESSES

A. American Series, 1860, 1862 or 1866 to 1880

Standard deviations, arranged in order of magnitude, of the relative deviations of the original data from lines of secular trend, corrected when necessary for seasonal variations.

Compiled from the Appendix to Persons, Tuttle and Frickey, "Business and Financial Conditions following the Civil War in the United States," *Review of Economic Statistics*, Preliminary vol. ii, Supplement, July, 1920.

	Standard Deviations
Call-loan rate on the New York Stock Exchange, monthly, 1866–80....	38.7
Clearings of the New York City banks, monthly, 1862–80............	24.8
Interest rates on prime commercial paper, New York City, monthly, 1866–80..	23.12
Interest rates on prime commercial paper, Boston, monthly, 1860–80..	23.0
Yield of U. S. Government 6's of 1881, monthly, 1862–80............	21.4
Price of ten common railroad stocks, monthly, 1866–80..............	18.1
Reserves of all National Banks, 5 calls yearly, 1866–80..............	11.7
Ratio of reserves to deposits, New York clearing-house banks, monthly 1866–80..	9.6
Loans and deposits of all National Banks, 5 calls yearly, 1866–80......	8.9
Loans of New York clearing-house banks, monthly, 1866–80..........	6.85
Wholesale price index (W. C. Mitchell), quarterly, 1860–80..........	5.63

TABLE 11—*Continued*

RELATIVE AMPLITUDE OF THE CYCLICAL-IRREGULAR FLUCTUATIONS OF VARIOUS
ECONOMIC PROCESSES

B. American Series, 1903–14 or 1903–18, by Months

Standard deviations, arranged in order of magnitude, of the relative deviations of the
original data from lines of secular trend corrected for seasonal variation.

Compiled from articles by Warren M. Persons, *Review of Economic Statistics*, Preliminary vol. i, pp. 36 and 191.

	Standard Deviations
Shares traded on the New York Stock Exchange	49.6
Unfilled orders of the U. S. Steel Corporation (quarterly before 1910)	32.3
Value of building permits issued for 20 American cities	20.4
Bank clearings in New York City	20.3
Interest rates on 60– to 90–day paper in New York City	19.66
Production of pig iron	19.15
Interest rates on 4– to 6–months paper in New York City	16.46
Average price of 12 industrial stocks	15.03
Dividend payments by industrial corporations	14.96
Number of business failures (Bradstreet's)	13.55
Imports of merchandise	11.91
Reserves of the New York clearing-house banks	10.83
Average price of 20 railroad stocks	10.18
Bank clearings outside of New York City	8.62
Deposits of New York clearing-house banks	8.20
Gross earnings of 10 leading railroads	6.07
Loans of New York clearing-house banks	5.37
Bradstreet's wholesale-price index	3.68
Interest yield on 10 railroad bonds	2.82
Bureau of Labor Statistics wholesale-price index	2.60

C. American Series, 1879–96 and 1897–1913

Standard deviations, arranged in order of magnitude, of the relative deviations of the
original data from lines of secular trend, corrected when necessary for seasonal variations.

From Warren M. Persons, "An Index of General Business Conditions, 1875–1913,"
Review of Economic Statistics, January, 1927, vol. ix, p. 28.

	Standard Deviations	
	1879–1896	1897–1913
New York bank clearings	24.55	18.21
Interest rates on prime commercial paper, New York	21.71 *	17.53 *
Pig-iron production	19.30	15.65
Industrial stock prices	14.11	15.07
Bank clearings outside New York City	12.03	7.98
Average of industrial and railroad stock prices	11.91	11.94
Railroad stock prices	10.89	10.12
Wholesale commodity prices (J. L. Snider's series)	7.78	3.77
Loan-deposit ratios of New York clearing-house banks	5.93	3.19
Loan-liability ratios of National Banks outside New York City	2.22	1.84

* Computed from percentage deviations from 5 per cent, adjusted for seasonal variations.

TABLE 11—*Continued*

RELATIVE AMPLITUDE OF THE CYCLICAL-IRREGULAR FLUCTUATIONS OF VARIOUS ECONOMIC PROCESSES

D. American National Banking Series, 1901–14, by 5 "calls" yearly

Standard deviations of percentage deviations from trend, corrected for seasonal variation.

From Allyn A. Young, "An Analysis of Bank Statistics for the United States," *Review of Economic Statistics*, January and April, 1925, vol. vii, pp. 36 and 101–104.

Standard Deviations

	New York City	Outside New York City	Boston	Chicago	San Francisco
Lawful money held.....	11.62	4.25			
Net deposits.........	9.64	3.41			
Investments..........	9.59	4.59			
Individual deposits.....	9.12	3.14	5.51	5.40	17.2
Loans and discounts...	6.80	2.96	3.84	4.02	17.0

	Individual deposits less clearing-house exchanges	Loans and discounts	Investments, except securities against notes and U. S. deposits
Pacific states............................	7.09	7.96	7.29
Southern states.........................	5.49	5.06	7.16
Western states..........................	5.36	4.92	3.62
New England states.....................	2.98	1.98	7.55
Eastern states, excluding New York City.	2.34	2.77	4.19
Middle Western states..................	2.30	2.62	6.97
Money in National Banks...............		5.9	
Money in circulation not in banks.......		3.74	

E. Velocity of Bank Deposits in American Cities, by Months, 1919–February, 1923

Standard deviations of the monthly velocity after adjustment for seasonal variation. From W. Randolph Burgess, "Velocity of Bank Deposits," *Journal of the American Statistical Association*, June, 1923, vol. xviii, p. 738.

	Standard Deviations		Standard Deviations
New York City.....................	5.98	Chicago.................	2.79
Syracuse...........................	4.74	San Francisco............	2.23
Albany............................	4.36	Buffalo..................	1.79
Boston............................	3.64	Rochester...............	1.22

TABLE 11—*Continued*

RELATIVE AMPLITUDE OF THE CYCLICAL-IRREGULAR FLUCTUATIONS OF VARIOUS
ECONOMIC PROCESSES

F. American Series Showing Volume of Wholesale and Retail Trade by Months 1919–1925

Standard deviations of percentage deviations from secular trends corrected for seasonal
variations.

From Simon S. Kuznets, *Cyclical Fluctuations: Retail and Wholesale Trade*, pp. 37,
41, 102, 114.

	Standard Deviations Retail Sales	Deviations Wholesale Sales
Mail-order houses.....................................	16.4	....
Music-store chains....................................	11.8	....
Dry goods...	11.5	16.5
Grocery-store chains.................................	10.6	14.4
Shoe-store chains....................................	9.6	18.1
Tobacco- and cigar-store chains.......................	7.9	....
Candy-store chains...................................	7.9	14.7
Department stores....................................	6.3	15.8
Five- and ten-cent store chains.......................	5.1	....
Drug-store chains....................................	4.4	6.2
Hardware..	....	13.4
General index..	....	14.8

Series "Deflated" by Dividing Dollar Volume of Sales by Appropriate Index
Number of Prices

	Standard Deviations Retail Trade	Wholesale Trade	Production
Shoe-store chains.........................	9.9	14.6	19.3
Department store chains....................	6.3	....	....
Grocery-store chains......................	4.5	7.6	10.8
Dry Goods...............................	...	13.3	....
Hardware................................	....	10.0	
Drugs...................................	....	5.1	
General index............................	....	6.7	

G. British Series, by Quarters, before 1850

Standard deviations, arranged in order of magnitude, of the percentage deviations
from the line of secular trend, adjusted when necessary for seasonal variations.

From Norman J. Silberling, "British Prices and British Cycles, 1779–1850," *Review
of Economic Statistics*, October, 1923, Preliminary vol. v, Supplement 2, pp. 254–257.

	Standard Deviations
Quarterly average market rate of discount in London, best bills, 1824–1850	30.3
General commodity prices at wholesale, by quarters, 1779–1850..........	5.3

TABLE 11—*Continued*

RELATIVE AMPLITUDE OF THE CYCLICAL-IRREGULAR FLUCTUATIONS OF VARIOUS
ECONOMIC PROCESSES

H. British Series, by Quarters, 1903–June 30, 1914

Standard deviations of the percentage deviations from secular trends.
Compiled from Persons, Silberling, and Berridge, "An Index of British Economic
Conditions," *Review of Economic Statistics*, Preliminary vol. iv, Supplement 2, June, 1922,
p. 189.

	Standard Deviations
Stores of Cleveland pig-iron in public warehouses	64.8
Percentage unemployed in all trades	43.8
Discount rate on 3–months paper in London	27.2
London bank clearings on stock-settling days	13.3
Exports of iron and steel (quantities)	13.2
Number of blast furnaces in blast	8.1
Exports of British produce (values)	7.50
Imports of raw materials, excluding cotton (values)	7.41
Bank clearings in 5 provincial cities	5.99
Sauerbeck Statist index number of wholesale prices of "all materials"	5.68
Market value of securities yielding variable incomes, Bankers' Magazine	4.3
Market value of selected British railway ordinary stocks	3.62
County bank clearings through London	3.34
Market value of local-government bonds	2.14

I. British Series, by Years, various dates—1913

Standard deviations of the percentage deviations from secular trends.
From Dorothy S. Thomas, *Social Aspects of the Business Cycle*, London, 1925, pp. 187,
200, 203 and 211.

	Standard Deviations
Percentage unemployed, "all trades," 1860–1913	54.6
Emigrants of British origin leaving U. K. for U. S. A., 1870–1913	21.3
Total emigrants of British origin from U. K., 1862–1913	19.1
Casual pauperism, 1883–1913	10.5
Production of pig iron, U. K., 1865–1913	8.77
Exports of British produce, 1854–1913	8.08
Sauerbeck's index number, wholesale prices of "all materials," 1854–1913	7.40
Indoor pauperism, 1857–1913	6.45
Provincial bank clearings, 1887–1913	5.25
Outdoor pauperism, 1857–1913	4.33
Per-capita consumption of spirits, 1856–1913	4.08
Per-capita consumption of beer, 1856–1913	3.83
Production of coal, 1865–1913	3.59
Railway freight traffic receipts, 1881–1913	2.69

TABLE 11—*Continued*

RELATIVE AMPLITUDE OF THE CYCLICAL-IRREGULAR FLUCTUATIONS OF VARIOUS
ECONOMIC PROCESSES

J. British Series, by Quarters, various dates to 1914

Standard deviations of the percentage deviations from secular trend corrected for
seasonal variations.

From Dorothy S. Thomas, unpublished data.

	Standard Deviations
Unemployed iron founders, 1855–1914	60.52
Unemployment, "all trades," 1887–1914	45.20
Value of total exports of British produce, 1855–1914	9.25
Sauerbeck's wholesale-price index number, "all materials," 1885–1914	6.44
Blast furnaces in blast, 1897–1914	6.30
Provincial bank clearings (Manchester and Birmingham), 1887–1914	6.03
Railway freight traffic receipts, 1881–1914	3.93

K. German series by Quarters or Months, various dates to 1913–14

Standard deviations, arranged in order of magnitude, of the percentage deviations
from lines of secular trend adjusted when necessary for seasonal variations.

Compiled from Emerson W. Axe and Harold M Flinn, "An Index of General Business Conditions for Germany, 1898–1914," *Review of Economic Statistics*, October, 1925,
vol. vii, p. 287.

	Standard Deviations
Market discount rates in Berlin, 1868–1914	27.90
Discounts and advances of the Reichsbank, 1872–1914	10.65
Ten-commodity price index of business cycles, 1898–1913	9.43
Index of stock prices on the Berlin Bourse, 1900–1914	8.45
Receipts from the *Wechselstempelsteuer*, 1900–1913	7.66
Value of commodities imported into Germany, 1892–1914	7.06
German bank clearings, 1898–1914	6.83
German pig-iron production, 1882–1914	6.64
Value of commodities exported from Germany, 1892–1914	5.53
Males enrolled in employees' insurance plan, 1904–1913	3.32
Monthly quotation of German *Reichsanleihung*, 1899–1914	2.36

Proceeding to particulars, we may set out certain conclusions which the figures suggest in quasi-tabular form. Regarding the volume of trade and production, the table indicates that

Retail trade shows fluctuations of smaller amplitude than wholesale trade in the same commodities.

Wholesale trade shows fluctuations of smaller amplitude than production of the same commodities, so far as our very limited evidence goes.

Judged by bank clearings, the volume of payments made in the great financial centers is far more variable than the volume of payments made in smaller towns.

The volume of foreign trade seems to be subject to wider fluctuations than domestic business outside the financial centers.

The volume of construction work in the United States, as shown by building permits, varies about as much as New York clearings.

Regarding prices we have no standard deviations for retail index numbers, which would presumably be small; but it does appear that

The cyclical-irregular fluctuations of wholesale-price index numbers have low standard deviations when many commodities are included, and moderate standard deviations (approaching 10.0) only when the indexes are made on purpose to exhibit cyclical fluctuations in a clear light. The "general level of wholesale prices" is one of the relatively stable factors in business, when monetary systems are not subject to grave disturbances, such as those caused by paper standards and great wars.

Stock prices are highly variable as compared with wholesale commodity prices, at least in the United States. (The British and German materials in the table do not admit of satisfactory comparisons with other series.)

Bond prices are even more stable than wholesale commodity prices, if we exclude the bonds of debtors whose credit is doubtful.

Regarding interest rates on short loans in the financial centers, for which alone the table gives data, we find that

The standard deviations are always rather high.[1] They range from 16.5 to 38.7. The London and Berlin rates in 1903-14

[1] It does not follow that the interest rates paid by most commercial borrowers are subject to wide variations. See Carl Snyder, "The Influence of the Interest Rate on the Business Cycle," *American Economic Review*, December, 1925, vol. xv, pp. 684-699.

fluctuate even more than the New York rates, a statistical result which may or may not be significant.

Regarding banking operations we have relatively full results for the National Banks as a whole, and by sections of the United States.

In all the operations for which the standard deviations of cyclical-irregular fluctuations have been computed, the New York figures are more than double the "outside" figures.

As among different operations, lending seems to be the least variable. The most variable item outside New York is the volume of investments; in New York it is the amount of lawful money held.

Another conclusion of theoretical importance is that the volume of coin and paper money held by the banks has larger standard deviations than the volume of coin and paper money in the hands of the public.

2. The Time Sequence of Cyclical-Irregular Fluctuations.

When several time series from which the secular trends and the seasonal variations have been eliminated are plotted by months one above another on the same time scale for a considerable period, the business cycles of that period can usually be traced in most if not all of the curves. But it is highly improbable that all the curves will reach the crests and troughs of their successive cycles in the same months. As a rule the crests and the troughs of the various curves are distributed over periods of several months—often over periods of more than a year.

Closer inspection shows that the order in which the curves reach their crests and decline, or reach their troughs and rise, presents that mixture of uniformity and differences with which economic statistics commonly confront us. The crests of a given curve may precede those of a second curve in some cycles and follow those of the latter curve in other cycles. But other comparisons show tolerably regular time relations over long periods. That is, the cyclical changes in certain economic processes appear to lead or lag behind the corresponding changes in certain other economic processes by intervals of time which are fairly constant.

This feature of the behavior of time series has been turned to account by statisticians interested in business forecasting. Indeed, it forms the corner-stone of several forecasting systems. If certain changes in banking operations regularly preceded certain other changes in discount rates by a regular interval, the latter changes could be foretold as soon as the former changes had been reported. Further, if an invariable series of such time relations between the cyclical fluctuations of different economic processes could be discovered, and if this series returned upon itself in the sense that the last set of changes in one cycle preceded the first set of changes in the next cycle by a regular interval, then business forecasting could be raised to a quasi-mechanical level. Needless to say, no such chain of events with links of unchanging length has been discovered. Perhaps no statistician has expected to find such a chain. But it has been a leading aim of statistical research to determine the time sequence in which important series pass through the successive phases of business cycles, to find cases in which this sequence is fairly regular, and in such cases to measure the average intervals by which certain series or groups of series lead or lag behind others.

The standard procedure in studying the time relationships among cyclical-irregular fluctuations is to start by plotting each series to be studied on a strip of translucent paper laid off with a uniform time scale. Any one of these strips can then be placed above any other and shifted to right or left until that position is found which seems to make the two series of cyclical-irregular fluctuations match best with each other. This matching may be closest when the same dates on the two strips are put together, or it may be closest when one series is made to lag behind the other by several months, by a year, or even more. Sometimes the best matching can be determined with confidence; sometimes it is so uncertain that two trained observers will differ in their opinions.

To test the conclusions suggested by this simple procedure, and to decide the doubtful cases, which are numerous, the statisticians resort to a more objective method. They compute several coefficients of correlation between two series, pairing the items in different ways. For example, if visual comparison of the curves suggests that the cyclical fluctuations of series A agree best with those of series B when A lags two months behind B, the investigator may compute (say) seven coefficients between the two series, one coefficient when

TABLE 12

TIME SEQUENCE IN THE CYCLICAL-IRREGULAR FLUCTUATIONS OF VARIOUS ECONOMIC SERIES

A. American Series, by Months, January, 1903–July, 1914

Compiled from Warren M. Persons, "An Index of General Business Conditions," *Review of Economic Statistics*, April, 1919, Preliminary vol. i, pp. 129, 182.

All the series included in each group have maximum coefficients of inter-correlation when concurrent months are paired, and these coefficients are of significant size. The coefficients are computed from cyclical-irregular fluctuations after elimination of secular trends, and, when necessary, of seasonal variations.

Groups based upon Time Sequence of Cyclical-Irregular Fluctuations	Comparison with Bradstreet's price index	
	Lead or lag in months	Coefficient of correlation
I Series which precede other groups in time sequence		
Yield of 10 railroad bonds	leads 10	− .72
Price of 20 railroad stocks	leads 10	+ .76
Price of industrial stocks	leads 10	+ .63
II Series which lag behind Group I by 2–4 months		
Shares traded in the N. Y. Stock Exchange	leads 12	+ .44
Value of building permits in 20 American cities	leads 6	+ .61
New York bank clearings	leads 6	+ .60
III Series which lag behind Group II by 2–4 months		
Production of pig iron	leads 2	+ .75
Bank clearings outside of New York City	leads 2	+ .70
Imports of merchandise	leads 2	+ .77
Business failures	leads 2	− .67
IV Series which lag behind Group III by 2–4 months		
Bradstreet's index of wholesale prices	concurrent	+1.00
Bureau of Labor Statistics index of wholesale prices	concurrent	....
Gross earnings of railroads	concurrent	+ .77
Reserves of New York City banks	lags 2	− .78
V Series which lag behind Group IV by 4–6 months		
Dividend payments	concurrent	+ .65
Loans of New York City banks	lags 4	− .67
Rate on 4- to 6-months paper	lags 4	+ .80

the Augusts in series A are paired with the Junes in series B, the Septembers in A with the Julys in B, the Octobers with the Augusts, and so on; a second coefficient when the Julys in A are paired with the Junes in B, etc.; a third when the Junes in A are paired with the Junes in B, etc.; a fourth pairing Mays in A with Junes in B, etc.; a fifth, sixth, and seventh when the Septembers, Octobers and Novembers in A are paired successively with the Junes in B. When all these coefficients have been computed, the investigator concludes that the closest time relationship between the cyclical-irregular fluctuations in the two series is that indicated by the highest of the co-

TABLE 12—*Continued*

TIME SEQUENCE IN THE CYCLICAL-IRREGULAR FLUCTUATIONS OF VARIOUS
ECONOMIC SERIES

B. American Series, by Months, January, 1902, to December, 1908

Compiled from Alvin H. Hansen, *Cycles of Prosperity and Depression in the United States,
Great Britain and Germany*, Madison, Wisconsin, 1921, pp. 26, 30, 33, 38, 39

Groups based upon Time-Sequence of Fluctuations	Comparison with Series Chosen as Standard for the Group Lead or lag in months	Coefficient of correlation
I Banking Group which precedes other groups in timing		
Cash reserves of N. Y. Clearing-house banks—		
Standard	concurrent	+1.000
Call-loan rates, New York	concurrent	− .477
Deposits N. Y. Clearing-house banks	concurrent	+ .956
Loans N. Y. Clearing-house banks	concurrent	+ .889
* Commercial paper rates New York	lags 3	− .686
II Investment Group, lags 12 months behind Banking Group		
* Prices of 10 railroad bonds	leads 2	+ .808
Liabilities of business failures	leads 1	− .542
Prices of 10 investment stocks. *Standard*	concurrent	+1.000
Prices of 40 common stocks	concurrent	+ .904
Shares traded on New York Stock Exchange	concurrent	+ .580
* Total bank clearings in the U. S.	lags 3	+ .557
* Building permits in 20 American cities	lags 3	+ .482
* Railroad net earnings	lags 6	+ .473
III Industrial Group, lags 8 months behind Investment Group		
* Railroad net earnings	leads 4	+ .756
* Unemployment (Hornell Hart)	leads 3	− .719
Pig iron production	leads 1	+ .797
Imports of merchandise	leads 1	+ .905
Bureau of Labor Statistics index of wholesale prices. *Standard*	concurrent	+1.000
Railroad gross earnings	concurrent	+ .857
Immigration	concurrent	+ .696
* Exports of merchandise	lags 4	+ .758
Commercial paper rates (see Group I) compared with Industrial Group	lags 5	+ .688

* Series omitted from Group indexes because of lead or lag.

efficients. If the coefficient is highest when the Septembers in A are
paired with the Junes in B, the investigator will say that series A
lags behind series B by three months; if the coefficient is highest when
the Mays in A are compared with the Junes in B, he will say that

series A leads series B by one month; if the coefficient is highest when the Junes in both series are paired, he will say that the two series fluctuate synchronously.

Table 12 shows two sets of results reached in this way by Professors Warren M. Persons and Alvin H. Hansen. Both these men publish the coefficients for several monthly pairings of each set of series, but only the maximum coefficients which they take to indicate leads or lags are entered in the table. Often the maximum coefficients are but little greater than those for a somewhat longer or shorter lead or lag. This fact raises a problem which requires illustration and discussion.

A rather elaborate illustration may be borrowed from Dr. Frederick C. Mills, who has worked out not less than twelve coefficients of correlation for different monthly pairings of an index of prices of industrial stocks and the index of "general business activity" compiled by the statistical division of the American Telephone and Telegraph Company. Dr. Mills gives these twelve coefficients for two separate periods and shows that the results differ considerably—a point to which we shall presently recur. The point of immediate interest is that in both periods the coefficients are much alike for no less than five different pairings. In the first period, with stock prices leading "general business" by 3, 4, 5, 6, and 7 months the coefficients

TABLE 13

COEFFICIENTS OF CORRELATION BETWEEN THE CYCLICAL-IRREGULAR FLUCTUATIONS OF INDUSTRIAL STOCK PRICES AND AN INDEX OF "GENERAL BUSINESS"

Based upon American data, by Months, 1903–14, and 1919–23
From Frederick C. Mills, *Statistical Methods*, New York, 1924, pp. 424 and 426

	Coefficient of correlation	
	1903–14	1919–23
Stock prices concurrent with business index.............	+.55	+.75
Stock prices preceding general business by 1 mo........	+.65	+.83
" " " " " " 2 mos........	+.70	+.87
" " " " " " 3 "........	+.73	+.88
" " " " " " 4 "........	+.76	+.85
" " " " " " 5 "........	+.76	+.82
" " " " " " 6 "........	+.76	+.77
" " " " " " 7 "........	+.74	+.72
" " " " " " 8 "........	+.71	+.66
" " " " " " 9 "........	+.67	+.57
" " " " " " 10 "........	+.61	+.46
" " " " " " 11 "........	+.54	+.33

range between +.73 and +.76. In the second period, the coefficients range between +.82 and +.88, when stock prices lead by 1, 2, 3, 4, and 5 months.

Whenever a close relation like this is found between the co-efficients computed for several different pairings, the statement that one series lags behind another by some definite interval, such as five months, hardly suggests the facts, and may suggest quite false ideas. The definite lag should be thought of as the central tendency of an elaborate array of time relations between the fluctuations of two variables. When we speak of a lag of say five months we should accustom ourselves to bear in mind the other intervals which may show agreements nearly as close. And when, as sometimes happens, the array of coefficients for lags of different length shows no central tendency, but varies in an irregular fashion, we should be extremely cautious about saying that there is a definite lag.

The importance of the full array of time relations becomes clearer when we consider the causal interpretation of leads and lags. A theorist in thinking about the relations between changes in the price and changes in the production of a commodity does not suppose that an increase in prices made in January will affect production in just one future month, say June. On the contrary, he supposes that the January increase will begin to influence production policies, and per-haps actual output, as soon as it is announced, which may be in ad-vance of the actual change in prices; or, rather, as soon as it is anticipated, which may be in advance of the announcement. The increase in prices actually made in January may have influenced pro-duction in the preceding December. Nor is the influence of the price change upon output likely to exhaust itself quickly; it may grow stronger for several months, reach a maximum, and then gradually decline. Conversely, the price influences upon the production of a given month, say, June, are not the result of changes made in some one preceding month, say, January; but the net resultant of price changes made in many preceding months, combined perhaps with price changes which are anticipated in the months to follow—changes which may not take place. Finally, the theorist does not trace the causal relationship in one direction only. He realizes that production reacts upon prices. The January change in prices, of which we have spoken, was probably influenced by the production of many months which preceded, and by anticipation of the production in months still to come.

So complicated a set of causal interrelationships can hardly be followed by statistical methods. But Professor Irving Fisher has shown how to take one step in advance by replacing a fixed lag with a lag which is distributed over many months. On comparing the rate of change from month to month in the wholesale-price index of the Bureau of Labor Statistics with Professor Persons' index of the physical volume of trade from August, 1915, to March, 1923, Fisher found that the usual methods gave the highest coefficient of correlation ($+.727$) for a lag of seven months in volume of trade. Six and eight months, however, gave coefficients nearly as high ($+.719$ and $+.715$). Giving a causal interpretation to the relation between price change and volume of trade, Fisher conceived the hypothesis that the effects of a given price change in one month upon volume of trade are distributed over succeeding months in accordance with the probability curve. He set himself to find out by experiment just what probability distribution of the price changes over time gives the index that correlates best with the volume of trade. As the result of many trials, he concluded that the best fit is obtained when the price changes are distributed along a "normal" curve having a logarithmic time axis, a mode lagging $9\frac{1}{2}$ months behind the change in prices, and "probable error points" lagging about 5 and 18 months. When the price changes of 1915-23 were redistributed in this way, the coefficient of correlation between the new index and the volume of trade index proved to be $+.941$.[1]

[1] Irving Fisher, "Our Unstable Dollar and the So-called Business Cycle," *Journal of the American Statistical Association,* June, 1925, vol. xx, pp. 179-203.

Our present concern is with the method of treating lags which Professor Fisher has devised; not with the time relations between fluctuations in prices and "trade." But we should note that statisticians interested in the latter problem have questioned the comparability of the two series which Fisher uses, and the interpretation which he gives of the results.

Mr. Carl Snyder points out that the index of physical volume of trade which Fisher borrows from Persons represents essentially fluctuations in basic industrial activity, while his price index is very heavily weighted by agricultural prices. That is, Fisher compares the price changes of one list of commodities with the trade in a decidedly different list.

Dr. Willford I. King suggests that the lag may be explained as follows: wholesale prices are made when orders are placed or contracts drawn; goods are manufactured at a later date; shipments and transfers come later still. Price indexes are based upon current quotations. Volume of trade indexes are based mainly upon manufacturing output and deliveries. Thus volume-of-trade indexes are "post-dated" in comparison with the price indexes. If we could take both price and volume-of-trade records at the same stage of given transactions—that is, if we could take volume of transactions entered into at the time prices are made, or if we could take the prices at which current output and deliveries are being made—the relations between changes in prices and changes in volume of trade might appear in a new light. As matters stand, what is more natural than that the changes in a price index should precede in date the changes in a trade index? But does this lead due to post-dating justify the conclusion that price change causes changes in volume of trade?

As Professor Fisher suggests, the principle involved in this study of time relationship "would seem to be a general and useful one." In practical application to any case, however, the method is exceedingly laborious and costly, because there is no way of determining, except by actual computation, precisely what form of the probability distribution applied to the curve which leads will turn it into the form which correlates best with the curve which lags. Until some far quicker way of distributing lags is devised, the method will have but limited use.[2]

The problem still remains of treating statistically the influence of the variable which lags upon the variable which leads. To apply this remark to Professor Fisher's problem: economic theory suggests that changes in the physical volume of trade react upon prices. Can this reaction be demonstrated and measured by the use of time series? So far as the writer knows, no statistician has attacked this problem. It would be interesting to see what results could be obtained, for example, by treating the volume-of-trade index, or some derivative of it, as the variable which leads, and the price-change index, or some derivative of it, as the variable which lags, presumably choosing a period in which monetary disturbances were less extraordinary than in the years which Professor Fisher took as the base for his experiments. If a significant relation were shown to exist not only between price-change and volume of trade, but also between changes in volume of trade and subsequent changes in prices, the statistician would have come nearer presenting the complicated relations which the theorist contemplates as real.

Time sequence among the cyclical-irregular fluctuations of different series is no more constant than are secular trends or seasonal variations. One illustration of change has already been given in

[2] Professor Fisher himself suggests a "short cut."

"By this method the influence of any given price-change is assumed to begin at a maximum immediately (i.e., at the very next month or quarter following the given price-change), and then to taper off by equal reductions for each successive interval of time. . . . By having only *one* parameter to vary . . . the labor is reduced by at least four-fifths. The only variable becomes the number of months in which the influence tapers off to zero."

This short method yielded somewhat higher coefficients of correlation than the long method in all cases which Fisher worked out in both ways. For example, in 1915-23, the short method, with a tapering off period of 25 months, when compared with the physical volume of trade, gave a coefficient of +.95, against +.94 for the long method. On Professor Fisher's own logic, the short method seems to be better as well as shorter. But, though taking only one-fifth as much time as the long method, it is still laborious.

See the paper referred to above, p. 198, note.

Table 13. While the period covered by the second column of that table (1919-23) is too brief to yield final conclusions,

> The results indicate that since the war the movements of general business have followed more closely behind stock-price movements than during the pre-war days. A maximum correlation is secured when stock prices precede the business index by 3 months (instead of 4-6 months as in 1903-14).[3]

So, too, Professor Persons found that the time sequences shown in section A of Table 12 were not maintained in 1914-18.

> The systematic relation of the fluctuations which held during the pre-war period was shattered by the outbreak of war.[4]

Apart from such catastrophic events, the improvement of communication and transportation speeds up many effects which economic processes exert upon each other. Statistically this quickening means a gradual reduction of the intervals by which certain time series lag behind others, as well as a shifting of seasonal variations.

A formal discrepancy between the two parts of Table 12 may have troubled the reader's mind. According to Professor Persons, in 1903-14 New York City bank loans and deposits belonged in the group of series which fluctuated last in the sequence, while the reserves of these banks belonged in the group which was next to the last. On the contrary, according to Professor Hansen, in 1902-08 these three banking series belong in the group which preceded all other groups in the time sequence. To reconcile these opposing results is easy on the theory that business fluctuations have the character of recurrent cycles. One can break into a round of events which keeps repeating itself in time at any point and follow the sequence back to its starting point. A second investigator can follow the sequence equally well by starting where the first man stopped. Our two authorities have merely chosen different starting points for their analyses of time sequence. By linking Professor Persons' last group to his first, one gets Professor Hansen's start; by linking Hansen's last group to his first, one gets Persons' ending.

Another point which requires notice here has already been mentioned in discussing the correlation of time series;[5] but it is so im-

[3] Frederick C. Mills, *Statistical Methods,* New York, 1924, p. 426.
[4] Warren M. Persons, "An Index of General Business Conditions," *Review of Economic Statistics,* April, 1919, Preliminary vol. i, p. 116.
[5] See section iv, i, above.

portant and so seldom attended to that repetition is in order. The time sequence of two series sometimes changes from phase to phase of business cycles. For example, one series may lead a second in reviving after depression, but lag behind the second in declining after prosperity. In such cases a coefficient of correlation computed in the usual fashion will conceal in an average two opposite sequences which may be highly significant. To guard against such misfortunes, the computation of coefficients of correlation to determine time relations should always be preceded by close study of the plotted curves to see whether the sequence of fluctuations changes during the cycles. If such changes do occur it may be feasible to compute separate coefficients for the periods of revival and recession, of prosperity and depression.

Finally, we should recall in connection with the study of time sequences what was said in the preceding section about hunting for the particular phase of one economic process which affects a second process, and for the particular phase of the second process which experiences the causal effects of the first. Economic theorists, like economic statisticians, have been prone to argue from chronological priority to causal relationship, without intensive analysis of the way in which the causal influence is exerted. To illustrate the danger of drawing hasty conclusions: A decline in one activity generally precedes, and so seems to cause, a decline in a second activity; but changes in the volume of the first activity may be controlled by changes in the rate of growth in the second. In that case, throwing the second time series into the form of first derivatives will show that changes in its rate of growth regularly precede the changes observed in the first series, and reverse the inference concerning cause and effect. No feature of business cycles presents more misleading cues than does the apparent chronological order among the cyclical fluctuations of different processes, and no other feature requires from the investigator a finer blend of theoretical insight with statistical skill.[6]

[6] A concrete example may make clearer the type of issues involved in such work. Mr. Karl G. Karsten's paper, "The Harvard Business Indexes—A New Interpretation," (*Journal of the American Statistical Association*, December, 1926) will serve.

The Harvard indexes in question, more fully described in the next section, are represented by three curves: Curve A showing changes in speculation; Curve B showing changes in general business, and Curve C showing changes in discount rates. Index A moves first. Index B, lagging six months behind A, shows a coefficient of correlation with A of +.77 in the pre-war period and of +.73 in the post-war period. Index C, lagging four months behind B, shows a coefficient of correlation with B of +.80 in the pre-war period and (according to Karsten) of +.36 in the post-war period.

Mr. Karsten develops a new set of working hypotheses concerning the causal rela-

VI. Indexes of Business Conditions.

So far we have been dealing with the statistical analysis of time series taken one at a time, or with statistical comparisons of time series taken in pairs. In ascertaining secular trends and seasonal variations, in isolating cyclical-irregular fluctuations, in turning series into new forms, and in computing the standard deviations of cyclical-irregular fluctuations, the investigator treats each series by itself. In computing coefficients of correlation, and in studying leads and lags, he works with two series at a time.

The chief value of statistical methods and results for the theory of business cycles lies in these intensive studies of the fluctuations of particular processes and of their relations to each other. But the theorist can profit also by a further stage in the statistician's program —the effort to combine time series representing different economic processes into general indexes of business conditions. If such indexes can really be made, they should help to solve many theoretical problems.

To find what the indexes of general business mean, what they do and do not tell about business cycles, it is necessary to examine the

tionships among the activities represented by these indexes. (1) He supposes changes in the security prices of Curve A to be determined primarily by the amount of "money" which in dull times flows out of business into the stock market for investment, and which in brisk times is withdrawn from the stock market for business use. (2) What counts in this causal relationship is not the volume of money flowing into or out of the stock market in a given month, but the fund accumulated in the stock market by the net influx and efflux of past months—just as the amount of a bank deposit account is determined by cumulated withdrawals and deposits over a period. (3) On this hypothesis, the movements of Index B should lead the movements of Index A, not lag behind the latter, as the Harvard interpretation holds. (4) Also, the causal relation between general business and speculation is inverse. Dull business tends to produce stock-market activity; active business to produce stock-market dullness. (5) Discount rates are controlled by the cumulated demand for loan funds from both general business and the securities market. The volume of the former demand exceeds that of the latter, perhaps by three to one.

Computations which Mr. Karsten made to test these hypotheses show that the cumulation of Index B, inverted, and given a lead of two and one-half months over Index A, yields coefficients of correlation with A of +.94 in the pre-war period and of +.96 in the post-war period. Similarly, by cumulating Indexes A and B, weighted one and three respectively, Karsten gets an index which yields coefficients of +.85 and +.94 when correlated with Index C in the pre-war and post-war periods.

Since these coefficients are on a decidedly higher level than those obtained by the Harvard Committee of Economic Research, Mr. Karsten argues that his interpretation of the causal and chronological relationships among the three Harvard indexes has more theoretical justification and affords a better basis for forecasting than the Harvard interpretation.

That Mr. Karsten's results cannot be regarded as definitely established until they have been subjected to critical examination, makes his paper all the better as an illustration of the argument in the text.

leading specimens, beginning with simple devices and **advancing toward** more elaborate constructions.

1. A Collection of Indexes of Business Conditions.

(1) Beveridge's Chart of "The Pulse of the Nation," Great Britain, 1856-1907.

Sir William H. Beveridge's chart of "The Pulse of the Nation," made in 1908 and reproduced on the next page, was one of the early efforts to present graphically that "remarkable phenomenon . . . the . . . cyclical fluctuation of industrial activity." Seven important variables are represented:—foreign trade, the bank rate, employment, marriage rate, indoor pauperism, consumption of beer, and capital of new companies registered. Sir William puts the trade-union employment returns in the central position, but he reverses the figures,

> so as to represent an unemployed percentage of 2.5 as an employed percentage of 97.5 and so on. Lines drawn through the successive lowest points of this curve—1868, 1879, 1885, 1894, 1904—cut it up into waves of unequal length, representing successive industrial cycles. The crest of each wave is at about 98; the depressions are anywhere between 89 and 94. The point of the chart is this, that the same lines cut up every one of the other curves into corresponding waves.[1]

No adjustments are practiced upon the data beyond reducing all the series, except the percentage figures, to a per-capita basis. Of course there are differences in the movements of the seven curves; but these differences are matters of detail, and Sir William concludes his picture of business cycles by remarking,

> It would be possible to extend almost indefinitely the . . . review of economic statistics and almost everywhere to meet the same familiar phenomenon. . . . It is hardly too much to say that, apart from the death rate, the only prominent social and economic records in which the pulsation of the nation's aggregate activities cannot be traced as a significant factor, whether cause or symptom, are the price of Consols and the price of wheat.[2]

[1] Sir William H. Beveridge, *Unemployment, a Problem of Industry*, 2d ed., London, 1910, p. 41.

[2] The same, pp. 50, 51.

CHART 9.

Sir William H. Beveridge's Chart of "The Pulse of the Nation."

Great Britain, by Years, 1856-1907.

(Reproduced from the chart in *Unemployment, a Problem of Industry*, 2d ed., London, p. 44.)

The scales at the left-hand side indicate respectively the actual Bank Rate of discount per cent, the percentage of trade union members not returned as unemployed, the number of marriages in England and Wales per 1000 of the population, the number of indoor paupers in England and Wales per 10,000 of the population, the gallons of beer consumed, and the nominal capital of new companies registered, in pounds, per head of the population. No scale is given for the Foreign Trade Curve. Unless the contrary is stated, all figures apply to United Kingdom generally.

292

With such a picture before them and with such materials to handle, statisticians wished to get results better adapted to analytic work than a collection of separate curves. Index numbers which reduce the price fluctuations of many commodities to a single series, raised the question whether it is possible to get a single curve to represent business cycles. And since business cycles cover but a few years, the year seemed too large a unit of measurement.

(2) Persons' "Index of General Business Conditions," United States, 1903-14.

By developing a more elaborate technique, Professor Warren M. Persons was able to draw a simpler chart of business cycles in 1919. He first isolated the cyclical-irregular fluctuations in a considerable number of time series in monthly form by the methods described above, and expressed these fluctuations as percentage deviations from the ordinates of secular trend corrected for seasonal variations. Since these deviations presented wide differences of amplitude from series to series, differences which seemed irrelevant for his purposes, Persons next reduced the cyclical-irregular fluctuations of each series to terms of their standard deviation. Then he made elaborate studies of the timing of the fluctuations of his various series expressed in this form, using coefficients of correlation to determine what series varied concurrently, what series lagged behind others, and how long were the lags. Finally, he averaged together the series which varied concurrently. In this way Persons reduced thirteen series to three indexes which he presented as "The Index of General Business Conditions." One index he called an "index of speculation," the second "an index of physical productivity and commodity prices combined," the third "an index of the financial situation in New York." [1]

[1] Warren M. Persons, "An Index of General Business Conditions," *Review of Economic Statistics*, April, 1919, Preliminary vol. i, pp. 111-114.
The series combined to make the three curves are as follows:
Index of speculation: yields of ten railroad bonds, prices of industrial stocks, prices of twenty railroad bonds, bank clearings in New York City.
Index of physical productivity and commodity prices: pig-iron production, outside clearings, Bradstreet's price index, Bureau of Labor Statistics price index, reserves of New York City banks.
Index of the financial situation in New York: rate on 4 to 6 months paper, rate on 60 to 90 day paper, loans of New York City banks, deposits of New York City banks.
For the revised form of this chart used for the post-war period, 1919 to date, see W. L. Crum, "The Interpretation of the Index of General Business Conditions," *Review of Economic Statistics*, Supplement, 1925, vol. vii, p. 226.
Recently Professor Persons has made a similar three-curve index which covers a much longer period than his first one. See his article, "An Index of General Business Conditions, 1875-1913," *Review of Economic Statistics*, January, 1927, vol. ix, pp. 20-29.

Although Persons called his chart "The Index of General Business Conditions," his aim was less to picture business cycles graphically, than to provide a basis for forecasting business changes. The merit of his index for this purpose was that, during the pre-war period, the cyclical fluctuations of the index of speculation systematically preceded in time those of the index of physical productivity and commodity prices, and that the cyclical fluctuations of the latter index systematically preceded those of the index of financial conditions.[2]

CHART 10.

PERSONS' "INDEX OF GENERAL BUSINESS CONDITIONS."

BI-MONTHLY AVERAGES, 1903 TO JUNE, 1914.

From *Review of Economic Statistics*, April, 1919, Preliminary vol. i, pp. 112-113.

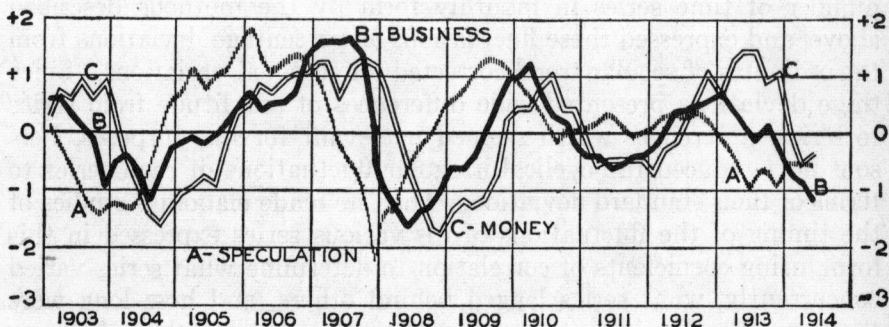

(3) The American Telephone and Telegraph Company's "Index of General Business Compared with Normal," United States, 1877 to date.

Later investigators have used Professor Persons' technique to combine numerous time series into a single index of business conditions. Of such constructions the one which covers the longest period of American business is the chart of "General Business Compared with Normal," 1877 to date, made by the statistical division of the American Telephone and Telegraph Company. In carrying their chart back to 1877 by months, the statisticians of the telephone company had to use such data as they could find. From 1877 to 1884 pig-iron output was the only series available. In 1885, bank clearings outside New York City and blast-furnace capacity were added. In 1892 Brad-

[2] See Professor Persons' paper, cited above, p. 114. Persons' latest statements concerning these lags are quoted below in this section, 2, (4) "Forecasting Sequences."

street's wholesale price index came in. Further changes were made in 1903, 1909, 1913, 1919 and 1921; but the compilers believed that

> Variation in the number of series used and in weights is of little importance, since all the series move together in the business cycle.[1]

Finally in April, 1922, it was decided to drop all data which contained a price factor, and to add several series of recent origin. As Colonel M. C. Rorty explained in publishing the chart,

> . . . it includes no measure of agricultural activity or retail trade, except as such items are indirectly reflected in freight movements and bank clearings, and it includes only a very limited list of non-agricultural raw materials. It is, therefore, primarily a measure of manufacturing activity and the physical movements of commodities. Nevertheless, with all these limitations, it represents, perhaps, as serviceable an approach as can be made to a single "all purpose" business index.[2]

In making this index, secular trends and seasonal variations were eliminated, the cyclical-irregular fluctuations were expressed as multiples of their standard deviations, in this form the several series were weighted according to their values as representatives of business conditions, and weighted totals were cast.

(4) Snyder's "Index of the Volume of Trade," United States, 1919-25.

While the telephone company's statisticians desired to cover as long a period as is feasible in their index, in the first of his indexes Mr. Carl Snyder of the Federal Reserve Bank of New York sought to cover a brief period as thoroughly as possible. For the years 1919 to 1923 Snyder was able to find no less than 56 series in monthly form

---

[1] *Method of Construction of "General Business" Curve.* American Telephone and Telegraph Company, Office of the Chief Statistician. New York, July 8, 1921, p. 3. (Manuscript.)

[2] M. C. Rorty, "The Statistical Control of Business Activities," *Harvard Business Review,* January, 1923, vol. i, pp. 159, 160. After the revisions of 1922 the items included in the index, and their weights, were as follows:

	Weight		Weight
Pig-iron production	20	Cotton consumption	10
Unfilled orders, U. S. Steel Corporation	10	Activity of wool machinery	10
		Paper production	10
Freight-car demand	10	Lumber production	5
Car loadings	5	Leather production	5
Net freight ton miles	5	Power production	5
Coal production	5		

which reflected some aspect of the fluctuations in the volume of trade. These series he arranged in 28 groups, which he classified in turn under five general heads, namely: productive activity, primary distribution, distribution to consumers, general business, and financial

CHART 11.

THE AMERICAN TELEPHONE AND TELEGRAPH COMPANY'S INDEX OF "GENERAL BUSINESS COMPARED WITH NORMAL."

By Months, 1877 to Date.

OLD SERIES DISCONTINUED FEB. 1925
NEW SERIES JAN.1923-DEC.1926 OVERLAPS OLD
CHANGE IN COMPOSITION OF INDEX

business. In working up his materials, Mr. Snyder divided the series expressed in dollars by appropriate index numbers of prices to eliminate the wild price perturbations of his period, computed secular trends and seasonal variations where necessary, expressed the cyclical-irregular fluctuations as percentages of the trends, and weighted each series according to the importance of the element which it represents

in the country's trade. He did not reduce the percentage deviations
from trends to multiples of their standard deviations; but averaged
them as they stood. For each of his five general heads and for each
of his 28 groups Mr. Snyder computed an index, which can be compared with his index for all of the series. Chart 12 gives his leading
results as revised and extended to 1925.[1]

(5) Persons' "Index of Trade," United States, 1903-25.

Valuable for comparison both with the American Telephone and
Telegraph Company's index, which covers so many years, and with
Snyder's index, which covers so many processes, is the "Index of
Trade" which Warren Persons made in 1923. This series is

designed to give a view of the combined fluctuations of trade,
transportation, manufacturing activity and industrial employment in the United States, month by month, since 1903.

[1] Carl Snyder, "A New Index of the Volume of Trade," *Journal of the American Statistical Association*, December, 1923, vol. xviii, pp. 949–963, and "The Revised Index of
the Volume of Trade," the same, September, 1925, vol. xx, pp. 397–404.

The 28 series or groups of series included in the revised form of the index and their
weights are as follows:

	Weights		Weights
Productive Activity		Distribution to Consumers	
Producers' goods.............	9%	Department store sales........	8%
Consumers' goods............	8	Chain store sales............	3
Employment................	6	Chain grocery sales...........	6
Motor vehicles..............	2	Mail order sales.............	3
Building permits.............	4	Life insurance written.........	2
	—	Real estate transfers..........	2
	29	Advertising..................	2
Primary Distribution			—
Merchandise car loadings.....	5		26
Other car loadings...........	2		
Wholesale trade..............	8	Financial Business	
Exports.....................	3	New securities issued.........	2
Imports....................	2	Stock sales.................	2
Cereal exports...............	1	Grain sales..................	1
Panama Canal...............	1	Cotton sales.................	1
	—		—
	22		6
General Business			===
Debits outside N. Y..........	8		100
Debits in N. Y..............	5		
Postal receipts..............	1		
Electrical power.............	2		
Series not published..........	1		
	—		
	17		

Since this chapter was written, Mr. Snyder has assembled in a book his various
studies in this field: *Business Cycles and Business Measurements*, New York, 1927.

CHART 12.

CARL SNYDER'S INDEX OF THE VOLUME OF TRADE

United States, by Months, 1919–April, 1925.

I
TOTAL VOLUME OF TRADE
(WEIGHT 100%)

II
(a) PRIMARY DISTRIBUTION (GROUP WEIGHT 22%)
(b) TOTAL VOLUME OF TRADE

III
(a) PRODUCTIVE ACTIVITY (GROUP WEIGHT 29%)
(b) TOTAL VOLUME OF TRADE

IV
(a) DISTRIBUTION TO CONSUMER (GROUP WEIGHT 26%)
(b) TOTAL VOLUME OF TRADE

V
(a) FINANCIAL (GROUP WEIGHT 6%)
(b) TOTAL VOLUME OF TRADE

VI
(a) GENERAL BUSINESS (GROUP WEIGHT 17%)
(b) TOTAL VOLUME OF TRADE

The technical methods employed are modifications of those used in constructing the three-curve "Index of General Business Conditions." Changes in the materials available for different parts of his period, and changes in economic conditions led Persons to make his index in three overlapping segments, 1903-15, 1915-19, and 1919-23. Before the war Persons thought it safe to use materials containing a price factor (outside clearings and values of imports); but from 1915 onward he excluded all series expressed in dollars.[1] Chart 13 shows his results.

(6) Miss Thomas' Quarterly Index of "British Business Cycles," 1855-1914.

Indexes of business cycles similar in character to the American series reviewed above are available for Great Britain and Germany.

The British index made by Dr. Dorothy Swaine Thomas, is a mean of percentage deviations from secular trends corrected for seasonal variations and expressed in units of standard deviations. The number of series included rises from two in 1855-80 to six in 1887-96, and seven in 1897 to 1914. Chart 14 shows the quarterly averages for the full 60 years covered.[1]

[1] Warren M. Persons, "An Index of Trade for the United States," *Review of Economic Statistics*, April, 1923, Preliminary vol. v, pp. 71–78.

The materials and methods used were as follows:

Series used	Character of average
1903–15: Bank clearings outside New York Imports of merchandise Gross earnings of leading railroads Production of pig iron Industrial employment	Simple arithmetic means of the percentage deviations from ordinates of secular trend corrected for seasonal variations, expressed in terms of standard deviations. The averages were multiplied by 8.62, the standard deviation of outside clearings.

Weights

1915–19: Net ton-miles of freight carried by railroads . . . . 2 Production of pig iron . . . . 1 Raw cotton consumed . . . . . . 1 Industrial employment 2	Weighted arithmetic means of percentage deviations from linear trends corrected for seasonal variations.

Weights

1919–23: Total railroad car loadings . . . . 6 Production of pig iron . . . . 1 Production of steel ingots . . . . 1 Raw cotton consumed . . . . . . 1 Industrial employment 3	Weighted arithmetic means of percentage deviations from linear trends corrected for seasonal variations.

[1] The series used are as follows:

Value of total exports of British produce, average of monthly items, 1855-1914.
Percentages of iron founders unemployed, inverted, 1855-1914.
Railway freight traffic receipts, 1881-1914.

(Continued on p. 302.)

CHART 13.

PERSONS' INDEX OF TRADE.
United States, by Months, 1903-26.

.... OVERLAPPING INDICES BASED UPON REVISED STATISTICS

CHART 14.

MISS THOMAS' INDEX OF "BRITISH BUSINESS CYCLES."

By Quarters, 1855 to June, 1914.

* CHANGE IN COMPOSITION OF CURVE

301

(7) Axe and Flinn's "Index of General Business Conditions for Germany, 1898-1914."

This is a three-curve index, covering the years 1898 to June, 1914, bi-monthly, corresponding in character to Persons' "Index of General Business Conditions in the United States" (number 2 above). It was made by Emerson Wirt Axe and Harold M. Flinn from nine series chosen to represent the fluctuations of "speculation," "business," and "money." The results are averages of percentage deviations from secular trends corrected for seasonal variations and expressed in units of standard deviations. In time sequence the speculation index precedes the business index, and the latter precedes the money-market index—relations corresponding to those found by Persons in America.[1] The three curves are shown in Chart 15.

(8) Annual Indexes of Business Cycles.

In addition to the monthly, bi-monthly, and quarterly indexes of business cycles made by averaging the cyclical-irregular fluctuations of more or less numerous series, several indexes have been made by similar methods from annual data. The most valuable of these series are:

Sauerbeck's wholesale price index, "all materials," 1885-1914.
Provincial bank clearings, Manchester and Birmingham, 1887-1914.
Percentage unemployed,—"all trades," 1887-1914.
Blast furnaces in blast, averages of monthly items, 1897-1914.

Dr. Thomas kindly put her quarterly index at the disposal of the National Bureau in advance of its publication. ("An Index of British Business Cycles," *Journal of the American Statistical Association*, March, 1926, vol. xxi, pp. 60-63). A chart of all the seven series which compose the index forms the frontispiece of her *Social Aspects of the Business Cycle*, London, 1925.

Another "Index of British Economic Conditions," covering the years 1902-14 by quarters, has been made by W. M. Persons, Norman J. Silberling, and W. A. Berridge. It is a three-curve construction, corresponding to number 2 above and to number 7 below. See *Review of Economic Statistics*, Preliminary vol. iv, Supplement, June, 1922, pp. 158-189.

[1] Emerson Wirt Axe and Harold M. Flinn, "An Index of General Business Conditions for Germany, 1898-1914," *Review of Economic Statistics*, October, 1925, vol. vii, pp. 263-287.

The series used in making the three curves of the index are:

Speculation:	Industrial stock prices.
Business:	10-commodity price index, averaged with a volume of business index, made from the following series:
	Pig-iron production.
	Domestic-bill tax receipts.
	Value of merchandise exports.
	Value of merchandise imports.
Money:	Berlin open-market discount rates.
	Discounts and advances of the Reichsbank.
	Bond prices.

CHART 15.

AXE AND FLINN'S "INDEX OF GENERAL BUSINESS CONDITIONS FOR GERMANY."

I.

The Adjusted Index of German Economic Conditions, A—Speculation, B—Business, and C—Money: Bi-Monthly, 1898-1914.

(Cycles).

II.

Volume of Business Activity: Monthly, 1898-1914.

An index of business cycles in the United States, 1870-1920, compiled by William F. Ogburn and Dorothy S. Thomas. Based upon 9 series.

An index of business cycles in Great Britain, 1854-1913, compiled by Dorothy S. Thomas. Based upon 7 series.

"Industrial Composites" for Great Britain, Germany and Italy, 1870-1913, compiled by Harry Jerome. Based upon 5, 4 and 2 series respectively.[1]

[1] For detailed methods of construction and results see Ogburn and Thomas, "The Influence of the Business Cycle on Certain Social Conditions," *Journal of the American Statistical Association*, September, 1922, vol. xviii, pp. 324-340. Reprinted, without the tables, in the book next cited, pp. 53-77. Thomas, *Social Aspects of the Business Cycle*, London, 1925, pp. 12-19, and 166-188. Jerome, *Migration and Business Cycles*, National Bureau of Economic Research, New York, 1926, p. 175.

While annual indexes are well adapted to certain uses, and while they may be employed in business-cycle work when data for briefer intervals cannot be had, they frequently give misleading indications of the trend of developments. When business activity declines rapidly in one year from a high to a low point, and recuperates less rapidly in the next year, annual averages may betray an investigator into thinking of the first year as fairly prosperous and the second year as very dull. Thus cyclical fluctuations get not merely obscured but actually distorted in the annual indexes. And of course no satisfactory measurement of periods so short as business cycles can be made with a unit so large as 12 months. Hence the annual business indexes may be passed by without more ado.

(9) Snyder's "Clearings Index of Business," United States, 1875-1924.

There remain the "single-factor" indexes, that is, the indexes made by treating some time series showing the fluctuations of an economic process which is affected by so many types of business activity as to become itself more or less representative of the general trend. The statistical case for accepting such an index has been presented by Mr. Carl Snyder.

After making his comprehensive "Index of the Physical Volume of Trade" in 1919-23 (number 4 above), Snyder sought some method of getting comparable results for earlier years. He thought that the record of bank clearings outside of New York, which can be followed by months back to 1875, might serve as a basis, provided he could eliminate the influence of price fluctuations. Of course the volume of clearings is affected by changes in the prices of all the goods men pay for in checks—commodities at wholesale and retail, securities, real estate, labor, and so on. For the chief categories of prices, Mr. Snyder could find, or make, fairly good index numbers. The problem was how to weight the several indexes so that they would yield an index of "the general price level," which could be used to transform clearings into a record of changes in the physical volume of goods exchanged. His criterion was that the best scheme of weights would be the one which, when applied to "outside debits," would yield the curve agreeing most closely with his comprehensive index of trade in 1919-23. After much experimenting, he concluded that the best results were given by weighting his index of commodity prices at wholesale by 2, his "composite of wage payments" by 3.5, his series showing "elements in the cost of living" by 3.5, his index of rents by 1, and by omitting security prices.[1]

Finding that "outside debits" divided by an "index of the general price level," made on this plan, gave a curve which agreed closely with the "index of the volume of trade" in 1919-23, Mr. Snyder felt justified in switching from "outside debits" to "outside clearings," and carrying his computations backward for 45 years. The construction of the index of the general price level by months for so long a period involved a bold use of scanty data. Even wholesale price indexes were not then available on a monthly basis before 1900, and the records of living costs, wages, salaries, and rents are meager indeed. But Mr. Snyder drove through his computations with the best materials he could gather, interpolated freely, and published his index for every month from 1875 to 1924.[2]

With his price index in hand, Snyder compiled the record of outside clearings from *The Public* and the *Commercial and Financial Chronicle,* and divided the total for each month by the corresponding item in the price index. To the resulting series, which he interpreted as showing fluctuations in the physical volume of trade, he fitted a parabolic trend. The percentage deviations from the trend, corrected for seasonal variations, and smoothed by a three-months moving average, constitute the "Clearings Index of Business," which is presented in Chart 16.[3]

(10) Frickey's Index of Outside Clearings, United States, 1875-1914.

On the same chart is presented a second index of outside clearings made upon a different plan by Mr. Edwin Frickey. Believing that, in the period before 1903, the introduction of new clearing houses at irregular dates appreciably distorted the series, Frickey decided to base his index upon the clearings in seven cities for which substantially complete figures can be had monthly since 1875, and which in the test period 1903-14 give totals agreeing closely in their cyclical-irregular fluctuations with the aggregates for all clearing houses outside of New York. The cities selected are Baltimore, Chicago, Cincinnati, Cleveland, Philadelphia, Pittsburgh, and San Francisco.

[1] It may be noted that these weights differ widely from those which our data concerning the volume of wholesale and retail trade, and wage payments would suggest. See Chapter II, section v.
[2] Carl Snyder, "A New Index of the General Price Level from 1875," *Journal of the American Statistical Association,* June, 1924, vol. xix, pp. 189-195.
[3] Carl Snyder, "A New Clearings Index of Business for Fifty Years," *Journal of the American Statistical Association,* September, 1924, vol. xix, pp. 329-335.

CHART 16.

SNYDER'S "CLEARINGS INDEX OF BUSINESS" AND FRICKEY'S "INDEX OF OUTSIDE CLEARINGS."

United States, by Months, 1875-1926 and 1875-1914.

A—Frickey's "Index of Outside Clearings" (Aggregate Bank Clearings for 7 Selected Cities): Relatives to ordinates of trend, adjusted for seasonal variations.

B—Snyder's "Clearings Index of Business" (Bank Clearings Outside New York City, 1875-1918; Debits Outside New York City, 1919-1926): Three-months' moving averages of relatives to ordinates of trend, adjusted for seasonal variations and price changes.

*Change in composition of index.

Casting up their total clearings each month, Mr. Frickey fitted a line of secular trend, made corrections for seasonal variations, and found the percentage deviations from the moving base thus obtained. Unlike Mr. Snyder, he attempted no correction for changes in prices; but broke off his index in 1914, just before the great price revolution began.[1]

(11) Snyder's "Index of Deposits Activity," United States, 1875-1924.

From data collected by the Federal Reserve Bank of New York, Dr. W. Randolph Burgess showed that the rate of turnover of bank deposits in eight reporting cities is subject to a wide cyclical swing.[1] A comparison of the individual deposits in about 760 banks belonging to the Federal Reserve System with clearings in 141 leading centers confirmed this conclusion. Further, the fluctuations in the turnover rate of the deposits in these banks, duly adjusted, agreed closely with the fluctuations of Snyder's comprehensive index of the physical volume of trade in 1919-23.

These facts suggested to Mr. Snyder that the velocity of bank deposits constitutes another index of business conditions, an index which he determined to carry back by months to 1875 as a check upon his Clearings Index. As data Snyder used the total bank clearings of the country, and the individual deposits of all National Banks. The latter figures are given at slightly irregular intervals five (now four) times a year. Resorting to interpolation, Mr. Snyder made up a table of individual deposits by months, divided these figures into monthly clearings, used seven-year moving averages as a trend, found the percentage deviations of his ratios from this trend, corrected the percentages for seasonal variations, and finally smoothed his curve by three-months moving averages. Thus he got an "Index of Deposits Activity," which he thought showed a gratifying correspondence with his Clearings Index. The two curves are compared in Chart 17.[2]

2. A CRITIQUE OF THE INDEXES OF BUSINESS CONDITIONS.

Before making use of the indexes assembled in the preceding section, we must examine them critically.

[1] Edwin Frickey, "Bank Clearings Outside New York City, 1875-1914," *Review of Economic Statistics*, October, 1925, vol. vii, pp. 252-262.
[1] See above, Chapter II, section iv, 4.
[2] Carl Snyder, "A New Index of Business Activity," *Journal of the American Statistical Association*, March, 1924, vol. xix, pp. 36-41, and "Deposits Activity as a Measure of Business Activity," *Review of Economic Statistics*, October, 1924, vol. vi, pp. 253-259.

CHART 17.

SNYDER'S "INDEX OF DEPOSITS ACTIVITY" COMPARED WITH HIS "CLEARINGS INDEX OF BUSINESS."

United States, by Months, 1875-1926.

A—Index of Deposits Activity: three-months' moving averages adjusted for seasonal variations and moving average trend.

B—Clearings Index of Business (bank clearings outside New York City, 1875-1918; debits outside New York City, 1919-1926): three-months' moving averages of deviations from trend, adjusted for seasonal variations and price changes.

At the outset, it should be noted that none of the indexes give, or are meant to give, an adequate picture of business cycles. For, as has been said several times, business cycles are congeries of cyclical fluctuations in a large number of economic activities, fluctuations which differ widely in amplitude and considerably in timing. Such intricate phenomena cannot be presented adequately by any simple device. A real chart of one business cycle would be a hopelessly complex tangle of hundreds of curves. Doubtless the shading produced in such a chart by the concentration of lines in certain areas and their dispersion in others would give an interesting total effect. A faint impression of this effect may be gathered by plotting on a large scale for one cycle 27 of the series, or groups of series, which Carl Snyder uses in the construction of his volume-of-trade index.

Anyone who dwells upon the intricacies of Chart 18, made in this way, will grant not only that the business indexes fail to picture business cycles, but also that faithful pictures would be of doubtful value. In dealing with price fluctuations we have learned to use index numbers which represent in a single time series the net resultants of very many dissimilar changes. These price indexes are far from adequate to show all we need to know about price fluctuations; but they are an indispensable tool even to those investigators who are beginning to go back of them in order to study the successive arrays of price changes which the index numbers condense into a single set of averages. Business fluctuations are far more complicated than price fluctuations; for they include the latter as just one strand interwoven with fluctuations in employment, incomes, consumption, production, transportation, commerce, and finance. Precisely because the full facts are so complicated, we need a device, or devices, for showing simply the general drift of all the changes. Such "indexes of general business conditions" may mislead us, of course, just as price indexes may mislead the unwary; but they may also prove a most useful instrument for gaining clear insights, if we remember their limitations. They will not enable us to dispense with more elaborate studies of the interrelationships among particular series, but they should supplement and summarize what we can learn by more intensive analysis.

Do the existing indexes meet our need? Do they show the general drift of business cycles accurately? How can they be improved?

It may seem that the neatest way to treat indexes of business conditions is to define the purpose they serve, to show what materials and methods are appropriate to that purpose, and to evaluate

CHART 18.

One Business Cycle, United States, 1919-21, Shown by a Plot of 27 of Its
Components.

Twelve of the Components Used in Snyder's Volume-of-Trade Index to Represent
Productive Activity and *Primary Distribution*.

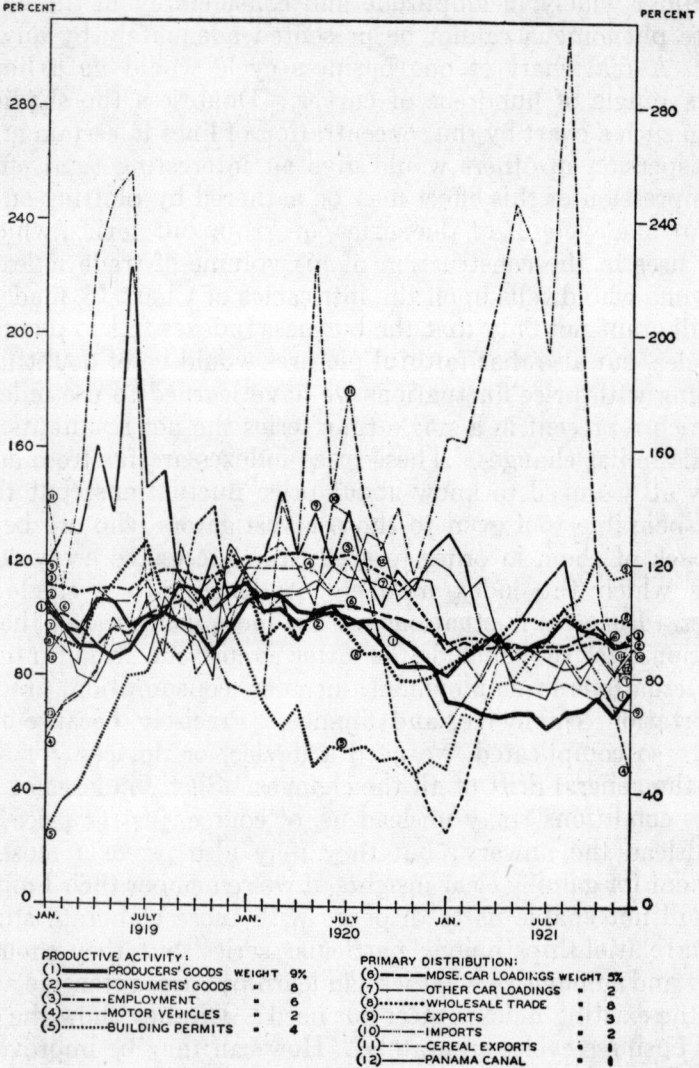

PRODUCTIVE ACTIVITY:
(1) PRODUCERS' GOODS   WEIGHT 9%
(2) CONSUMERS' GOODS   "   8
(3) EMPLOYMENT   "   6
(4) MOTOR VEHICLES   "   2
(5) BUILDING PERMITS   "   4

PRIMARY DISTRIBUTION:
(6) MDSE. CAR LOADINGS WEIGHT 5%
(7) OTHER CAR LOADINGS "   2
(8) WHOLESALE TRADE   "   6
(9) EXPORTS   "   3
(10) IMPORTS   "   2
(11) CEREAL EXPORTS   "   1
(12) PANAMA CANAL   "   1

CHART 18 (*Continued*).

ONE BUSINESS CYCLE, UNITED STATES, 1919-1921, SHOWN BY A PLOT OF 27 OF ITS
COMPONENTS.

Fifteen of the Components Used in Snyder's Volume-of-Trade Index to Represent
Distribution to Consumers, Finance, and *General Business.*

PER CENT   PERCENT

DISTRIBUTION TO CONSUMER:
(13) DEPARTMENT STORES	WEIGHT	8%
(14) CHAIN STORES	"	3
(15) CHAIN GROCERIES	"	6
(16) MAIL ORDER	"	3
(17) LIFE INSURANCE	"	2
(18) REAL ESTATE TRANSFERS	"	2
(19) ADVERTISING	"	2

FINANCIAL:
(20) NEW SECURITIES	WEIGHT	2%
(21) STOCK SALES	"	2
(22) GRAIN SALES	"	1
(23) COTTON SALES	"	1

GENERAL BUSINESS: *
(24) DEBITS OUTSIDE N.Y.C.	WEIGHT	8 %
(25) DEBITS N.Y.C.	"	5
(26) POSTAL RECEIPTS	"	1
(27) ELECTRICAL POWER	"	2

* ONE OF THE SERIES IN THIS GROUP (WEIGHT 1%) UNAVAILABLE.

the existing indexes by the canons thus provided. But that procedure assumes some single purpose to be served by business-cycle indexes, a purpose so definite that it dictates an ideal set of materials and an ideal set of methods. This assumption is no more valid in our field than in the better-explored field of wholesale-price indexes. Certainly the purposes for which the statisticians whose indexes we have reviewed designed their series were not all the same, and certainly there is a use to which every one of their series can be put.

We can accomplish more by reversing the procedure. Instead of starting with some single purpose to be served and criticizing the existing indexes for their ill adaptation to this use, we shall start with the materials and methods employed in making the existing indexes, and consider what the results mean and to what uses they may be put. Constructive suggestions of practical value in future work are more likely to come out of a discussion which regards divergent purposes and limited data than out of a speculation spun from some definition.

Round the technique of making index numbers of prices an extensive literature has grown up. This literature warns us that we are entering a field where none but statistical experts feel comfortable. On the making of business indexes there has been but little critical discussion so far, unless we put under that head the preliminary processes of eliminating secular trends and seasonal variations. Our problem stands now much as the price-index problem stood in Jevons' youth. Having little to guide me, I cannot go far, and I may readily go wrong.

The chief conclusion to which analysis leads is that the various methods used in making indexes of business conditions produce, not rival measures of the same variable, but indexes of different variables. If we can become clear just what the variable is which each index relates to, we can tell for what uses the several indexes are adapted.

(1) Indexes of the Pecuniary Volume of Business.

Of the variables to which the indexes relate, the most comprehensive, and yet the simplest, is the pecuniary volume of business transactions. We conceive of it as the aggregate made up of all the values exchanged in a country month by month—not merely commodities in the usual sense, but also real estate, securities, funds loaned and repaid, interest, rents, services of all sorts from manual labor to professional advice, transportation, storage, publicity—to repeat, every good exchanged for a price, counted at every exchange.

The only *measure* of this variable is its own aggregate value. In the United States we now have data which enable us to fix the order of magnitude attained by the dollar volume of payments, and even to venture rough estimates of how many billions it comes to. Such estimates, indeed, have already been given on an annual basis in Chapter II.[1]

To these rough estimates we might add a monthly *index* of changes in the dollar volume of payments, built up from series showing bank debits, retail sales, payroll disbursements, amusement receipts, and the like. We could argue that such series, when properly selected and combined with an eye to their relative importance and to overlaps, give partial totals whose monthly variations probably represent approximately the variations in the aggregate volume.

If we felt sufficient confidence in the figures to elaborate still further, we might tie the monthly index to the annual estimates of the aggregate volume of payments, and say that we were approximating the monthly aggregates. Finally, we might eliminate the secular trend and seasonal variations of our series, if we had data for a sufficient period, and present the results in billions of dollars or in percentages, as showing the cyclical-irregular fluctuations of the pecuniary volume of transactions.

Only one of the business indexes reviewed above relates directly to this variable—Mr. Frickey's series for bank clearings in seven American cities from 1875 to 1914. In technical parlance, however, Frickey's results are not index numbers, but a series of relatives computed on a moving base (each month the ordinate of secular trend, adjusted for seasonal variation, equals 100). Mr. Frickey calls them "a continuous monthly index of business activity as indicated by the fluctuations of bank clearings." [2] The only form of business activity which bank clearings show directly, is the amount of payments made.

Doubtless, this partial record of payments is the best single indicator of the pecuniary volume of trade for the years before bank debits were compiled. But we are not sure whether bank clearings,

[1] See Table 9 above, Chapter II, section v, 4, "The Flow of Payments Among Business Enterprises."
[2] Edwin Frickey, "Bank Clearings Outside New York City, 1875-1914," *Review of Economic Statistics,* October, 1925, vol. vii, p. 252.

even with New York City omitted, give a just impression of the amplitude of the cyclical-irregular fluctuations in the aggregate of payments. For the fluctuations of clearings probably have a larger amplitude than the fluctuations of payments in coin and paper money. And it must be recalled that the volume of payments made does not parallel closely the dollar volume of goods exchanged day by day. Many of the checks cleared are "cash" payments for goods just bought; a few are advance payments for goods to be received in the future, but the majority are payments for goods received some time in the past.[3] Much business is done three times over so to speak, advance orders are placed, or contracts for future performances are made; somewhat later the goods ordered are shipped or the contract work is performed; later still the payments are made. When borrowed funds are used, the scheme is still more complicated, and the pecuniary volume of exchanging growing out of a given operation is enhanced by the making and repaying of loans. We have little information about the volume of the several types of operations, or about the average lags of deliveries behind orders, and of payments behind deliveries. An ideally complete index of pecuniary transactions would have at least three curves, one showing commitments entered into each month, one showing current transfers of goods in dollar values, and one showing payments. The third curve is the only one we can draw with any confidence. But it is important to remember that the two curves we cannot draw represent actual processes of great moment, which certainly differ in timing, and probably differ in amplitude of fluctuation from the process typified by bank clearings.

The reason why few investigators have dealt with the pecuniary volume of trade must be that they have believed other aspects of business activity to be more significant. Almost all of the business indexes have been compiled since the price revolution of the war produced violent oscillations in the pecuniary volume of trade. Even Mr. Frickey, it will be noticed, did not think it worth while to continue his series beyond 1914. While economists have been deeply interested in measuring price changes, they have sought to measure the reaction of prices, not on the amount of exchanging done in dollars, but on the physical volume of goods exchanged.

---

[3] Compare Chapter II, section iv, 5, above; "The Quantity Theory and Business Cycles."

(2) Indexes of the Physical Volume of Trade or of Production.

Like the pecuniary volume of trade, the physical volume of trade is a definite quantity. It consists of all the goods exchanged in a country, during specified intervals, reckoned in physical units—hours of labor, cubic feet of buildings occupied under leases, numbers of securities transferred, ton miles of freight carried one mile, lines of advertising printed, and so on. Conceivably one might make an inventory of the goods exchanged each month, expressed in such units. But to make from the inventories totals which could be compared month by month, it is necessary to assign each good a money price. If the prices are kept fixed month after month, the aggregates, though expressed in billions of dollars, will show changes in the physical volume of trade weighted by dollar values.

While we lack data to approximate even roughly the physical inventories of goods exchanged annually in the United States, we might build up from series now published an aggregative index of the physical volume of trade which would possess much interest. Such an index would correspond in character to the U. S. Bureau of Labor Statistics index number of wholesale prices. That price index shows changing prices weighted by fixed physical quantities; the volume-of-trade index would show changing physical quantities weighted by fixed prices. With this series in hand, we might eliminate the secular trend and seasonal variations (if any), and thus get an index of the cyclical-irregular fluctuations in the physical volume of trade, expressed in dollars, or converted into ratios of the adjusted trend values.

The current indexes of the cyclical-irregular fluctuations in the physical volume of trade are not made on this simple plan. Instead of starting with an index of the volume of trade and ascertaining its trend, the compilers ascertain the trend of each time series separately, turn the original data into relatives of their trends, weight these relatives, and compute their arithmetic means. Snyder's index of the volume of trade in 1919-25, and the two later segments of Persons' index of the volume of trade (the segments for 1915-19, and 1919-23) are made in this way. Thus they are not quite what their names suggest, indexes of the volume of trade, but weighted arithmetic means of the percentage deviations of certain time series from their adjusted trends. Their analogues among price indexes would be a new type:—weighted arithmetic means of relative prices, computed on the base: ordinates of secular trends, corrected for seasonal variations, equal 100.

It is now generally recognized that weighted arithmetic means of relatives are less desirable price indexes for most uses than relatives made from aggregates of actual prices weighted by physical quantities.[1] If we wish to make an index of changes in the physical volume of trade, we can apply this conclusion with confidence, and say that the aggregative form of index is more serviceable, on the whole, than the weighted mean of relative quantities. But does it follow that an index of the cyclical-irregular fluctuations in the volume of trade is better made by the aggregative method than by weighting and averaging the relatives of the constituent series?

It is clear from their formulas that the two methods do not yield identical results.[2] In seeking to choose between them we get

[1] Of course, the averages of relatives have their advantages; but I think the conclusion stated in the text is valid.

On the relative merits of different forms of price indexes, see Irving Fisher, *The Making of Index Numbers*, Boston and New York, 1922, and Truman L. Kelley, *Statistical Method*, New York, 1924, chapter xiii. A summary of the chief findings is given by Frederick C. Mills, *Statistical Methods*, New York, 1924, pp. 207-221.

[2] The formula for an index of deviations from a secular trend made by the aggregative method, may be written:

$$\frac{\Sigma q_1\, p_w}{T_1} \qquad (1)$$

Here q_1 represents the quantities of the goods exchanged in time "1"; p_w represents the fixed prices used as weights, and T_1 represents the adjusted ordinate of the secular trend of $\Sigma q\, p_w$ in time 1. We may regard this trend as itself the aggregate of the trends of the constituent series, each weighted by its appropriate price, provided that the trends fitted to all the constituent series and to the aggregate are straight lines, or (perhaps) if some single type of curve other than a straight line is fitted throughout. Then the formula becomes:

$$\frac{\Sigma q_1\, p_w}{\Sigma t_1\, p_w} \qquad (2)$$

The formula for a similar index made by averaging relatives weighted by fixed values (v_w) is:

$$\frac{\Sigma\left(\dfrac{q_1}{t_1}\right)v_w}{\Sigma v_w} \qquad (3)$$

But the values used as weights are products of quantities and prices. Therefore we may replace v_w by $q_w p_w$ and write:

$$\frac{\Sigma\left(\dfrac{q_1}{t_1}\right)q_w p_w}{\Sigma q_w p_w} \qquad (4)$$

If $q_w = t_1$, formula (4) reduces to formula (1). That is, the two methods yield identical results only when the quantities used in the value-weights applied to the relalittle help from the discussions of price indexes, for they deal with the problem of comparing the relative values of the same variables in different periods, and our problem is to compare two values of the same variable at the same periods—the values shown by averaging deviations from the adjusted trends of the individual series and the values shown by computing deviations from the adjusted trend of the group aggregate.[3] But by falling back upon broader considerations we can justify a choice. Ease of computation, and, what is more important, ease of comprehension, speak for the aggregative method. That method requires the computation of but one trend and one set of seasonal variations, while the method of averaging relatives requires the computation of as many trends and sets of seasonals as there are component series. An aggregative index of physical volume of trade is relatively easy to conceive; so are its trend, its seasonal variations, and the deviations from its trend adjusted for seasonals. When one tries to think what reality is represented by a weighted average of many sets of deviations made in this way, the conception grows more complicated. Finally, we have need of an index of the physical volume of trade, as well as need of an index of its cyclical-irregular fluctuations. The method of aggregates gives us the first index as well as the second. The average of relatives gives us the second index, but not the first, though in compensation it offers the cyclical-irregular fluctuations of all the component series, for which we can find use. An ideal procedure would be to deal with our quantity series as the federal Bureau of Labor Statistics deals with price series—make the general index from weighted aggregates, but also publish relatives for each series separately, and, of course, add indexes

tives equal the adjusted ordinate of secular trend at the time for which the computation is made. This coincidence may well happen once in a period for which two indexes are made from identical materials by the two methods; but it is most unlikely to happen twice.

When the trend-lines used do not make the ordinates of the trend of the aggregate equal to the sum of the ordinates of the trends of the constituent series, there is no assurance that the two methods will give identical results. This is the commoner case in statistical practice. But the differences between the two sets of results may be small.

[3] For example, in our problem the time bias of arithmetic means of relative prices and of various systems of weighting does not enter. Nor is the "circular test" applicable in the usual way, if at all. The "factor reversal" test can be used, but it is inconclusive, because neither method can pass it. Kelley's test of reliability is pertinent: one might divide a body of data into two samples, compute indexes for both samples by both methods, and see which pair of indexes showed the higher coefficient of correlation. But the test would be laborious, and trial with one set of data might not prove conclusive.

Mathematical statisticians have in this problem a promising field for work.

of the cyclical-irregular deviations from adjusted trends both for the aggregates and for all the components.[4]

The practice of expressing cyclical-irregular fluctuations in terms of their standard deviations is not proper in making volume-of-trade indexes. For differences in the amplitude of these variations are present in the inventories to which such indexes relate. To cover up the differences by reducing the fluctuations of all the series used to a common scale, is to make measurement of changes in the aggregate volume impossible. A series constructed in this way may have some interest as indicating the time at which cyclical-irregular fluctuations have occurred, and as indicating the relative amplitude of successive cycles as pictured by the series in question, so long as it is made of uniform materials; but it is of little value for comparing the amplitude of fluctuations in the physical volume of trade with that of fluctuations in production, employment, prices, or any other variable.

To get reliable indexes of the physical volume of trade and of its cyclical-irregular fluctuations we need representative samples drawn from all parts of the field. Even for recent years in the United States, the materials are not ample. The trading done by farmers is most inadequately covered. There is reason to suspect that the best

The only practical test of the agreement between the two methods of which I know is the following:

In making his "index of physical production for all manufacture" in the United States by years since 1899, Dean Edmund E. Day started with 33 time series showing the output of various types of goods. These series he arranged in 10 industrial groups.

(1) For each group he made an "unadjusted index" by reducing the annual items of the component series to relatives on the base, production in 1909 equals 100, weighting these relatives, computing geometric means, and making certain corrections on the basis of Census data which do not now concern us. Next he weighted the 10 group indexes, and used their geometric means as an "unadjusted index of physical production for manufacture."

(2) To measure the cyclical fluctuations of manufacturing, Day returned to his 33 original series, fitted a trend line to each, expressed the actual figures as percentages of the corresponding trend values, weighted these relatives, computed averages (this time arithmetic) for each of the 10 industries, then weighted these group averages, and finally took their arithmetic means as his "adjusted index."

Day found two objections to the latter procedure. The determination of the lines of secular trend for the 33 original series involved difficult choices of period and line. The computations were laborious. For both reasons he sought a simpler method.

(3) This method was to fit a trend line directly to the "unadjusted index," and turn its annual values into percentages of the corresponding ordinates of this trend. The differences between the results of methods (2) and (3) in the 21 years 1899-1919 did not exceed three points in the percentage scale in any year. Dean Day concluded that the "case for the simpler method of getting the adjusted index is conclusive." I should be inclined to argue that the simpler method is preferable on logical grounds, as well as on practical grounds.

See Edmund E. Day, "An Index of the Physical Volume of Production," *Review of Economic Statistics*, November and December, 1920, Preliminary vol. ii, pp. 310, 311, 332-337, 362-365.

totals we can now make show variations somewhat in excess of the truth; for the types of trading not represented at all, particularly the retail sales of the great mass of small, independent shops, are probably rather steady. By long odds the most comprehensive index we have is Snyder's series for 1919-25.

When compilers go back to pre-war years, they are forced to resort to one of two undesirable shifts. Either they must change the composition of their indexes from time to time, accepting less satisfactory and smaller samples as they work backward, or they must use materials which do not show the physical volume of trade. Mr. Snyder chose the latter alternative in making his "clearings index of business." Instead of treating bank clearings outside of New York City as a sample of fluctuations in the pecuniary volume of transactions, Snyder sought to transmute these dollars figures into a physical-volume index. Of course, it is always questionable how accurately division of such data by a price index really shows the corresponding changes in physical quantities. Mr. Snyder was able to test his procedure more adequately than is often possible in such cases, by making sure that his price index when applied to outside bank debits in 1919-23 gave results which fitted closely his physical-volume index   Yet a doubt remains whether a "deflating series" adjusted to bank debits in the period of violent price fluctuations just after the war is well adapted to deflating bank clearings for distant years, when prices were relatively stable. And at best, clearings is only one sample of volume of trade—though the best single sample.[5]

What has been said about methods of making indexes of the physical volume of trade and its cyclical-irregular fluctuations applies also to indexes of physical production. Production is not limited to the output of tangible commodities; it includes such services as fabrication, transportation, storage, and distribution, which suggests that production indexes should be made on a "value-added" basis. For example, if we have data showing retail sales of shoes in pairs and dollars, wholesale sales, and manufacture in the same double form, leather used by shoemakers in physical units and value, and hides and skins tanned into shoe leather, we can include the output of all these agencies in an index of physical production. Starting with the

[5] These doubts about the reliability of long-period indexes made from changing materials or by deflating clearings are shared by the compilers. It is necessary to note them, but it is also just to add that the criticisms apply to the data, and not to the men who have sought to learn all they can from what records the past provides.

pairs of shoes sold at retail, we can weight the service of the shopkeepers by the average value which they add to the wholesale price,
and work back in this way to the fresh hides. Of course, to make the
result show changes in physical production, we must keep constant
the "values added" which we use as weights. Constructed in this
way from exhaustive data, production indexes would cover most of
the transactions included in the volume-of-trade indexes; but the
weights of the two indexes would differ widely. For example, in a
trade index the retail sales of shoes in pairs would be multiplied by
the full retail price, instead of by the retailers' margin. Both indexes
would run in billions of dollars, but the trade index would show many
more billions. There would also be differences in timing. In a trade
index the aim is to record exchanges when they are made; in a production index the aim is to record productive services when they are
rendered. Manufacturers make goods before they exchange them,
and merchants render their productive service to the community
from the time they buy goods to the time they deliver packages to
the ultimate consumer. These time relations are of great moment in
the theory of business cycles.

As we should like three indexes of the pecuniary volume of trade
showing commitments entered into, goods transferred, and payments
made, so we should like three indexes of production in physical terms,
—one showing goods ordered, one showing productive services rendered, and one showing goods delivered. To complete our modest requirements, add that these three indexes should be made to show separately for each industry the operations of retail dealers, wholesale
merchants, manufacturers of consumers' and producers' goods, producers of raw materials, and builders of industrial equipment. In all
this work adequate samples should be used, the aggregative method
followed, and the cyclical-irregular fluctuations taken in their original
amplitudes, not in units of their standard deviations.

(3) Indexes of "General Business Conditions."

Most of the indexes under review relate neither to the pecuniary
nor to the physical volume of trade, but to the "general condition of
business." This concept is much less definite than the others. It
corresponds to no sum in dollars, to no inventory of goods, to nothing
we can count. By nature it is not an aggregate amount, but a syn-
thesis of relatives. We can say that retail sales in dollars are larger
now than they were last month or last year, that the percentage of

unemployment is less, that more tons of steel are being produced, railway traffic is heavier, prices are higher, "money is tighter," and so on. Or we can compare each of these variables with the standard we have made from its secular trends and seasonal variations. But when we combine these series we are not measuring any quantity, or the variations in any quantity. We are merely summarizing our observations upon the values of certain variables from time to time in terms of other values of the same variables. And these variables in their original form are largely incommensurable, or rather are divided among incommensurable groups, prices, physical quantities of many sorts, values, ratios.

Of course, there is no technical difficulty in combining or averaging time series of any sort when they are expressed as relatives, percentage deviations from trends, or multiples of standard deviations. Combinations of incommensurable series are frequently made in the business indexes. The American Telephone and Telegraph Company's index for a time included Bradstreet's price series, the production of pig iron in tons, and bank clearings outside of New York, though it is now made of more homogeneous materials. Persons also used these three series, among others, in making one of the curves in his "Index of General Business Conditions." In her British index, Miss Thomas went even further; she combined unemployment percentages with series expressed in price relatives, physical units, and pounds sterling.

In defense of this practice, it can be urged that the phenomena of business cycles include changes in prices, physical quantities, pecuniary volumes, and ratios—for example, the ratio of bank reserves to demand liabilities. Not only do these four types of variables coexist; they also act and react upon one another. When the statistician combines measurements of the changes in these variables, he is merely trying to represent in one series of figures the net resultants of changes which are genuine and which do interact. Anyone who can conceive of business cycles as congeries of fluctuations in many processes should be able to grasp what is meant by an index made from sample fluctuations. It is true that indexes confined to one type of changes, such as prices, pecuniary volume of trade, or physical production, have a more definite meaning. But what they gain in definiteness they lose in breadth. No business index deserves the term "general" unless it includes samples of the various types of business activities.

By considering the method of weighting the series used in a "general business" index, we can put this elusive problem in the clearest light. Conceivably, a logical basis for weighting even the series which belong to incommensurable groups might be found in the relation which every business series bears to the pecuniary volume of trade.[1] But do we wish such a scheme of weights? Certainly we do not make an index of general business conditions as an indirect way of showing fluctuations in the pecuniary volume of business transactions. As said above, the condition of business is not itself an aggregate of goods or of values, and the components we use in making an index do not derive their importance from the influence they exercise upon anything which can be counted. But to what other criterion can we appeal to make sure that every series we use shall have due chance to influence the results?

In practice, statisticians have not lingered long upon this question. They usually proceed promptly to turn the original data into percentage deviations from their adjusted secular trends, to express each set of deviations in units of its standard deviation, and to take arithmetic means of the series in this form. Sometimes they apply rough weights, but more often not.[2] Reduction of the several sets of deviations to multiples of their own standard deviations is itself a scheme of weighting that gives each series a chance to influence the results in inverse proportion to its variability in terms of its standard deviation; applying different weights to the multiples gives each series an

[1] Many series are fractions of that aggregate—bank debits, railway receipts, pay-roll disbursements, import and export values, and the like. Price data become fractions of the aggregate when multiplied by physical volume of trade; physical-volume and production data become similar fractions when multiplied by prices. A place can be made even for the ratios:—unemployment percentages, for instance, can be related to payroll disbursements, and bank-reserve ratios to the volume of financial transactions. The elaboration of a scheme of weights upon this basis would require much ingenuity, and many conjectural estimates. Not only are there gaps in the data, but there is also much overlapping to be allowed for, particularly between bank debits and other factors. Yet the task is not an impossible one.

[2] For example, for some time the American Telephone and Telegraph Company's "General Business Curve" was made from the following series and weights:

	Weights
Outside clearings	25
Pig-iron production	20
Railroad traffic	15
Failures (number)	10
Copper production	5
Cotton consumption	10
Coal production	5
Commodity prices	10
	100

influence upon the results proportioned to the investigator's rating of its relative importance. That is, the original differences among the series as components of averages are wiped out, and new differences are written in. No single criterion of the importance of the several series is set up; but statisticians easily agree upon the more important and less important business indicators in any list of series, and agree also that the rankings within these groups must be rather arbitrary. In some lists they judge that even weighting is quite as good as differential weighting.

Of course such general agreement upon schemes of weights for practical use is not a satisfactory solution of the problem how to make an index of general business conditions; but it is the nearest approach to a solution which has been worked out. The need of further methodological research at this point is pressing.

Indexes made in the way described are clearly more representative of general business conditions when they are based upon large and varied lists of series than when the lists are small or one-sided. The rule is sometimes laid down that only series in which the cyclical-irregular fluctuations are synchronous should be included. This rule is proper if the compiler wishes merely to exhibit the cyclical element in business changes; it is not proper if he wishes an index of general business conditions. For we have seen how considerably and how systematically the cyclical-irregular fluctuations of certain processes lag behind those of other processes. To exclude any series from the index merely because it differs in timing from others, and therefore blurs the cycles, is to distort the general business index in the interests of symmetry. The only way to observe the rule and remain faithful to fact is to give up the plan of making a single index, and follow Persons in making a three-, possibly a four-, or a five-curve index, including as many trustworthy series as possible, but throwing them into groups on the basis of synchronous fluctuations. It is not consonant with the aim of representing general business conditions to exclude even series which show no cyclical characteristics.

Granted that general-business indexes combining the changes in many economic activities are not irrational, the question remains, What are they good for? One use at least can be claimed for them. So long as such a series is made from uniform materials by uniform methods, it enables one to compare successive cycles with respect to duration, amplitude and the character of their several phases. The wider the range of materials included and the longer the period covered, the more significant these comparisons become. For intensive theoretical work they are of slight value. As said before, they do not measure any magnitude. And their value for the extensive work to which they are adapted is compromised by the small number and changing character of the data available for the long periods which they should cover.[3]

(4) Forecasting Sequences.

While the three-curve charts which Professor Persons and his co-workers have made for the United States, Great Britain and Germany are called "Indexes of General Business Conditions," they are made primarily as forecasting sequences. That is, the series used in each curve were chosen for the regularity with which their cyclical-irregular fluctuations are synchronized, and for the regularity with which their cyclical-irregular fluctuations precede or follow those of the series used in the other curves. Such constructions are to be judged on principles somewhat different from those laid down concerning general business indexes proper.

[3] Dr. Frederick C. Mills points out that when standard deviations are used as units in which to measure cyclical deviations from trend lines, they cannot be interpreted in the usual fashion. The standard deviation of a "normal distribution" has a precise meaning; we know what percentage of the total number of cases in such a distribution will deviate from the mean by more (or less) than any given multiple of the standard deviation; we know also what the odds are that a given deviation from the mean will be exceeded by a random observation. These precise rules of the normal distribution apply approximately to a wider variety of actual distributions. But they are frequently violated by the distribution of deviations of time series from their secular trends.

(1) A deviation equal to 6 standard deviations below the mean would occur in a normal frequency distribution once in 1,000,000,000 times. Deviations of that order occur not infrequently among deviations from a secular trend, in consequence of such disturbances as strikes, railway embargoes, wars, panics.

(2) Such extraordinary deviations are particularly common among deviations measured from projected trends. For example, in the publications of the Harvard Committee on Economic Research we find the Bureau of Labor Statistics index number of prices at wholesale represented by a positive deviation of 15.5 times the standard deviation in February, 1920, and Bradstreet's price index represented by a negative deviation of 10.6 times the standard deviation in July, 1921. Deviations reaching or exceeding 4.5 times the standard deviation are somewhat common in this valuable source. In a normal distribution, a deviation of this size occurs three times in a million.

(3) Since these extreme deviations are commoner in some series than in others, we do not quite get away from the danger of distorting our averages by using the standard deviations of the series as units.

In short, Professor Warren M. Persons' argument concerning the non-applicability of the concept of the probable error to time series seems to apply to the use of the standard deviation for measuring departures from a projected trend, if not to its use in measuring departures from a fitted trend. (For the argument see above section iv, 1, "The Correlation of Time Series and Its Pitfalls," note 2.)

A forecasting sequence cannot be expected to utilize all the materials which are available for making a general business index, and which should be included in the latter to render it "general." Comparatively few of the series lead or lag behind others with sufficient regularity to give reliable forecasts. But it may be argued that slenderness of materials is no defect in a forecasting sequence; it is better to limit the series rigidly to those showing the closest approach to perfect regularity of sequence than to gain comprehensiveness at the cost of uncertainty. If it does not matter what is to be forecasted, this view is valid. Strictly speaking, all that can be inferred from a three-curve chart is the movements of the particular series represented by the curves which lag. Both for practical and for theoretical purposes the whole operation is highly important or a curiosity, according as the curves whose movements are forecasted represent activities of large or of slight significance.

As for technical methods, the only criterion applicable to the making of forecasting sequences is supplied by the results. The original data can be made into aggregates, treated as relatives to some base period, computed as deviations from adjusted trends, expressed in units of their standard deviations, or thrown into any other form which brings out most clearly the regularity of the time sequences. The methods developed by Professor Persons serve well, and have been accepted as models by many other investigators.

The chief difficulty in applying these methods lies in securing indexes which maintain fairly regular relationships in the timing of their movements. For the period 1903 to 1914, Professor Persons finds:

first, that the cyclical fluctuations of curve B, business, lagged eight months, on the average, after those of curve A, speculation; second, that the cyclical fluctuations of curve C, money rates, lagged four months, on the average, after those of curve B, business, and third, that the cyclical fluctuations of curve C, money rates, lagged twelve months, on the average, after those of curve A, speculation.

To complete the full round of events, it is necessary to ascertain the average period by which the movements of curve A, speculation, in one cycle, lag behind the movements of curve C, money rates, in the preceding cycle. Supplemental computations made for the purpose show that the interval of lag of speculation after money rates was extremely variable and averaged 6-12 months. . . .[1]

All these averages are ascertained by finding the period of lag which yields the highest coefficient of correlation between the indexes paired. The maximum coefficients are not exceedingly high. They run for curves B and A +.81; for curves C and B +.83; for curves C and A +.74; for curves A and C —.67. Moreover, every pairing shows one or two other lags with coefficients nearly equal to the maximum.[2] Of course, this means that the time relationships among the three indexes of the Harvard sequence are not sufficiently regular to afford an assured mechanical forecast of the successive movements which occur within a cycle and which form the transition from one cycle to the next. What is claimed for the sequence is that,

> Although the *lag*—the time by which the movements of one curve lag behind those of another—is not invariable in length, it is much more nearly uniform than is the length of the cycle itself. Furthermore, variations in the duration of lag can in a measure be foreseen by a careful examination of the relations subsisting between the curves at the time of forecast.[3]

3. What the Indexes of Business Conditions Show About Business Cycles.

A classification of certain business indexes according to the economic processes to which they relate will summarize the preceding

[1] See Warren M. Persons and Edwin Frickey, "Money Rates and Security Prices," *Review of Economic Statistics*, January, 1926, vol. viii, pp. 30 and 32.

[2] The full array of coefficients given by Professor Persons in the article quoted (pp 30 and 32) is as follows:

COEFFICIENTS OF CORRELATION BETWEEN CURVES A, B, AND C, OF THE INDEX OF GENERAL BUSINESS CONDITIONS. BI-MONTHLY, 1903–JUNE, 1914

Curves Correlated	0	2	4	Lag in Months 6	8	10	12	14	16
B follows A	..	..	.72	.80	.81	.76	..	..	..
C " B	..	.75	.83	.81	.70	..	..	..	..
C " A	..	..	..	..	..	.69	.74	.71	.62
A " C	−.29	−.44	−.58	−.63	−.67	−.65	−.62	..	..

Somewhat different results concerning the lags between curves A and B, A and C, and B and C of the "revised index," are given by Professor W. L. Crum, in "The Pre-War Indexes of General Business Conditions," *Review of Economic Statistics*, January, 1924, vol. vi, p. 19. But since Professor Persons uses the results obtained from the old index in the latest issue I have seen, I follow his example. See W. M. Persons, "An Index of General Business Conditions, 1875–1913," *Review of Economic Statistics*, January, 1927, vol. ix, p. 26.

[3] W. L. Crum, "The Interpretation of the Index of General Business Conditions," *Review of Economic Statistics*, Supplement, September, 1925, vol. vii, p. 223.

critique in part, and prepare for the following constructive comparisons. The indexes selected all refer to the same country, cover relatively long periods by months, and present their results in readily comparable form.

INDEX RELATING TO THE PECUNIARY VOLUME OF TRANSACTIONS.

Edwin Frickey's "Index of Outside Clearings," United States, 1875-1914.

Relatives (not strictly an index) of bank clearings in seven cities (used as a sample of all clearings outside of New York), computed on the base, monthly ordinate of secular trend, adjusted for seasonal variation, equals 100.

The transactions which give rise to the drawing of checks cover many types of economic relations, but small transactions in general and rural transactions in particular are under-represented. The exclusion of New York City reduces the representation of financial and of speculative transactions. In time, the clearings of a particular day cover transactions ranging from the re-payment of debts incurred years before to the advance of funds to be returned years later. On the average, clearings probably lag some weeks behind the exchange of goods to which they relate.

INDEXES RELATING TO THE PHYSICAL VOLUME OF TRADE.

Carl Snyder's "Clearings Index of Business," United States, 1875-1924.

Relatives (not strictly an index) of all outside clearings, "deflated" by an index of the "general price level," computed on the base, monthly ordinate of secular trend equals 100, corrected for seasonal variations, and smoothed by a three-months moving average.

What is said above concerning the activities represented by outside clearings applies here. It is, of course, questionable how far an aggregate in dollars can be made to show fluctuations in physical volume through division by a price index.

Warren M. Persons' "Index of Trade," United States, 1903-23.

First segment, 1903-15.

A mixed index of physical and pecuniary volume of trade.

Simple arithmetic means of relatives of seven series computed on the base, monthly ordinate of secular trend, corrected for seasonal variations, equals 100, expressed in multiples of their several standard deviations. The arithmetic means are multiplied by the standard deviation of outside clearings (8.62).

Second and third segments, 1915-19 and 1919-23.

Indexes of physical volume only.

Weighted arithemtic means of relatives of four (1915-19) and of five (1919-23) series, computed on the base, monthly ordinate of linear trend, corrected for seasonal variation, equals 100.

INDEXES RELATING TO GENERAL BUSINESS CONDITIONS.

American Telephone and Telegraph Company's index of "General Business Compared with Normal," United States, 1877-1925.

From 1877 to 1884, when pig-iron output is the only series used, this index relates to physical volume of production. From 1922, when all "dollar series" are dropped, to date, it relates to physical volume of production and of trade. In the intervening years, 1885-1921, it relates to "general business conditions."

Weighted arithmetic means of relatives computed on the base, monthly ordinate of secular trend, corrected for seasonal variations, equals 100, expressed in multiples of standard deviations. The arithmetic means are finally put into percentage form through multiplying by 10 (the approximate weighted average of the standard deviations of the constituent series in percentages).

Carl Snyder's "Index of Deposits Activity," United States, 1875 to 1924.

Relatives (not strictly an index) of the ratios of individual deposits in all National Banks to total clearings, computed on the base, monthly ordinate of secular trend equals 100, corrected for seasonal variations, and smoothed by three-months moving averages.

This interesting series is best classed as relating to general business conditions. The inclusion of New York City clearings (as well as New York City deposits) gives dealings in securities far more weight in this series than they have in Frickey's and Snyder's relatives of outside clearings.

None of the series here described is comprehensive enough to pass as an index of business cycles. Each series relates to but one or a few economic activities, and these activities differ widely. In every case the representative character of the data used is open to question, and the methods of isolating cyclical-irregular fluctuations lack precision. Two series change character from period to period. Three series are relatives measuring the fluctuations of a variable about its adjusted trend; two series show arithmetic means of such relatives reduced to units of their standard deviations. By no means uniform materials, one would say.

If these series made by different hands, with different methods, from different data, to show different things, agree with each other in large measure, it must be that business cycles manifest themselves in much the same way over a wide variety of economic activities, that these fluctuations are recorded with reasonable accuracy in numerous time series, and that the diversities of method make no great difference in the results. So far as the series differ, we may infer that variety of method does make some difference in the results; that the data are unreliable in different ways; or that the activities to which the series relate have characteristically different fluctuations. Perhaps all these explanations, and others too, are applicable to every difference.

Thus in comparing the five indexes of business conditions in the United States which cover by months the longest periods of time, we shall be testing the underlying statistics, testing the methods of isolating cyclical-irregular fluctuations, and testing the hypothesis that similar cycles occur in different economic activities. Of course, we should prefer to test these matters separately, but must content ourselves with testing them in combination. Further, we shall be testing in one country for about 50 years the regularity of business cycles in respect to duration and amplitude.

(1) The "Saw-Tooth" Contour of the Business Indexes.

All five of our indexes present business cycles, not as sweeping smoothly upward from depressions to a single peak of prosperity and then declining steadily to a new trough, but as moving in a jerky fashion. Even the two curves which Snyder smoothed by moving averages are made up of serrated segments.

Counting shows that the indexes change direction on the average every three months, every two months, or even oftener.[1] We cannot

[1] The following table gives details.

FREQUENCY OF CHANGES IN DIRECTION OF THE CURVES TRACED BY FIVE MONTHLY INDEXES OF BUSINESS CONDITIONS IN THE UNITED STATES, 1877–1922

1877–1922	Number of Times Curves Change Direction		Total changes of direction	No. of months covered	Proportion of months in which curves change direction
	From rise to fall or from fall to rise	From rise or fall to horizontal, or *vice versa*			
A. T. and T. Index.......	178	134	312	550	57%
Frickey's Clearings Index*	222	59	281	456	62
Snyder's Clearings Index..	103	87	190	552	34
Snyder's Deposits Index..	127	141	268	552	49
1903–1922					
Persons' Trade Index.....	95	61	156	238	66
A. T. and T. Index......	91	39	130	240	54
Frickey's Clearings Index*	69	18	87	144	60
Snyder's Clearings Index..	36	86	121	240	50
Snyder's Deposits Index..	47	69	116	240	48

* To 1914 only.

be sure that these frequent minor irregularities are due wholly to the failure of random influences to cancel each other. They may be due in part to the averaging together of series which differ in timing. And perhaps the cyclical movements themselves keep producing and overcoming small checks.

Reversals of direction are more frequent near the climax of prosperity and in the trough of depression than during the transitions between these extreme states. Charts 11 to 17 suggest that business has a ceiling and a floor, both somewhat elastic or irregular. Between these limiting planes it can glide up or down on a slant rather smoothly. But when business nears the ceiling or the floor it bumps up and down in a jerky fashion for a while before it goes off on the next glide.

(2) Month-to-Month Changes.

A second resemblance among the five indexes concerns the amplitude of their month-to-month changes. The "points" in which the monthly changes are expressed are relatives to ordinates of secular trend, averages of such relatives reduced to percentage form, or averages of such relatives multiplied by the standard deviations of "outside" clearings. In practice, the scales cover similar ranges.

Chart 19 shows the distribution of these monthly changes in percentages of the total number of cases covered by each series.[1]

[1] The data from which the chart is drawn are as follows:

FREQUENCY DISTRIBUTION OF THE MONTH-TO-MONTH CHANGES IN FIVE INDEXES OF BUSINESS ACTIVITY

Unit in each case is one point in the scale of deviations from adjusted trends. These scales differ somewhat from each other. See text.

Percentage Basis

Direction and magnitude of month-to-month changes	A. T. and T. Index 1877–1925	Frickey's Clearings Index 1875–1914	Snyder's Clearings Index 1875–1923	Snyder's Deposits Index 1875–1923	Persons' Index of Trade 1903–1924
+17		.2			
+16		.2			
+15		.2			
+14		.2			
+13		.6			
+12		.2		.2	
+11				.5	
+10	.2	.6			
+ 9		.8		.3	.4
+ 8	.3	1.9	.2	1.2	.7
+ 7	.8	1.7		1.7	1.5
+ 6	1.2	4.0	.5	1.9	1.5

As economic data go, these distributions are remarkably symmetrical and show a high degree of concentration around their central tendencies, most marked in Snyder's Clearings Index and least marked in Frickey's series. The difference between the two clearings indexes in this respect is probably due to the facts (1) that Snyder smoothed his index by a three-months moving average, thus reducing the amplitude of the extreme movements and increasing the number of minor movements, and (2) that Frickey used data from only seven cities, while Snyder took all outside clearings. In each case, the distribution is slightly elongated toward the left; that is, the most violent declines exceed the most considerable advances. The abrupt declines

FREQUENCY DISTRIBUTION OF THE MONTH-TO-MONTH CHANGES IN FIVE INDEXES OF BUSINESS ACTIVITY

Direction and magnitude of month-to-month changes	A. T. and T. Index 1877–1925	Frickey's Clearings Index 1875–1914	Snyder's Clearings Index 1875–1923	Snyder's Deposits Index 1875–1923	Persons' Index of Trade 1903–1924
+ 5	3.2	5.2	1.7	2.2	2.7
+ 4	3.6	5.0	2.2	4.1	6.1
+ 3	7.2	7.7	6.2	6.1	7.6
+ 2	12.8	10.5	10.4	11.3	12.2
+ 1	14.3	7.3	18.3	11.6	13.3
0	17.5	8.8	24.0	13.8	13.3
− 1	13.5	7.3	16.9	15.0	11.8
− 2	9.0	7.3	8.5	9.9	7.6
− 3	6.5	8.4	6.0	8.2	6.5
− 4	3.7	5.0	2.1	4.6	6.1
− 5	2.6	4.6	.9	3.1	2.7
− 6	1.7	4.4	.9	1.5	1.9
− 7	.5	2.5	.3	1.0	.4
− 8	.8	1.3	.5	.7	2.3
− 9	.2	2.1	.2	.7	.4
−10		1.0		.2	.4
−11	.2	.2			
−12		.2	.2		.7
−13					
−14		.2			
−15				.2	
−16					
−17	.2				
−18					
−19		.2			
....					
−27		.2			
	100.0	100.0	100.0	100.0	100.0

+ Indicates a rise.
− Indicates a fall.

CHART 19.

FREQUENCY DISTRIBUTION OF MONTH-TO-MONTH CHANGES IN FIVE INDEXES OF BUSINESS ACTIVITY.

FRICKEY'S CLEARINGS INDEX
1875 – 1914

SNYDER'S DEPOSITS INDEX
1875 – 1923

PERSONS' INDEX OF TRADE
1903 – 1924

A.T. & T. INDEX
1877 – 1925

SNYDER'S CLEARINGS INDEX
1875 – 1923

DEVIATION AND MAGNITUDE OF MONTH-TO-MONTH CHANGE

usually occur in crises; the greatest gains occur in periods of revival,
or come in other phases of the cycle as reactions after sudden drops.[2]
Except in Snyder's deposits index, the number of declines is smaller
than the number of advances, but the average magnitude of the
declines is greater.[3] Business contraction seems to be a briefer and
more violent process than business expansion. Why Snyder's deposits
index give opposite indications will appear presently. But most of
the monthly changes in both directions have small amplitudes. Less

[2] The dates of the largest month-to-month changes in each of the series have some
interest. As above, + indicates an advance, − a decline. Readers whose recollection
of business chronology is hazy may care to use the "Conspectus of Business Conditions,"
given in the next chapter to interpret this table.

A. T. and T. Index	Frickey's Clearings Index	Snyder's Clearings Index
−17 Nov., 1907	−27 Nov., 1907	−12 Aug., 1893
−11 Aug., 1893	−19 June, 1884	− 9 March 1884
− 9 Nov., 1890	−14 July, 1881	− 8 Sept., 1876
		− 8 Nov., 1907
		− 8 Dec., 1907
+10 June, 1886	+17 Nov., 1880	+ 8 June 1881
+ 8 July, 1891	+16 June, 1881	+ 6 Nov., 1875
+ 8 Aug., 1894	+15 Oct., 1875	+ 6 Nov., 1879
		+ 6 May, 1890

Snyder's Deposits Index	Persons' Index of Trade
−15 July, 1901	−12 Jan., 1921
−10 June, 1901	−12 June, 1924
− 9 Aug., 1875	−10 Nov., 1907
− 9 June, 1880	− 9 Dec., 1907
− 9 May, 1907	
− 9 Sept., 1914	
+12 April, 1901	+ 9 March, 1918
+11 Dec., 1880	+ 8 July, 1919
+11 Dec., 1898	+ 8 Nov., 1922
+11 Dec., 1900	+ 7 Feb., 1904
+ 9 Feb., 1876	+ 7 Oct., 1912
+ 9 July, 1897	+ 7 Dec., 1919
	+ 7 Dec., 1924

[3] The details are as follows:

NUMBER AND AVERAGE MAGNITUDE OF ADVANCES AND DECLINES IN THE MONTH-TO-MONTH CHANGES IN FIVE INDEXES OF BUSINESS CONDITIONS

	Number of cases of			Average magnitude of	
	Advance	No Change	Decline	Advance Points	Decline Points
A. T. and T. business index	256	103	228	2.5	2.7
Frickey, clearings	222	42	215	4.0	4.2
Snyder, clearings	231	141	213	2.0	2.2
Snyder, deposits	241	81	264	3.0	2.8
Persons, trade	121	35	107	2.8	3.3

than half exceed two points in the scales used, except in Frickey's index, and, with the same exception, only a tenth exceed five points.[4]

(3) On Identifying Business Cycles by Use of the Business Indexes.

The irregularities of contour in the business indexes cause considerable difficulty when one tries to count the number of business cycles in a given period. The memorable cycles which culminated in 1882, in 1893, in 1907, in 1917, and in 1920 stand out clearly in all our curves. But in all the curves there are stretches when the cyclical fluctuations are less easy to identify; for example, the later 1880's, the middle 1890's, the early 1900's, the years 1910-13, and 1923-24. While the five monthly indexes agree in presenting this contrast between major and minor fluctuations, it would be hard from study of the curves to lay down rules for determining precisely what movements of an index shall be counted a business cycle. In the less pronounced cycles, the period of greatest activity occasionally (2 times out of 56) remains below the base line in some one of the indexes. In other cycles, the period of least activity occasionally (2 times out of 55) remains above the base line in some index. Often there are double or triple peaks, and double or triple troughs. At times one suspects that irregular fluctuations are dominating the cyclical factors. Nor is the duration of business cycles uniform enough to be used as a criterion in doubtful cases. But one who studies all five curves with care can draw up a list of business cycles which anyone else can identify with confidence in every curve.

Such a list is best made by noting the successive turning points in the business indexes. One may count either the successive crests, or the successive troughs of the waves. These two ways of reckoning usually give different measurements of duration for particular cycles; but the average duration over a period of considerable length must

[4] Once more the details are of interest:

PERCENTAGES OF THE MONTH-TO-MONTH CHANGES IN FIVE INDEXES OF BUSINESS CONDITIONS WHICH FALL WITHIN CERTAIN LIMITS

	± 1 point	± 2 points	± 5 points	± 10 points
A. T. and T. business index.....	45.3%	67.1%	93.9%	99.6%
Frickey's clearings index........	23.4	41.2	77.1	97.4
Snyder's clearings index........	59.2	78.1	97.2	99.8
Snyder's deposits index.........	40.4	61.6	89.9	99.1
Persons' trade index............	38.4	85.2	89.9	99.4

come out nearly the same whether one counts from trough to trough or from crest to crest.

Table 14 shows that 13 business cycles occurred in the United

TABLE 14

DATES OF THE TROUGHS AND THE CRESTS OF AMERICAN BUSINESS CYCLES IN 1878–1924
ACCORDING TO FIVE MONTHLY INDEXES OF BUSINESS ACTIVITY

	A. T. and T. business index	Frickey's clearings index	Snyder's clearings index	Snyder's deposits index	Persons' trade index
Trough....	Dec. '78– Apr. '79	Dec. '78	May '78	June and Dec. '78	
Crest......	June-Aug. '81	June '81	Aug. '81	Feb. '81	
Trough....	Feb., May '85	Nov. '84	Apr. '85	Nov. '84	
Crest......	March '87	June '87	June '87	Nov., Dec. '86	
Trough....	March '88	March '88	March '88	Feb. '88	
Crest......	May, Oct. '90	July '90	July '90	June '90	
Trough....	May '91	March '91	March '91	Jan., Feb. '91	
Crest......	Feb. '92	June '92 Jan. '93	Jan. '93	Feb. '93	
Trough....	June '94	Aug. '93	Oct. '93	Oct. '94	
Crest......	Oct. '95	Oct. '95	Dec. '95	June '95	
Trough....	Oct. '96	May '97	Mar. '97	Apr. '97	
Crest......	Dec. '99 Feb. '00	March '99	June '99	Feb. '99	
Trough....	Nov., Dec. '00	Sept. '00	Sept. '00	Sept. '00	
Crest......	Sept. '02	May '01 Sept. '02 July '03	June '01	Apr. '01 May '01	
Trough....	Dec. '03	May '04	July '04	Apr., May '04	July '04
Crest......	May, July '07	May '07	Feb. '06	Jan. '06	May '07
Trough....	May, June '08	Dec. '07	Jan. '08	Dec. '07	March '08
Crest......	Jan., March '10	March '10	Apr. '10	Feb. '10	March '10
Trough....	April '11	Oct. '11	Dec. '11	Sept. '10	April '11
Crest......	Jan. '13	Oct. '12	Feb. '13	March., Apr. '12	Oct. '12
Trough....	Dec. '14	Nov. '14	Dec. '14	Sept., Oct. '14	Nov. '14
Crest......	Nov. '16 Jan. '17		Dec. '16 Jan. '17	Oct., Nov. '16	May '17
Trough....	March '19		March '19	March '19	June '19
Crest......	Jan. '20		Aug., Sept. '19	July '19	March '20
Trough....	Apr., May, July '21		March '21	Mar., July '21	July '21
Crest......	May '23		May '23	March '23	May '23
Trough....	June '24				June '24

States between 1878 and 1923. Each of these cycles is traced by each of our indexes. The table gives the dates both of the crests and the troughs, as they appear in the several curves. Closer agreement among the dates could be secured by smoothing out their serrations with free-hand curves, and making a single crest and trough for each successive cycle. That process is legitimate; but it is well to show how frequent are the multiple peaks.

(4) Time Relationships Among the Business Indexes.

Of the several comparisons which Table 14 suggests, the simplest concerns the time sequence in which the five indexes reach their turning points. For this purpose, we need to replace the multiple peaks and troughs by single dates. The method followed is arbitrary and does nothing to lessen the differences among the curves: we place the crest midway between the months showing the highest points revealed by a given wave of activity, and date the troughs in corresponding fashion.[1] With this simplification, we can manage the data easily.

On no occasion do all of our indexes reach the crest or the trough of a given wave in the same month. Four times three out of four series then available agree; [2] but there is always one series which leads or lags behind the others by a month or more. Seemingly, we should think, not of turning points in business cycles, but of turning periods. As a rule, these turning periods are relatively long in the violent cycles and relatively short in the mild cycles. If we count from the date when the first of our indexes turns a given corner to the date when the last one turns the same corner, we get periods which run from one month in the trough of 1888, or two months in the trough of 1914 and in the crests of 1890, 1910, and 1923, to 14 months in the trough of 1893-94, 15 months in the trough of 1910-11, 16 months in the crests of 1901-02, and 17 months in the crest of 1906-07. On the average these turning periods are longer at the crest (8.0 months) than in the troughs (6.1 months).

Snyder's deposits index is the first to reach the crest 12 times out of 13 (the exception occurred in 1892-93). It also leads 8 times out of 13 in reaching the troughs. It will be recalled that this index is made by dividing individual deposits in all National Banks into total clearings. Of total clearings, the New York City figures make

[1] If there is a double crest in two adjacent months (for example, October and November, 1916), we choose the later month to avoid fractions. Similarly, in dealing with a double crest in May and October, 1890, we put the single crest in August, instead of July. There are 23 double or multiple crests or troughs among 111 turning points in Table 14.

[2] These dates are March, 1888, September, 1900, March, 1919, and May. 1923.

roughly half, and the New York City figures are influenced largely by the current volume of transactions on the Stock Exchange. In the other indexes this type of business activity counts for little. We may infer, then, that the pecuniary volume of trading in stocks almost always reaches its peak and begins to decline in a business cycle, before other types of business have culminated. With decidedly less regularity, trading in stocks also precedes other types of business in recovering from a depression.

As for the other indexes, their average order in reaching peaks and troughs is (2) Snyder's clearings index, (3) Frickey's clearings index, (4) the American Telephone and Telegraph Company's general business index, and (5) Person's index of trade. In each of these cases the lags average longer at the crests than in the troughs.[3]

(5) Duration of Periods of Expansion and Contraction.

Since all five indexes never reach the crests or the troughs of cyclical waves at the same time, and since neither the time sequences among the indexes nor the lags are constant, we find considerable differences among our measurements of the duration of periods of rising and declining activity. Table 15 presents the details.

Here we have a double complexity—five different measures of phenomena which themselves vary widely from case to case. But when we strike averages we approach uniformity. According to four of the indexes, periods of business expansion have lasted about two years on the average (23-25 months); while periods of business contraction have averaged little more than a year and a half (18, 18, 19 and 21 months according to the several indexes). That the longest periods of decline are greater than the longest periods of advance makes this average the more striking. It links with what has already been said about the greater number and smaller average value of the upward month-to-month changes. The average (and the modal) American ·cycle seems to be made up of two unequal segments, a two-year period of gradually increasing activity, and a period, four to six months shorter, of less gradually shrinking activity.

[3] The average lags of the several indexes behind the leaders are as follows:

	A. T. and T.	Frickey	Snyder clearings	Snyder deposits	Persons
In troughs	3.7 mo.	3.2 mo.	3.0 mo.	2.4 mo.	4.2 mo.
At crests	5.8 "	6.1 "	4.2 "	0.9 "	6.5 "
Number of cases	26	21	26	26	12

TABLE 15

Duration of Alternate Periods of Business Expansion and Business Contraction in the United States, 1878–1923, According to Five Indexes of Business Activity.

Based upon Table 14

Business Cycles of	A. T. and T. business index Months		Frickey's clearings index Months		Snyder's clearings index Months		Snyder's deposits index Months		Persons' trade index Months	
	Rise	Fall	Rise	Fall	Rise	Fall	Rise	Fall	Rise	Fall
1878–85 Rise	29		30		39		29			
Fall		45		41		44		45		
1885–88 Rise	23		31		26		25			
Fall		12		9		9		14		
1888–91 Rise	29		28		28		28			
Fall		9		8		8		8		
1891–94 Rise	9		19		22		24			
Fall		28		10		9		20		
1894–97 Rise	16		26		26		8			
Fall		12		19		15		22		
1897–00 Rise	39		22		27		22			
Fall		11		18		15		19		
1900–04 Rise	21		22		9		8			
Fall		15		22		37		36		
1904–08 Rise	42		36		19		20		34	
Fall		12		7		23		23		10
1908–11 Rise	20		27		27		26		24	
Fall		14		19		20		7		13
1911–14 Rise	21		12		14		19		18	
Fall		23		25		22		30		25
1914–19 Rise	24				25		25		30	
Fall		27				26		28		25
1919–21 Rise	10				6		4		9	
Fall		16				18		22		16
1921–23 Rise	24				26		22		22	
Maximum Rise	42		36		39		29		34	
Fall		45		41		44		45		25
Minimum Rise	9		12		6		4		9	
Fall		9		7		8		7		10
Average Rise	24		25		23		20		23	
Fall		19		18		21		23		18

Snyder's deposits index gives a different result. As it almost always leads the other indexes in attaining the crest of a business wave, and less uniformly leads them in reaching the trough, so it makes the periods of increasing activity relatively brief, and the periods of declining activity relatively long. Combined with what we know of its composition and its month-to-month changes, this suggests (though it does not prove) that the cycles in financial activity differ from those characteristic of general business in being made up of a shorter section of relatively rapid advance, and a longer section of decline.

All that has just been said applies strictly to the five indexes under consideration, for one country, in the years 1878-1923. Whether the generalizations are applicable to other indexes, other countries, and other periods remains an open question. In view of the diversity of the items which enter into the averages, we cannot judge the representative value of the averages themselves until a wider array of data is available. In the meanwhile, we may note that in respect to variability, our measures of the durations of business cycles compare not unfavorably with the measures made of many other social phenomena. The period of decline in business cycles is decidedly more variable in duration than the period of advance; the latter period in turn is appreciably more variable in duration than are whole cycles. For the latter measurements, our materials show a coefficient of variation of 29.4 per cent.[1]

(6) The Duration of Business Cycles.

In Table 16 the lengths of the American cycles of 1878-1925 are measured by adding together first each period of advance and its subsequent period of decline, secondly each period of decline and its subsequent period of advance. From what we have already seen about the variability of these periods, it is clear that the two ways of measuring seldom give identical results. No reason appears for regarding one set of measurements as more significant than the other.

[1] Using all of the observations given in Table 15, we get the following coefficients of variation (that is, standard deviations as percentages of the corresponding arithmetic means):

	Number of observations	Mean duration	Standard deviation	Coefficient of variation
Period of advance..........	55	22.75 mo.	8.34 mo.	36.7%
Period of decline...........	51	19.82 "	10.10 "	51.0%
Whole cycles..............	101	42.02 "	12.37 "	29.4%

Further, our five indexes often given five different measurements for a given cycle counted in the same way. The differences range from

TABLE 16

Duration of Business Cycles in the United States, 1878–1925, According to Five Indexes of Business Activity

Based upon Table 15

	A. T. and T. business index Months		Frickey's clearings index Months		Snyder's clearings index Months		Snyder's deposits index Months		Persons' trade index Months	
	T–T	C–C	T–T	C–C	T–T	C–C	T–T	C–C	T–T	C–C
Trough-trough 1878–85	74		71		83		74			
Crest-crest 1881–87		68		72		70		70		
Trough-trough 1885–88	35		40		35		39			
Crest-crest 1887–90		41		37		37		42		
Trough-trough 1888–91	38		36		36		36			
Crest-crest 1890–92		18		27		30		32		
Trough-trough 1891–94	37		29		31		44			
Crest-crest 1892–95		44		36		35		28		
Trough-trough 1894–97	28		45		41		30			
Crest-crest 1895–99		51		41		42		44		
Trough-trough 1897–00	50		40		42		41			
Crest-crest 1899–02		32		40		24		27		
Trough-trough 1900–04	36		44		46		44			
Crest-crest 1902–07		57		58		56		56		
Trough-trough 1904–08	54		43		42		43		44	
Crest-crest 1907–10		32		34		50		49		34
Trough-trough 1908–11	34		46		47		33		37	
Crest-crest 1910–12		35		31		34		26		31
Trough-trough 1911–14	44		37		36		49		43	
Crest-crest 1912–17		47				47		55		55
Trough-trough 1914–19	51				51		53		55	
Crest-crest 1917–20		37				32		32		34
Trough-trough 1919–21	26				24		26		25	
Crest-crest 1920–23		40				44		44		38
Trough-trough Maximum	74		71		83		74		55	
Crest-crest "		68		72		70		70		55
Trough-trough Minimum	26		29		24		26		25	
Crest-crest "		18		27		24		26		31
Trough-trough Average	42		43		43		43		41	
Crest-crest "		42		42		42		42		38

2 to 18 months, and average nearly 10 months. Yet even a period of about 45 years is long enough to make the average length of busi-

ness cycles come out nearly the same whatever index is used, and whether the measurements are taken from crest to crest or from trough to trough. The eight averages covering this period all come out 42 or 43 months. Even Persons' index, which overs only 20 years, gives averages of 38 months from crest to crest and 41 months from trough to trough.

Once more we must note the limited scope of the data under analysis and question the representative value of the averages. But these are the most precise measurements of the duration of business cycles we can get for the present; they refer to the country and the period which interests us most, and they come from five different sources. We may therefore consider the distribution of the measurements in some detail. We shall treat each measurement given by each series for each cycle, whether taken from crest to crest or from trough to trough, as one observation upon the duration of business cycles.

The 101 observations which this procedure lets us count are scattered over a range which runs from 18 to 83 months.[1] Half of the

---

[1] The full arrays, tabulated from Table 16, may be given.

OBSERVATIONS UPON THE DURATION OF BUSINESS CYCLES IN THE UNITED STATES, 1878–1923, MADE FROM FIVE INDEXES OF BUSINESS ACTIVITY

Duration in Months	Number of Cases Trough to Trough	Number of Cases Crest to Crest	Total	Duration in Months	Number of Cases Trough to Trough	Number of Cases Crest to Crest	Total
18		1	1	45	1		1
24	1	1	2	46	2		2
25	1		1	47	1	2	3
26	2	1	3	49	1	1	2
27		2	2	50	1	1	2
28	1	1	2	51	2	1	3
29	1		1	53	1		1
30	1	1	2	54	1		1
31	1	2	3	55	1	2	3
32		5	5	56		2	2
33	1		1	57		1	1
34	1	4	5	58		1	1
35	2	2	4	68		1	1
36	5	1	6	70		2	2
37	3	3	6	71	1		1
38	1	1	2	72		1	1
39	1		1	74	2		2
40	2	2	4	83	1		1
41	2	2	4		—	—	—
42	2	2	4		51	50	101
43	3		3				
44	5	4	9				

(Note continued on p. 342.)

observations, however, are concentrated between 34 and 47 months, an interval of little more than a year.

As often happens in dealing with a frequency table, we get more significant results by grouping the intervals. Here we may combine months into quarters. This we can do in three ways, treating each month as the end, the middle, or the beginning of a quarter. Thus our time scales might be based upon any of these groupings:

1st grouping	2d grouping	3d grouping
22–24 mo.	23–25 mo.	24–26 mo.
25–27 "	26–28 "	27–29 "
28–30 "	29–31 "	30–32 "
etc.	etc.	etc.

These three groupings give appreciably different distributions, as the following figures show:

	Crude Primary Mode	Crude Secondary Mode
1st grouping (22–24 mo., etc.)	15 observations at 34–36 mo.	13 observations at 43–45 mo.
2d " (23–25 " ")	16 observations at 35–37 mo.	12 observations at 44–46 mo.
3d " (24–26 " ")	16 observations at 42–44 mo.	14 observations at 36–38 mo.

Such shifting in the positions of the crude mode as the grouping of the months is altered from one arbitrary scheme to another, makes us wish for an average of the three groupings. In averaging, we can once more arrange the items in three ways, putting (say) the 26-28 month interval first in a combination with 27-29, and 28-30 months; second in a combination with 25-27 and 27-29 months; or last in a combination with 24-26 months and 25-27 months. As before, we have no reason for preferring any of these arrangements to the others. We may therefore use an average of all three. That plan will give as our final distribution of the 101 observations a distribution in which the class-frequencies are weighted averages of the frequencies secured in nine different groupings of the observations. The central

---

Two measures of the central tendencies of the arrays may be added.

	Observations taken		
	From trough to trough	From crest to crest	In both ways
Arithmetic means............	42.5 months	41.5 months	42.0 months
First Quartile................	36	32	34
Median......................	41	39	40
First Quartile................	46	49	47

points of the intervals used are 16 months, 19 months, 22 months, etc.[2]

Chart 20, in which the results appear, shows that all our averaging of different arrangements does not completely smooth out the irregularities. The two modes persist in the intervals centering on 37 and 43 months. They are separated by a lower point at 40 months, which happens to be the median of the series.

The conclusion is clear that within the period and country represented by our indexes, business cycles, while varying in length from a year and a half to nearly seven years, have a modal length in the neighborhood of three to three and one half years. They are far from uniform in duration, but their durations are distributed about a well marked central tendency in a tolerably regular fashion. This distribution differs from the type described by the "normal curve" in being prolonged toward the upper end of the time scale somewhat farther than toward the lower end.

There we may leave the topic for the present, planning to return to it in the next chapter, when we shall have for analysis observations upon a larger number of business cycles, over a longer period, and from seventeen countries instead of one.

(7) The Amplitude of Business Cycles.

All our indexes measure the amplitude of business fluctuations in percentage deviations from base lines, which represent the loci of the ordinates of secular trend corrected for seasonal variation.[1] We have noted certain technical differences in methods of construction, but have found that the average magnitudes of the published figures are of the same order in all the indexes. The greatest differences, indeed, are between two indexes which are alike in method of construction—Snyder's series for clearings and for deposits.

Table 17 assembles all the measurements of extreme deviations from the base line at the troughs and crests of successive business

[2] Under this plan, the average for the interval centering on 19 months, for example, is made from the observations for 16-18 months weighted 1, the observations for 17-19 months weighted 2, the observations for 18-20 months weighted 3, the observations for 19-21 months weighted 2, and the observations for 20-22 months weighted 1. By months, this arrangement weights the observation at 16 months 1, at 17 months 3, at 18 months 6, at 19 months 7, at 20 months 6, at 21 months 3, and at 22 months 1.

[1] For the present purpose, Snyder's practice of eliminating the seasonal variations *after* the deviations from secular trends have been computed is not an important departure from the methods followed by Persons, Frickey, and the statisticians of the American Telephone and Telegraph Company.

cycles, and Table 18 shows the magnitude of the successive swings from trough to crest and from crest to trough.

CHART 20.

FREQUENCY DISTRIBUTION OF 101 OBSERVATIONS UPON THE DURATION OF BUSINESS CYCLES: UNITED STATES, 1878-1923.

Based upon Table 16.

Averages obtained by combining several different groupings of the observations. See text

CENTRAL MONTHS OF THE INTERVALS

NUMERICAL VALUES

Central Months of the intervals	Average Number of observations	Central months of the intervals	Average Number of observations
16	.3	52	4.2
19	.7	55	5.1
22	.8	58	2.4
25	5.0	61	.1
28	5.7	64	.9
31	8.4	67	2.9
34	11.9	70	2.5
37	12.7	73	.7
49	9.4	76	..
43	13.3	79	.7
46	7.8	82	.3
49	5.1		
			100.9

The highest pitch of prosperity in the whole period covered was attained in 1881 according to Frickey's and Snyder's clearings indexes, in 1901 according to Snyder's deposits index, in 1907 according to the American Telephone and Telegraph Company's index, and in 1917 according to Persons' index (which does not go back of 1903). These differences are not to be regarded as discrepancies, but rather as probably reliable indications that the processes to which the indexes specifically relate really attained their highest levels above their base lines in different cycles.

The most interesting case is the maximum shown by Snyder's deposits index in 1901,—a moderate crest according to the two clearings indexes, and the lowest crest in the list according to the American Telephone and Telegraph Company's series. That year saw the great "Northern Pacific corner" on the New York Stock Exchange. Financial activity in New York did perhaps rise higher above its trend then than at any other time between 1878 and 1923. The series which is much influenced by New York City clearings reflects this feverish activity. Outside clearings were stimulated in moderate degree. But "general business," as shown by the telephone company's series, expanded only a little.

The deepest depressions occurred in 1878 and 1896 according to Frickey's index, in 1894 and 1896 according to Snyder's clearings index, in 1914 according to Snyder's deposits index, and in 1921 according to the telephone company's and Persons' indexes. All these were unquestionably periods of extreme hardship, and the differences among the several indexes concerning their relative severity need give us no concern.

The periods of maximum and minimum advance and decline in business activity according to the five indexes are best presented in tabular form. The greatest "boom" in the whole period was that which followed the prolonged period of depression in the 1870's if we consider outside clearings, that which culminated in the Northern Pacific corner of 1901 if we give metropolitan clearings their share in the national total, and that which accompanied or followed the World War if we take the trade indexes. Similarly the most catastrophic declines were those which followed on the greatest booms; for even Snyder's deposits index makes the drop of 1881-1884 slightly larger than that following the Northern Pacific corner. The mildest periods of expansion, on the other hand, were those which culminated in 1895, 1902, and 1912-13, while the mildest depressions came in 1886-88, 1900, and 1910-11. The decline in 1895-97 was also slight; but that was because the preceding period of activity was mild, not because the depression lacked severity. All this is quite consistent with what is known from other sources concerning the major and minor business cycles of the period.

TABLE 17

PERCENTAGE DEVIATIONS FROM THEIR BASE LINES OF FIVE INDEXES OF BUSINESS ACTIVITY AT THE CRESTS AND TROUGHS OF SUCCESSIVE BUSINESS CYCLES, UNITED STATES: 1878–1923.

		A. T. and T. business index		Frickey's clearings index		Snyder's clearings index		Snyder's deposits index		Persons' trade index	
		Trough	Crest	Trough	Crest	Trough	Crest	Trough	Crest	Trough	Crest
'78	Trough	−13		−29		−14		−14			
'81	Crest		+13		+27		+26		+30		
'84–'85	Trough	−19		−20		−19		−23			
'86–'87	Crest		+ 9		+19		+11		+ 7		
'88	Trough	− 7		− 3		− 4		− 7			
'90	Crest		+17		+22		+21		+14		
'91	Trough	− 7		+ 4		+ 3		− 1			
'92–'93	Crest		+14		+20		+18		+13		
'93–'94	Trough	−20		−17		−20		−18			
'95	Crest		+ 6		− 2		− 3		+ 3		
'96–'97	Trough	−17		−29		−20		−11			
'99	Crest		+11		+10		+ 7		+21		
'00	Trough	− 4		−11		− 5		−15			
'01–'02	Crest		+ 6		+ 8		+15		+34		
'03–'04	Trough	−14		−11		− 2		−17		− 9	
'06–'07	Crest		+18		+15		+16		+19		+13
'07–'08	Trough	−17		−22		−12		−20		−19	
'10	Crest		+12		+ 8		+ 6		+11		+ 8
'10–'11	Trough	− 3		− 8		− 2		− 7		− 4	
'12–'13	Crest		+10		+ 8		+ 3		+ 5		+ 9
'14	Trough	−18		−17		−17		−28		−18	
'16–'17	Crest		+17				+10		+13		+25
'19	Trough	− 8				− 2		− 6		− 3	
'19–'20	Crest		+13				+ 9		+11		+15
'21	Trough	−25				−10		− 7		−22	
'23	Crest		+10				+11		+ 6		+17
Minimum		− 3	+ 6	+ 4	− 2	+ 3	− 3	− 1	+ 3	− 3	+ 8
Maximum		−25	+18	−29	+27	−20	+26	−28	+34	−22	+25
Average		−13.2	+12.0	−14.8	+13.5	− 9.5	+11.5	−13.4	+14.4	−12.5	+14.5

By far the most important difference among the indexes is that Snyder's clearings series, and less clearly Frickey's companion piece, suggest that business cycles have been growing progressively milder decade by decade, whereas the other indexes show no such cheering

TABLE 18

AMPLITUDE OF THE RISE FROM TROUGH TO CREST AND OF THE DECLINE FROM CREST TO TROUGH IN THE AMERICAN BUSINESS CYCLES OF 1878–1923 AS SHOWN BY FIVE INDEXES OF BUSINESS ACTIVITY.

	A. T. and T. business index		Frickey's clearings index		Snyder's clearings index		Snyder's deposits index		Persons trade index	
	Rise	Fall	Rise	Fall	Rise	Fall	Rise	Fall	Rise	Fall
Rise 1878–'81.........	26		56		40		44			
Fall 1881–'84, '85......		32		47		45		53		
Rise 1884, '85–'86, '87..	28		39		30		30			
Fall 1886, '87–'88......		16		22		15		14		
Rise 1888–'90..........	24		25		25		21			
Fall 1890–'91.........		24		18		18		15		
Rise 1891–'92, '93......	21		16		15		14			
Fall 1892, '93–'93, '94..		34		37		38		31		
Rise 1893, '94–'95......	26		15		17		21			
Fall 1895–'96, '97......		23		27		17		14		
Rise 1896, '97–'99......	28		39		27		32			
Fall 1899–'00..........		15		21		12		36		
Rise 1900–'01, '02......	10		19		20		49			
Fall 1901, '02–'03, '04..		20		19		17		51		
Rise 1903, '04–'06, '07..	32		26		18		36		22	
Fall 1906, '07–'07, '08..		35		37		28		39		32
Rise 1907, '08–'10......	29		30		18		31		27	
Fall 1910–'11.........		15		16		8		18		12
Rise 1911–'12, '13......	13		16		5		12		13	
Fall 1912, '13–'14......		28		25		20		33		27
Rise 1914–'16, '17......	35				27		41		43	
Fall 1916, '17–'19......		25				12		19		28
Rise 1919–'19, '20......	21				11		17		18	
Fall 1919, '20–'21......		38				19		18		37
Rise 1921–'23.........	35				21		13		39	
Minima...............	10	15	15	16	5	8	12	14	13	12
Maxima...............	35	38	56	47	40	45	49	53	43	37
Average rise...........	25		28		21		28		27	
Average fall...........		25		27		21		28		27

drift. If we confine attention to the most violent cycles of 1878–1923 (including the cycle of 1900–04 in Snyder's deposits index), and com-

TABLE 19

DATES OF THE MOST AND THE LEAST VIOLENT CYCLICAL FLUCTUATIONS IN AMERICAN
BUSINESS, 1878–1923, ACCORDING TO FIVE INDEXES OF BUSINESS ACTIVITY

	A. T. and T. business index	Frickey's clearings index	Snyder's clearings index	Snyder's deposits index	Persons' trade index
Greatest rise...	1914–17 1921–23	1878–81	1878–81	1900–01	1914–17
Greatest fall...	1920–21	1881–84	1881–85	1881–84	1920–21
Smallest rise...	1900–02	1893–95	1911–13	1910–12	1911–12
Smallest fall....	1899–00 1910–11	1910–11	1910–11	1886–88 1895–97	1910–11

bine the points of rise and fall shown in Table 18, we get the following
results:

TABLE 20

AMPLITUDE OF COMBINED RISE AND FALL IN VIOLENT BUSINESS CYCLES, ACCORDING
TO FIVE INDEXES OF BUSINESS ACTIVITY

Based upon Table 18

Business Cycles of	A. T. and T. business index	Frickey's clearings index	Snyder's clearings index	Snyder's deposits index	Persons' trade index
1878–85..........	58	103	85	97	
1891–94..........	55	53	53	45	
1900–04..........	..	..	..	100	
1904–08..........	67	63	46	75	54
1914–19..........	60		39	60	71
1919–21..........	59		30	35	55

On the face of the returns we must conclude that, since the early
1880's, the cyclical fluctuations of outside clearings have been greatly
reduced; but that the lessened fluctuations of outside clearings have
not led to greater stability in other types of business.[2] It does not
necessarily follow, however, that business processes of any one of the
many types which affect outside clearings have become more stable.
In the periods covered by Snyder's and Frickey's indexes, checks have
come into wider use in retail trade, and in paying rents, salaries, and
even wages. Transactions of this type have cyclical-irregular fluctuations of notably smaller amplitude than the wholesale transactions
which have long been settled with checks. Further, Mr. Snyder's
series, which includes all outside clearings, tends to become stabler

[2] It may be remarked that the evidence of the A. T. and T. index on this point cannot be thrown out because of the many changes in the series used in making it. For
these changes have been mainly of a sort which tend to render the averages less variable.

from the addition of new clearing houses to the list. In view of these considerations and of the contrary evidence borne by other business indexes, it is rash to say that business cycles are growing milder because the cyclical fluctuations of outside clearings are less now than they were some 40 years ago. The severity of the crisis of 1920 and the depression of 1921 is attested by abundant evidence.

By way of summary we may assemble our 111 observations upon the extreme amplitudes of the crests and troughs of business cycles in another frequency table.[3] Again the question arises how the observations made at successive points shall be grouped to bring out their significance. Taking a span of 5 points in the scale of deviations, I have made groups centered around deviations of 0, 5, 10 . . . points; 1, 6, 11 . . . points; 2, 7, 12 . . . points; 3, 8, 13 . . . points; and 4, 9, 14 . . . points. In all of these groupings, the distributions of the maximum deviations at the troughs of cycles show two crude modes. One or both of these modes shift their locations and their relative prominence on every change in the groupings of the observations. On the other hand, all 5 of the distributions of the maximum deviations at the crests of cycles rise step by step to a

[3] The full array is as follows:

Scale of deviations from base lines in Points		Number of Observations		Scale of deviations from base lines in Points		Number of Observations	
Troughs	Crests	Troughs	Crests	Troughs	Crests	Troughs	Crests
+ 4	− 4	1		−16	+16		1
+ 3	− 3	1	1	−17	+17	6	3
+ 2	− 2		1	−18	+18	3	2
+ 1	− 1			−19	+19	3	2
0	0			−20	+20	5	1
− 1	+ 1	1		−21	+21		2
− 2	+ 2	3		−22	+22	2	1
− 3	+ 3	3	2	−23	+23	1	
− 4	+ 4	3		−24	+24		
− 5	+ 5	1	1	−25	+25	1	1
− 6	+ 6	1	4	−26	+26		1
− 7	+ 7	5	2	−27	+27		1
− 8	+ 8	2	4	−28	+28	1	
− 9	+ 9	1	3	−29	+29	2	
−10	+10	1	4	−30	+30		1
−11	+11	3	5	−31	+31		
−12	+12	1	1	−32	+32		
−13	+13	1	5	−33	+33		
−14	+14	3	2	−34	+34		1
−15	+15	1	3				
					Totals	56	55

single mode and decline again step by step. Only once is this mode
shifted to a new position by altering the groupings. If the observations analyzed are representative, the crests of business cycles are
more regularly distributed about their central tendency than are the
troughs.

On adding together the groupings for troughs and crests, we get
five total distributions which are not quite so regular as the distributions of the crests, but decidedly more regular than the distributions
of the troughs. In two cases there are two crude modes separated by
a lower interval; in one case two adjacent intervals show the same
maximum figure; in the other two cases there is a single mode coin-
ciding in position with the mode of the distribution of crests.

Perhaps the best way to establish the broad characteristics of these
distributions is to strike averages of all five groupings. Table 21 shows
the results of that operation. The number of observations recorded
at each point in the scale of deviations from the trend lines of the
series appear five times in as many different combinations. In dividing these interlocking combinations for averaging I have used a scale
which centers the successive groups around deviations from the trends
of 2 points, 7 points, 12 points, etc. Since two troughs are found
slightly above and two crests slightly below the trend lines, the first
group in the scale centers around + 8 for the troughs and — 3 for the
crests.

It will be seen that the double mode persists in the averaged distribution of the troughs. The primary mode is in the group centering
about 17 per cent below the trend lines, the secondary mode in the
group centering about minus 7 per cent. The intermediate interval,
12 per cent, is the point of greatest concentration of the crests. The
distribution which combines crests and troughs has almost equal
values at 7, 12 and 17 per cent deviations from trend values.

On the whole, there is no clear evidence of the existence of two
distinct types of business cycles—major and minor, or violent and
mild—in these observations concerning extreme deviations from the
trends. Of course there are major business cycles and minor ones,
just as there are tall men and short men in every race; but when all
the deviations at the crests and troughs of business cycles are put
together they suggest a homogeneous group of phenomena rather
than a mixture of two species. Yet the volume of data is not sufficient
to close the question.

TABLE 21

FREQUENCY DISTRIBUTIONS OF 111 OBSERVATIONS UPON THE AMPLITUDE OF THE PERCENTAGE DEVIATIONS OF FIVE BUSINESS INDEXES FROM THEIR RESPECTIVE TRENDS AT THE TROUGHS AND CRESTS OF AMERICAN BUSINESS CYCLES: 1878–1923.

Data from Table 17

Averages of five groupings of the observations. See text

Scales of Percentage Deviations		Number of Observations					
Central points of the groups averaged		Actual Numbers			Percentages of Totals		
Troughs	Crests	Troughs	Crests	Both	Troughs	Crests	Both
+ 8	− 8	0.2	...	0.2	0.4	...	0.2
+ 3	− 3	2.0	1.8	3.8	3.6	3.3	3.4
− 2	+ 2	8.6	3.0	11.6	15.4	5.5	10.5
− 7	+ 7	11.4	13.8	25.2	20.4	25.1	22.7
−12	+12	7.8	16.0	23.8	13.9	29.1	21.4
−17	+17	14.2	11.0	25.2	25.4	20.0	22.7
−22	+22	8.0	5.0	13.0	14.3	9.1	11.7
−27	+27	2.8	2.8	5.6	5.0	5.1	5.0
−32	+32	1.0	1.2	2.2	1.8	2.2	2.0
−37	+37	...	0.4	0.4	...	0.7	0.4
	Totals	56.0	55.0	111.0	100.2	100.1	100.0

	Arithmetic Means	Medians	Standard deviations	Coefficients of variation
Troughs........	12.6	13.5	7.88	63%
Crests..........	13.0	12.0	7.54	58%
Both...........	12.8	12.7	7.92	52%

FREQUENCY DIAGRAMS
PERCENTAGE BASIS

Additional evidence upon this important point can be obtained by analyzing in similar fashion the figures given in Table 18 concerning the percentage amplitude of the swings from crest to trough, and from trough to crest of successive cycles. Of course, the same materials underlie this table and the one we have just been using; but the deviations, instead of being taken always with reference to the base lines, are combined in two new ways: first a deviation in a trough is added (without regard to signs) to the next deviation at a crest; then the latter deviation is added to that at the following trough, and so on. Such re-groupings of data are most useful in trying to determine whether multiple modes reveal features which are accidental or characteristic of the series in which they occur.

Again I have used a span of 5 points; centered my groups successively around movements of 2, 7, 12 . . ., 3, 8, 13 . . ., 4, 9, 14 . . ., 5, 10, 15 . . ., and 6, 11, 16 . . . per cent of trend values, and finally averaged all the groupings together. Double modes appear in most of the groupings; but they shift location as the groupings change, and they dwindle when the five groupings are combined in a general average.

Thus Table 22, which presents the final outcome of these operations, confirms the impression made by Table 21. The diagram for the declines from crest to trough shows a slight secondary mode at 34 per cent separated from the primary mode by a wider interval than appeared in Table 21, while the diagram for the advances from trough to crest shows almost equal frequencies at 19 and 29 per cent, and a slight increase from 34 to 39 per cent. But the diagram which includes both declines and advances rises rapidly to a single mode and then falls gradually step by step with one slight arrest in the descent. On the whole our frequency distributions of the amplitudes of cyclical fluctuations are somewhat more regular than our distributions of their durations, and afford even less basis for supposing that there are two or more distinct species of business cycles.

That business cycles bring enormous economic losses upon a country is clear from this study of their amplitudes. Reckoned in percentages of ordinates of secular trend, the declines from the crests to the troughs of business cycles in the United States from 1878 to 1923 averaged more than a fifth in Snyder's clearings index, and more than a quarter in all the other series. The grand average of all the observations is 25.5 per cent. In extreme cases, these declines exceeded

TABLE 22

FREQUENCY DISTRIBUTIONS OF 106 OBSERVATIONS, MADE FROM FIVE INDEXES OF BUSI-
NESS CONDITIONS, UPON THE AMPLITUDE OF THE RISE FROM TROUGH TO CREST AND
THE DECLINE FROM CREST TO TROUGH IN AMERICAN BUSINESS CYCLES, 1878–1923,
RECKONED IN PERCENTAGES OF TREND VALUES.

Data from Table 18

Averages of five groupings of the observations. See text

Scale of percentage rise or decline	Number of Observations					
	Actual Numbers			Percentages of Totals		
Central points of the groups averaged	Decline	Rise	Both	Decline	Rise	Both
4	0.2	0.8	1.0	0.4	1.5	0.9
9	2.0	2.6	4.6	3.9	4.7	4.3
14	9.8	8.8	18.6	19.2	16.0	17.5
19	11.8	10.0	21.8	23.1	18.2	20.6
24	6.2	8.8	15.0	12.2	16.0	14.1
29	5.6	9.8	15.4	11.0	17.8	14.5
34	6.4	4.4	10.8	12.5	8.0	10.2
39	5.0	5.4	10.4	9.8	9.8	9.8
44	1.2	2.4	3.6	2.4	4.4	3.4
49	1.6	1.0	2.6	3.1	1.8	2.5
54	1.2	0.6	1.8	2.4	1.1	1.7
59	...	0.4	0.4	...	0.7	0.4
Totals	51.0	55.0	106.0	100.0	100.0	99.9

	Arithmetic means	Medians	Standard deviations	Coefficients of variation
Decline.........	25.5	23	10.99	43%
Rise............	25.6	25	10.97	43%
Both..........	25.5	24.2	10.89	43%

FREQUENCY DIAGRAMS
PERCENTAGE BASIS

DECLINES ADVANCES BOTH

AMPLITUDE OF DECLINE IN PERCENTAGES OF TREND AMPLITUDE OF ADVANCE IN PERCENTAGES OF TREND AMPLITUDE OF ADVANCE AND DECLINE IN PERCENTAGES OF TREND

35, 45, and even 50 per cent of the levels indicated by the trends. Perhaps the data from which these indexes are made overweight the activities which are particularly susceptible to the business-cycle hazard; that is another question which requires the study of elaborate evidence which would be confusing here. But one might make large reductions on this score and still leave a huge charge against depressions, without counting the lasting impairment of efficiency produced by business demoralization and unemployment.

(8) The Distinctive Character of Each Business Cycle.

As one analyzes successive business cycles in various ways, one finds evidence, even in the bleak statistical records here used, that each cycle has special characteristics of its own, or rather a special combination of characteristics. More intensive study carried over a wider range in time and space would strengthen this impression. Strictly speaking, every business cycle is a unique historical episode, differing in significant ways from all its predecessors, and never to be repeated in the future. Of course, the theory of business cycles aims primarily to find generalizations which can be applied to all cases. But it is wise for those on theory bent to realize clearly the multi-faceted variability of their cases. Such knowledge may even help them in the process of establishing generalizations. For one who is familiar with the idiosyncrasies of particular cycles will sometimes see that a given rule does apply to cases which at first sight seem to form exceptions. Both as a contribution to our general understanding of business cycles and as an aid to our later inquiries, we may note briefly some of the salient characteristics of the American cycles of 1878 to 1923.

(1) The cycle of 1878-85 followed an exceptionally long and exceptionally severe period of depression. When it finally started, revival was rapid; prosperity was sustained at a high level for an unusually long time; the recession was gentle, and the decline long drawn out. The only season of acute financial strain in this cycle came, not at the downward turning point, but late in the decline—the so-called "crisis of 1884."

(2) While the period of expansion was decidedly shorter than the period of contraction in the cycle of 1878-85, the reverse was true in the cycle of 1885-88. Again the recession was mild, there was no period of acute financial stress, and the depression was not severe.

(3) In the cycle of 1888-91 prosperity attained a higher pitch than in its predecessor, though not so high as in 1881. The recession of 1890 was accompanied by more financial strain than occurred in 1882 or 1887; but the difficulties seem to have been due largely to foreign influences connected with the collapse of Baring Brothers in London. The period of decline was even briefer and milder than in the preceding cycle, being cut short by an unusual harvest situation. The world crop of wheat was poor in 1891, the American crop abundant. Hence our farmers sold a large amount of grain at prices high for that period. Their prosperity, shared by the "granger" railroads and distributors in the agricultural districts, contributed powerfully to an early resumption of activity.

(4) The next period of expansion, 1891-93, was briefer than any of its predecessors shown by our indexes. It was terminated by the great panic of 1893, one of the longest and severest crises in American business history. While this business wave had not risen to a high crest, its trough was very low.

(5) We may call the fluctuations of 1894-97 a submerged cycle. Although the amplitudes of the rise and the decline were not far from the average amplitudes shown by Table 18, the preceding and the following troughs were so low that the crest of the wave did not quite reach the base line in two of our indexes, and barely rose above the base line in two others.

(6) Rising slowly from the low point of 1897, business had not attained a very high level when it was interrupted by the mild reaction of 1900. As in 1890, foreign difficulties seem to have been largely responsible for the recession. The period of contraction was both brief and mild.

(7) The cycle of 1900-04 contained the Northern Pacific corner of 1901, and the peculiar "rich-man's panic" of 1903. In financial circles the fluctuations were of great amplitude, as Snyder's deposits index shows. But business of other sorts was affected relatively little. The American Telephone and Telegraph Company's index makes this cycle the mildest in our list, while Snyder's deposits index makes it the most intense.

(8) Perhaps better than any other case in our period, the fluctuations of 1904-08 answer to the generalized conception of a business cycle presented in the theoretical treatises. From the depression of 1904, business made a fine recovery in 1905, maintained a high pitch of prosperity for some two years, passed through a severe crisis in the

autumn of 1907, and plunged into a new depression in 1908. All the familiar phenomena appeared in standard succession and sharply defined.

(9) and (10) The next two cycles (1908-11 and 1911-14), on the other hand, were mild affairs. While the revival from the depression of 1908 was vigorous, it did not lead to a boom; the recession in 1910 was not sharp, the depression of 1911 was not severe, and the succeeding period of expansion of 1912-13 was terminated early by another mild recession. But the depression which closed the second of these cycles gained dramatic intensity when it was accentuated by the outbreak of war at the end of July, 1914.

(11) Of course the war-time cycle of 1914-18 was distinguished by unusual features—extraordinary price fluctuations, a not less extraordinary shift in the character of production, extreme scarcity of labor, abundance of loan funds, and, toward the end, by government intervention in business on an unprecedented scale.

(12) Hardly less exceptional was the first post-war cycle of 1918-21. After the brief and mild depression ushered in by the Armistice of November, 1918, business started on a boom so sudden that the period which can be labeled "revival" was very brief. Again the price fluctuations were extremely violent. The crisis was of exceptional severity so far as industry was concerned, and, while the Federal Reserve System bore the financial strain with marked success, the subsequent depression was one of the worst in American experience. Yet one who realizes how profoundly economic activities in the United States were affected by the great war, from the time when its sudden onset shattered confidence to the time when industry won back to a peace basis, must wonder that it altered the usual round of business cycles so little. A person who did not know when the great war occurred, could not date it from inspection of our five business indexes, though it would stand out clearly in indexes made largely from price series.

(13) During the cycle of 1921-24, American business gradually returned to more settled conditions. While price fluctuations continued greater than they had been from 1878 to 1914, the price system attained a new equilibrium. After a rather slow recovery from the depression of 1921, business had a short period of almost feverish activity early in 1923, suffered a check, recovered in the opening months of 1924, and then entered upon a sharper decline.

(14) From this trough in the middle of 1924 we may date the

beginning of the cycle in the later stages of which this account is written.

VII. The Need of Combining Theory, Statistics, and History.

From the outset of this inquiry into business cycles, the need of statistical work has been clear. The first demonstration came from a quarter which few might expect—a review of theories made on non-statistical lines. By showing how many processes are involved in business cycles, these theories raised a series of essentially quantitative problems. Which of the causes of cyclical fluctuations stressed by different theorists are the most important? How considerable are the effects produced by these causes, directly and indirectly? What changes occur simultaneously? In what sequence, and after what intervals do other changes follow? How regular are cyclical fluctuations? All these are obviously questions which call for measured observations—very many measured observations upon diverse processes, systematically made in numerous markets over long series of years—in short, the type of observations which constitute statistics. Indeed, the idea suggested itself at the close of Chapter I, that the whole inquiry might shift from a search for causes conducted in the light of common reason to a quasi-mathematical study of the interrelations among a number of complex variables.

Again in Chapter II, when discussing the economic organization within which business cycles run their course, we found ourselves facing quantitative issues at every turn. From the section which dealt with the proportions of "real" income which families produce for themselves and the proportions which they buy with money, to the section on international differences of organization, we had to answer as best we could questions of how much and how often.

But now that in the present chapter we have surveyed the statistical materials and methods of particular concern to students of business cycles, we see that there are grave limitations upon the help we can expect from this source. Rapid progress has been made by the last generation in gathering and in utilizing statistical data; yet we are far from the goal of establishing the study of business cycles upon a strictly statistical basis.

On the technical side, our methods of determining both the secular trends and the seasonal variations of time series are rough. So far, no one has segregated irregular from cyclical fluctuations. While a method of approximating that result was suggested above and will be elaborated in Chapter V, it yields only averages, and is applicable only to series which cover a considerable number of cycles. Neither the visual study of charts nor the coefficient of correlation are wholly satisfactory methods of determining the relationships among fluctuations. In precisely what forms series should be expressed to bring out their most significant relationships is a problem which statisticians have posed rather than solved. Little systematic work has been done toward measuring the amplitude of the cyclical-irregular fluctuations characteristic of different processes. More attention has been given to the problems of time sequence, but the results are neither comprehensive nor secure. Finally, we have no index numbers of business cycles, nor any definite program for making them. As substitutes we must use a somewhat haphazard collection of indexes relating to such processes as happen to have been recorded in statistical form for considerable periods.

Yet graver limitations are imposed by the paucity of statistical materials. Of the various processes which the theories reviewed in Chapter I represent as of crucial importance, we have satisfactory data concerning not one. Wholesale prices, foreign trade, banking, railway transportation, the metropolitan money and securities markets are the fields best covered in the United States; but the investigator who works on any of these subjects develops many problems for which he cannot get solutions from his data. About profits, savings, advance orders and other future commitments, the production of consumers' goods and industrial equipment, the amount of income disbursed to consumers and their spending, our information is fragmentary. In certain respects other countries offer better data than the United States—the British unemployment returns, and the German receipts from the tax on domestic bills of exchange are examples; but broadly speaking the foreign records are more deficient than our own.

To overcome this handicap so far as possible, the National Bureau of Economic Research has made a systematic collection of economic and social statistics for the United States, Great Britain, France and Germany, which it hopes to publish in the near future for the benefit of all workers in the social sciences. Each series is described, annotated, and presented by months or quarters, if possible, for the full period since its start. The collection covers in considerable detail all types of economic activity, and the leading indicia of social changes.

By enlisting the coöperation of foreign experts, the compilers, Dr. Willard L. Thorp and Mr. Harold Villard, hope to keep errors of omission and commission to a minimum. In addition, the National Bureau is compiling various new series of data which throw light upon salient aspects of business cycles. Dr. Frederick R. Macaulay's studies of bond yields and interest rates since 1857, Dr. Harry Jerome's monograph upon *Migration and Business Cycles*, Dr. Leo Wolman's critical investigations of the labor market, Dr. Frederick C. Mills' intensive work upon the interrelations among price fluctuations, and Dr. Simon S. Kuznets' study of secular trends all promise contributions of importance. Incidental use can be made also of our earlier studies of unemployment, and of Dr. Willford I. King's continuing estimates of income. By utilizing the general collection of statistics, together with the special studies made by the National Bureau and other agencies, we shall be doing what we can to give our inquiry a secure foundation of measurements.

One other source we have, intermediate between statistics and casual observation. This is the collection of *Business Annals*, recently published by the National Bureau. Diligent ransacking and critical comparison of many reports, periodicals, and pamphlets enabled Dr. Thorp to trace the course of business cycles over a longer period and a wider area than is covered by any but the most meager statistics. From his systematic records we can learn certain broad facts about the characteristics of recent cycles in countries of varying culture, and of early cycles in the countries which concern us most. These annals give the best opportunity for studying the international relationships of business fluctuations. They enable us even to make crude measurements of the duration of business cycles, which by covering many more cases supplement and broaden the conclusions drawn above from the business indexes. Exploiting this fresh source is our next task.

Just as a review of theories of business cycles made us see the need of statistics, so our review of statistics makes us see the need of economic history. Of course our historical survey must be condensed, like our summary of theories. When that survey has been completed, we shall not dwell upon the limitations of business annals —they will be obvious.

It is wise to face the shortcomings of each of these approaches to one problem—the theoretical, the statistical, and the historical. But critical though we must be of all our materials and methods, we can put the criticisms to constructive uses. What has just been said concerning the limitations of statistics should not check, but guide our dealings with tables and charts. The diversity of theories sketched in Chapter I, all plausible and each claiming to reveal the cause of most importance, seemed rather disconcerting. But from each explanation we may get some suggestion of value, and certainly neither our statistics nor our condensed business histories will enable us to do without much reasoning of the sort relied upon by economic theorists. To win as much knowledge as we can of business cycles, we must combine all that we can learn from theory, statistics, and history.

CHAPTER IV.

THE CONTRIBUTION OF BUSINESS ANNALS.

I. The National Bureau's Collection of Business Annals.

Several of the theorists whose writings were laid under contribution in Chapter I—notably Tugan-Baranovski, Bouniatian and Lescure—have devoted much attention to the history of crises and depressions. Similarly, some of the statisticians referred to in Chapter III—for example, Warren M. Persons and his colleagues—have supplemented their time series on occasion by preparing annual summaries of business conditions. But the histories have dealt largely with what was common in the episodes treated, and the summaries have been confined to rather brief periods in a few countries. For theoretical uses, there is needed a systematic record of cyclical alternations of prosperity and depression, covering all countries in which the phenomena have appeared, and designed to make clear the recurrent features of the alternations. If the view taken in Chapter II of the circumstances under which business cycles occur is valid, it may not be impracticable to make a modest descriptive record of this sort which approximates completeness.

While the National Bureau of Economic Research has not been able to perform this whole task, it has sought to form a larger collection of what we may call "business annals" than has been available hitherto. Dr. Willard L. Thorp, who directed the work of compilation, ransacked the rich resources of the New York Public Library for official documents, reports, pamphlets, periodicals, and books dealing systematically or incidentally with business conditions in various countries. The generous coöperation of several foreign scholars brought additional materials and special knowledge to the work.[1] For every year and every country covered, the plan required a digest

[1] Professor Albert Aftalion of Paris reviewed the French annals, Dr. Robert R. Kuczynski of Berlin the German annals, Dr. F. A. von Hayek of Vienna the Austrian annals, Dr. Robert F. Foerster the Italian annals, Dr. E. H. D. Arndt of Transvaal University the South African annals, and Drs. N. D. Kondratieff, A. L. Vainstein and M. B. Ignatieff of the Conjuncture Institute, Moscow, the Russian annals.

of contemporary opinions concerning (1) industrial, commercial and labor conditions, (2) conditions in the markets for loans, securities, and foreign exchange, (3) agricultural production and prices, and (4) non-economic occurrences, such as political events, epidemics, floods or earthquakes, which seem to have influenced business appreciably. From such information as he could gather upon these four heads, Dr. Thorp formed his own opinion concerning the phase of the business cycle through which the country in question was passing each year, and expressed his opinion in a brief caption.

Annals of this sort for the United States have been carried back to 1790, the first year after the adoption of the Constitution. To make possible international comparisons from the beginning of the American record, English annals have been compiled for the same 136 years. Lack of accessible sources, or lack of economic unity, made it difficult to go back of 1840 in France, 1853 in Germany, and 1867 in Austria. To show the geographical spread of business fluctuations in recent times, several other countries were added to the five covered in the long-period studies. With 1890 as the starting-point in all cases, Italy, the Netherlands, Sweden, and Russia were chosen to show diversified conditions in Europe. Next, three great English-speaking colonies on three continents were taken—Canada, Australia, and South Africa. To represent South America, Argentina and Brazil seemed fittest. Finally the foremost Oriental civilizations were included—British India, Japan and China. Needless to say, the sample might well have been enlarged, both by carrying the annals back to earlier dates in several of the nations covered, and by including at least a dozen other countries. The National Bureau hopes that what it lacked means to accomplish may be done by men who have access to the fullest records available for the periods and the countries it has omitted.

Limited as it is in scope, our collection of annals attained proportions and a promise of usefulness which called for independent publication. In the present book, we can use the volume of *Business Annals* much as we use the coördinate statistical series.[2]

---

[2] See *Business Annals*, by Willard Long Thorp, Publications of the National Bureau of Economic Research, No. 8, New York, 1926.

The present chapter consists mainly of the "Introduction" which I contributed to Dr. Thorp's book, with such omissions, emendations, and additions as are suggested by its relation to earlier chapters, or by sober second thoughts. Once more I may thank the National Bureau's staff, especially Dr. Frederick C. Mills and Dr. Thorp, for much help in analyzing the material contained in the annals.

II. The Trustworthiness of Business Annals.

1. Sources and Methods of Compilation.

The materials with which compilers of business annals work lack the objectivity, as well as the formal precision, of statistics. A man's opinion concerning the fortunes of business in a given year is affected by his personal interests, his training, his opportunities for making observations himself and collecting the observations of others, his aptitude for generalizing, and the care with which he studies his evidence.

One who begins sampling contemporary opinions concerning business conditions in any country with this reflection in mind, will be impressed less by the differences among the conclusions reached by various observers than by their consensus. In the majority of years, business developments are dominated by a trend so clear that it impresses every thoughtful observer, whatever his personal equation may be. Of course, there are years in the record of every country when such is not the case. When the investigator finds serious discrepancies among his sources, he must sometimes ascribe them to bias or incompetence on the part of one or more writers; but more often he discovers that the writers who seem to disagree referred to different industries or different sections of a country—industries or sections which had divergent fortunes.

As the activities of a people get more definitely organized on the basis of business economy, the sources of information concerning business become more numerous, more reliable, and more alike in tenor. On the one hand, different industries and different sections of the country are tied more closely together, so that prosperity or depression in one affects more, and is more affected by, prosperity or depression in others. We shall have occasion to observe, for example, that the American annals reveal greater similarity of fortunes in the opening years of the 20th century than in the closing years of the 18th century. On the other hand, business reporting becomes a profession, and undergoes a development comparable in character to the contemporary development in gathering statistics. Indeed, these two developments foster one another. Since about the middle of the 19th century in England and the United States, and since later dates in other countries, there have been established an increasing number of periodicals which report business developments weekly or monthly to critical circles of subscribers. Government agencies, especially the consular offices, render similar services to the whole business public. In recent years, it is possible to find for all the countries included in our annals several sources of information, domestic or foreign, which can be checked against each other. In default of local periodicals, British, French and American consular reports can be drawn upon for information concerning trade in every quarter of the world. And besides the reports made at regular intervals for every country, there is a much longer list of pamphlets and books which throw light upon business affairs at different times. The bibliography appended to Dr. Thorp's report shows how numerous and how varied are the sources upon which a diligent compiler of business annals can draw.

In proportion as his sources multiply, an alert compiler, like an alert historian, realizes that his own work has its subjective side. The few sentences he writes to summarize the mass of material are colored by his personal equation, compounded of his preconceptions, his knowledge and his ignorance, his technical training, and all the other characteristics which enter subtly into his appreciation of various bits of evidence. From the same set of sources, no two compilers will make quite the same summaries. In most years, the differences will be slight in comparison with the similarities; but in the years when business conditions as seen by contemporaries are confused, two compilers may get appreciably different impressions concerning the situation as a whole.

Perhaps the gravest danger lurking in the statistical treatment of social problems is that, once data have been compiled into neatly published tables, the figures gain a pontifical authority over many minds. Field statisticians who provide the original data usually retain a prudent skepticism concerning the representative value of the precise-seeming results toward which they have contributed. But "arm-chair statisticians," who have never filled in a questionnaire from interviews, deciphered a factory payroll, audited the accounts of a business enterprise, or assessed the value of a stock of merchandise, are prone to put unmerited confidence in tables they wish to analyze. Business annals have not yet won undeserved credit. But it is not premature to point out that the crisp phrases, in which a compiler of annals sets down his conclusions for country after country and year after year, are as much subject to a margin of error as are statistical summaries. The compiler, like the statistical field worker, is sure that the width of this margin varies from entry to entry; but, again like the field statistician, he cannot feel much confidence in his own estimate of his probable error.

2. A Comparison of Business Annals and Business Indexes.

Fortunately, there is a way of testing two samples of the National Bureau's annals objectively. As seen in the preceding chapter, we have statistical indexes of business conditions in the United States and England which cover considerable periods. If these series deserve their name, the fluctuations which they show in economic activity and the business changes which our annals describe may be expected to run similar courses.

While Dr. Thorp and his assistants have made some use of statistical tables in compiling their annals, and while the writers whose observations constitute their sources have done likewise, it is by no means a foregone conclusion that the annals and the indexes of business activity will agree closely. For the data used in making the indexes cover a much narrower range of economic activities than are represented in the annual business reviews of such sources as consular reports, the London *Economist,* Raffalovich's *Marché Financier,* or the *Financial Review.* Moreover, in so far as consuls, or editors, or our own compilers have used statistics in drawing their conclusions, they have used the data in unadjusted, or but slightly altered form. The statisticians who make business indexes, on the other hand, subject their data to the elaborate series of transformations described in Chapter III. They compute and eliminate secular trends; often they eliminate also seasonal variations; in some cases they seek to eliminate the effects of price fluctuations. When they are combining several series, they may reduce the fluctuations of each to units of its standard deviation, and "weight" their averages as best they can. As a final step they often "smooth" their curves. All these operations are quite different from those which a financial editor performs when he passes through his mind reports from many cities and many industries, and sets down his broad conclusion concerning the course of business as a whole. The statistical operations are more objective and more precise; but they deal with more limited data, and deal with them in a more circumscribed and mechanical fashion.

To all acquainted with the making of the two types of summaries, it will be clear that a comparison between the annals of business and the statistical indexes of business activity is quite as much a test of the latter as of the former. The makers of the statistical indexes are usually careful to point out the limitations of their results, and eager to compare them with the results of other investigations. They recognize (1) that the original data are subject to varying margins of error; (2) that the technical methods of eliminating secular trends, seasonal fluctuations, and the effects of price variations are far from perfect; (3) that the residuals left in time series by these eliminations contain not merely the cyclical fluctuations, but also the effects of random factors peculiar to the series used. Even if a statistician had relatively abundant raw materials to work up, he would not claim that his results formed a strictly accurate record of changes in business conditions. In his eyes the best results he can get remain approximations, limited by the errors of the underlying data and the uncertainties of his technical methods.

But the most serious limitation is that the statistician who seeks to cover a considerable period can find but few time series fit for his purpose. The indexes of general business or volume of trade which run back of the great war must be made on one of two plans. Either they must be records of a single type of activity—like Mr. Carl Snyder's "clearings index of business"—or they must be made by averaging the fluctuations of groups of series which themselves change from time to time—like the American Telephone and Telegraph Company's "index of general business conditions," or Professor Warren M. Persons' "index of trade."

Now, no single type of transactions—not even such an inclusive type as the volume of checks cleared in all reporting towns outside of New York—can be taken to represent all the important phases of business activity. The payments made by check in the towns which have no clearing houses, and the payments made in coin and paper money may undergo fluctuations which differ in amplitude and timing from the fluctuations of clearings. That is merely a doubt concerning the faithfulness with which clearings represent changes in total payments. Far more important is the certainty that the volume of payments made by check within a given period undergoes fluctuations materially different from the fluctuations which are taking place in the volume of goods produced, shipped, or consumed, and different from the fluctuations in employment, the disbursing of income, and the purchasing of consumers' goods. Yet the latter processes are quite as much a part of business as is paying bills by check.

The indexes made by averaging the fluctuations of several series represent a wider range of activities. But the activities which can be included are those for which a statistical record happens to have been made for a relatively long period—not the activities which a statistician would choose were he planning an index. Moreover, the changes in the lists of series which are available for successive decades raise grave questions about the comparability of the results for the earlier and the later years covered. Finally, there are puzzling questions about the interpretation of a composite made by averaging the fluctuations of series so different as (say) price indexes, values of goods imported, and tons of pig iron produced.

What we have in our business annals and our indexes of general business conditions, then, are different approaches to the problem of recording the fluctuations of economic activities—approaches each of which has its uncertainties as well as its merits. We cannot expect them to agree perfectly. When they disagree we cannot say that the discrepancy necessarily means error in one or all; it may mean merely that the different activities reflected by the various approaches really did not change in quite the same way. But if we find a general consilience among the results we shall feel increased confidence in the reliability of both approaches, and may regard the occasional discrepancies as presenting genuine problems from the study of which fresh knowledge may be gained.

The charts which follow offer as graphic a comparison as can well be made between our annals and the leading American and British indexes of general trade which cover considerable periods. In the column for each year is entered a brief characterization of business conditions drawn from the annals, and above are plotted the index curves.[1] The curves show cyclical fluctuations above and below the moving base traced by the monthly ordinates of the secular trends of

[1] For the methods followed in making the two American indexes used in Chart 21, see M. C. Rorty, "The Statistical Control of Business Activities." *Harvard Business Review*, January, 1923, vol. 1, pp. 154-166, and Carl Snyder, "A New Clearings Index of Business for Fifty Years," *Journal of the American Statistical Association*, September, 1924, vol. xix, pp. 329-335.

For the recent items in the two series, we are indebted respectively to Mr. Seymour L. Andrew, Chief Statistician of the American Telephone and Telegraph Company, and to Mr. Snyder of the Federal Reserve Bank of New York.

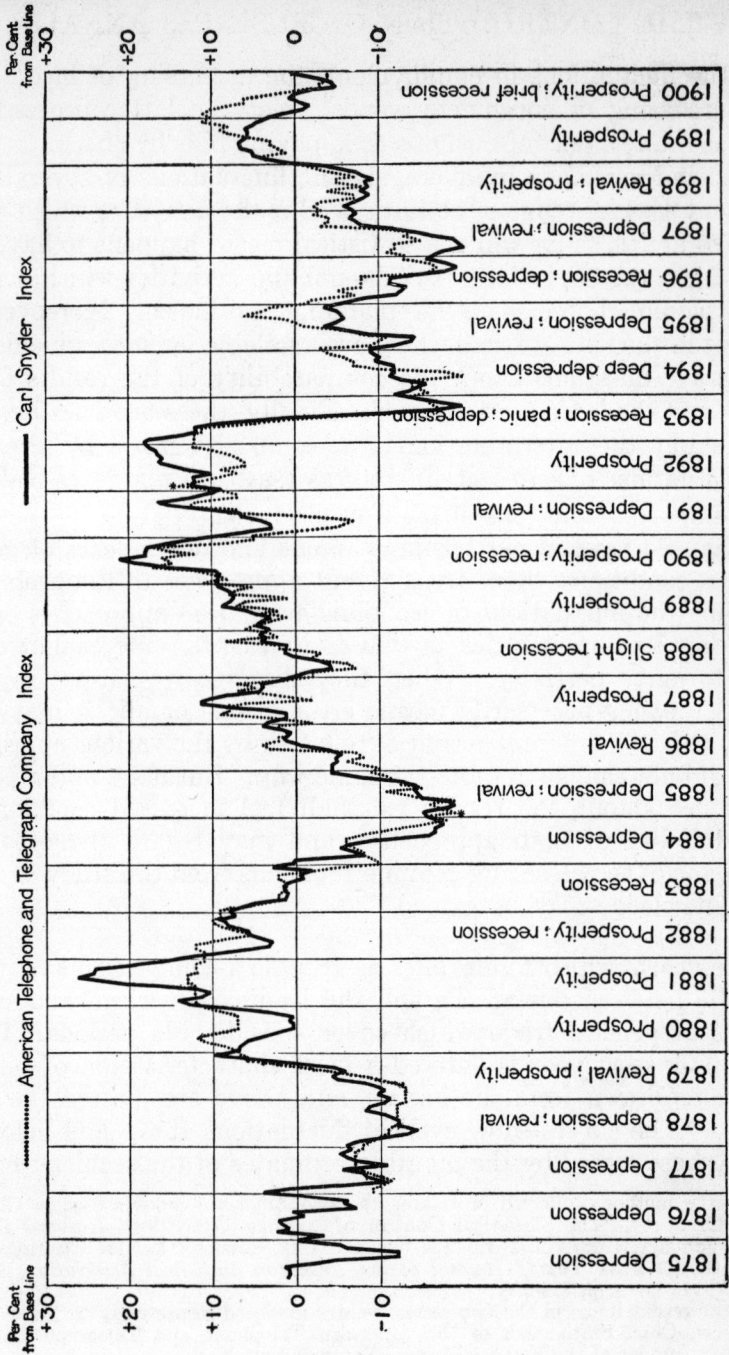

CHART 21. Business Fluctuations in the United States, as shown by the Annals and by Two Statistical Indexes, 1875-1925.

.... American Telephone and Telegraph Company Index   ——— Carl Snyder Index

* Change in composition of curve

CHART 21. Business Fluctuations in the United States, as shown by the Annals and by Two Statistical Indexes, 1875-1925.— (*Continued*)

.... American Telephone and Telegraph Company Index   ———— Carl Snyder Index

* Change in composition of curve

Year	Phase
1901	Prosperity
1902	Prosperity
1903	Prosperity : recession
1904	Mild depression · revival
1905	Prosperity
1906	Prosperity
1907	Prosperity: panic, recession, depression
1908	Depression
1909	Revival : mild prosperity
1910	Recession
1911	Mild depression
1912	Revival : prosperity
1913	Prosperity : recession
1914	Depression
1915	Revival, prosperity
1916	Prosperity
1917	Prosperity · war activity
1918	War activity · recession
1919	Revival : prosperity
1920	Prosperity : recession : depression
1921	Depression
1922	Revival : prosperity
1923	Prosperity : recession
1924	Mild depression · revival
1925	Prosperity

Per Cent from Base Line: +30, +20, +10, 0, -10

369

the time series used (corrected when necessary for seasonal variations). Since these ordinates are assigned the value of zero or 100 in the computations, they fall in the chart upon a horizontal line, which may be called the base.

In studying the charts, we must bear in mind that they do not do full justice either to the statistical method of presenting changes in business or to the annals. It is a commonplace that no statistical average represents adequately the array of data from which it is computed. Just so, the catchwords used to summarize the annals do not represent adequately Dr. Thorp's records. Much more than the charts show can be learned by examining the series combined to make the indexes of business conditions, and by reading the fuller form of the annals. In confining our comparison to the most abstract and symbolic summaries of the two sets of materials, we are imposing a severe test of conformity.

On the American chart the correspondence between the annals and the two statistical indexes is very close. Indeed, there are no serious discrepancies. To be more specific, the annals show 13 business recessions, mild or severe, between 1875 and 1924. Every one of these recessions is marked in both of the statistical indexes by a decline in the curve. These declines are slight in the recessions which the annals describe as mild, and abrupt in the recessions which the annals (in their fuller form) describe as crises or panics.[2] Further, the two curves give joint evidence of no recessions other than those mentioned by the annals. Similarly with other phases of the successive cycles. When the annals report revivals the curves ascend; when the annals report prosperity the curves fluctuate on levels decidedly higher than in the preceding or following depressions; when the annals report depressions the curves are relatively low

The chief difference between the two records is that the annals show but vaguely and irregularly the degrees of prosperity and depression attained in successive cycles, whereas the curves necessarily deviate from the horizontal base by definite distances. Finally, there are indications in the American chart that business commentators are influenced in their use of the terms prosperity and depression by recent experience. From such subjective waverings, the statistical indexes are exempt. But this point comes out more clearly in the British chart, and will be discussed in that connection.

[2] On the use of these three terms in the annals to suggest the varying character of the transitions from prosperity to depression, see below, section iii, 4, "Crises" and "Recessions."

For opportunity to compare the British annals with a British index, the National Bureau is indebted to Dr. Dorothy Swaine Thomas, who generously put at our disposal before publication a series showing changes in business conditions from 1855 to 1913 by quarters.[3] This index, like the American Telephone and Telegraph Company's index for the United States, is a composite made from a list of series which reflect various types of economic activity. Since these materials have grown more abundant with the years, Dr. Thomas' index represents British business as a whole more faithfully in the later decades than in the earlier ones. But of course the introduction of a new series with a numerical value different from the average of the other components of the index produces changes which may not correspond with the changes in business conditions.

On the whole, the correspondence between the British annals and the British index is close, though not so close as in the American comparison. Dr. Thomas' curve usually rises when the annals report revival, stands high when the annals report prosperity, sinks when the annals report recession, and runs on a low level when the annals report depression. But there are exceptions to the rule which require comment.

(1) Judging from the curve, one would expect the annals to report a recession of British business in 1860-61. These years present an unusually mixed state of affairs. As a result of the American Civil War, the cotton textile industry suffered severely from scarcity of raw material. But reports from other trades do not indicate that there was a general recession of activity. On the contrary, most industries seem to have been very active. In the fuller form of the annals these facts are succinctly stated. For his two-word summary Dr. Thorp could find no phrase which seemed more accurate than "uneven prosperity," a phrase which he uses in all cases when most industries are thriving, but one or more important trades are depressed by special circumstances. The statistics available to Dr. Thomas for the 1860's are data in which the cotton industry counts heavily. Hence her curve drops abruptly. Most of the other English series covering these years which the National Bureau has collected confirm the index rather than the business commentators. In our later statistical work we shall have to recognize the cycles which the consensus of statistical evidence shows. But it would be conceal-

[3] See "An Index of British Business Cycles," by Dorothy S. Thomas, *Journal of the American Statistical Association*, March, 1926, vol. xxi, pp. 60-63.

CHART 22. Business Fluctuations in England, as shown by the Annals and Dr. Dorothy S. Thomas' "Quarterly Index of British Cycles," 1855-1914.

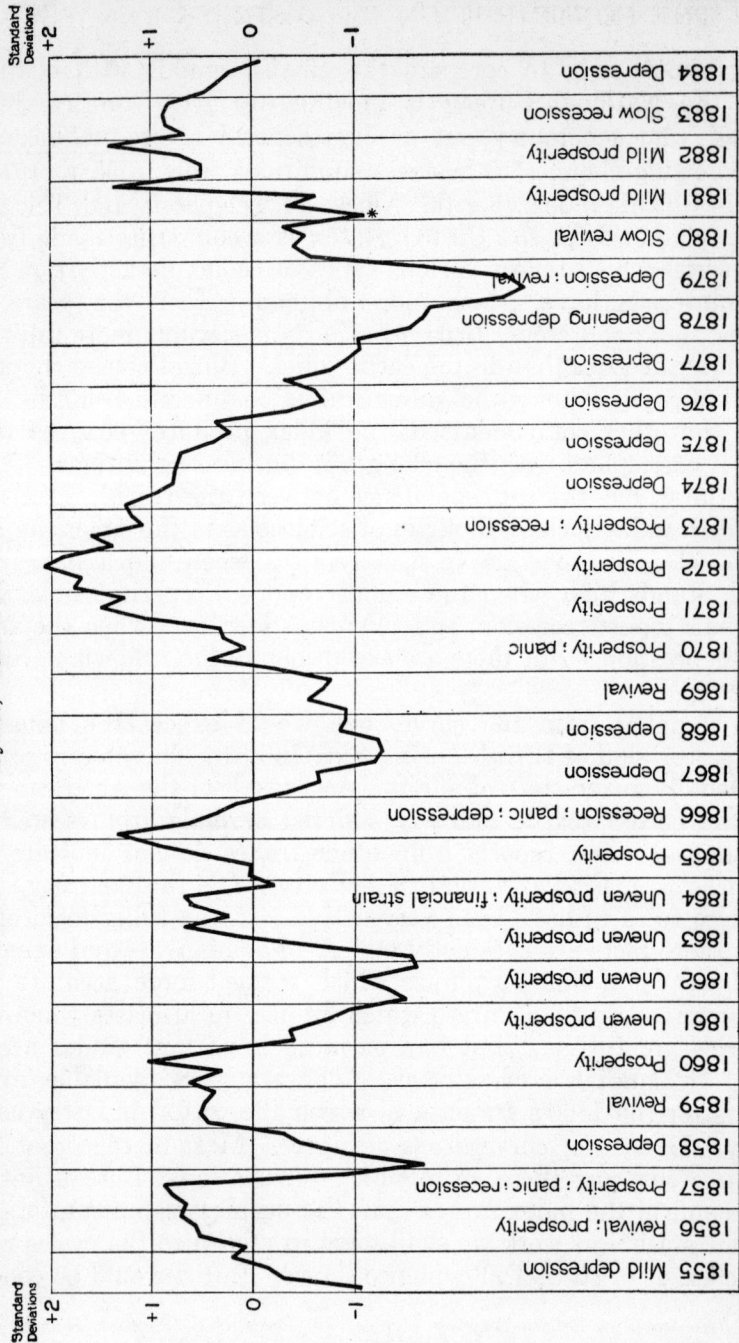

* Change in composition of curve

CHART 22. Business Fluctuations in England, as shown by the Annals and Dr. Dorothy S. Thomas' "Quarterly Index of British Cycles," 1855-1914.—(Continued)

* Change in composition of curve

ing, rather than overcoming, a difficulty to make our interpretation of contemporary opinions fit the surviving figures.

(2) In 1874-75 the annals report depression while Dr. Thomas' curve, though declining, is still above the base line. In 1881, 1897-98 and 1910-11 the annals report "mild prosperity" or "prosperity," while Dr. Thomas' curve is slightly below or but slightly above the base line. Perhaps these differences between the statistical record and the annals are due in part to defects in the data at Dr. Thomas' disposal, or to the technical difficulties of eliminating secular trends. But it is probable that they indicate one of the defects characteristic of business annals. In judging current business conditions, everyone is influenced by comparisons with recent experience. When business has been notably good for several years, as it had been in England during the early 1870's, and then grows slack, a commentator will say that business is depressed, though the volume of trade still remains large. Similarly, after business has passed through a period of hard times, commentators are likely to hail as prosperity any substantial increase of activity. In short, men's judgments upon business conditions belong among the social phenomena which are influenced by business cycles. As a summary of current opinion about the state of trade, our annals reflect these subjective changes in the use of terms.

The preceding comparisons cover periods and countries in which business reporting is well developed. Presumably the annals for earlier years in the United States and England, and the annals for countries with a less integrated organization, contain a wider margin of error. But usually there is such a consensus of judgment among the sources as to leave little doubt about the general tenor of affairs. In years when differences of opinion appear among contemporary writers, Dr. Thorp has consulted every source available to him and has weighed the evidence with care. He has endeavored also to use the technical terms employed in characterizing different states of business as consistently as possible. Yet the results are subject to emendation, and readers who discover errors of any sort are urged to let the National Bureau of Economic Research benefit by their acumen.

Despite the difficulties dwelt upon in the preceding chapter, the most satisfactory materials for studying business cycles are statistical data—not mere business indexes, like those shown in the preceding charts, but series showing month by month the fluctuations of many types of economic activity. But we have found that the periods and the places for which such data can be had in abundance are few. Hence we have been forced to recognize that narrow limits of time and of space are drawn around the quantitative study of business fluctuations. We cannot trace back business cycles to their beginnings in any country of Europe by the aid of figures. Nor can we trace in figures the spread of business cycles to countries which are just beginning to standardize their economic life on the European pattern. For the compilation of abundant statistics of business activities does not begin in any country until the business activities themselves have become highly organized. That comes later than business cycles.

According to the logic of the statistical method, this limitation of the number of cycles for which data have been preserved is most serious. The statistician's art, as practiced in the social sciences, consists in establishing generalizations about variable phenomena by the analysis of an array of cases. When his cases are few, no elaboration of technique can enable the statistician to generalize with security. Business cycles are both highly complex and highly variable phenomena, and statistical inferences concerning them must be taken as tentative until the number of cases available for analysis has grown decidedly larger than at present.

Under these circumstances it is well to learn all that we can from the annals of business. In countries like the United States and England these annals cover at least twice as many cycles as are covered by more than a few statistical series. In countries where statistics are in their infancy, the annals give us some insight into the course of developments. Precision, of course, cannot be had from descriptive accounts; but the annals speak in terms of more and less, they mark off turning points in business trends, they compare in general terms the contemporary fortunes of different countries. Taken, not as a rival, but as a supplement of statistical analysis, an attempt to find the characteristics of business cycles as shown by the longer and wider record of the annals has its value. Indeed, as was said near the close of the preceding chapter, there are certain fundamental problems concerning business cycles which can be answered more certainly by studying the annals than by analyzing the statistics now available.

III. The Cyclical Character of Business Fluctuations.

1. The "Normal State of Trade" a Figment.

The broadest conclusion established by the long and wide experience covered by the annals is that there is no "normal state of trade." The phrase is common both in treatises upon economic theory and in the talk of business men. Yet the historical record shows no reality corresponding to this figment of the imagination.

If "normal" is interpreted to mean usual, prevailing, that which exists in the absence of grave "disturbing causes," the annals show that the only normal condition is a state of change—which is not what the phrase means to those who use it. From England in 1790 to China in 1925, from Sweden to Australia, the tables reveal incessant fluctuations. Frequently the word "prosperity" is used in the annals of some country for several years in succession. But "depression" occurs in series perhaps as often. And in a less condensed summary both of these catchwords would be qualified always, as they often are qualified even in these tables, by adjectives indicating that the prosperity or depression is waxing or waning.

If "normal" means, not that which usually does prevail, but that which we think should prevail, it is equally a figment—though one of a useful kind. There are good reasons for trying to decide what phase of business cycles is most conducive to social welfare; for seeking ways to make that phase last longer and to mitigate departures from it. But when such is the meaning in mind, a less ambiguous word than "normal" should be used.

Of course, the economic theorist's "normal state," that which corresponds to the conditions assumed for purposes of analysis, is not to be looked for in an historical record. Nor can we take for granted the existence of a moving "normal state of trade," of such a nature that departures from it tend to correct themselves. That idea, if needed, can be less ambiguously expressed in terms of economic equilibria.

An additional source of confusion and therefore an additional reason for avoiding the word is supplied by the slipshod practice of business-cycle statisticians, who sometimes write "normal" when they mean a long-period average, and sometimes write "normal" when they mean the course marked by the ordinates of a secular trend.

2. Use of the Term "Cycles."

While the annals show that business is subject to continual fluctuations, they also show that in no country are the alternations of expansion and contraction highly regular. Is it justifiable, then, to speak of these fluctuations as business "cycles"?

That of course is a question regarding the proper use of a technical term. In 1922, President John C. Merriam of the Carnegie Institution called "A Conference on Cycles," in which representatives of several sciences discussed the cyclical phenomena with which they deal. To prevent misunderstandings the conferees needed a definition of cycles applicable alike in meteorology, botany, geology, paleontology, astronomy, geography and economics. Subsequent discussion showed that the definition given by the first speaker, Dr. F. E. Clements, commended itself to the others.

> In general scientific use (said Dr Clements) the word (cycle) denotes a recurrence of different phases of plus and minus departures, which are often susceptible of exact measurement. It has no necessary relation to a definite time interval, though this is frequently a characteristic of astronomical cycles. Apart from the familiar cycles of the day, the lunar month, and the year, the one best known is the sun-spot recurrence, to which the term cycle is almost universally applied. This furnishes convincing evidence that the significance of the term resides in the fact of recurrence rather than in that of the time interval, since the sun-spot cycle has varied in length from 7 to 17 years since 1788, while the minimum-maximum phase has ranged from 3 to 5 years and the maximum-minimum phase from 6 to 8 years since 1833. In consequence, it seems desirable to use cycle as the inclusive term for all recurrences that lend themselves to measurement, and period or periodicity for those with a definite time interval, recognizing, however, that there is no fixed line between the two.[1]

Now our annals show beyond doubt "a recurrence of different phases" in business activity, and these recurrences "lend themselves to measurement." Hence we have ample warrant in the usages of other sciences than economics for applying the term "cycles" to

[1] "Report of a Conference on Cycles," *The Geographical Review,* Special Supplement, October, 1923, vol. xiii, pp. 657, 658.

business fluctuations. But the term "periodicity" we should not use with reference to business cycles, or with reference to crises. For the time intervals between crises are far from regular. They vary, as will appear presently, even more than the length of sun-spot cycles.

3. THE PHASES OF BUSINESS CYCLES.

The different phases which recur in business activity are sometimes treated as only two—depression and prosperity. More often there are said to be three phases which recur in the order prosperity, crisis, depression.[1] But if the transition from prosperity to depression is recognized as a separate phase, it seems logical to give similar recognition to the transition from depression to prosperity. Then we have a four-phase cycle of prosperity, crisis, depression, and revival.[2] Professor Warren M. Persons goes further still. By dividing the transition from prosperity to depression into "financial strain" and "industrial crisis," he gets five phases.[3]

This process of subdivision can be carried further indefinitely as statistics with brief time intervals become more abundant. And as knowledge of the subject grows and its practical applications become more important, there may be call for such refinements. As matters stand, however, four phases satisfy the needs of systematic inquiry. The separation of the phase of "financial strain" from that of "industrial crisis" rests on logical quite as much as upon chronological grounds, and is somewhat confusing in a cycle of recurrence in time. Cases will be cited presently of financial strain occurring at other stages of the cycle than the transition from prosperity to depression, and industrial reactions frequently occur when it is difficult to find any trace of preceding financial strain, for example, in the United States in 1923. But we are trenching upon a topic which requires separate treatment.

4. "CRISES" AND "RECESSIONS."

Two quite distinct conceptions of business crises are current in recent books. Professor Aftalion, for example, defines the crisis as

[1] Compare for example, Dr. E. H. Vogel's description of a cycle, *Die Theorie des volkswirtschaftlichen Entwickelungsprozesses und das Krisenproblem*, Vienna, 1917, pp. 31, 32.

[2] These four phases were recognized and separately described as long ago as 1867 by John Mills, "On Credit Cycles, and the Origin of Commercial Panics," *Transactions of the Manchester Statistical Society*, 1867-68, pp. 5-40.

[3] See Professor Persons' numerous articles in the *Review of Economic Statistics*, and his *Measuring and Forecasting General Business Conditions*, New York, 1920, p. 34.

"the point of intersection . . . at which prosperity passes over into depression." [1] Professor Bouniatian, to give a corresponding example of the second usage, applies the term "to an organic disturbance of economic life, bringing upon a large number of enterprisers loss of fortune and income or complete economic ruin." [2]

From this difference of definition there follow differences in the lists of crises recognized in various books, and hence differences in the average intervals asserted to lie between crises. Professor Lescure, who antedated Aftalion in defining crisis as the point of intersection between prosperity and depression, includes the crisis of 1913 in his historical section. But Bouniatian admits no crisis between 1907 and 1920, and quite consistently; for, as Lescure himself explains, there was no epidemic of bankruptcies in 1913.[3] Tugan-Baranovski goes even further than Bouniatian in stressing the violence of crises, and consequently in shortening his list of crisis dates. A crisis "breaks out like a tempest" in the midst of prosperity, "bringing bankruptcies, unemployment, misery, etc." With this conception in mind, he quite rightly says that England escaped a crisis in 1873, in 1882, in 1890, in 1900 and in 1907—though the "industrial cycle" shows itself in the evolution of English business in these later times "with the same neatness and clarity as before." [4]

Which of these two conceptions of the crisis fits better in a discussion of business cycles is easy to decide. What concerns such a discussion is the recurrence of certain phases of business activity. The transition from prosperity to depression is one of the regularly recurring phases, whether it is marked by "an organic disturbance of economic life," in Bouniatian's phrase, or whether financial strain is conspicuous by its absence.

But while there is no doubt about the reality of these transitions, there is grave doubt whether the word crisis should be retained to describe them. For with that word there is associated in the public mind, as in the minds of writers like Bouniatian and Tugan-Baranovski, the idea of financial strain. When such strain is scarcely perceptible, it is confusing to call the transition a crisis. Close study of the annals shows that transitions free from strain are frequent—

[1] Albert Aftalion, *Les Crises Périodiques de Surproduction*, Paris, 1913, vol. i, Preface, p. vi.
[2] Mentor Bouniatian, *Les Crises Économiques*, Paris, 1922, p. 31.
[3] Lescure, *Des Crises Générales et Périodiques de Surproduction*, 3rd ed., Paris, 1923, pp. 2 and 238-253; Bouniatian, as cited above, pp. 43, 44.
[4] Michel Tugan-Baranovski, *Les Crises Industrielles en Angleterre*, Paris, 1913, pp. 34, 150, 152, 166, 167, 174.

perhaps more frequent than violent transitions. And there are cheering indications that the preponderance of mild transitions is growing greater.

To make the confusion worse, the annals report numerous cases of financial strain, not at the moment when prosperity is passing into depression, but in other phases of the cycle. "Financial stringency" and "bourse panics" are common phenomena in "booms," often occurring a year or two before the phase of expansion in general business ends Less remembered, but not less important, are the cases of financial strain coming in periods of depression. To cite a dozen examples, the annals make such reports for France in 1861, Germany in 1877, England in 1878, Argentina in 1891, Australia and Russia in 1892, Italy and the Netherlands in 1893, the United States in 1896 (as well as in 1819 and 1884), South Africa in 1898, Japan in 1901, and China in 1912. Often the sources from which the annals are drawn use the words "crisis" or "panic" in describing these episodes of depression, and sometimes they use "crisis" as equivalent to depression itself.

"Crisis," then, is a poor term to use in describing one of the four phases of business cycles. If it is to be retained, it must be defined in the colorless fashion of Lescure and Aftalion—as the mere point of intersection between prosperity and depression. But sad experience shows how much misunderstanding comes from the effort to use familiar words in new technical senses. Scientific writers can hardly expect that readers will purge their minds of old associations and form new ones at a terminologist's bidding.

One remedy for the ambiguity of "crisis" is to apply a qualifying adjective whenever the word is used. Thus Mr. Joseph Kitchin distinguishes between major and minor crises. But his major crises are in some cases such mild transitions that many writers refuse to call them crises at all. Such is the case with the American crises of 1882 and 1899 (1900 is a better date), and the English crisis of 1913, all of which Mr. Kitchin labels "major." [5] Thus his conception of a major crisis is even more confusing to non-technical readers than the use of the unqualified term. If the ambiguity is to be remedied by applying adjectives, it seems best to use a pair that bear directly upon the ambiguous point. Thus the common expressions "mild crisis" and "severe crisis" are clear in intent and safe

[5] See the "Dates of Major Crises" in Mr. Kitchin's paper, "Cycles and Trends in Economic Factors," *Review of Economic Statistics*, January, 1923, Prel. vol. v, pp. 10-16.

to use in descriptive work, such as business annals, provided there are not too many cases on the borderline between mildness and severity.

But no set of adjectives can make "crisis" a suitable name for the fourth phase of business cycles. Hardly can one say "depression, revival, prosperity, mild or severe crisis." The choice lies between retaining "crisis" defined in an unfamiliar way, or replacing it by some word corresponding to "revival," which is used to designate the upward turn of the cycle. This second alternative seems the lesser evil, especially in view of the fact that our theoretical and practical interests lie increasingly in those mild transitions from prosperity to depression which have been little attended to by theorists.

In this discussion, accordingly, business cycles are treated as having four phases—depression, revival, prosperity and recession. The word "crisis" is not dropped, but is used like the words "panic" or "boom" to indicate degrees of intensity. Every business cycle includes a phase of recession; this recession may or may not be marked by a crisis; the crisis, if there is one, may or may not degenerate into a panic. All the old and most of the recent books on the subject deal chiefly with crises, panics and severe depressions; these annals endeavor to show also the mild recessions and the periods of dull business.

We have, indeed, gone far—we hope not too far—in calling attention to the mild recessions. Our aim has been to include all cases in which the evidence indicates a general slackening of activity, even though the slackening lasted but a few months, and did not reach grave proportions. Cases in point may be found in the American annals for 1888, 1900 and 1923. Other illustrations are Italy in 1900, England in 1803 and 1854, and the brief reaction in the majority of our 17 countries after the Armistice of 1918. On the other hand, we have tried not to include cases in which only a few branches of business suffered a setback—such as the English case of 1860-61 already referred to, or the financial difficulties caused in London by the outbreak of war between France and Prussia in 1870.

5. "Prosperity" and "Depression."

A somewhat different criticism may be made of the terms used for two other phases of business cycles. In comparing the annals with business indexes, we had occasion to note that the words "prosperity" and "depression" are themselves subject to cyclical fluctuations in meaning. Their significance is relative rather than fixed. The more active phase of a given cycle is called prosperous, and the less active phase is called depressed, though both phases may be very mild. We must not suppose that business conditions are almost identical in the prosperous phases of successive cycles, even in the same country—or in the depressed phases.

This relativity of meaning appeared in the review of business indexes in Chapter III, though little was said about it at the time. The crests of business cycles sometimes reach but a little way above the base lines of the index charts. On rare occasions they remain below these lines. The like is true, *mutatis mutandis,* of the troughs. Statistically, prosperity and depression are variables, distributed in a fairly regular fashion over a considerable range.[1]

Perhaps we might develop quantitative definitions for prosperity and depression by saying, for example, that business is prosperous when certain indexes have attained a given percentage height above their corrected trends. The time may come when that shift in practice will appear both feasible and desirable. Or we might substitute for the words in question other terms whose relativity of meaning is patent. For example, we might speak of the phase of business expansion and the phase of business contraction, or of the phase of rising and declining activity. Of course these two proposals are quite compatible with each other. But our business indexes are not yet sufficiently perfect, and they do not yet cover a sufficient range of times and places, to afford satisfactory measurements of degree of prosperity and depression. The second proposal presents no such difficulties, and is often followed in this discussion. Yet the misunderstandings to which the words in question may give rise seem scarcely grave enough to justify discarding them entirely. Few people are likely to think of prosperity and depression as definite states. When their application to business cycles involves a serious stretching of the vague popular usage, a reminder of their technical meaning may be sufficient safeguard.

6. The Uniformity and the Variability of Business Cycles.

Recurrence of depression, revival, prosperity and recession, time after time in land after land, may be the chief conclusion drawn from

---

[1] See Chapter III, section vi, 3 (3) "On Identifying Business Cycles by the Use of the Business Indexes," and (7) "The Amplitudes of Business Cycles."

the experience packed into our annals; but a second conclusion is that no two recurrences in all the array seem precisely alike. Business cycles differ in their duration as wholes and in the relative duration of their component phases; they differ in industrial and geographical scope; they differ in intensity; they differ in the features which attain prominence; they differ in the quickness and the uniformity with which they sweep from one country to another.

This mixture of uniformity and variability in business cycles may seem disconcerting when stated so baldly. But we confront a similar mixture of fundamental similarity and detailed differences when we visualize men's faces, or consider their characters, or study any social phenomena. In all such cases, variability presents conceptual difficulties not to be glossed over, and difficulties of explanation not surmounted as yet. But uncounted ages ago men found that they could think of pines despite difference in the size, shape, location, color, roughness, and hardness of particular specimens; they could think of trees despite the differences among pines, maples and palms, and the difficulty of delimiting trees from shrubs. And within the past hundred years men have developed a technique for studying variations about a central tendency, a technique which reveals the existence of formerly unsuspected uniformities among variations themselves.

Differences among business cycles, then, afford no reason for doubting that these cycles constitute a valid species of phenomena. But the existence of such differences should put us on our guard against using concepts and methods of analysis appropriate only in work where differences among individuals of a given species either do not exist or can be precisely defined (as in geometry), or are not significant for the problems under consideration (as in certain branches of physics and chemistry). The student of business cycles should picture their characteristic differences as clearly as may be, measure them with what precision he can, and find how these differences are distributed around their central tendencies. While the annals are not quantitative in form, they can be used to some extent in treating this statistical problem.

IV. The Duration of Business Cycles.

1. CURRENT ESTIMATES OF AVERAGE LENGTH.

The differences among business cycles which have attracted most attention are differences in duration. Quite naturally, the discoverers of the recurrence overstressed its uniformity in this respect as in others. Influenced by the dominant type of economic theory, these discoverers thought of a "normal" cycle and so simplified their problem—a practice still common. To cite an extreme example: in 1867 John Mills described the "credit cycle" as lasting ten years—three years of declining trade, three years of increasing trade, three years of over-excited trade, and one year of crisis.[1] Even the early statistical workers yielded to the lure of "normality." They were eager to establish the "periodicity of crises," which was suggested by such crisis dates as 1815, 1825, 1836, 1847, 1857 and 1866. This desire warped their selection and treatment of data. Jevons had an admirably candid mind; yet in 1875, when the sun-spot cycle was supposed to last 11.1 years, he was able to get from Thorold Rogers' *History of Agriculture and Prices in England* a period of 11 years in price fluctuations, and when the sun-spot cycle was revised to 10.45 years he was able to make the average interval between English crises 10.466 years.[2] To get this later result, Jevons purposely left out from his list of crises "a great commercial collapse in 1810-11 (which will not fit into the decennial series)"; he also omitted the crisis of 1873, and inserted a crisis in 1878, which other writers do not find.[3]

Jevons' way of reckoning the length of cycles by the intervals between crises, and of counting as crises periods of financial strain coming after booms, or recessions followed by long depressions, is still common among theoretical writers. The results they get are not in close agreement. Tugan-Baranovski takes 7 to 11 years as the limits of variation in the length of cycles and 10 years as the average duration. Bouniatian says that "under normal conditions" cycles last from 9 to 11 years, but adds that there is "a tendency toward a normal period of about 10 years." Cassel takes 1873, 1882, 1890, 1900, and 1907 as crisis years in Europe, and 1873, 1882, 1893, 1903, and 1907 as crisis years in the United States. Cassel himself strikes no average, but his dates give limits of 4 to 11 years and an average of 8½ years. Lavington accepts 8 years as the average duration.

[1] "On Credit Cycles and the Origin of Commercial Panics," *Transactions of the Manchester Statistical Society*, 1867-68, pp. 5-40. Compare the diagram of a cycle which Jevons gives in his *Primer of Political Economy*, New York, 1882, p. 121.

[2] Jevons withdrew his first paper from publication when he discovered "that periods of 3, 5, 7, 9, or even 13 years would agree with Professor Rogers' data just as well as a period of 11 years." See his *Investigations in Currency and Finance*, London, 1884, pp. 207, 225.

[3] See the three papers on crises reprinted in Jevons' *Investigations in Currency and Finance*, especially pp. 200-203, 225, 233.

Slightly different is the method of reckoning cycles by the intervals between depressions. Otto C. Lightner records 18 depressions in American business from 1808 to 1921, not counting "minor" cases, with intervals ranging from 3 to 12 years and averaging 6⅔ years. George H. Hull, denying that depressions are periodic, counts 17 "industrial crises" in the United States from 1814 to 1907. His dates differ somewhat from Lightner's, having intervals ranging from 1 to 11 years, and averaging a little less than 6 years apart.

With these results may be given two others of the same order of magnitude, but reached by quite different methods. Pigou, using British unemployment returns and measuring intervals between both the crests and the troughs of the industrial waves, gets a trifle less than 8 years as his average length. Henry L. Moore also gets 8 years as the standard length both of "generating" and of "derived economic cycles," but gets it from periodogram analysis of time-series.[4]

Other statistical workers have recently reached quite different conclusions. Thus Professor W. L. Crum made a periodogram analysis of monthly interest rates upon commercial paper in New York from 1866 to 1922 and found (somewhat doubtful) evidence of a period of 39-40 months in their fluctuations. At the same time Mr. Joseph Kitchin, after analyzing bank clearings, interest rates, and wholesale prices in Great Britain and the United States from 1890 to 1922, suggested that the cyclical fluctuations of trade are composed of minor cycles averaging 40 months in length, and major cycles, which are aggregates of two or less often, of three minor cycles.[5] Since the publication of these two papers in January, 1923, "the 40-month cycle" has enjoyed a considerable vogue among statisticians. Forty months is also the median value of the observations upon the duration of American cycles in 1878-1923, derived in Chapter III from five indexes of business conditions, while the mean value is 42 months.

[4] See M. Tugan-Baranovski, *Les Crises Industrielles en Angleterre*, 1913, pp. 247, 248; M. Bouniatian, *Les Crises Économiques*, 1922, p. 42; G. Cassel, *The Theory of Social Economy*, 1924, p. 508; A. Aftalion, *Les Crises Périodiques de Surproduction*, 1913, vol. i, pp. 8-14; F. Lavington, *The Trade Cycle*, 1922, p. 14; O. C. Lightner, *History of Business Depressions*, 1922, table of contents; G. H. Hull, *Industrial Depressions*, 1911, pp. 54-57, and the chronological table, pp. 50, 51; A. C. Pigou, *The Economics of Welfare*, 1920, p. 804; Henry L. Moore, *Generating Economic Cycles*, 1923, pp. 15, 64.
[5] See W. L. Crum, "Cycles of Rates on Commercial Paper," *Review of Economic Statistics*, January, 1923, preliminary vol. v, pp. 17-28; Joseph Kitchin, "Cycles and Trends in Economic Factors," the same, pp. 10-16.

2. Measurements Based upon the Annals.

It is not necessary to examine narrowly the discrepancies among the results obtained by measuring the intervals between years of crisis or years of depression. They run back partly to differences in the countries and the periods covered, and partly to differences of opinion concerning the severity which entitles a particular disturbance to be called a true crisis or depression. Granted each author his own conception of what constitutes a cycle, his measurements are presumably correct for the land and period covered. By using the present annals, anyone so disposed might validate, and anyone so disposed might question any of the averages and limits of variations which have been derived in this way.

But anyone who reads the annals closely, whatever the definition of crisis in his mind, will see that there is grave question regarding the unity of many of the 6-, or 8-, or 10-year cycles. Take as the simplest example Professor Cassel's list of crisis years in the United States: 1873, 1882, 1893, 1903 and 1907. Perhaps one may argue that the annals justify these dates from Cassel's viewpoint, though it is not clear why he should omit 1888 if he includes 1903. But the important point is that the cycle from 1882 to 1893 was punctuated by the recessions of 1888 and 1890, and that the cycle from 1893 to 1903 was punctuated by recessions both in 1896 and in 1900.

Now, the differences of opinion concerning the length of American cycles in this period turn less on the facts of business expansion and contraction than on what movements of expansion and contraction should be selected for treatment as business cycles. The older writers fastened upon the salient phenomena—severe crises and the rather long intervals between them—as requiring explanation. This tradition still rules in theoretical treatises. But as knowledge of business cycles grows, and as men seek to use this knowledge more effectively in interpreting current developments month by month, a more intensive treatment becomes both feasible and useful. Without denying the graver importance of the wider swings, we find ourselves involved much of the time in dealing with fluctuations of less amplitude, fluctuations which the theorists have passed over lightly. The same developments which make it wise to substitute the concept of recession for the concept of crisis make it wise to recognize the shorter segments into which the long swings are frequently divisible.

This change reduces the typical duration of American cycles to roughly one-half of the estimate commonest among theoretical writers.

By way of illustration, we may compile from the American annals a list of recessions in the United States since 1790. In this list the recessions are characterized by phrases which indicate their severity, and leading features. Financial troubles occurring in the middle of depressions are not counted as recessions, but cases of this sort which have commonly been listed as crises are noted in the table. In the early years the business fortunes of the northern states alone are followed; sometimes conditions were quite different in the agricultural south and west. Since the annals seldom permit a precise dating of recessions, the duration of successive cycles is reckoned to the nearest whole year.

TABLE 23

BUSINESS RECESSIONS IN THE UNITED STATES AND APPROXIMATE DURATION OF BUSINESS CYCLES, 1790–1925

		Duration of Cycles in Years			Duration of Cycles in Years
1796 *	Financial crisis, spring.....		1865	Recession, second quarter, close of Civil War	5
1802	Recession early in year....	6	1870	Recession, January	5
1807 *	Recession late in year.....	6	1873 *	Violent panic, September..	4
1812	Brief recession, June, War with England	5	1882	Recession late in year, financial panic in 1884 *....	9
1815 *	Crisis, March, following peace	3	1888	Slight recession, early in year	5
1822	Mild recession, May.......	7	1890	Financial crisis, autumn....	3
1825 *	Panic, autumn	3	1893 *	Severe panic, May........	2
1828	Recession, summer	3	1896	Recession early in year, financial stringency	3
1833	Recession, panic, autumn..	5			
1837 *	Panic, spring	4	1900	Brief and slight recession, spring	4
1839 *	Panic, October	3			
1845	Brief recession, May	6	1903 *	Financial strain, spring....	3
1846	Mild recession early in year, War with Mexico	1	1907 *	Severe crisis, autumn......	4
			1910	Mild recession, January....	2
1847 *	Recession, financial panic, November	2	1913 *	Recession, summer	3
1853	Recession, last quarter....	6	1918	Recession after Armistice, November	5
1857 *	Recession, late spring, panic in August	4	1920 *	Severe crisis, May	2
1860	Recession late in year, prospect of Civil War	3	1923	Mild recession, summer....	3

* The dates thus marked show the commonly accepted crisis years. Other dates frequently listed are 1819, a case of financial strain in a business depression, and 1890. The "rich man's panic" of 1903 is omitted in some lists.

To show the usual way of reckoning the length of cycles, the commonly accepted dates of crises in the United States are marked with asterisks. Anyone who checks these dates against those given in other books will find different ways of counting; for example, 1837-1839 is sometimes put down as a single crisis. But, taking the dates as marked, we have 14 cycles between 1796 and 1920, ranging from about 2 years (1837-39) to about 16 years (1857-1873) in length, and averaging 8⁶⁄₇ years. We can raise this average by omitting or combining some of the crises counted here, or reduce it by counting some of the other recessions as crises. At best there is a considerable margin for admissible difference of opinion.

When we drop the effort to discriminate the degrees of severity among crises and count all recessions, this margin of uncertainty becomes narrower, though it does not vanish. It is easier to recognize a change of direction in business movements than it is to determine how serious a change for the worse has been. Yet, another compiler drawing off a list of recessions from the most detailed form of our annals might give a slightly different set of dates, and one who made a fresh set of annals from the original sources might increase these differences somewhat. The broad results, however, seem well assured.

Counting business cycles now as the intervals between recessions, noting the quarters in which the turns came, and reckoning to the nearest whole year, we get the following results:

1	cycle about	1	year long		(1845-46)
4	cycles "	2	years "		
10	" "	3	"	"	
5	" "	4	"	"	
6	" "	5	"	"	
4	" "	6	"	"	
1	" "	7	"	"	(1815-1822)
0	" "	8	"	"	
1	" "	9	"	"	(1873-1882)

In all we have 32 cycles in 127 years, which yields an average length of not quite 4 years. The commonest length is about three years; and two-thirds of the cases fall within the limits of three to five years.

These results may be compared with similar summaries from the other country for which we have annals covering 136 years. The dates given in Bouniatian's list of English crises are starred to show the conventional view of cycle chronology. His 16 dates mark off 15 cycles in the 127 years from 1793 to 1920—an average length of almost 8½ years. If 1913 be added to the list of crises and it seems to belong there quite as much as certain dates which Bouniatian admits as turning points unaccompanied by severe financial strain, there are 16 cycles, ranging in length from about 4 to about 13 years, and averaging not quite 8 years.

Of the cycles marked off by recessions, 22 are shown. Perhaps we should add recessions in 1814 after the first abdication of Napoleon, in 1861 when the American Civil War upset the cotton trade, in 1864 when financial strain was marked, in 1870 when the Franco-Prussian War brought confusion to the financial markets, in 1897 and 1911 when the rising tides of activity were checked. But in none of these cases does the evidence of contemporary business reports indicate a general slackening of trade. Even if these cases were counted, it would still appear that English business has experienced fewer recessions than American business during the same period of four generations. Hence English cycles have been longer on the average than American cycles. Taking the dates entered in the table we get an average duration of 5¾ years in England against 4 years in the United States.

But these averages are even less a guide to business forecasting in England than in America. It is difficult to find any regular order in the lengths of the successive cycles in either Table 23 or Table 24. When we tabulate the frequency of English cycles according to duration we find less concentration at the mode than in the corresponding American table. From 1793-1920 there were

2 cycles about 2 years long (1829-31, and 1918-20)
1   "   "   3   "   "   (1807-10)
5   "   "   4   "   "
2   "   "   5   "   "
4   "   "   6   "   "
2   "   "   7   "   "
3   "   "   8   "   "
1   "   "   9   "   "   (1873-83)
2   "   "   10   "   "   (1837-47, and 1890-1900)

Four-year cycles are most common in England, three-year cycles in the United States. One-half of the English cases are 4-6 years in length, while two-thirds of the American cases are grouped at 3-5 years.

TABLE 24

BUSINESS RECESSIONS IN ENGLAND AND APPROXIMATE DURATION OF BUSINESS CYCLES, 1790–1925

		Duration of Cycles in years			Duration of Cycles in years
1793	Recession, February, following financial pressure in 1792 *	....	1854	Recession, January, Crimean War	7
1797 *	Panic, February	4	1857 *	Financial panic, November	4
1803	Recession, May, renewal of war	6	1866 *	Severe financial crisis, first quarter, Overend-Gurney failure	8
1807	Mild recession	4	1873 *	Recession late in year.....	8
1810 *	Severe crisis, July.........	3	1883	Slow recession, early in year, perhaps beginning in 1882 *	9
1815 *	Crisis, autumn, following end of war	5	1890 *	Recession following financial crisis in November........	8
1819 *	Recession, early spring.....	4	1900 *	Recession, summer	10
1825 *	Recession, spring, followed by financial panic.........	6	1907 *	Recession, autumn, financial stringency	7
1829	Recession, first quarter....	4	1913	Recession, last quarter.....	6
1831	Recession	2	1918	Recession on Armistice, November	5
1837	Recession early in year, following financial panic in 1836 *	6	1920 *	Severe crisis, second quarter	2
1847 *	Financial panic, April, recession, summer	10			

* The dates thus marked show the crises recognized by Mentor Bouniatian, *Les Crises Économiques*, Paris, 1922, p. 43. Most authorities would include 1913, also, on the same grounds that lead Bouniatian to list crises in 1882 and 1900, although these years were not marked by severe financial strain.

On applying the same methods of analysis to the three other countries for which we have annals running back to the 1860's, 1850's, and 1840's, we find that in average duration their cycles are intermediate between the English and the American patterns. The average length works out as follows:

> 1838-1920—82 years
>> France, 15 cycles, average length 5½ years.
>> England, (1837-1920), 12 cycles, average length nearly 7 years.
>> United States, (1837-1920), 22 cycles, average length 3¾ years.

1848-1925—77 years
> Germany, 15 cycles, average length 5 years.
> England (1847-1920), 11 cycles, average length 6⅔ years.
> United States (1847-1923), 19 cycles, average length 4 years.

1866-1922—56 years
> Austria, 10 cycles, average length 5.6 years.
> England (1866-1920), 8 cycles, average length 6¾ years.
> United States (1865-1923), 15 cycles, average length not quite 4 years.

3. FREQUENCY DISTRIBUTIONS OF THE MEASUREMENTS BASED UPON THE ANNALS.

A systematic summary of our evidence concerning the duration of business cycles is provided by the following exhibits. Table 25 is a companion piece to Tables 23 and 24. It shows the dates of recessions in fifteen countries as accurately as Dr. Thorp can determine them from the annals, and shows also the approximate duration of successive cycles reckoned to the nearest whole year. Chart 23 is a graphic version of Tables 23, 24, and 25. It uses lines of varying length to show the duration of business cycles in each of our countries, in chronological order.

TABLE 25

DATES OF BUSINESS RECESSIONS IN FIFTEEN COUNTRIES: VARIOUS YEARS TO 1925

		Duration of Cycles in years			Duration of Cycles in years			Duration of Cycles in years
	France		1900	late summer	11	1873	autumn	3
1838			1908	early	7	1878	early	4
1847	early	9	1913	early summer	5	1880	early	2
1854	March	7	1918	November	5	1882	summer	3
1857	autumn	3	1920	summer	2	1890	early	8
1860	autumn	3				1900	August	10
1867	early	6				1904	summer	4
1870	July	3		Germany		1907	summer	3
1873	early	3	1848			1913	summer	6
1876	early	3	1857	autumn	9	1918	November	5
1882	early	6	1866	June	9	1922	summer	4
1890	early	8	1870	July	4	1925	summer	3

TABLE 25—(*Continued*)

DATES OF BUSINESS RECESSIONS IN FIFTEEN COUNTRIES

		Dura-tion of Cycles in years			Dura-tion of Cycles in years			Dura-tion of Cycles in years
Austria			**Italy**			1913	....	10
1866			1888	early		1918	late	5
1869	late	3	1900	spring	12	1920	autumn	2
1873	summer	4	1907	last quarter ..	8			
1884	early	11	1913	second half...	6	**Australia**		
1892	early	8	1918	October	5	1890	January	
1894	early	2	1920	early	1	1901	January	11
1900	early	6				1908	January	7
1908	early	8	**Argentina**			1913	January	5
1912	autumn	5	1890	first quarter		1914	autumn	2
1918	October	6	1892	autumn	3	1920	November ...	6
1922	autumn	4	1900	early	7	1924	January	3
			1908	early	8			
			1911	early	3	**India**		
Russia			1913	early	2	1889		
1891	early		1920	December ...	8	1896	summer	7
1899	third quarter.	8				1900	summer	4
1904	February	5	**Brazil**			1907	autumn	7
1908	early	4	1889	November		1914	August	7
1914	early	6	1896	early	6	1918	November ...	4
1917	March	3	1900	autumn	5	1920	May	2
1923	October	7	1907	autumn	7			
1925	late	2	1912	late	5	**Japan**		
			1918	November ...	6	1890	January	
			1920	autumn	2	1894	August	5
Sweden			1924	second half ...	4	1897	autumn	3
1892	early					1905	September ...	8
1901	early	9	**Canada**			1907	spring	2
1907	late autumn..	7	1888			1914	spring	7
1913	autumn	6	1893	early	5	1918	November ...	5
1917	....	4	1900	autumn	7	1920	March	1
1920	summer	3	1907	autumn	7			
			1913	second half ..	6	**China**		
			1918	November ...	5	1888		
Netherlands			1920	autumn	2	1897	....	9
1891	early		1924	spring	4	1900	May	3
1901	early	10				1906	....	6
1907	autumn	7	**South Africa**			1910	....	4
1913	late	6	1890	September		1920	midyear	10
1917	early	3	1895	autumn	5			
1920	autumn	4	1899	October	4			
			1903	early	3			

White inset figures indicate approximate duration in years.

UNITED STATES

Period	Years
1796–1802	6
1802–1807	6
1807–1812	5
1812–1815	3
1815–1822	7
1822–1825	3
1825–1828	3
1828–1833	5
1833–1837	4
1837–1839	3
1839–1845	6
1845–1846	1
1846–1847	2
1847–1853	6
1853–1857	4
1857–1860	3
1860–1865	5
1865–1870	5
1870–1873	4
1873–1882	9
1882–1888	5
1888–1890	3
1890–1893	2
1893–1896	3
1896–1900	4
1900–1903	3
1903–1907	4
1907–1910	2
1910–1913	3
1913–1918	5
1918–1920	2
1920–1923	3

ENGLAND

Period	Years
1793–1797	4
1797–1803	6
1803–1807	4
1807–1810	3
1810–1815	5
1815–1819	4
1819–1825	6
1825–1829	4
1829–1831	2
1831–1837	6
1837–1847	10
1847–1854	7
1854–1857	4
1857–1866	8
1866–1873	8
1873–1883	9
1883–1890	8
1890–1900	10
1900–1907	7
1907–1913	5
1913–1918	5
1918–1920	2

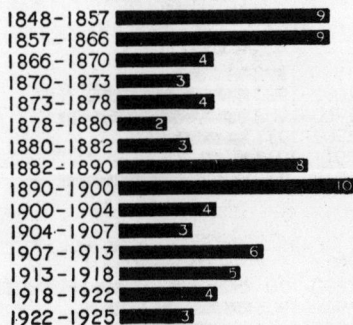

GERMANY

Period	Years
1848–1857	9
1857–1866	9
1866–1870	4
1870–1873	3
1873–1878	4
1878–1880	2
1880–1882	3
1882–1890	8
1890–1900	10
1900–1904	4
1904–1907	3
1907–1913	6
1913–1918	5
1918–1922	4
1922–1925	3

FRANCE

Period	Years
1838–1847	9
1847–1854	7
1854–1857	3
1857–1860	3
1860–1867	6
1867–1870	3
1870–1873	3
1873–1876	3
1876–1882	6
1882–1890	8
1890–1900	11
1900–1908	7
1908–1913	5
1913–1918	5
1918–1920	2

AUSTRIA

Period	Years
1866–1869	3
1869–1873	4
1873–1884	11
1884–1892	8
1892–1894	2
1894–1900	6
1900–1908	8
1908–1912	5
1912–1918	6
1918–1922	4

CHART 23. Approximate Duration of Business Cycles, arranged in Chronological Sequence—*Continued.*

White inset figures indicate approximate duration in years.

RUSSIA
1891–1899	8
1899–1904	5
1904–1908	4
1908–1914	6
1914–1917	3
1917–1923	7
1923–1925	2

CANADA
1888–1893	5
1893–1900	7
1900–1907	7
1907–1913	6
1913–1918	5
1918–1920	2
1920–1924	4

SWEDEN
1892–1901	9
1901–1907	7
1907–1913	6
1913–1917	4
1917–1920	3

NETHERLANDS
1891–1901	10
1901–1907	7
1907–1913	6
1913–1917	3
1917–1920	4

ITALY
1888–1900	12
1900–1907	8
1907–1913	6
1913–1918	5
1918–1920	1

CHINA
1888–1897	9
1897–1900	3
1900–1906	6
1906–1910	4
1910–1920	10

ARGENTINA
1890–1892	3
1892–1900	7
1900–1908	8
1908–1911	3
1911–1913	2
1913–1920	8

SOUTH AFRICA
1890–1895	5
1895–1899	4
1899–1903	3
1903–1913	10
1913–1918	5
1918–1920	2

AUSTRALIA
1890–1901	11
1901–1908	7
1908–1913	5
1913–1914	2
1914–1920	6
1920–1924	3

INDIA
1889–1896	7
1896–1900	4
1900–1907	7
1907–1914	7
1914–1918	4
1918–1920	2

BRAZIL
1889–1896	6
1896–1900	5
1900–1907	7
1907–1912	5
1912–1918	6
1918–1920	2
1920–1924	4

JAPAN
1890–1894	5
1894–1897	3
1897–1905	8
1905–1907	2
1907–1914	7
1914–1918	5
1918–1920	1

394

We can treat the observations upon the duration of business cycles assembled in this table and chart as the data of an historical inquiry, or as the data of a theoretical problem. In the first case we ask: What has been the duration of business cycles in the countries and during the periods for which we have annals? In the second case we ask: What expectations regarding the duration of business cycles are justified by the sample observations in hand?

As historical data, our observations probably contain inaccuracies. Conceiving a business recession as a decline in economic activity which follows a period of expansion and spreads over most of a country's industries, we have sought to find and date every recession which occurred in certain countries during certain periods. On the basis of these recession dates, we have measured the duration of successive cycles to the nearest whole year. Finally, we have struck averages from these measurements. Mistakes may have occurred in any of these steps. We may have omitted some recessions; we may have included some cases which do not fit our definition of recessions; we may have blundered in measuring or averaging. But so long as we are trying merely to report what has taken place in the past, these doubts concerning the accuracy of our work are all that need concern us. The historical record is fixed; it has its unique features and interest; in studying it we can indulge in no speculations.

A subtler problem and doubts of another order are presented when we treat our observations as data for drawing theoretical conclusions regarding the duration of business cycles at large. For this purpose, we must ask, not merely whether our observations are historically dependable, but also whether they constitute a representative sample of the phenomena measured. Are the observations sufficiently numerous? Are they sufficiently independent of each other? Ought we to discard the observations upon cycles which we think have been cut short or prolonged by factors which have no organic relation to business activity?

In the sense in which the term is used here—recurrences of prosperity, recession, depression and revival in the business activities of countries taken as units—the total number of past business cycles may well be less than a thousand. For business cycles are phenomena peculiar to a certain form of economic organization which has been dominant even in Western Europe for less than two centuries, and for briefer periods in other regions. And the average cycle has lasted five years, if we may trust our data. Of the whole number of cases to date, the 166 cycles we have measured fcrm a significant fraction. By compiling business annals for Norway, Belgium, Switzerland, Denmark, Spain, New Zealand and Chile we could probably get additional observations as satisfactory as some of those already included. Perhaps we could trace business cycles in Greece, Egypt, Turkey, some of the Balkan States, possibly Mexico, and additional countries in Spanish America. Doubtless we might carry our observations further back in most of the seventeen countries which we have studied. But after we had pushed our investigations everywhere into the twilight zone where business cycles are doubtfully recognizable, we should still be dealing with relatively small numbers. A strict standard would bar out not only most of the extensions suggested, but also some of the cases we now include. It is not certain that the Chinese fluctuations should be treated as business cycles proper. At best, they represent conditions only in the coast cities having a large foreign trade. Also, our early American observations are open to question, even on the understanding that they refer only to the most highly organized of the thirteen original states.

The observations are not all independent of each other. We shall see presently that the duration of business cycles in every country influences, and is influenced by, the duration of business cycles in other countries. Moreover, the non-business factors which affect the duration of business cycles often produce uniform results in several countries. To cite one example: 7 of our 17 countries had a two-year cycle at the end of the World War. One hundred and sixty-six observations, many of which come in clusters, are likely to show a less regular distribution around their central tendency than would 166 observations strictly independent of each other.

If we wish to find out what we can about the probable duration of future business cycles, we should discard observations upon cycles whose duration has been determined by factors of a kind not likely to be influential in the future. If the data for any country show unequivocal evidence of a change in the length of cycles, the later data are likely to be a safer guide to expectations than the earlier data, or the full array. But we have no warrant for discarding cases in which cycles seem to have been cut short or prolonged by wars, civil disorders, exceptional harvest conditions, or any other factor, unless we believe that such "disturbing circumstances" will not recur in the future as in the past. Even the man who has supposed that business cycles "tend" to have some standard period will probably conclude upon studying the present charts that he had better take the data as they come.

In fine, our observations form a fairly satisfactory basis for studying the duration of business cycles. Like all observations, their accuracy is open to question; but they have been made with care and their number is sufficient to allow errors to offset each other in some measure. We should be glad to have a larger sample; but the present one constitutes an appreciable fraction of its "universe." We need not reject any of the observations on the ground that the duration of certain cycles has been affected by "disturbing circumstances"; for we are interested in actual cycles in the actual world where "disturbing circumstances" are always present. We might expect a more regular distribution if all our observations were strictly independent of each other. But once again, as the world is constituted, interdependence in duration is characteristic of business cycles in different countries. A complete array of measurements for all past cycles would resemble our sample in this respect, and future cycles seem likely to show increasing interdependence in duration. Perhaps we should conceive of our distributions as made from a number of independent measurements smaller than the nominal count, but with the use of "weights" which total 166. Many cycles are weighted by one, while other cycles, which began and ended on the same dates in countries with close business relations, or dominated by the same non-business factors, are weighted by numbers running as high as seven.

To put our data in shape for analysis, we must disregard the chronological sequence of cycles of varying length, shown in Chart 23, and rearrange all the cases in frequency tables of the sort already given for American and English cycles—tables which show the number of cycles of each recorded duration. That step is taken in Table 26. But the tabulations by separate countries have slight significance except for England and the United States, because the number of cases is small (5-15 cycles). Hence Table 27 is made from Table 26, by combining the observations from single countries into various groups. To facilitate comparisons among the two dozen distributions here shown, all the samples are put in percentages. Chart 24 is a graphic form of these percentage distributions.

TABLE 26.

FREQUENCY DISTRIBUTION OF BUSINESS CYCLES ACCORDING TO DURATION IN YEARS

Data from Seventeen Countries. Various Dates to 1925.

Based upon Tables 23, 24 and 25.

Duration in Years	England 1793–1920	France 1838–1920	Germany 1848–1925	Austria 1866–1922	Italy 1888–1920	Netherlands 1891–1920	Sweden 1892–1920	Russia 1891–1925
1 year	..	..	..	..	1	..	..	..
2 years	2	1	1	1	..	..	..	1
3 "	1	5	4	1	..	1	1	1
4 "	5	..	4	2	..	1	1	1
5 "	2	2	1	1	1	..	..	1
6 "	4	2	1	2	1	1	1	1
7 "	2	2	..	..	.	1	1	1
8 "	3	1	1	2	1	..	..	1
9 "	1	1	2	..	..	..	1	..
10 "	2	..	1	..	..	1	..	..
11 "	..	1	..	1	..	..	..	..
12 "	..	..	..	..	1	..	..	..
Total number	22	15	15	10	5	5	5	7
Average duration in years	5.8	5.5	5.1	5.6	6.4	5.8	5.6	4.9

Duration in years	United States 1796–1923	Canada 1888–1924	Australia 1890–1924	South Africa 1890–1920	Argentina 1890–1920	Brazil 1889–1924	India 1889–1920	Japan 1890–1920	China 1888–1920
1 year	1	..	..	..	..	..	..	1	..
2 years	4	1	1	1	1	1	1	1	..
3 "	10	..	1	1	2	..	..	1	1
4 "	5	1	..	1	..	1	2	..	1
5 "	6	2	1	2	..	2	..	2	..
6 "	4	1	1	..	..	2	..	..	1
7 "	1	2	1	..	1	1	3	1	..
8 "	..	..	..	..	2	..	..	1	..
9 "	1	..	..	..	..	..	..	..	1
10 "	..	..	..	1	..	..	..	..	1
11 "	..	..	1	..	..	..	..	..	..
Total number	32	7	6	6	6	7	6	7	5
Average duration in years	4.0	5.1	5.7	5.0	5.0	5.0	5.2	4.3	6.4

TABLE 27.

Frequency Distribution of Business Cycles According to Approximate Duration in Years: by Countries, Groups of Countries and Periods

(Based upon Table 26)

Duration in Years	United States		England		United States and England		United States, England, France, Germany and Austria						Duration in Years
							Before 1873		After 1873		Full Period		
	Num-ber	Per Cent	Num-ber	Per Cent	Num-ber	Per Cent	Num-ber	Per Cent	Num-ber	Per Cent	Num-ber	Per Cent	
1	1	3.1	..	...	1	1.9	1	2.1	..	...	1	1.1	1
2	4	12.5	2	9.1	6	11.1	2	4.3	7	14.9	9	9.6	2
3	10	31.2	1	4.5	11	20.4	12	25.5	9	19.1	21	22.4	3
4	5	15.6	5	22.7	10	18.5	10	21.3	6	12.8	16	17.0	4
5	6	18.8	2	9.1	8	14.8	5	10.6	7	14.9	12	12.8	5
6	4	12.5	4	18.2	8	14.8	8	17.0	5	10.6	13	13.8	6
7	1	3.1	2	9.1	3	5.6	3	6.4	2	4.3	5	5.3	7
8	..	...	3	13.6	3	5.6	2	4.3	5	10.6	7	7.4	8
9	1	3.1	1	4.5	2	3.7	3	6.4	2	4.3	5	5.3	9
10	..	...	2	9.1	2	3.7	1	2.1	2	4.3	3	3.2	10
11	..	...	..	...	..	...	..	...	2	4.3	2	2.1	11
Totals	32	100.0	22	100.0	54	100.0	47	100.0	47	100.0	94	100.0	Totals

Duration in Years	Countries with close business relations [2]		Countries relatively independent of each other [2]		Countries with average duration of 5.5 years or more [3]		Countries with average duration of 5.2 years or less [4]				Countries with average duration of 5.0 to 5.7 [5] years		Duration in Years
							Excluding United States		Including United States				
	Num-ber	Per Cent	Num-ber	Per Cent	Num-ber	Per Cent	Num-ber	Per Cent	Num-ber	Per Cent	Num-ber	Per Cent	
1	..	...	1	2.6	1	1.4	1	1.6	2	2.2	..	...	1
2	4	10.3	5	13.2	5	6.9	8	13.1	12	12.9	11	10.5	2
3	7	18.0	5	13.2	11	15.4	9	14.8	19	20.4	16	15.2	3
4	6	15.4	8	21.0	10	13.7	10	16.4	15	16.1	17	16.2	4
5	4	10.3	6	15.8	7	9.6	10	16.4	16	17.2	13	12.4	5
6	5	12.8	6	15.8	13	17.8	5	8.2	9	9.7	14	13.3	6
7	2	5.1	3	7.9	7	9.6	9	14.8	10	10.8	13	12.4	7
8	6	15.4	2	5.3	7	9.6	5	8.2	5	5.4	9	8.6	8
9	1	2.6	1	2.6	4	5.5	2	3.3	3	3.2	5	4.8	9
10	2	5.1	1	2.6	4	5.5	2	3.3	2	2.2	4	3.8	10
11	2	5.1	..	...	3	4.1	..	...	..	...	3	2.9	11
12	..	...	..	...	1	1.4	..	...	..	...	..	...	12
Totals	39	100.0	38	100.0	73	100.0	61	100.0	93	100.0	105	100.0	Totals

TABLE 27—*Continued*

FREQUENCY DISTRIBUTION OF BUSINESS CYCLES ACCORDING TO APPROXIMATE DURATION IN YEARS: BY COUNTRIES, GROUPS OF COUNTRIES AND PERIODS—(*Continued*)

Duration in Years	Eight European Countries		Nine Non-European Countries		Five English-Speaking Countries [1]		Twelve Non-English-Speaking Countries		All Countries except United States		All Countries		Duration in Years
	Number	Per Cent	Number	Per Cent	Number	Per Cent	Number	Per Cent	Number	Per Cent	Number	Per Cent	
1	1	1.2	2	2.4	1	1.4	2	2.2	2	1.5	3	1.8	1
2	6	7.1	11	13.4	9	12.5	8	8.6	13	9.7	17	10.2	2
3	14	16.7	16	19.5	13	17.8	17	18.3	20	14.9	30	18.1	3
4	14	16.7	11	13.4	12	16.4	13	14.0	20	14.9	25	15.1	4
5	8	9.5	15	18.3	13	17.8	10	10.8	17	12.7	23	13.9	5
6	13	15.5	9	11.0	10	13.7	12	12.9	18	13.4	22	13.3	6
7	7	8.3	10	12.2	6	8.2	11	11.8	16	11.9	17	10.2	7
8	9	10.7	3	3.7	3	4.1	9	9.7	12	9.0	12	7.2	8
9	5	6.0	2	2.4	2	2.7	5	5.4	6	4.5	7	4.2	9
10	4	4.8	2	2.4	3	4.1	3	3.2	6	4.5	6	3.6	10
11	2	2.4	1	1.2	1	1.4	2	2.2	3	2.2	3	1.8	11
12	1	1.2	..	...	..	...	1	1.1	1	0.7	1	0.6	12
Totals	84	100.0	82	100.0	73	100.0	93	100.0	134	100.0	166	100.0	Totals

RECENT CYCLES ONLY: ABOUT 1890 TO 1925

Duration in Years	European and Non-European Countries				Industrial and Non-Industrial Countries				Totals excluding and including United States				Duration in Years
	Eight European Countries		Eight Non-European Countries [2]		Seven Industrial Countries [3]		Ten Non-Industrial Countries [4]		Excluding United States		Including United States		
	Number	Per Cent	Number	Per Cent	Number	Per Cent	Number	Per Cent	Number	Per Cent	Number	Per Cent	
1	1	2.2	1	2.0	..	...	2	3.2	2	2.1	2	1.9	1
2	3	6.7	7	14.0	5	11.6	8	12.9	10	10.5	13	12.4	2
3	6	13.3	6	12.0	9	20.9	7	11.3	12	12.6	16	15.2	3
4	7	15.6	6	12.0	8	18.6	7	11.3	13	13.7	15	14.3	4
5	6	13.3	9	18.0	5	11.6	11	17.7	15	15.8	16	15.2	5
6	8	17.8	5	10.0	6	14.0	7	11.3	13	13.7	13	12.4	6
7	5	11.1	9	18.0	4	9.3	10	16.1	14	14.7	14	13.3	7
8	3	6.7	3	6.0	1	2.3	5	8.1	6	6.3	6	5.7	8
9	1	2.2	1	2.0	1	2.3	1	1.6	2	2.1	2	1.9	9
10	3	6.7	2	4.0	3	7.0	2	3.2	5	5.3	5	4.8	10
11	1	2.2	1	2.0	1	2.3	1	1.6	2	2.1	2	1.9	11
12	1	2.2	..	...	..	...	1	1.6	1	1.1	1	1.0	12
Totals	45	100.0	50	100.0	43	100.0	62	100.0	95	100.0	105	100.0	Totals

[1] England, United States, Canada, Australia, South Africa.
[2] Not including United States.
[3] England, France, Germany, Austria, Netherlands, Sweden, United States.
[4] All other countries included in *Annals*.

The first six figures in the chart deal with the five countries for which we have annals covering relatively long periods. The peculiarities of the American distribution stand out clearly—the pronounced mode, almost a "spike," at three years, and the relatively slight dispersion, indicated by a standard deviation and a coefficient of variation which are respectively the lowest and next the lowest in the list. In the English distribution, there is a curious predominance of cycles lasting 2, 4, 6, 8 and 10 years over cycles lasting 3, 5, 7 and 9 years. In view of the small number of observations (only 22), it is uncertain whether this feature is significant. However that may be, the irregularities in the American and English distributions compensate each other for the most part, so that Figure C is more regular than either of the arrays from which it is made.

Next, the French, German and Austrian observations are combined with the English and American. Advantage is taken of the larger number of cases to compare earlier with later cycles. By using 1873 as the dividing point, we get two groups each of which contains 47 observations. From 1873 to the end of the late war, the business fortunes of these countries, particularly of the European countries, ran more similar courses than in earlier years. That is, the observations in the later period are less independent of each other than the earlier observations—a fact which may explain the lesser regularity of Figure E as compared with Figure D. As a test of this suggestion we have made a distribution of the cycles in the four countries in our list which seem to have the closest business ties with each other for the period in which we have annals for all four. The results, shown in Figure G, constitute one of the least regular distributions in the whole twenty-four. As a companion piece we have made up a random group of similar size from observations which must be nearly independent of each other, taking English cycles in 1793-1825, American cycles in 1825-57, German cycles in 1857-90, Canadian cycles in 1888-1924, and Russian cycles in 1891-1925. In this comparison the 38 independent observations (Figure H) yield a much more regular distribution than the 39 observations which are inter-correlated with each other. Indeed, the contrast in regularity is more striking than we would expect from other comparisons of the sort.

There follow ten figures in which all of the observations are broken into parts on the basis of four criteria. First, the countries are grouped according to the average duration of their business

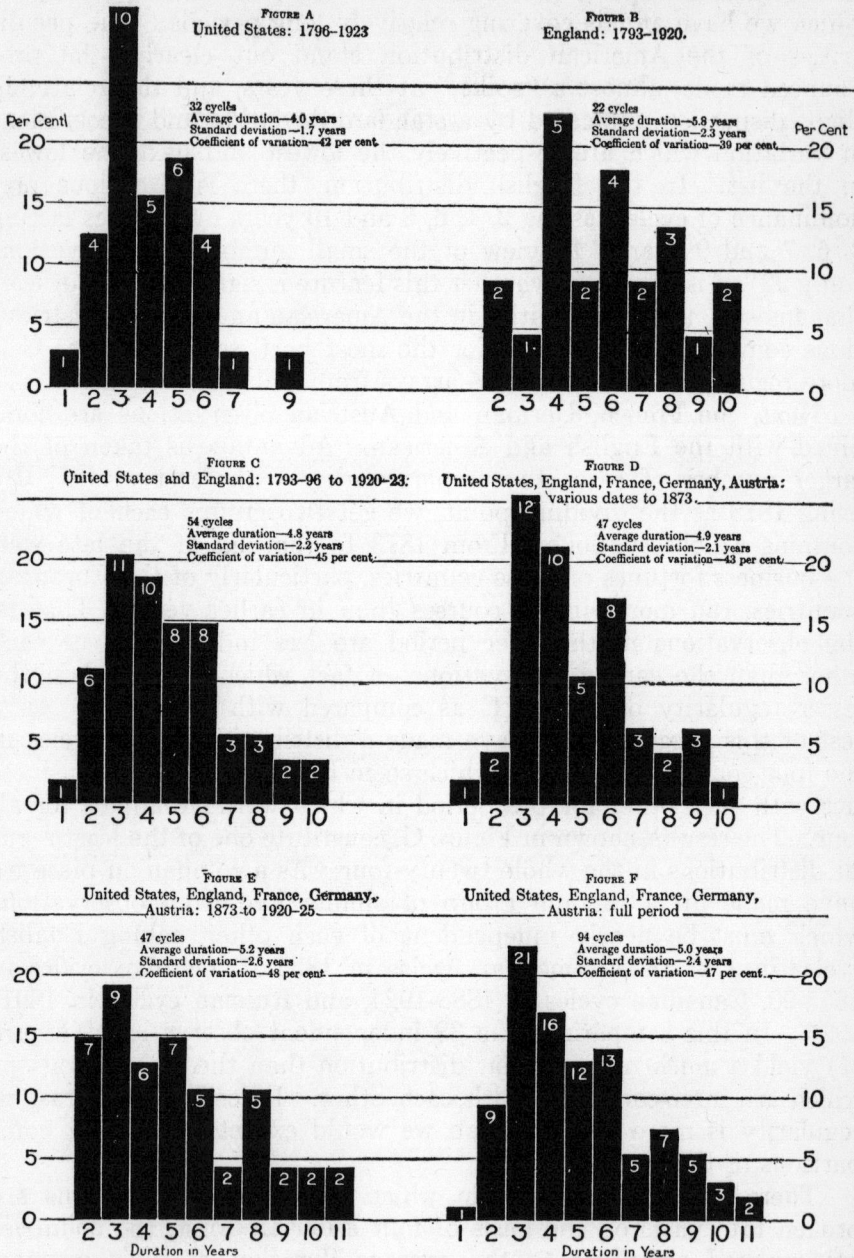

CHART 24. Percentage Distribution of Business Cycles in Various Countries and Various Periods According to their Approximate Duration in Years.

FIGURE A
United States: 1796–1923

32 cycles
Average duration—4.0 years
Standard deviation—1.7 years
Coefficient of variation—42 per cent

FIGURE B
England: 1793–1920.

22 cycles
Average duration—5.8 years
Standard deviation—2.3 years
Coefficient of variation—39 per cent

FIGURE C
United States and England: 1793–96 to 1920–23.

54 cycles
Average duration—4.8 years
Standard deviation—2.2 years
Coefficient of variation—45 per cent

FIGURE D
United States, England, France, Germany, Austria: various dates to 1873.

47 cycles
Average duration—4.9 years
Standard deviation—2.1 years
Coefficient of variation—43 per cent

FIGURE E
United States, England, France, Germany, Austria: 1873 to 1920–25.

47 cycles
Average duration—5.2 years
Standard deviation—2.6 years
Coefficient of variation—48 per cent

FIGURE F
United States, England, France, Germany, Austria: full period.

94 cycles
Average duration—5.0 years
Standard deviation—2.4 years
Coefficient of variation—47 per cent

Duration in Years

FIGURE G
Countries with Close Business Relations—England, France, Germany, Austria: 1866–1920.

FIGURE H
Observations Relatively Independent of Each Other—England, 1793–1825; United States, 1825–1857; Germany, 1857–1890; Russia, 1891–1825; Canada, 1888–1924.

Per Cent

39 cycles
Average duration—5.5 years
Standard deviation—2.6 years
Coefficient of variation—47 per cent

38 cycles
Average duration—4.7 years
Standard deviation—2.1 years
Coefficient of variation—43 per cent

Per Cent

FIGURE I
Countries Having Cycles with Average Duration of 5.5 Years or More—France, Austria, Sweden, England, Australia, Netherlands, Italy, China: various dates to 1920–24.

FIGURE J
Countries Having Cycles with Average Duration of 5.2 Years or Less, excluding United States—Japan, Russia, South Africa, Argentina, Brazil, Canada, Germany, India: various dates to 1920–25.

73 cycles
Average duration—5.8 years
Standard deviation—2.5 years
Coefficient of variation—43 per cent

61 cycles
Average duration—5.0 years
Standard deviation—2.2 years
Coefficient of variation—44 per cent

FIGURE K
Countries Having Cycles with Average Duration of 5.2 Years of Less—Countries listed in Figure J, United States added: various dates to 1920–25.

FIGURE L
Countries Having Cycles with Average Duration of 5.0–5.7 Years—South Africa, Argentina, Brazil, Canada, Germany, India, France, Austria, Sweden, England, Australia: various dates to 1920–25.

93 cycles
Average duration—4.7 years
Standard deviation—2.1 years
Coefficient of variation—45 per cent

106 cycles
Average duration—5.4 years
Standard deviation—2.4 years
Coefficient of variation—44 per cent

Duration in Years

Duration in Years

403

FIGURE M
Eight European Countries: various dates to 1920–25.

FIGURE N
Nine Non-European Countries: various dates to 1920–24.

84 cycles
Average duration—5.6 years
Standard deviation—2.5 years
Coefficient of variation—45 per cent

82 cycles
Average duration—4.7 years
Standard deviation—2.2 years
Coefficient of variation—46 per cent

FIGURE O
Five English-Speaking Countries—England, Canada, Australia, South Africa, United States: various dates to 1920–24.

FIGURE P
Twelve Non-English-Speaking Countries: various dates to 1920–25.

73 cycles
Average duration—4.9 years
Standard deviation—2.2 years
Coefficient of variation—46 per cent

93 cycles
Average duration—5.4 years
Standard deviation—2.5 years
Coefficient of variation—47 per cent

FIGURE Q
All Countries except United States: various dates to 1920–25.

FIGURE R
All Countries: various dates to 1920–25.

134 cycles
Average duration—5.4 years
Standard deviation—2.5 years
Coefficient of variation—45 per cent

166 cycles
Average duration—5.2 years
Standard deviation—2.4 years
Coefficient of variation—47 per cent

404

FIGURE S
Eight European Countries: 1888–92 to 1920-25.

FIGURE T
Eight Non-European Countries, excluding United
States: 1888–1890 to 1920–24.

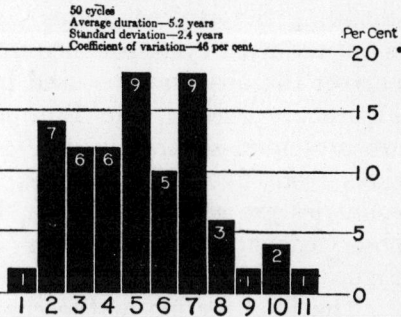

45 cycles
Average duration—5.6 years
Standard deviation—2.5 years
Coefficient of variation—45 per cent

50 cycles
Average duration—5.2 years
Standard deviation—2.4 years
Coefficient of variation—46 per cent

FIGURE U
Seven Industrial Countries—England, France,
Germany, Austria, Netherlands, Sweden, United
States, 1890–92 to 1920–25.

FIGURE V
Ten Non-Industrial Countries—Russia, Italy, Ar-
gentina, Brazil, Canada, South Africa, India,
Australia, Japan, China: 1888–91 to 1920–25.

43 cycles
Average duration—5.0 years
Standard deviation—2.4 years
Coefficient of variation—48 per cent

62 cycles
Average duration—5.3 years
Standard deviation—2.5 years
Coefficient of variation—47 per cent

FIGURE W
All Countries except United States: 1888–92 to
1920–25.

FIGURE X
All Countries: 1888–92 to 1920–25.

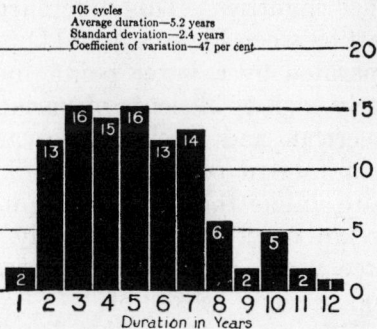

95 cycles
Average duration—5.4 years
Standard deviation—2.5 years
Coefficient of variation—44 per cent

105 cycles
Average duration—5.2 years
Standard deviation—2.4 years
Coefficient of variation—47 per cent

Duration in Years

Duration in Years

cycles as given in our annals. Figure I shows the observations from countries with relatively long cycles, Figures J and K the observations from countries with relatively short cycles (excluding and including the United States), and Figure L the observations from countries with cycles of medium length. The latter group contains part of the observations used in Figure I and part of those used in Figure J. Second, the European and non-European observations are presented separately in Figures M and N. Third, the observations from five English-speaking and twelve non-English-speaking countries are shown. Fourth, Figure Q gives all the non-American observations for comparison with the American distribution of Figure A. Figure R sums up the whole body of data.

The final section of the chart is confined to recent cycles—those occurring since about 1890. Again the data are divided into groups: observations from European and non-European countries, from industrial and non-industrial countries; from all countries except and all including the United States.

When we review the whole array of distributions, we see that the diagrams and the differences among the diagrams are of a sort common in studies of social phenomena. As usually happens in such work, the small samples, especially when they contain inter-correlated observations, are rather irregular. But with increase in the size of the samples and in the independence of the observations, the distributions grow fairly regular, though not symmetrical.

The materials appear to be fairly homogeneous, with the important exception already noted—the distribution of American business cycles in respect to length differs from the distribution of cycles in other countries. This difference stands out most sharply in the contrast between Figures A and Q. It is responsible for the double modes, separated by a lower point, in Figures O and X, and for the relatively high coefficients of variation in most of the groups combining American and foreign observations. In the samples drawn solely from foreign countries, the diagrams usually have a rounded top quite unlike the spike of Figure A. Combining the American with foreign observations generally produces an unambiguous mode at three years, but twice (Figures O and X) it produces the double mode already spoken of.

Barring out the twelve distributions into which American observations enter does not reduce the variety in the position of the crude modes. Two of the remaining dozen figures have modes at three years (G and P); two at three and four years (M and Q); and eight at 4, 5, or 6 years, if we may include here one double mode at 5 and 7 years (Figure T). By way of generalization we can hardly be more specific than to say that two-thirds of the foreign cycles are concentrated in the interval three to seven years.

All of the distributions have rather high coefficients of variation. In other words, the observations do not cluster closely around their averages. These coefficients are least in the two distributions confined to single countries (Figures A and B), and greatest in the distributions made from American, British, French, German and Austrian observations since 1873 (Figure E). But the difference between the lowest and highest coefficients (39 and 48 per cent) is not great, and 14 of the 24 round off at 45, 46 or 47 per cent.

All the distributions are skewed positively. The range runs farther above the arithmetic mean than below it in every case, and in every case but Figure T the range also runs farther above the crude mode than below it. Moreover, the crude mode is less than the arithmetic mean in 16 cases, about equal to it in 7 cases, and clearly higher than the mean only in Figure T. One of the most significant distributions, Figure W, which includes all cycles since about 1890 in countries other than the United States, approaches symmetry; but the very broadest groups, Figures X (all recent cycles), Q (all foreign cycles), and R (all cycles) are decidedly, though not extremely, skewed.

Before attempting to interpret these frequency distributions, it is advisable to consider the relative duration of periods of prosperity and depression, the bearing of long-period trends of wholesale prices and secular changes in cycle lengths.

4. THE RELATIVE DURATION OF PROSPERITY AND DEPRESSION.

Dr. Thorp has made a special study of the annals to determine as accurately as possible how many months of the record for each country can be classed as prosperous and how many as depressed. Needless to say, this task involved the continuous exercise of personal judgment.

As pointed out in the comparison between the annals and certain statistical indexes of business activity, contemporary observers are always influenced by recent experience in their use of the terms depression and prosperity. Hence, no rigid criterion of what constitutes business prosperity and depression can be evolved from, or read into, our sources. But that fact does not obstruct, it really facilitates, the task in hand. For we seek to compare the duration of the prosperous phase with that of the depressed phase within each cycle treated as a unit. That the prosperous phases of successive cycles in the same country and of synchronous cycles in different countries attain different degrees of intensity is a matter of deep interest, both practically and theoretically; but it is beside the present point.

Dr. Thorp's chief difficulty was that his sources seldom date the transitions from one phase of a cycle to the next phase. In trying to supply that omission in every case, he had to rely upon indications which are often faint. In detail his decisions must be subject to a wider margin of error than his measurements of the durations of whole cycles, since the recessions on which the latter measurements are based, are the phases which have attracted most attention. Hence it will be advisable to confine ourselves to his averages covering several or many cycles, and to draw only broad conclusions.

Table 28 shows the form and drift of Dr. Thorp's tabulations. It

TABLE 28

RELATIVE DURATION OF DIFFERENT PHASES OF BUSINESS CYCLES IN SEVENTEEN COUNTRIES, 1890–1925

	Months	Percentages
Months of prosperity	2,888	39.3
Months of recession and revival.............	1,756	23.9
Months of depression	2,700	36.8
Total	7,344	100.0

Years of prosperity per year of depression: 1.07.

appears that the phases of recession and revival put together make up rather less than one-quarter of the duration of recent cycles. But in view of the difficulty of saying just when revival has blossomed into prosperity, and just when recession has merged into depression, this conclusion should not be stressed heavily. However, if these decisions can be made on a substantially consistent basis, the comparison between the relative duration of the prosperous and depressed phases of the cycles will not be compromised.[1] What the table indicates is that in this period of 36 years the prosperous

[1] Chart 27, below, shows for every cycle the quarters and years which Dr. Thorp has taken as marking off revival and recession.

phases averaged somewhat longer than the depressed phases. A similar conclusion was drawn from American business indexes in Chapter III. Business contraction was found to be "a briefer and more
violent process than business expansion." A crude average of over
50 measurements of the duration of the ascending phase of the cycles
since 1878 gives 23 months. The corresponding average for the de-
scending phase is about 19 months.[2]

Similar averages showing the relative duration of prosperity and
depression for particular countries and periods are given in Table 29.
To get comparable results it has been necessary both to take periods
which comprise whole cycles, and to make these periods as nearly
synchronous as may be. For the results in any one country vary
considerably from one period to another. For example, the English
and American averages come out in three different periods as follows:

	Years of Pros-perity per Year of Depression		Years of Pros-perity per Year of Depression
England 1790–1925.........	1.11	United States 1790–1925....	1.50
1890–1913.........	1.24	1890–1913....	1.57
1890–1920.........	1.71	1890–1923....	1.79

As a guide to future expectations, the averages which include the
years of the great war seem less significant than the averages which
we have for longer periods of time in five countries, or than the averages for 17 countries in the period from about 1890 to 1913.

The wide differences between the averages for the countries at the
the bottom and the top of the list in Table 29 show how much business
conditions are affected by political turmoil and stability. Brazil,
China, Russia and South Africa had grave troubles in the period for
which we have compiled their annals, and Austria suffered from her
proximity to the Balkan volcanoes. The other figures speak for themselves. But we should remember that the figures for each country
speak that country's language. Swedish prosperity may differ from
Canadian prosperity—the comparison made is between the prosperous
and the depressed phases of Swedish cycles in one case, and between
the prosperous and the depressed phases of Canadian cycles in the
other case. It is risky to say that one of these countries has been more
prosperous than the other, even in the period here covered. And it

[2] See Chapter III, section vi, (2) "Month-to-Month Changes," and (5) "Duration of
Periods of Expansion and Contraction."

is easy to conceive that any country might change its ranking in such a list radically within a decade or two.

TABLE 29.

RELATIVE DURATION OF THE PROSPEROUS AND DEPRESSED PHASES IN THE BUSINESS CYCLES OF SEVENTEEN COUNTRIES DURING VARIOUS PERIODS

	Period	Years of Prosperity per Year of Depression
United States	1790–1925	1.50
England	1790–1925	1.11
France	1840–1925	1.18
Germany	1853–1925	1.18
Austria	1866–1925	0.70

	Period	Years of Prosperity per Year of Depression	Period	Years of Prosperity per Year of Depression
Canada	1888–1924	1.86	1888–1913	2.08
United States....	1890–1923	1.79	1890–1913	1.57
England	1890–1920	1.71	1890–1913	1.24
France	1890–1920	1.70	1890–1913	1.47
Australia	1890–1920	1.69	1890–1913	1.37
Sweden	1892–1920	1.67	1892–1913	1.89
Netherlands	1891–1920	1.61	1891–1913	1.59
India	1889–1920	1.43	1889–1914	1.26
Argentina	1890–1920	1.07	1890–1913	1.06
Japan	1890–1920	1.05	1890–1914	.75
Germany	1890–1925	1.03	1890–1913	1.14
Italy	1888–1920	.98	1888–1913	.90
South Africa	1890–1920	.89	1890–1913	.66
Russia	1891–1925	.81	1891–1914	1.09
China	1888–1920	.65	1888–1910	.57
Austria	1892–1922	.63	1892–1912	.73
Brazil	1889–1924	.45	1889–1912	.29
Seventeen Countries		1.14		1.08

One of the main reasons why these ratios of years of prosperity to years of depression are unstable is revealed by a further analysis of the long records for England and the United States. From various index numbers of prices, it is known that the long-period trend of the wholesale price level changed direction four times in the 130 years, 1790 to 1920. The turning points came at nearly the same dates in this country and England, save that our greenback prices reached their highest point just before the end of the Civil War in

1865, whereas in gold-standard nations prices continued to rise until 1873. Thus we have in both countries five periods of alternately declining and advancing price trends. From 1790 to 1814 wholesale prices rose unsteadily; from 1814 to 1849 they declined unsteadily; from 1849 to 1865 in the United States and to 1873 in England they rose unsteadily; from 1865 in the United States and 1873 in England they declined unsteadily until 1896; from 1896 to 1920 they rose unsteadily. For the periods thus marked off, Dr. Thorp has obtained the following ratios of years of prosperity to years of depression:

TABLE 30

RELATIVE DURATION OF THE PROSPEROUS AND THE DEPRESSED PHASES OF BUSINESS CYCLES IN PERIODS OF RISING AND DECLINING TRENDS OF WHOLESALE PRICES: ENGLAND AND THE UNITED STATES, 1790–1925

England	Years of Prosperity per Year of Depression	United States	Years of Prosperity per Year of Depression
1790–1815 Prices rising	1.0	1790–1815 Prices rising	2.6
1815–1849 Prices falling	.9	1815–1849 Prices falling	.8
1849–1873 Prices rising	3.3	1849–1865 Prices rising	2.9
1873–1896 Prices falling	.4	1865–1896 Prices falling	.9
1896–1920 Prices rising	2.7	1896–1920 Prices rising	3.1

These results are so uniform and so striking as to leave little doubt that the secular trend of the wholesale price level is a factor of great moment in determining the characteristics of business cycles. That is no novel conclusion; but Dr. Thorp's data lend it new force and precision.

A final point established by study of the relative duration of the prosperous and the depressed phases of business cycles is that the very long cycles usually owe their length primarily to prolongation of depression. Among the 166 cycles we have measured there are 17 which lasted 9 years or more. The average of all our observations, it will be remembered, is 5.2 years. Dr. Thorp has made a special examination of these long cycles to determine when the revivals occurred, and how long were the periods of declining and of increasing activity. His results appear in Table 31.

Whereas the most inclusive average in Table 29 gives a ratio of 1.14 years of prosperity per year of depression, the present table gives a ratio of 0.79. In 11 of the 17 cycles the phase of depression is longer than the phase of prosperity. The longest period of prosperity found is 72 months; the longest periods of depression run 72, 76 and 100 months. Finally, the average phase of depression in these long cycles is nearly a year longer than the average phase of prosperity.

TABLE 31.

RELATIVE DURATION OF PHASES OF DEPRESSION AND PHASES OF PROSPERITY IN BUSINESS CYCLES LASTING NINE YEARS OR MORE

Length in Years	Country	Periods Covered by the Cycles	Year of Revival	Months of Depression	Months of Prosperity
12	Italy	1888, early–1900, early	1897	100	30
11	France	1890, early–1900, late	1895	60	42
11	Austria	1873–1884	1880	72	36
11	Australia ...	1890–1901	1896	62	48
10	England	1837, early–1847, April	1843	68	44
10	England	1890, Nov.–1900	1895	42	48
10	Germany ...	1890, early–1900, summer..	1894, late	44	51
10	Netherlands .	1891–1901	1896	48	48
10	South Africa.	1903–1913	1909	60	36
10	China	1910–1920	1916	60	48
9	United States	1873–1882	1878	57	42
9	England	1873, late–1883, early	1880	69	24
9	France	1838–1847	1840	24	72
9	Germany ...	1848–1857	1853	54	42
9	Germany ...	1857–1866	1860	18	66
9	Sweden	1892–1901	1895	30	60
9	China	1888–1897	1895	76	12
			Total	944	749
			Average	55	44

Years of prosperity per year of depression: 0.79.

5. SECULAR CHANGES IN THE AVERAGE DURATION OF BUSINESS CYCLES.

Another matter which demands attention is the differences between the average duration of business cycles in various countries revealed by Table 26. In particular, why do American cycles average only 4 years in length, while English cycles during the same period average nearly 5 years and 10 months?

A possible clew to this puzzle is suggested by the hypothesis, developed in Chapter II, that business cycles are associated with a particular form of economic organization, here called "business economy."

If that hypothesis be valid, the characteristics of business cycles may be expected to change as economic organization develops. We have historical evidence to support this supposition in respect to at least one characteristic: violent panics are giving way to recessions. May not the average intervals between recessions also vary from generation to generation?

In the introduction to *Business Annals* I noted that secular changes in duration have occurred in certain countries for which Dr. Thorp has compiled annals covering an extended period. But I failed to develop the full significance of the data. Dr. Frederick C. Mills of the National Bureau's staff has made a more extended study of the problem, and suggested a tentative explanation, not only of the secular changes which he finds in the average duration of business cycles in the United States, England, France, and Germany, but also of the differences in the average length of business cycles in our 17 countries.[1]

Dr. Mills formulates his hypothesis as follows:

. . . the duration of business cycles in a given country is a function of the stage of industrial development which that country has attained. More specifically: When the modern type of economic organization is in the initial stage of development, the average duration of business cycles is relatively long. During the stage of rapid growth, when modern types of business enterprise and modern forms of industrial organization are being applied extensively, business cycles are of relatively short average duration. With the decline in the rate of economic change and the attainment of comparative stability, business cycles increase again in length.

To test this hypothesis adequately Dr. Mills recognizes that he needs, not only a larger body of observations, but also an "objective criterion for distinguishing the stages in a country's industrial development, or for classifying countries according to their present state of development." On the view developed in this book, the factor in economic organization critically important for the understanding of business cycles is not the "stage of industrial development" as such, but the proportion of the people who are depending mainly upon making and spending money incomes, and the proportion of total business that is done by large-scale enterprises. Needless to say, we

[1] "An Hypothesis concerning the Duration of Business Cycles," *Journal of the American Statistical Association*, December, 1926, vol. xxi, pp. 447-457.

have neither an "index of industrialization," nor an index of business economy. Under these circumstances, Dr. Mills is forced to make a somewhat arbitrary division of Dr. Thorp's materials into the periods suggested by his hypothesis—a division based partly on the evidence of the annals themselves and partly on other information. Thus he takes the early stage of industrialization in the United States to last from the beginning of the annals to 1822, since which time the country has been in the stage of rapid economic transition. In England he supposes that the first stage had been passed before our annals begin, that the second stage extended from 1793 to 1831, and the third from 1831 to date. The countries which he assigns to this third stage of decreasing rate of progress are England since 1831, France since 1876, Austria since 1873, the Netherlands and Sweden since the beginning of their annals in 1890. Germany he puts into the first stage until 1866, and into the second stage since then.[2]

---

[2] Mills' full classification of the materials is as follows:

A. Countries in the early stages of industrialization:

United States	to 1822	(Annals begin 1796)*
Germany	to 1866	" " 1848
Italy	to 1907	" " 1888
Canada	to 1913	" " 1888
Australia	to 1913	" " 1890
South Africa	to 1913	" " 1890
China	to date	" " 1888
India	to date	" " 1889
Russia	to date	" " 1891
Argentina	to date	" " 1890
Brazil	to date	" " 1889

B. Countries in the stage of rapid economic transition:

England	to 1831	(Annals begin 1793)
United States	1822 to date	
France	to 1876	" " 1838
Germany	1866 to date	
Austria	to 1873	" " 1866
Italy	1907 to date	
Canada	1913 to date	
Australia	1913 to date	
South Africa	1913 to date	
Japan	to date	" " 1890

C. Countries in which the transition is going forward at a decreasing rate:

England	1831 to date	
France	1876 to date	
Austria	1873 to date	
Netherlands	to date	(Annals begin 1891)
Sweden	to date	" " 1892

* The dates given as marking the beginning of the *Annals* are the dates of the first recorded recessions. In cases where the beginning of a stage is not defined in the above table, that stage is assumed to date from a period prior to the beginning of the *Annals*.

On this basis, Dr. Mills gets the following results:

	Early stages of industrialization	Stage of rapid economic transition	Stage of relative economic stability
Number of observations	51 cycles	77 cycles	38 cycles
Mean duration	5.86 years	4.09 years	6.39 years
Standard deviation	2.41 "	1.88 "	2.42 "

He computes that differences as great as those between the averages of the first and second periods and between the averages of the second and third periods would arise as the result of sampling fluctuations about one time out of 50,000 and 1,000,000 trials respectively. The explanation for the relatively short duration of American cycles suggested by these results is "an exceptional prolongation of the period of industrial transition in this country."

There can be little doubt that the average duration of business cycles has undergone secular changes in the countries for which Thorp has compiled the longest records. If our annals are valid, this conclusion is definitely established for England, and made highly probable for France and the United States. Mills gives the following averages for periods which differ in the case of one country from those used in his systematic classification of all the materials:

England	1793–1831	9 cycles	Average duration 4.22 years
"	1831–1920	13 "	" " 6.85 "
France	1854–1876	6 "	" " 3.67 "
"	1876–1920	7 "	" " 6.32 "
United States	1796–1822	5 "	" " 5.20 "
" "	1822–1860	11 "	" " 3.50 "
" "	1860–1888	5 "	" " 5.50 "
" "	1888–1923	11 "	" " 3.20 "

Thus English and French cycles have grown longer, while American cycles have gone through a curious double swing, first decreasing in length, then increasing, then decreasing again.

But, granting the statistical significance of these averages, and their value as a summary of past experience, what theoretical importance can we attach to them? From the empirical viewpoint they show the existence of secular trends in the duration of business cycles. We have seen that purely empirical trends can be used only in the most tentative fashion as a basis for forming future expectations, or as a basis for giving explanations. But if trends can be developed from rational hypotheses, they become far more useful. Thus we come back to a critical consideration of the evidence for Mills' hypothesis concerning the connection between the average duration of business cycles and the state of industrialization.

It is doubtful if any half-dozen economic historians, given Mills' necessarily vague definitions of three stages of industrialization, and asked to date the close of each stage in the 17 countries for which we have business annals, would undertake the task, or find themselves in substantial agreement if they did. It is easy to question many of the dates assigned by Mills, and hard either to establish or to disprove their validity. To canvass the pertinent evidence in detail would be an enormous task, and would lead to no conclusive result unless prefaced, first by a more precise statement of the hypothesis than Mills has given, and second by the development of objective standards by which to rate the significance of what facts might be established.

Our best hope for further light upon the hypothesis which Mills makes so interesting lies in further analytic work upon secular trends in economic history. Few problems are more fascinating, more important, or more neglected than the rates at which economic development proceeds in successive generations and in different countries. It is conceivable that men who combine the requisite statistical technique with the requisite historical knowledge can develop effective methods of utilizing the scattered figures which survive in little known sources, and the abundant descriptive materials, in such fashion as to show at least the broad stages in the recent economic development of the leading commercial nations. If they do, sidelights upon changes in various characteristics of business cycles will be a not unimportant gain from their labors.

6. Conclusions.

1. Our measurements of the intervals between recessions do not bear precisely upon the obsolescent debate concerning the periodicity of crises. But measurements made from the annals upon the old plan would be as fatal to the hypothesis of periodicity as the measurements which I prefer. Indeed, counting from crisis to crisis would make the limits within which cycles vary even wider than does counting from recession to recession. The longest cycle shown by the annals

—the Italian case of 1888-1900—would be extended from 12 to 19 years if we skipped the mild recession of 1900 and passed on to the crisis of 1907. Perhaps still longer cycles might be found, were this method of counting systematically applied to all countries. Nor could the extension of the range in one direction be compensated by reduction at the other end of the scale. The shortest cycle could not be prolonged beyond two or three years, except by such violent procedures as telescoping the American panics of 1837 and 1839 into a single crisis.

Nor can I confirm the ingenious suggestion made by Professor H. S. Jevons and Mr. Joseph Kitchin, that long cycles are multiples of two or three short ones.[1] Were such the case, and were the short cycles 3⅓ or 3½ years long as these writers suppose, one would expect our frequency diagrams to show modes, primary or secondary, at 3, 7, and 10, or 11 years. None of them do so. There are diagrams with modes, pronounced or faint, at 3 and 7 years, and 4 and 8 years. But there are also diagrams with modes, pronounced or faint, at 3 and 4 years; 3 and 5 years; 3 and 6 years; 3 and 8 years; 3, 4, 6, and 8 years; 3, 5, and 7 years; 3, 5, and 10 years; 3, 6, and 10 years; 4 and 5 years; 4 and 6 years; 5 and 7 years, etc. More significant is the fact that as the size of the samples increases the minor modes tend to disappear, instead of tending to grow clearer. In the most inclusive sample of all (Figure R of Chart 24), there are no secondary modes.

While few if any recent writers maintain the hypothesis of periodicity in any form, many of them do give some average figure to represent the duration typical of business cycles. Such averages are adequate for certain purposes. But the present results show that no average can suggest the facts about the duration of cycles which are most significant for theory and practice.

2. If there is any regularity in the sequence of cycles of different lengths, I have failed to find it. Chart 23, which represents the duration of cycles taken in chronological order, shows the hazard of attempting to forecast how long the next cycle will last in any of our countries. Neither modal length, nor the duration of the preceding cycle is a safe guide.

3. A semblance of regularity does appear, however, when we disregard chronological sequence and group our observations in fre-

---

[1] See Herbert Stanley Jevons, *The Sun's Heat and Solar Activity*, London, 1910, and Joseph Kitchin, "Cycles and Trends in Economic Factors," *Review of Economic Statistics*, January, 1923, Preliminary vol. v, pp. 10-16.

quency tables. And the regularity becomes more marked as the size of the sample increases, that is, as the number of independent observations upon the duration of business cycles becomes greater.

The regularity which emerges, consists, not in the preponderance of cycles of any given duration, but in the way in which cycles of different durations group themselves about their central tendency. The distribution is of a type found in many studies of biological and social phenomena. It is not symmetrical, but skewed positively. In all the groups into which we have divided the observations for analysis, the range runs farther above than below the arithmetic mean, and in two-thirds of the groups the crude mode is less than the arithmetic mean.

4. American cycles have a shorter average duration than those of any other country studied. The averages of 32 American and of 134 foreign measurements are 4.0 and 5.4 years respectively. The shortest average duration found in any foreign country is 4.3 years in Japan, where 7 cycles occurred in approximately the period covered by 10 American cycles. The American distribution shows a pronounced mode at 3 years; the most inclusive of the foreign distributions shows a rounded top with equal numbers of cases at 3 and 4 years, and no marked decline in numbers before 8 years.

5. Secular changes in the average duration of business cycles can be traced in countries for which business annals have been compiled for long periods. In England and France the duration has increased; in the United States the duration averaged 5.2 years in 1796-1822, 3.5 years in 1822-60, 5.5 years in 1860-88, and 3.2 years in 1888-1923. This fact makes it difficult to adapt the physical-cause theories of economic fluctuations to business cycles.

The most interesting hypothesis concerning these changes in secular length, and concerning the differences in the average duration of cycles in different countries at a given period, is that offered by Dr. Frederick C. Mills, who suggests tentatively that business cycles tend to be relatively long in a country during the early stages of industrialization, relatively short during the stage of rapid economic transition, and relatively long again when the rate of transition decreases.

6. While our frequency distributions lack the symmetry of the Gaussian normal curve, their form suggests fitting "a logarithmic normal curve; that is a Gaussian curve in which the successive units [standard deviations] of the horizontal scale are readjusted to dis-

tances having a constant ratio rather than a constant difference." [2] This experiment has been tried upon Figure R of Chart 24—the distribution which includes all of our 166 observations. Chart 25 shows that the fit of the logarithmic normal curve to the data is on the whole rather close.[3]

CHART 25. Logarithmic Normal Curve Fitted by Davies' Method to the Frequency Distribution of 166 Observations upon the Duration of Business Cycles.

From this fact we infer that, like other biological and social phenomena whose distributions are well described by some form of the normal curve, the durations of business cycles may be regarded as the net resultants of a multitude of factors which are largely inde-

[2] See George R. Davies, "The Logarithmic Curve of Distribution," *Journal of the American Statistical Association*, December, 1925, vol. xx, pp. 467-480. Dr. Thorp has adopted Professor Davies' method in making the chart on this page.

[3] When the cycles now running in our 17 countries are ended, the new batch of observations promises to modify the distribution of Chart 25 somewhat. Five years have already elapsed since the latest recession in three of our countries, and six years in seven countries.

pendent of each other. If there is any dominant factor or set of factors, which tends to produce cycles of uniform duration, its influence is greatly modified by a host of other factors combined in ways which vary endlessly. This conclusion has an important bearing upon the theory of business cycles and the methods by which that theory may be improved.[4]

7. Regarding the relative duration of the several phases which make up business cycles, the annals yield certain fragmentary, but significant, results.

As we interpret them on the basis of current business reports, the phases of recession and revival are relatively brief.[5] Put together, they account for only one-quarter of the duration of business cycles on the average. Of the remaining three-quarters, the prosperous phase occupies a somewhat longer time than the phase of depression. But the ratio of months of prosperity to months of depression varies widely from country to country, and within any country it varies widely from cycle to cycle. Consequently, the average ratios ap-

---

[4] Dr. Oskar Morgenstern has kindly allowed me to read the manuscript of a paper on "Internationale vergleichende Konjunkturforschung" (soon to appear in the *Zeitschrift für die gesammte Staatswissenschaft*), in which he questions the propriety of my averaging together measurements of the duration of business cycles which have occurred in communities of widely different economic organization. As Dr. Morgenstern points out, the hypothesis that there is an intimate connection between the form of economic organization and business cycles implies that radical differences in economic organization are associated with corresponding differences in cyclical fluctuations. Since I work with the hypothesis in question, am I justified in assembling in a single array measurements of cycles in communities so unlike in organization as contemporary England and China, or the United States of the 20th and of the 18th centuries?

As said in the text, I take the Chinese reports to represent conditions in the coast cities only. Similarly, in dealing with the earlier American annals, I use only the reports from the northern and eastern states, paying no attention to the reports from the southern states and western settlements, which are frequently quite different in tenor. There is evidence that business economy, as defined in Chapter II, had become established (though not highly developed) by 1790 from Pennsylvania to Massachusetts, and by 1890 in the coast cities of China. If that opinion is valid, I seem justified in treating the fluctuations of economic fortune experienced by these two communities as business cycles.

Granted so much, is not something to be learned by studying the available measurements of these highly variable phenomena as a whole, as well as in a variety of small groups? Of course, it would be easy to over-stress the significance of my grand average of the duration of business cycles. I do not attach much importance to the arithmetic mean of the total array; but I do think the distribution of the observations around their central tendency is a matter of much theoretical interest.

Finally, I agree with Dr. Morgenstern that the relation between the duration of business cycles and changes in the form of economic organization was not adequately treated in my introduction to Thorp's *Business Annals*. Since that book was published, Mills' hypothesis has put the problem in a clearer form, and indicated how much work may be required to reach a satisfactory solution.

[5] When it is necessary to define revivals and recessions as the periods within which all of the statistical series in a large collection turn up or turn down, these two phases become relatively long. But more of that matter in the volume to follow.

proach stability only when long periods of time and many countries are included. Perhaps the most significant figures are those for the United States and England in 1790-1925, and for all our 17 countries in 1890-1913. These three results come out respectively 1.50, 1.11 and 1.08 years of prosperity per year of depression.

Both the English and the American records indicate that the relative duration of the prosperous and depressed phases of business cycles is dominated by the secular trend of wholesale prices. In the three periods of rising price trends since 1790, the prosperous phases of the cycles have been prolonged and the depressed phases have been relatively brief. In the three periods of declining price trends, the prosperous phases of the cycles have been relatively brief and the depressed phases prolonged. While the observations upon which these conclusions rest are subject to a margin of uncertainty in every cycle considered, random errors could hardly produce such uniform results as we find.

Finally, it appears that the depressed phases of business cycles are susceptible of greater prolongation than the prosperous phases. Whereas our averages including many cycles all show a slight preponderance of years of prosperity over years of depression, our long cycles as a group show a marked preponderance of years of depression over years of prosperity.

In weighing the conclusions drawn in this section, one should bear in mind certain features of the data and methods used.

No selection or "adjustment" has been practiced upon the observations. The "abnormal cases"—if that phrase has an intelligible meaning—are included with the "normal." Every reader of the annals will note how frequently foreign wars and domestic turmoil, harvest fluctuations, epidemics, floods and earthquakes have checked or reënforced the tides of business activity. A tendency toward alternations of prosperity and depression must have considerable constancy and energy to stamp its pattern upon economic history in a world where other factors of most unequal power are constantly present, and where one or other of these factors, singly or in combination, rises to dominance at irregular intervals.

Our measurements are based solely upon the intervals between recessions. It would be desirable to check the results by a second set, based on the intervals between revivals. We have not attempted such a check, because business commentators have paid less attention to the upward than to the downward turning points of business cycles. The materials for making the second set of measurements are less full and reliable than the materials we have exploited. If a second set as satisfactory as the first could be made, the frequency distributions it yielded would doubtless differ in numberless details from the frequency distributions here presented. But we have no reason to believe that the broad conclusions suggested by the new frequency distributions would run counter to the conclusions we have drawn.

The year is too large a unit for measuring business cycles. Our results have the crudity of an effort to ascertain the stature distribution of men, women and children from measurements made in feet. In statistical work with time series, it is often possible to substitute the more appropriate unit of a month. But such investigations of business fluctuations are confined to those narrow limits of time, place, and type of business for which elaborate numerical data have been collected.

The best we could do when we were seeking to determine the duration of business cycles by using monthly statistics was to make numerous measurements of a dozen cases in one country. Five business indexes, covering by months part or all of the last half century in the United States, together with the plan of counting durations both from crest to crest and from trough to trough, enabled us to accumulate 101 observations upon the lengths of what the annals represent as 12 cycles (or 12½ if we start with the trough of 1878). That the results obtained in this way agree with the results obtained from the same period of the annals appears from Chart 21. For that chart shows that the most significant of the statistical indexes which run back to 1875 give the same recession dates as do the annals.

It may be worth while, however, to compare the 101 statistical measurements of the 12½ cycles of 1878 to 1923 with the 32 measurements of 32 cycles made from the annals of 1796 to 1923. To that end, we may condense the quarterly figures made from the statistical observations which ran originally by months, into yearly figures, assigning each quarter to that year into which it presumably would fall were the reckoning made from annals. For example, we count the cycles lasting approximately two years as those included in the four quarters centering on 19, 22, 25 and 28 months—that is, the quarters which run from 1½ years to 2 years and five months. Chart 26 gives the results.

CHART 26

Percentage Distribution of Measurements of the Duration of Business Cycles in the United States Based upon Business Indexes, 1875–1925, and Business Annals, 1790–1925.

By using 5 business indexes, and counting intervals both from trough to trough and crest to crest of the cycles, 101 measurements were made of the duration of 12½ cycles. The measurements, originally expressed in months, were grouped first by quarters, and later by years. See Table 16, Chart 20, and context in Chapter III.

The Annals yield a single set of measurements of the duration of 32 cycles. See Table 27.

■ Measurements made from Business Indexes

▨ Measurements made from Business Annals

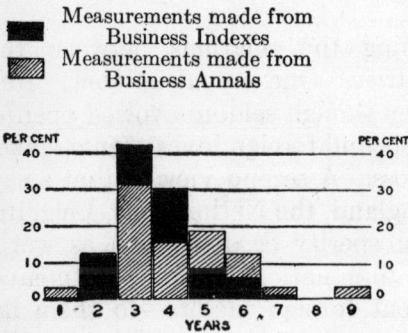

	Percentage Distribution of the Measurements made from	
	Business Indexes 1875–1925	Business Annals 1790–1925
1 year	.3	3.1
2 years	12.1	12.5
3 "	42.0	31.2
4 "	30.1	15.6
5 "	8.4	18.8
6 "	6.0	12.5
7 "	1.0	3.1
8 "	....	....
9 "	....	3.1
	100.0	100.0

The similarity of the two figures on this chart is patent. If the measurements based on statistics show an even greater concentration at three years than do the measurements made from the annals (42 per cent of the observations as compared with 31 per cent), it is because of the difference in the years covered by the two sets of data. If we take only that part of the annals covered by the business indexes, we find 5 of the 12 cycles lasting 3 years, and 5 is 42 per cent of 12. Similar explanations apply to the other differences between the two figures:—for example, the lack of very short and very long cycles in 1875-1925 as compared with 1790-1925, accounts for the margins between the lines at 1 and 9 years.

In view of the agreement between the two sets of measurements, it seems safe to say (1) that if our business indexes extended back to 1790, they would show less concentration of cycles at 3 years, and a wider spread in the measurements; (2) that if we could elaborate the measurements made from the annals, by counting in months, and reckoning duration not merely from recession to recession, but also from revival to revival, we should find the modal length to be more than 36 months, as Chart 20 indicates, though less than three and a half years.

V. International Relationships Among Business Cycles.

1. A CONSPECTUS OF BUSINESS CONDITIONS IN DIFFERENT COUNTRIES.

Opinions differ widely concerning the relations between the economic fortunes of different countries. One prevalent view, often implied in discussions of public policy though seldom avowed openly, is that competition for foreign markets and foreign investments makes one nation's gain another nation's loss. A second view is that small countries with a vast commerce—England, the Netherlands, Belgium, Sweden and Norway—experience prosperity or depression as world business quickens or slackens; but that nations with a continental spread need feel slight concern about foreign factors—to them internal development is of overshadowing importance. There is still a third view, that business enterprise has been silently establishing a "world economy," a "commercial league of nations," in which all the members prosper or suffer together.

Needless to say, the annals do not give clear proof or disproof of any of these contentions. But they do indicate a trend in the direction of "world economy."

To facilitate international comparisons of economic fortunes, the annals of all the countries studied have been compressed into a single table. This conspectus begins with the United States and England in 1790, adds France in 1840, Germany in 1853, Austria in 1867, and 12 other countries in 1890. For the last generation it affords a fair view of world experience. The entries have the bleakness of statistical averages; they do not indicate the complexity of conditions prevailing every year within each country. For most purposes the fuller form of the annals given in Dr. Thorp's book should be used rather than the conspectus. But it is only as we concentrate in each country upon the net resultant of its diverse conditions that we can gain a clear view of the international similarities and diversities. Even the conspectus is not simple enough to tell its own story; it needs to be analyzed and summarized, as the reader who looks it over will agree.

TABLE 32

CONSPECTUS OF BUSINESS FLUCTUATIONS IN VARIOUS COUNTRIES

	1790	1791	1792	1793
United States	Revival; prosperity	Prosperity	Prosperity; financial distress	Prosperity
England.....	Moderate prosperity	Prosperity	Prosperity; financial strain	Recession; panic; depression

	1794	1795	1796	1797
United States	Uneven prosperity	Prosperity	Recession; depression	Depression; panic
England.....	Depression	Revival	Uneven prosperity	Recession; panic; depression

	1798	1799	1800	1801
United States	Depression	Revival	Prosperity	Mild prosperity
England.....	Depression	Depression	Depression	Depression; revival

	1802	1803	1804	1805
United States	Recession	Mild depression	Revival	Prosperity
England.....	Prosperity	Prosperity; recession	Mild depression	Revival

	1806	1807	1808	1809
United States	Prosperity	Prosperity; recession	Depression	Depression
England.....	Prosperity	Recession	Mild depression	Revival; prosperity

	1810	1811	1812	1813
United States	Revival	Moderate prosperity	Brief recession; uneven prosperity	Prosperity
England.....	Prosperity; recession	Deep depression	Revival	Prosperity

	1814	1815	1816	1817
United States	Prosperity; financial distress	Prosperity; panic; recession	Depression	Mild depression
England.....	Uneven prosperity	Boom; recession	Deep depression	Depression; revival

	1818	1819	1820	1821
United States	Mild depression	Severe depression; financial panic	Depression	Depression; revival
England.....	Prosperity	Recession; depression	Depression; slight revival	Slow revival

TABLE 32—(*Continued*)

CONSPECTUS OF BUSINESS FLUCTUATIONS IN VARIOUS COUNTRIES

	1822	1823	1824	1825
United States	Mild recession	Revival	Prosperity	Prosperity; panic; recession
England.....	Revival; prosperity	Prosperity	Prosperity	Prosperity; recession; panic

	1826	1827	1828	1829
United States	Depression; revival	Moderate prosperity	Prosperity; recession	Depression; revival
England.....	Depression	Revival	Prosperity	Recession; depression

	1830	1831	1832	1833
United States	Moderate prosperity	Prosperity	Moderate prosperity	Prosperity; panic; recession
England.....	Slow revival	Recession; depression	Depression	Revival

	1834	1835	1836	1837
United States	Mild depression	Revival; prosperity	Prosperity	Prosperity; panic; recession; depression
England.....	Prosperity	Prosperity; stock exchange panic	Prosperity; financial panic	Recession; panic; depression

	1838	1839	1840	1841
United States	Depression; slight revival	Revival; panic; recession	Depression	Depression
England.....	Depression	Depression	Depression	Depression
France.......	....	....	Revival	Prosperity

	1842	1843	1844	1845
United States	Depression	Depression; revival	Revival; prosperity	Prosperity; brief recession
England.....	Depression	Revival	Mild prosperity	Prosperity
France.......	Prosperity	Prosperity	Prosperity	Prosperity; bourse panic

	1846	1847	1848	1849
United States	Recession; mild depression	Revival; prosperity; panic; recession	Mild depression; revival	Prosperity
England.....	Prosperity	Prosperity; panic; recession	Depression	Depression; revival
France.......	Prosperity	Recession; panic	Depression; panic	Depression

	1850	1851	1852	1853
United States	Prosperity	Prosperity	Prosperity	Prosperity; recession
England.....	Prosperity	Prosperity	Prosperity	Prosperity
France.......	Depression	Depression	Revival	Prosperity
Germany....	....	....	....	Revival

TABLE 32—(*Continued*)

CONSPECTUS OF BUSINESS FLUCTUATIONS IN VARIOUS COUNTRIES

	1854	1855	1856	1857
United States	Recession; depression	Depression; revival	Prosperity	Prosperity; panic; recession; depression
England.....	Recession	Mild depression	Revival; prosperity	Prosperity; panic; recession
France.......	Prosperity; brief recession	Prosperity	Brief recession	Moderate prosperity; panic; recession
Germany....	Prosperity	Prosperity	Prosperity; bourse panic	Prosperity; panic; recession

	1858	1859	1860	1861
United States	Depression	Revival	Prosperity; recession	Mild depression; revival
England.....	Depression	Revival	Prosperity	Uneven prosperity
France.......	Depression	Revival	Prosperity; recession	Recession
Germany....	Recession; depression	Depression	Revival	Mild prosperity

	1862	1863	1864	1865
United States	War activity	War activity	War activity	Boom; recession
England.....	Uneven prosperity	Uneven prosperity	Uneven prosperity; financial strain	Prosperity
France......	Mild depression	Uneven depression	Depression; financial panic	Depression
Germany....	Uneven prosperity	Moderate prosperity	Moderate prosperity	Prosperity

	1866	1867	1868	1869
United States	Mild depression	Depression	Revival	Prosperity; monetary difficulties
England.....	Recession; panic; depression	Depression	Depression	Revival
France.......	Revival	Recession; mild depression; bourse panic	Depression; revival	Prosperity; Prosperity bourse panic
Germany....	Prosperity; recession; depression	Depression; revival	Revival	
Austria......	....	Revival	Moderate prosperity	Prosperity; panic; recession

TABLE 32—(*Continued*)

CONSPECTUS OF BUSINESS FLUCTUATIONS IN VARIOUS COUNTRIES

	1870	1871	1872	1873
United States	Recession; mild depression	Revival; prosperity	Prosperity	Prosperity; panic; recession
England.....	Prosperity; panic	Prosperity	Prosperity	Prosperity; recession
France.......	Prosperity; recession; depression	Depression; panic	Revival	Recession; depression
Germany....	Prosperity; brief recession	Prosperity	Prosperity	Prosperity; panic; recession; depression
Austria......	Slow recession	Mild depression	Revival; prosperity	Prosperity; panic; recession

	1874	1875	1876	1877
United States	Depression	Depression	Depression	Depression
England.....	Depression	Depression	Depression	Depression
France.......	Mild depression	Revival	Gradual recession	Mild depression
Germany....	Depression	Depression	Depression	Slow revival
Austria......	Deep depression	Depression	Depression	Depression

	1878	1879	1880	1881
United States	Depression; revival	Revival; prosperity	Prosperity	Prosperity
England.....	Deepening depression	Depression; revival	Slow revival	Mild prosperity
France.......	Depression	Revival; bourse panic	Prosperity	Moderate prosperity
Germany....	Recession; depression	Depression; revival	Recession; mild depression	Renewed revival
Austria......	Depression	Depression	Revival	Mild prosperity

	1882	1883	1884	1885
United States	Prosperity; slight recession	Recession	Depression	Depression; revival
England.....	Mild prosperity	Slow recession	Depression	Depression
France.......	Recession; panic	Depression	Depression	Depression
Germany....	Prosperity; recession	Mild depression	Depression	Depression
Austria......	Moderate prosperity; bourse panic	Prosperity	Recession	Mild depression

	1886	1887	1888	1889
United States	Revival	Prosperity	Brief recession	Prosperity
England.....	Depression; slight revival	Revival	Moderate prosperity	Prosperity
France.......	Depression	Revival	Moderate prosperity	Moderate prosperity; financial strain
Germany....	Depression; revival	Revival	Moderate prosperity	Prosperity
Austria......	Depression; revival	Revival	Prosperity	Prosperity

TABLE 32—(*Continued*)

CONSPECTUS OF BUSINESS FLUCTUATIONS IN VARIOUS COUNTRIES

	1890	1891	1892	1893
United States	Prosperity; recession	Depression; revival	Prosperity	Recession; panic; depression
England.....	Prosperity; panic; recession	Industrial recession; financial prostration	Depression	Deep depression
France.......	Recession; mild depression	Mild depression	Depression	Depression
Germany....	Recession	Depression	Depression	Depression
Austria......	Uneven prosperity	Prosperity	Recession	Revival
Russia.......	Mild prosperity	Recession, depression	Depression	Revival
Sweden......	Prosperity	Prosperity	Recession, mild depression	Depression
Netherlands..	Mild prosperity	Recession	Depression	Depression
Italy........	Depression	Depression; panic	Depression	Depression; panic
Argentina....	Recession; depression	Depression; panic	Revival, recession	Mild depression
Brazil........	Depression	Depression	Uneven depression	Depression
Canada......	Mild depression	Depression; revival	Mild prosperity	Recession; depression
South Africa.	Prosperity; recession; depression	Depression	Rapid revival	Prosperity
Australia.....	Recession; depression	Depression	Depression	Depression; panic
India........	Mild depression	Depression	Uneven depression	Depression
Japan.......	Recession; depression	Depression	Depression	Mild depression
China.......	Mild depression	Mild depression	Depression deepens	Depression

TABLE 32—(*Continued*)

CONSPECTUS OF BUSINESS FLUCTUATIONS IN VARIOUS COUNTRIES

	1894	1895	1896	1897
United States	Deep depression	Depression; revival	Recession; depression	Depression; revival
England.....	Depression	Depression; revival last half-year	Revival; prosperity	Prosperity
France.......	Depression	Depression; revival	Revival	Moderate prosperity
Germany....	Depression; revival	Revival	Prosperity	Prosperity
Austria......	Recession; mild depression	Mild depression	Mild depression	Mild depression
Russia.......	Prosperity	Prosperity	Prosperity	Prosperity
Sweden......	Mild depression	Revival	Prosperity	Prosperity
Netherlands..	Depression	Depression	Revival	Mild prosperity
Italy.........	Depression	Depression	Depression; slight revival	Revival
Argentina....	Depression	Lessening depression	Revival	Revival retarded
Brazil........	Revival	Mild prosperity	Recession; panic; depression	Depression; panic
Canada......	Acute depression	Depression	Lessening depression	Revival
South Africa.	Prosperity	Prosperity; recession	Depression	Depression
Australia....	Depression	Depression; slight revival	Strong revival	Mild prosperity; agricultural depression
India........	Uneven revival	Mild prosperity	Recession	Depression
Japan........	Revival; recession	Revival	Prosperity	Prosperity; recession
China.......	Depression	Revival	Prosperity	Gradual recession

TABLE 32—(*Continued*)

CONSPECTUS OF BUSINESS FLUCTUATIONS IN VARIOUS COUNTRIES

	1898	1899	1900	1901
United States	Revival; prosperity	Prosperity	Prosperity, brief recession	Prosperity
England.....	Prosperity	Prosperity	Prosperity; recession, summer	Mild depression
France.......	Prosperity	Prosperity	Prosperity; recession	Depression
Germany....	Prosperity	Prosperity	Prosperity; recession; depression	Depression
Austria......	Mild depression; revival	Mild prosperity	Recession; depression	Depression
Russia.......	Prosperity	Prosperity; panic; recession	Recession; depression	Depression
Sweden......	Prosperity	Prosperity	Prosperity	Recession; depression
Netherlands..	Prosperity	Prosperity	Prosperity	Recession; mild depression
Italy........	Uneven prosperity	Mild prosperity	Prosperity; brief recession	Prosperity
Argentina....	Mild prosperity	Prosperity	Recession; depression	Depression
Brazil.......	Depression deepens	Depression; revival	Revival; panic; recession	Mild depression
Canada......	Prosperity	Prosperity	Prosperity; slight recession	Revival; prosperity
South Africa.	Depression	Revival; recession	Depression	Revival
Australia....	Prosperity	Prosperity	Prosperity	Recession
India........	Slow revival	Moderate prosperity	Recession	Depression
Japan.......	Depression	Depression	Deeper depression	Depression; financial panic, spring
China.......	Mild depression	Revival; prosperity	Prosperity; recession; depression	Depression; revival

TABLE 32—(*Continued*)

CONSPECTUS OF BUSINESS FLUCTUATIONS IN VARIOUS COUNTRIES

	1902	1903	1904	1905
United States	Prosperity	Prosperity; recession	Mild depression; revival	Prosperity
England.....	Lessened depression	Depression deepens	Revival	Revival; prosperity
France.......	Depression	Revival	Moderate prosperity	Prosperity
Germany....	Depression	Revival	Mild prosperity; recession	Revival; prosperity
Austria......	Depression	Depression; revival	Revival	Mild prosperity
Russia.......	Depression	Depression; revival	Recession; depression	Depression
Sweden......	Depression	Revival	Mild prosperity	Prosperity
Netherlands..	Depression	Depression	Revival; prosperity	Prosperity
Italy........	Moderate prosperity	Prosperity	Prosperity	Prosperity
Argentina....	Depression; revival	Prosperity	Prosperity	Prosperity
Brazil.......	Mild depression	Depression deepens	Depression	Depression
Canada......	Prosperity; financial distress	Prosperity	Uneven prosperity	Full prosperity
South Africa.	Prosperity	Recession	Depression	Depression
Australia....	Mild depression	Deepening depression	Revival	Mild prosperity
India........	Revival	Prosperity	Prosperity	Prosperity
Japan.......	Slow revival	Revival	Prosperity	Prosperity; recession; depression
China.......	Mild prosperity	Mild prosperity	Mild prosperity	Mild prosperity

TABLE 32—(*Continued*)

CONSPECTUS OF BUSINESS FLUCTUATIONS IN VARIOUS COUNTRIES

	1906	1907	1908	1909
United States	Prosperity	Prosperity; panic; recession; depression	Depression	Revival; mild prosperity
England.....	Prosperity	Prosperity; recession	Depression	Revival
France.......	Prosperity	Prosperity	Recession; mild depression	Revival
Germany....	Prosperity	Prosperity; recession; depression	Depression	Depression; revival
Austria......	Prosperity	Prosperity	Recession; depression	Depression
Russia.......	Depression; slight revival	Revival	Recession; depression	Depression; revival
Sweden......	Prosperity	Prosperity; recession; panic	Depression	Depression
Netherlands..	Prosperity	Prosperity	Depression; revival	Revival; prosperity
Italy........	Prosperity	Prosperity; recession	Depression	Depression
Argentina....	Prosperity	Prosperity	Mild recession	Revival; prosperity
Brazil........	Slow revival	Revival; recession, autumn	Depression	Revival
Canada......	Prosperity peak	Prosperity; panic; recession	Depression; revival	Revival
South Africa.	Depression	Depression deepens	Depression lessens	Revival
Australia....	Prosperity	Prosperity	Recession; mild depression	Rapid revival; prosperity
India........	Prosperity	Prosperity; recession	Depression	Depression; slight revival
Japan.......	Revival; prosperity	Prosperity; panic; recession	Depression	Depression; revival
China.......	Recession	Depression	Depression	Revival

TABLE 32—(*Continued*)

CONSPECTUS OF BUSINESS FLUCTUATIONS IN VARIOUS COUNTRIES

	1910	1911	1912	1913
United States	Recession	Mild depression	Revival; prosperity	Prosperity; recession
England.....	Prosperity	Prosperity	Prosperity	Prosperity; recession, last quarter
France.......	Prosperity	Prosperity	Prosperity	Prosperity; recession
Germany....	Revival; prosperity	Prosperity	Prosperity	Prosperity; recession
Austria......	Depression	Revival	Prosperity; recession; depression	Depression; panic
Russia.......	Prosperity	Prosperity	Prosperity	Prosperity except on bourse
Sweden......	Revival	Prosperity	Prosperity	Prosperity; slight recession
Netherlands..	Prosperity	Prosperity	Prosperity	Recession
Italy........	Mild depression	Revival halted, autumn	Uneven prosperity	Mild prosperity; recession
Argentina....	Prosperity	Recession; mild depression	Depression; revival, autumn	Recession
Brazil........	Prosperity	Prosperity	Prosperity	Uneven prosperity
Canada......	Prosperity	Prosperity	Prosperity	Prosperity; recession
South Africa.	Prosperity	Prosperity	Prosperity	Uneven recession
Australia....	Prosperity	Prosperity	Prosperity	Mild recession
India........	Revival	Prosperity	Prosperity	Uneven prosperity
Japan.......	Revival; prosperity	Prosperity	Prosperity	Prosperity
China.......	Recession	Depression	Depression	Depression

TABLE 32—(*Continued*)

CONSPECTUS OF BUSINESS FLUCTUATIONS IN VARIOUS COUNTRIES

	1914	1915	1916	1917
United States	Depression	Revival; prosperity	Prosperity	Prosperity; war activity
England.....	Mild depression, deepens with war	War activity	War activity	War activity
France.......	Depression	War activity	War activity	War activity
Germany....	Mild depression; revival	War activity	War activity	War activity
Austria......	Depression	War activity	War activity	War activity
Russia.......	Recession; panic; depression	Uneven depression	War activity	Recession; depression
Sweden......	Recession; depression	Revival, prosperity	Prosperity	Recession
Netherlands..	Recession; panic; depression	Revival; uneven prosperity	Moderate prosperity	Recession
Italy........	Recession; panic; depression	Uneven depression	War activity	War activity
Argentina....	Depression; panic	Uneven depression	Depression; slow revival	Revival
Brazil........	Depression deepens	Depression; revival	Revival; prosperity	Prosperity
Canada......	Depression deepening with war	Depression; revival	War activity	War activity
South Africa.	Recession; depression	Slow revival	Rapid revival	Prosperity
Australia.....	Revival; recession	Mild depression; revival	War activity	War activity
India........	Prosperity: recession	Depression	Revival	Prosperity
Japan.......	Recession; depression	Revival; prosperity	Prosperity	Uneven prosperity
China........	Depression deepens	Depression	Revival; prosperity	Uneven prosperity

TABLE 32—(*Continued*)

CONSPECTUS OF BUSINESS FLUCTUATIONS IN VARIOUS COUNTRIES

	1918	1919	1920	1921
United States	War activity; recession	Revival; prosperity	Prosperity; recession; depression	Depression
England.....	War activity; recession	Revival; prosperity	Prosperity; recession; depression	Deep depression
France.......	War activity; stagnation	Depression; revival; boom	Prosperity; recession; depression	Depression; revival
Germany....	War activity; disorganization, November	Depression	Depression	Revival, spring
Austria......	War activity; chaos	Depression	Slow revival	Revival
Russia.......	Depression	Depression	Depression	Depression
Sweden......	Depression	Depression; revival	Boom; recession; depression	Depression
Netherlands..	Depression	Revival; prosperity	Prosperity; recession; depression	Depression
Italy........	War activity; slight recession	Mild depression; revival	Recession; depression	Depression; panic
Argentina....	Moderate prosperity	Prosperity	Prosperity; recession	Depression
Brazil........	Prosperity; brief recession	Prosperity	Prosperity; recession; depression	Severe depression
Canada......	War activity; recession	Revival; prosperity	Prosperity; recession	Depression
South Africa.	Prosperity; recession	Revival; prosperity	Prosperity; recession; depression	Deep depression
Australia.....	War activity	Prosperity	Prosperity; recession	Depression
India........	Prosperity; recession	Revival; prosperity	Prosperity; recession; depression	Depression
Japan.......	Uneven prosperity; recession	Depression; revival; prosperity	Prosperity; recession; depression	Depression
China.......	Uneven prosperity	Prosperity	Prosperity; recession; depression	Depression

TABLE 32—(*Continued*)

CONSPECTUS OF BUSINESS FLUCTUATIONS IN VARIOUS COUNTRIES

	1922	1923	1924	1925
United States	Revival; prosperity	Prosperity; recession	Mild depression; revival	Prosperity
England.....	Depression	Depression	Lessening depression	Depression
France.......	Revival	Prosperity	Prosperity	Prosperity
Germany....	Revival checked, summer; disorganization	Depression	Revival; temporary check, summer	Halting revival; recession
Austria......	Uneven recession	Depression	Depression; financial strain	Depression
Russia.......	Depression; slight revival	Revival; recession, October	Mild depression; revival	Uneven prosperity; recession
Sweden......	Depression; revival	Revival	Mild prosperity	Mild prosperity
Netherlands..	Depression	Depression	Revival	Mild prosperity
Italy........	Depression	Depression; revival	Moderate prosperity	Prosperity
Argentina....	Depression	Lessening depression	Revival	Prosperity
Brazil.......	Lessening depression	Revival	Mild prosperity; recession	Depression
Canada......	Depression; revival	Moderate prosperity	Recession; mild depression	Revival; prosperity
South Africa.	Depression	Revival	Mild prosperity	Prosperity
Australia.....	Slow revival	Revival; mild prosperity	Mild recession	Revival; prosperity
India........	Depression	Slow revival	Revival; mild prosperity	Mild prosperity
Japan.......	Depression	Depression	Depression	Depression; revival
China.......	Depression	Depression	Depression	Depression

2. How Closely the Cycles in Different Countries Agree.

Concerning the fact of fundamental interest in this inquiry, the conspectus of business conditions gives an exaggerated impression of century-long and world-wide similarity. Periods of prosperity, recession, depression and revival are here pictured as recurring in much the same way in every country and during every decade. The fuller form of the annals makes it clear, not only that this recurrence is nowhere the whole story of economic fluctuations, but also that it is farther from being the whole story in some countries than in others. The importance of business cycles as a factor in national life was less during the closing decades of the 18th century than during the opening decades of the 20th century in England and the United States. There is a similar difference between these two countries and China, Russia or Brazil at present. The more highly organized a country's business, the larger the proportion of its people who live by making and spending money incomes, the more important become the recurrent cycles of activity. Let us, however, take cyclical oscillations for granted, disregard their relative amplitudes, and inquire what influence the cycles in one country exercise upon cycles in other countries.

It has long been recognized that the great financial crises have an international sweep. Thus the conspectus shows that England and the United States shared in the crises of 1815, 1825 and 1837; that England, the United States and France (which now is represented in the annals) shared in the crisis of 1847; that these three countries, and Germany also, shared in the panic of 1857; that England, the United States, France, Germany and Austria shared in varying degrees the crisis of 1873. To these familiar facts our annals add that all five countries had mild recessions in 1882-84. Of the 17 countries included in the annals after 1890, 10 had recessions in 1890-91, 15 had recessions in 1900-01, 15 in 1907-08, 12 in 1912-13, 11 in 1918, and 14 in 1920. Further, the countries which escaped a share in these world reactions usually owed their exemption to an earlier turn for the worse. Thus South Africa and Japan had no recession in 1900-01 because they were already suffering from depression. The three countries of our 17 which escaped in 1920 were Germany, Austria and Russia.

Of course the experiences of the several countries were not identical in the years of crises and recessions. In the whole record there is no crisis which was equally severe everywhere. In 1873, for example, the United States, Germany and Austria suffered far more severely than England and France. In 1890, on the contrary, the financial strain was more severe in London than in New York or Berlin, while Vienna deferred its recession until 1892. The center of disturbance in 1900 seems to have been Germany; countries like the United States and Italy felt but repercussions of a foreign shock. In 1907 the gravest difficulties appeared in the United States. Probably the nearest approach to a severe world-wide crisis was made in 1920, and that case was obviously dominated by post-war readjustments. It is clear, however, that a financial crisis breaking out in any country of commercial importance produces financial strains in other countries, and that even mild recessions like those of 1882-83 and 1913 spread widely.

It has been less noticed that other phases of business cycles also propagate themselves. The long depressions of the 1870's, the checkered fortunes of the 1880's, the revival of the middle 1890's, the boom of 1906-7, the calmer prosperity of 1912, the hectic activity of the war years, and the severe depression after 1920 had much the same international character as the crises to which attention is often restricted.

Yet business cycles do not run a strictly parallel course in any two countries. Perhaps the best way to bring out the degree of likeness and difference in contemporary fortunes is to note the proportion of years in which conditions in different countries are described by the same terms in the conspectus, and the proportion of years in which conditions are described in unlike terms. An effort to carry out this plan shows that many years do not fall into either category. Business may be reviving in one country and already prosperous in another, depressed in one and entering depression in another; or conditions may be similar during the early part of a year and divergent in the closing months, or different at the start and convergent at the close. In such cases one cannot call the conditions quite similar or decidedly unlike. Thus it is necessary to recognize at least three types of relations between the synchronous phases of business cycles in different countries—agreement, partial agreement and opposition. Arbitrary definitions may be adopted, and a statistical tabulation made of these relationships.[1]

Such a comparison of business conditions in the five countries for which we have annals running back of 1890 is provided by Table 33. Most of the comparisons here made show a preponderance of years in which the business cycles of the countries paired were passing through the same phases over years in which they were passing through opposite phases. The intimacy of relations is probably understated by the table; for it takes no account of the shifting relations of lead and lag in the influence exercised by business conditions in one country upon business conditions in the other country with which it is compared. As one would expect from England's position in international trade and finance, English cycles are more highly correlated with the cycles of other countries, than the cycles of other countries are correlated with each other. The closest agreements are found between English and French or English and German cycles; the loosest agreements are between Austrian and American cycles.

From the third section of the table, it appears that the international similarity of phase in business cycles increased on the whole with the passage of time. The breaking of economic bonds by the war, and the tardiness of their restoration after the Armistice, interfered with this process of synchronizing cycles. But the non-economic factors, which played so large a rôle after 1914, had much the same character and influenced business among all the belligerents in much the same way, so long as hostilities lasted. Since 1918, economic

---

[1] The rules followed by Dr. Thorp in preparing the data for the following table are as follows:

Agreement includes

1. Years in which two countries pass through the same phase or phases of a cycle.
2. Years in which two countries pass through at least two corresponding phases, though one may enter a third phase. Example: "Prosperity; recession" in one country, and "Prosperity; recession; depression" in another.

Partial agreement includes

Years in which two countries pass through phases of the cycle which succeed one another. Example: "Revival" in one country, and "Prosperity" in another; or "Recession" in one country, and "Recession; depression" in another.

Opposition of phases includes

Years in which opposite phases of cycles occur, whatever intermediate phases are noted. Example: "Prosperity; recession; depression" in one country, and "Depression; revival" in a second.

War activity is interpreted in this tabulation as corresponding to prosperity.
The relative severity of recessions in different countries is not taken into account.

TABLE 33.

AGREEMENT AND DIFFERENCE OF PHASE IN ENGLISH, FRENCH, GERMAN, AUSTRIAN AND
AMERICAN BUSINESS CYCLES

Various Periods

	Period Covered		Number of Years of			Percentage of Years of		
	Dates	Number of Years	Agreement in Phase	Partial agreement	Opposition in Phase	Agreement in Phase	Partial agreement	Opposition in Phase
I								
English and French cycles.	1867–1925	59	32	20	7	54	34	12
English and German cycles	" "	59	33	22	4	56	37	7
English and Austrian cycles	" "	59	27	21	11	46	36	19
English and American cycles	" "	59	28	18	13	47	31	22
French and German cycles.	" "	59	27	25	7	46	42	12
French and Austrian cycles	" "	59	19	21	19	32	36	32
French and American cycles	" "	59	23	23	13	39	39	22
German and Austrian cycles	" "	59	23	24	12	39	41	20
German and American cycles	" "	59	21	20	18	36	34	31
Austrian and American cycles	" "	59	18	23	18	31	39	31
II								
England and four other countries	1867–1925	236	120	81	35	51	34	15
Germany and four other countries	" "	236	104	91	41	44	39	17
France and four other countries	" "	236	101	89	46	43	38	19
United States and four other countries	" "	236	90	84	62	38	36	26
Austria and four other countries	" "	236	87	89	60	37	38	25
III								
English and American cycles	1790–1857	68	21	28	19	31	41	28
	1857–1925	68	33	21	14	49	31	21
English and French cycles..	1840–1882	43	12	17	14	28	40	33
	1883–1925	43	28	11	4	65	26	9
English and German cycles.	1853–1888	36	19	15	2	53	42	6
	1889–1925	37	21	13	3	57	35	8
English and Austrian cycles.	1867–1895	29	14	12	3	48	41	10
	1896–1925	30	13	9	8	43	30	27

fortunes have diverged widely. Presumably the business forces tending toward convergence are gradually resuming their wonted sway.

In treating the period when the annals include 17 countries, a more significant method of presenting the relations among their business cycles is feasible. For the cycles since 1890 have an international pattern simple enough to be carried in mind, and applied to the experience of one country after another. This pattern may be sketched as follows:

1st cycle, 1890-91 to 1900-01
> Recession in 1890-91; depression in 1891-95; revival in 1895-96; prosperity in 1896-00; recession in 1900-01.

2nd cycle, 1900-01 to 1907-08
> Recession in 1900-01; depression in 1901-03; revival in 1903-04; prosperity in 1905-07; recession in 1907-08.

3rd cycle, 1907-08 to 1913-14
> Recession in 1907-08; depression in 1908-09; revival in 1909-10; prosperity in 1910-13; recession in 1913-14.

4th cycle, 1913-14 to 1918
> Recession in 1913-14; depression in 1914-15; revival in 1915; prosperity in 1915-18; recession in 1918.

5th cycle, 1918 to 1920
> Recession in 1918; very brief and mild depression early in 1919; quick revival in 1919; prosperity in 1919-20; recession in 1920.

6th cycle, 1920 to —— (unfinished)
> Recession in 1920; severe depression in 1921-22; revival in 1922-23; mild prosperity in 1924-25.

During this period, of our 17 countries

Six have had 5 cycles and are now in a 6th: England, France, the Netherlands, Sweden, Italy and China.

Five have had 6 cycles and are now in a 7th: Austria, South Africa, Australia, Argentina and India.

Five have had 7 cycles and are now in an 8th: Germany, Russia, Canada, Brazil, and Japan.

One has had 10 cycles and is now in an 11th: the United States.

Thus no country in our list has had fewer business cycles since 1890 than the international pattern calls for; but the majority of countries have had one or two more than that number. These additional cycles seldom result from failure to participate in the international movements of activity and depression, but rather from the intercalation of what we may call domestic recessions between the dates of international recessions. To take the most striking case: the United States had its share in all the recessions of the international pattern; but it also had domestic recessions in 1893, 1896, 1903, 1910, and 1923. When a country skips an international recession, it is usually because that country has recently suffered a domestic recession. Thus business was already depressed in Japan and South Africa when the international recession of 1900 began; South Africa and China escaped the international recession of 1907 for similar reasons; so too the European neutrals had recessions in 1917 and not in 1918.

The countries whose business cycles diverge most from the international pattern are Italy before say 1907, Russia, South Africa, Brazil and China—all countries rather backward in economic organization and predominantly agricultural. The countries whose cycles have followed the international pattern most closely, on the other hand, are countries of highly developed industry, trade, and finance— England, France, Germany (until 1919), Sweden, and the Netherlands. Australia and Canada lag but a little behind these European powers in conformity. Austrian cycles were being assimilated closely to those of her western and northern neighbors in the decade before the war. Even British India and Japan have followed the European pattern of cycles without very striking divergencies.

Another way of summing up the international relationships of business cycles since 1890 is to run down the columns of entries in Table 32 for each year. There is no year of the 36 covered in which the same phase of the cycle prevailed in all of the 17 countries. Uniformity is approached, however, in 1893, 1899, 1906, 1908, 1912, 1916, 1920, and 1921; and in most years there is a marked preponderance of entries of similar tenor.

A graphic presentation of these facts is given by Chart 27. The irregular bands of white and of black which run vertically across the chart are not quite continuous in any year from 1890 to 1925. But the existence of a general trend toward uniformity of business fortunes is plain.

CHART 27. Conspectus of Business Cycles in Various Countries, 1790 to 1925.

CHART 27. Conspectus of Business Cycles in Various Countries, 1790-1925—(Continued)

PROSPERITY   RECESSION   DEPRESSION   REVIVAL   W WAR ACTIVITY

UNITED STATES, ENGLAND, FRANCE, GERMANY, AUSTRIA, RUSSIA, SWEDEN, NETHERLANDS, ITALY, ARGENTINA, BRAZIL, CANADA, SOUTH AFRICA, AUSTRALIA, INDIA, JAPAN, CHINA

445

3. Domestic and Foreign Factors in Business Cycles.

Possibly this tendency to synchronize their phases, found in the business cycles of different countries, arises from some cosmic cause which affects all quarters of the globe in much the same way each year. Upon that daring hypothesis, our annals throw no light. But the annals do suggest certain tamer explanations, which account not only for the general resemblance among cycles in different countries, but also for their differences. These tamer explanations are not inconsistent with the cosmic hypothesis, but they do not depend upon it.

Whatever the causes of the recurrent fluctuations in economic activity may be, the annals suggest that these causes become active in all communities where there has developed an economic organization approximating that of western Europe. There appears to be a rough parallelism between the stage attained in the evolution of this organization by different countries, and the prominence of business cycles as a factor in their fortunes.

One characteristic of the type of organization in question is the wide area over which it integrates and coördinates economic activities. Bare as they are and short their span, the annals reveal a secular trend toward territorial expansion of business relations and a concomitant trend toward economic unity. For example, the American annals show how often the fortunes of the North, the South and the West diverged from one another in the earlier decades after the adoption of the Constitution, and how these divergencies have diminished in later decades. Not that business is ever equally prosperous or equally depressed in all states of the Union even now: always there are perceptible differences, and at times the differences are wide, particularly among the great farming "belts." Yet the annals picture the vastly·greater population of to-day, spread over a vastly greater territory, as having more unity of fortune than had the people of the thirteen original states and the frontier settlements in 1790-1820.

Broadly speaking, the annals support a similar conclusion concerning the world at large. The network of business relations has been growing closer and firmer at the same time that it has been stretching over wider areas. The annals allow us to catch some glimpses of this double trend within the borders of a few countries besides the United States, and they show it clearly in the relations among different countries. As American business is coming to have one story, diversified by agricultural episodes, so, before the war shattered international bonds for a time, world business seemed to be approaching the time when it too would have one story, diversified by political and social as well as agricultural episodes in different countries.

The basis of this trend toward unity of economic fortunes among communities organized on the European model is that each phase in a business cycle, as it develops in any area, tends to produce the same phase in all the areas with which the first has dealings.

Prosperity in one country stimulates demand for the products of other countries, and so quickens activities in the latter regions. Prosperity also lessens the energy with which merchants, financiers, and contractors seek competitive business in neutral markets, and so gives a better chance to the corresponding classes in countries where the domestic demand is less active. Further, prosperity, with its sanguine temper and its liberal profits, encourages investments abroad as well as at home, and the export of capital to other countries gives an impetus to their trade. A recession checks all these stimuli. A severe crisis in any important center produces quicker and graver results. Demands for financial assistance raise interest rates and reduce domestic lending power in other centers; apprehensions regarding the solvency of international houses may start demands for liquidation in many places; the losses which bankruptcies bring are likely to be felt by business enterprises the world over. So, too, with depressions and revival; wherever they prevail, they exert influences upon business elsewhere which tend to produce depressions or revivals in all regions with which the center of disturbance trades.

Nor are these relations one-sided. The condition of business in every country not only influences, but is influenced by conditions in other countries. The trend toward international similarity of business cycles is enforced by an endless series of actions and reactions among the influences exerted and experienced by all the nations which deal with each other.

Of course, the degree of influence exerted by business conditions in a given area upon business elsewhere depends upon the importance of that area in international commerce and finance. Similarly, the sensitiveness of business in a given area to the influence of business conditions elsewhere is least in communities like interior China, whose economic activities are mainly self-contained, and greatest in communities which depend largely upon foreign markets, foreign investments, and foreign sources of supply, like England. It is also clear that a country of the latter type will reflect world conditions more faithfully, the more widely its foreign interests are distributed.

While this line of analysis explains the tendency of business cycles in different countries to synchronize their phases, it does not hide the obstructions which this tendency meets.

In so far as the people in any country buy and sell, lend and borrow only among themselves, they are likely to have economic vicissitudes all their own. Agricultural communities which live largely on what they produce suffer more from acts of nature than farming populations which trade extensively; but they have little share in the world dislocations of business. Even in countries where farmers are more business-like, we have noted that agriculture has a story of its own, dictated by the weather at home and abroad—a story which often differs from the story of mining, manufactures, transportation, wholesale trade, and finance.[1] Of course the agricultural story modifies the general tale. Fluctuations in the cost of raw materials and of foods, as well as fluctuations in the buying power of farm families, react upon the prosperity of other industries in proportion to the relative weight of agriculture in the country's total business. Hence, the larger the agricultural element in a given nation, the less likely are that nation's business cycles to fit neatly into the international pattern over a long series of years. For two nations with large farming interests are not likely to have closely similar harvest fluctuations year after year. The one development touching agriculture which most clearly tends toward unifying business fortunes is the decline in the proportion of families which depend on farming, and the concomitant increase in the proportion following industrial pursuits. Dr. Thorp's prefaces to the chapters of *Business Annals* show that this decline is world-wide.

While the rise of large-scale industry within a nation of cultivators, craftsmen and petty traders links its economic life to that of other nations, there may be a stage in this development when international influences seem to recede and domestic influences to grow more important. The first modern mines, factories, railways, and banks in such a country are likely to be foreign enterprises,

---

[1] In one way, the development of a "world market" for the great agricultural staples even increases the hazards of farming. A scanty yield of wheat in Canada, for example, does not always cause a compensatory rise of prices.

dependent upon foreign investors for their capital and perhaps upon foreign customers for their markets. During that stage, such business as the outside world recognizes in the new-old country will be peculiarly sensitive to foreign fluctuations in finance and commerce. Meanwhile, if the new ventures prosper, natives of the country will learn to practice modern methods and to consume modern products. Alongside the foreign-owned enterprises, domestic enterprises will multiply, drawing their capital from home sources and selling largely in the home market. After a time perhaps most of the early enterprises will be sold by their foreign owners to native business men. During this stage the country's business will seem to be emancipating itself from the domination of outside influences, and its business cycles will diverge more widely from the international pattern. But if the process of modernizing economic life continues until a considerable fraction of the population is affected, then a gradual re-approach toward world conditions will begin. Some such series of changes probably explains in part, but in part only, a curious feature of our Russian annals. In the earlier years covered by this record, Russian cycles followed the international pattern more closely than in the later years of the Tsarist régime.[2] Perhaps Chinese business will pass through similar stages in the not-distant future.

Besides differences in economic organization, in the proportion of people engaged in farming, and in harvest conditions, there is a host of more obvious causes of divergencies among business cycles, whether we consider successive cycles in the same country or synchronous cycles in different countries. Wars and civil disturbances play a prominent rôle in business annals, and that rôle is most erratic. Many of the differences of business fortune which the annals show seem ascribable to such factors; but we have had occasion to note that during its earlier stages, at least, the World War had a unifying effect upon conditions among both belligerents and neutrals. The after-effects of this war, however, were far from uniform in different nations. In the cycles of every country we can trace also the influence of changes in monetary conditions, banking organization and tariff acts domestic or foreign, if not the influence of changes in taxation, internal improvement plans and public regulation of business enterprises. Besides these governmental matters, it seems probable that

[2] For a fuller discussion of the relations between business cycles in Russia and in Western Europe, see S. A. Pervushin, *The Business Conjuncture*, Moscow, 1925, pp. 209-213. I am indebted to Dr. Simon S. Kuznets for a synopsis of Professor Pervushin's analysis.

differences of national habit in respect to enterprise and thrift affect the frequency and violence of business oscillations. Still other matters which may count are changes in the methods of managing investments, the integration of industry, the organization of labor, the development of social insurance. But there is little point in extending a list of factors whose relative importance we cannot weigh.

This much seems clear: business activity is influenced by countless developments in the realms of nature, politics and science, as well as by developments within the realm of business itself; few of these developments occur at the same time, in the same form and on the same scale in all countries. Thus there is no difficulty in understanding why business cycles vary in many ways from nation to nation, though it is quite impossible as yet to assign its relative importance to each (perhaps to any) cause of divergence. One's final reflection may be that the quiet business forces working toward uniformity of fortunes must be powerful indeed to impress a common pattern upon the course of business cycles in many countries. And the increasing conformity to an international pattern which the annals reveal in recent years shows that the international influences are gaining in relative importance.

CHAPTER V.

RESULTS AND PLANS.

I. The Concept of Business Cycles.

1. EVOLUTION OF THE CONCEPT.

To the early workers in our field the pressing problem was to account for the dramatic events which they called "commercial crises." Not only did they confine themselves mainly to this single phase of business fluctuations; also they confined themselves mainly to excogitating explanations. The occurrence of crises was known to everyone. What need was there of elaborate factual investigations? And why need one explain prosperity?

This approach led to a discussion which centered in the validity of rival doctrines, rather than in the characteristics of business fluctuations. The participants debated with each other on the basis of common knowledge, reënforced by occasional citations of evidence. Even in using evidence, their aims were oftener dialectical than positive. A second consequence was that the discussion tended to drift away from the main body of economic theory and to become a "specialty." For when crises are taken out of their setting in a continuous process of change, they appear to be "abnormal" phenomena. As such they lie on the edge, rather than in the center, of the theoretician's domain. In discussions of what were taken to be the leading problems of economics, changes in business activity were among the matters hidden from sight under the blanket assumption, "other things remaining the same." While chapters on the cause of crises appeared in some of the standard treatises which applied economic principles to practical issues, the topic had no place in "pure theory." Most of the contributions were monographs, and many of the writers had but slender knowledge of economics. As late as 1898, Böhm-Bawerk thought it necessary to argue that a theory of crises "should always form the last, or next-to-the-last, chapter in a system of eco-

nomic theory, written or unwritten." [1] The converse view, that ideas
developed in the study of business fluctuations may lead to reformu-
lations of economic theory, still strikes most economists as strange.[2]

A broader conception of the problem was implied by John Wade's
casual observation, made in 1833, that "the commercial cycle," with
its "alternate periods of prosperity and depression," had been running
its course in England "during the last seventy years." [3] Probably
the notion that trade fluctuations are cyclical occurred independently
to other men; certainly it spread rapidly. Clement Juglar made
this conception his own, and in 1860 sought to show the relations
between the "three periods of prosperity, crisis, and liquidation,"
which "always follow one another in the same order." More than
that, Juglar threw himself energetically into factual investigations,
basing his conclusions largely upon analyses of changes in commodity
prices, interest rates, and bank balances, supplemented by a history of
crises since 1696.[4] His work marks a critical ·turning point in the
study. But, though Juglar grasped the need of dealing with business
cycles, he called his book *Des Crises Commerciales*. If to this day
many writers (especially Europeans) follow his precedent. in choosing
titles for their books, they also follow his other precedent by making
their theories of crises include a discussion of prosperity and depressions, if not also of revivals.[5]

Most of the changes made since Juglar's time in the conception
of the problem have resulted from doing the kind of work he did on
a larger scale and more intensively. Ideas implicit in his notions
have become clear; matters which he passed over lightly have been
emphasized; better methods of analyzing time series have been invented; terms have come into use which Juglar would not have under-

[2] See Böhm-Bawerk's review of Eugen von Bergmann's *Geschichte der Nationalökonomischen Krisentheorien*, in *Zeitschrift für Volkswirtschaft, Sozialpolitik und Verwaltung*, vol. vii, p. 112.
    [2] Compare Dr. Adolf Löwe's elaborate argument that the problem of cyclical fluctua-
tions cannot be treated by the "variation methods" of pure economics, and that it,
among other problems, calls for the development of a dynamic theory, in which the
concept of equilibrium will be replaced by the concept of cyclical oscillations. "Wie ist
Konjunkturtheorie überhaupt möglich?" *Weltwirtschaftliches Archiv*, October, 1926, vol.
xxiv, pp. 165-197.
    [3] See Chapter I, section iii.
    [4] To appreciate the scope of Juglar's long-continued labors, one must examine the
second edition of his book, *Des Crises Commerciales*, Paris, 1889. The phrases quoted
in the text are from p. 21.
    [5] For example, see Mentor Bouniatian's remarks concerning the ground which should
be covered by a theory of crises: *Les Crises Économiques*, Paris, 1922, p. 28.

stood. Both in seeming and in truth, the whole discussion is on a different plane; yet one can read many of the ideas which seem to us fresh between the lines of Juglar's book, if not in the text itself.

Juglar did not realize clearly that the intervals between crises frequently contain two, and sometimes contain three, alternations of prosperity and depression. Nor is this important fact firmly grasped by contemporary writers upon crises. It stands out sharply only when one analyzes appropriate time series, or reads business reviews with care. Of course, the reason why these brief cycles are overlooked by writers upon crises is that the cycles in question include no crises, in the traditional meaning of the term. A man who composes a treatise upon "Commercial Crises" may entertain the idea of "commercial cycles," plan to treat them, and yet not recognize a goodly part of the cycles revealed by his own materials. To minimize the danger of being thus misled, statistical investigators, who plume themselves upon following faithfully the indications of their data, have discarded what seemed to be the most firmly established term in the whole discussion. They call the transition from prosperity to depression a recession. It follows that the cycles which they recognize are briefer on the average than the cycles of the books on crises. Instead of thinking about periods seven or eight years long, they think of three- or four-year cycles as typical. But they are also concerned to find how the longer and shorter cycles are distributed about this mode, and how the average duration of cycles varies from period to period and from one country to another.

In word, at least, Juglar held that crises are "periodic": his full title runs *Des Crises Commerciales et de leur Retour Périodique en France, en Angleterre et aux États-Unis.* But his own history of crises in these three countries shows that in no one of them have the intervals between crises been regular. Theoretical writers frequently follow this inexact precedent, calling crises periodic in their titles and showing in their texts that the period varies widely.[6] Statistical

---

[6] Compare the titles of the following books with the passages cited in each: A Aftalion, *Les Crises Périodiques de Surproduction,* Paris, 1913, vol. i, pp. 8-14; M. Bouniatian, *Les Crises Économiques—Essai de Morphologie et théorie des crises économiques périodiques,* Paris, 1922, pp. 42-45; J. Lescure, *Des Crises Générales et Périodiques de Surproduction,* 3d ed., Paris, 1913, pp. 1-288 (note the intervals between the dates of the crises described); Ludwig Pohle, *Bevölkerungsbewegung, Kapitalbildung, und periodische Wirtschaftskrisen,* Göttingen, 1902, statistics in the appendix, especially pp. 89-90.

This may be one more case in which we should explain what seems to be a verbal contradiction by observing that what a theorist takes to be "normally" true he does not expect to find historically true.

workers have avoided this loose use of a term which in other sciences implies strict regularity of timing. What they find to be regular is the recurrence of prosperity, recession, depression and revival, in that sequence. One of their leading aims, as said above, is to find out just how business cycles, and their constituent phases, vary in duration. Yet to this day an occasional critic treats the word "cyclical" as synonymous with "periodic," and imputes belief in the periodicity of fluctuations to writers upon business cycles.

John Wade spoke confidently of "the" commercial cycle; on occasion Juglar used the corresponding French phrase;[7] there are recent books upon "the" business cycle and "the" trade cycle.[8] Possibly the misleading implications which can be read into these phrases would have been accepted by their early users. John Wade may have conceived the commercial cycle as a single movement, or as a succession of grand, unitary swings from prosperity to depression and back again. Maybe a ghost of this dim notion still haunts the minds of some who trace business cycles to a single cause. But most of those who now speak of "the" business cycle, mean by it, not one phenomenon, but a congeries of interrelated phenomena. Increasing emphasis upon the diversities in respect to amplitude and timing found among the cyclical fluctuations of different processes is highly characteristic of recent work. Statistics provide no direct evidence of the existence of "the" business cycle; what they provide is evidence of cyclical fluctuations in hundreds of time series. Indeed, it is difficult to construct from the data, or even to conceive of constructing, any single index of "the general trend" in business activity.[9] But the more thoroughly investigators anatomize the business cycle, the more they need a general term to designate the whole.

Yet the words we use set traps for us. Starting with a vague conception of a group of seemingly related phenomena which we wish to study, we name it. That step is necessary, but dangerous. The definiteness of the name may conceal from us the indefiniteness of our knowledge. If the name is a compound of words familiar in other uses, we may take their implications for facts. Assuming tacitly that

[7] For example, "Le cycle est parcouru dans le monde entier sur toutes les places de commerce;" *Des Crises Commerciales*, 2d ed., p. 17.
[8] For example, Miss Dorothy S. Thomas calls her valuable study *Social Aspects of the Business Cycle*, and Mr. F. Lavington uses *The Trade Cycle* as a title.
[9] Compare Chapter III, section vi, 2 "A Critique of the Indexes of Business Conditions."

we know what we have named, we may begin contriving explanations, when we should be trying to find out what our words mean.[10]

All this was said at the beginning of the book. It explains why no definition of business cycles was given there. It explains why even the review of theories was made to emphasize a fundamental feature of business cycles, to indicate what detailed facts should be looked for, and how those facts should be studied. It explains the long chapters on economic organization, statistical methods, and business annals. It explains the present section on the evolution of the concept of business cycles. Even now, we can do no more than frame a working definition to use in trying to learn more—a definition which presumably will require modification as knowledge grows.

2. A Working Concept of Business Cycles.

To find out what business cycles are, we have looked at them through the eyes of economic theorists, through the eyes of economic statisticians, and through the eyes of business reporters. Each group of workers helps us to appreciate features of the common object which the other groups take for granted, or fail to see. It is by combining the three sets of observations that we can form the mental picture of business cycles most useful in the constructive work which lies before us.

(1) Elements derived from Business Reports.

Treated in one way, business reports give a most confusing view of business fluctuations; but treated in another way, they give the simplest view. When we wade through the commercial histories printed in financial papers or consular documents, we may get no general impression except that of infinite detail. But by careful planning and hard work, we can put these records in such form that they afford a view over wide areas and through decades. Then the details fade, and the broad features of commercial history become clear. Among these broad features, one of the most prominent is a pattern in the changes taking place in time—a pattern common to all countries which can be said to have a business history. Again and

---

[10] It seems to me that as a name for our subject "the business cycle" exposes us to these dangers rather more than does "business cycles." On that ground, I prefer the latter term in most contexts. Surely it is safer usage to speak of "commercial crises" than to speak of "the commercial crisis."

again in many lands, a period of active trade ends in a relapse; then dull times prevail; afterwards comes a quickening, and presently trade is active once more. This frequently recurring sequence, of which there are so many examples in the record slowly built up by the coöperation of numberless business reporters, is what men have in mind when they speak of the business cycle.

But business annals give us much more than this bare skeleton of a concept.

(1) Current commercial histories usually take nations as their units, but they make it clear that a given wave of prosperity or depression does not always sweep over all parts of a country, and that such a wave sometimes sweeps over the commercial world. So unequal are the areas affected by different waves that we cannot associate business cycles with any given geographical or political unit. For convenient discussion it seems wise to abide by the convention of our sources, and think of (say) Japanese cycles, Swedish cycles and Brazilian cycles. There is the more reason for this practice in that the record of business cycles in every country has its own peculiarities. But we must conceive of the phenomena as international, not only in the sense that they occur in many countries, but also in the sense that the state of trade prevailing in any country at any time actively promotes the development of a similar condition in all other countries with which the first has important business relations. On the other hand, we must recognize that in a large country whose economic organization is not highly integrated different sections sometimes have cyclical fluctuations more divergent than those of neighboring nations.

(2) The conception of prosperity or depression within a given country has the character of an average. Seldom does a detailed survey show that all branches of business are active, or all dull, at the same time. As a rule, the reporters are clear and unanimous concerning the "prevailing tone"; but sometimes they picture conditions as so mixed that it is hard to discover the trend. And sometimes when reporters agree concerning the prevailing tone, they agree also that certain industries present striking exceptions. In other words, a reader of commercial histories conceives of business cycles as a sequence of phases each of which is a highly complex aggregate of conditions in different industries—conditions which are never strictly uniform, and which are at times markedly divergent.

(3) Another characteristic of business cycles as pictured by com-

mercial histories is that they vary in intensity. The writers tell of
wild panics and of quiet recessions, of sensational booms and of mild
prosperity, of complete prostration and of mere dullness, of dramatic
revivals and of long-drawn-out recuperations. These descriptive
terms and their hundred variants cannot be interpreted with precision. We cannot even rank successive or contemporary cycles in
the order of their intensities,—to say nothing of measuring degrees of
intensity. But neither can we doubt the fact that cycles run the
gamut from violent fluctuations to moderate swings. And if we
follow these sources faithfully, we must drop crises from our conception of business cycles, for in the moderate swings no phase occurs
which is fitly designated by that word.

(4) Concerning the wave-length of business cycles, commercial
histories give us more definite impressions. We can measure approximately the intervals between successive recessions. There are doubtful cases, because the industrial complexity just referred to sometimes makes it hard to say whether a given set of difficulties was
general enough to be called a recession; but these cases are not sufficiently numerous to cut much figure in the results.

Some cycles are found in the record which appear to have been
nearer one year than two years in length. At the other extreme, we
find a few cycles lasting 11 or 12 years. But the bulk of the cases fall
within the three- to six-year range. And when a goodly number of
observations are put together the measurements distribute themselves about their central tendency in a fairly regular, though not
symmetrical, fashion.

Further, it appears that the phases of revival and recession, as
reported in the sources from which business annals are compiled, are
brief in comparison with the phases of prosperity and depression;
that on the average prosperity lasts a little longer than depression; that this relation of prosperity to depression is accentuated when
wholesale prices have a rising secular trend, and reversed when that
trend declines; that the very long cycles are due more to the prolongation of depression than to the prolongation of prosperity.

(5) On reading the business records of any country year after
year, one is impressed by the continuity of cyclical changes. In the
sequence of prosperity, recession, depression and revival, any stage
can be treated as the end of one cycle and the beginning of another.
Yet it seems wiser to say that there is no beginning and no end; or
better still, that there is a continuous movement which passes through

certain phases in an established order, but at a pace which varies from time to time and country to country.

(6) Current business commentators say many hasty things about the causes of changes in conditions which we cannot incorporate into a working conception of business cycles. But for one generalization along this line we have use: business cycles are highly sensitive phenomena, influenced by a host of factors not of business origin. Among such factors, wars, civil disturbances, inequalities in harvests, and epidemics play prominent rôles.

(7) Finally, a survey of business annals of countries at different stages of development, and of the business annals of the same country through successive stages, suggests that business cycles are associated with a certain form of economic organization. This suggestion is confirmed by a longer-range study of economic history.[1] While commercial and financial crises can be traced back a long time in England, the Netherlands, France, Southern Germany, and northern Italy, these early modern and late medieval crises appear to have been due far more largely to non-business factors than are modern recessions, and to have been less general in their incidence. Business cycles which affect the fortunes of the mass of people in a country, which succeed each other continuously, and which attain a semblance of regularity, do not become prominent in the economic history of a country until a large proportion of its people are living mainly by making and spending money incomes. Also, there is evidence that business cycles keep changing character as economic organization develops. The most violent manifestations are brought under control. Panics subside into crises, and crises into recessions. It seems probable that the average length of cycles grows shorter at one stage of institutional development, and at a later stage grows longer again. In fine, we must think of the recurrence of prosperity, recession, depression and revival as characteristic of economic activity only when economic activity is organized on the basis of what is here called "business economy."

Thus the conception of business cycles obtained from a survey of contemporary reports starts with the fundamental fact of rhythmical fluctuations in activity, and adds that these fluctuations are peculiar to countries organized on a business basis, that they appear in all

---

[1] See Chapter II, section i, "The Historical Connection between Business Cycles and the Use of Money."

such countries, that they tend to develop the same phase at nearly the same time in different countries, that they follow each other without intermissions, that they are affected by all sorts of non-business factors, that they represent predominant rather than universal changes in trend, and that, while they vary in intensity and duration, the variations are not so wide as to prevent our identifying different cases as belonging to a single class of phenomena.

(2) Elements Derived from Theories of Business Cycles.

What alterations in this concept are suggested by studying the theories of business cycles?

Read one after another in full detail, these theories are scarcely less confusing than are commercial reviews. It is feasible, however, to deal with the theories in much the same way as we have dealt with the business reports. Chapter I presents a collection of theoretical accounts, which can be set against the historical accounts summarized in Chapter IV. Treating one collection as we did the other, we can ask, What do the theories as a whole tell us about the phenomena?

First, the theories put fresh emphasis upon the exceeding complexity of cyclical fluctuations. But the complexity revealed by the theories is complexity of an order different from that revealed by commercial reports. While the latter deal with business conditions in different areas and different industries, the theories deal with different processes—processes which are supposed to run their course in, or to affect, all industries and all communities organized upon a business basis.

Among the processes so intimately involved in cyclical fluctuations that they have been made to yield explanations of business cycles, we noted the following:

Banking operations—particularly the processes of expanding or contracting bank loans, with their effects in enlarging or reducing the volume of credit currency; fluctuations in discount rates, and the fluctuations of bank reserves which result from changes in the public's use of coin and paper money, and from the banks' efforts to maintain solvency.

Saving and investing in their relation to the amount of construction work undertaken, the supply of consumers' goods sent to market, and the volume of retail buying.

The process of adjusting the current supply of goods of all sorts to the demand for them, as that process affects business commitments, or is affected by (1) the uncertainties incident to all business planning, (2) changes in the marginal utilities of consumers' goods and the marginal utility of money, on the one hand, and, on the other hand, by changes in the demand for and in the operation of industrial equipment.

Disbursing money incomes to consumers and spending money by consumers, in relation to the processes of making and selling goods—relations which may be treated with reference to the influence of price fluctuations upon the incomes and purchasing power of different classes, with reference to the effect of saving by corporations and individuals upon the demand for consumers' goods, or with reference to the difficulty of providing liquid capital for business enterprises without reducing the demand for goods in general below the volume sent to market.

Making profits out of industrial operations—a process which is held to breed illusions concerning the volume of demand, to magnify the moderate fluctuations of retail buying into violent oscillations in production, or to cause the alternate marking up and writing down of the capital values at which business enterprises are rated and upon which loan credits are based.

Promoting new business ventures, or making revolutionary changes in business methods.

"Progress" at large, a characteristic of the age which makes it impossible to keep the rates at which different factors grow properly adjusted to each other.

In addition to these economic processes our attention has been called to:

Waves of optimism and pessimism, which are held by one writer to "give birth to one another in an endless chain," and by another writer to result from fluctuations in birth-, death-, and morbidity-rates.

Cyclical changes in weather, which affect business on one line of analysis because they affect crop yields, on a second line of analysis because they affect health and mental attitudes, and on a third line because they give the industries using organic materials a rhythm different from that of the industries using inorganic materials.

Of course not all of these theories of business cycles can be valid in the sense of their authors. Indeed, if any one theory really shows

the chief cause of cyclical fluctuations, none of the rival theories
shows the chief cause. But we can take all of the theories into our
working conception of business cycles in the sense that we can conceive of the recurrent sequences of prosperity, recession, depression
and revival as involving cyclical fluctuations in each of the economic
processes listed, and as affected by emotional and climatic conditions.
Nor can we limit our view to the processes and conditions on which
theories of business cycles have been erected. In working, we must
be prepared to study any feature of modern life which appears to be
intimately related to business fluctuations. But with every factor in
the complex, whether suggested by others or discovered in our inquiry,
we must deal critically. Among other things, this means that our
conception of a multiplicity of processes involved in business cycles
does not commit us in advance to any conclusion about the number
of causes at work. If the evidence we find points in that direction,
we can conclude that some single cause produces, directly and indirectly, the cyclical fluctuations in an uncounted list of processes.

While adding a significant feature to our conception of business
cycles, the survey of theories sheds little light upon the suggestions
derived from the survey of business annals. For the cycles explained
by economic theorists are not the cycles recorded by business historians. Interested in establishing generalizations, a theorist passes
lightly over the differences among successive cycles in the same country and synchronous cycles in different countries. He contemplates an
ideal, or a typical, case, supposedly modeled on real cases and summing up all their really essential features. Nor is that procedure open
to criticism, provided the theorist takes care to test his ideal construction for conformity to fact. Some modern theorists do so explicitly
and at length; doubtless others believe that they have made adequate
tests privately, though they spare their readers the heavy task of as-
sessing their evidence. In any case, concentration upon an ideal
case by a theorist does not mean that he denies the variability of the
phenomena, but that he sets the variations aside in order to get a
clearer view of what seem to him fundamentals.

On two points, however, most of the theories of business cycles
are at variance with the concept derived from commercial reviews.
These points were discussed in Chapter IV, and noted in the preceding
section; but they must be mentioned in the present connection.
(1) Most theorists take crises to be one of the phases of all business

cycles, though a few writers define "crisis" in a way which makes it equivalent to "recession." (2) By taking cycles as the intervals between crises, and not counting mild recessions as crises, most theorists make the duration typical of business cycles roughly twice the length we deduce as typical. On both these points, the conception suggested by business annals, confirmed as it is by statistical analysis, is more useful in constructive work than its rival.

Nor can the idea presented in many theories that business cycles represent an alternate rupture and restoration of economic equilibrium be included in our working conception. Men who take as their point of departure the theorem that economic forces tend to establish a stable equilibrium may conceive the main problem to be, how this fundamental tendency is overcome at times and how it presently reasserts itself. I have not chosen that point of departure. Hence it is no part of my task to determine how the fact of cyclical oscillations in economic activity can be reconciled with the general theory of equilibrium, or how that theory can be reconciled with facts.

Yet this does not dispose of the matter. Whatever his methodological assumptions, anyone who deals with crises is likely to think of a balance of forces, particularly if his explanation centers in some single process. "Over-saving," "over-production," "under-consumption," "a rate of interest higher than that economically justified," "optimistic error," "excess capacity,"—all such phrases imply the idea of an equilibrium which has been disturbed. They may or may not be conscious applications of a general economic theorem. But when we enlarge our problem to include numerous processes and all phases of the cycle, the idea of equilibrium becomes less helpful in conceiving the whole movement than in dealing with details. Provided we interpret equilibrium, not in the mechanical, but in the bookkeeping sense, as suggested in the closing section of Chapter II, we may compare one set of factors or forces with an opposing set, note which set exceeds the other for the time being, and inquire what consequences that excess produces. But in what useful way can we conceive of the equilibrium of the whole system we must contemplate, when that system includes factors which cannot be combined into two opposing totals—quantities of goods in physical terms, prices, pecuniary aggregates? If we could reduce every factor to its money value, the feat might be accomplished; but in the process we should bury qualitative distinctions of great moment. While we can relate all the qualitatively unlike factors in the problem to each other through their bearing upon prospective profits, we cannot add them all together and get results which are illuminating.

(3) Elements Derived from Statistical Analysis.

Our collection of statistics is like our collection of business annals, and unlike our collection of theories, in that it deals with the cycles of history—fluctuations which have occurred in certain countries between certain dates. Hence the statistics can be used to test elements in our concept which are derived from commercial reviews. The tests confirm, with a welcome increase of definiteness, the view that business cycles run a continuous round; that they vary, but vary after the fashion characteristic of most social phenomena, in intensity, in duration and in the intensity and duration of their constituent phases; that the synchronous fluctuations in countries having business relations with one another tend to have a common pattern, and that the course of business changes is frequently altered by factors not of business origin.

On the other hand, our collection of statistics resembles our collection of theories, and differs from our collection of business annals, in that it deals with economic processes rather than with the fortunes of different industries. Hence, the impression derived from the theories, that a business cycle is a highly complex congeries of fluctuations in different processes, can be made clearer by appeal to statistics. And though statistics deal with historical cycles, to a limited extent we can combine the different cases they present in such a way as to test theoretical conceptions of what features of the historical cycles are typical, and what are exceptional.

Besides confirming certain elements in the concept derived from our other sources, the collection of statistics brings forcibly to our attention two elements which are traceable, rather than prominent, in business annals and in certain theories.

Time series show that the cyclical fluctuations characteristic of various economic processes differ in amplitude and timing; they show approximately how much these fluctuations differ in amplitude, and what order they follow in time.

Time series also show that the cyclical fluctuations of most (not all) economic processes occur in combination with fluctuations of several other sorts:—secular trends, primary and secondary, seasonal variations, and irregular fluctuations.

By developing special methods for segregating secular trends and seasonal variations, statisticians have enabled us to get a clearer view of cyclical fluctuations, though they have accomplished little toward isolating the irregular changes in their series. Thus we are forced to deal with materials, which, at best, show cyclical-irregular fluctuations in combination. Even so, we can sort the series into groups, based upon the regularity and the measure of agreement among their movements. There are some time series whose fluctuations, mild or violent, show slight traces of any rhythm. But there are enough series which show tolerably regular cyclical fluctuations, agreeing with one another and with our business annals in tenor, to give us confidence in the basic element of our conception—the recurrence of the prosperity-recession-depression-revival sequence.

3. Two Criticisms Considered.

One element in our working concept has been rejected by Dean Arthur B. Adams, who holds:

> It is a mistake to think that cyclical movements are continuous. . . . Each business cycle is, in a large measure, separate and distinct from the one preceding it and the other succeeding it. Considerable time may elapse between the ending of one cycle and the beginning of another.

Adams illustrates this contention by reference to American experience:

> No period of prosperity developed from 1893 until the industrial expansion of 1905-07. Again, following the Panic of 1907 no period of prosperity developed until the World War expansion of 1915-20.

Our annals, on the contrary, and the business indexes with which we have compared them, show between 1893 and 1907 a "submerged cycle" terminated by a recession early in 1896, a second period of somewhat greater activity terminated by a very mild reaction in 1900, and a third movement of expansion ending in the "rich man's panic" of 1903. Between 1907 and 1920, also, our annals and indexes show three cycles, marked off by recessions in 1910, 1913 and 1918.

Yet the difference between Dean Adams' view and the one taken here is more a difference in the use of terms than a difference concerning facts. For Adams recognizes that between 1893 and 1905, and again between 1907 and 1915, there was "some oscillation of prices, credit and profits." He thinks, however, that

these slight movements occurring within a few months were far too inconsequential to be designated as cyclical fluctuations.

What are here called business cycles of small amplitude, Dean Adams calls "periods of time covered by oscillating business equilibria." [1] In his terminology, no fluctuation is a business cycle unless the prosperous phase develops into a "boom."

Perhaps it does not matter greatly which of these contrasting usages is adopted, so long as the facts are kept in mind. On either view, one must face the problem why some revivals grow into intense and prolonged prosperity, and why in other cases prosperity is mild and brief. But one who takes the trouble to measure the amplitudes of successive fluctuations in many time series throughout considerable periods, finds his observations so distributed about their central tendency that he has no basis for contrasting business cycles and what Dean Adams calls "oscillating business equilibria." [2] Our inquiry will be more orderly if we treat all cyclical oscillations as belonging to one species of phenomena, and inquire into the variations characteristic of the species in respect to amplitudes, duration, and other measurable features.

Professor Irving Fisher doubts the validity of the whole conception with which we are concerned, and asks whether "the" business cycle is not a myth. His chief argument runs as follows:

if by the business cycle is meant merely the statistical fact that business does *fluctuate* above and below its average trend, there is no denying the existence of a cycle—and not only in business but in any statistical series whatsoever! If we draw any smooth curve to represent the general trend of population, the actual population figures must necessarily rise sometimes above and sometimes below this mean trend line. . . . In the same way weather conditions necessarily fluctuate about their own means; so does the luck at Monte Carlo. Must we then speak of "the population cycle," "the weather cycle" and "the Monte Carlo cycle"?

[1] Arthur B. Adams, *Economics of Business Cycles,* New York, 1925, pp. 195-197, and 213.
[2] See "The Amplitude of Business Cycles" in Chapter III, sections vi, 3 (7).

I see no more reason to believe in "the" business cycle. It is simply the fluctuation about its own mean. And yet the cycle idea is supposed to have more content than mere variability. It implies a regular succession of *similar* fluctuations, constituting some sort of *recurrence*, so that, as in the case of the phases of the moon, the tides of the sea, wave motion, or pendulum swing, we can forecast the future on the basis of a pattern worked out from past experience, and which we have reason to think will be copied in the future. We certainly cannot do that in predicting the weather, or Monte Carlo luck. Can we do so as to business? Not so long as business is dominated by changes in the price level! [3]

Professor Fisher has rendered a wholesome service to students of business cycles by challenging their basic concept in this vigorous fashion. To discuss the issue in full would involve repeating once again many of the facts set forth in the preceding chapters and summarized in the preceding sections. That is not feasible; but it is well to recall what groups of facts the challenge must face.

Even when economic time series are reduced to percentage deviations from their secular trends adjusted for seasonal variations, the fluctuations in some cases still seem as irregular as the fluctuations of the weather, or of "Monte Carlo luck." But there are many series of which this cannot be said. When charted, the fluctuations of pig-iron production, unemployment percentages, bank clearings, and building permits, to cite but a few examples, prove to be decidedly less irregular than the fluctuations of a weather chart, a chart of net gold shipments, or of potato crops. In no case are the fluctuations highly regular; but in many cases they are far from haphazard, despite the inability of statisticians to free what they call "cyclical" changes from what they call "irregular" perturbations. Further, the cyclical-irregular fluctuations of the series which individually show semblance of regularity are found to have tolerably regular relations with one another in respect to time, duration, and amplitude of movement—relations many of which have been suggested by economic theory. Finally, in timing and direction these inter-correlated fluctuations agree closely with the evidence given by business annals concerning a long-continued and wide-spread recurrence of prosperity, recession, depression and revival.

[3] Irving Fisher, "Our Unstable Dollar and the So-called Business Cycle," *Journal of the American Statistical Association*, June, 1925, vol. xx, pp. 191, 192.

To ascertain how regularly this sequence recurs, to learn all they can about its characteristics, causes, and consequences, is the problem upon which students of business cycles are working. They speak of cyclical fluctuations, instead of periodic fluctuations, just because the first term does not imply strict regularity of recurrence. To them "the cycle idea" does "have more content than mere variability"; but it does not have the content of periodicity. Anyone who makes business forecasts on the basis of a fixed time schedule is not applying their concept, but violating it. What they know about the recurrence does not yet enable them to make consistently successful business forecasts. But in that fact they see reason, not for giving up their work, but for pressing it further.

No competent judge questions the desirability of studying economic fluctuations in an objective fashion. Professor Fisher himself is one of the distinguished workers in the field. But he thinks that the subdivision of this broad problem which is called "business cycles" in America and "trade cycles" in England would flourish better under some other name. Perhaps a new name can be found which is equally apt and less subject to misconstruction. If so, it should be adopted. But no such blanket term as "economic undulations," "industrial fluctuations," "business oscillations," or "theory of conjunctures" will meet the needs of current research. For we have seen that various investigators believe they have discovered several different types of fluctuations in time series—secular trends, "long waves," secondary trends, generating cycles, commercial cycles (the commonest name for inter-crisis changes), business cycles, seasonal variations, irregular perturbations. Probably each of these types which withstands critical examination will become the object of intensive study by economic statisticians and by economic theorists, or better by men who unite these too-often separated interests. As knowledge grows, there will be increasing need of specific names to characterize each type of fluctuations and to differentiate each from the other types. To drop the name now widely used for one of the best established of these types, before a better substitute has been supplied, might cause more confusion than is now caused by misunderstanding of the word "cycles." Meanwhile, the general adoption of this word in other sciences to designate recurrent, but non-periodic, phenomena is familiarizing the intelligent public with its meaning.[4] Perhaps the

---

[4] See above, Chapter IV, section iii, 2; "Use of the Term 'Cycles.'"

course which will make the least trouble is for critics to observe what those who treat of business cycles mean by that term.

4. A Definition of Business Cycles.

In a systematic investigation of business cycles, all of the characteristics developed in the preceding pages by analyzing business annals, theoretical hypotheses and statistical data should be considered. But it is useful to have a brief definition summarizing those characteristics which show the generic type of the phenomena in question, and those characteristics which mark off business cycles from the other phenomena just mentioned with which they may be confused.

Business cycles are a species of fluctuations in the economic activities of organized communities. The adjective "business" restricts the concept to fluctuations in activities which are systematically conducted on a commercial basis. The noun "cycles" bars out fluctuations which do not recur with a measure of regularity.

The phenomena with which business cycles may be confused are (1) changes in business conditions which occur between the dates of "crises," (2) fluctuations which affect a minor portion of the economic activities of a business community, (3) fluctuations which recur every year, and (4) the less definitely established secondary trends and "long waves." From the first of these related species, business cycles are distinguished by the fact that each cycle includes one wave of rising and falling, or falling and rising activity, whereas the intervals between "crises" often include two and some times include three such waves. From the second species, business cycles are distinguished by their wider inclusiveness. From the third species they are distinguished by not recurring annually. From the fourth species they are distinguished by their briefer time-span.

Following the lines of this analysis, we indicate both the generic features and the distinguishing characteristics of business cycles by saying that they are recurrences of rise and decline in activity, affecting most of the economic processes of communities with well-developed business organization, not divisible into waves of amplitudes nearly equal to their own, and averaging in communities at different stages of economic development from about three to about six or seven years in duration.

Seldom can the interrelated species of social (or natural) phenomena be marked off from one another with such precision as to leave no doubtful cases. Certainly our business annals and statistical indexes show some fluctuations which are difficult to classify on any scheme. If the definition suggested makes clear what is typical of the phenomena in question, it will serve its purpose.

II. Tentative Working Plans.

To give an intelligible account of business cycles, as we have come to conceive them, is the task of the second volume. The cycles with which the discussion will deal are neither the cycles of history, nor the cycles of some speculative construction, but cycles of an inter-- mediate order. We shall seek to find what features have been characteristic of all or of most cycles, and to concentrate attention upon them, paying less attention to features which have been peculiar to one or a few cases. In this respect, our aim will be like that of economic theorists, and different from that of economic historians, commercial journalists, and business forecasters, who are concerned with particular cycles. But our way of finding what is typical and what is exceptional will be the way of the statistician and the historian who ventures to generalize. Of course, concentrating upon what is typical involves considering the way in which the various phenomena treated are distributed around their central tendencies. What this procedure shows to be typical may at times be equivalent to what many economic theorists would call "normal" features of business cycles; but there is no assurance that such correspondence will be common.

Materials for the discussion are supplied by the three collections from which our working conception of business cycles has been derived—the collection of business annals, the collection of statistical series, and the collection of theories. These are formal, objective sources which any student can exploit. In addition, like every other student of economic behavior, I shall draw upon my own store of experiences and observations—a queer mixture of generic and individual elements, the latter determined largely by chance and by personal equation.

The methods employed must be methods which make it possible to weave these diverse materials into a single fabric. We must be ready to consider concrete events such as historians treat; but we must array them in groups after the fashion of statisticians, and interpret them in the light of what we know about economic behavior, after the fashion of economic theorists. Similarly, we must be ready to apply the mathematical technique of statisticians; but we must guide our statistical investigations by rational hypotheses, and eke out our statistical observations by recourse to historical records. So, too, while we must be ready on occasion to analyze imaginary cases with the theorists, these cases should be arranged whenever possible with an eye upon the historical and statistical data by which speculative conclusions may be tested. Of course, it is an error to think that free use of factual materials reduces the need for careful reasoning. In our effort to give an intelligible account of business cycles, reasoning must be our chief concern; but it should be reasoning which deals, and squares, with observations, and the observations should have as wide a sweep as we can get from history, as much precision as we can get from statistics, and as much subtlety as we can get from personal experience.

The concept of business cycles developed in this volume suggests that the leading question of the second volume be put in the form "How do business cycles run their course?" rather than in the form "What causes business cycles?" What we are seeking to understand is a complex of recurrent fluctuations in numerous interrelated processes. To learn what we can about the workings of these processes in their relations to one another and as a whole is the next step. When we have taken that step, it will be time to see what the question about the cause of business cycles means, and in what sense it can be answered.

Meanwhile, we need not hesitate to speak about causal relationships among the numerous factors in the processes whose fluctuations we are tracing, whenever such language seems appropriate. Men phrase their statements concerning economic relations in various ways. One may say that under certain circumstances an increase of orders for goods is followed by a rise of prices, or that it permits sellers to raise prices, or that it tends to produce a rise of prices, or that it occasions a rise, or that it causes prices to rise. Each of these phrases has implications somewhat different from the others—implications of which we seldom stop to think in the midst of our constructive work. The only statement in the list which we can test adequately is the colorless statement that one event is followed by another. We should be on the safest ground if we confined ourselves strictly to tested allegations concerning past sequences. Yet in our searches for sequences to test, and in our thinking about probable future developments, it would be foolish to contend against the settled habit of thinking in terms of cause and effect. Many of our keenest guesses at new truth come to mind in this dubious form, just as many stimulating insights are suggested by analogies. We avail ourselves of analogies both in making investigations and in stating their results, though we all know that analogy is not proof. So we think and write in causal terms, though we admit the impossibility of establishing a necessary connection between antecedent and consequent.

Whatever causal connections we may work into our account of business cycles, that account will remain an analytic description of interrelated processes. Of necessity, the causal relationships will appear most complicated. A phenomenon which crops up first as an effect turns presently into a cause, and since we shall be following a continuous process we must treat it first as the one and then as the other. Even that is a simplified version of the facts: in truth every factor in the situation at every moment is being influenced by, and is influencing, other factors—it is not first cause and then effect, but both cause and effect all the time. Further, we cannot follow single chains of causal influence. The interactions among economic processes are so important that we cannot set them aside. Almost every effect with which we deal will appear to be the joint product of numerous causes, and to be one among several causes of numerous effects. In view of these complications, it will prove more helpful to treat our problem at large in terms of the relations among a number of complex variables, rather than in terms of cause and effect.

A cardinal illustration of our difficulties, and of the way out, is provided by Chapter II. To avoid getting lost in the maze of processes which Chapter I showed we must follow, we sought to find some general scheme for viewing these processes in systematic relation to one another. The scheme suggested was to relate every factor to the current and prospective profits of business enterprises. Profits are net mathematical resultants of many plus and minus items in a computation. We do not analyze profit and loss statements in terms of cause and effect, though we often give causal explanations of changes in certain items. So, when we put the scheme of Chapter II to use in the second volume, we shall concentrate attention upon the net resultants of interrelated changes in many variables and relegate causal analysis to incidental uses.

The best framework for a discussion of how business cycles run their course is that provided by the phases of these cycles—prosperity, recession, depression, and revival. Our collections of business annals and of theories lend themselves readily to this plan; for the annals mark changes in the tides of activity, and most current theories explain crises by what happens in prosperity and revivals by what happens in depression. But statistical time series are continuous. How shall we break them into parts for use in a discussion which treats first all periods of prosperity as a unit, then all periods of recession, and so on?

Most of the statistics which the National Bureau is collecting come from the United States, England, France and Germany—countries included in our volume of *Business Annals*. For each of these countries Dr. Thorp has drawn up a table which marks off, not only successive cycles, but also the successive phases of each cycle. As they stand, or with such modifications as prove advisable when we enter into full detail, his divisions will be used as a basis for breaking up the time covered by each series used, first into cycles, second into periods of prosperity, recession, depression and revival. That is, we plan to analyze all the time series for a given country on the basis of a standard pattern derived from the business annals of that country, not on the basis of the various patterns which might be derived from study of the several series themselves. In most cases we anticipate that the cycles and phases of the individual series will correspond fairly well with the standard patterns of the countries from which they come. But there will be cases of notable divergence in timing— cases which our plan will throw into high relief, and from which we shall learn much of interest.

The cycles with which we are working run from trough to trough; that is, they show a business cycle as a wave which rises, breaks and subsides. We might equally well have taken the cycles from peak to peak, representing each as a decline, followed by a rise. Our chief reason for preferring the former plan is that it may enable us to include a few more recent cases than would its rival.

When a series has been divided into cycles on this basis, we plan to ascertain its mean value in each cycle, and to turn the original figures for every month or quarter of each cycle into relatives on the basis of this mean value as 100. This step will put all the series into comparable form, and give us numerical results which can be used in many ways. Then each cycle in each series will be repre-

sented by four charts, one showing its relative fluctuations during the
prosperous phase, one during the phase of recession, a third during
depression, and a fourth during revival. These charts will be drawn
with overlaps at either end; for example, the charts for revivals of
activity will include the latter part of the preceding depression and
the earlier part of the succeeding prosperity.

Charts drawn in this manner, with logarithmic vertical scales, can
be used in many combinations. We can compare the fluctuations of
a given series in a given country in successive periods of given phase,
and contrast its fluctuations in opposite phases. We can study the
movements of similar series from different countries in the same
phases of the same cycles. We can take different series from the same
country in the same phase of the same cycle. And so on.

By using the average value of each series during each cycle as the
base for computing relatives, we eliminate most of the secular trend.
Otherwise, the plan involves a minimum of "adjustments" in presenting data. But though simple, it can be elaborated at will. At need,
the seasonal variations of series can be ascertained by any of the
standard methods, and eliminated. Or a series can be turned into
percentage deviations from its secular trend before it is broken up
into cycles. Our percentage fluctuations about the mean values of
a series in a given cycle can be reduced to multiples of their own
standard deviations. Indeed, we can utilize almost any technical device which the work of other investigators, or our own experience,
shows to be helpful.

A special advantage of the plan is that it helps us to deal with
the most baffling problem encountered in analyzing time series—the
problem of segregating cyclical from irregular fluctuations. In no
single case will our procedure effect such a segregation; but when we
assemble charts showing the movements of some variable during (say)
the prosperous phase of numerous cycles in several countries, we
should be able to make out with some confidence what changes are
characteristic and what are exceptional. In some cases we may be
able to go further, and connect deviations from the common course
with disturbing factors of which we read in non-statistical sources.

Of course, our fundamental problem in using statistics will be to
find out what relations subsist between the cyclical fluctuations characteristic of different economic processes. As pointed out in Chapter
III, the possible relationships are of many types. We are accustomed
to asking whether it is the total magnitude of one variable which

affects a second, a change in the direction of its movement, or the amount of change from one date to the next, or the percentage rate of change. We are learning to ask whether it is the changes accumulated over a period of time that should be looked into, or the amount of the variable in excess of a critical range, or its ratio to some other variable. These are but a few of the possibilities which statisticians may soon be considering. Moreover, the effects upon the second variable may be changes in total amount, in direction of movement, in amount of movement, in percentage rise or fall, or in any of the other indefinitely numerous possibilities. Again, a given variable may affect a second variable in one way while it affects a third and fourth in other ways. So, too, a given variable may be affected in unlike ways by two or more processes which bear upon it. All these problems are further complicated by the need of finding how promptly an effect is exercised, how that effect is distributed through time, and whether the effect is constant in character through all phases of business cycles, or whether it changes from phase to phase.

There are important problems relating to business cycles which cannot be treated within the framework which has been sketched. Hence the analysis of what happens in periods of prosperity, recession, depression and revival must be supplemented by discussions in which certain hypotheses are tested with reference to long periods of time, in which business annals are considered in their wider sweep, and in which statistical series are taken as wholes instead of in segments. But these problems will stand out far more clearly after the successive phases of business cycles have been analyzed in detail than they do at present.

No group of workers in the present generation can hope to cover the field marked out by these suggestions. The task of finding, case by case, the best form of stating the relations among different economic processes is a task on which an increasing number of increasingly skillful investigators will be working for a long time to come —how long no one can guess. But what our successors can accomplish will depend upon the stage at which we pass on the problem. Our task is to use as best we can the means at our disposal—the insights given by economic theory as it now stands, the statistical and historical data now available, and all the suggestions we can get.

ADDENDA

Work upon business cycles is progressing so rapidly in so many quarters that a manuscript falls somewhat behind date while it is passing through the press. As partial remedy, I add notes on a few developments of which I have learned too late for mention in the proper place. Before the volume reaches its first readers, doubtless I shall be wishing that I might supplement these addenda. Not all the omissions are items of recent date. Probably the most serious are matters of which I should have known long ago, but of which I am still ignorant.

A Russian paper by Albert Wainstein on *Harvests, Meteorological and Economic Cycles, and the Problem of Economic Forecasting,* Moscow, 1926, reviews the recent literature upon weather theories of business cycles. Among the contributions noticed is a series of articles, otherwise unknown to me, published by Axel F. Enström in the *Teknisk Tidskrift* (Veckoupplagen), 1916. From the French synopsis of Wainstein's paper, supplemented by notes which Dr. Kuznets has made, I judge Enström's investigations to merit more attention than they have received. By repeated smoothing and differentiation of numerous time series, most of which run back to 1830, Enström finds non-synchronous cycles of 8 to 9 years in wholesale prices, crops, production, temperature and sunspots. Between sunspot and temperature cycles he gets a correlation coefficient of —.94. He attributes the lagging cycles in economic activities to the cycles in temperature, and believes that the sequences are sufficiently regular to afford a basis for forecasting economic cycles from solar observations.

In the new volume of *Der moderne Kapitalismus,* "Das Wirtschaftsleben im Zeitalter des Hochkapitalismus" (Munich and Leipzig, 1927), Professor Werner Sombart gives a fresh exposition of his theory of business cycles, showing the relation between the factor which he stresses (the different conditions under which organic and inorganic goods are produced) and other processes.

475

This discussion, Chapter xxv, also throws light upon the historical connection between business cycles and the form of economic organization. In treating that theme, I ought to have referred to Chapters xvi and xvii in the second volume of *Der moderne Kapitalismus,* 3rd ed., Munich and Leipzig, 1919. Sombart there points out the characteristics which differentiate the economic perturbations of the 16th, 17th and 18th centuries from the business cycles of the 19th and 20th centuries.

Professor A. C. Pigou's treatise on *Industrial Fluctuations,* mentioned in Chapter I as forthcoming, has been published in London. A hasty examination of the copy I have just received suffices to show that the book fulfills the high expectations with which it has been awaited.

Mr. R. G. Hawtrey's article in the May, 1927, issue of the *Quarterly Journal of Economics* on "The Monetary Theory of the Trade Cycle and Its Statistical Test" contains not only a concise statement of his own views, but also a criticism of Pigou's "psychological theory," which Hawtrey seems to regard as the only serious "rival" of the "monetary theory."

An interesting variant of the "profits theory" has been suggested by Professor F. Schmidt of the University of Frankfurt in *Die Industriekonjunktur—ein Rechenfehler*. (Zeitschrift für Betriebswirtschaft, 2. Sonderheft, Berlin and Vienna, 1927.)
The gist of Schmidt's contention is that illusions concerning current profits arise from a technical defect in bookkeeping. When the price level rises, profits are overstated, because no allowance is made for the increasing unit costs of replacing the raw materials, current supplies, and other goods which enterprises are continually using up. The whole difference between aggregate buying prices and aggregate selling prices is set down as profits, although the replacement of the necessary working supplies will absorb a larger part of the receipts than in the preceding turnover period. When the price level is falling, profits are minimized, or losses magnified, because no account is taken of the diminished unit costs of replacing the goods used up. This illusory element in profits leads to over-borrowing, over-confidence, and over-extension of industrial equipment in the one case, and to their opposites in the other case.

Dr. Matsuyo Takizawa's *Penetration of Money Economy in Japan and its Effects upon Social and Political Institutions* has now been published by the Columbia University Press.

The American estimate, cited in Chapter II, that savings have averaged about one-seventh of national income, may be compared with the new British estimate by Professor Bowley and Sir Josiah Stamp. "Total savings expressed as a proportion of total social income was . . . 16 per cent in 1911, and 12 or 13 per cent in 1924. If the unemployed are absorbed in industry, and we reach a year of good trade, the pre-war proportion of saving may well be again attained." *The National Income, 1924,* by Arthur L. Bowley and Sir Josiah Stamp, Oxford, 1927, p. 57.

A study of secondary trends, by Dr. Charles A. R. Wardwell of the University of Pennsylvania, will soon be published in Philadelphia under the title, *An Investigation of Economic Data for Major Cycles.* I have seen only the first draft of the manuscript. Dr. Wardwell uses methods different from those of de Wolff, Kondratieff, or Kuznets, and gets from his American data, which run by quarters from 1866 or later to the present, "major cycles" averaging about 15 years in duration. Smaller samples of English and German series also give "major cycles," but somewhat briefer ones.

My remark in Chapter I, that "no one has yet devised a satisfactory method of measuring . . . cyclical fluctuations directly," has been made questionable by Dr. Martin Allen Brumbaugh. His doctoral dissertation, published at the University of Pennsylvania and in New York in 1926, is entitled *Direct Method of Determining Cyclical Fluctuations of Economic Data.*

"The method developed arrives at the relatives of cyclical differences in two major operations, first, the division of each item of data by the item of the same season of the preceding year, and secondly, the correction for trend residue. The first step removes the seasonal variations, reduces the data to relative form and, since it is a chain index, removes the normal growth. The second step removes the small residual trend element which represents the increase of one year. . . .

"In the final result we have not measured cycles but cyclical differences. . . . We have demonstrated that the relative cyclical differences lead to a wave curve whose periodic changes conform to those of a curve of relative cycles. Further, that the amplitudes of the curve of cyclical differences express rapidity of change whereas the amplitudes of the curve of relative cycles express amounts which are the results of such change." (Pp. 71, 72.)

Dr. Brumbaugh recognizes that the final test of his method "must come from an appeal to business conditions." In his judgment, the method "has satisfactorily fulfilled every reasonable requirement for the cases to which it has been applied." (P. 73.)

Mr. A. W. Flux publishes a valuable paper upon "Indices of Industrial Productive Activity" in the latest issue of the *Journal of the Royal Statistical Society*, vol. xc, part ii, pp. 225-271.

Mr. Carl Snyder has brought together in one volume his numerous studies of cyclical fluctuations (of which such free use is made in Chapters III and IV), and added valuable new results to the papers already published. *Business Cycles and Business Measurements: Studies in Quantitative Economics*, by Carl Snyder, New York, 1927.

In "The Summation of Random Causes as the Source of Cyclic Processes" (*Problems of Economic Conditions*, vol. iii, part i, published by the Conjuncture Institute in Russian with an English summary, Moscow, 1927), E. E. Slutsky presents two theses:

> (a) that cyclic . . . processes may originate owing to a summation of mutually independent chance causes, and (b) that these chance waves may show a certain regularity, being an imitation in lesser or greater degree, of strictly periodical fluctuations.

The first thesis, which is supported by a most interesting analysis of a random series from numbers drawn in a lottery, has a bearing upon my inference from the distribution of cycle durations (see above pp. 419, 420). But Mr. Slutsky thinks that I am not justified in treating the variability of cycle durations

> as a reason for denying the regular periodicity of cycles . . . for a similar result could be obtained also for many curves composed from regular sine curves.

The preliminary annals for 1926, prepared by Dr. Willard L. Thorp and published in the National Bureau's *News-Bulletin* for May 20, 1927, indicate that recessions occurred last year in France, Italy, and Argentina. These reports add three new observations upon the duration of business cycles to the collection analyzed in Chapter IV. All three of the cycles just terminated lasted about 6 years.

INDEX

ADAMS, A. B., 41, 42n, 51, 90n, 255n, 464, 465n.
Addenda, 475-478.
Advertising, as means of controlling demand, 155, 165
AFTALION, ALBERT, 7n, 29n, 52, 55, 90n, 361n., 379n., 380, 385n., 453n.
Aggregative Indexes of Trade, 316, 317
Agriculture
  Business-cycle, hazard in, 87-89
  Capitalization of, 97
  Relative importance in different countries, 175-177
  Savings in, 153
ALTSCHUL, EUGEN, 196n.
AMERICAN BUREAU of METAL STATISTICS, 95, 96n.
American Telephone and Telegraph Company's Index of "General Business," 284, 287, 288, 294-296, 321, 328, 329-348, 366, 368, 369.
Amplitudes of Cyclical Fluctuations, 45, 46, 87-89, 95, 100, 123, 124, 141-146, 150, 153, 174, 261, 270-280, 343-354, 457, 463.
ANDREW, S. L., 367n.
ANGELL, J. W., 139n.
Annals of Business, 82, 358-360, 361-450, 455-459.
Analytic description, 2, 54, 55.
Argentina, 176, 177, 362, 380, 392, 394, 398, 410, 414n, 429, 437, Addenda.
ARKWRIGHT, RICHARD, 159.
ARNDT, E. H. D., 361n
"Arts of Production," 92-94.
ARTMAN, C. E., 109n
Australia, 99n, 176, 177, 179, 362, 380, 392, 393, 394, 398, 410, 412, 414n, 429-437.
Austria, 176, 202, 362, 391, 392, 393, 398, 410, 412, 414n, 427-437, 438-445.
Automobile Production, 235.
AXE, E. W., 278, 302n, 303.
Axe and Flinn's Business Index for Germany, 302, 303.

BABBAGE, CHARLES, 236n.
BACON, N. T., 194n.
BAINES, SIR ATHELSTANE, 195n.
Bank Clearings, 210, 211, 247, 264, 279, 280, 304-306, 313, 314, 327, 329-348, 385.

Bank Currency, 117-139.
Bank Reserves, 31-34, 133-135, 247, 288.
Banking and Business Cycles, 31-34, 51, 52, 102, 133-135, 280, 288.
Bankruptcies, 247, 258.
BEAN, L. M., 64n.
Belgium, 5, 396.
BELLERBY, J. R., 44n, 53.
BERGMANN, EUGEN VON, 7 n., 452n.
BERRIDGE, W. A., 277, 302.
BEVERIDGE, SIR WILLIAM, 13n., 14, 15n., 51, 206n., 259n., 260n., 291n., 292.
Beveridge's Chart of "The Pulse of the Nation," 293, 294.
BILGRAM, HUGO, 47n.
Birth Rates and Business Cycles, 20, 50.
BÖHM-BAWERK, EUGEN VON, 450, 451n.
Bond yields, 210, 211, 219, 222.
BOUNIATIAN, MENTOR, 3n., 29n., 52, 57n., 81n., 90n., 361, 379n., 384, 385n., 390n., 452n., 453n.
BOWLEY, A. L., 239n., 240n., 242n., 243n., 245, Addenda.
BRADLEY, HARRIETT, 70n.
Brazil, 82, 176, 362, 392, 394, 398, 410, 414n., 429-437, 442-445.
BREWSTER, SIR DAVID, 4, 5.
BRUMBAUGH, M. A., Addenda.
BUCKLE, H. T., 193.
Building Permits, 218, 247, 258, 279.
BUREAU of INTERNAL REVENUE (TAX DIVISION), 141, 142, 145.
BUREAU of LABOR STATISTICS, 94n., 146, 147n., 207n., 282, 286, 293n., 315, 317, 324n.
BURGESS, W. R., 123n., 124n., 126, 275, 307.
Business Annals, 82, 358-360; 361-450, 455-459.
Business Cycles, Concept of, 455-469.
Business Cycles, Definition of, 468, 469.
Business Cycles, Development of, 75-82, 182, 395, 396, 412-416, 418, 420n., 446-450, 458.
Business Cycles, Early Recognition of, 10, 11, 452.
Business Cycles and Economic Theory, 3, 4, 451, 452.
Business-cycle Hazard, 87-89, 157, 173.

Business-cycle Theories, Summaries of, 11, 12, 459-461.

Business Economy, 63-74, 116, 154-157, 171-173, 174-180, 182, 185, 396, 412-416, 418, 420n., 446-450, 458.

Business Enterprises, 71, 72, 86-90, 100-105, 111, 112, 149-151.

Business Failures, 247, 258.

Business Forecasting, 201, 251, 252, 324-326, 466, 467.

Business Indexes, 200, 202, 284, 287, 288, 290-354, 365-375.

Business Management, 157-159, 169-173, 185.

Business Reporting, 363, 455, 456.

Business Statistics, 155, 160.

Calendar and Seasonal Variations, 237.

Canada, 176, 362, 392, 394, 398, 410, 414n., 429-437, 442-445, 448n.

Capitalism and Business Cycles, 8, 9, 24, 55-57, 61, 62, 169-173. (See Business Economy).

Capitalization and Business Cycles, 43, 44, 51.

Cassel, Gustav, 44n., 48n., 53, 90n., 93, 115n., 154n., 384, 385n., 386

Catchings, Waddill, 37, 39, 40n., 51, 90, 117n.

Causal Theories of Business Cycles, 1, 2, 49n., 54-57, 460, 461, 470, 471.

Causation and Correlation, 267-269, 285-289.

Cement Production, 234, 246.

Chalmers, George, 191.

Changing Seasonal Variations, 241, 243-245, 248, 252.

Charts of Time Series, Development of, 191.

Checks, as Means of Payment, 117-128, 149, 184.

China, 66, 82, 176, 177, 178, 362, 380, 392, 394, 396, 398, 410, 412, 414n., 420n., 429-437, 442-445, 447, 449.

Cigar consumption, 234.

Cigarette Production, 246.

Circulating Medium, 117-139.

Circulation, Velocity of, 122-128.

Clare, George, 199.

Clark, Hyde, 10.

Clark, J. M., 44, 45n., 48n., 53, 90n., 170.

Clearings, 210, 211, 247, 264, 279, 280, 304-306, 313, 314, 327, 329-348, 385.

Clements, F. E., 377.

Climatic Seasonal Variations, 236-239.

Classification of Business-Cycle Theories, 11, 12, 49-53, 459-461.

Coal Production, 227, 246.

Coefficient of Correlation, 262-270, 282, 283, 284, 326.

Coefficient of Variation, 79, 339n., 351, 353, 407.

Coin and Paper Money, 117-128, 149.

Coinage, Invention of, 66.

"Commercial Crises," 1-11, 451-455.

Commercial Relations among Business Enterprises, 102.

Commitments and Business Cycles, 28, 52.

Commons, J. R., 71, 232n., 238n.

Commutation, 69.

Competition and Business Cycles, 17n., 52.

Competition and Prices, 114.

Complexity of Business Cycles, 1-3, 47-49, 58, 59, 180, 181, 204, 205, 291, 309-311, 455-462.

Construction Work and Business Cycles, 26-28, 52, 90, 100.

Consumers' Demand and Business Cycles, 6, 8, 24, 25, 30, 35-42, 45, 51, 52, 139, 150, 151, 155, 163-167, 185.

Consumers' Goods, 108, 109, 164, 165.

Consumers' Goods, Stock of, 94, 95.

Continuity of Business Cycles, 457, 458, 463-465.

Conventional Seasons, 236-239.

Co-operation in the Business Economy, 171, 172.

Copper, 95, 96, 210, 211.

Correlation, Theory of, 197, 262-270.

Cost of Business Cycles, 353, 354.

Cotton Statistics, 246.

Cournot, Augustin, 194.

Credit and Business Cycles, 9, 32-34, 51, 52.

Credit men, 162.

Crests and Troughs of American Cycles, 334-337, 343-354.

Crises, Relation to Business Cycles, 75-82, 378-381.

"Crises" and "Recessions," 378-381.

Crises in Periods of Depression, 78, 380.

Crisis Years, 384, 387, 390-392, 438, 439.

Crum, W. L., 213n., 214n., 240n., 244n., 245n., 259n., 293n., 326n., 385n.

"Cycles," Scientific Meaning of, 377, 378, 466, 467.

Cyclical Fluctuations in Time Series, 123-125, 199, 255-261, 290-354, Addenda.

Dates of American Cycles, 334-337, 387.

Dates of Crises, 384, 387, 390-392, 438, 439.

Davenport, H. J., 115n.

Davies, G. R., 419n.

Day, E. E., 213n., 249n., 318n.

Death rates and Business Cycles, 20, 50.

Declining Industries, 225.

Deduction and Statistical Method, 192, 193.
Definition of Business Cycles, 468, 469.
DENNISON, H. S., 51, 95.
DEPARTMENT of COMMERCE, 83n., 200n.
Deposit Currency, 117-139.
Depressions
Amplitude of, 343-354, 457.
Duration of, 337-343, 407-412, 420, 421, 457.
Interpretation of, 381, 382, 456.
DIBBLEE, G. B., 166n.
Distinctive Character of Each Cycle, 354-357.
Distributed lags, 266, 267, 285-287.
Dividends, Income from, 142-146, 247, 258.
"Domestic Recessions," 443.
DOREN, ALFRED, 80n.
DOUGLAS, C. H., 41n.
DRAPER, E. G., 238n.
Duration of Business Cycles, 79, 339-343, 384-424, 453, 457, Addenda.

Early Crises, 75-82.
Early Theories of Business Cycles, 4-11.
Easter and Seasonal Variations, 237, 239, 245.
Economic Cost of Business Cycles, 353, 354.
Economic Equilibrium and Business Cycles, 9, 186-188, 462.
Economic Organization and Business Cycles, 5, 6, 8, 16, 17, 22-25, 42-46, 51, 52, 55-57, 61-188, 363, 364, 412-416, 418, 420n., 446-450, 458.
Economic Resources, 90-100.
Economic Theory and Business Cycles, 3, 4, 451, 452.
Economic Welfare, 65, 66.
EDEN, SIR F. M., 191.
EDGEWORTH, F. Y., 10, 195n., 196n., 197n., 204n., 250, 262.
EDWARDS, ALBA M., 84n., 85n.
Education, Expenditure upon, 92-94.
EHRENBERG, RICHARD, 80n.
Elasticity of Circulating Medium, 119-122.
Emotional Factor in Business Cycles, 9, 17-20, 44, 50.
Employees, 87-89, 141-146, 153.
Employment, 87-89, 198, 210-212, 238, 239, 240n., 241, 385.
Employment, Statistics of, 198, 210, 211, 238, 239, 240n.
Engineering Professions, Development of, 159-162.
Engineers and Industrial Management, 159-162, 185.
ENGLAND, MINNIE T., 22, 50, 93.

England
Agriculture, 176.
Business annals, 4, 5, 362, 363, 371-374, 376, 379, 380, 385, 390, 393, 398, 402, 409-415, 421, 425-437, 438-445.
Business reporting, 201, 202.
Crises of 16th-18 Centuries, 3-5, 10, 12, 13, 75-81.
Crises of 19th and 20th Centuries, 388-390.
Employment statistics, 210, 211, 238, 239, 240n., 241, 291, 292.
Enterprise and thrift, 177.
Evolution of business economy, 68-73, 185.
Government regulation of business, 179.
Index of business cycles, 299, 301, 371-374.
Wealth and income, 99n.
Wholesale prices, 210, 211, 219, 222.
ENSTRÖM, AXEL F., Addenda.
Enterprisers, 89, 90, 153, 157-159, 183.
Equation of Exchange, 128-139.
Equilibrium and Business Cycles, 9, 186-188, 462.
Expenditures, Family, 146-149, 163-167.

"Fact" and "Theory," 59n., 357-360, 469, 470.
FAULKNER, ROLAND P., 195, 196n.
Family budgets, 94, 147.
Family expenditures, 94, 147, 163-167.
Farmers, 87-89, 97, 153, 175-177.
FAULKNER, HELEN D., 242n.
FEDDER, J. (J. VAN GELDEREN), 227n., 228.
FEDERAL RESERVE BANK of NEW YORK, 123, 124, 307.
Federal Reserve System, 136n., 178, 179.
FEDERAL TRADE COMMISSION, 91n., 92n., 97n., 98n., 99n., 148n., 150n.
FELDMAN, H., 238n.
FETTER, FRANK A., 90n.
FIELD, J. A., 209n.
Financial Relations among Business Enterprises, 101-103.
FISHER, IRVING, 22, 35n., 117n., 118n., 123n., 126n., 127, 128, 129n., 130, 134, 138, 209n., 266n., 267n., 268n., 286n., 287n., 316n., 465n., 466n., 467.
FLEETWOOD, BISHOP, 191.
FLINN, HAROLD M., 244n., 278, 302n., 303.
FLUX, A. W., 202, Addenda.
FOERSTER, R. F., 361n.
Forecasting of Business Conditions, 201, 251, 252, 324-326, 466, 467.
Forecasting Sequences, 324-326.
"Forty-month Cycle," 343, 385.
FOSTER, W. T., 37, 39, 40n., 51, 90, 117n.
FOURIER, JOSEPH, 191.

France, 14, 80, 99n., 176, 177, 178, 179, 185, 202, 227, 228, 362, 380, 390, 391, 393, 398, 410, 412, 414n., 415, 426-437, 438-445, Addenda.

FRANK, L. K., 45, 46n., 51, 56, 95, 233n., 272n.

Frequency Distributions, 205n., 332, 344, 351-353, 399-407, 418, 419.

FRICKEY, EDWIN, 244n., 273, 305, 306, 307, 313n., 314, 326n., 327, 328, 329n., 330n., 331, 332, 333n., 334n., 335, 337, 338, 340, 343n., 344, 345, 346, 347, 348.

Frickey's "Index of Outside Clearings," 305, 306, 313, 314, 327, 329-348.

FRIDAY, DAVID, 153.

FUNK, W. C., 64.

Gainful Workers, 83-85.

GALTON, SIR FRANCIS, 197n., 262.

GAUSS, K. F., 193, 254n.

GAY, E. F., 74n.

GELDEREN, J. VAN, 227n., 228, 229.

"General Business" Indexes, 284, 287, 288, 290, 293, 294, 320-324.

Germany, 5, 80, 99n., 176, 177, 179, 185, 202, 227, 278, 302, 303, 362, 380, 391, 393, 398, 410, 412, 414n., 426-437, 438-445.

GILBERT, J. W., 236n.

GINI, CORRADO, 202.

Gold, Monetary Stock of, 119-121.

Gold, Supply of and Demand for, 119-121, 135, 136, 138, 228, 410, 411.

Gompertz Curves and Trends, 224-226.

Goods in process, 95, 96.

Government and Production, 167-169, 179, 180, 185.

Graphic Methods, Development of, 191, 209.

Great Numbers, Law of, 194.

GRESSENS, O., 244n., 245n.

Growth Factor in Time Series, 93, 195, 200, 212-236.

Guidance of Production, 154-173, 184, 185.

HALE, R. L., 65n.

HALL, L. W., 214n., 242n.

HANSEN, A. H., 31, 32n., 33n., 53, 283, 284, 288.

HARAP, HENRY, 166n.

HARDY, C. O., 16, 17n., 18, 52, 156.

Harmonic Analysis, 191, 200, 259-261 (See Periodogram Analysis).

HART, W. L., 242n.

HARVARD COMMITTEE on ECONOMIC RESEARCH, 200, 201, 324n., 326.

HASTINGS, HUDSON B., 37, 40n., 51.

HAWTREY, R. G., 33, 34n., 53, 139n., Addenda.

HAYEK, F. A. VON, 202, 361n.

HAYES, H. G., 164n.

Health and Business Cycles, 15, 50.

HERSCHEL, SIR WILLIAM, 12.

HEXTER, M. B., 19, 20n., 50, 236n.

HILDEBRAND, BRUNO, 63n.

History and Business Cycles, 55-57, 232, 354-360, 361, 412-416, 420n., 446-450. (See Business Annals).

HOBSON, J. A., 24, 25n., 52, 90, 151.

HOOKER, R. H., 200n.

HOOKSTADT, CARL, 90n.

HOOVER, HERBERT, 94n.

Housewives, 64, 83-85, 165, 166.

HULL, C. H., 190n.

HULL, G. H., 27, 28n., 29, 52, 90, 385n.

HUNTINGTON, ELLSWORTH, 15n., 20, 50.

HURLIN, R. G., 85n.

IGNATIEFF, M. B., 361n.

Illusion and Business Cycles, 46, 47, 51.

Imports of Merchandise, 227, 235, 247.

Improvements upon Land, 97.

Incomes
    Aggregate of prices, 116.
    Expenditure of, 146-149.
    Received in money, 140, 141.

Incomes and Business Cycles, 35-42, 51.

Individualism in the Business Economy, 170.

Industrial Equipment and Business Cycles, 8, 27, 29-31, 44, 51, 52, 90, 96, 97, 182.

Industrial Relations among Business Enterprises, 101.

Industrial Technique, 92-94, 159-162.

Industry and Business, 105-107.

Index Numbers of Prices, 191, 193n., 195, 196, 204, 206-208, 210, 211, 218, 220, 222, 235, 266, 267, 279.

Indexes of Business Conditions, 200, 202, 284, 287, 288, 290-354, 365-375.

India, 66, 82, 176, 177, 362, 392, 394, 398, 410, 414n., 429-437, 442-445.

INGALLS, W. R., 91n., 92n., 96n., 153, 154n.

INGRAHAM, OLIN, 214n., 216n.

Inter-crisis Cycles, 78, 79, 229, 384-390, 416, 417, 453, 461, 462, 468, 469.

Interdependence of Business Enterprises, 100-105.

International Aspect of Business Cycles, 438-450, 456.

International Differences in Economic Organization, 174-180.

Interrelations among Prices, 113-115.

Induction in Economic Theory, 192, 193.

"Industrialization" and Business Cycles, 412-416, 418, 420n.

Inflation Theory of Business Cycles, 9, 44, 52, 53.

Innovations and Business Cycles, 20-22, 51, 156.

Investing and Business Cycles, 23-25, 52.
Investors, 162, 163, 185.
Interest Rates and Business Cycles, 31-34, 35n., 44, 52, 210, 211, 219, 241, 247, 248, 265, 279.
Irregular Fluctuations, 212, 249-255, 257, 463, 473.
Iron Production, 210, 211, 217, 222, 227, 235, 248.
Isolation Methods, 212, 255-261, 473.
Italy, 68, 80, 176, 202, 362, 380, 392, 394, 398, 410, 412, 414n., 417, 429-437, 442-445, Addenda.

Japan, 75n., 176, 177, 185, 362, 380, 392, 394, 398, 410, 414n., 429-427, 438, 442-445.
JEROME, HARRY, 303n., 359.
Jerome's "Industrial Composites," 303.
JEVONS, HERBERT STANLEY, 13, 50, 90n.
JEVONS, W. STANLEY, 9, 10, 12, 13n., 53, 81n., 194, 195n., 199, 209n., 236n., 310, 384n., 417n.
JOHANNSEN, N., 25n.
Joint-stock Companies, 72, 102-104, 157, 158.
JONES, E. D., 7n.
JUGLAR, CLEMENT, 10, 11, 452n., 453, 454.

KARSTEN, KARL G., 265, 266n., 267n., 270n., 289n., 290n.
KELLEY, T. L., 268n., 316n., 317n.
KEMMERER, E. W., 123n.
KING, W. I., 64, 88n., 89, 90n., 92n., 94n., 97, 140, 141n., 147, 152, 153n., 154, 168n., 214n., 244n., 245n., 256n., 286n., 359.
KINLEY, DAVID, 117, 118n., 123, 127, 150n.
KITCHIN, JOSEPH, 380n., 385n., 417n.
KNIGHT, F. H., 156n.
Knowledge and Income, 92-94.
KONDRATIEFF, N. D., 201, 227n., 228, 229, 230, 361n., Addenda.
KOREN, JOHN, 195n., 199n.
KUCZYNSKI, R. R., 361n.
KUZNETS, S. S., 46n., 48n., 51, 95 200n., 213n., 221, 225, 226, 229, 235n., 276, 359, Addenda.
KIRK, HAZEL, 166n.

"Lacking" and Business Cycles, 25n., 26n.
"Lags," 264-269, 280-289, 324-326, 336, 337.
Land, Value of, 97, 99n.
LANGTON, WILLIAM, 10.
LAPLACE, P. S., 191, 192, 193, 194, 197, 254n.
LAVINGTON, F., 44n., 53, 384, 385n., 464n.
Least-squares Method, 193.
LEDERER, EMIL, 36, 37n., 51.
LEICHTER, OTTO, 9n.
Lenders, 162, 163, 185.

Length of Business Cycles, 79, 339-343, 384-424, 453, 457.
LESCOHIER, D. 238n.
LESCURE, JEAN, 7n., 42n., 44n., 51, 57n., 361, 379n., 380, 453n.
LEVEN, MAURICE, 90n., 168n.
LEVY, L. E., 47n.
LEWISOHN, SAM A., 238n.
LEXIS, WILHELM, 196n.
LIGHTNER, O. C., 385n.
"Link-relative" Method, 240.
Live-stock, 97, 99n., 246.
Logarithmic Scale in Charts, 209.
Logistic Curves as Trends, 225, 226.
"Long Waves," 226-230, 468, 469, Addenda.
Losses caused by Business Cycles, 353, 354.
LÖWE, ADOLF, 7n., 59n., 452n.
LOYD, S. J., (LORD OVERSTONE), 10, 11n.

MACAULAY, F. R., 242, 246, 359.
Making Money and Business Cycles, 42-47, 51, 105-107, 142-146, 162, 172, 173.
Major Cycles, See "Long Waves."
MALTHUS, T. R., 8n., 166n., 191.
MANN, L. B., 147, 148n.
Manorial Economy, 67, 69.
MANSFIELD, CHIEF JUSTICE, 71.
Manufacturing
    Business-cycle hazard, 87, 89.
    Capitalization compared with agriculture, 97.
MARSHALL, ALFRED, 3, 4n.
MARSHALL, JOHN, 191.
MARX, KARL, 8, 9n., 232.
MARTIN, P. W., 40, 41n., 51, 139.
MAY, R. E., 35, 36n., 51.
McCRACKEN, H. L., 232n.
McCULLOCH, J. R., 193n.
Merchandise Inventories, 95, 96.
MERRIAM, JOHN C., 377.
Meteorological Theory of Business Cycles, 9, 12-16, 50, Addenda.
Method, Problems of, 1-3, 47-49, 53-59, 59n., 61, 62, 66, 106, 107, 129n., 138, 139, 180, 181, 186-188, 192, 193, 205, 229, 230-233, 357-360, 395-397, 451, 452, 454, 455, 460-463, 469-474.
MILL, JOHN STUART, 3, 4n., 8n., 106n., 192n.
MILLER, H. E., 7n., 11n.
MILLS, F. C., 108n., 189n., 213n., 263n., 284, 285, 288n., 324n., 359, 362n., 413, 414, 415, 416, 418, 420n.
Mills' Hypothesis concerning Duration of Business Cycles, 412-416, 418.
MILLS, JOHN, 9, 11, 378n., 384.
MITCHELL, T. W., 46, 51, 95, 157, 272.
MOMBERT, PAUL, 48n.
Monetary Mechanism, 117-139.
Monetary Stock, U. S., 98.

Money, Definitions of, 117.
Money and Business Cycles, 33, 34, 38, 40, 41, 51, 52, 128, 133-139, 182.
Money Economy and Business Cycles, 31, 44, 51, 61-63, 66-74, 182, 185.
Money Economy, Evolution of, 66-74, 171.
Money Incomes and Business Cycles, 35-42, 51, 64-66, 140-151, 146-149.
Month-to-month Changes in Business Indexes, 330-333.
"Monthly-means" Method, 242.
MOORE, HENRY L., 13, 14n., 50, 189, 200, 259n., 385n.
MORGENSTERN, OSKAR, 420n.
Multiple-cycle Hypothesis, 417.

NATIONAL BUREAU of ECONOMIC RESEARCH, 64n., 75, 87, 89n., 92, 97n., 108n., 140, 141n., 142, 147n., 148n., 153n., 168n., 199n., 210n., 238n., 302, 303n., 358, 359, 361, 362n., 365, 371, 374, 413, 472.
National Income, 64, 65, 92, 140, 141.
NATIONAL INDUSTRIAL CONFERENCE BOARD, 160, 161n.
NATIONAL MONETARY COMMISSION, 117, 118n., 123.
National Wealth, 90, 91.
Netherlands, 80, 81, 176, 362, 380, 392, 394, 398, 410, 412, 414n., 429-437, 442-445.
NEWCOMER, MABEL, 93n.
NEWTON, SIR ISAAC, 190.
NEYMARCH, A., 178n.
"Normal," Uses of the Term, 129n., 254n., 376.
"Normal" State of Trade, 376.
NORTON, J. P., 200, 262.
NYSTROM, P. H., 147, 148n.

Occupations of the American Population, 82-85, 88, 89, 161n.
OGBURN, W. F., 303n.
Ogburn and Thomas' Annual Index of Business, 303.
Organic and Inorganic Industries, 15, 16, 50, Addenda.
"Outside" Clearings, 264, 280, 305, 306, 313, 314, 327, 329-348.
Overproduction Theory of Business Cycles, 7, 8, 29-31, 38, 52, 139.
Over-saving and Business Cycles, 6, 24, 25, 52, 90.
OVERSTONE, LORD, 10, 11n.
OWEN, ROBERT, 8, 159.

Paper Money, 117, 121, 184.
PATTERSON, E. M., 49n.
PATTON, A. C., 213n.
Parallelism of Cycles in Different Countries, 438-450, 456.

Payments
  Among business enterprises, 149-151.
  Estimated total volume in U. S., 149.
  How made, 117-128, 184.
  Timing of sales and payments, 131, 132.
  Volume of payments and production, 140.
  (See Bank Clearings, Indexes of Business Conditions, Pecuniary Volume of Business).
PEARSON, KARL, 197, 254n., 262.
Peculiarities of Successive Cycles, 354-357.
Pecuniary Volume of Business, 312-314, 327.
"Period of Gestation," 30.
Periodicity, Scientific Use of the Term, 377, 378, 466, 467.
Periodicity of Commercial Crises, 10, 11, 13-15, 384, 416, 417, 453, 454, 466, 467.
Periodogram Analysis, 251, 259-261, 385.
Personal Effects, Wealth in, 94.
PERSONS, W. M., 49n., 58n., 197n., 200, 201, 213n., 240n., 242n., 243, 247, 252n., 253n., 254n., 263n., 264n., 266, 273, 274, 277, 282, 284, 288n., 293n., 294n., 297, 299n., 300, 302n., 315, 321, 324n., 325, 326n., 327, 329n., 330n., 331, 332, 333n., 334n., 335, 337, 338, 340, 341, 343n., 345, 346, 347, 348, 361, 366, 378n.
Persons' "Index of General Business," 293, 294, 324-326.
Persons' "Index of Trade," 297, 300, 315, 327, 329-348, 366.
PERVUSHIN, S. A., 255n.
PETTY, SIR WILLIAM, 190.
Phases of Business Cycles, 58, 78-80, 378. (See Crises, Depression, Prosperity, Revival).
Pig-iron Production, 210, 211, 217, 222, 227, 235, 248.
PIGOU, A. C., 17, 18, 19n., 20, 30n., 31n., 44n., 50, 157, 385n., Addenda.
PLAYFAIR, WILLIAM, 191, 209n.
POHLE, LUDWIG, 47n., 453n.
POISSON, S. D., 193.
"Political Arithmetic" 190, 191.
POLLAK FOUNDATION for ECONOMIC RESEARCH, 37, 40n., 139.
PORT of NEW YORK AUTHORITY, 109n.
POYNTING, J. H., 200n.
PRESCOTT, R. B., 224.
PRICE, RICHARD, 190.
Price fluctuations and Business Cycles, 29, 30, 32-34, 36-42, 107.
Price Indexes, 191, 193n., 195, 196, 204, 206-208, 210, 211, 218-220, 222, 235, 266, 267, 279.
Price Trends and Business Cycles, 135, 136, 138, 228, 230, 233, 263, 264, 407-412.

Prices, System of, 108-115.
Prices and the "Quantity of Money," 128-139.
Probabilities, Theory of, 191, 192, 195, 196, 250, 251, 419, 420.
Producers' Goods, 110, 111. (See Industrial Equipment.)
Production, Indexes of, 315-320, Addenda.
Profits and Business Cycles, 41-47, 51, 105-107, 142-146, 162, 172, 173, 182, 183, 471.
Progress and Business Cycles, 22, 23, 50, 93.
"Progressive Link-relative" Method, 244, 245, 248.
Prolongation of Depressions, 411, 412, 421.
Promotion and Business Cycles, 22, 50, 159.
Property, Income from, 142-146.
Prosperity
    Amplitude of, 343-354, 457.
    Duration of, 337-343, 407-412, 420, 421, 457.
    Interpretation of, 381, 382, 456.
"Psychological Theory" of Business Cycles, 9, 17-20, 50, Addenda.
Publicity and Statistics, 198, 199.
Purchasing Power and Business Cycles, 31, 32, 35-42, 51, 90, 139, 140.

Quantitative Analysis, 10, 53, 54, 189-360. (See Statistical Method and Business Cycles).
Quantity Theory of Money, 128-139.
QUETELET, ADOLPHE, 193, 195.

RAGUET, CONDY, 11.
Railway Statistics, 210, 211, 218-220, 222, 234, 247, 265.
Random Fluctuations, 212, 249-255, 258.
Ratio Charts, 209.
"Ratio-to-ordinate" Method, 242.
Real Income, 64-66.
Recessions, 378-371.
Relationships, Measures of, 261-270, 473, 474.
Rents, Income from, 142-146.
Resources, 90-100.
Retail trade, 45, 46, 71, 74, 87-89, 108, 109, 147-149, 198, 234, 279.
RICARDO, DAVID, 3, 4n., 157, 167, 189, 193n.
RIETZ, H. L., 240n., 263n.
ROBERTSON, D. H., 26n., 27n., 30n., 31n., 48n., 53, 90n.
RODBERTUS, K. J., 8.
ROGERS, THOROLD, 384.
RÖPKE, WILHELM, 35n., 47n.
RORTY, M. C., 28, 29n., 52, 261n., 295n., 367n.

ROSCHER, WILHELM, 9.
Russia, 82, 176, 177, 201, 362, 392, 394, 398, 410, 414n., 429-437, 439, 442-445, 449.

Salaries, 142-146.
SANFORD, H. W., 48n.
SAUERBECK, AUGUSTUS, 195, 196n., 219, 302.
Savings and Business Cycles, 23-25, 52, 90, 151-154, 184, Addenda.
Scale of Operations, 86-90, 172.
SCHÄFFLE, A. E. F., 8.
Schmidt, F., Addenda.
School Attendance, 83-85, 93, 94.
SCHUCKBURG-EVELYN, SIR GEORGE, 191.
SCHUMPETER, JOSEPH, 20, 21, 22n., 93, 156.
SCHWABE, HEINRICH, 12.
Science and Wealth, 92-94.
SCOTT, W. R., 75, 76, 77, 78n., 79n., 80n., 81n., 82.
Seasonal Variations, 123, 124, 195, 199, 212, 234-249, 463, 468, 469.
"Secondary Trends," 226-230, 463, 468, 469, Addenda.
Secular Changes in Duration of Business Cycles, 412-416, 418, 420n., 458.
Secular Trends, 93, 195, 200, 212-236, 252, 410-412, 463, 468n., 469.
Securities, Prices of, 111, 112.
Services, Income from, 142-146.
SILBERLING, N. J., 276, 277, 302.
SIMMEL, GEORG, 75n.
SISMONDI, J. C. L. SIMONDE DE, 4, 5, 6, 7n., 8n., 16, 53, 155, 157, 166n., 189.
Size of Enterprises, 86-90, 172.
SLUTSKY, E. E., Addenda.
SMITH, ADAM, 3, 4n., 72, 168, 190.
SMITH, K. C., 239n., 240n., 242n., 243n., 245.
SNYDER, CARL, 124, 125n., 127, 149n., 279n., 286, 296, 297n., 298, 304, 305n., 306, 307, 308, 309, 310, 311, 315, 319, 327, 328, 329n., 330n., 331, 332, 333n., 334n., 335, 337, 338, 339, 340, 343n., 344, 345, 346, 347, 348, 352, 355, 366, 367n., 368, 369, Addenda.
Snyder's "Clearings Index of Business," 304-306, 319, 327, 329-348, 366, 368, 369.
Snyder's "Index of Deposits Activity," 307, 308, 328, 329-348.
Snyder's "Index of Volume of Trade," 295, 296, 298, 309-311, 315, 319.
SOETBEER, ADOLF, 195, 196n.
SOMBART, WERNER, 15, 16n., 50, 86n., Addenda.
South Africa, 82, 176, 362, 380, 392, 394, 398, 410, 412, 414n., 429-437, 438, 442-445.
Speculation and Business Cycles, 8, 17.
Spending Money, 94, 147, 163-167.
SPIETHOFF, ARTHUR, 27n., 29, 48n., 52, 90n., 151

Spurious Correlation, 263, 264.
STAMP, SIR JOSIAH, 99n., Addenda.
Standard Deviation, 271-280, 318, 324n., 339n., 351, 353, 402-405.
Standardization and Production, 155.
Standardization and Statistics, 198, 199.
Statistical Data, Growth of, 54, 190, 191, 197-199, 203-205.
Statistical Method and Business Cycles, 10, 53, 54, 189-360, 364, 453, 454, 463, 464.
STINE, O. C., 64n.
Stock-Exchange Statistics, 218, 279.
STONE, N. I., 238n.
STUCKEN, RUDOLF, 25n., 26n.
Sugar Meltings, 246.
Sun-spot Theory of Business Cycles, 12, 13, 50, 384, Addenda.
Sweden, 154n., 176, 362, 392, 394, 398, 410, 412, 414n., 429-437, 442-445.
Switzerland, 5, 176, 396.
Synchronism of Cycles in Different Countries, 438-450.

TAKIZAWA, MATSUYO, 75n., Addenda.
Technical Experts, 159-162, 185.
Theories of Business Cycles, 3-53, 189.
Theories of Business Cycles, Summaries of, 11, 12, 49-53, 459-461.
"Theory" and "Fact," 59n., 357-360, 469, 470.
THOMAS, DOROTHY S., 277, 278, 299, 301, 302n., 303, 321, 371n., 372, 373, 374, 454n.
Thomas' Index of "British Business Cycles," 299, 301, 321, 371-374.
THORP, W. L., 5n., 75, 77, 78, 79, 81, 82, 103n., 176n., 359, 361, 362n., 364, 365, 370, 371, 374, 391, 407, 408n., 411, 414, 420n., 424, 440n., 448, Addenda.
Time Sequence of Cyclical Fluctuations, 264-269, 280-289, 324-326.
Time Series, Analysis of, 199-354.
TOOKE, THOMAS, 191.
Trade Associations and Statistics, 155.
"Trade Cycles" (See Business Cycles).
Trade, Volume of, 128-139, 266, 267, 286, 287, 295-300, 312-320, 327, 329-348.
Transformations of Time Series, 265-269, 473, 474.
Troughs and Crests of American Cycles, 334-337, 343-354.
TSCHUPROW, A. A., 263n.
TUGAN-BARANOVSKI, MICHEL, 10, 23, 24n., 26, 29, 52, 53, 55, 57n., 90, 151, 361, 379n., 384, 385n.
TUGWELL, R. G., 65n., 170n.
TUTTLE, P. M., 273.

Unemployment, 87-89, 198, 210-212, 238, 239, 240n., 241, 385.
Uncertainty and Business Cycles, 5, 6, 16, 17, 52, 87-89, 156, 157.
"Under-consumption Theory" of Business Cycles, 6, 7, 8, 51, 52.
"Under-saving" and Business Cycles, 23, 24, 52.
United States
    Amplitudes of business cycles, 343-353.
    Business annals, 362-370, 386-389, 393, 398, 399, 402, 409-411, 414, 415, 418, 422-424, 425-437, 438, 441-446.
    Business forecasting, 200, 201.
    Business indexes, 293-308, 326-354.
    Character of business cycles of 1878-1924, 354-357.
    Crises and recessions, 334, 355, 354-357, 387.
    Development of statistical data, 197, 198.
    Duration of bsuiness cycles, 337-344, 383-424.
    Estimated savings, 151-154.
    Estimated volume of payments, 149-151.
    Evolution of economic organization, 73, 74, 363, 414, 415, 446.
    Expenditures in retail trade, 146-149.
    Government regulation of business, 168, 179.
    Monetary mechanism, 116-128.
    National income, 64, 65, 140, 141.
    Occupations, 82-85, 161n., 176.
    Standard deviations of cyclical fluctuations, 273-276.
    Taxable incomes, 141-146.
    Time sequences of cyclical fluctuations, 282, 283.
    Time series, 210, 211, 216-220, 222, 223, 234, 235, 241, 246-248, 258.
    Wealth and income, 90-100.
    Wholesale prices, 204n., 205n., 210, 211.

VAINSTEIN, A. L., 361n.
Variability of Business Cycles, 354-357, 382, 383, 465-467.
VEBLEN, THORSTEIN, 42, 43, 44, 49n., 51, 90n., 101n., 255n.
Velocity of Circulation, 122-128.
VIALLES, PIERRE, 47n.
VILLARD, HAROLD, 359.
VOGEL, E. H., 22, 23n., 50, 93, 378n.
Volume of Payments, U. S., 149.
Volume of Trade, 128-139, 266, 267, 286, 287, 295-300, 312-320, 327, 329-348.

WADE, JOHN, 10n., 452, 454.
WAGEMANN, ERNST, 202.
Wages and Business Cycles, 6, 7, 8, 9, 24, 35, 51, 141-146.

WAINSTEIN, ALBERT, Addenda.
WALKER, AMASA, 11.
WALRAS, LEON, 115n.
WAR INDUSTRIES BOARD, 204n., 208n.
WARDWELL, C. A. R., Addenda.
Wealth and Income, 90-100, 182.
Weather, Theory of Business Cycles, 9, 12-16, 50, Addenda,
Wheat, 210, 211, 246.
WIEDENFELD, K., 177n.
WIRTH, MAX, 10.
WOLFF, S., DE, 227n., 228n., 229, Addenda.

WOLMAN, LEO, 89n., 90n., 359.
WORKING, HOLBROOK, 214n.
World Economy and Business Cycles, 446-450, 456.

Yields of Bonds, 210, 211.
YOUNG, A. A., 189n., 216n., 264n., 275.
YOUNG, ARTHUR, 190.
YULE, G. U., 197, 200, 262.

ZEUCH, W. B., 232n.

NATIONAL BUREAU PUBLICATIONS ON
BUSINESS CYCLES

I Books on Business Cycles

Business Cycles and Unemployment (1923)
Committee on Unemployment and Business Cycles of the
President's Conference on Unemployment, and a Special
Staff of the National Bureau
448 pp., $4.10

Employment, Hours and Earnings in Prosperity and Depression, United States, 1920-1922 (1923)
W. I. King
150 pp., 3.10

Business Annals (1926)
W. L. Thorp, with an introductory chapter, Business Cycles
as Revealed by Business Annals, by Wesley C. Mitchell
382 pp., 2.50

Migration and Business Cycles (1926)
Harry Jerome
258 pp., 2.50

Business Cycles: The Problem and Its Setting (1927)
Wesley C. Mitchell
514 pp., 5.00

Planning and Control of Public Works (1930)
Leo Wolman
292 pp., 2.50

The Smoothing of Time Series (1931)
F. R. Macaulay
174 pp., 2.00

Strategic Factors in Business Cycles (1934)
J. M. Clark
256 pp., 1.50

German Business Cycles, 1924-1933 (1934)
C. T. Schmidt
308 pp., 2.50

Public Works in Prosperity and Depression (1935)
A. D. Gayer
482 pp., 3.00

Prices in Recession and Recovery (1936)
Frederick C. Mills
602 pp., 4.00

*Some Theoretical Problems Suggested by the Movements of
Interest Rates, Bond Yields and Stock Prices in the United
States Since 1856* (1938)
F. R. Macaulay
612 pp., 5.00

Consumer Instalment Credit and Economic Fluctuations
(1942)
Gottfried Haberler
262 pp., 2.50

Measuring Business Cycles (1946)
A. F. Burns and Wesley C. Mitchell
592 pp., 5.00

Price-Quantity Interactions in Business Cycles (1946)
Frederick C. Mills
158 pp., 1.50

Changes in Income Distribution During the Great Depression (1946)
Horst Mendershausen
192 pp., 2.50

American Transportation in Prosperity and Depression
(1948)
Thor Hultgren
432 pp., 5.00

II Books Partly Concerned with Business Cycles

The Behavior of Prices (1927)   598 pp., 7.00
Frederick C. Mills

Recent Economic Changes in the United States (1929)
                       2 vol., 990 pp., 7.50
  Committee on Recent Economic Changes of the President's
Conference on Unemployment, and a Special Staff of the
National Bureau

Seasonal Variations in Industry and Trade (1933)   480 pp., 4.00
Simon Kuznets

Production Trends in the United States Since 1870 (1934) 396 pp., 3.50
A. F. Burns

Industrial Profits in the United States (1934)   692 pp., 5.00
R. C. Epstein

Ebb and Flow in Trade Unionism (1936)   272 pp., 2.50
Leo Wolman

The International Gold Standard Reinterpreted, 1914-1934
(1940)   2 vol., 1474 pp., 12.00
William Adams Brown, Jr.

National Income and Its Composition, 1919-1938 (1941) 1012 pp., 5.00
Simon Kuznets

Financing Small Corporations in Five Manufacturing In-
dustries, 1926-36 (1942)   192 pp., 1.50
C. L. Merwin

The Financing of Large Corporations, 1920-39 (1943) 160 pp., 1.50
Albert R. Koch

Corporate Cash Balances, 1914-43: Manufacturing and
Trade (1945)   148 pp., 2.00
Friedrich A. Lutz

National Income: A Summary of Findings (1946) 160 pp., 1.50
Simon Kuznets

Value of Commodity Output since 1869 (1947) 320 pp., 4.00
W. H. Shaw

Business Incorporations in the United States, 1800-1943
(1948)   196 pp., 6.00
G. Heberton Evans, Jr.

III Papers on Business Cycles

Testing Business Cycles (Bulletin 31, March 1, 1929)
Wesley C. Mitchell

*The Depression as Depicted by Business Annals (Bulletin
43, September 19, 1932)*
Willard L. Thorp

*Gross Capital Formation, 1919-1933 (Bulletin 52, Novem-
ber 15, 1934)*   .50
Simon Kuznets

* *The National Bureau's Measures of Cyclical Behavior* (Bulletin 57, July 1, 1935)   .50
Wesley C. Mitchell and Arthur F. Burns

Production during the American Business Cycle of 1927-1933 (Bulletin 61, November 9, 1936)   .50
Wesley C. Mitchell and Arthur F. Burns

Technical Progress and Agricultural Depression (Bulletin 67, November 29, 1937)   .50
Eugen Altschul and Frederick Strauss

* *Statistical Indicators of Cyclical Revivals* (Bulletin 69, May 28, 1938)   .25
Wesley C. Mitchell and Arthur F. Burns

Commodity Flow and Capital Formation in the Recent Recovery and Decline 1932-1938 (Bulletin 74, June 25, 1939)   .25
Simon Kuznets

* *A Significance Test for Time Series and Other Ordered Observations* (Technical Paper 1, September 1941)   .50
W. Allen Wallis and Geoffrey H. Moore

Railway Freight Traffic in Prosperity and Depression (Occasional Paper 5, February 1942)   .25
Thor Hultgren

* *Wartime 'Prosperity' and the Future* (Occasional Paper 9, March 1943)   .35
Wesley C. Mitchell

Railroad Travel and the State of Business (Occasional Paper 13, December 1943)   .35
Thor Hultgren

Railway Traffic Expansion and Use of Resources in World War II (Occasional Paper 15, February 1944)   .35
Thor Hultgren

Economic Research and the Keynesian Thinking of Our Times (Twenty-sixth Annual Report, June 1946)
Arthur F. Burns

The Role of Inventories in Business Cycles (Occasional Paper 26, May 1948)   .50
Moses Abramovitz

The Structure of Postwar Prices (Occasional Paper 27, July 1948)   .75
Frederick C. Mills

Out of print.

NATIONAL BUREAU OF ECONOMIC RESEARCH

1819 Broadway, New York 23, N. Y.